—— **CHAPTER FOUR** ——————————————

DERIVATIVES

First derivative

$$f'(x_0) \approx \frac{f(x_0 + h) - f(x_0)}{h}$$

INTERPOLATORY QUADRATURE

$$\int_a^b f(x)\, dx \approx \sum_{k=1}^n f(x_k)A_k, \tag{4.13}$$

with

$$A_j = \int_a^b l_j(x)\, dx, \qquad l \le j \le n,\ l_j(x) \text{ is as in } (3.11)$$

COMPOUND QUADRATURE

Trapezoidal rule

$$\int_a^b f(x)\, dx \approx t_N = h[\tfrac{1}{2}f(x_1) + f(x_2) + f(x_3) + \cdots + f(x_{N-1}) + \tfrac{1}{2}f(x_n)] \tag{4.21}$$

for $h = \dfrac{b - a}{N},\ x_j = a + jh,\ j = 0, 1, \ldots, N.$

Simpson's rule

$$\int_a^b f(x)\, dx \approx s_M = \frac{h}{3}[f(x_0) + 4f(x_1) + 2f(x_2) + 4f(x_3) + \cdots + 2f(x_{M-2})$$
$$+ 4f(x_{M-1}) + f(x_M)], \tag{4.22}$$

where $h = \dfrac{b - a}{M}$, and for $j = 0, 1, \ldots, M,\ x_j = a + jh.$

$x_4 = 0 + 4\frac{2}{2}$

$x_u = 2$

—— **CHAPTER FIVE** ——————————————

BISECTION METHOD

$$x_M = \frac{x_L + x_R}{2} \tag{5.4}$$

SECANT METHOD

$$x_{k+1} = x_k - \frac{f(x_k)(x_k - x_{k-1})}{f(x_k) - f(x_{k-1})} \qquad (k \ge 1) \tag{5.7}$$

NEWTON'S METHOD

$$x_{k+1} = x_k - \frac{f(x_k)}{f'(x_k)} \tag{5.10}$$

—— **CHAPTER SIX** ——————————————

LEAST-SQUARES APPROXIMATION

Polynomial coefficients

$$\sum_{k=0}^m \left(\sum_{i=1}^n x_i^{k+j} \right) a_k = \sum_{i=1}^n f_i x_i^j, \qquad (0 \le j \le m) \tag{6.6}$$

—— **CHAPTER SEVEN** ——————————————

EULER'S METHOD

$$y_{j+1} = y_j + hf(x_j, y_j)$$
$$h = x_{j+1} - x_j \tag{7.7}$$

CLASSICAL RUNGE–KUTTA METHOD

$$k_1 = f(x_j, y_j)$$
$$k_2 = f(x_j + \tfrac{1}{2}h, y_j + \tfrac{1}{2}hk_1)$$
$$k_3 = f(x_j + \tfrac{1}{2}h, y_j + \tfrac{1}{2}hk_2) \tag{7.21}$$
$$k_4 = f(x_j + h, y_j + hk_3)$$

$$y_{j+1} = y_j + \frac{h}{6}(k_1 + 2k_2 + 2k_3 + k_4)$$

An Introduction to Numerical Computations

An Introduction to Numerical Computations

SECOND EDITION

Sidney Yakowitz

Systems and Industrial Engineering Department
University of Arizona
Tucson, Arizona

Ferenc Szidarovszky

Department of Mathematics and Computer Science
Karl Marx University of Economics
Budapest, Hungary

Macmillan Publishing Company
New York
Collier Macmillan Publishers
London

Macmillan Publishing Company
866 Third Avenue, New York, New York 10022
Collier Macmillan Canada, Inc.

Library of Congress Cataloging in Publication Data

Yakowitz, Sidney (date)
  An introduction to numerical computations.

  Includes index.
  1. Numerical analysis.   I. Szidarovszky, Ferenc.
II. Title.
QA297.Y35   1989   519.4   88-31512
ISBN 0-02-430821-8

Printing: 4 5 6 7 8   Year: 9 0 1 2 3 4 5 6 7 8

Preface ▬▬▬▬▬▬▬▬▬▬▬▬▬

THE INTENDED READER

This book, now in its second edition, is an outgrowth of class notes for a numerical methods course required of most engineering students at the University of Arizona. The prerequisites are a course in either FORTRAN or Pascal, and a standard calculus sequence. Past or concurrent study of an introductory differential equations course is encouraged but is not essential. This course in numerical computations constitutes the only systematic training most of our graduates will receive, and this book is written with that fact in mind. On the other hand, a portion of the students do take a senior/graduate course in numerical analysis. *An Introduction to Numerical Computations* provides a solid foundation for such further study. It gives the motivations, fundamental methods, basic principles, and applications of the subject, and is rife with subroutines, computational examples, and "experiments," but leaves rigorous development of theoretical superstructure and error analysis to future coursework or outside reading. Toward aiding those wishing to obtain a full mathematical picture, references pointing to advanced material are offered at points where our analysis leaves off. Much of the theoretical superstructure is to be found in our intermediate-level book (F. Szidarovszky and S. Yakowitz: *Principles and Procedures of Numerical Analysis*, New York, Plenum Publishing Corporation, 1978). Hereafter, we refer to that book simply as "S & Y."

We believe that the backgrounds and educational requirements of computer scientists, mathematicians, physicists, and operations research specialists are not essentially different from the backgrounds and needs of engineers: The subjects treated here are foundational and appropriate for all quantitative disciplines. The applications in this book are from elementary physics, circuit theory, and population dynamics, but they are meaningful and worthy of consideration no matter what the student's career goals happen to be. Although there are many uses, there is only one discipline of numerical methods; it serves the routine needs of every subject area. The present book covers this subject, and our contention is that such coverage cannot be done properly with less background or reader participation than we ask.

THE ORIENTATION OF THIS BOOK

With some exceptions, we find other introductory textbooks more authoritarian and pedantic than we would like. In *An Introduction to Numerical Computations*, we aim to build intuition and self-reliance through an experimentalist viewpoint more akin to physics than to mathematics. The topical developments follow a systematic pattern of inquiry:

1. We first present a motivational statement and an application requiring some numerical computation.
2. Then a "commonsense," readily understood algorithm is devised.
3. In exploring the primitive algorithm, in some cases we find that trouble arises: The answer computed may not be sufficiently accurate to warrant the processing time, or the method may fail to provide any answer at all.
4. We examine the sources of the failure and call upon theory, which suggests that approximation polynomials or other analytic devices point the way to more sophisticated algorithms.
5. The refined algorithms are tested and found to be comparatively effective.
6. Before passing to new investigations, we look for checks and error bounds, to gain assurance that the refined methods are, in fact, working reliably, and to delimit their range of proper application.

Thus we follow this pattern of pushing simplistic procedures beyond their limits, showing through concrete case studies that in some reasonable circumstances, elementary techniques cannot deliver the required accuracy. By this plan, we provide incentive for seeking higher-order methods. We do not settle for a more sophisticated rule without evidence that it does indeed significantly outperform more primitive ones. This book is unique in its steadfast effort to compare features of various methods for a given problem area. Our aim in such analysis and computational experimentation is not just to provide a progression of techniques but to encourage and guide the student in developing a critical eye for computational matters.

Although we aim to cultivate the reader's computational intuition, mathematical principles are at the forefront of this exposition. The theoretical bases and fundamental properties of the various methods are carefully described. The reader will find this to be an honest and demanding work: We do give a solid foundation for numerical analysis but leave completion of the edifice to future study.

FEATURES OF THE SECOND EDITION

Some fundamental changes have been incorporated into this edition. They are based on our teaching experience and on commissioned reviews by instructors at other institutions where this textbook is assigned. Most of all, this new edition reflects the evolving nature of the subject and the evolving needs and backgrounds of our readers. The main direction of these changes has been to include more illustrational applications as well as additional motivational and explanatory material. Some highlights of the second edition follow.

- An orientation chapter giving perspective on how numerical computations fits into the broader field of computer science and the role it plays in modeling and analysis activities in engineering.
- Number representation and roundoff are now presented in terms of a hypothetical computer decimal word instead of binary representation. This vastly simplifies explanation of the origins and propagation of roundoff error without burdening the reader with an unfamiliar number system.

- The linear equation chapter has been moved forward to become the first subject area after the general topics of roundoff and error propagation.
- In helping to fortify the student for grasping the subtle concepts behind Taylor's interpolatory and piecewise polynomials as well as interpolatory and compound quadrature, the general derivations are preceded by simple motivational explanation in terms of constant and linear polynomials.
- The exposition of Gauss quadrature has been revised toward making the book more self-contained. We found that our secant algorithm was quite adequate for computing Gauss points to great accuracy. The result is that now the origin of these points is a fairly simple code rather than reference to a table of mysterious origin.
- Reflecting recent developments in computational practice, we have augmented the eigenvalue section. It turns out that a code based on Rayleigh quotients (the idea at the heart of the effective, but extremely complicated, QR algorithm) is adequate for computing the eigenvalues and eigenvectors of fairly large matrices.
- The section on the discrete Fourier transform has been elaborated, giving explanations and filtering applications.
- The needs of advanced students and practitioners have been further recognized. For example, we now include an explanation of how transfer functions can be transcribed to differential equations of a form conveniently solved by our multivariate Runge–Kutta code. Then (following an illustrative application to a simple *RLC* circuit), we offer a procedure for passing directly from a system of block diagrams, so familiar to practicing engineers, into a form ready for numerical solution by the multivariate Runge–Kutta subroutine. By this device, the usually arduous task of combining blocks into one big transfer function is entirely sidestepped. Apparently, these elementary developments are not widely discussed in the literature, but we are convinced that they could be very helpful.
- The problem sets are larger, more diverse, and more oriented toward applications.

Generally speaking, the first edition of *An Introduction to Numerical Computations* was successful with regard to acceptance as well as critical review. Our intention in this second edition has been to enhance the good qualities of the first, while striving to make the material as accessible and relevant to our readers as we possibly can.

PROGRAMMING ASPECTS

Developments in computer technology have assisted us in our dialectic and experimental pedagogic orientation. The students now use an interactive computer. Because of various capabilities and rapid throughput times on these machines, the students avoid much of the drudgery of earlier days, and concentrate their efforts on performing and interpreting their computational experiments. For example, they are able to copy the subroutines of this book directly into their file areas; the only coding required, therefore, is the (usually brief) problem-specific calling program. To assist the student in concentrating on essentials, this book supplies simple but adequate VAX-11 FORTRAN 77 subroutines for virtually all the methods described. These codes are so elementary and fully documented that they could well be viewed as pseudocodes, and thus serve as a basis for implementation in C, Basic, or other languages. A Pascal version is provided in the Instructor's Solution Manual for this book.

In composing these subroutines, we have held clarity and simplicity above all else, including efficiency, elegance, and safeguards. Most of the subroutines are accompanied by calling programs, output, and discussion of sample numerical studies that show, by example, the experimental and pragmatic view toward computation, which we believe to be most healthy and valuable. In addition to providing a direct link from theory to action, our approach to programming and use of subroutines exemplifies the modular top-down philosophy that has proved so effective over the past decade.

The VAX-11/FORTRAN 77 compiler has a nonstandard feature utilized in our codes: namely, "DO WHILE" loops. By availing ourselves of this feature, we have avoided use of "GO TO" statements. Hopefully, it will be apparent to readers how to convert these loops to standard FORTRAN 77 loops with conditional branches. In any event, versions of our codes in standard ANSI FORTRAN 77 as well as Pascal are available as explained below.

Software Distribution

The codes in this book are available from the first author on either IBM-PC DOS disks or VAX/VMS-readable tape. Alternatively, a version in standard ANSI FORTRAN 77 or Pascal can be supplied by disk. These codes have been tested on MS FORTRAN and Turbo Pascal compilers, respectively, on an IBM PC. The *Instructor's Solution Manual for an Introduction to Numerical Computations*, 2nd ed., contains standard Pascal versions of the programs and subroutines. We have compiled and run these codes under VAX-11 Pascal and on PCs running Turbo-Pascal.

PLANS OF STUDY

The "unstarred" sections of this book constitute our basic numerical computations course. We have taken great pains to make these sections, which include the

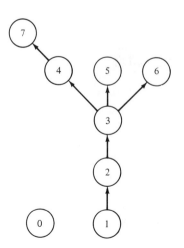

traditional fare of introductory numerical methods courses, readily accessible to our students. The "starred" sections contain material we regard as important but not essential in a first course. The instructor can order the material in any fashion within the prerequisite chapter constraints shown in the figure on page viii.

ACKNOWLEDGMENTS

We are deeply grateful for encouragement and support for this effort from the Systems and Industrial Engineering Department and the Engineering College of the University of Arizona. Also, we are indebted to innumerable students, secretaries, and graduate assistants, who provided help beyond the call of duty in refining early versions of the book. Thomas Hassett, T. Jayawardena, Karen Markey, and Brian Rutherford particularly deserve our deep gratitude. We appreciate, also, the helpful suggestions of our reviewers: Steven Rosencrans of Tulane University, Henry King of the University of Maryland, Leroy D. Sturges of Iowa State University, Donald M. Esterling of George Washington University, Theodore J. Weidner of Rensselaer Polytechnic Institute, Betty Shepherd of Louisiana State University, and David Dougherty of the University of California, Irvine.

We take great pride in the style and workmanship evident in Macmillan's production of these editions. Particularly, Production Supervisor Elaine Wetterau has earned our admiration, respect, and deep gratitude. Finally, we mention that it was through various National Science Foundation grants that the authors met and enjoyed a productive and happy 15 years of collaboration.

Sidney Yakowitz
Tucson, Arizona

Ferenc Szidarovszky
Budapest, Hungary

Contents ━━━━━━━━━━━━━

An Introduction to Numerical Computations

Introduction: An Overview of Numerical Computations

Our primary concern in this book is to introduce students and professionals to the quantitative side of the computer and information revolution. These foundations must be understood in order for the reader to appreciate and contribute to the ongoing renovation and revitalization of the practice of science, engineering, mathematical economics, and, in general, of all fields of applied mathematics. The discipline of numerical computations particularly influences the practice of engineering modeling and design methodology. The aim of this orientation segment is to offer an historical and intellectual perspective on numerical methods.

WHAT COMPUTERS ARE USED FOR

Presumably, the reader has learned the rudiments of computer programming. It is time now to consider how this skill can be used to advantage. As we see it, computational activity can be categorized into three different empires:

1. Data-base management.
2. Numerical computations.
3. Artificial intelligence.

We remark briefly next on the nature of each of these categories.

Data-Base Management

Data-base management includes methods for managing large information files for banking, airline reservations, and other bookkeeping and practical financial and inventory tasks. These activities are of prime economic importance, but they do not have much mathematical content and, at present, seem less relevant to missions of engineers and scientists. A prototype data-base management task is the keeping of records of expenditures and receipts in a business. The file should be readily and easily accessible with regard to various questions, such as "What is the current balance?", "Did Mr. Jones pay his bill?", "How much did we spend on electricity last summer?", and so on.

Numerical Computations

Of course, numbers are a central concern in data-base management and are often fundamental to artificial intelligence. A feature that distinguishes numerical computations from these other areas is that on a mathematical level, calculus, linear algebra, and mathematical analysis (differential equations, complex variables, etc.) are the foundations. Derivative and Taylor's series ideas are the backbone of almost everything in this book. As a consequence of this tie to the real number system, floating-point variables are essential to virtually all programs for numerical computations. On the other hand, integer representations are sufficient for most applications in the other two computer realms. A prototypical numerical computations task is that of finding the roots of a tenth-degree polynomial. Numerical computations is an old field and has a venerable tradition. The bulk of our methods bear illustrious names, including Gauss, Newton, and Lagrange; indeed, most of the methods in this book were invented by these giants to perform heroic computational tasks centuries before digital computers appeared.

Almost all classical quantitative analyses rely on calculus-based models. At the research level, especially in computer science, procedures based on abstract algebra and logic are gaining prominence, but still, numerical computations are the standard tools of the trade in engineering, applied mathematics, physics, and management information systems.

Artificial Intelligence

Artificial intelligence is concerned with using computers to solve decision problems involving models that are not calculus based. A standard computation in this realm involves a time sequence of choices (presumably machine-made, according to some algorithm). At each decision time in the sequence there are only finitely many selections that can be made. Typically, one can get by with integer or symbolic variables; differentiation does not enter the picture. Computer chess programming is a fundamental artificial intelligence activity. At each board position, a finite set of moves is available. Chess programs explore the value of each move by looking ahead at possible responses, and responses to responses, and so on, as permitted by time and CPU limitations. A characteristic of this realm is that the number of combinations possible in a realistic problem (e.g., trying to find an optimal chess move) are way beyond a computer's power to explore. One has to be content with a suboptimal decision. The realm of artificial intelligence is modern and is the focus of intense research. The mathematical underpinnings are few and not entirely satisfying. Ideas from logic, abstract algebra, and graph theory give most of the foundation.

THE USES OF NUMERICAL COMPUTATIONS

Numerical Computations in Problem Solving

For our purposes, a *model* is a mathematical expression relating (physical, engineering, economic, etc.) measurables. To mention a famous example, Newton's law of motion,

$$m \frac{d^2}{dt^2} x(t) = F(t) \tag{1}$$

relating linear position $x(t)$ to applied force $F(t)$, is a model. Numerical computations come into the picture when one wishes to use the model for prediction, experimentation, or to obtain information from observations. For example, it is possible to use this relation to determine what forces impinged on a body on the basis of the record of positions $x(t)$.

If the model has a known closed-form solution, one may want to use the computer to evaluate it at times of interest. Equation (1) does have a closed-form solution of position, in response to force $F(t)$, if the second integral of $F(t)$ is known. In the absence of neat solutions, $x(t)$ can be accurately approximated computationally by integration techniques revealed in Chapter 4.

──── **EXAMPLE** ────

As explained in Lin and Segel (1974, Sec. 2.1), by painstaking calculations (four years worth!) by hand, Kepler was able to demonstrate convincingly that his law for planetary motion explained observations. In terms of the radius R and angle θ, as shown in Figure 1, Kepler's law can be phrased precisely as, for all time t,

$$R(t)^2 \frac{d}{dt} \theta(t) = \text{constant.} \tag{2}$$

This model, as validated with measurements, was a triumphal contribution to science, and it served (but not quickly) to dispel the teaching and impression of the time that the earth was the center of the solar system. Also, importantly, Kepler's law influenced Isaac Newton in his derivations of the laws of motion [equation (1)] and gravitation, two of the most important models of all times.

To get back to computational use of the model (2), one can deduce from it that planets follow an elliptical trajectory. That is, the locus $(x(\theta), y(\theta))$ of a planet's motion about the sun must satisfy

$$x(\theta) = A \cos (a\theta), \qquad y(\theta) = B \sin (a\theta) \tag{3}$$

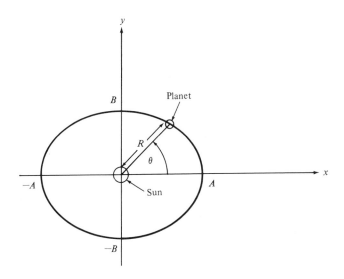

FIGURE 1 Planetary Motion

for some constants a, A, and B. Now if one wished to solve the problem of finding a planet's orbit, on the basis of a few location measurements, one could use these measurements to calibrate the parameters a, A, and B, and then evaluate equation (3) over a range of the angular variable θ. This problem demands only elementary computational methods. It turns out to be somewhat tricky to find the planetary position as a function of time, and thereby predict eclipses. The trouble is that from model (2) the rate of phase-angle change $\dot{\theta}$ varies with radius. Yet prediction calculations were successfully undertaken by hand centuries ago. Now we have the privilege of living at a time when most of the drudgery of numerical computations problems can be assigned to an automatic computer. This book is intended to give you the means for using the computer effectively for model analysis.

Newton's laws of motion and gravitation, as applied to the solar system, have been used to predict eclipses, tides, return of comets, and so on.

Now, through the powers of numerical computation, much more lavish modeling efforts than Newton's are undertaken. A model for the flow of fluids can be the basis of scientific design of hulls for boats, fuselages of airplanes, and profiles of submarines, to optimize performance in terms of speed, energy consumption, or noise emission. The subject of fluid dynamics has been revitalized by computing power and practice. Wind tunnels are being replaced by computers as design tools for the tasks just mentioned. As illustration, it has been argued (Letcher et al., 1987) that such modeling and analysis applied to hull design was the key to the Challenger's victory in the 1987 America's Cup yacht race.

Numerical Computations in Modeling

Numerical computations play an indispensable role in modeling itself. We have mentioned that Kepler spent years making painstaking computations with Tycho Brahe's data. Most of this effort was not to solve problems involving his model but just to infer and verify that (2) was indeed the right model. Such chores could have been done cleanly and quickly had Kepler done his work on a computer (in 1600!). For example, having entered the Brahe measurements of a certain planet into a data file, he might have tried different conjectured laws:

$$(1) \quad R\,\frac{d\theta}{dt} = \text{constant}$$

$$(2) \quad R^2\,\frac{d\theta}{dt} = \text{constant}$$

$$(3) \quad R^3\left(\frac{d\theta}{dt}\right)^2 = \text{constant}$$

$$\vdots$$

and checked discrepancies with the Brahe astronomical data. The point is that modeling itself usually means comparing motions implied by conjectured relations to observed numbers. The art of conjecturing requires first-class scientists. But the testing can and should be automated, using principles such as those offered in this book.

It turns out that modeling is a task that is subject to continuing refinement. Kepler's law (2) does not hold exactly within the framework of Newton's model [gravitation and equation (1)] because it does not account for interplanetary gravitational attraction. Even accounting for such attraction, Newton's laws do not perfectly describe planetary motion because the effects of general relativity (discovered by Einstein) have an influence that can now be observed. Errors in the Brahe data stemming from his primitive telescope probably led to greater inaccuracies than even the second-order effect of planetary interaction.

The point of this discussion is that modeling, data quality, and computation proceed hand in hand. An overly refined model cannot be verified or calibrated with crude data or inadequate computer power. On the other hand, a model that is more simplistic than necessary might have limited usefulness or lead to erroneous decisions.

WHAT YOU WILL GAIN FROM THIS BOOK

In earlier sections we spoke of the role that numerical computations play within the general framework of modeling and problem solving. Here we discuss specific learning objectives addressed in this book.

Numerical Computations Literacy

The principal components of the field of numerical computations are

- Computer representation of numbers, and the origin and propagation of computational error.
- Function approximation and curve fitting of data.
- Numerical differentiation and integration.
- Solution of linear, nonlinear, and differential equations.
- Fourier methods and filtering.

All these subjects will be studied in detail. The ideas will be reinforced by a multitude of hand- and machine-computation examples and a number of applications to models from engineering and physics. Among the benefits of this textbook are the following:

1. The computational viewpoint and experimentation will help you to *understand principles of applied mathematics* and the implications of various physical and engineering models. The mere task of transcribing formulas and model relations into computer programs often *brings to life the theory* you have studied elsewhere.

2. Application of computational techniques to case studies in this text and to your homework will *enhance your skill in problem solving*. You will gain a better understanding of what is easy and what is challenging.

3. Through study of material in this book, you will come to think of technical questions in terms of programming and computational demands. Through such *development of your intuition*, you will increase your ability to find the most suitable methodology for practical problems you confront in your career.

4. The universality of computers has engendered an industry of software aids. The industry has provided software packages that seem to automate the application of numerical methods. In applying such software, the user is typically presented with a menu from which the general problem area is to be selected. Then another

menu appears which invites the user to supply needed parameters and particulars about the problem to be solved. This done, the program attempts to supply the desired answers. Control over methodology and algorithms is frequently maintained by the package, and in fact, is typically hidden from the user. The advantages must be weighted against the dangers of relinquishing control. This book aims at preparing you, the reader, to be an *informed and intelligent user* of modern software technology.

5. Most practical engineering problems cannot be properly solved immediately simply by application of a commercial program. The knowledge of numerical methodology that you obtain from this book and the programming skill you acquire through homework or self-study will guide you in developing your own programs for tasks that you confront. In addition, you will build a *background for understanding the rationale behind commercial programs* and be able to employ them wisely, in modular fashion if necessary, for the purposes at hand.

CHAPTER 1

Computer Number Representation and Roundoff

1.1
PRELIMINARIES

In applications, calculations typically depend on some ''input'' values. Such inputs may be measured data, physical constants, or results of earlier computations. In the vast majority of cases, these inputs are inexact. In the course of computations, these inexact values are propagated in place of the ideal values. Furthermore, for reasons discussed in this chapter, even more error will be induced because of inherent limitations of digital computers. In some cases, the output resulting from imperfect computations on inexact inputs will be accurate enough for practical purposes. In other cases, the final result may be worthless. This chapter is intended to give the reader insight into the origins and patterns of error accumulation. Some notions about how to bound and minimize the effects of error are presented.

The intention of the following example is to impress on the reader that as marvelous as computers are, they are not perfect. The slight error induced by their inability to represent real numbers exactly will turn out to have amazingly strong repercussions in certain practical cases.

EXAMPLE 1.1

It is possible, in fact customary, for a computer to store a number different from that presented as input, and to commit this error without warning. We perform the simple experiment of reading the number $x = 0.1234567890123$ into a VAX-11 computer, and then printing out the number actually stored. The program for doing this is shown in Table 1.1. The first of the numbers listed in Table 1.2 is the number stored in the input file, and the second is the representation received in the output file. Note that the format field length is adequate and is not the cause of the discrepancy. The difference between these numbers, which is about 2×10^{-9}, is termed ''roundoff'' error. We will learn more about this as the chapter progresses.

7

TABLE 1.1   Program to Illustrate Roundoff Error

```
C       PROGRAM STORE
C
C       **************************************************
C       THIS PROGRAM WILL READ A NUMBER FROM ONE FILE AND
C       WRITE IT TO ANOTHER
C       INPUT: X
C       OUTPUT: X
C       **************************************************
C
        READ(11,1) X
        WRITE(10,1) X
      1 FORMAT(2X,F15.13)
        STOP
        END
```

TABLE 1.2   Input and Output

Input:	0.1234567890123
Output:	0.1234567910433

To appreciate the concerns of "numerical computations," one must understand what a computer can and cannot do with numbers. Within limits to be discussed in this chapter, the computer has two fundamental capabilities:

CAPABILITY 1.   The computer can store numbers.

CAPABILITY 2.   The computer can perform arithmetic (addition, subtraction, multiplication, and division), and it can compare the magnitudes of any two stored numbers x and y. That is, it can decide whether x is greater than, equal to, or less than y.

For reasons to be disclosed in this chapter, neither Capability 1 nor Capability 2 can be achieved exactly. There are only a fixed finite number of distinct computer words available for representing numbers. Thus regardless of what scheme is used to map the infinite set of real numbers into computer numbers, error will usually occur. Such error is referred to as *roundoff error*. In several sections of this chapter, origins, bounds, illustrations, and remedies for roundoff error are presented. Example 1.1, just presented, illustrated roundoff error.

Capability 2, says, in essence, that the only mathematics that computers can do is arithmetic. Every computational solution to a numerical problem must ultimately be built up of operations in which stored numbers are compared or operated on arithmetically and the resultant stored. Most problems of interest cannot be solved by a finite sequence of such operations. We must be content with some program that yields an approximation to the solution and accept that there will typically be approximation error. Such error resulting from replacing a desired mathematical operation by a realizable computation is referred to as *truncation error*. Techniques for bounding this error or assuring a specified accuracy should accompany a computational method.

Whereas roundoff error and its properties are somewhat independent of application area, truncation error can only be analyzed in the context in which it occurs.

We delay such discussions, therefore, until later chapters specializing in specific computational areas.

But the effects of truncation error can be seen without much introduction. Example 1.2 illustrates a typical numerical computations dilemma: If any answer is sought with too much precision, roundoff becomes a limiting factor. Otherwise, lack of mathematical accuracy (truncation error) prevails. Together, roundoff and truncation error constitute a limit to how accurately a desired quantity can be computed by a given algorithm.

─────── **EXAMPLE 1.2** ───

Recall from calculus that the derivative $f'(x)$ of a function $f(x)$ at x_0 is defined to be the limit of

$$D(h) = \frac{f(x_0 + h) - f(x_0)}{h}$$

as h converges to 0. This formula for $D(h)$, which we have illustrated in Figure 1.1, is representative of finite difference methods, to be presented in Chapter 4 to approximate derivatives numerically. The true derivative is the slope of the tangent line, in Figure 1.1, and the approximation is the slope of the line connecting $[x_0, f(x_0)]$ and $[x_0 + h, f(x_0 + h)]$.

If the magnitude of h is "too large," $D(h)$ is inaccurate because h is not sufficiently close to the limit. This error is the truncation error associated with using the "realizable" arithmetic formula $D(h)$ for approximating an unrealizable limiting operation, the derivative. Such error would occur even if $f(x)$ and $D(h)$ could be evaluated exactly. This error, then, is of mathematical origin. For reasons to be discussed in Section 1.5, as h becomes small, inaccuracies due to roundoff error dominate. The error in computing the difference $f(x_0 + h) - f(x_0)$ is large relative to the actual value of this difference. Roundoff error would not be present if $D(h)$ could somehow be computed perfectly.

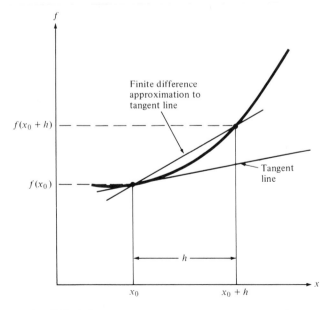

FIGURE 1.1 Finite Difference Approximation

The program and printout displayed in Tables 1.3 and 1.4 give clear evidence that there is a limit to how well the derivative of exp (x) at $x_0 = 1$ can be approximated by the finite difference formula $D(h)$. The approximation error is

TABLE 1.3 Program for Derivative Approximation

```
C       PROGRAM DERIVAPPROX
C
C       ********************************************************
C       THIS PROGRAM DEMONSTRATES ERRORS IN NUMERICAL
C       APPROXIMATION OF THE DERIVATIVE OF THE
C       EXPONENTIAL FUNCTION
C       OUTPUT: H=THE MAGNITUDE OF THE CHANGE IN INDEPENDENT
C                 VARIABLE USED IN THE FINITE DIFFERENCE
C                 APPROXIMATION
C               ERR=THE DIFFERENCE BETWEEN THE TRUE VALUE
C                 OF THE DERIVATIVE AS COMPUTED BY THE
C                 LIBRARY FUNCTION EXP AND THE APPROXIMATION
C       ********************************************************
C
        X=1.
        TRUE=EXP(1.0)
        H=0.5
        B=EXP(X)
        DO WHILE(H.GT.1.E-8)
           APPROX=(EXP(X+H)-B)/H
           ERR=TRUE-APPROX
           WRITE(10,*)H,ERR
           H=H/2.0
        END DO
        STOP
        END
```

TABLE 1.4 Printout Showing Errors in Numerical Approximation of a Derivative

h	exp $(1) - D(h)$	
0.5000000	-0.8085327	
0.2500000	-0.3699627	
0.1250000	-0.1771994	
6.2500000E-02	-8.6745262E-02	Mathematical
3.1250000E-02	-4.2918205E-02	approximation too coarse
1.5625000E-02	-2.1357536E-02	(truncation error)
7.8125000E-03	-1.0661125E-02	
3.9062500E-03	-5.3510666E-03	
1.9531250E-03	-2.6655197E-03	
9.7656250E-04	-1.4448166E-03	
4.8828125E-04	-9.5653534E-04	
2.4414063E-04	-4.6825409E-04	
1.2207031E-04	-4.6825409E-04	
6.1035156E-05	-4.6825409E-04	
3.0517578E-05	-4.6825409E-04	
1.5258789E-05	-4.6825409E-04	Failure due to computer
7.6293945E-06	-4.6825409E-04	inaccuracies
3.8146973E-06	-3.1718254E-02	(roundoff error)
1.9073486E-06	-3.1718254E-02	
9.5367432E-07	-3.1718254E-02	
4.7683716E-07	-0.2817183	
2.3841858E-07	-0.2817183	
1.1920929E-07	-1.281718	
5.9604645E-08	-5.281718	
2.9802322E-08	2.718282	
1.4901161E-08	2.718282	

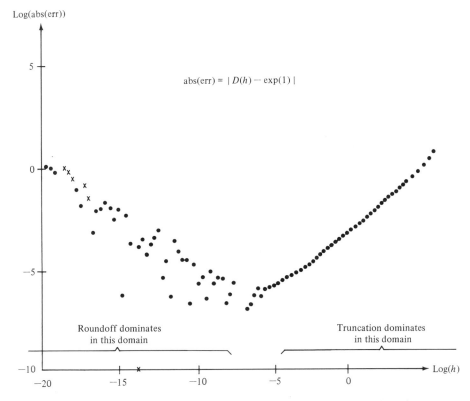

FIGURE 1.2   Error Versus Step Size in Derivative Approximation

graphed against step size h in Figure 1.2. (The scales are logarithmic and additional step values h were used.)

In view of the foregoing remarks, computers might seem to be unexpectedly limited instruments. But one should note that compared to human beings, computers can do those operations in Capability 2 very quickly. Therein lie the beauty and power of digital computation. But exploitation of this power ultimately requires that someone approximate more complicated operations [such as evaluating $\sin (x)$] by a sequence of arithmetical operations and comparisons.

1.2
CONCEPTS OF COMPUTATION ERROR

Toward surveying the ground to be covered in this book, let us sharpen some notions introduced informally in Section 1.1. We will view a *program* as a finite sequence of instructions involving only comparisons and arithmetic operations on stored numbers, and conditional branches from one place to another in the sequence of instructions. For a concrete example, think of FORTRAN. We disallow library functions such as $\sin (x)$ and $\exp (x)$ until Chapter 3, where their rationale is revealed. Also, input and output facilities are of little concern to us.

With this notion of "program" in mind, we summarize the concepts of roundoff and truncation errors:

ROUNDOFF ERROR.   The error introduced in approximating a given number by a computer number.

TRUNCATION ERROR.   The error introduced by approximating some ideal mathematical operation by computations directed by a program. It is presumed that computations are done without roundoff error.

The term *truncation error* stems from recognition that many numerical methods are constructed by first finding a Taylor's series representation $\sum_{j=0}^{\infty} a_j x^j$ of the mathematical operation, and then computing a truncation [i.e., an initial (polynomial) segment $\sum_{j=0}^{n} a_j x^j$] of this series. We will find that polynomial approximations and power series expansions lie behind a large proportion of the computational methods to be encountered. Analysis of truncation error is strongly dependent on the application area and computational methodology under consideration. Meaningful discussion must therefore await the special topics of later chapters.

Roundoff error has its origins in computer operations regardless of problem area. In this chapter we describe these origins and examine some frequently encountered settings in which its effects can be distressing if not confronted intelligently.

Roundoff error tends to become a bothersome and perhaps a limiting factor when at some point in a computation, small changes of an input parameter to a calculation result in relatively large deviations of the calculated output. Linear equations, the subject of Chapter 2, have the form

$$x_{i1}x_1 + a_{i2}x_2 + \cdots + a_{in}x_n = b_i, \qquad 1 \le i \le m,$$

and arise quite naturally from engineering considerations. In many cases linear equations have solutions that depend sharply on the coefficient values a_{ij}. For such equations, roundoff error often causes unacceptable computational inaccuracies.

Regardless of its source, error is usually quantified in two different but related ways. Let x denote an exact value and x^* its computer approximation. Then the absolute difference $|x - x^*|$ is known as the *absolute error*. In many cases, absolute error does not properly reflect its influence. For instance, an error of 0.01 m in measuring the distance to the moon would seem negligible, but it might be disastrous in designing a piston to fit into a cylinder of a car motor. In view of the effect of scale, the concept of *relative error*, that is, $|x - x^*|/|x|$, is helpful. In summary,

---

absolute error $= |\text{true value} - \text{approximation}|$

relative error $= \dfrac{\text{absolute error}}{|\text{true value}|}$

Any number $\delta(x^*)$ satisfying the inequality

$$\delta(x^*) \ge |x - x^*|$$

is called an *error bound*, or alternatively, an *absolute error bound* for the error of x^* as an approximation of x. Note that all numbers larger than $\delta(x^*)$ also serve as error bounds. Similarly, any number Rel (x^*) satisfying

$$\text{Rel } (x^*) \geq \frac{|x - x^*|}{|x|}$$

is called a *relative error bound*. If an absolute error bound is known, then we may select Rel $(x^*) = \delta(x^*)/|x|$. If $\delta(x^*)$ is a small number compared to $|x^*|$, then

$$\frac{\delta(x^*)}{|x^*|}$$

is a good approximation for Rel (x^*). This follows because

$$\frac{\delta(x^*)}{|x^*|} = \frac{\delta(x^*)}{|x|} \cdot \frac{|x|}{|x^*|}$$

$$= \frac{\delta(x^*)}{|x|} \cdot \frac{|x^* + x - x^*|}{|x^*|}$$

$$\leq \frac{\delta(x^*)}{|x|} \cdot \frac{|x^*| + |x - x^*|}{|x^*|}$$

$$\leq \frac{\delta(x^*)}{|x|} \cdot \left[1 + \frac{\delta(x^*)}{|x^*|} \right].$$

Under our assumption $\delta(x^*)/|x^*| \ll 1$. Hence the second term in the brackets is negligible, and

$$\frac{\delta(x^*)}{|x^*|} \approx \text{Rel } (x^*).$$

Let x denote any real number. We say that a k-digit approximation x^* of x is obtained by *rounding* if x^* is constructed as follows:

1. If the $(k + 1)$st significant digit of x is 4 or less, then all digits following that digit are replaced by zeros.
2. Otherwise, all digits following the kth are replaced by zeros and a one is added to the kth significant place.

For example, letting d_j, $j = 1, \ldots, 4$, denote digits, if $x = d_1d_2.d_3d_4$ is to be rounded to three places,

$$x^* = \begin{cases} d_1d_2.d_3 & \text{if } d_4 < 5 \\ d_1d_2.d_3 + 0.1 & \text{if } d_4 \geq 5. \end{cases}$$

The addition of 1 at the kth place will cause a change in other digits of x if that digit happened to be a 9. The examples below illustrate this construct.

EXAMPLE 1.3

Let $x = 123.476$. One rounds x to four significant figures by raising the fourth leading digit by 1 if the fifth digit is greater than 5. Here it is 7. Thus the rounded value of x is $x^* = 123.5$. If $x = 1.99$, then x rounded to two significant figures is 2.0. In rounding with 9's, more than one figure may need to be altered.

Let $\text{Round}_k(x)$ denote the number x^* obtained by rounding x to the kth digit. The definition of "rounding" implies that

$$|\text{Round}_k(x) - x| \leq 0.5 \cdot 10^{-k} \cdot 10^E,$$

where E is an integer satisfying

$$10^{E-1} \leq |x| < 10^E.$$

The concept of correct significant figures (or digits) is useful in specification of error. We say that the decimal representation of an approximation x^* of x has *k correct significant figures* if

$$\text{Round}_k(x^*) = \text{Round}_k(x).$$

EXAMPLE 1.4

Suppose that $x^* = 125.172$ is an approximation of x. If x^* is known to be correct to three significant figures, we know that $124.5 \leq x < 125.5$. In this case $\text{Round}_3(x) = 125.$ and $|x - 125.| \leq 0.5$. In this example, $k = 3$ and $E = 3$. If $x^* = 0.00231$ is correct to two significant figures, it must be that $0.00225 \leq x < 0.00235$. That is, in this case $\text{Round}_2(x) = 0.0023$ and $|x - 0.0023| \leq 0.5 \cdot 10^{-4}$. Here $k = 2$ and $E = -2$.

In the next section it will be seen that computers do rounding on inputted and computed numbers as an unavoidable consequence of their design. Roundoff error tends to become a bothersome and perhaps a limiting factor when at some point in a computation, small changes of an input parameter to a calculation result in relatively large deviations of the calculated output. Regardless of problem area, roundoff error limits the accuracy to which a solution can be computed. Assume that x^* and $x^* + \Delta$ are two successive computer numbers. Then any number x between x^* and $x^* + \Delta$ will be represented by either x^* or by $x^* + \Delta$. Thus, if the computer approximates x by the closest computer number, clearly we cannot count on being able to locate x more closely than $\Delta/2$. We have illustrated this

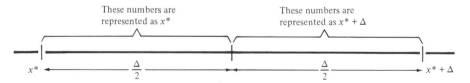

FIGURE 1.3 Illustration of Computer Roundoff

in Figure 1.3. In the next section it will be seen that the gap length Δ depends on x^* as well as on computer hardware and software.

　　Toward understanding the source and magnitude of roundoff error, we need to have a more detailed notion of how computers store numbers. This topic is considered next.

1.3
COMPUTER REPRESENTATION OF NUMBERS

1.3.1　Normal Forms and Computer Words

Computer representation of numbers is most readily introduced by use of normal form notation. If x is any real number, its *normal form* representation is

$$x = f \cdot 10^E \tag{1.1}$$

where for $x \neq 0$,

$$\frac{1}{10} \leq |f| < 1,$$

and E is an integer. For example,

$$125.32 = 0.12532 \cdot 10^3$$
$$-125.32 = -0.12532 \cdot 10^3$$
$$0.65 = 0.65 \cdot 10^0$$
$$-0.65 = -0.65 \cdot 10^0$$
$$0.0546 = 0.546 \cdot 10^{-1}$$
$$-0.0546 = -0.546 \cdot 10^{-1}.$$

The convention is that the number 0 has the normal form representation $0 \cdot 10^0$.

　　The number f of the normal form representation is termed the *mantissa* and E is the *exponent*. The mantissa, then, can be obtained by shifting the point in a decimal representation of x to the position just left of the first significant figure. Then let E denote how many positions the point had to be shifted. Shifts to the right are negative counts, and to the left, positive counts.

　　Now we tie this terminology to "computer representation." A *bit* (short for "BInary digiT") is a variable that takes on only two values, 0 or 1. A computer's memory is segmented into strings of bits, called *words*. Each such string has the same length, depending on computer construction. All information in the "fast" memory—program instructions, data, operating system commands, and so on— must somehow be encoded into computer words. The reason for words being based on bits has to do with hardware convenience. Bit-valued variables are easily stored by "flip-flop" circuits embedded into computer chips. However, for our purposes, there is little advantage to explaining computer words in terms of bits as opposed to digits. Thus for most of this book it is imagined that digits (i.e., values in the set $\{0, 1, \ldots , 9\}$) rather than bit values are stored in each location of a computer word.

d_1	d_2	d_3	d_4	d_5	d_6	d_7	d_8

FIGURE 1.4 A Word of Our Hypothetical Decimal Machine

We introduce here a hypothetical computer with words being strings of digits rather than bits. It is presumed that the length of each string is eight digits, as shown in Figure 1.4. We describe the major computer number representations—integer, floating point, and double precision—in terms of this decimal word, and at the close of this section, show how easy it is to construct a binary counterpart that exhibits the same properties and is an exact model of operations in real computers.

1.3.2 Integer Representation

The *signed-magnitude* integer representation encodes an integer by placing the decimal representation of the magnitude of that integer into the rightmost positions of the word, in their correct order. Zeros fill in the places to the left of the integer, up to the leading digit of the word. If the number is zero or positive, the leftmost digit (d_1) in Figure 1.4 is set to zero, and if the number represented is negative, $d_1 = 1$. Thus in the signed-magnitude representation, the only possible values for the leading "box" are 0 or 1.

─────── **EXAMPLE 1.5** ───────

In our machine, the number 1229 is encoded as

0	0	0	0	1	2	2	9

and -1229 is

1	0	0	0	1	2	2	9

∎

Of course, because of the specification of computer word as above, there are only a finite number (i.e., $2 \cdot 10^7 - 1$) of distinct computer integers. An integer greater than 9999999 or less than -9999999 must necessarily result in overflow or misrepresentation. If integer representation is used to approximate any real number, clearly the error need never be greater than 0.5, since the given number is rounded to the nearest integer. The distribution of signed-magnitude integers representable by our hypothetical decimal word is illustrated in Figure 1.5. As we see, they form a uniform grid in the interval $[-(10^7 - 1), 10^7 - 1]$.

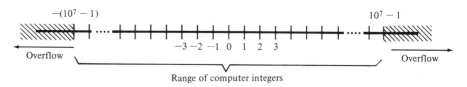

FIGURE 1.5 Distribution of Computer Integers

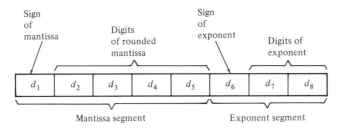

FIGURE 1.6 Computer Storage of a Floating-Point Number

In practice, a slightly more complicated method than signed magnitude is used for representing negative integers. Problems 6 and 7 outline the idea.

1.3.3 Floating-Point Representation

In *floating-point representation*, part of the computer word is blocked off to encode the mantissa, and part of it represents the exponent. The leading digit gives the sign of the number, as before. For our machine, we presume the pattern is as shown in Figure 1.6. Presume that the number x has been represented in normal form [as in equation (1.1)],

$$x = f \cdot 10^E.$$

The exponent E is encoded in signed-magnitude fashion in the positions d_6, d_7, and d_8, as indicated. That is, $d_6 = 0$ if the exponent is zero or positive and is 1 if the exponent is negative. After rounding f to four significant digits, these digits are stored in positions d_2, d_3, d_4, and d_5, in order of decreasing significance. As with computer integers, $d_1 = 0$ implies that the number is "zero" or "positive," and $d_1 = 1$ means "negative."

――― **EXAMPLE 1.6** ―――――――――――――――――――――

Let $x = 125.32$. Then

$$x = 0.12532 \cdot 10^{+3} = f \cdot 10^E.$$

Then f, rounded to four places, is 0.1253 and the floating-point representation is

0	1	2	5	3	0	0	3

The number $x = -0.0325475$ is, in normal form,

$$x = (-0.325475) \cdot 10^{-1}.$$

Rounded to four significant places, the mantissa becomes -0.3255 and the floating-point word for x, then, is

1	3	2	5	5	1	0	1

■

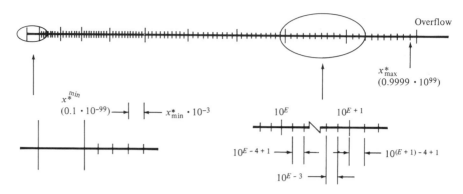

FIGURE 1.7   Distribution of Nonnegative Floating-Point Numbers

In Figure 1.7 we have illustrated the placement of our floating-point numbers on the positive real line. It is a characteristic that they are more densely placed near the origin and more sparse near the extremes of their range. Regardless of the magnitude of the number x, its floating-point approximation always preserves the first four significant figures. The distance between successive floating-point numbers is 10^{E-4}, E being the value of the normal form exponent. Numbers with small magnitudes have small E values, and large numbers imply large E values and thus larger gaps between successive machine numbers. By encoding the rounded value of the mantissa, we assure that we approximate any number x by its closest machine number, x^*; this will be at most half the larger distance of δ_1 and δ_2 between the two machine numbers closest to x. We illustrate the situation in Figure 1.8 when $\delta_1 = \delta_2 = \delta$.

Thus, when $\delta_1 = \delta_2 = \delta$, we can bound the error of floating-point approximation by

$$\delta(x^*) = \tfrac{1}{2} \cdot 10^{E-4}.$$

Since by definition of normal form (1.1),

$$|x| \geq \tfrac{1}{10} \cdot 10^{E} = 10^{E-1},$$

we conclude that the relative error in floating-point approximation of x satisfies

$$\text{Rel}\,(x^*) \leq \frac{\delta(x^*)}{|x|} \leq \frac{\tfrac{1}{2} \cdot 10^{E-4}}{10^{E-1}} = \varepsilon, \qquad \text{where } \varepsilon = \tfrac{1}{2} \cdot 10^{-3}.$$

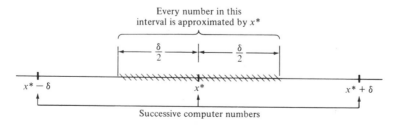

FIGURE 1.8   Computer Number Approximation

This value above is termed *machine epsilon*. Machine epsilon is a bound to the relative error of floating-point approximation. The designation "machine" reminds us that the value is machine dependent. For a more general decimal machine, with s being the number of significant digits in the rounded mantissa, the definition of machine epsilon generalizes to

$$\text{machine epsilon} = \varepsilon = \tfrac{1}{2} \cdot 10^{-s+1}. \qquad (1.2)$$

Equation (1.2) is important; data presented to a computer may not be remembered more accurately than (1.2) suggests. After each step of any numerical computation, intermediate values must be stored; They cannot be relied on to have less relative error than ε. Intuitively, $1 + \varepsilon$ is the smallest number greater than 1 that the computer in question will distinguish from 1. More generally, $|x| \cdot \varepsilon$ is a good estimate of the absolute error bound of the computer number that represents x.

It is good practice to design programs that are "portable" in the sense that their performance does not depend on which computer is being used. We will see in Table 1.6 that the length s of the mantissa, and hence machine epsilon, can vary widely. Therefore, it is often advisable to include in a program a code that automatically estimates machine epsilon. In Table 1.5, subroutine EPS for computing machine epsilon is offered. Certain subroutines will require the user to supply a "stopping rule" threshold. The choice of such a value should be based on an estimate of machine epsilon.

───── **EXAMPLE 1.7** ─────

Machine epsilon of the VAX computer was obtained by means of subroutine EPS. To three significant decimal places, the output was $5.96 \cdot 10^{-8}$. This number was actually 2^{-24}, which seems contradictory to the entry $s = 23$ in Table 1.6 for this machine. It will be explained later that the VAX effectively gets an extra bit of storage in the mantissa by using the fact that the leading bit of a binary normal form representation is always 1.

TABLE 1.5 Subroutine EPS for Finding Machine Epsilon

```
      SUBROUTINE EPS(E)
C
C  ***************************************************************
C  *   FUNCTION: THIS SUBROUTINE COMPUTES THE MACHINE EPSILON   *
C  *   USAGE:                                                   *
C  *        CALL SEQUENCE: CALL EPS(E)                          *
C  *   PARAMETERS:                                              *
C  *        INPUT:                                              *
C  *             NONE                                           *
C  *        OUTPUT:                                             *
C  *             E=MACHINE EPSILON                              *
C  ***************************************************************
C
      E=1.0
      DO WHILE(E+1.0.GT.1.0)
         E=E/2.0
      END DO
      E=2.0*E
      RETURN
      END
```

With regard to the experiment described in Example 1.1, examination of the output Table 1.2 reveals that the observed roundoff error in the number actually stored for input $x = 0.1234567890123$ was $2.03 \cdot 10^{-9}$. By the considerations in this section this error should be less than $\varepsilon \cdot |x| \approx 7.36 \cdot 10^{-9}$. Thus machine epsilon did lead to a reasonably close upper bound for the observed roundoff error.

In examining Figure 1.7, the reader will notice a gap from the origin to x_{min}^*. This reflects the fact that smallest positive floating-point number is $0.1000 \cdot 10^{-99}$ (we call it x_{min}^*) and the next larger number is $0.1001 \cdot 10^{-99}$. Thus x_{min}^* is 1000 times larger than the gap to the next number.

In comparing the error properties of integer representation with those of floating point, we conclude that integers preserve absolute error bound in the sense that the absolute error is never greater than 0.5, no matter what the number, and floating point preserves the relative error bound, namely machine epsilon. For most numerical purposes, relative error, or equivalently, the number of correct significant figures, is the more valuable criterion.

In *double-precision* representation, two or more computer words are used to represent a single floating-point number. Usually, the second word is devoted entirely to storing mantissa digits. Thus one can count on double-precision numbers of any given computer to have at least twice as many significant figures as single-precision floating-point representation. Our idealized eight-digit word computer stores values in double precision as shown in Figure 1.9. Here, 16, rather than 8, digits are available for storage, and we have allotted the extra digits to the mantissa. Consequently, 12, rather than 4, leading mantissa digits are stored.

1.3.4 Binary Computers and Their Number Representation

Our preceding discussions have been based on decimal computer words, whereas in fact, actual computer words use binary storage. Thus the contents of each box in an idealized word as in Figure 1.4 is restricted to 0 or 1, instead of 0 through 9. In Table 1.6 we have presented binary word lengths of some of the better-known computers. Notice that the word lengths vary from computer to computer. Most of them are much longer than our idealized eight-digit decimal word. But it takes over three bits (binary digits) to give the same information as that in one (decimal) digit since $10 > 2^3$.

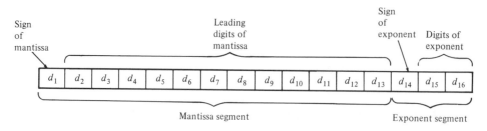

FIGURE 1.9   Computer Storage of Floating Point Number in Double Precision

TABLE 1.6 Floating-Point Characteristics of Some Computers

Computer	Word Length	Single Precision		Double Precision	
	l	s	e	s	e
Control Data Corporation	60	48	11	96	11
CDC 6000, 7000, and CYBER series					
IBM Corporation					
IBM 360/370 series and 303X and	32	24	7	56	7
308X series					
IBM PC,[a] AT, and XT	16	24	7	56	7
Digital Equipment Corporation					
DEC-10	36	27	8	63	8
PDP-11 series[a]	16	23	8	55	8
VAX-11 series	32	23	8	55	8
Prime computers	32	23	8	47	15
AT&T 3B Series	32	23	8	55	8

[a]Uses two computer words for a single-precision floating-point number.

For most practical purposes, it makes little difference to the user that the machine is actually binary instead of decimal. The binary integers and floating-point representations have the same rationale as their decimal counterparts.

The analysis surrounding equation (1.2) for determining machine epsilon carries over to binary floating-point words. The modification is that base 2 is substituted for base 10 in (1.2), so for binary machines with a mantissa length of s bits,

$$\text{machine epsilon} = 2^{-s} \qquad (1.3)$$

[In transcribing (1.2) to obtain this formula, we used the fact that $\frac{1}{2} \cdot 2^{-s+1} = 2^{-s}$.]

We close this discussion with mention of some fine points. Almost all computers use the "two's-complement technique" (described, for example, in Knuth, 1969, p. 170), rather than signed magnitude, to represent negative integers. Also, they use a variation of the plan we described for representation of the exponent E of floating-point numbers. Problems 8 through 14 are intended to give the reader further introduction to arithmetic in binary and other bases, and supplement this discussion with particulars of actual computer operation. These differences should not have a bearing on the computer user. One thing that might have relevance is that the VAX computer as well as some others make use of the observation that the leading bit of the mantissa of a nonzero floating-point number must always be 1, and therefore need not be remembered. Thus the VAX effectively represents $s + 1$ significant bits from a mantissa storage area of s bits. This property has been illustrated in Example 1.7.

In Table 1.6 we tabulated the word length l and the numbers s and e of bits assigned to the mantissa and the exponent, respectively, and those of floating-point double precision in various computers. IBM PCs allow s and e to be determined by the compiler. Our values refer to Microsoft FORTRAN.

1.4
EFFECTS OF ROUNDOFF ERROR

1.4.1 Computer Arithmetic and Roundoff

Provided that no overflow occurs, addition, subtraction, and multiplication of integer variables are done without error. Integer division is also done perfectly if the remainder is zero (i.e., assuming that the denominator exactly divides the numerator). Otherwise, error can be anticipated, since the result of the operation is not itself an integer. In FORTRAN, the result is taken to be the integer part of the quotient.

In floating-point arithmetic, it is correct to suppose that given any two floating-point variables, the arithmetical operation is performed perfectly, and then the result is rounded, as necessary, so that the result fits into a floating-point computer word. The floating-point variables to which the operations are applied have limited precision, and as we will explain, subtraction can therefore lead to large relative error.

───── **EXAMPLE 1.8** ───

Addition with our hypothetical eight-digit floating-point word would result in the following calculations (FP = "floating point"):

$$
\begin{array}{ll}
 & 0.1685 \cdot 10^2 \\
+ & 0.3210 \cdot 10^2 \\
\hline
\text{Perfect answer} \quad & 0.4895 \cdot 10^2 \\
\text{FP answer} \quad & 0.4895 \cdot 10^2
\end{array}
\qquad
\begin{array}{ll}
 & 0.6342 \cdot 10^2 \\
+ & 0.4964 \cdot 10^2 \\
\hline
\text{Perfect answer} \quad & 1.1306 \cdot 10^2 \\
\text{FP answer} \quad & 0.1131 \cdot 10^3
\end{array}
$$

Note that in the second case, some roundoff error results. Similarly, some examples of multiplication are:

$$
\begin{array}{ll}
 & 0.2500 \cdot 10^4 \\
\times & 0.5000 \cdot 10^2 \\
\hline
\text{Perfect answer} \quad & 0.1250 \cdot 10^6 \\
\text{FP answer} \quad & 0.1250 \cdot 10^6
\end{array}
\qquad
\begin{array}{ll}
 & 0.2534 \cdot 10^4 \\
\times & 0.1657 \cdot 10^2 \\
\hline
\text{Perfect answer} \quad & 0.4198838 \cdot 10^5 \\
\text{FP answer} \quad & 0.4199 \cdot 10^5
\end{array}
$$

And here is a division calculation:

$$
\begin{array}{ll}
 & 0.2346 \cdot 10^2 \\
\div & 0.5678 \cdot 10^1 \\
\hline
\text{Perfect answer} \quad & 0.4131736 \ldots \cdot 10^1 \\
\text{FP answer} \quad & 0.4132 \cdot 10^1
\end{array}
$$

Similarly, by the principle of perfect arithmetic and then floating-point rounding, an example of floating-point subtraction is as follows:

$$
\begin{array}{ll}
 & 0.1234 \cdot 10^3 \\
- & 0.7231 \cdot 10^0 \\
\hline
\text{Perfect answer} \quad & 0.1226769 \cdot 10^3 \\
\text{FP answer} \quad & 0.1227 \cdot 10^3
\end{array}
$$

But floating-point subtraction can induce a special phenomenon: It is possible that under perfect arithmetic on floating-point variables, some mantissa positions are left unspecified. These are filled by arbitrary digits having no relation to the data given. The manner in which "missing" digits are supplied depends on computer design and software. For example:

$$
\begin{array}{r}
0.1234 \cdot 10^0 \\
- \; 0.1233 \cdot 10^0 \\
\hline
0.0001 \cdot 10^0
\end{array}
$$

Perfect answer $0.0001 \cdot 10^0$

FP answer $0.1ddd \cdot 10^{-3}$

Here the d's indicate arbitrary digits. Because of this filling, the relative error of subtraction can be arbitrarily large. This phenomenon occurs if two nearly equal numbers are subtracted. Such *subtractive cancellation* is to be avoided if at all possible. ∎

EXAMPLE 1.9

We performed a simple calculation on an IBM PC in the BASIC mode. According to the machine,

$$0.1234567 - 0.1234566 = 0.1043081 \cdot 10^{-6},$$

whereas the correct difference is, of course, $0.1 \cdot 10^{-6}$. ∎

To summarize the situation, roughly speaking, significant figures are preserved in addition (of numbers of like sign), multiplication, and division, but subtraction of nearby numbers can result in serious loss of precision, and without any warning from the computer.

1.4.2 Roundoff Error in Action

Here we present two examples illustrating common situations in which a computed solution is needlessly inaccurate as a result of roundoff error. These examples show further that mathematical and computational reasoning can be beneficial. For in each instance, once we see the origin of the problem, we are able to devise a more cunning computational strategy and thereby achieve an accurate answer. The ultimate source of difficulty in these examples is clearly roundoff error. Were computers able to store and operate on real numbers, rather than floating-point approximations, these difficulties would not arise. A moral is that when computational error occurs, it can often be circumvented by thinking about the particulars of the problem.

EXAMPLE 1.10

We here examine a common "trapdoor" known as *subtractive cancellation*. In Section 1.4.1 we have seen that this arises when two nearly equal floating-point numbers are subtracted from one another.

For convenience of notation, assume that we have a machine with decimal words of mantissa length $s = 4$, as in the case of our hypothetical decimal computer. Suppose that we are to estimate the difference of square roots of two given integers

$$y = \sqrt{1985} - \sqrt{1984}$$

and we are given the rounded approximations

$$\sqrt{1985} \approx 0.4455 \cdot 10^2$$
$$\sqrt{1984} \approx 0.4454 \cdot 10^2.$$

Then blind subtraction would have us estimate y by

$$y^* = 0.4455 \cdot 10^2 - 0.4454 \cdot 10^2 = 0.1 \cdot 10^{-1} = 0.01.$$

The correct answer to the accuracy shown is 0.011224. Could we have done better with the given approximations? Yes! The basic trouble is that the definition of y has us subtract two very nearly equal numbers, and the only information about their difference resides in their unequal digits, which in this case is only the last digit. There are several paths that bypass this subtractive cancellation problem. One way is as follows. Recall from algebra that

$$\sqrt{A} - \sqrt{B} = \frac{A - B}{\sqrt{A} + \sqrt{B}}. \tag{1.4}$$

Here we presume that A and B are exact, so no cancellation occurs in the numerator of (1.4), and the denominator retains nearly four significant digits of accuracy. Specifically, by use of the right side of (1.4), we compute the new estimate

$$y^{**} = \frac{1}{0.4455 \cdot 10^2 + 0.4454 \cdot 10^2} = \frac{1}{0.8909 \cdot 10^2} = 0.1122 \cdot 10^{-1}.$$

Here the answer resulting from using the rounded values is exact, up to the accuracy of number representation in our hypothetical computer. ∎

EXAMPLE 1.11

This example is due to Henrici (1982). From Taylor's series developments in calculus books (and as we learn in Chapter 3), it is known that

$$e^x \approx S(x) = 1 + \frac{x}{1!} + \frac{x^2}{2!} + \cdots + \frac{x^n}{n!}. \tag{1.5}$$

The error of this approximation does not exceed

$$\frac{|x|^{n+1}}{(n+1)!} \max \{1, e^x\}.$$

Recall that

$$(n + 1)! = (n + 1) \cdot n \cdot (n - 1) \cdot \ldots \cdot 2 \cdot 1.$$

A sensible computational procedure would seem to be to sum terms $x^j/j!$ until the magnitude of the addends is less than machine epsilon. The program listed in Table 1.7 follows this strategy and on a VAX, computes an approximation, which we denote by $S(-8)$, of e^{-8} to be $0.319328 \cdot 10^{-3}$. The correct value, to the accuracy shown, is $0.3354626 \cdot 10^{-3}$.

The error of the estimate $S(-8)$ is $1.6 \cdot 10^{-5}$, and the answer is correct only in the first significant digit. In our calculation, n turned out to be 36. The approximation bound is $|-8|^{37}/37! \approx 2 \cdot 10^{-10}$, so truncation was not the source of this error. The fundamental trouble is that whereas the magnitude of the final sum is relatively small, as shown in Table 1.8, several of the terms $(-8)^j/j!$ are large, and these large terms, while eventually canceling, determine the number of significant places. Henrici (1982) has termed this phenomenon *smearing*. Smearing can be anticipated whenever magnitudes of individual terms in a summation are considerably larger than the sum itself. Since the error in a stored number x is in the neighborhood of $\varepsilon|x|$, in the notation of (1.2), the error in computing a sum is typically at least as large as ε times the magnitude of the largest addend. If the sum itself is much smaller than the largest addend, smearing will almost surely occur, as in this example. The moral: Beware of summing a series with mixed signs.

For the particular case of evaluating exp (-8), smearing can be sidestepped by observing that for $x = -1$, for instance, the largest addends have the same order of magnitude as the sum. Thus the procedure in Table 1.7 should be accurate

TABLE 1.7   Program for Approximation of Exponential Function

```
C       PROGRAM TAYEXP
C
C       ***********************************************************
C       COMPUTE THE TAYLOR SERIES APPROXIMATION OF EXP(X), (X=-8.)
C       OUTPUT: S=THE TAYLOR SERIES APPROXIMATION
C                   TRUE=THE VALUE OF EXP(X) AS COMPUTED BY THE
C                       LIBRARY FUNCTION EXP
C                   ERR=THE DIFFERENCE BETWEEN THE TRUE VALUE
C                       AND THE TAYLOR SERIES APPROXIMATION
C       ***********************************************************
C
        S=0.
        A=1.
        X=-8.
        J=0
C
C       *** THIS LOOP WILL COMPUTE THE TAYLOR SERIES APPROX.    ***
C       *** UNTIL ADDEND IS NEAR MACHINE EPS                   ***
C
        DO WHILE(ABS(A).GT.1.E-9)
          S=S+A
          A=A*(X/(J+1))
          J=J+1
        END DO
        TRUE=EXP(X)
        ERR=TRUE-S
        WRITE(10,*)S,TRUE,ERR
        STOP
        END
```

TABLE 1.8   Addends in Series for exp (-8)

j	$\dfrac{(-8)^j}{j!}$
0	1.000000
1	-8.000000
2	32.00000
3	-85.33334
4	170.6667
5	-273.0667
6	364.0889
7	-416.1017
8	416.1017
9	-369.8681
10	295.8945
11	-215.1960
12	143.4640
13	-88.28555
14	50.44889
15	-26.90608
16	13.45304
17	-6.330842
18	2.813707
19	-1.184719
20	0.4738875
21	-0.1805286

for finding an approximation $S(-1)$ of e^{-1}. In fact, with $x = -1.0$ the program in Table 1.7 computes the estimate 0.36787945, which is correct in all but the last decimal place. Then, since $e^{-8} = (e^{-1})^8$, one may offer $S(-1)^8$ as an estimate. The error in following this tactic is only about $2 \cdot 10^{-9}$, whereas direct use of the algorithm resulted in an error of $1.6 \cdot 10^{-5}$. Thus by this alternative computation plan, which avoids subtractive cancellation, we have gained six significant figures in our approximation.

1.5
ERROR PROPAGATION

The goal of the preceding portions of this chapter is to show how and why computer number representation inevitably induces error. In the remaining sections we investigate how error passes through various stages of computation and influences the final output. We follow the customary path in such investigations of seeing how slight inaccuracies (or *perturbations*, as they are often termed) in the input of an operation influence the output. This sort of study is common in engineering and is useful, regardless of whether the source of error is in roundoff, measurement error, or some other contamination. In fact, such perturbation study (or *sensitivity analysis*, as it is called) is useful even in cases when roundoff error is insignificant but data error is present. By the example below, we hope to orient the reader to this activity.

Application 1.1

Here we illustrate the effects of slight inaccuracies, which are essentially unavoidable. They stem from roundoff and from inexact input due to measurement error.

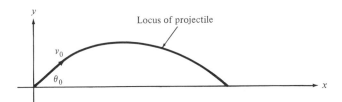

FIGURE 1.10   Trajectory of a Projectile

We will find that computation necessarily adds to the error, and that through systematic error analysis, the error can be anticipated and bounded.

   This example is motivated by ballistics. Ballistics, the theory for projectiles (usually cannon shells), has a position of great significance in the history of computing. For instance, the first digital computer was built at the University of Pennsylvania under contract with the U.S. Army and essentially, its only capability was to solve ballistics equations. [See Metropolis et al. (1980) for elaboration and for other points of historical interest.]

   From Newtonian mechanics, as a first approximation and neglecting air resistance, the height $y = y(x)$ of a projectile, as a function of the distance x traveled, is determined by

$$y(x) = \tan(\theta_0) \cdot x - \frac{g}{2[v_0 \cos(\theta_0)]^2} \cdot x^2. \tag{1.6}$$

Here v_0 is the initial velocity and θ_0 is the angle of the initial slope. The setting is illustrated in Figure 1.10. Assume that nominal values of these quantities are: $\theta_0 = \pi/4$, $v_0 = 400$ m/s, and $g = 9.81$ m/s². (At this velocity, neglecting air resistance is a crude approximation, which will be corrected in later example.)

   With these values, at the position of 10,000 m, the height as determined by (1.6) is

$$y(10{,}000) = 10{,}000 - \frac{9.81}{2(400 \cdot 0.7071)^2} \cdot 10{,}000^2 = 3868.75 \text{ m.}$$

What happens if some of the parameters are in error? As a first cut at examining this issue, we decrease each of the values, separately, by 1%, and recalculate the corresponding value of y. The results of this study are tabulated in Table 1.9.

TABLE 1.9   Deviations in Height Due to Parameter Perturbations

Variable Changed	Changed to:	Change in Percent	New y Value	Change in y Value	
θ_0	0.7775	−1%	3807.71	−61.04	−1.6%
v_0	396	−1%	3744.26	−124.49	−3.2%

We see that the more influential change was that of the initial velocity v_0.

A trial-and-error experiment such as Application 1.1 leaves many issues unresolved. What happens if error occurs simultaneously among several parameters? Can we sidestep the task of recomputing the height for each possible perturbation? From developments to follow, we will see that we can answer these questions elegantly. Whereas computers really had nothing to do with this particular problem, since every stage of computation potentially adds to propagated error, sensitivity to error is a fundamental issue in numerical computations. Thus the section to follow is of broad importance.

1.5.1 Propagation of Error in a Single Computation

We now derive upper bounds for the errors that result from computing functional values using inexact data. Assume that x^* is an approximation of x. If the functional value $f(x)$ is desired, and only the approximating value x^* of x is known, we approximate $f(x)$ by $f(x^*)$. Here we assume that $f(x^*)$ can be computed exactly. Assume that $\delta(x^*)$ is an absolute error bound for $|x - x^*|$ and that the function $f(x)$ is differentiable. Then the mean-value theorem of calculus (Appendix B, property 19) implies that

$$f(x) - f(x^*) = f'(\zeta)(x - x^*), \tag{1.7}$$

where ζ is some number in the interval with endpoints x and x^* and $f'(\zeta)$ is the derivative of $f(x)$ at ζ. Since the value of ζ is unknown, equation (1.7) cannot be used directly. To obtain practical formulas, we have to make further assumptions about function f.

Assume first that for arbitrary t between x^* and x, and for some fixed number D,

$$|f'(t)| \leq D.$$

Then (1.7) implies that

$$|f(x) - f(x^*)| = |f'(\zeta)| \cdot |x - x^*| \leq D\,\delta(x^*);$$

consequently, the quantity $D\,\delta(x^*)$ can be accepted as an error bound for $f(x^*)$. That is, for the interval I containing all points between x^* and x,

$$\delta(f(x^*)) = \max_{t \in I} |f'(t)|\,\delta(x^*). \tag{1.8}$$

This error bound has the disadvantage that an upper bound for the derivative $f'(x)$ of $f(x)$ must be determined. This is sometimes a difficult task.

Assume next that $\delta(x^*)$ is small, $f'(x^*) \neq 0$, and $f'(t)$ is nearly constant near x^*. Then $D \approx |f'(x^*)|$. Consequently,

$$\boxed{\delta(f(x^*)) \approx |f'(x^*)|\,\delta(x^*).} \tag{1.9}$$

Figure 1.11 illustrates the error-bound construct (1.9).

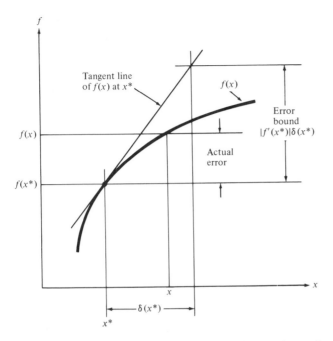

FIGURE 1.11   Error Bound for Operation of Inexact Data

EXAMPLE 1.12

Let $f(x) = \sqrt{x}$ and assume that x^* is an approximation of x with an error bounded by $\delta(x^*)$. Then (1.9) implies that

$$\delta(\sqrt{x^*}) \approx \frac{1}{2\sqrt{x^*}}\, \delta(x^*).$$

If, for example, $x^* = 4.00$ and $\delta(x^*) = 0.005$, then

$$\delta(\sqrt{4.00}) \approx \frac{1}{2\sqrt{4.00}} \times 0.005 = 0.00125.$$

In fact, if $x = x^* - \delta(x^*) = 3.995$, then

$$\sqrt{x} - \sqrt{x^*} = -0.0012504.$$

In this case, the approximation (1.9) does give an accurate error estimate. ∎

Application 1.2

In Application 1.1 we related a model for the trajectory of a projectile fired at an angle θ_0 and with initial velocity v_0. We related that the height $y(x)$ at a given range x is

$$y(x) = \tan(\theta_0) \cdot x - \frac{g}{2[v_0 \cos(\theta_0)]^2} \cdot x^2,$$

and we took interest in the height at $x = 10,000$ m when the nominal values of the angle and velocity were, respectively, $\pi/4$ and 400 m/s. In that example, from ballistics theory, we found deviations in height resulting from perturbations in these parameters. Armed with our sensitivity formula (1.9), we can pose analytic formulas for the height deviations:

$$\delta(y^*) = \left| \frac{x}{\cos^2(\theta_0)} - \frac{g \cdot 2 \cdot \cos(\theta_0) \cdot \sin(\theta_0)}{2 \cdot v_0^2 \cdot \cos^4(\theta_0)} \cdot x^2 \right| \cdot \delta(\theta_0^*). \quad (1.10)$$

Here the application of (1.9) needs explanation. Function y plays the role of f, but the perturbation is with respect to angle θ_0, not x. Thus θ_0 plays the role of x, and the error bound is given by

$$\delta(y^*) = \left| \frac{\partial y}{\partial \theta_0} \right| \delta(\theta_0^*).$$

Differentiating the right-hand side of (1.6) with respect to θ_0, we have the expression (1.10). The experimental perturbation in Application 1.1 was $\delta(\theta_0^*) = 0.00785$ and the deviation observed was -61.04. When the nominal parameters are substituted into (1.10), we calculate that

$$\delta(y^*) = 60.72(\text{m}),$$

so we see that the magnitudes agree well. In summary:

Magnitude of Experimental Deviation	Theoretical Deviation
61.04	60.72

The sensitivity of height to initial velocity is similarly calculated to be

$$\delta(y^*) \approx \left| \frac{g \cdot 2v_0 \cdot x^2}{2 \cos^2(\theta_0) \cdot v_0^4} \right| \cdot \delta(v_0^*),$$

and when the nominal parameters are substituted, we find that

$$\delta(y^*) \approx 122.63 \text{ (m)}$$

and recall that the magnitude of the experimental deviation was 124.49.

The gist of the situation is that for small to midrange errors, the sensitivity formula (1.9) does, in this case, give a very accurate prediction of the error in the output.

◇

Error bounds for functions of two or more variables can also be obtained by the approach described above. Consider a real-valued function $f(x, y)$ of two variables x and y. Assume that the "true" values x and y are unknowns but their approximations, x^* and y^* are given. Then the desired value $f(x, y)$ is approximated by $f(x^*, y^*)$. Assume again that f is differentiable, the error bounds $\delta(x^*)$ and $\delta(y^*)$ are small, and the first partial derivatives are not both zero and change slowly. (Partial derivatives are defined in Section 4 of Appendix B.) Then

$$f(x, y) - f(x^*, y^*) = f(x, y) - f(x^*, y) + f(x^*, y) - f(x^*, y^*).$$

Consequently, relation (1.9) implies that

$$|f(x, y) - f(x^*, y^*)| \leq |f(x, y) - f(x^*, y)| + |f(x^*, y) - f(x^*, y^*)|$$

$$\approx \left|\frac{\partial f}{\partial x}(x^*, y)\right| \cdot |x - x^*| + \left|\frac{\partial f}{\partial y}(x^*, y^*)\right| \cdot |y - y^*|$$

$$\approx \left|\frac{\partial f}{\partial x}(x^*, y^*)\right| \cdot |x - x^*| + \left|\frac{\partial f}{\partial y}(x^*, y^*)\right| \cdot |y - y^*|$$

$$\leq \left|\frac{\partial f}{\partial x}(x^*, y^*)\right| \cdot \delta(x^*) + \left|\frac{\partial f}{\partial y}(x^*, y^*)\right| \cdot \delta(y^*).$$

Hence analogously to (1.9),

$$\delta(f(x^*, y^*)) \approx \left|\frac{\partial f}{\partial x}(x^*, y^*)\right| \delta(x^*) + \left|\frac{\partial f}{\partial y}(x^*, y^*)\right| \delta(y^*). \qquad (1.11)$$

Generalization of this approach to more variables should be evident. If x_i^* is an estimate of x_i, $1 \leq i \leq n$, and $\delta(x_i^*)$ denotes a bound for $|x_i - x_i^*|$, $1 \leq i \leq n$, and if the first-order partial derivatives are not zero and change slowly, then with $x^* = (x_1^*, \ldots, x_n^*)$, we have

$$\boxed{\begin{aligned} \delta(f(x_1^*, \ldots, x_n^*)) &\approx \left|\frac{\partial f(x^*)}{\partial x_1}\right| \delta(x_1^*) + \left|\frac{\partial f(x^*)}{\partial x_2}\right| \delta(x_2^*) \\ &+ \cdots + \left|\frac{\partial f(x^*)}{\partial x_n}\right| \delta(x_n^*). \end{aligned}} \qquad (1.12)$$

This expression answers a question raised earlier about the effects of perturbing several variables at once. It is also the foundation for the analysis of error propagation in arithmetic, which follows.

1.5.2   Error Propagation in Arithmetic

Recall an observation stated many times now: A computer can only do arithmetic. Thus a particularly important type of error accumulation is propagation through a sequence of arithmetic operations. Bounds for error in arithmetic can be derived from the general rule (1.12), as the following example illustrates.

EXAMPLE 1.13

Assume that $f(x, y) = x + y$. Then

$$\frac{\partial}{\partial x} f(x^*, y^*) = \frac{\partial}{\partial y} f(x^*, y^*) = 1,$$

so, by (1.12),

$$\delta(f(x^*, y^*)) = \delta(x^* + y^*) = 1 \times \delta(x^*) + 1 \times \delta(y^*) = \delta(x^*) + \delta(y^*).$$

In addition, then, the error bounds are added.
  Assume next that $f(x, y) = x - y$. Then

$$\delta(f(x^*, y^*)) = \delta(x^* - y^*) = 1 \times \delta(x^*) + 1 \times \delta(y^*) = \delta(x^*) + \delta(y^*).$$

Hence in subtraction the error bounds also add.
  If we define $f(x, y) = xy$, then

$$\delta(f(x^*, y^*)) = \delta(x^*y^*) \approx |y^*| \, \delta(x^*) + |x^*| \, \delta(y^*),$$

and if $f(x, y) = x/y$, then

$$\delta(f(x^*, y^*)) = \delta\left(\frac{x^*}{y^*}\right) \approx \frac{1}{|y^*|} \delta(x^*) + \frac{|x^*|}{|y^*|^2} \delta(y^*) = \frac{|y^*| \, \delta(x^*) + |x^*| \, \delta(y^*)}{|y^*|^2}.$$

EXAMPLE 1.14

Consider the function

$$f(x, y, z) = xy + z,$$

where

$$x \approx x^* = 2.20, \qquad \delta(x^*) = 0.005$$
$$y \approx y^* = 1.15, \qquad \delta(y^*) = 0.005$$
$$z \approx z^* = 3.05, \qquad \delta(z^*) = 0.005.$$

Then repeated application of the developments above gives that

$$\delta(x^*y^*) \approx |1.15| \times 0.005 + |2.20| \times 0.005 = 0.01675$$

and therefore

$$\delta(x^*y^* + z^*) \approx \delta(x^*y^*) + \delta(z^*) = 0.02175.$$

  In Tables 1.10 and 1.11 we collect the absolute and relative error bounds induced by performing arithmetic on approximating data.

TABLE 1.10   Absolute Error Bounds for Arithmetic Operations on Inexact Data

$$\delta(x^* + y^*) = \delta(x^*) + \delta(y^*)$$

$$\delta(x^* - y^*) = \delta(x^*) + \delta(y^*)$$

$$\delta(x^*y^*) \approx |x^*| \, \delta(y^*) + |y^*| \, \delta(x^*)$$

$$\delta\left(\frac{x^*}{y^*}\right) \approx \frac{|x^*| \, \delta(y^*) + |y^*| \, \delta(x^*)}{|y^*|^2}$$

———— **EXAMPLE 1.15** ————

We derive the entry in Table 1.11 for Rel $(x^* + y^*)$, with x and y having the same sign:

$$\text{Rel } (x^* + y^*) = \frac{\delta(x^*) + \delta(y^*)}{|x + y|}.$$

Suppose, by exchanging labels if necessary, that

$$\frac{\delta(x^*)}{|x|} = \text{Rel } (x^*) \geq \text{Rel } (y^*) = \frac{\delta(y^*)}{|y|}.$$

Then $\delta(x^*)|y| \geq \delta(y^*)|x|$ and

$$\delta(x^*)|x + y| = \delta(x^*)(|x| + |y|) \geq |x|(\delta(x^*) + \delta(y^*)),$$

which gives the relation

$$\frac{\delta(x^*)}{|x|} \geq \frac{\delta(x^*) + \delta(y^*)}{|x + y|}$$

or

$$\text{Rel } (x^*) \geq \text{Rel } (x^* + y^*).$$

The expression for Rel $(x^* - y^*)$ in Table 1.11 deserves special note. If $x \approx y$, then the denominator is very small, and thus Rel $(x^* - y^*)$ can be very large, even when the absolute and relative errors of x^* and y^* are small. This is in keeping with subtractive cancellation developments in Section 1.4.2.

TABLE 1.11   Relative Error Bounds for Arithmetic Operations on Inexact Data

Rel $(x^* + y^*) = \max \{(\text{Rel } (x^*), \text{Rel } (y^*)\}$, for x, y having same sign

$$\text{Rel } (x^* - y^*) = \frac{\delta(x^*) + \delta(y^*)}{|x - y|}, \text{ any } x, y$$

Rel $(x^* y^*) \approx \text{Rel } (x^*) + \text{Rel } (y^*)$, any x, y

Rel $(x^*/y^*) \approx \text{Rel } (x^*) + \text{Rel } (y^*)$, any x, and any $y \neq 0$

★1.5.3   Propagation of Errors Through a Computation

In our discussion of bounds for propagated error, we assumed that all operations and computation of function values are done exactly. But in fact, at each stage of a computation, errors are introduced through truncation and rounding. Thus, typically, each stage of a lengthy program operates on faulty data and is itself a source of new errors.

Figure 1.12 illustrates the distinction between an ideal sequence of computations and its computer-realizable counterpart. In this figure the exact input to the first stage is represented by x_1. After the first stage of computation, ideally the output should be $y_1 = F_1(x_1)$. This output serves as input to the next computational stage or module. In the realizable computation, the input x_1^* is an approximation of the desired input x_1. Whereas ideally, we wished the output of the first stage to be $F_1(x_1)$, in the actual computation, it will be $y_1^* = F_1(x_1^*)$. Added to this faulty output is an undesired error e_1, which can represent effects of inexact calculation of the operator F_1 as well as roundoff error accumulated in the first stage of computation. The sum of y_1^* and e_1 serves as input to the next computational stage or module, and this process continues, with error propagating and accumulating at each segment of the computation.

Armed with an understanding from the preceding section about how error propagates through an arithmetical operation, and assuming that the relative error introduced by roundoff after each such operation F_j is e_j, we are in a position to analyze the overall accumulated error in any program-directed computation. Such analysis is seldom undertaken for lengthy programs because, while conceptually straightforward, it involves excruciating detail due to all the many operations and branches in a typical computation. Moreover, such "worst-case" analysis tends to lead to pessimistic bounds if carried out over many stages. However, for relatively small computations that occur repeatedly within a larger program, error bounding is frequently useful.

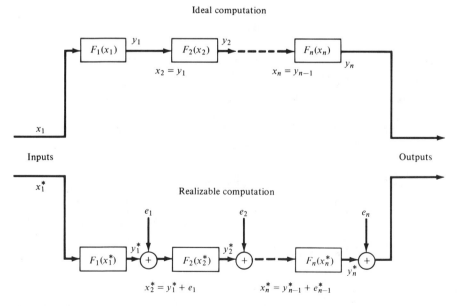

FIGURE 1.12   Comparison of Ideal and Realizable Computations

──────── **EXAMPLE 1.16** ────────

To illustrate the principle involved, let us bound the relative error in computing $xy + z$ using a machine with epsilon value ε. Further, presume that the floating-point numbers x^*, y^*, and z^*, which approximate x, y, and z, are positive. Then, according to Table 1.11,

$$\text{Rel}\,(x^*y^*) \approx \text{Rel}\,(x^*) + \text{Rel}\,(y^*). \tag{1.13}$$

Now the number $(x^*y^*)^*$, stored as the computed x^*y^*, is subject to roundoff error with relative error bound ε. This error is added directly to the propagated error. We then have that

$$\text{Rel}\,((x^*y^*)^*) = \frac{\delta(x^*y^*) + \varepsilon|xy|}{|xy|} = \text{Rel}\,(x^*y^*) + \varepsilon$$

$$\approx \text{Rel}\,(x^*) + \text{Rel}\,(y^*) + \varepsilon.$$

Now again by Table 1.11,

$$\text{Rel}\,((x^*y^*)^* + z^*) = \max\,\{\text{Rel}\,((x^*y^*)^*,\ \text{Rel}\,(z^*)\},$$

and after approximating $(x^*y^*) + z^*$ by the floating-point number $((x^*y^*)^* + z^*)^*$ and again accounting for roundoff, we obtain the relative error bound of the output approximation $((x^*y^*)^* + z^*)^*$ for $xy + z$, as

$$\text{Rel}\,(((x^*y^*)^* + z^*)^*) = \max\,\{\text{Rel}\,(x^*) + \text{Rel}\,(y^*) + \varepsilon,\ \text{Rel}\,(z^*)\} + \varepsilon.\ \blacksquare$$

The block diagram of this computation is shown is Figure 1.13. It is a particular case of the abstract illustration in Figure 1.12.

──────── **EXAMPLE 1.17** ────────

Suppose that in using the hypothetical computer word shown in Figure 1.6, two numbers of different orders of magnitude are added. Let $x = 0.2315 \cdot 10^8$ and $y = 0.1372 \cdot 10^4$. Then the value of $x + y$ becomes $0.23151372 \cdot 10^8$ and the floating-point representation of $x + y$ becomes $(x + y)^* = 0.2315 \cdot 10^8 = x^*$. Thus y has absolutely no effect on the result. Note that y was not large enough to change the floating-point representation after addition. $\blacksquare$

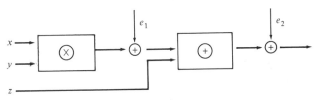

FIGURE 1.13 Block Diagram for Example 1.16

Although the error resulting from a single arithmetic operation is usually insignificant in itself, over the course of a long computation, the cumulative effect of many such errors can make itself felt.

━━━ **EXAMPLE 1.18** ━━━━━━━━━━━━━━━━━━━━━━━━━━━━━━━━━━━━━

We perform the experiment of forming a sum by adding the number $A = 10^{-6}$ one million times. The program and outcomes on a VAX are given in Tables 1.12 and 1.13. Note that the sum is correct only to two significant digits, whereas from Table 1.5, or direct computation of machine epsilon, we are assured that the number A itself was stored with an accuracy of seven or eight significant digits.

TABLE 1.12   Program for Accumulating a Sum

```
C       PROGRAM ADDALOT
C
C
C       ********************************************************
C       THIS PROGRAM DEMONSTRATES THE CUMULATIVE EFFECT OF
C       ADDING NUMBERS OF DIFFERENT MAGNITUDES MANY TIMES
C       OUTPUT: SUM=SUM OF THE VARIABLE A 1000000 TIMES
C       ********************************************************
C
        A=1.E-6
        SUM=0.
        DO 1 I=1,1000000
            SUM=SUM+A
      1 CONTINUE
        WRITE(10,2) SUM
      2 FORMAT(33X,'SUM=',F10.7)
        STOP
        END
```

TABLE 1.13   Output for Accumulating a Sum

```
        SUM= 1.0090389
```

TABLE 1.14   Program for Accumulating a Sum

```
C       PROGRAM ADD
C
C
C       ********************************************************
C       THIS PROGRAM ILLUSTRATES HOW MORE ACCURACY IS OBTAINED
C       WHEN CARE IS TAKEN TO ADD NUMBERS OF SIMILAR MAGNITUDE
C       OUTPUT: SUM=SUM OF THE VARIABLE A COMPUTED AS THE SUM
C                   OF 1000 SUMS OF 1000 A'S
C       ********************************************************
C
        DIMENSION S(1000)
        A=1.E-6
        SUM=0.
        DO 1 J=1,1000
            S(J)=0.
            DO 1 I=1,1000
                S(J)=S(J)+A
      1     CONTINUE
        DO 2 J=1,1000
            SUM=SUM+S(J)
      2 CONTINUE
        WRITE(10,3) SUM
      3 FORMAT(33X,'SUM=',F10.7)
        STOP
        END
```

The major cause of this loss of precision is error accumulation in adding a relatively small number to the much larger sum, as the number of terms increases. This is the phenomenon illustrated in Example 1.11. To some extent this loss of significance can be sidestepped by accumulating the sums in a great many smaller partial sums, and then adding these partial sums together. The program shown in Table 1.14 follows this idea, accumulating the sums of the small number A in a thousand different partial sums S(J), which are later added to one another to achieve an answer (Table 1.15) with five correct significant digits.

TABLE 1.15   Output for Accumulating a Sum

SUM= 0.9999985

1.6
SUPPLEMENTARY NOTES AND DISCUSSIONS

During the period from 1940 to 1955, ideas and methodology for computer number representation underwent lively and innovative development, as indeed this was the period of the emergence of the electronic digital computer. Prior to this period, computers were mechanical and, with the exception of experimental devices, strictly decimal. The arithmetic mode was equivalent to integer representation. Metropolis et al. (1980) give ample documentation of the evolution of floating-point representations. The advantage of this representation was clearly foreseen by the pioneers of modern computers, but in the first machines there was a tendency to force the programmer to encode the number representation. In early computer designs, essentially all user conveniences were sacrificed for the sake of computational speed. Since the advent of FORTRAN in the late 1950s, automatic floating-point representation seems to have become firmly established as the medium for numerical calculations. Many implementations of BASIC, for example, allow only such representation. The evolution will undoubtedly continue. For instance, some experimental computers have variable-length floating-point mantissas.

For details of number representation and the actual operations involved in computer arithmetic, the assembly language manual of the computer in question should be consulted. Knuth (1969, Chap. 4) provides additional details and illustrates the principles of computer number representation and arithmetic with a hypothetical assembly language.

We have described situations such as subtractive cancellation and smearing in which numerical error leads to large or intolerable "loss of significance." As illustrated in our examples, sometimes these difficulties can be circumvented through more careful computational and analytical thinking. Stegun and Abramowitz (1956), Henrici (1982), and Rice (1983) provide further examples and insights along these lines. Our plan is to delay until later chapters (especially Chapter 2 on linear equations) a discussion of "ill-conditioned" problems in which slight roundoff or measurement error on input parameters can lead to devastating error in the computed output.

At the close of this chapter we sketched principles involved in finding the absolute bound of propagated error. For full-scale computations, such analysis, in addition to being excruciatingly tedious, tends to result in pessimistic answers.

Early in the computer age, scientists occasionally concluded from such calculations that a given problem could not possibly be solved on present-day computers, only to find that somebody else had indeed found and verified the solution. At present, absolute bound analysis finds use in small-scale tasks such as bounding the effect of computer word roundoff in a library function routine. For large-scale computations, the tendency is to push ahead with the calculations but provide accuracy checks at key points along the way. For example, it may be possible to substitute a proposed solution back into an equation to be solved and to check that the equation is indeed satisfied. Alternatively, a method may be checked on prototypical problems having known closed-form solutions.

At the outset of this chapter we described the goals of numerical analysis as including construction of computer-realizable approximations for unrealizable mathematical operations, and derivation of error bounds for these constructs. A further theme that will come to the fore in subsequent chapters is that methods should be efficient. If one method is essentially as accurate as another but requires only half the computation time, it is clearly the method of choice.

PROBLEMS

Section 1.3

1. Experimentally find the largest integer N such that $(10.0)^N$ can be represented in floating point in your computer. (**HINT:** Compute 10.0^N for $N = 1, 2, \ldots$, until overflow occurs.)

2. Experimentally, find the largest integer number M that your computer can store in integer arithmetic. [**FACT:** Many computers (not VAXen running VMS) do not give overflow messages, but instead store meaningless integers, often negative, after overflow occurs.]

3. How many distinct floating-point numbers can be represented by our hypothetical decimal representation shown in Figure 1.6?

4. Give the computer representations (in terms of the decimal representations in Sections 1.3.2 and 1.3.3).
(a) 2531, -2531, 48, -48, as integer variables.
(b) 315.4, -315.4, 0.03154, -0.03154, as floating-point variables.

5. Experimentally find machine epsilon for an actual computer. Also find the minimum positive computer number x^*_{min} (as in Figure 1.7). Compare these to the theoretical formulas for these quantities for mantissa length s of your computer. Similarly, find or approximate the largest floating-point number, and compare with theory and the exponent capacity of your computer. Redo this experiment using double precision (if your compiler allows it). Double precision is always available in FORTRAN and can be called in VAX VMS-11 Pascal.

6. We have mentioned that in practice, computers usually use the two's-complement method for representing negative integers. On our hypothetical decimal machine, this is the same as the 10's complement. The negative number is stored as the 10's complement of its magnitude (which, of course, is positive). The *10's com-*

plement of a positive integer represented in the decimal number system can be obtained by subtracting that number from 10^t, where t is the word length ($t = 8$ for our hypothetical computer). Determine the 10's-complement representation of -1986, -1990, -1, and -23. Note that in this manner we can get 10^8 distinct integers from our eight-digit computer word.

7. **(Continuation of Problem 6.)** One can tell, given a stored integer, whether it is representing a positive number, or alternatively, is the 10's-complement representation of a negative number (ignoring the possibility that too large a positive number might have been presented). The test would be whether the stored number exceeds a certain magnitude. What is the magnitude?
   (a) Give a formula for converting back from the (positive) 10's-complement numbers to the negative integers they presumably encoded.
   (b) What negative numbers are represented by the following 10's-complement numbers: 73,000,000; 90,000,000; 53,000,212?

8. In the decimal system, the *base* is 10, and the "string" 357, for example, is really a code that designates the number

$$3 \cdot 10^2 + 5 \cdot 10^1 + 7 \cdot 10^0.$$

With the use of various bases other than 10 now being standard in the computer world, one sometimes designates the number system in mind by enclosing the string in parentheses, and writing the base as a subscript. Thus 357, as above, would appear as $(357)_{10}$. More generally, for any positive integer N, the code

$$(q_k \, q_{k-1} \, q_{k-2} \, \cdots \, q_0)_N$$

has meaning, provided that $0 \le q_j < N$, namely,

$$q_k N^k + q_{k-1} N^{k-1} + \cdots + q_0 N^0.$$

Thus, in binary,

$$(1 \ 0 \ 1)_2 = 1 \cdot 2^2 + 0 \cdot 2^1 + 1 \cdot 2^0 = 5.$$

With these thoughts in mind, convert the following binary numbers to decimal.
   (a) $(1 \ 1 \ 0 \ 0 \ 0 \ 1 \ 1)_2$, $\quad (1 \ 1 \ 1 \ 1 \ 1 \ 1 \ 1)_2$, $\quad (1 \ 0 \ 1 \ 0 \ 1 \ 0 \ 1)_2$.
   (b) $(1 \ 0 \ 1.0 \ 0 \ 1 \ 1)_2$, $\quad (0.0 \ 1 \ 1 \ 1 \ 1 \ 1)_2$, $\quad (1.0 \ 1 \ 0 \ 0 \ 1 \ 1)_2$.

9. One can convert an integer from decimal to binary by setting $b_0 = 0$ or 1, according to whether the number is even or odd, and then successively dividing by 2, and then assigning the next bit to be 0 or 1, according to whether the remainder is 0 or 1. For example, if $[M]$ denotes the "integer part of M," we convert $(456)_{10}$. The number 456 is even, so $b_0 = 0$. $[456/2] = 228$ is even and $b_1 = 0$; $[228/2] = 114$ and $b_2 = 0$; $[114/2] = 57$ is odd, so $b_3 = 1$; $[57/2] = 28$, so $b_4 = 0$; $[28/2] = 14$, so $b_5 = 0$; $[14/2] = 7$ is odd, so $b_6 = 1$; $[7/2] = 3$, so $b_7 = 1$; $[3/2] = 1$, so $b_8 = 1$; in summary,

$$(456)_{10} = (b_8 \, b_7 \, \ldots \, b_0)_2 = (1 \ 1 \ 1 \ 0 \ 0 \ 1 \ 0 \ 0 \ 0)_2.$$

Find the binary numbers representing $(34)_{10}$ and $(554)_{10}$.

10. **(Continuation of Problem 8.)** Write a computer program for converting positive integers from binary to decimal representation. Test it on the numbers given in Problem 8, part a.

11. (**Continuation of Problem 8.**) Generalize to find an algorithm for converting from any base N into decimal. Find the decimal numbers coded in the octal (base 8) system by
(a) $(34561)_8$.
(b) $(3256)_8$.

12. The *two's-complement* representation of a negative number in the binary system is found by subtracting the magnitude of that number from 2^t, where t is the given binary word length of the computer in question. Find the two's-complement representation of the binary integers

$$-110011, \quad -1, \quad -11, \quad -1011101.$$

Take $t = 32$.

★**13.** (**Continuation of Problem 12.**) Assuming that (in the spirit of Figure 1.4) a binary integer representation is encoded into the computer word as shown below, verify that the integer part of the two's complement of $N/2$, for any positive binary integer N, can be obtained by shifting the bits storing the coefficients of N to the right one "box" and keeping the sign bit fixed.

14. Some computers use the hexidecimal base (in the terminology of Problem 8, $N = 16$) for number representation. The symbols in the hexadecimal system are

$$\{0, 1, 2, \ldots, 9, A, B, C, D, E, F\}.$$

Here $A = 10, B = 11, C = 12, D = 13, E = 14, F = 15$. Thus

$$(A\ 3\ B)_{16} = 10 \cdot 16^2 + 3 \cdot 16^1 + 11 \cdot 16^0 = 2560 + 48 + 11 = 2619.$$

Find the decimal representations of
(a) $(29BC)_{16}$.
(b) $(0.98A)_{16}$.
(c) $(29.ABC)_{16}$.

15. As explained in Section 1.3 and illustrated in Figure 1.7, there is a gap between zero and the smallest positive floating-point number.
(a) Try to find s and e (in the terminology of Table 1.6) for your computer. Then calculate the size of this gap. If you cannot find the data for your computer, use the VAX partition (effectively, $s = 24, e = 8$).
(b) Write a program to estimate this gap by experiment.

(**Hint:** Keep in mind that binary systems are used in most real-world computers.)

Section 1.4
16. Define

$$x = 7{,}555{,}555 - 7{,}555{,}554.$$

Compute this difference in integer and floating-point arithmetic and compare. Assume that our hypothetical decimal computer is used.

17. Define

$$x(n) = 10^n - (10^n - 1),$$

with $n = 1, 2, \ldots$, and use your computer to evaluate $x(n)$ as a floating-point variable. Explain what is happening when your computed solution differs from 1.

18. Assume that our hypothetical decimal computer is used to evaluate the following expressions:
(a) $493.5 * 3.975$.
(b) $465.4 + 0.03252$.
(c) $0.073454 * 1.2450 + 123.6$.
(d) $125.3/0.001252 + 0.2543$.

What numbers will the decimal computer actually store as the operation result, and what are the exact answers?

19. Consider the expressions

$$(a + b) + c \qquad \text{and} \qquad a + (b + c).$$

Find values for a, b, c such that the operations performed in the order indicated above yield different numbers on your computer. (**HINT:** Take a and b to be very large, and of opposite signs, so that $a + b$ is in the same order of magnitude as c.)

20. Problem 19 is intended to illustrate that the computed sum of numbers may depend on the order in which the operations are done. Here we ask the reader to show that, in contrast to theory, the distributive law may fail in computer arithmetic. Find numbers A, K, and L such that in floating point,

$$(K + L) * A \neq (K * A) + (L * A).$$

Section 1.5

21. From calculus (Taylor's theory) it is known that for all x,

$$\sin x = x - \frac{x^3}{3!} + \frac{x^5}{5!} + \cdots + \frac{(-1)^{n+1}x^{2n-1}}{(2n-1)!} + \cdots$$

Using a computer, approximate sin (x) for $x = 0, 2\pi, 3\pi, 5\pi$. [Of course, the theoretical value of sin (x) equals 0 in all these cases.] Take $n = 1, 5, 10$, and 20 and approximate the series by their initial polynomials of degree $2n - 1$.

22. Derive error-bound formulas for the following expressions:
(a) $x + y + x^2 - xy + y^2$.
(b) $\sqrt{x^2 - y^2}$.
(c) $2 \cos (x) \cdot \cos (y) + \sin (x) \cdot \sin (y)$.
(d) $\dfrac{\sin (x)}{\cos (y)} + z^2 - 1$.
(e) $(x - y)e^{2x+y^2}$.

23. Set $x = 3.25$, $y = 2.45$, and $z = 5.73$ and suppose that $\delta(x) = \delta(y) = \delta(z) = 0.005$. Bound the error of the following expressions.
    (a) $x + y + x^2 - xy + y^2$.
    (b) $\sqrt{x^2 - y^2}$.
    (c) $2 \cos(x) \cdot \cos(y) + \sin(x) \cdot \sin(y)$.
    (d) $\dfrac{\sin(x)}{\cos(y)} + z^2 - 1$.
    (e) $(x - y)e^{2x + y^2}$.

24. **(Continuation of Problem 23.)** Find relative error bounds for the expressions in parts (a) through (e).

25. Derive absolute error bounds for the following expressions:
    (a) $x^2 - xy + y^2$.
    (b) $\sqrt{x^2 + y^2}$.
    (c) $x \cdot \sin(y) - \cos(x) \cdot y$.
    (d) xe^y.
    (e) $(x + y)^2 e^{x + y}$.

26. For the nominal values $x^* = 3.75$, $y^* = 4.24$, and with $\delta(x^*) = \delta(y^*) = 0.005$, bound the errors in calculating the following expressions:
    (a) $x^2 - xy + y^2$.
    (b) $\sqrt{x^2 + y^2}$.
    (c) $x \cdot \sin(y) - \cos(x) \cdot y$.
    (d) xe^y.
    (e) $(x + y)^2 e^{x + y}$.

27. **(Continuation of Problem 26.)** Give relative error bounds for the expressions in parts (a) through (e) at the values indicated.

28. On your computer, find a root of the quadratic equation

$$ax^2 + bx + c = 0$$

using the quadratic formula

$$x = \frac{-b + \sqrt{b^2 - 4ac}}{2a} \tag{1.14}$$

with the values $b = 1$ and $a = c = 10^{-n}$. Assess the accuracy of your answers by seeing how closely the equation is satisfied for $n = 2, \ldots, 10$. If you can, think of a clever way to avoid subtractive cancellation, and improve your answer. (Going to high precision does not count!)

29. The following (decimal) numbers are approximated within a relative error bound of 1%. In each case, give the smallest intervals that can be assured to contain the exact values.

    (a) 111.1.
    (b) 0.01111.
    (c) 43.1234.
    (d) 0.0431234.

30. **(a)** Compute the sum

$$\sum_{k=1}^{\infty} \frac{1}{k^2} \tag{1.15}$$

to four significant decimals. Compare this approximation to the exact answer, which is $\pi^2/6$. (**HINT:** To determine how many terms to sum, use the fact that for any n,

$$\sum_{k=n+1}^{\infty} \frac{1}{k^2} < \frac{1}{n}.$$

If you want to impress your instructor and yourself, prove this inequality.)

(b) Try to compute the sum (1.15) as accurately as you can by summing for 1 to n, and alternatively, from n to 1. You had better let k be a floating-point number. Which direction of summation gives the more accurate answer?

31. Find some trick in each case to avoid subtractive cancellation in the following expressions (Assume that x, y are positive integers.)
(a) $\sqrt{x} - \sqrt{y}$.
(b) $\ln(x) - \ln(y)$.
(c) $\sin(x) - \sin(y)$.

32. A charge of q coulombs is uniformly distributed throughout a nonconductive spherical volume with radius r. Let x be a distance of a point from the center. Then the potential at this point is given by

$$V = \frac{q(r^2 - x^2)}{8\pi e r^3},$$

where e is the permittivity constant. Suppose that nominal values

$$q^* = 6.52, \quad r^* = 3.15, \quad x^* = 1.12, \quad \pi^* = 3.14, \quad e^* = 8.85 \cdot 10^{-12}$$

are given and assume that all numbers are accurate to the number of figures given. That is, the values have been rounded to three digits. Bound the associated error in computing V.

33. In the figure, the area of the shaded region is determined by

$$T = \frac{r^2}{2} [\alpha - \sin(\alpha)]$$

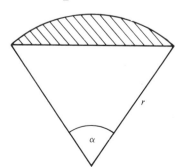

α being in radians. Suppose that r is known exactly but that α is imperfectly approximated by α^*. If T must be known to an accuracy of 0.01 and $r = 10$, how much error is tolerable if the approximation is $\alpha^* = 0.2$ rad?

34. A crude population growth model is that if the population is $P(0)$ at time 0, at time t it will be

$$P(t) = P(0) \exp (\theta t),$$

for some fixed constant θ. This model does give a reasonable approximation for the growth of an animal species (including human beings) with unlimited food and resources, no predators, and so on. Suppose that the error in initial population estimate is $\delta(P(0))$ and the error in estimating θ is bounded by $\delta(\theta^*)$. Give an error bound for the approximation of $P^*(t)$ in terms of estimates $P^*(0)$ and θ^*.

35. Consider the recursion

$$x_0 = 1$$

and

$$x_{k+1} = 5.0x_k + b, \qquad k = 0, 1, \ldots .$$

Suppose that the nominal value is $b^* = 1.22$ and $\delta(b^*) = 0.005$.
(a) Find a recursive formula for the error bound $\delta(x_k^*)$.
(b) HARDER: Find a closed-form (not recursive) expression for $\delta(x_k^*)$.

36. The area of a triangle is

$$A = \frac{ab \sin (\theta)}{2},$$

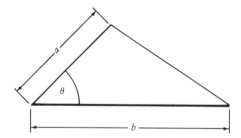

where a and b are the lengths of two sides and θ is the angle of intersection (in radians). Assume that a^*, b^*, and θ^* are approximations of a, b, and θ, respectively, and that $a^* = b^* = 10$ cm and $\theta^* = \pi/4$. If

$$\delta(a^*) = \delta(b^*) = 0.01 \text{ cm}$$

and

$$\delta(\theta^*) = 0.01 \text{ rad},$$

bound the error in the estimate A^*.

37. **(Continuation of Problem 36.)** Find a relative error bound for A.

38. The downward velocity $v(t)$ of a falling object under the influences of gravity and air resistance is given by

$$v(t) = \frac{gm}{c}\left[1 - \exp\left(\frac{-ct}{m}\right)\right],$$

where g, m, and c are, respectively, gravity, mass, and drag coefficient. Suppose that there is a relative error bound of 5% in the measurement of c. For values

$$g = 9.81 \text{ m/s}^2, \qquad m = 85 \text{ kg}, \qquad c = 11 \text{ kg/s},$$

find the associated relative error bound in $v(t)$ for $t = 10$ and 50 s.

39. In a diatomic molecule, the potential energy $U(x)$ resulting from the force fields between two atoms a distance x apart is given by

$$U(x) = \frac{a}{x^{12}} - \frac{b}{x^6},$$

where a and b are positive but not perfectly known. Let a^* and b^* denote approximations of a and b. Presume that e is a given positive error tolerance, and error bounds are denoted by

$$\delta(a^*) = \delta(b^*) = \delta.$$

Find what the common value of δ must be so that $\delta(U(x)) = e$. Sketch $\delta(U(x))$ as a function of separation x.

40. Consider the following resistive circuit:

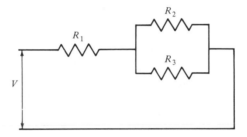

The formula for the net resistance is

$$R = R_1 + \frac{R_2 \cdot R_3}{R_2 + R_3}.$$

Suppose that the nominal values are $R_j^* = j$ ohms for $j = 1, 2, 3$, and $\delta(R_j) = 0.1$. Bound the range of possible values for R about

$$R^* = R_1^* + \frac{R_2^* \cdot R_3^*}{R_2^* + R_3^*}.$$

41. The period of a "linearized" pendulum is given by

$$t = 2\pi\sqrt{\frac{l}{g}}$$

with l the pendulum length, which we take to be nominally 3 m. The error bound $\delta(l) = 0.01$ m. As usual, π is the ratio of a circle circumference to its diameter. In evaluating π by the trigonometric formula

$$\pi = 4 \cdot \tan^{-1}(1),$$

one can approximate π on a computer with error about $\pi^* \times$ (machine epsilon). Gravity g at the 45° latitude is nominally 9.80 m/s², with $\delta(g) = 0.02$. Bound the error in estimating t. How long will it be until a clock using this pendulum might be 1 min in error?

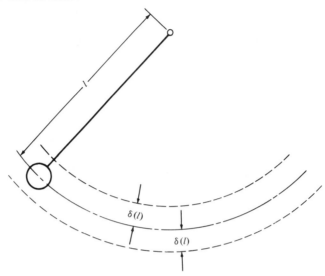

42. Refer to Figure 1.2. Notice that in the region in which truncation error dominates, the error has the form of a straight line with slope close to 1.0. Conclude from this that the truncation error varies with step size h in a regular fashion. That is, letting $D(0)$ denote the ideal limit of $D(h)$, as $h \rightarrow 0$,

$$\log (|D(h) - D(0)|) \approx a + \log (h). \tag{1.16}$$

After exponentiating both sides, conclude that for constant $k = e^a$ it must be true that to the extent that (1.16) is correct,

$$D(0) = D(h) + K * h.$$

(a) Justify formula (1.17) below for finding $D(0)$ from $D(h_1)$ and $D(h_2)$, two different evaluations of $D(h)$.

$$D(0) \approx \frac{h_2\,D(h_1) - h_1\,D(h_2)}{h_2 - h_1}. \tag{1.17}$$

(b) Using the following table, show that the approximation (1.17) is more accurate by far than either $D(h_1)$ or $D(h_2)$. [**HINT:** Formula (1.17) is based on the idea of using two values of $D(h)$ to eliminate k and solve (1.16) for $D(0)$.]

Table for Problem 42

j	h_j	$D(h_j) = \dfrac{\exp\,(1 + h_j) - \exp\,(1)}{h_j}$
1	0.2	3.009175
2	0.1	2.858842

This idea lies at the heart of "correction formulas," to be encountered later (Chapters 3 and 7).

CHAPTER 2

Simultaneous Linear Equations

2.1
PRELIMINARIES

Simultaneous linear equations are equations of the form

$$
\begin{aligned}
a_{11}x_1 + a_{12}x_2 + \cdots + a_{1n}x_n &= b_1 \\
a_{21}x_1 + a_{22}x_2 + \cdots + a_{2n}x_n &= b_2 \\
&\;\;\vdots \\
a_{m1}x_1 + a_{m2}x_2 + \cdots + a_{mn}x_n &= b_m.
\end{aligned}
\tag{2.1}
$$

The coefficients a_{ij} and b_i are given real or complex numbers. Equation (2.1) is a system of m equations with n variables, or "unknowns," $x_1, x_2, \ldots, x_n$. Our job is to determine their values.

We will see that many numerical techniques require, as a key step, solving simultaneous linear equations. For example, linear equations will be encountered in the construction of natural cubic splines, the determination of weights in numerical differentiation and interpolatory-type quadrature (4.13). We will also find in later chapters that the solution of systems of nonlinear equations, the method of least squares for function approximation, and popular methods for solving certain types of differential equations also entail simultaneous linear equation problems. Many engineering and economic applications, such as current response to fixed-frequency voltage sources in electric networks, heat transfer in static thermal models, and equilibrium problems of economic sectors involve linear equations. More can be said: Linear equations are fundamental to virtually every field of numerical computation and, as a consequence, to every scientific and engineering discipline, even (and sometimes, especially) those which on the surface seem most remote from "linearity." In brief, it is virtually impossible to overestimate the value of mastery of the theoretical and computational aspects of linear algebra.

47

Application 2.1 ──

Ohm's law, a primary law of circuit theory, tells us that the voltage V across a resistor is related to the current i passing through it, and the resistance value R, by

$$V = iR.$$

As illustrated in Figure 2.1, the voltage drop is in the direction of current flow. Two famous circuit theory laws, Kirchhoff's laws, tell us that the net voltage drop around a closed path in a circuit must be zero, and that the net current flow into a junction connecting circuit components must be zero. From these laws one can determine the currents and voltages at any location in a configuration of resistors, voltage sources, and current pumps, once one is given the interconnection diagram and the values of the resistances and current and voltage sources. In fact, these laws lead to a linear system of equations for the unknown voltages and currents.

In Figure 2.1 we have presented a simple resistor and battery circuit. The implication of Kirchhoff's and Ohm's laws are that the currents i_1, i_2, and i_3 must satisfy the following relations:

$$(R_1 + R_2 + R_4)i_1 \qquad -R_2 i_2 \qquad\qquad -R_4 i_3 = 0$$
$$-R_2 i_1 + (R_2 + R_3)i_2 \qquad\qquad -R_3 i_3 = V_1$$
$$-R_4 i_1 \qquad -R_3 i_2 + (R_3 + R_4 + R_5)i_3 = V_2.$$

This is actually a system of three equations with three unknowns, which can be solved by using methods known from high school algebra. However, in the case of more equations and unknowns, computer-oriented methods are needed. ◇

──

Some familiar methods for solving "textbook-sized" linear equations by hand calculations are totally inadequate for higher-order systems. For example, the solution of a 20-variable ($m = n = 20$) system by the popular Cramer's rule

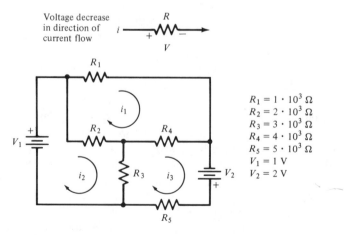

$$R_1 = 1 \cdot 10^3 \ \Omega$$
$$R_2 = 2 \cdot 10^3 \ \Omega$$
$$R_3 = 3 \cdot 10^3 \ \Omega$$
$$R_4 = 4 \cdot 10^3 \ \Omega$$
$$R_5 = 5 \cdot 10^3 \ \Omega$$
$$V_1 = 1 \ \text{V}$$
$$V_2 = 2 \ \text{V}$$

FIGURE 2.1   Resistive Network

requires about 5×10^{19} multiplications, and such an effort would require on the order of 1 million years by a modern computer. Yet people routinely solve systems having several hundred variables by techniques described in this chapter.

Equation (2.1) can be written compactly in matrix form as

$$\mathbf{Ax} = \mathbf{b}, \tag{2.2}$$

where $\mathbf{A} = (a_{ij})$ is an $m \times n$ matrix of coefficients, and $\mathbf{b} = (b_i)$ and $\mathbf{x} = (x_j)$ are column vectors of dimension m and n, respectively. The usual case of interest is when m, in (2.1), equals n. In this standard case, the *order* of the linear system is n. Appendix A supplies the elementary definitions and results of matrix theory needed for understanding the material of this chapter.

In many cases, "naive" codes are sufficient for solving fairly large ($n > 100$) order systems of linear equations. But, solution of some important linear equations is subject to ill-conditioning effects. By way of illustration, we shall see in Chapter 4 that linear equations for weights in Newton–Cotes quadrature characteristically are unstable, and this instability leads to deterioration of accuracy for orders n as low as 20, even with double-precision number representation. Thus in the course of this chapter, we are obliged to cast an eye toward the effects of roundoff error and partial remedies of its effects.

2.2
GAUSSIAN ELIMINATION

2.2.1 An Example of Elimination

The most popular linear equation methods are the different variants of the Gaussian elimination algorithm. By "elimination" here we refer to a procedure for adding multiples of one equation in (2.1) to other equations so as to set the coefficients of one of the variables, say x_j, in these other equations to zero. This is repeated until the resulting system of equations is characterized by having its coefficient matrix in upper triangular form. That is (Appendix A, property 3), all the elements a_{ij}, $i > j$, are zero. When the linear system is in this form, it is very simple to solve for the unknowns x_j.

Because it is a purely arithmetic process, Gaussian elimination has the interesting feature that in contrast to other major computational methods to be discussed, there is no truncation error. Limitations on accuracy are due solely to roundoff error. The mathematical formulas of Gaussian elimination are given in the next section. But this technique is one of those procedures most readily understood by example, and with this conviction in mind, let us examine such an example.

───────── **EXAMPLE 2.1** ─────────────────────────

We now solve the system of equations

$$
\begin{aligned}
2x_1 + x_2 + 3x_3 &= 1 \\
4x_1 + 4x_2 + 7x_3 &= 1 \\
2x_1 + 5x_2 + 9x_3 &= 3.
\end{aligned}
\tag{2.3}
$$

By subtracting the multiple 2 of the first equation from the second equation and the first equation from the third equation, the first "derived system" is obtained:

$$2x_1 + x_2 + 3x_3 = 1$$
$$2x_2 + x_3 = -1$$
$$4x_2 + 6x_3 = 2.$$

Let us look in detail at the computation of the second or middle equation above. The first equation, after being multiplied by 2, becomes

$$4x_1 + 2x_2 + 6x_3 = 2.$$

Subtract this from the middle equation in (2.3) to see that the result is

$$(4 - 4)x_1 + (4 - 2)x_2 + (7 - 6)x_3 = 1 - 2.$$

After performing the arithmetic indicated by the parenthetical expressions above, we have the second equation of the first derived system. The same rationale yields the third equation in the first derived system.

Continue the computation by subtracting the multiple 2 of the second equation of the first derived system from the third equation to obtain the second derived system:

$$2x_1 + x_2 + 3x_3 = 1$$

$$2x_2 + x_3 = -1$$

$$4x_3 = 4.$$

The derivation of this upper triangular system of equations is called the *forward elimination process*.

From the third equation of the system above, we immediately calculate

$$x_3 = \frac{4}{4} = 1.$$

Then the second equation, with 1 substituted for x_3, implies that

$$x_2 = \frac{-1 - 1}{2} = -1.$$

Finally, from the first equation, with their numerical values replacing x_2 and x_3, we see that $x_1 = \dfrac{1 - 3 - (-1)}{2} = -\dfrac{1}{2}$, and thereby obtain the solution, which is

$$x_1 = -\tfrac{1}{2}, \qquad x_2 = -1, \qquad x_3 = 1.$$

The computation of the unknowns from the upper triangular system is known as *back substitution*.

2.2.2 Naive Gaussian Elimination

We now formalize the elimination and back-substitution algorithms illustrated in Example 2.1.

Let us assume that in equations (2.1) the matrix of coefficients is nonsingular; that is, assume $m = n$, and that a solution exists and is unique. Then (2.1) can be rewritten as

$$
\begin{aligned}
a_{11}x_1 + a_{12}x_2 + \cdots + a_{1n}x_n &= a_{1,n+1} \\
a_{21}x_1 + a_{22}x_2 + \cdots + a_{2n}x_n &= a_{2,n+1} \\
&\vdots \\
a_{n1}x_1 + a_{n2}x_2 + \cdots + a_{nn}x_n &= a_{nn+1}.
\end{aligned}
\tag{2.4}
$$

where, for later notational convenience, we have defined $a_{i,n+1} = b_i$ ($1 \le i \le n$). Assume that $a_{11} \ne 0$, and subtract the multiple a_{i1}/a_{11} of the first equation from the ith equation for $i = 2, \ldots, n$. The coefficient of x_1 in the ith equation then becomes 0, and we thereby obtain the first derived system, which has the form

$$
\begin{aligned}
a_{11}x_1 + a_{12}x_2 + \cdots + a_{1n}x_n &= a_{1,n+1} \\
a_{22}^{(1)}x_2 + \cdots + a_{2n}^{(1)}x_n &= a_{2,n+1}^{(1)} \\
&\vdots \\
a_{n2}^{(1)}x_2 + \cdots + a_{nn}^{(1)}x_n &= a_{n,n+1}^{(1)},
\end{aligned}
\tag{2.5}
$$

where

$$
a_{ij}^{(1)} = a_{ij} - \frac{a_{i1}}{a_{11}} a_{ij} \qquad (2 \le i \le n, \, 2 \le j \le n + 1).
\tag{2.6}
$$

There is no loss of generality in making the assumption that $a_{11} \ne 0$, since in any nonsingular matrix A there is at least one nonzero entry in the first column. If $a_{11} = 0$ but for index i, $a_{i1} \ne 0$, then the first and ith equations may be interchanged.

One can see intuitively that if $x_1, \ldots, x_n$ is the solution to (2.1) and some multiple of the first ($i = 1$) equation is added to the jth equation, then $x_1, \ldots, x_n$ is also the solution of the new system. More justification is offered in Appendix A, property 23.

Note that in the first derived system, the variable x_1 has been "eliminated" in all but the first equation of (2.4). The matrix of coefficients of the first derived system (2.5) is nonsingular, since row operations such as interchanging rows or adding a multiple of one row to another, as in (2.5), cannot make the matrix singular (Appendix A, property 23).

Assume next that $a_{22}^{(1)} \ne 0$, and subtract the multiple $a_{i2}^{(1)}/a_{22}^{(1)}$ of the second equation of (2.5) from the ith equation ($i = 3, \ldots, n$). We thereby obtain the second derived system:

$$a_{11}x_1 + a_{12}x_2 + a_{13}x_3 + \cdots + a_{1n}x_n = a_{1,n+1}$$

$$a_{22}^{(1)}x_2 + a_{23}^{(1)}x_3 + \cdots + a_{2n}^{(1)}x_n = a_{2,n+1}^{(1)}$$

$$a_{33}^{(2)}x_3 + \cdots + a_{3n}^{(2)}x_n = a_{3,n+1}^{(2)} \qquad (2.7)$$

$$\vdots \qquad \qquad \vdots \qquad \vdots$$

$$a_{n3}^{(2)}x_3 + \cdots + a_{nn}^{(2)}x_n = a_{n,n+1}^{(2)}.$$

By repeating this process until the $(n-1)$st derived system has been constructed, we obtain

$$a_{11}x_1 + a_{12}x_2 + a_{13}x_3 + \cdots + a_{1n}x_n \quad = a_{1,n+1}$$

$$a_{22}^{(1)}x_2 + a_{23}^{(1)}x_3 + \cdots + a_{2n}^{(1)}x_n \quad = a_{2,n+1}^{(1)}$$

$$a_{33}^{(2)}x_3 + \cdots + a_{3n}^{(2)}x_n \quad = a_{3,n+1}^{(2)} \qquad (2.8)$$

$$\vdots \qquad \qquad \vdots$$

$$a_{nn}^{(n-1)}x_n = a_{n,n+1}^{(n-1)},$$

where the relation for obtaining the coefficients of the kth derived system from the coefficients of the preceding system has the general form

$$a_{ij}^{(k)} = a_{ij}^{(k-1)} - \frac{a_{ik}^{(k-1)}}{a_{kk}^{(k-1)}} a_{kj}^{(k-1)} \qquad (2.9)$$

$$(i = k + 1, \ldots, n; j = k + 1, \ldots, n + 1).$$

In (2.9) k ranges from 1 to $n - 1$. The process is started by assigning

$$a_{ij}^{(0)} = a_{ij} \qquad (i = 1, \ldots, n; j = 1, \ldots, n + 1).$$

By inspection of (2.8), we see that the coefficient matrix of the $(n-1)$st derived system is in upper triangular form. The remaining step in solving this system is easy. The value of x_n can be obtained from the final equation of (2.8) since nonsingularity of A implies that necessarily $a_{nn}^{(n-1)} \neq 0$. Specifically,

$$x_n = \frac{a_{n,n+1}^{(n-1)}}{a_{nn}^{(n-1)}},$$

and the (backward) recursive formula for obtaining the values of the unknowns x_k in terms of the previously calculated values x_j $(j > k)$ is

$$x_k = \frac{1}{a_{kk}^{(k-1)}} \left[a_{k,n+1}^{(k-1)} - \sum_{j=k+1}^{n} a_{kj}^{(k-1)}x_j \right] \qquad (k = n - 1, \ldots, 1). \qquad (2.10)$$

This relation is obtained from the kth equation of system (2.8). Formula (2.10) is called *back substitution*. Process (2.9) is referred to as *forward elimination*. The entire process of forward elimination and back substitution is called *Gaussian elimination*. The adjective "naive" is sometimes applied to this procedure since as will be seen in our discussion of pivoting, modifications are often advised for improving accuracy in the face of roundoff error. The subroutine for Gaussian elimination, which is deferred to the next section, will employ a pivoting strategy.

───── **EXAMPLE 2.2** ─────────────────────────

The coefficients of the successive derived systems associated with Example 2.1 are given in Table 2.1.

TABLE 2.1   Derived Systems in Forward Elimination

	2	1	3	1
Original system	4	4	7	1
$A^{(0)}$	2	5	9	3
	2	1	3	1
First derived system		2	1	-1
$A^{(1)}$		4	6	2
	2	1	3	1
Second derived system		2	1	-1
$A^{(2)}$			4	4

■

2.2.3   Gaussian Elimination with Pivoting

Because of the effect of propagated rounding errors, naive Gaussian elimination is sometimes unsatisfactory. This fact can be illustrated by the following example.

───── **EXAMPLE 2.3** ─────────────────────────

Assume that in the absence of roundoff error, the last two equations of the $(n - 2)$nd derived system are

$$0x_{n-1} + x_n = 1$$

$$2x_{n-1} + x_n = 3,$$

where the zero coefficient is obtained from previous calculations. The solution is $x_n = x_{n-1} = 1$. As we have seen in Chapter 1, resultants of arithmetic operations usually have roundoff errors: Therefore, the computed derived system of equations is actually

$$\varepsilon x_{n-1} + x_n = 1$$

$$2x_{n-1} + x_n = 3.$$

Here ε is a number having small magnitude, and the roundoff errors of the other coefficients have been neglected. Since $\varepsilon \neq 0$, in the computation of the $(n - 1)$st derived system the naive elimination process is continued with the nonzero element ε, and the last two equations of the final derived system are

$$\varepsilon x_{n-1} + x_n = 1$$

$$\left(1 - \frac{2}{\varepsilon}\right) x_n = 3 - \frac{2}{\varepsilon}.$$

Back substitution applied to these equations results in the values

$$x_n = \frac{3 - 2/\varepsilon}{1 - 2/\varepsilon}$$

$$x_{n-1} = \frac{1 - x_n}{\varepsilon}.$$

For values of ε near zero, the values $3 - 2/\varepsilon$ and $1 - 2/\varepsilon$ are both very close to $-2/\varepsilon$, and the value of x_n is very close to 1, which is the correct value. But the value of x_{n-1} will have considerable error because x_n, being very close to 1, will induce subtractive cancellation (Section 1.4) in the numerator. The method of back substitution (2.10) implies that the values of all the other unknowns $x_{n-2}, \ldots, x_1$ obtained by the use of the erroneous value of x_{n-1} are also suspect.

We performed the calculations above with $\varepsilon = 4.321 \cdot 10^{-9}$ using a TRS-80 pocket computer having about nine-place accuracy. The calculated value of x_{n-1} was 0.995; the answer was accurate only to two decimal places. We will later see how partial pivoting succeeds in improving the answer. It is to be emphasized that the error arises because of roundoff error, not because this problem is inherently unstable. A curiosity is that larger values of ε do not induce so much error. ∎

The difficulty in the system discussed above is not due simply to ε being small but rather to its being small relative to other coefficients in the same column. The element $a_{kk}^{(k-1)}$ used for elimination is termed a *pivot*. The subtractive cancellation difficulty just observed can be remedied if we choose as the kth pivot element the coordinate $a_{i^*j^*}^{(k-1)}$ having the largest magnitude among all $a_{ij}^{(k-1)}$, $k \leq i \leq n$, $k \leq j \leq n$. The element $a_{i^*j^*}^{(k-1)}$ is then put in the diagonal position by interchanging rows i^* and k and columns j^* and k. That is, equations i^* and k, and unknowns x_{j^*} and x_k are interchanged. This operation is called *pivoting for maximal size* or, more simply, *maximal pivoting* (see Figure 2.2). We need to find the maximum of $(n - k + 1)^2$ numbers before computing the kth derived system.

At the expense of some increase in roundoff error propagation, a popular alternative procedure is to perform *partial pivoting*, where the maximal element is chosen from only the kth column. That is, we choose the kth pivot element, to be any coordinate $a_{i^*k}^{(k-1)}$ that maximizes $|a_{ik}^{(k-1)}|$, $i \geq k$. Then the kth and i^*th rows are interchanged to put the pivot element in the diagonal position. Figure 2.2 illustrates the partial and maximal pivoting strategies.

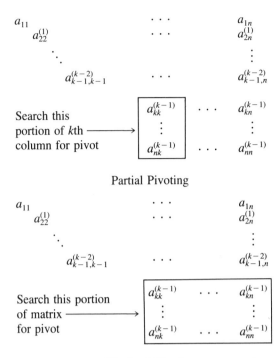

Partial Pivoting

Maximal Pivoting

FIGURE 2.2   Partial and Maximal Pivoting

—— **EXAMPLE 2.4** ——

The partial pivoting strategy is now illustrated in the case of the linear equations of Examples 2.1 and 2.2. The system of equations under consideration is

$$2x_1 + x_2 + 3x_3 = 1$$
$$4x_1 + 4x_2 + 7x_3 = 1$$
$$2x_1 + 5x_2 + 9x_3 = 3.$$

In Example 2.1 the first coefficient 2 of the first equation was used for eliminating x_1 from the second and third equations. In partial pivoting, we select the largest coefficient of the first column. In our example this maximal coefficient is the 4 in the second row. By interchanging the first and second rows, the modified system becomes

$$4x_1 + 4x_2 + 7x_3 = 1$$
$$2x_1 + x_2 + 3x_3 = 1$$
$$2x_1 + 5x_2 + 9x_3 = 3.$$

After this interchange has been made, the first derived system is obtained by an elimination, as before: The multiple $\frac{1}{2}$ of the first equation is subtracted from the second and third equations, giving

$$4x_1 + 4x_2 + 7x_3 = 1$$
$$- \ x_2 - \tfrac{1}{2}x_3 = \tfrac{1}{2}$$
$$3x_2 + \tfrac{11}{2}x_3 = \tfrac{5}{2}$$

as the first derived system. There are two coefficients $a_{i2}^{(1)}$ in the second column satisfying $i \geq 2$. They are -1 and 3 in the second and third rows. The larger is 3. Partial pivoting calls for interchanging the second and third rows. We get the modified system

$$4x_1 + 4x_2 + 7x_3 = 1$$
$$3x_2 + \tfrac{11}{2}x_3 = \tfrac{5}{2}$$
$$- \ x_2 - \tfrac{1}{2}x_3 = \tfrac{1}{2}.$$

By subtracting the multiple $-1/3$ of the second row from the third row, we obtain the second derived system:

$$4x_1 + 4x_2 + 7x_3 = 1$$
$$3x_2 + \tfrac{11}{2}x_3 = \tfrac{5}{2}$$
$$\tfrac{4}{3}x_3 = \tfrac{4}{3}.$$

Now back substitution is performed as in naive elimination. The third equation implies that

$$x_3 = \frac{\frac{4}{3}}{\frac{4}{3}} = 1.$$

Then from the second equation we get

$$x_2 = \frac{\frac{5}{2} - \frac{11}{2} \cdot 1}{3} = -1,$$

and finally, the first equation implies that

$$x_1 = \frac{1 - 4 \cdot (-1) - 7 \cdot 1}{4} = -\tfrac{1}{2}.$$

The computation is summarized in Table 2.2.

TABLE 2.2 Derived System in Partial Pivoting

Original system	2	1	3	1
	4	4	7	1
	2	5	9	3
Modified original system	4	4	7	1
	2	1	3	1
	2	5	9	3
First derived system	4	4	7	1
		-1	$-\frac{1}{2}$	$\frac{1}{2}$
		3	$\frac{11}{2}$	$\frac{5}{2}$
Modified first derived system	4	4	7	1
		3	$\frac{11}{2}$	$\frac{5}{2}$
		-1	$-\frac{1}{2}$	$\frac{1}{2}$
Second derived system	4	4	7	1
		3	$\frac{11}{2}$	$\frac{5}{2}$
			$\frac{4}{3}$	$\frac{4}{3}$

The partial pivoting strategy in this present form has a theoretical weakness, since by rescaling the equations of the derived systems (i.e., by multiplying them by sufficiently large scalars), any nonzero element could be made to satisfy the pivot condition. A heuristic procedure known as *equilibration* is sometimes used to sidestep this problem. In equilibration, at each step of elimination, before choosing the pivot element, we scale each of the remaining ($i \geq k$) rows by scalars α_i so that, for example,

$$\alpha_i(|a_{i,k}| + |a_{i,k+1}| + \cdots + |a_{in}|) = 1.$$

Although this is sometimes found to be useful, there exist cases when equilibration makes roundoff effects even worse.

EXAMPLE 2.5

Let us examine what happens in the situation of Example 2.3 under the partial pivoting regime. In constructing the $(n - 1)$st derived system, we examine the last two rows of the $(n - 1)$st column,

$$\varepsilon x_{n-1} + x_n = 1$$
$$\textcircled{2} x_{n-1} + x_n = 3$$

and find that the encircled term has the largest magnitude. Then this encircled term is selected as the pivot, and the equations are rearranged as

$$2x_{n-1} + x_n = 3$$
$$\varepsilon x_{n-1} + x_n = 1.$$

Now proceeding with elimination, we calculate

$$2x_{n-1} + x_n = 3$$

$$\left(1 - \frac{\varepsilon}{2}\right) x_n = 1 - \frac{3\varepsilon}{2}.$$

Now for small ε, $x_n \approx 1.0$, and

$$x_{n-1} = \frac{3 - x_n}{2} \approx 1.0,$$

and our answer is accurate.

The calculations of Example 2.3 were redone with partial pivoting. As before, $\varepsilon = 4.321 \cdot 10^{-9}$, and the same TRS-80 was used. Following the formula above, we found that $x_{n-1} = 1.0$, to nine decimal places. Partial pivoting overcame the earlier instability. ∎

Subroutine GAUSS, which performs Gaussian elimination with partial pivoting, is listed in Table 2.3. The calling parameter M represents the number of linear systems with the same coefficient matrix to be solved and should not be confused with m in (2.1). If, as is the usual case, only one linear system of equations is to be solved, as in (2.1), then $M = 1$. The calling parameter DELT is the positive threshold below which the pivot element is regarded as zero and

TABLE 2.3   Subroutine GAUSS for Gauss Elimination with Partial Pivoting

```
      SUBROUTINE GAUSS(N,M,A,DELT)
C
C     ***************************************************************
C     *  FUNCTION: THIS SUBROUTINE COMPUTES THE SOLUTIONS FOR M    *
C     *            SYSTEMS WITH N EQUATIONS AND N UNKNOWNS USING    *
C     *            GAUSSIAN ELIMINATION                             *
C     *  USAGE:                                                     *
C     *     CALL SEQUENCE: CALL GAUSS(N,M,A,DELT)                   *
C     *  PARAMETERS:                                                *
C     *     INPUT:                                                  *
C     *        N=NUMBER OF EQUATIONS AND UNKNOWNS                   *
C     *        M=NUMBER  OF SYSTEMS (RIGHT HAND SIDE VECTORS)       *
C     *        A=N BY M+N (USUALLY,M=1) ARRAY OF COEFFICIENTS       *
C     *          AUGMENTED WITH EACH RIGHT SIDE VECTOR              *
C     *        DELT=ESTIMATE OF ERROR BOUND (MACHINE EPSILON)       *
C     *     OUTPUT:                                                 *
C     *        A(1,N+J),...,A(N,N+J)                                *
C     *          =SOLUTION OF THE J-TH SYSTEM (J=1,...,M)           *
C     ***************************************************************
C
      DIMENSION A(N,M+N)
      IF(N.GT.1) THEN
         DO 1 K=1,N-1
            PIV=ABS(A(K,K))
            KK=K+1
            IN=K
```

TABLE 2.3.   (Continued)

```
C       *** SEARCH FOR INDEX IN OF MAXIMUM PIVOT VALUE ***
                DO 2 I=KK,N
                    IF(ABS(A(I,K)).GT.PIV) THEN
                        PIV=ABS(A(I,K))
                        IN=I
                    END IF
        2       CONTINUE
                IF(K.NE.IN) THEN
C       *** INTERCHANGE ROWS K AND INDEX IN ***
                DO 3 J=K,M+N
                    X=A(K,J)
                    A(K,J)=A(IN,J)
                    A(IN,J)=X
        3       CONTINUE
                END IF
C       *** CHECK IF PIVOT TOO SMALL ***
                IF(PIV.LT.DELT) THEN
                    WRITE(6,4)
        4           FORMAT(2X,'THE MATRIX IS SINGULAR. GAUSSIAN'
        1           ' ELIMINATION CANNOT BE PERFORMED.')
                    RETURN
                END IF
C       *** FORWARD ELIMINATION STEP ***
                DO 5 I=KK,N
                DO 5 J=KK,M+N
                    A(I,J)=A(I,J)-A(I,K)*A(K,J)/A(K,K)
        5       CONTINUE
        1   CONTINUE
            IF(ABS(A(N,N)).LT.DELT) THEN
                WRITE(6,4)
                RETURN
            END IF
C       *** BACK SUBSTITUTION ***
            DO 6 K=1,M
                A(N,K+N)=A(N,K+N)/A(N,N)
                DO 6 IE=1,N-1
                    I=N-IE
                    IX=I+1
                    DO 7 J=IX,N
                        A(I,K+N)=A(I,K+N)-A(J,K+N)*A(I,J)
        7           CONTINUE
                    A(I,K+N)=A(I,K+N)/A(I,I)
        6       CONTINUE
            RETURN
            ELSE IF(ABS(A(1,1)).LT.DELT) THEN
                WRITE(6,4)
                RETURN
            END IF
            DO 8 J=1,M
                A(1,N+J)=A(1,N+J)/A(1,1)
        8   CONTINUE
            RETURN
            END
```

the system declared singular. Machine epsilon as described in Section 1.3.3 is probably a sensible value for DELT.

The structure of subroutine GAUSS is as follows. The DO loop with label 1 computes the derived systems 1 through $N - 1$, and the DO loop with label 6 performs back substitution. The DO loop with label 2 finds the row index IN and value PIV of the element of the largest magnitude among A(K.K), . . . , A(N,K), and the DO loop with label 3 interchanges rows K and IN.

──── **EXAMPLE 2.6** ──

We call on subroutine GAUSS to solve our example problem,

$$2x_1 + x_2 + 3x_3 = 1$$

$$4x_1 + 4x_2 + 7x_3 = 1$$

$$2x_1 + 5x_2 + 9x_3 = 3.$$

Here $N = 3$ and $M = 1$. We take the singularity threshold DELT to be approximately machine epsilon. The calling program and output are given in Tables 2.4 and 2.5. The calling program copies the original matrix into array **B**, and **B** is subsequently passed on to GAUSS. This matrix is altered as GAUSS performs eliminations. Then the solution computed by GAUSS (and stored in the fourth column of the returned matrix **B**) is checked. The simple check of comparing $A\tilde{x}$ with **b**, $\tilde{x}$ being the computed solution, is a popular test. The difference $A\tilde{x} - b$

TABLE 2.4   Calling Program for a Linear Equation Solution

```
C      PROGRAM RESIDUAL
C
C      *************************************************************
C      THIS PROGRAM SOLVES A 3 BY 3 SYSTEM OF LINEAR EQUATIONS,
C      AND COMPUTES RESIDUALS ASSOCIATED WITH THE SOLUTION
C      CALLS:   GAUSS
C      OUTPUT: A=3 BY 4 ARRAY CONTAINING COEFFICIENTS AND RIGHT
C                   HAND SIDE VECTOR
C              B(I,4)=3 BY 1 SOLUTION VECTOR
C              R=1 BY 3 ARRAY OF RESIDUALS ASSOCIATED WITH
C                   COMPUTED SOLUTION OF THE SYSTEM
C      *************************************************************
C
       DIMENSION A(3,4),B(3,4),R(3)
       DATA A /2,4,2,1,4,5,3,7,9,1,1,3/
C
C      *** COPIES THE ORIGINAL MATRIX INTO B                    ***
       DO 1 I=1,3
          DO 1 J=1,4
             B(I,J)=A(I,J)
     1 CONTINUE
     4 FORMAT(4X,4F9.5)
       EPS=1.E-7
C
C      *** SUBROUTINE GAUSS COMPUTES SOLUTION OF THE LINEAR     ***
C      *** SYSTEM                                               ***
C
       CALL GAUSS(3,1,B,EPS)
     8 FORMAT(///)
       WRITE(10,8)
       WRITE(10,*)'ANSR ',(B(I,4),I=1,3)
       WRITE(10,8)
C
C      *** COMPUTES RESIDUALS ASSOCIATED WITH SOLUTION          ***
C
       DO 3 KK=1,3
          S=0
          DO 2 J=1,3
             S=S+A(KK,J)*B(J,4)
     2    CONTINUE
          R(KK)=S-A(KK,4)
          WRITE(10,*)'RESID',R(KK)
     3 CONTINUE
       STOP
       END
```

is called the *residual vector*, and it will be examined in Section 2.2.4. In our case we can see that the components of the residual vector are zero, up to machine accuracy.

TABLE 2.5   Results and Residuals for Example 2.6

ANSR	-0.5000000	-1.000000	1.000000

RESID	0.0000000E+00
RESID	0.0000000E+00
RESID	0.0000000E+00

A number of subroutines in this book call for GAUS1 instead of GAUSS, when a linear system of equations requires solution. GAUS1 is identical to GAUSS, except for the added calling parameter ND. The need for this alternative subroutine arises in cases in which the matrix of the linear system to be solved is not a calling parameter of the main program and consequently its dimension cannot be varied. In such cases, the subroutine calling GAUS1 sets ND to an appropriate application upper bound. The first few lines of GAUS1 are given in Table 2.6. Below the dimension declaration, GAUS1 and GAUSS are identical.

The consensus of experts is that among the alternative pivoting strategies—no pivoting, partial pivoting, and maximal pivoting—partial pivoting is the most attractive for solution of "routine" linear equations. Any sensible code should have some check to avoid zero pivots. Partial pivoting provides such a check and as the order n of the linear system increases, the relative expense of partial pivoting becomes inconsequential. For the reader may confirm that fewer than $\frac{1}{2}n^2$ comparisons need to be made during the course of a calculation, whereas in Section 2.2.5 we will see that the number of arithmetic operations grows as n^3. The

TABLE 2.6   Subroutine GAUS1

```
          SUBROUTINE GAUS1(N,M,ND,A,DELT)
C
C     ***********************************************************
C     *   FUNCTION: THIS SUBROUTINE COMPUTES THE SOLUTIONS FOR M  *
C     *             SYSTEMS WITH N EQUATIONS AND N UNKNOWNS USING  *
C     *             GAUSSIAN ELIMINATION                           *
C     *   USAGE:                                                   *
C     *       CALL SEQUENCE: CALL GAUS1(N,M,ND,A,DELT)             *
C     *   PARAMETERS:                                              *
C     *       INPUT:                                               *
C     *           N=NUMBER OF EQUATIONS AND UNKNOWNS               *
C     *           M=NUMBER  OF SYSTEMS (RIGHT HAND SIDE VECTORS)   *
C     *           ND=UPPER BOUND TO THE LINEAR EQUATION ORDER      *
C     *           A=N BY M+N (USUALLY,M=1) ARRAY OF COEFFICIENTS   *
C     *              AUGMENTED WITH EACH RIGHT SIDE VECTOR         *
C     *           DELT=ESTIMATE OF ERROR BOUND (MACHINE EPSILON)   *
C     *       OUTPUT:                                              *
C     *           A(1,N+J),...,A(N,N+J)                            *
C     *             =SOLUTION OF THE J-TH SYSTEM (J=1,...,M)       *
C     ***********************************************************
C
          DIMENSION A(ND,ND+M)
```

*Subroutine GAUS1 is identical to GAUSS, below dimension declaration.

number of comparisons by maximal pivoting is also proportional to n^3, so the effort of this alternative is commensurate with the computation time of the elimination process itself.

In theory (e.g., Stewart, 1973, p. 152), the roundoff error with partial pivoting can grow much faster with increasing number n of equations than with maximal pivoting (2^n versus $n^{1/2}$). But in practice, the error growth with partial pivoting is typically far smaller than its theoretical limit. The extra computing expense associated with maximal pivoting is significant for large matrices. For comparable additional expense, one can typically achieve much greater improvement in accuracy by performing Gaussian elimination with partial pivoting in double precision.

Application 2.2 ———————————————————————————

In the introduction of this chapter we have seen (Application 2.1) that the currents in a resistive network can be obtained by solving linear equations

$$(R_1 + R_2 + R_4)i_1 \quad - R_2 i_2 \qquad - R_4 i_3 = 0$$
$$- R_2 i_1 + (R_2 + R_3)i_2 \qquad - R_3 i_3 = V_1$$
$$- R_4 i_1 \qquad - R_3 i_2 + (R_3 + R_4 + R_5)i_3 = V_2.$$

Define the numerical values as

$$R_1 = 1 \cdot 10^3 \ \Omega$$
$$R_2 = 2 \cdot 10^3 \ \Omega$$
$$R_3 = 3 \cdot 10^3 \ \Omega$$
$$R_4 = 4 \cdot 10^3 \ \Omega$$
$$R_5 = 5 \cdot 10^3 \ \Omega$$
$$V_1 = 1 \ V$$
$$V_2 = 2 \ V.$$

Upon substituting numerical values, we have

$$7 \times 10^3 i_1 \quad -2 \times 10^3 i_2 \quad -4 \times 10^3 i_3 = 0$$
$$-2 \times 10^3 i_1 \quad +5 \times 10^3 i_2 \quad -3 \times 10^3 i_3 = 1$$
$$-4 \times 10^3 i_1 \quad -3 \times 10^3 i_2 \quad +12 \times 10^3 i_3 = 2.$$

A program too trivial to include calling subroutine GAUSS (Table 2.3) gives the solution that, to the accuracy shown,

$$i_1 = 0.486 \ mA. \qquad i_2 = 0.696 \ mA, \qquad i_3 = 0.503 \ mA,$$

where "mA" denotes 10^{-3} ampere.

2.2.4 Error Checks

In Section 2.2.3 we acknowledged that the cumulative effects of roundoff error in naive Gaussian elimination can be troublesome, although pivoting techniques can, to some extent, reduce these effects. Now rules for on-line assessment of error are offered.

A popular procedure for checking the computed solution of a linear system is to examine the residual. The *residual error* (or simply *residual*) associated with a computed solution $\tilde{\mathbf{x}}$ of (2.1) is defined in matrix notation by

$$\mathbf{r} = \mathbf{A}\tilde{\mathbf{x}} - \mathbf{b}. \tag{2.11}$$

Clearly, if $\tilde{\mathbf{x}}$ is the exact solution, $\mathbf{r}$ is zero. The residual gives some indication of how reliable a computed solution $\tilde{\mathbf{x}}$ is. If the coordinates of $\mathbf{r}$ are large, $\tilde{\mathbf{x}}$ is suspect. However, a small residual does not guarantee that $\tilde{\mathbf{x}}$ is accurate, as will be demonstrated in Section 2.4. On the positive side, it is possible (Section 2.4.2) to bound the error in terms of the residual.

Another accuracy check is the following. Suppose that we choose a vector $\mathbf{y} = (y_1, y_2, \ldots, y_n)^T$ to be a vector of 1's. That is, $y_i = 1$, for $i = 1, 2, \ldots, n$. Then define the vector $c = (c_1, c_2, \ldots, c_n)^T$ by the condition that

$$c_i = \sum_{j=1}^{n} a_{ij}, \qquad 1 \le i \le n, \tag{2.12}$$

By construction, therefore, the solution of

$$\mathbf{Ay} = \mathbf{c} \tag{2.13}$$

is the vector of $y = (1, 1, \ldots, 1)^T$. Now by setting $M = 2$ and defining $a_{i,n+2} = c_i$, $i = 1, \ldots, n$, one may employ subroutine GAUSS (Table 2.3) to solve both equations $\mathbf{Ax} = \mathbf{b}$ and $\mathbf{Ay} = \mathbf{c}$ at essentially the same expense as either one of them, since forward elimination (2.9) needs to be performed only once. When the solution $\tilde{\mathbf{y}}$ is returned, one can see whether the computed solution of (2.13) is close to the known solution vector $\mathbf{y} = (1, 1, \ldots, 1)^T$. A rule of thumb is that if for a given matrix $\mathbf{A}$, the solution of $\mathbf{Ax} = \mathbf{b}$ is sensitive to roundoff, it will be sensitive for every coefficient vector $\mathbf{b}$. The procedure of solving equation (2.13) allows us to assess this sensitivity. (The use of 1's here is arbitrary. Any vector $\mathbf{y}$ could be chosen, with the understanding that $\mathbf{c} = \mathbf{Ay}$.)

We compare some results based on computational experimentation in the next two examples.

───── **EXAMPLE 2.7** ─────────────────────────────────────

By means of the calling program in Table 2.7, subroutine GAUSS is used to solve a linear equation of order 80. We assess the accuracy by the measures just discussed. The coordinates of the coefficient matrix $\mathbf{A}$ and the vector $\mathbf{b}$, in the equation $\mathbf{Ax} = \mathbf{b}$ are chosen by a VAX/VMS random number generator. The vector $\mathbf{A}(j, 82)$, $1 \le j \le 80$, is defined as $\mathbf{c}$ in (2.12). The program in Table 2.7 executes the calculation the results of which are given in Table 2.8. The 80 components of the outputted residual $A\tilde{x} - b$ were of the order of 10^{-6} or 10^{-7}, and the computed coordinates of y were all equal to 1, to at least four significant digits. In view of this evidence, we feel confident that the computed solution vector $\tilde{x}$ was accurate to at least three significant decimals.

TABLE 2.7   Calling Program for a Linear Equation of Order 80

```
C       PROGRAM RAN
C
C       ***************************************************************
C       GENERATES A SYSTEM OF 80 LINEAR EQUATIONS WITH RANDOM
C       COEFFICIENTS, SOLVES THE SYSTEM AND COMPUTES THE RESIDUALS
C       ASSOCIATED WITH THE SOLUTION
C       CALLS:  GAUSS
C       OUTPUT: A=80 BY 1 ARRAY CONTAINING THE SOLUTION TO THE
C               SYSTEM
C               R=80 BY 1 ARRAY OF RESIDUALS
C       ***************************************************************
C
        DIMENSION A(80,82),B(80,82),R(80)
C
C       *** GENERATE THE INPUT DATA AND STORE IT IN B              ***
C
        KSEED=12345
        DO 1 I=1,80
        DO 1,J=1,81
           A(I,J)=RAN(KSEED)
           B(I,J)=A(I,J)
      1 CONTINUE
C
C       *** GENERATES A DATA VECTOR SO THAT Y(J)=1.0 IS           ***
C       *** A SOLUTION                                           ***
C
        DO 2 I=1,80
        DO 2 J=1,80
           A(I,82)=A(I,82)+A(I,J)
      2 CONTINUE
        EPS=1.E-7
C
C       *** SUBROUTINE GAUSS COMPUTES SOLUTION OF THE LINEAR      ***
C       *** SYSTEM                                               ***
C
        CALL GAUSS(80,2,A,EPS)
C
C       *** COMPUTES RESIDUALS ASSOCIATED WITH SOLUTION           ***
C
        DO 3 I=1,80
           S=0.
           DO 4 J=1,80
              S=S+B(I,J)*A(J,81)
      4    CONTINUE
           R(I)=S-B(I,81)
      3 CONTINUE
        DO 5 I=1,40
           J=I+40
           WRITE(10,6)I,A(I,82),R(I),J,A(J,82),R(J)
      6    FORMAT(1X,I3,2X,F10.6,2X,E12.5,6X,I3,2X,F10.6,2X,E12.5)
      5 CONTINUE
        STOP
        END
```

TABLE 2.8   Application of GAUSS to a System of 80 Variables

Coordinate Number, k	Computed Test Coordinate, $\tilde{y}_k$	Residual, r_k	k	$\tilde{y}_k$	r_k
1	0.999992	0.17881E-06	41	1.000012	-0.14901E-05
2	0.999998	-0.21458E-05	42	0.999997	-0.65565E-06
3	0.999981	0.36359E-05	43	1.000014	-0.26822E-05
4	1.000000	-0.54464E-05	44	1.000028	-0.29802E-06
5	1.000007	0.45896E-05	45	1.000001	0.17881E-05
6	1.000007	0.26822E-05	46	0.999999	0.15795E-05
7	1.000005	0.22650E-05	47	1.000009	-0.59605E-06
8	0.999990	0.71526E-06	48	1.000003	-0.19148E-05
9	1.000020	-0.15199E-05	49	0.999998	0.46492E-05
10	1.000002	-0.10729E-05	50	0.999996	-0.10282E-05
11	0.999992	-0.51260E-05	51	1.000016	-0.50664E-06
12	1.000010	0.26822E-05	52	0.999998	-0.41723E-06
13	1.000011	-0.15795E-05	53	0.999993	-0.13411E-06
14	1.000029	-0.10878E-05	54	0.999998	0.13113E-05
15	1.000016	0.65565E-06	55	1.000006	-0.29802E-05
16	0.999991	0.41723E-06	56	1.000013	-0.55432E-05
17	1.000001	0.30994E-05	57	1.000006	0.26822E-06
18	1.000007	0.28610E-05	58	0.999994	0.24252E-05
19	0.999998	-0.39935E-05	59	0.999993	-0.23842E-06
20	0.999994	-0.26226E-05	60	1.000010	0.11325E-05
21	0.999994	-0.67055E-06	61	0.999991	0.25332E-06
22	1.000004	-0.41723E-06	62	1.000011	0.51036E-05
23	1.000009	-0.32634E-05	63	0.999992	-0.29802E-05
24	0.999993	-0.15497E-05	64	1.000002	0.49472E-05
25	0.999999	0.16093E-05	65	0.999993	-0.67949E-05
26	1.000010	0.13560E-05	66	1.000003	0.10133E-05
27	0.999991	0.15497E-05	67	0.999992	0.27418E-05
28	0.999997	0.25034E-05	68	1.000006	-0.28461E-05
29	0.999997	-0.15423E-05	69	0.999997	-0.95367E-06
30	0.999993	-0.21160E-05	70	0.999979	-0.42617E-05
31	0.999993	0.39935E-05	71	0.999996	-0.16391E-05
32	0.999982	0.10431E-05	72	1.000000	-0.23842E-05
33	1.000011	0.23842E-06	73	1.000011	-0.16391E-05
34	1.000016	-0.14305E-05	74	0.999993	0.59605E-07
35	1.000003	0.24438E-05	75	0.999998	-0.25034E-05
36	1.000000	-0.19073E-05	76	0.999994	-0.81658E-05
37	0.999994	0.71526E-06	77	0.999980	-0.83447E-06
38	0.999992	0.17881E-06	78	0.999986	0.47088E-05
39	0.999984	-0.46492E-05	79	1.000005	0.21383E-05
40	1.000001	-0.20862E-05	80	0.999985	-0.39339E-05

──────────── **EXAMPLE 2.8** ────────────

We shall see that Newton–Cotes integration (Section 4.3) and polynomial interpolation with equally spaced abscissas x_i both entail solution of linear equations with coefficient matrices of the form

$$
\mathbf{A} = \begin{bmatrix}
1 & 1 & \cdots & 1 \\
x_1 & x_2 & \cdots & x_n \\
\vdots & \vdots & & \vdots \\
x_1^{n-1} & x_2^{n-1} & \cdots & x_n^{n-1}
\end{bmatrix}. \tag{2.14}
$$

In Chapter 4 (Example 4.13) it will be seen that this matrix leads to large numerical error. Actually, this matrix (2.14) shows up in many engineering and physical contexts, and is known as the *Vandermonde matrix*.

The Vandermonde matrix (2.14) is famous not only for the regularity of its occurrence in applications, but also for its tendency toward instability. This instability, or ill-conditioning, as we will call it in Section 2.4, gives us an opportunity to investigate the relative effectiveness of different pivoting strategies in Gauss elimination. We took

$$x_i = ih, \qquad 1 \le i \le n,$$

with $h = 0.1$, and took n to be 8. The coefficients of the vector **b** were chosen randomly. We compared:

1. No pivoting (naive elimination).
2. Partial pivoting (subroutine GAUSS).
3. Maximal pivoting.
4. Partial pivoting in double precision.

The error was assessed by the root-mean-square (rms) residual and rms difference defined, respectively, as

$$\text{rms residual} = \left(\frac{1}{n} \sum_{i=1}^{n} r_i^2 \right)^{1/2}$$

with $\mathbf{r} = (r_1, r_2, \ldots, r_n)^T = \mathbf{A\tilde{x}} - \mathbf{b}$ and

$$\text{rms difference} = \left[\frac{1}{n} \sum_{i=1}^{n} (1 - \tilde{y}_i)^2 \right]^{1/2} .$$

Here $\tilde{\mathbf{x}}$ is the computed solution to $\mathbf{Ax} = \mathbf{b}$ and $\tilde{\mathbf{y}}$ the computed solution to $\mathbf{Ay} = \mathbf{c}$, where, as in (2.12),

$$c_i = a_{i1} + a_{i2} + \cdots + a_{in}$$

(so the exact answer is $y_i = 1$, $1 \le i \le n$). Furthermore, r_i is the ith component of the residual vector **r**. We display the results of our study in Table 2.9. With the exception of the obvious benefits of partial pivoting in double precision, the relative merits of the pivoting strategies are inconclusive. The calculations were done on a VAX machine.

TABLE 2.9 Observed Root-Mean-Square (RMS) Error Under Different Pivoting Strategies

RMS Errors	No Pivoting	Partial Pivoting	Maximal Pivoting	Partial Pivoting in Double Precision
Rms residual	$8.6 \cdot 10^{-5}$	$2.1 \cdot 10^{-4}$	$9.0 \cdot 10^{-4}$	$9.2 \cdot 10^{-14}$
Rms difference	$1.6 \cdot 10^{-3}$	$2.0 \cdot 10^{-3}$	$3.4 \cdot 10^{-3}$	$4.4 \cdot 10^{-14}$

★2.2.5 Analysis of Computational Effort

Here we calculate the total number of operations needed for the solution of the linear system (2.4) by Gauss elimination. Forward elimination [equation (2.9)] for fixed i, j, and k requires one multiplication and one addition. (We are regarding subtraction as addition with possibly negative summands.) If k is fixed, there are $n - k$ values for i and $n + 1 - k$ values for j, so the number of additions and multiplications is $(n - k)(n + 1 - k)$. There are $(n - k)$ divisions, one for each value of i. The total number of additions and multiplications are both given by summing over the range of k:

$$\sum_{k=1}^{n-1} (n - k)(n + 1 - k) = \sum_{k=1}^{n-1} [(n^2 + n) - k(2n + 1) + k^2]$$

$$= (n - 1)(n^2 + n) - (2n + 1) \sum_{k=1}^{n-1} k + \sum_{k=1}^{n-1} k^2$$

$$= (n - 1)(n^2 + n)$$

$$- (2n + 1)\frac{n(n - 1)}{2} + \frac{(n - 1)n(2n - 1)}{6}$$

$$= \frac{n^3}{3} - \frac{n}{3}.$$

$$(2.15)$$

We have used the facts that for $n \geq 2$,

$$1 + 2 + \cdots + (n - 1) = \frac{n(n - 1)}{2}$$

and

$$1^2 + 2^2 + \cdots + (n - 1)^2 = \frac{(n - 1)n(2n - 1)}{6}.$$

These identities can be proven by induction (Problem 8). The number of divisions equals

$$\sum_{k=1}^{n-1} (n - k) = (n - 1) + (n - 2) + \cdots + 1 = \sum_{k=1}^{n-1} k = \frac{n(n - 1)}{2}.$$

In back substitution as defined by (2.10), for each value of k we require one division, $n - k$ additions, and $n - k$ multiplications. By summing over the range of k, one can conclude that the number of additions and multiplications equals

$$\sum_{k=1}^{n} (n - k) = \frac{n(n - 1)}{2}$$

and only n divisions are needed. Thus the effort required for forward elimination dominates, and we can conclude that the number of multiplications and additions grows proportionally to $n^3/3$. Thus, as the order n becomes large, the relative

TABLE 2.10   Computational Effort for Gauss Elimination*

	Forward Elimination	Back Substitution
Additions	$\dfrac{n^3}{3} - \dfrac{n}{3}$	$\dfrac{n(n-1)}{2}$
Multiplications	$\dfrac{n^3}{3} - \dfrac{n}{3}$	$\dfrac{n(n-1)}{2}$
Divisions	$\dfrac{n(n-1)}{2}$	n

*n, order of the system.

cost of back substitution becomes negligible. For that reason, the sensitivity check of recovering the known solution y described in connection with (2.12) and (2.13) is economical. We summarize the findings of this section in Table 2.10.

★2.2.6   Solution of General Systems of Linear Equations

In the previous sections we assumed that the matrix **A** of coefficients is a square matrix and is nonsingular. The matrix **A** can be $m \times n$, $m \neq n$. If one applies maximal pivoting, the process terminates if no further nonzero elements can be found for pivoting. In the general case, the final derived system has the form

$$a_{11}x_1 + a_{12}x_2 + a_{13}x_3 + \cdots + a_{1k}x_k + a_{1,k+1}x_{k+1} + \cdots + \quad a_{1n}x_n = a_{1,n+1}$$
$$a_{22}^{(1)}x_2 + a_{23}^{(1)}x_3 + \cdots + a_{2k}^{(1)}x_k + a_{2,k+1}^{(1)}x_{k+1} + \cdots + \quad a_{2n}^{(1)}x_n = a_{2,n+1}^{(1)}$$
$$\cdot \quad \quad a_{kk}^{(k-1)}x_k + a_{k,k+1}^{(k-1)}x_{k+1} + \cdots + a_{kn}^{(k-1)}x_n = a_{k,n+1}^{(k-1)}$$
$$0x_{k+1} + \cdots + \quad 0x_n = a_{k+1,n+1}^{(k)}$$
$$\vdots \quad\quad\quad \vdots \quad \vdots$$
$$0x_{k+1} + \cdots + \quad 0x_n = a_{m,n+1}^{(k)}$$

If any of the elements $a_{k+1,n+1}^{(k)}, \ldots, a_{m,n+1}^{(k)}$ on the right side differ from zero, no solution exists, since the corresponding equation itself leads to a contradiction. Otherwise, the variables $x_{k+1}, \ldots, x_n$ can be selected arbitrarily: They are *free parameters*. For any particular selection of these variables, the remaining variables $x_1, \ldots, x_k$ are uniquely determined by back substitution, after substituting the free parameters $x_{k+1}, \ldots, x_n$ into the first k equations.

As an illustration of this procedure consider the following example.

──────── **EXAMPLE 2.9** ────────────────────────────────────

The linear system of equations

$$x_1 - x_2 + 2x_3 + x_4 = 3$$

$$2x_1 + 3x_2 + x_3 - x_4 = 5$$

$$3x_1 + 2x_2 + 3x_3 = 8$$

$$x_1 + 4x_2 - x_3 - 2x_4 = 2$$

will be solved. The elimination is shown in Table 2.11.

TABLE 2.11   Solution of a General System of Linear Equations

Original system	1	-1	2	1	3
	2	3	1	-1	5
	3	2	3	0	8
	1	4	-1	-2	2
First derived system	1	-1	2	1	3
		5	-3	-3	-1
		5	-3	-3	-1
		5	-3	-3	-1
Second derived system	1	-1	2	1	3
		5	-3	-3	-1
			0	0	0
			0	0	0

For the sake of simplicity we did not use maximal pivoting. Since the numbers in the final column of the last two rows are all zeros, solutions exist. Here $k = 2$, and unknowns x_3 and x_4 are free parameters. From the second equation of the last system we get

$$5x_2 = 3x_3 + 3x_4 - 1.$$

That is,

$$x_2 = \tfrac{3}{5}x_3 + \tfrac{3}{5}x_4 - \tfrac{1}{5}.$$

The first equation then implies that

$$x_1 = x_2 - 2x_3 - x_4 + 3$$

$$= \tfrac{3}{5}x_3 + \tfrac{3}{5}x_4 - \tfrac{1}{5} - 2x_3 - x_4 + 3$$

$$= -\tfrac{7}{5}x_3 - \tfrac{2}{5}x_4 + \tfrac{14}{5}.$$

These formulas for x_1 and x_2 give the general solution. Particular solutions are obtained by any selection of values for x_3 and x_4.

If we select $x_3 = 1$, $x_4 = 0$, then

$$x_1 = -\tfrac{7}{5} + \tfrac{14}{5} = \tfrac{7}{5}$$

$$x_2 = \tfrac{3}{5} - \tfrac{1}{5} = \tfrac{2}{5}.$$

If we select $x_3 = 0$, $x_4 = 1$, then

$$x_1 = -\tfrac{2}{5} + \tfrac{14}{5} = \tfrac{12}{5}$$

$$x_2 = \tfrac{3}{5} - \tfrac{1}{5} = \tfrac{2}{5}.$$

One can check that $x_1 = \tfrac{7}{5}$, $x_2 = \tfrac{2}{5}$, $x_3 = 1$, and $x_4 = 0$, and also $x_1 = \tfrac{12}{5}$, $x_2 = \tfrac{2}{5}$, $x_3 = 0$, and $x_4 = 1$ satisfy the original system. All solutions can be obtained by the proper selection of x_3 and x_4.

2.3
MATRIX INVERSION, DETERMINANTS, AND BAND SYSTEMS

2.3.1 Gauss Elimination for Matrix Inversion

The elimination method can be used to find inverses of matrices. Let $\mathbf{A}$ be an nth-order nonsingular matrix, and let the n columns of the inverse matrix be denoted by $\mathbf{x}^{(1)}, \ldots, \mathbf{x}^{(n)}$. That is, $\mathbf{A}^{-1} = (\mathbf{x}^{(1)}, \mathbf{x}^{(2)}, \ldots, \mathbf{x}^{(n)})$. Then (Appendix A, property 21)

$$\mathbf{A}\mathbf{A}^{-1} = \mathbf{A}(\mathbf{x}^{(1)}, \ldots, \mathbf{x}^{(n)}) = (\mathbf{A}\mathbf{x}^{(1)}, \ldots, \mathbf{A}\mathbf{x}^{(n)}). \tag{2.16}$$

On the right of (2.16), $\mathbf{A}\mathbf{x}^{(j)}$ ($j = 1, \ldots, n$) denotes the column vector obtained after the matrix $\mathbf{A}$ has been multiplied by vector $\mathbf{x}^{(j)}$. The columns of the identity matrix will be represented by $\mathbf{e}^{(1)}, \ldots, \mathbf{e}^{(n)}$. That is, the jth coordinate of $\mathbf{e}^{(j)}$ is 1 and the other coordinates are 0, for $j = 1, \ldots, n$. Now, by definition of matrix inverse (Appendix A, property 17),

$$\mathbf{A}\mathbf{A}^{-1} = \mathbf{I} = (\mathbf{e}^{(1)}, \ldots, \mathbf{e}^{(n)}).$$

That is,

$$(\mathbf{A}\mathbf{x}^{(1)}, \ldots, \mathbf{A}\mathbf{x}^{(n)}) = (\mathbf{e}^{(1)}, \ldots, \mathbf{e}^{(n)}).$$

By matching the columns of the left- and right-hand sides of the equation above, we assemble the set of linear equations

$$\mathbf{A}\mathbf{x}^{(1)} = \mathbf{e}^{(1)}, \ \mathbf{A}\mathbf{x}^{(2)} = \mathbf{e}^{(2)}, \ldots, \ \mathbf{A}\mathbf{x}^{(n)} = \mathbf{e}^{(n)}. \tag{2.17}$$

Observe that the coefficient matrix $\mathbf{A}$ of each of the systems above is the same. The forward elimination process, therefore, needs to be done only once. Back substitution has to be repeated n times, once for each of the vectors $\mathbf{x}^{(j)}$. Specifically, the first derived system is obtained by operating on the array

a_{11}	a_{12}	$\cdots$	a_{1n}	1	0	$\cdots$	0
a_{21}	a_{22}	$\cdots$	a_{2n}	0	1	$\cdots$	0
$\vdots$	$\vdots$		$\vdots$	$\vdots$	$\vdots$		$\vdots$
a_{n1}	a_{n2}	$\cdots$	a_{nn}	0	0	$\cdots$	1

according to the rule

$$a_{ij}^{(1)} = a_{ij} - \frac{a_{i1}}{a_{11}} a_{1j} \qquad (2 \leq i \leq n, \, 2 \leq j \leq 2n),$$

where the elements of the right-hand vectors (i.e., the elements of the identity matrix) are now placed in the positions $a_{ij}(i = 1, \ldots, n$ and $j = n + 1, \ldots, 2n)$. Further derived systems are obtained by (2.9), with the modification that j ranges from $k + 1$ to $2n$, in constructing the elements $a_{ij}^{(k)}$ for each value of k.

In the notation of (2.17), one obtains the column vectors $\mathbf{x}^{(j)}$ of the inverse matrix by performing back substitution but with the values $a_{k,n+j}^{(k-1)}$ replacing $a_{k,n+1}^{(k-1)}$ in (2.10).

──────── **EXAMPLE 2.10** ────────────────────────────────────

Let $\mathbf{A}$ be the matrix of coefficients of the system given in Example 2.1:

$$\mathbf{A} = \begin{bmatrix} 2 & 1 & 3 \\ 4 & 4 & 7 \\ 2 & 5 & 9 \end{bmatrix}.$$

The inverse of $\mathbf{A}$ will be now determined. The calculations of the derived systems are given in Table 2.12.

TABLE 2.12   Computations of Example 2.10

	2	1	3	1	0	0
Original system	4	4	7	0	1	0
	2	5	9	0	0	1
	2	1	3	1	0	0
First derived system	0	2	1	-2	1	0
	0	4	6	-1	0	1
	2	1	3	1	0	0
Second derived system	0	2	1	-2	1	0
	0	0	4	3	-2	1

By the successive use of back substitution we find that

$$\mathbf{A}^{-1} = \begin{bmatrix} \frac{1}{16} & \frac{3}{8} & -\frac{5}{16} \\ -\frac{11}{8} & \frac{3}{4} & -\frac{1}{8} \\ \frac{3}{4} & -\frac{1}{2} & \frac{1}{4} \end{bmatrix}.$$

For example, the first column is obtained by using back substitution on the $(n + 1)$st column of the second derived system. Thus according to (2.10), with $a_{ij}^{(-1)}$ denoting the (i, j) coordinate of $\mathbf{A}^{-1}$,

$$a_{31}^{(-1)} = \frac{3}{4}$$

and continuing recursively,

$$a_{21}^{(-1)} = \frac{-2 - 1 \cdot \frac{3}{4}}{2} = -\frac{11}{8}$$

$$a_{11}^{(-1)} = \frac{1 - 3 \cdot \frac{3}{4} - 1 \cdot (-\frac{11}{8})}{2} = \frac{1}{16}.$$

The second and third columns of $\mathbf{A}^{-1}$ are obtained in similar fashion from the $(n + 2)$nd and $(n + 3)$rd columns of the second derived system.

Note that if $\mathbf{A}^{-1}$ is known, the solution $\mathbf{x}$ of equation (2.2) can be obtained according to

$$\mathbf{x} = \mathbf{A}^{-1}\mathbf{b}, \tag{2.18}$$

which is verified as property 18 in Appendix A. However, solution of (2.2) by computing the inverse of the matrix of coefficients and the use of (2.18) is relatively expensive. The computation of an inverse requires about three times as many operations as the Gauss elimination method given in Section 2.2.4 for solving (2.2). Moreover, the effects of roundoff error in inverting $\mathbf{A}$ and multiplying as in (2.18) tend to be more pronounced. In short, the technique given here should be reserved for cases in which the matrix inverse is actually needed.

TABLE 2.13   Subroutine INVG for Matrix Inversion

```
        SUBROUTINE INVG(N,A,B,DELT,C)
C
C   ****************************************************************
C   *   FUNCTION: THIS SUBROUTINE COMPUTES THE INVERSE MATRIX     *
C   *             BY GAUSS ELIMINATION                            *
C   *   USAGE:                                                    *
C   *       CALL SEQUENCE: CALL INVG(N,A,B,DELT,C)                *
C   *       EXTERNAL FUNCTIONS/SUBROUTINES: SUBROUTINE GAUSS      *
C   *   PARAMETERS:                                               *
C   *       INPUT:                                                *
C   *           N=ORDER OF THE MATRIX                             *
C   *           A=N BY N ARRAY OF MATRIX VALUES                   *
C   *          DELT=ERROR BOUND                                   *
C   *       OUTPUT:                                               *
C   *           B=N BY N ARRAY, THE COMPUTED INVERSE OF A         *
C   *           C=N BY 2*N ARRAY, A WORK MATRIX                   *
C   ****************************************************************
C
        DIMENSION A(N,N),B(N,N),C(N,2*N)
C       *** COMPUTE WORKING MATRIX C FROM MATRIX A ***
C       ***     AND THE APPENDED IDENTITY MATRIX   ***
C       ***  NUMBER OF COLUMNS OF MATRIX C IS 2*N  ***
        DO 1 I=1,N
          DO 1 J=1,N
            C(I,J)=A(I,J)
            C(I,N+J)=0.0
            IF(I.EQ.J) C(I,N+J)=1.0
      1 CONTINUE
C       *** COMPUTE MATRIX INVERSE BY GAUSSIAN ELIMINATION ***
        M=N
        CALL GAUSS(N,M,C,DELT)
        DO 2 I=1,N
          DO 2 J=1,N
            B(I,J)=C(I,J+N)
      2 CONTINUE
        RETURN
        END
```

Subroutine INVG for matrix inversion is given in Table 2.13. A professional-level code would require about half the memory but would be more difficult to understand. In writing a driver program for INVG, the user must be careful to dimension $\mathbf{A}$, $\mathbf{B}$, and the work space matrix $\mathbf{C}$ to be, respectively, $n \times n$, $n \times n$, and $n \times 2n$.

EXAMPLE 2.11

By using the result of Example 2.10 the solutions of equations

$$2x_1 + x_2 + 3x_3 = 1$$
$$4x_1 + 4x_2 + 7x_3 = 1$$
$$2x_1 + 5x_2 + 9x_3 = 3$$

will be determined from (2.18).

In our case $\mathbf{b} = (1, 1, 3)^T$. Consequently, relation (2.18) implies that

$$\mathbf{x} = \begin{bmatrix} x_1 \\ x_2 \\ x_3 \end{bmatrix} = \mathbf{A}^{-1}\mathbf{b} = \begin{bmatrix} \frac{1}{16} & \frac{3}{8} & -\frac{5}{16} \\ -\frac{11}{8} & \frac{3}{4} & -\frac{1}{8} \\ \frac{3}{4} & -\frac{1}{2} & \frac{1}{4} \end{bmatrix} \begin{bmatrix} 1 \\ 1 \\ 3 \end{bmatrix}$$

$$= \begin{bmatrix} \frac{1}{16} + \frac{3}{8} - \frac{15}{16} \\ -\frac{11}{8} + \frac{3}{4} - \frac{3}{8} \\ \frac{3}{4} - \frac{1}{2} + \frac{3}{4} \end{bmatrix} = \begin{bmatrix} -\frac{1}{2} \\ -1 \\ 1 \end{bmatrix}.$$

This coincides with the solution obtained in Examples 2.1 and 2.4.

We remark that if $\mathbf{B}$ is an $n \times n$ matrix with columns $[\mathbf{b}^{(1)}, \mathbf{b}^{(2)}, \ldots, \mathbf{b}^{(n)}]$ and $\mathbf{X}$ now is a matrix of vectors $\mathbf{X} = (\mathbf{x}^{(1)}, \mathbf{x}^{(2)}, \ldots, \mathbf{x}^{(n)})$, the technique of this section can be used to find the matrix $\mathbf{X}$ satisfying

$$\mathbf{AX} = \mathbf{B}. \tag{2.19}$$

The idea is to perform the preceding elimination technique on the $n \times (2n)$ tableau

$$[\mathbf{a}^{(1)}, \mathbf{a}^{(2)}, \ldots, \mathbf{a}^{(n)} : \mathbf{b}^{(1)}, \mathbf{b}^{(2)}, \ldots, \mathbf{b}^{(n)}].$$

Then perform Gaussian elimination as we have just described, the difference being that the identity matrix in the initial tableau is to be replaced by matrix $\mathbf{B}$.

EXAMPLE 2.12

To illustrate the matrix technique for solving (2.19), we take

$$\mathbf{A} = \begin{bmatrix} 2 & 1 & 3 \\ 4 & 4 & 7 \\ 2 & 5 & 9 \end{bmatrix} \quad \text{and} \quad \mathbf{B} = \begin{bmatrix} 1 & 4 & 6 \\ 1 & 7 & 15 \\ 3 & 6 & 16 \end{bmatrix}.$$

The elimination process is summarized in Table 2.14.

TABLE 2.14   Computation of Example 2.12

Original system	2	1	3	1	4	6
	4	4	7	1	7	15
	2	5	9	3	6	16
First derived system	2	1	3	1	4	6
		2	1	−1	−1	3
		4	6	2	2	10
Second derived system	2	1	3	1	4	6
		2	1	−1	−1	3
			4	4	4	4

Back substitution shows that

$$x_{31} = \frac{4}{4} = 1, \qquad x_{32} = \frac{4}{4}, \qquad x_{33} = \frac{4}{4} = 1$$

$$x_{21} = \frac{-1 - 1 \cdot 1}{2} = -1, \qquad x_{22} = \frac{-1 - 1 \cdot 1}{2} = -1,$$

$$x_{23} = \frac{3 - 1 \cdot 1}{2} = 1, \qquad x_{11} = \frac{1 - 3 \cdot 1 - 1(-1)}{2} = -\frac{1}{2}$$

$$x_{12} = \frac{4 - 3 \cdot 1 - 1 \cdot 1}{2} = 1, \qquad x_{13} = \frac{6 - 3 \cdot 1 - 1 \cdot 1}{2} = 1.$$

Consequently,

$$\mathbf{X} = \begin{bmatrix} -\frac{1}{2} & 1 & 1 \\ -1 & -1 & 1 \\ 1 & 1 & 1 \end{bmatrix}$$

■

★2.3.2   Evaluation of Determinants

The concept of determinants is firmly embedded in classical matrix theory books, and determinants are used in many application areas. On the other hand, they play a minor role in computational methodology, and they are not simple to define. For that reason we elected not to discuss them in Appendix A. Instead, we refer the reader to standard linear algebra texts such as that by Nering (1963, Chap. 3) for the definition and elementary properties of determinants. Determinant evaluation is a relatively simple extension of the Gaussian elimination method, as we now demonstrate.

Let det (**A**) denote the determinant of matrix **A**. The forward elimination op-

TABLE 2.15 Subroutine DETC for Calculating Determinants

```
          SUBROUTINE DETC(N,A,D,DELT)
C
C       ****************************************************************
C       *   FUNCTION: THIS SUBROUTINE COMPUTES THE DETERMINANT OF A  *
C       *             MATRIX USING GAUSSIAN ELIMINATION              *
C       *   USAGE:                                                   *
C       *       CALL SEQUENCE: CALL DETC(N,A,D,DELT)                 *
C       *   PARAMETERS:                                              *
C       *       INPUT:                                               *
C       *           N=ORDER OF THE MATRIX                            *
C       *           A=N BY N ARRAY OF MATRIX ELEMENTS               *
C       *         DELT=ERROR BOUND                                   *
C       *       OUTPUT:                                              *
C       *           D=DETERMINANT OF THE MATRIX                     *
C       ****************************************************************
C
          DIMENSION A(N,N)
C       *** TEST IF MATRIX A CONTAINS A SINGLE ELEMENT ***
          IF(N.LE.1) THEN
             D=A(1,1)
             RETURN
C       *** IF NOT PERFORM INITIALIZATION ***
          ELSE
             D=1.0
          END IF
          DO 1 K=1,N-1
C       *** PERFORM PARTIAL PIVOTING ***
             U=ABS(A(K,K))
             IN=K
             DO 2 I=K+1,N
                IF (ABS(A(I,K)).GT.U) THEN
                   U=ABS(A(I,K))
                   IN=I
                END IF
    2        CONTINUE
C            *** EXCHANGE ROWS K AND IN IF NEEDED ***
             IF (K.NE.IN) THEN
                D=-D
                DO 3 J=K,N
                   X=A(K,J)
                   A(K,J)=A(IN,J)
                   A(IN,J)=X
    3           CONTINUE
             END IF
             IF (U.LT.DELT) THEN
                D=0.0
                RETURN
             END IF
             D=D*A(K,K)
C            *** PERFORM GAUSSIAN ELIMINATION ON MATRIX ELEMENTS ***
             DO 4 I=K+1,N
                DO 4 J=K+1,N
                   A(I,J)=A(I,J)-A(I,K)*A(K,J)/A(K,K)
    4        CONTINUE
    1     CONTINUE
C       *** COMPUTE MATRIX DETERMINANT ***
          D=D*A(N,N)
          RETURN
          END
```

erations (2.9) do not change the value of the determinant of a matrix and the interchange of two rows (as required in pivoting) has the effect of multiplying the determinant by the factor (-1). The reader may verify by expansion along the diagonal that because it is an upper triangular matrix, the determinant of the coefficient matrix of the $(n - 1)$st derived system is equal to the product of its diagonal elements $a_{11}, a_{22}^{(1)}, a_{33}^{(2)}, \ldots, a_{nn}^{(n-1)}$. Therefore, the determinant of **A** is given by

$$\det (\mathbf{A}) = (-1)^p a_{11} a_{22}^{(1)} a_{33}^{(2)} \cdots a_{nn}^{(n-1)}, \tag{2.20}$$

p being the number of times the row-interchange operation has been used during the entire computation of the derived systems. Table 2.15 gives subroutine DETC for determinant calculation.

──────── **EXAMPLE 2.13** ────────

To obtain the determinant of the matrix in Example 2.1, observe that after forward elimination

$$\det \begin{bmatrix} 2 & 1 & 3 \\ 4 & 4 & 7 \\ 2 & 5 & 9 \end{bmatrix} = (-1)^0 \det \begin{bmatrix} 2 & 1 & 3 \\ 0 & 2 & 1 \\ 0 & 0 & 4 \end{bmatrix} = (-1)^0 (2 \times 2 \times 4) = 16.$$

■

★2.3.3 Band Systems

In certain numerical procedures, especially those for computation of spline functions as discussed in Chapter 4, and solution of boundary-value problems of differential equations by difference equations (S & Y, 1978, Sec. 8.2.3), linear systems having a *band structure* arise. The special case of tridiagonal matrices has special significance. For such matrices the nonzero elements must be on the main diagonal or on the two diagonals just above and below the main diagonal. The tridiagonal matrices are therefore characterized by the property that $a_{ij} = 0$ if $|i - j| \geq 2$. In general, a square matrix $\mathbf{A} = (a_{ij})$ is called a *band matrix* if there is a positive integer k substantially smaller than the order n of the matrix such that $a_{ij} = 0$ if $|i - j| \geq k$. In the case of tridiagonal matrices, $k = 2$. The number of k is said to be the *width* of the band matrix.

It may be seen that the storage requirements for band matrices are much less than for general matrices of the same order. For instance, an $n \times n$ tridiagonal matrix has at most $n + 2(n - 1) = 3n - 2$ nonzero elements. This property is very important if the band matrices are associated with large order n.

To conserve storage capacity, represent the tridiagonal coefficient matrix equation as follows, the elements outside the band shown being zero:

$$\begin{aligned}
d_1 x_1 + c_1 x_2 &= b_1 \\
a_1 x_1 + d_2 x_2 + c_2 x_3 &= b_2 \\
a_2 x_2 + d_3 x_3 + c_3 x_4 &= b_3 \\
&\;\vdots \\
a_{n-2} x_{n-2} + d_{n-1} x_{n-1} + c_{n-1} x_n &= b_{n-1} \\
a_{n-1} x_{n-1} + d_n x_n &= b_n.
\end{aligned} \tag{2.21}$$

Now, instead of storing an $n \times n$ matrix, we need only to store the vectors $\mathbf{a} = (a_i)$, $\mathbf{d} = (d_i)$, $\mathbf{c} = (c_i)$ with dimensions $n - 1$, n, and $n - 1$, respectively. By choosing the diagonal element d_1 as a pivot for the first derived system, we need to eliminate x_1 from the second equation only, and all the other equations will remain the same. The first derived system is therefore the following:

$$
\begin{aligned}
d_1 x_1 + c_1 x_2 &= b_1 \\
d_2^{(1)} x_2 + c_2 x_3 &= b_2^{(1)} \\
a_2 x_2 + d_3 x_3 + c_3 x_4 &= b_3 \\
&\ \ \vdots \\
a_{n-2} x_{n-2} + d_{n-1} x_{n-1} + c_{n-1} x_n &= b_{n-1} \\
a_{n-1} x_{n-1} + d_n x_n &= b_n,
\end{aligned}
$$

where

$$
d_2^{(1)} = d_2 - \frac{a_1}{d_1} c_1, \qquad b_2^{(1)} = b_2 - \frac{a_1}{d_1} b_1. \tag{2.22}
$$

By choosing the diagonal element $d_2^{(1)}$ for computing the second derived system, we need to eliminate x_2 from the third equation only. Now the second derived system has the form

$$
\begin{aligned}
d_1 x_1 + c_1 x_2 &= b_1 \\
d_2^{(1)} x_2 + c_2 x_3 &= b_2^{(1)} \\
d_3^{(2)} x_3 + c_3 x_4 &= b_3^{(2)} \\
a_3 x_3 + d_4 x_4 + c_4 x_5 &= b_4 \\
&\ \ \vdots \\
a_{n-2} x_{n-2} + d_{n-1} x_{n-1} + c_{n-1} x_n &= b_{n-1} \\
a_{n-1} x_{n-1} + d_n x_n &= b_n.
\end{aligned}
$$

We continue in this fashion, proceeding from one equation to the next according to

$$
\boxed{\ d_{k+1}^{(k)} = d_{k+1} - \frac{a_k}{d_k^{(k-1)}} c_k, \qquad b_{k+1}^{(k)} = b_{k+1} - \frac{a_k}{d_k^{(k-1)}} b_k^{(k-1)}\ } \tag{2.23}
$$

for $k = 1, 2, \ldots, n - 1$. By the procedure above, we obtain the upper triangular system

$$d_1 x_1 + c_1 x_2 \qquad\qquad = b_1$$
$$d_2^{(1)} x_2 + c_2 x_3 \qquad\qquad = b_2^{(1)}$$
$$d_3^{(2)} x_3 + c_3 x_4 \qquad\qquad = b_3^{(2)}$$
$$\cdot \quad \cdot \qquad\qquad\qquad\qquad \vdots$$
$$d_{n-1}^{(n-2)} x_{n-1} + c_{n-1} x_n = b_{n-1}^{(n-2)}$$
$$d_n^{(n-1)} x_n = b_n^{(n-1)}.$$

Back substitution also has an efficient form, since from the last equation above we get

$$x_n = \frac{b_n^{(n-1)}}{d_n^{(n-1)}},$$

and the preceding equations imply that

$$x_k = \frac{b_k^{(k-1)} - c_k x_{k+1}}{d_k^{(k-1)}} \qquad (k = n - 1, \ldots, 1). \qquad (2.24)$$

By the algorithm above, the total number of additions and multiplications equals

$$2(n - 1) + n - 1 = 3n - 3,$$

TABLE 2.16   Subroutine BAND for Band Matrices

```
      SUBROUTINE BAND(N,A,B,C,D)
C
C     ****************************************************************
C     *   FUNCTION: THIS SUBROUTINE COMPUTES THE SOLUTION OF A       *
C     *             BAND SYSTEM OF WIDTH 2 OF LINEAR EQUATIONS       *
C     *             USING A MODIFIED GAUSSIAN ELIMINATION            *
C     *   USAGE:                                                     *
C     *       CALL SEQUENCE: CALL BAND(N,A,B,C,D)                    *
C     *   PARAMETERS:                                                *
C     *       INPUT:                                                 *
C     *           A=N-1 BY 1 ARRAY OF SYSTEM 1-ST SUBDIAGONAL        *
C     *               COEFFICIENTS                                   *
C     *           C=N-1 BY 1 ARRAY OF SYSTEM 1-ST SUPERDIAGONAL      *
C     *               COEFFICIENTS                                   *
C     *           D=N BY 1 ARRAY OF SYSTEM DIAGONAL COEFFICIENTS     *
C     *           B=N BY 1 ARRAY OF RIGHT HAND SIDE VALUES           *
C     *       OUTPUT:                                                *
C     *           B=N BY 1 ARRAY OF THE COMPUTED SOLUTION VALUES     *
C     ****************************************************************
C
      DIMENSION A(N-1),B(N),C(N-1),D(N)
C     *** COMPUTE GAUSSIAN ELIMINATION FACTORS ***
      DO 1 I=2,N
        X=A(I-1)/D(I-1)
        D(I)=D(I)-X*C(I-1)
        B(I)=B(I)-X*B(I-1)
    1 CONTINUE
C     *** COMPUTE SYSTEM SOLUTION AND STORE IN VECTOR B ***
      B(N)=B(N)/D(N)
      DO 2 I=1,N-1
        B(N-I)=(B(N-I)-C(N-I)*B(N-I+1))/D(N-I)
    2 CONTINUE
      RETURN
      END
```

which for larger n is essentially nothing compared to the $n^3/3$ additions and multiplications required by conventional Gaussian elimination. The number of divisions is

$$(n - 1) + n = 2n - 1.$$

Table 2.16 presents subroutine BAND for implementing this method.

────── **EXAMPLE 2.14** ──────

We now solve the system of equations

$$x_1 + 2x_2 \qquad\qquad\quad = 2$$
$$x_1 + 3x_2 + 2x_3 \qquad\quad = 7$$
$$x_2 + 4x_3 + 2x_4 = 15$$
$$4x_3 + x_4 = 11.$$

TABLE 2.17   Solution of a Band System

Original system	1	2			2
	1	3	2		7
		1	4	2	15
			4	1	11
First derived system	1	2			2
		1	2		5
		1	4	2	15
			4	1	11
Second derived system	1	2			2
		1	2		5
			2	2	10
			4	1	11
Third derived system	1	2			2
		1	2		5
			2	2	10
				-3	-9

Then Table 2.17 shows the computational results. The method of back substitution leads to the solution:

$$x_4 = \frac{-9}{-3} = 3,$$

$$x_3 = \frac{10 - 2 \cdot 3}{2} = 2,$$

$$x_2 = \frac{5 - 2 \cdot 2}{1} = 1,$$

$$x_1 = \frac{2 - 2 \cdot 1}{1} = 0.$$

■

2.4
MATRIX CONDITIONING

2.4.1 A Qualitative Notion of Conditioning

In solving linear equations by computers, the effect of the accumulated errors on the computed solution should be estimated to check the accuracy of the results. As we have noted in Section 2.2.4, one common test involves finding the *residual vector* **r**, which is defined to be

$$\mathbf{r} = \mathbf{A}\tilde{\mathbf{x}} - \mathbf{b}, \tag{2.25}$$

where $\tilde{\mathbf{x}}$ is a computed approximating solution. Clearly, if $\tilde{\mathbf{x}}$ is actually the exact solution to $\mathbf{A}\mathbf{x} = \mathbf{b}$, the residual is the zero vector. On the other hand, if the residual is relatively large, one can be confident that $\tilde{\mathbf{x}}$ is not a very good approximation to the solution. Unfortunately, the plan of accepting a solution if the residual vector is small is not without some potential peril. In Example 2.15 the computation of the residual vector will be illustrated and following that, in Example 2.16, we will have an instance in which the residual is small but the proposed solution is nevertheless far from the correct solution.

─────── **EXAMPLE 2.15** ───────────────────────────────────

As an illustration of a residual computation, consider the equation

$$\begin{aligned} x_1 + x_2 &= 2 \\ 3x_1 - x_2 &= 2. \end{aligned} \tag{2.26}$$

Suppose, furthermore, that we computed the solution to be

$$\tilde{x}_1 = 0.999, \qquad \tilde{x}_2 = 1.002.$$

By substituting these calculated values into equation (2.25), we get the components of the residual vector:

$$r_1 = 0.999 + 1.002 - 2 = 0.001$$

$$r_2 = 3 \cdot 0.999 - 1.002 - 2 = -0.005.$$

Since these residuals 0.001 and -0.005 are small, we are tempted to think that the approximating solution is also very close to the exact solution, which is actually the case, for the exact solution of (2.26) is $x_1 = x_2 = 1$.
                                                                              ■

─────── **EXAMPLE 2.16** ───────────────────────────────────

Consider next the system of equations

$$\begin{aligned} x_1 + x_2 &= 2 \\ 1.001x_1 + x_2 &= 2.001, \end{aligned} \tag{2.27}$$

where the exact solution is again given by $x_1 = x_2 = 1$. Assume that the calculated solution is $\tilde{x}_1 = 0$, $\tilde{x}_2 = 2$. In computing the residual, we find that

$$r_1 = 0 + 2 - 2 = 0$$

$$r_2 = 1.001 \cdot 0 + 2 - 2.001 = -0.001.$$

The first equation is satisfied exactly and the second residual coordinate is small (-0.001). Note that the error in each term of the computed solution is 1; that is, their relative errors are 100%.

By way of Example 2.16 we see that a system of simultaneous linear equations can almost be satisfied by completely erroneous answers. Equations for which this is possible are spoken of as being *ill-conditioned*. As a guide to intuition concerning the ill-conditioned property, Figure 2.3 shows the lines associated with the equations of the previous examples.

The solution of the system is the value of x_1 and x_2 at the point of the intersection of the two straight lines that represent the equations. Thus the solution of system (2.26) is the point of intersection of lines ① and ②, and the solution of system (2.27) is given by the point of intersection of lines ① and ③. In the latter case we can see that the two lines are almost parallel, so it is hard to tell just where they really cross or, equivalently, just where the solution lies.

From this vantage point, one can sense why a slight change in coefficients can, when the lines are nearly parallel (or, what amounts to the same thing, when the linear system is nearly singular), shift the solution by an enormous amount in the case of (2.27). For if either the slope or the intercept between two nearly parallel lines such as ① and ③ is altered, it is clear that there will be a dramatic shift in their intersection point.

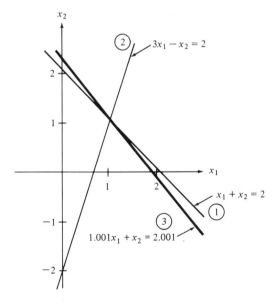

FIGURE 2.3   Graphs of Solutions to Linear Equations

★2.4.2   Quantification of Ill-Conditioning

To definitively relate the magnitudes of the coordinates of the residual vector to errors in the computed solution, it is necessary to introduce vector and matrix norms. The *norm* of a vector $\mathbf{x}$ is a nonnegative number, usually denoted as $\|\mathbf{x}\|$, which is intuitively a measure of vector length. There are a number of different vector norms, but they are characterized by the following properties:

    (a) $\|\mathbf{x}\| \geq 0$.
    (b) $\|\mathbf{x}\| = 0$ if and only if $\mathbf{x} = \mathbf{0}$.
    (c) $\|\alpha\mathbf{x}\| = |\alpha| \cdot \|\mathbf{x}\|$ for all vectors $\mathbf{x}$ and real or complex numbers α.
    (d) $\|\mathbf{x} + \mathbf{y}\| \leq \|\mathbf{x}\| + \|\mathbf{y}\|$ for all vectors $\mathbf{x}, \mathbf{y}$.

Similarly, the *norm* $\|\mathbf{A}\|$ of a square matrix $\mathbf{A}$ is a nonnegative number. Matrix norms satisfy properties analogous to (a) through (d). Also, for two $n \times n$ matrices $\mathbf{A}$ and $\mathbf{B}$,

    (e) $\|\mathbf{AB}\| \leq \|\mathbf{A}\| \cdot \|\mathbf{B}\|$.   (2.28)

For additional information about norms, see, for example, Lancaster (1969, Chap. 6). Regarding the norm $\|\mathbf{A}\|$ as a function of the matrix $\mathbf{A}$, and the vector norm $\|\mathbf{x}\|$ as a function defined over vectors $\mathbf{x}$, $\|\mathbf{A}\|$ and $\|\mathbf{x}\|$ are *consistent* if for all $\mathbf{A}$ and $\mathbf{x}$,

$$\|\mathbf{Ax}\| \leq \|\mathbf{A}\| \cdot \|\mathbf{x}\|.$$

EXAMPLE 2.17

For any column vector $\mathbf{x} = (x_1, \ldots, x_n)^T$ define

$$\|\mathbf{x}\| = \max_{1 \leq i \leq n} |x_i|.$$

This is called the *uniform norm*. The uniform matrix norm is defined for any $n \times n$ matrix $\mathbf{A} = (a_{ij})$ by

$$\|\mathbf{A}\| = \max_{1 \leq i \leq n} \sum_{j=1}^{n} |a_{ij}|$$

and it is consistent with the uniform vector norm. For

$$\|\mathbf{Ax}\| = \max_{1 \leq i \leq n} \left| \sum_{j=1}^{n} a_{ij} x_j \right| \leq \max_{1 \leq i \leq n} \sum_{j=1}^{n} |a_{ij}| \cdot |x_j|$$

$$\leq \left(\max_{1 \leq i \leq n} \sum_{j=1}^{n} |a_{ij}| \right) \max_{1 \leq i \leq n} |x_i| = \|\mathbf{A}\| \cdot \|\mathbf{x}\|.$$

    ■

EXAMPLE 2.18

The vector and matrix norms defined by

$$\|\mathbf{x}\| = \left(\sum_{i=1}^{n} |x_i|^2 \right)^{1/2}$$

and

$$\|\mathbf{A}\| = \left(\sum_{i=1}^{n} \sum_{j=1}^{n} |a_{ij}|^2 \right)^{1/2}$$

are consistent. The vector norm $\|\mathbf{x}\|$ is called the *Euclidean* norm, and $\|\mathbf{A}\|$ the *Frobenius* norm. ∎

An obvious but highly significant consequence of the definition of norm is that for $\tilde{\mathbf{x}}$ the computed approximation to the solution of $\mathbf{Ax} = \mathbf{b}$, and $\mathbf{r}$ the residual $\mathbf{r} = \mathbf{A}\tilde{\mathbf{x}} - \mathbf{b}$,

$$\|\tilde{\mathbf{x}} - \mathbf{x}\| \le \|\mathbf{A}^{-1}\| \cdot \|\mathbf{r}\| \qquad (2.29)$$

for any consistent vector and matrix norms.

This inequality can be verified as follows: The definition of the residual vector implies that

$$\mathbf{r} = \mathbf{A}\tilde{\mathbf{x}} - \mathbf{b} = \mathbf{A}\tilde{\mathbf{x}} - \mathbf{Ax} = \mathbf{A}(\tilde{\mathbf{x}} - \mathbf{x}).$$

By premultiplying this relation by the inverse $\mathbf{A}^{-1}$, we get

$$\tilde{\mathbf{x}} - \mathbf{x} = \mathbf{A}^{-1}\mathbf{r},$$

and by taking the norm of both sides and using the definition of consistent norms, we obtain

$$\|\tilde{\mathbf{x}} - \mathbf{x}\| = \|\mathbf{A}^{-1}\mathbf{r}\| \le \|\mathbf{A}^{-1}\| \cdot \|\mathbf{r}\|.$$

Formula (2.29) allows us to bound the error of the computed solution vector $\tilde{\mathbf{x}}$ in terms of the residual vector and the norm of the inverse of the coefficient matrix.

With the notion of matrix norm in hand, we define the *condition number* of a nonsingular matrix $\mathbf{A}$ by

$$\text{Cond } (\mathbf{A}) = \|\mathbf{A}\| \cdot \|\mathbf{A}^{-1}\|.$$

One says that a matrix is *ill-conditioned* if Cond $(\mathbf{A})$ is a large number. Now ill-conditionedness is not precisely defined, since it will depend on the matrix norm used as well as whatever one takes as "large." As a rule of thumb, for the norms above, if Cond $(\mathbf{A})$ is greater than 1000, one should be alert for trouble. Always, Cond $(\mathbf{A}) \ge 1$, which can be proven in the following way: Observe first that

$$\text{Cond } (\mathbf{A}) = \|\mathbf{A}\| \cdot \|\mathbf{A}^{-1}\| \ge \|\mathbf{AA}^{-1}\| = \|\mathbf{I}\|.$$

On the other hand, with any nonzero vector $\mathbf{x}$,

$$\|\mathbf{x}\| = \|\mathbf{Ix}\| \le \|\mathbf{I}\| \cdot \|\mathbf{x}\|,$$

and by dividing this inequality by $\|\mathbf{x}\| \neq 0$, we get

$$\|\mathbf{I}\| \geq 1.$$

The condition number allows compact expressions relating error in the solution of a linear equation to errors or perturbations in the coefficient matrix $\mathbf{A}$ or vector $\mathbf{b}$. Assume that the right-hand-side vector $\mathbf{b}$ is slightly modified to be $\tilde{\mathbf{b}}$. Let $\mathbf{x}^*$ be the solution of $\mathbf{A}\mathbf{x} = \mathbf{b}$, and $\tilde{\mathbf{x}}$ the solution of $\mathbf{A}\mathbf{x} = \tilde{\mathbf{b}}$. Then since $\|\tilde{\mathbf{x}} - \mathbf{x}^*\| \leq \|\mathbf{A}^{-1}\| \|\tilde{\mathbf{b}} - \mathbf{b}\|$ and $\|\mathbf{x}^*\| \geq \|\mathbf{b}\|/\|\mathbf{A}\|$, we see that

$$\frac{\|\tilde{\mathbf{x}} - \mathbf{x}^*\|}{\|\mathbf{x}^*\|} \leq (\|\mathbf{A}^{-1}\| \|\mathbf{A}\|) \frac{\|\tilde{\mathbf{b}} - \mathbf{b}\|}{\|\mathbf{b}\|}.$$

That is,

$$\frac{\|\tilde{\mathbf{x}} - \mathbf{x}^*\|}{\|\mathbf{x}^*\|} \leq \text{Cond } (\mathbf{A}) \frac{\|\tilde{\mathbf{b}} - \mathbf{b}\|}{\|\mathbf{b}\|}. \tag{2.30}$$

Formulas related to (2.30) are derived in S & Y (1978, Sec. 6.3). They are useful in bounding error in the solution resulting from roundoff in the coefficients. Golub and Van Loan (1983, p. 72) offer the rule of thumb that under the uniform norm, and with error in Gaussian elimination arising from roundoff only, for $\mathbf{x}^*$ the exact and $\tilde{\mathbf{x}}$ the computed solution of $\mathbf{A}\mathbf{x} = \mathbf{b}$,

$$\boxed{\frac{\|\mathbf{x}^* - \tilde{\mathbf{x}}\|}{\|\mathbf{x}^*\|} \approx \text{Cond } (\mathbf{A}) \cdot (\text{machine epsilon}).} \tag{2.31}$$

─── **EXAMPLE 2.19** ───

In Example 2.7 we found that if we chose the coefficients of the matrix $\mathbf{A}$ to be random numbers, then the matrix solution seemed stable, even with order $n = 80$. For the particular case of $n = 6$, and the coefficients picked randomly according to the program in Table 2.7, we computed that under the uniform norm, Cond $(\mathbf{A}) = 51.9$. Next we took $\mathbf{A} = (a_{ij})$ to be the Vandermonde matrix with elements $a_{ij} = (0.2j)^{i-1}$, which was seen in Example 2.8 to have unstable behavior. The order n was again taken to be 6, and after an obvious modification of the program in Table 2.18, we found the condition number to be about 79,000.

TABLE 2.18   Program to Calculate the Condition Number of a Matrix

```
C       PROGRAM CONDNO
C
C       ****************************************************************
C       GENERATES A 6 BY 6 MATRIX, INVERTS THE MATRIX, COMPUTES THE
C       UNIFORM NORM OF A AND A INVERSE AND COMPUTES THE CONDITION
C       NUMBER OF MATRIX A
C       CALLS:   INVG, GAUSS
C       OUTPUT: A=6 BY 6 ORIGIONAL MATRIX
C               ANORM =UNIFORM NORM OF MATRIX A
C               AINORM=UNIFORM NORM OF MATRIX A INVERSE
C               CONDNO=CONDITION NUMBER OF MATRIX A
C       ****************************************************************
C
```

TABLE 2.18   (Continued)

```
      DIMENSION C(6,12),B(6,6),A(6,6)
C
C     *** GENERATE THE ELEMENTS OF MATRIX A                 ***
C
      KSEED=12345
      DO 1 I=1,6
      DO 1 J=1,6
        A(I,J)=RAN(KSEED)
    1 CONTINUE
      WRITE(10,4)((A(I,J),J=1,6),I=1,6)
    4 FORMAT(2X,6F9.6,/)
      EPS=1.E-7
C
C     *** SUBROUTINE INVG COMPUTES THE INVERSE OF MATRIX A  ***
C
      CALL INVG(6,A,B,EPS,C)
C
C     *** COMPUTES THE UNIFORM NORM OF MATRIX A AND A INVERSE ***
C
      DO 3 J=1,6
        AN=0.
        AIN=0.
        DO 2 K=1,6
          AN=AN+ABS(A(J,K))
          AIN=AIN+ABS(B(J,K))
    2   CONTINUE
        ANORM=AMAX1(AN,ANORM)
        AINORM=AMAX1(AIN,AINORM)
    3 CONTINUE
C
C     *** COMPUTES THE CONDITION NUMBER OF MATRIX A         ***
C
      CONDNO=ANORM*AINORM
      WRITE(10,7)ANORM,AINORM,CONDNO
    7 FORMAT(//' NORMS AND CONDITION NUM.',//3E15.7)
      STOP
      END
```

Direct calculation of condition number by a technique such as in Table 2.18 is worthwhile if the order n of the linear system of equations is not large and if we feel any uneasiness at all about the computed solution. However, the expense of the computation is about three times that of solving the linear system itself, and for large systems, therefore, one would like to sidestep this expense. Golub and Van Loan (1983, Sec. 4.5), and Rice (1983, Sec. 6.6B) offer numerical approximations of the condition number, the computational effort of which grows only as n^2, instead of n^3, as exact calculation requires.

★2.5
LU DECOMPOSITION AND CHOLESKY'S METHOD

The professional linear equation codes (such as those in the IMSL[†] library) tend to be based on a scheme that is closely related to Gauss elimination, but is not quite so intuitive. This variation is called the *LU decomposition*; in our experience, it is just as fast, and noticeably more accurate than Gauss elimination. Furthermore, it is the basis for a very efficient way to factor positive definite

---

[†]IMSL designates the "International Mathematical and Statistical Libraries, Inc.," the mailing address of which is: Sixth Floor, NBC Building, 7500 Bellaire Boulevard, Houston, Texas 77036.

matrices, a task that recurs in modern engineering and statistics. The Dolittle reduction, which we discuss next, is an effective method for finding the LU decomposition.

★2.5.1   Dolittle Reduction

First we show the relation of the Gaussian elimination method to a special triangular factorization of square matrices. Assume that matrix $\mathbf{A}$ is square and nonsingular and that Gaussian elimination can be performed without pivoting. Let $\mathbf{A}_k$ denote the coefficient matrix determined by the kth derived system. That is, $\mathbf{A}_k$ is the same as $\mathbf{A}^{(k)} = (a_{ij}^{(k)})$, as determined by (2.9), except that the $(n + 1)$st column is omitted. One may then verify that $\mathbf{A}_k = L_k \mathbf{A}_{k-1}$, where

$$L_k = \begin{bmatrix} 1 & & & & & & \\ & \cdot & & & & & \\ & & 1 & & & & \\ & & -\dfrac{a_{k+1.k}^{(k-1)}}{a_{kk}^{(k-1)}} & 1 & & & \\ & & \cdot & & \cdot & & \\ & & \cdot & & & \cdot & \\ & & -\dfrac{a_{nk}^{(k-1)}}{a_{kk}^{(k-1)}} & & & & 1 \end{bmatrix} \tag{2.32}$$

(all elements not shown here are equal to zero).

Repeated application of this principle implies that

$$\mathbf{A}_{n-1} = \mathbf{L}_{n-1}\mathbf{A}_{n-2} = \cdots = \mathbf{L}_{n-1}\mathbf{L}_{n-2} \cdots \mathbf{L}_1 \mathbf{A}. \tag{2.33}$$

Since the inverse matrix

$$L_k^{-1} = \begin{bmatrix} 1 & & & & & & \\ & \cdot & & & & & \\ & & 1 & & & & \\ & & \dfrac{a_{k+1.k}^{(k-1)}}{a_{kk}^{(k-1)}} & 1 & & & \\ & & & & \cdot & & \\ & & \cdot & & & \cdot & \\ & & \dfrac{a_{nk}^{(k-1)}}{a_{kk}^{(k-1)}} & & & & 1 \end{bmatrix} \tag{2.34}$$

is lower triangular with unit diagonal elements, the matrix

$$\mathbf{L} = (\mathbf{L}_{n-1}\mathbf{L}_{n-2} \cdots \mathbf{L}_1)^{-1} = \mathbf{L}_1^{-1} \cdots \mathbf{L}_{n-2}^{-1}\mathbf{L}_{n-1}^{-1}$$

is also lower triangular with unit diagonal elements, and (2.33) implies that

$$\mathbf{A} = \mathbf{LU}, \tag{2.35}$$

where $\mathbf{U} = \mathbf{A}_{n-1}$. In this decomposition $\mathbf{U}$ is the upper triangular matrix produced in the final derived system of Gaussian elimination, and as we have seen, $\mathbf{L}$ is a lower triangular matrix with unit diagonal elements. Representation (2.35) is called the *Dolittle LU decomposition* of $\mathbf{A}$. (The Dolittle decomposition is very close to the well-known *Crout decomposition*. The only difference between the two is that in the Crout case, $\mathbf{U}$ has unit diagonal values, and the diagonal values of the lower-diagonal matrix $\mathbf{L}$ are unrestricted.) We will soon show that a linear system may quickly be solved once the LU decomposition is known. But first, let us see how to decompose efficiently.

Decomposition (2.35) can be computed directly, without performing Gaussian elimination. Let $\mathbf{A} = (a_{ij})$, $\mathbf{L} = (l_{ij})$, and $\mathbf{U} = (u_{ij})$. Then (2.35) implies that for all i and j,

$$a_{ij} = \sum_{k=1}^{\min\{i,j\}} l_{ik} u_{kj}, \tag{2.36}$$

since for $k > j$, $u_{kj} = 0$ and for $i < k$, $l_{ik} = 0$.

Now we may successively determine the elements of $\mathbf{U}$ and $\mathbf{L}$ as follows. If $i \leq j$, then by recalling that $l_{ii} = 1$ and by rearranging (2.36), we get

$$u_{ij} = a_{ij} - \sum_{k=1}^{i-1} l_{ik} u_{kj} \qquad (j = i, \dots, n). \tag{2.37}$$

Observe that the right-hand side depends only on the first $i - 1$ rows of $\mathbf{U}$ and $i - 1$ columns of $\mathbf{L}$. If $i > j$, then, similarly,

$$l_{ij} = \frac{1}{u_{jj}} \left(a_{ij} - \sum_{k=1}^{j-1} l_{ik} u_{kj} \right) \qquad (j = 1, \dots, i - 1). \tag{2.38}$$

In our subroutine, the actual computation begins by defining $u_{11} = a_{11}$, and $l_{ii} = 1$, $l_{i1} = a_{i1}/u_{11}$, $i = 2, \dots, n$. Then for each $j = 2, \dots, n$, we compute u_{ij} and l_{ij} by (2.37) and (2.38) for increasing i. By this procedure, each coefficient is available by the time it is needed. In brief, $\mathbf{U}$ and $\mathbf{L}$ are found, column by column. This rule for constructing the LU decomposition is called *Dolittle reduction*. Observe that the method can be used if and only if all diagonal elements $u_{11}, u_{22}, \dots, u_{nn}$ differ from zero. As in Gaussian elimination, partial pivoting for avoiding small values in the diagonal of $\mathbf{U}$ may be accomplished by row interchanges. We refer the reader to Stewart (1973, pp. 137–139) for details on pivoting and overwriting.

TABLE 2.19 Subroutine COMPLU for LU Decomposition

```
      SUBROUTINE COMPLU(N,A,L,U,DELT)
C
C **************************************************************
C *  FUNCTION: THIS SUBROUTINE COMPUTES THE LU DECOMPOSITION  *
C *            OF A GIVEN MATRIX A USING DOLITTLE REDUCTION    *
C *  USAGE:                                                    *
C *        CALL SEQUENCE: CALL COMPLU(N,A,L,U,DELT)            *
C *  PARAMETERS:                                               *
C *     INPUT:                                                 *
C *         N=ORDER OF THE MATRIX                              *
C *         A=N BY N ARRAY OF MATRIX ELEMENTS                  *
C *       DELT=ERROR BOUND                                     *
C *     OUTPUT:                                                *
C *         L=N BY N ARRAY OF LOWER TRIANGULAR MATRIX          *
C *           ELEMENTS (ALL ZERO ELEMENTS ABOVE DIAGONAL)      *
C *         U=N BY N ARRAY OF UPPER TRIANGULAR MATRIX          *
C *           ELEMENTS (ALL ZERO ELEMENTS BELOW DIAGONAL)      *
C **************************************************************
C
      DIMENSION A(N,N),U(N,N)
      REAL L(N,N)
      U(1,1)=A(1,1)
C     *** TEST IF MATRIX A CONTAINS A SINGLE ELEMENT ***
      IF(N.LE.1) THEN
         L(1,1)=1.0
         RETURN
      END IF
C     *** TEST IF MATRIX U'S (1,1) ELEMENT IS VERY SMALL ***
      IF(ABS(U(1,1)).LT.DELT) THEN
         WRITE(6,6)
         STOP
      END IF
      DO 1 I=2,N
         L(I,1)=A(I,1)/U(1,1)
    1 CONTINUE
      DO 2 J=2,N
         U(1,J)=A(1,J)
C     *** COMPUTE JTH COLUMN OF U ***
         DO 3 I=2,J
            SUM=A(I,J)
            DO 9 K=1,I-1
               SUM=SUM-L(I,K)*U(K,J)
    9       CONTINUE
      U(I,J)=SUM
    3 CONTINUE
         IF(J.NE.N) THEN
C     *** COMPUTE JTH COLUMN OF L ***
            DO 4 I=J+1,N
               SUM=A(I,J)
               DO 5 K=1,J-1
                  SUM=SUM-L(I,K)*U(K,J)
    5          CONTINUE
               L(I,J)=SUM
               IF(ABS(U(J,J)).LT. DELT) THEN
                  WRITE(6,6)
    6             FORMAT(2X,' THE METHOD CANNOT BE USED ')
                  STOP
               END IF
               L(I,J)=L(I,J)/U(J,J)
    4       CONTINUE
         END IF
    2 CONTINUE
      DO 7 J=1,N
         L(J,J)=1.0
    7 CONTINUE
      DO 8 I=2,N
         DO 8 J=1,I-1
            U(I,J)=0.0
            L(J,I)=0.0
    8 CONTINUE
      RETURN
      END
```

Subroutine COMPLU (Table 2.19) implements LU decomposition by (2.37) and (2.38). A more sophisticated code would save memory by "overwriting" **A** with **L** and **U**, instead of requiring separate arrays.

The computational effort required by the Dolittle reduction approach is essentially the same as that of Gauss elimination. One advantage of Dolittle reduction is that whereas by forward elimination, for fixed i, j, $a_{ij}^{(k)}$ is pulled in and out of storage as k goes from 1 to $n - 1$, with Dolittle reduction, the values u_{ij} and l_{ij} are computed once and for all according to (2.37) and (2.38), respectively. By this "one-pass" feature, we have the capability of accumulating sums in double precision and thereby reducing the effect of roundoff error, while avoiding the memory burden of declaring all storage locations to be double precision.

──────── **EXAMPLE 2.20** ────────────────────────────────

Consider again the matrix given in Examples 2.1 and 2.2. The triangular decomposition of the form

$$
\begin{bmatrix} 2 & 1 & 3 \\ 4 & 4 & 7 \\ 2 & 5 & 9 \end{bmatrix} = \begin{bmatrix} 1 & 0 & 0 \\ l_{21} & 1 & 0 \\ l_{31} & l_{32} & 1 \end{bmatrix} \begin{bmatrix} u_{11} & u_{12} & u_{13} \\ 0 & u_{22} & u_{23} \\ 0 & 0 & u_{33} \end{bmatrix}
$$

will now be calculated.

For $i = 1$, since $l_{11} = 1$, (2.37) implies that

$$u_{11} = a_{11} = 2$$

$$u_{12} = a_{12} = 1$$

$$u_{13} = a_{13} = 3.$$

Then equation (2.38) gives

$$l_{21} = \frac{a_{21}}{u_{11}} = \frac{4}{2} = 2, \qquad l_{31} = \frac{a_{31}}{u_{11}} = \frac{2}{2} = 1.$$

For $i = 2$, we find that

$$u_{22} = a_{22} - l_{21}u_{12} = 4 - 2 \cdot 1 = 2$$

$$u_{23} = a_{23} - l_{21}u_{13} = 7 - 2 \cdot 3 = 1$$

$$l_{32} = \frac{a_{32} - l_{31}u_{12}}{u_{22}} = \frac{5 - 1 \cdot 1}{2} = 2,$$

and finally, for $i = 3$,

$$u_{33} = a_{33} - l_{31}u_{13} - l_{32}u_{23} = 9 - 1 \cdot 3 - 2 \cdot 1 = 4.$$

Thus the LU decomposition of **A** is

$$
\begin{bmatrix} 2 & 1 & 3 \\ 4 & 4 & 7 \\ 2 & 5 & 9 \end{bmatrix} = \begin{bmatrix} 1 & 0 & 0 \\ 2 & 1 & 0 \\ 1 & 2 & 1 \end{bmatrix} \begin{bmatrix} 2 & 1 & 3 \\ 0 & 2 & 1 \\ 0 & 0 & 4 \end{bmatrix}.
$$

Note that matrix **U** and the coefficient matrix of the second derived system given in Example 2.1 are the same.

■

Once the triangular decomposition **A** = **LU** is known, the solution of **Ax** = **b** can be found in two steps. First, solve the equation

$$
\boxed{\mathbf{Lz} = \mathbf{b},} \tag{2.39}
$$

where **L** is the lower triangular matrix and **z** is the unknown vector. An obvious modification of back substitution can be used, where z_1 is calculated from the first (rather than the last) equation, then z_2 is determined from the second equation, and so on. Next solve the equation

$$
\boxed{\mathbf{Ux} = \mathbf{z},} \tag{2.40}
$$

where **x** is the unknown vector, and the result **z** of the previous step constitutes the coefficient vector. The solution **x** of this equation can be obtained by use of the original version (2.10) of back substitution. Then **x** is the solution of the original equations, since, by substitution, we have

$$
\mathbf{Ax} = (\mathbf{LU})\mathbf{x} = \mathbf{L}(\mathbf{Ux}) = \mathbf{Lz} = \mathbf{b}. \tag{2.41}
$$

EXAMPLE 2.21

By using the result of Example 4.20, we shall now solve the equations given in Example 2.1. In this case (2.39) has the particular form

$$
\begin{aligned}
z_1 \qquad\qquad &= 1 \\
2z_1 + z_2 \qquad &= 1 \\
z_1 + 2z_2 + z_3 &= 3,
\end{aligned}
$$

which implies that $z_1 = 1$, $z_2 = -1$, and $z_3 = 4$. Now (2.40) can be written as

$$
\begin{aligned}
2x_1 + x_2 + 3x_3 &= 1 \\
2x_2 + x_3 &= -1 \\
4x_3 &= 4,
\end{aligned}
$$

and after back substitution $x_3 = 1$, $x_2 = -1$, and $x_1 = -\frac{1}{2}$.

■

Increasingly, in the literature of numerical linear algebra, one finds mention of the *LDU decomposition*. This refers to the representation

$$\mathbf{A} = \mathbf{LDU},$$

where it is presumed that $\mathbf{L}$ and $\mathbf{U}$ are lower and upper triangular matrices both having 1's as diagonal elements. The matrix $\mathbf{D}$ is presumed diagonal. It is an easy matter to obtain this representation from the Dolittle form. Define

$$\mathbf{D} = \text{diag}\ (\tilde{u}_{11}, \tilde{u}_{22}, \ldots, \tilde{u}_{nn})$$

for $\tilde{u}_{jj}$ the diagonal elements of the Dolittle upper-triangular matrix, which is now denoted by $\tilde{\mathbf{U}}$. That is, $\mathbf{A} = \mathbf{L}\tilde{\mathbf{U}}$. Now take $\mathbf{U}$ to be that matrix obtained by dividing each element of the ith row of $\tilde{\mathbf{U}}$ by $\tilde{u}_{ii}$. Then check that

$$\mathbf{U} = \mathbf{D}^{-1}\tilde{\mathbf{U}}$$

and that $\mathbf{U}$ has 1's along its diagonal. Clearly,

$$\mathbf{A} = \mathbf{L}\tilde{\mathbf{U}} = \mathbf{LDU}.$$

The final form is the desired representation.

★2.5.2 Cholesky's Method

In the special case that $\mathbf{A}$ is real and symmetric (Appendix A, property 8), the LU decomposition can be modified so that the two factors are the transpose of each other. That is, the factorization

$$\mathbf{A} = \mathbf{U}^T\mathbf{U} \tag{2.42}$$

can be obtained, in which $\mathbf{U}$ is upper triangular. Specifically, by arguments leading to the Dolittle reduction (2.36), one can verify that the elements of $\mathbf{U}$ can be obtained by the recurrence relations

$$
\begin{aligned}
u_{ii} &= \left(a_{ii} - \sum_{k=1}^{i-1} u_{ki}^2 \right)^{1/2}, \qquad i = 1, 2, \ldots, n, \\
u_{ij} &= \frac{1}{u_{ii}} \left(a_{ij} - \sum_{k=1}^{i-1} u_{ki}u_{kj} \right) \qquad (j > i).
\end{aligned}
\tag{2.43}
$$

This decomposition is called *Cholesky's method* or the *method of square roots*.

EXAMPLE 2.22

Cholesky's method will be applied to the symmetric matrix

$$\mathbf{A} = \begin{bmatrix} 2 & 1 & 1 \\ 1 & 3 & 2 \\ 1 & 2 & 2 \end{bmatrix}$$

For $i = 1$, (2.43) yields

$$u_{11} = \sqrt{a_{11}} = \sqrt{2}$$

$$u_{12} = \frac{a_{12}}{u_{11}} = \frac{\sqrt{2}}{2}$$

$$u_{13} = \frac{a_{13}}{u_{11}} = \frac{\sqrt{2}}{2}.$$

For $i = 2$, we have

$$u_{22} = \sqrt{a_{22} - u_{12}^2} = \sqrt{3 - \frac{1}{2}} = \frac{\sqrt{10}}{2}$$

$$u_{23} = \frac{a_{23} - u_{12}u_{13}}{u_{22}} = \frac{2 - (\sqrt{2}/2)(\sqrt{2}/2)}{\sqrt{10}/2} = \frac{3\sqrt{10}}{10},$$

and finally, for $i = 3$, we find that

$$u_{33} = \sqrt{a_{33} - u_{13}^2 - u_{23}^2} = \sqrt{2 - \frac{1}{2} - \frac{9}{10}} = \frac{\sqrt{15}}{5}.$$

Thus

$$\mathbf{U} = \begin{bmatrix} \sqrt{2} & \dfrac{\sqrt{2}}{2} & \dfrac{\sqrt{2}}{2} \\ 0 & \dfrac{\sqrt{10}}{2} & \dfrac{3\sqrt{10}}{10} \\ 0 & 0 & \dfrac{\sqrt{15}}{5} \end{bmatrix}$$

Because the arguments of the square root in (2.43) can be negative, Cholesky's method can require complex arithmetic. In the important special case in which $\mathbf{A}$ is positive definite, that is, $\mathbf{x}^T\mathbf{A}\mathbf{x} > 0$ for all nonzero vectors $\mathbf{x}$, Cholesky's method requires only real numbers and pivoting is never needed for avoiding division by zero.

There is a strong relation between Cholesky's method and the LDU decomposition of matrices discussed at the end of Section 2.5.1. Toward showing the connection between these two decompositions, assume that $\mathbf{A}$ is a real symmetric matrix. Let the LDU decomposition of $\mathbf{A}$ be given by

$$\mathbf{A} = \mathbf{LDU}. \tag{2.44}$$

We shall first prove that in this case necessarily $\mathbf{U}^T = \mathbf{L}$. Consider matrix $(\mathbf{U}^{-1})^T\mathbf{A}\mathbf{U}^{-1}$, which is symmetric. The LDU decomposition of $\mathbf{A}$ implies that after left multiplication of (2.44) by $(\mathbf{U}^{-1})^T$, and right multiplication by $\mathbf{U}^{-1}$,

$$(\mathbf{U}^{-1})^T\mathbf{A}\mathbf{U}^{-1} = (\mathbf{U}^T)^{-1}\mathbf{LD}.$$

Since matrices U^T and L are lower triangular with unit diagonal elements, the same property holds for $(U^T)^{-1}$ and $(U^T)^{-1}L$. Thus $(U^T)^{-1}LD$ is lower triangular, and its symmetry then implies that it is diagonal. Therefore, $(U^T)^{-1}L$ is diagonal with unit diagonal elements. Consequently,

$$(U^T)^{-1}L = I,$$

which implies that

$$U^T = L,$$

or in other words,

$$A = U^TDU.$$

This decomposition is sometimes called the U^TDU decomposition of symmetric matrices.

From the U^TDU decomposition, Cholesky's method follows by multiplying the ith row of U by $\sqrt{d_{ii}}$, where $D = \text{diag}(d_{11}, d_{22}, \ldots)$. If the resulting upper triangular matrix is denoted by $\tilde{U}$, then $A = \tilde{U}^T\tilde{U}$ is the Cholesky's decomposition of A.

★2.6
ITERATIVE METHODS

For linear systems of small or moderate size (say, of order not exceeding 200), either Gaussian elimination or LU decomposition is effective and efficient, and these are the methods recommmended. For certain classes of high-order linear equations, which arise, for example, in solving differential equations, iterative methods are attractive. In this section some of the better-known iterative methods are described.

★2.6.1   Jacobi Iteration

Consider again (2.1) with $m = n$. Assume that A is nonsingular and the rows have been exchanged, as necessary, so that the diagonal elements are nonzero. Equations (2.1) can then be rewritten so that the ith equation is explicit for x_i:

$$x_1 = -\frac{1}{a_{11}}(a_{12}x_2 + a_{13}x_3 + \cdots + a_{1n}x_n - b_1)$$

$$x_2 = -\frac{1}{a_{22}}(a_{21}x_1 + a_{23}x_3 + \cdots + a_{2n}x_n - b_2) \tag{2.45}$$

$$\cdots\cdots$$

$$x_n = -\frac{1}{a_{nn}}(a_{n1}x_1 + a_{n2}x_2 + \cdots + a_{n,n-1}x_{n-1} - b_n).$$

Assume that an initial approximation of the solution has been given, or simply choose an arbitrary vector. Let $\mathbf{x}^{(0)} = (x_1^{(0)}, \ldots, x_n^{(0)})^T$ denote this initial approximation. Substitute it into the right-hand side of (2.45) and evaluate. The elements of the resulting vector give the next approximations of the unknowns. Let vector $\mathbf{x}^{(1)} = (x_1^{(1)}, \ldots, x_n^{(1)})^T$ denote these approximations, and then substitute the new vector $\mathbf{x}^{(1)}$ into the right side of (2.45) to get a further approximation, $\mathbf{x}^{(2)} = (x_1^{(2)}, \ldots, x_n^{(2)})^T$, and so on. The general step is given by

$$x_1^{(k+1)} = -\frac{1}{a_{11}}(a_{12}x_2^{(k)} + a_{13}x_3^{(k)} + \cdots + a_{1n}x_n^{(k)} - b_1)$$

$$x_2^{(k+1)} = -\frac{1}{a_{22}}(a_{21}x_1^{(k)} + a_{23}x_3^{(k)} + \cdots + a_{2n}x_n^{(k)} - b_2) \qquad (2.46)$$

$$\cdots\cdots$$

$$x_n^{(k+1)} = -\frac{1}{a_{nn}}(a_{n1}x_1^{(k)} + a_{n2}x_2^{(k)} + \cdots + a_{n,n-1}x_{n-1}^{(k)} - b_n).$$

Scheme (2.46) is called the Jacobi iteration method.

It can be proven that under certain conditions (see S & Y, 1978, Sec. 6.2), for $k \to \infty$, the sequence of vectors $\mathbf{x}^{(k)}$ converges to the exact solution of equations (2.1). One such condition is that each diagonal element of the matrix of coefficients satisfy the condition:

$$|a_{ii}| > \sum_{\substack{j=1 \\ j \neq i}}^{n} |a_{ij}|, \qquad i = 1, \ldots, n. \qquad (2.47)$$

If this condition is satisfied, then $\mathbf{A}$ is said to be *diagonally dominant*.

The criteria for stopping the iteration process are usually either:

1. The number of iterations has exceeded some predetermined maximum K, or
2. The difference between successive values of all x_i's are less than some predetermined tolerance ε.

One iteration step requires at most n divisions, n^2 multiplications, and n^2 additions (or subtractions), which implies that if the number of iteration steps to get the desired accuracy of the solution is less than $n/3$, this method needs fewer arithmetic operations than the Gaussian elimination.

───── **EXAMPLE 2.23** ──

We wish to apply the Jacobi method to the following system:

$$64x_1 - 3x_2 - x_3 = 14$$

$$x_1 + x_2 + 40x_3 = 20$$

$$2x_1 - 90x_2 + x_3 = -5.$$

The matrix of coefficients is not diagonally dominant, since in the second equation

$$|1| < |1| + |40|.$$

But by interchanging the second and third equations, a system with a diagonally dominant matrix of coefficients is obtained:

$$64x_1 - 3x_2 - x_3 = 14$$

$$2x_1 - 90x_2 + x_3 = -5$$

$$x_1 + x_2 + 40x_3 = 20.$$

For this case, the Jacobi iteration scheme (2.46) takes the particular form

$$x_1^{(k+1)} = 0.04688x_2^{(k)} + 0.01563x_3^{(k)} + 0.21875$$

$$x_2^{(k+1)} = 0.02222x_1^{(k)} + 0.01111x_3^{(k)} + 0.05556$$

$$x_3^{(k+1)} = -0.02500x_1^{(k)} - 0.02500x_2^{(k)} + 0.50000,$$

where all coefficients have been rounded to five decimal places. Let the error bound of the successive values of x_i be given as 10^{-5}, and take $\mathbf{x}^{(0)}$ to be the constant terms on the right-hand sides of the iteration scheme. The numerical results are presented in Table 2.20.

TABLE 2.20   Jacobi Iterations for Example 2.23

	k = 0	k = 1	k = 2	k = 3	k = 4	k = 5
$x_1^{(k)}$	0.21875	0.22916	0.22959	0.22955	0.22954	0.22954
$x_2^{(k)}$	0.05556	0.06598	0.06616	0.06613	0.06613	0.06613
$x_3^{(k)}$	0.50000	0.49592	0.49262	0.49261	0.49261	0.49261

★2.6.2   Gauss–Seidel Iteration

Consider again the recursive Jacobi iteration scheme (2.46). Observe that in calculating the "new" value of $x_2^{(k+1)}$, the previous value of $x_1^{(k)}$ is used on the right-hand side although the "new" value, $x_1^{(k+1)}$ is already known. Similarly, for obtaining the new value $x_3^{(k+1)}$, the "old" values $x_1^{(k)}$ and $x_2^{(k)}$ are used, although the new, and presumably more accurate values $x_1^{(k+1)}$ and $x_2^{(k+1)}$ of these variables are already available. A modification typically (but not always) giving faster convergence can be devised if in the calculation of $x_i^{(k+1)}(2 \le i \le n)$, the updated new values $x_1^{(k+1)}, \ldots, x_{i-1}^{(k+1)}$ are used in place of the earlier values $x_1^{(k)}, \ldots, x_{i-1}^{(k)}$, in (2.46). This modification results in the Gauss–Seidel iterative method, which is defined by the recursive scheme

$$x_1^{(k+1)} = -\frac{1}{a_{11}}(a_{12}x_2^{(k)} + a_{13}x_3^{(k)} + \cdots + a_{1n}x_n^{(k)} - b_1)$$

$$x_2^{(k+1)} = -\frac{1}{a_{22}}(a_{21}x_1^{(k+1)} + a_{23}x_3^{(k)} + \cdots + a_{2n}x_n^{(k)} - b_2)$$

$$\cdots \quad \cdots \cdots \cdots$$

$$x_n^{(k+1)} = -\frac{1}{a_{nn}}(a_{n1}x_1^{(k+1)} + a_{n2}x_2^{(k+1)} + \cdots + a_{n,n-1}x_{n-1}^{(k+1)} - b_n).$$

(2.48)

Conditions for the convergence of this method are discussed by S & Y (1978, Sec. 6.2) and Golub and Van Loan (1983, Chap. 10). Table 2.21 gives a computer subroutine for the Gauss–Seidel method.

TABLE 2.21   Subroutine SEID for Gauss–Seidel Iterations

```
          SUBROUTINE SEID(N,X0,X,A,B,EPS)
C
C    ****************************************************************
C    *   FUNCTION: THIS SUBROUTINE COMPUTES THE SOLUTION FOR A      *
C    *             SYSTEM OF N EQUATIONS IN N UNKNOWNS USING THE    *
C    *             GAUSS SEIDEL ITERATION METHOD                    *
C    *   USAGE:                                                     *
C    *         CALL SEQUENCE: CALL SEID(N,X0,X,A,B,EPS)             *
C    *   PARAMETERS:                                                *
C    *         INPUT:                                               *
C    *               N=NUMBER OF EQUATIONS AND UNKNOWNS (< 500)     *
C    *               X0=N BY 1 ARRAY OF INITIAL SOLUTION VALUES     *
C    *               A=N BY N ARRAY OF MATRIX COEFFICIENTS          *
C    *               B=N BY 1 ARRAY OF RIGHT HAND SIDE VECTOR       *
C    *             EPS=ERROR BOUND                                  *
C    *         OUTPUT:                                              *
C    *               X=N BY 1 ARRAY OF SOLUTION VALUES              *
C    ****************************************************************
C
          DIMENSION A(N,N),B(N),X0(N),X(N),U(500)
C    *** INITIALIZATION ***
          K=1
          M=1
          DO 1 I=1,N
             U(I)=X0(I)
             B(I)=B(I)/A(I,I)
             DO 5 J=1,N
                IF(I.NE.J) A(I,J)=A(I,J)/A(I,I)
        5    CONTINUE
             A(I,I)=0.0
        1 CONTINUE
          DO WHILE(M.LT.N+1)
C    *** COMPUTE SOLUTION VALUES X ***
             DO 2 I=1,N
                X(I)=0.0
                DO 3 J=1,N
                   X(I)=X(I)-A(I,J)*U(J)
        3       CONTINUE
                X(I)=X(I)+B(I)
                U(I)=X(I)
        2    CONTINUE
C    *** TEST IF SOLUTION VALUES X ARE CLOSE ***
             M=1
             DO WHILE(ABS(X(M)-X0(M)).LT.EPS.AND.M.LT.N+1)
                M=M+1
             END DO
C    *** IF NOT THEN RESET THE INITIAL X0 ***
C    ***    AND CONTINUE ITERATION PROCESS   ***
             IF(M.LT.N+1) THEN
                DO 4 I=1,N
                   X0(I)=X(I)
        4       CONTINUE
C    *** OTHERWISE SOLUTION VALUES X ARE GOOD ***
C    ***   CEASE ITERATION PROCESS AND RETURN   ***
                K=K+1
             END IF
          END DO
          RETURN
          END
```

─────── **EXAMPLE 2.24** ───────────────────────────────────────

Application of Gauss–Seidel iteration to the equation in Example 2.23 is summarized in Table 2.22. In comparison to the Jacobi iteration calculation (Table 2.20), fewer steps are needed to obtain the same accuracy.

TABLE 2.22   Gauss–Seidel Iterations for Example 2.24

	$k = 0$	$k = 1$	$k = 2$	$k = 3$
$x_1^{(k)}$	0.21875	0.22916	0.22955	0.22955
$x_2^{(k)}$	0.05556	0.06621	0.06613	0.06613
$x_3^{(k)}$	0.50000	0.49262	0.49261	0.49261

■

Iterative methods are particularly popular for solution of band systems arising in numerical methods for partial differential equations. For such equations, in many cases the width k (see Section 2.3.3) is relatively wide—often proportional to $n^{1/2}$—but the band itself has relatively few nonzero entries. Let p denote a bound to the number of nonzero elements in each row. The effort required by elimination for solution of banded systems is porportional to k^2n, and for iterative methods, proportional to $2pnM$, where M is the number of iterations necessary for acceptable accuracy. Thus iterative methods are preferable if

$$2pnM < k^2n,$$

that is,

$$M < \frac{k^2}{2p} \sim \frac{n}{p}.$$

Unfortunately, it is typically difficult to assess M until computations have already begun.

─────── **EXAMPLE 2.25** ───────────────────────────────────────

It is known (S & Y, 1978, Sec. 6.2) that the Gauss–Seidel method converges whenever the matrix **A** is positive definite, that is, whenever **A** is symmetric and $x^TAx > 0$ for all **x** except the zero vector. In Table 2.23 we have called on subroutine SEID to solve a 100-variable equation with a positive definite coefficient matrix. The lower diagonal coefficients were chosen at random, as was the coefficient vector **b**. The upper diagonal elements were then determined by the condition that the matrix be symmetric, and the diagonal elements were set to 100, a number large enough to ensure that the matrix is positive definite. The maximum residual value was printed out at each iteration (Table 2.24). The run was made on a VAX.

TABLE 2.23   Calling Program for the Gauss–Seidel Algorithm

```
C      PROGRAM SEIDEL
C
C      ****************************************************************
C      THIS PROGRAM WILL GENERATE A SYSTEM OF RANDOM NUMBERS
C      FOR THE COEFFICIENT MATRIX A AND THE RIGHT HAND SIDE VECTOR B
C      IT THEN CALLS SUBROUTINE SIED TO SOLVE THE SYSTEM
C      CALLS:    SEID
C      OUTPUT(FROM MODIFIED SUBROUTINE):
C                  K=NUMBER ITERATION
C                  EMAX=MAXIMUM (FOR ALL EQUATIONS)  ABSOLUTE
C                       ERROR
C      ****************************************************************
C
       DIMENSION A(100,100),B(100),X0(100),X(100)
       N=100
       KSEED=12345
C
C      *** FIRST THE SYSTEM IS GENERATED USING THE RANDOM NUMBER ***
C      *** GENERATOR RAN                                        ***
C
       DO 1 I=1,N
          DO 2 J=1,I
             A(I,J)=RAN(KSEED)
             A(J,I)=A(I,J)
    2     CONTINUE
          A(I,I)=N*1.
          B(I)=RAN(KSEED)
    1  CONTINUE
       EPS=1.E-9
C
C      *** SUBROUTINE SEID WILL SOLVE THE SYSTEM USING GAUSS    ***
C      *** SEIDEL ITERATION. PRINTING IS DONE IN THE SUBROUTINE ***
C
       CALL SEID(N,X0,X,A,B,EPS)
       STOP
       END
```

TABLE 2.24   Application of the Gauss–Seidel Algorithm

k	Maximum Absolute Value of Coordinate in Residual After Iteration k
1	8.9787366E-03
2	2.2037476E-03
3	3.6594970E-04
4	2.3348257E-05
5	1.6423874E-06
6	3.8836151E-07
7	1.1175871E-08
8	3.2596290E-09
9	4.6566129E-10

★2.7
EIGENVALUES

★2.7.1 Preliminaries

Let A be an $n \times n$ matrix. An *eigenvalue* for A is a (perhaps complex) number λ which, for some nonzero vector x, satisfies

$$Ax = \lambda x. \tag{2.49}$$

The vector x as above is the *eigenvector* associated with the eigenvalue λ. A matrix A may have complex eigenvalues and eigenvectors with complex coefficients, even in cases in which all coefficients of A are real.

APPLICATION 2.3 ━━━

A preponderance of classical engineering models are, mathematically speaking, linear differential equations. For example, resistor/inductor/capacitor circuits in electrical engineering, dynamic models based on Newton's equations in mechanical engineering, and linear reservoir models for river flow in civil engineering fall into this category. Eigenvalue problems are prominent whenever linear differential equations are employed. As an important instance, in the case of one independent variable, say time, linear differential equations are called *ordinary*, and can be expressed in matrix notation as

$$\dot{x}(t) = Ax(t) + bu(t), \tag{2.50}$$

where

$$x(t) = \begin{bmatrix} x_1(t) \\ \vdots \\ x_n(t) \end{bmatrix}$$

is a vector of time functions, and $\dot{x}(t)$ denotes the vector of functions obtained by differentiating the corresponding coordinate of $x(t)$. That is,

$$\dot{x}(t) = \begin{bmatrix} \dot{x}_1(t) \\ \vdots \\ \dot{x}_n(t) \end{bmatrix},$$

$\dot{x}_j(t)$ being the derivative of $x_j(t)$ with respect to t.

For a concrete illustration of how eigenvalue problems show up in the context of differential equation models, consider the force/spring/damper/mass config-

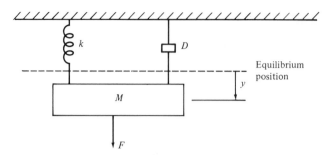

FIGURE 2.4   Mechanical Oscillation Problem

uration of Figure 2.4. At rest, $y = 0$. In general, at all t, $y(t)$ denotes the distance of the mass M from the equilibrium position.

The force balance equation for this arrangement is

$$\dot{y}(t) = v(t) \tag{2.51}$$
$$M\dot{v}(t) = -ky(t) - Dv(t) + F(t),$$

where M is the mass, D the damping coefficient, and k the constant for Hooke's law. The force $F(t)$ is regarded as the input to the model, and the position $y(t)$ is the response. One can immediately rewrite this system in form (2.50):

Let

$$\mathbf{x}(t) = \begin{bmatrix} y(t) \\ v(t) \end{bmatrix}$$

and then from (2.51), evidently,

$$\dot{\mathbf{x}}(t) = \begin{bmatrix} v(t) \\ -\dfrac{k}{M}\, y(t) - \dfrac{D}{M}\, v(t) + \dfrac{F(t)}{M} \end{bmatrix}$$

$$= \begin{bmatrix} 0 & 1 \\ \dfrac{-k}{M} & \dfrac{-D}{M} \end{bmatrix} \mathbf{x}(t) + \begin{bmatrix} 0 \\ \dfrac{1}{M} \end{bmatrix} F(t) \tag{2.52}$$

$$= \mathbf{A}\mathbf{x}(t) + \mathbf{b}u(t).$$

Eigenvalue problems arise, for example, when one seeks the ''natural modes'' of the system. That is, suppose that no external force is applied, and movement results solely from the mass being released from a point below its rest position at time 0. It is then known (Rabenstein, 1970, Chap. 5) that the solution $y(t)$ has the form

$$y(t) = c \exp(\lambda_1 t) + d \exp(\lambda_2 t),$$

where λ_1 and λ_2 are the eigenvalues (here presumed distinct) of $\mathbf{A}$, and c and d are constants, determined by the initial conditions. Such representations apply to the general case (2.50) also.

Suppose, for example, that $M = 1, D = 4$, and $k = 3$, in the units appropriate to the MKS system. Then

$$\mathbf{A} = \begin{bmatrix} 0 & 1 \\ -3 & -4 \end{bmatrix}, \tag{2.53}$$

and as one may confirm by direct substitution into (2.49), $\lambda = -1$ is an eigenvalue and $(1, -1)^T$ is an eigenvector. Moreover,

$$y(t) = \exp(-t), \qquad v(t) = -\exp(-t)$$

is a solution of (2.51) associated with the mode $\lambda = -1$, and $F(t) \equiv 0$.

★2.7.2 Determination of Eigenvalues and Eigenvectors

Our discussion of eigenvalues and their computation will be devastatingly abridged. It is intended for the reader who has already some introduction to the theory [such as is offered by Bellman (1970) or Nering (1963)]. We merely offer an elementary algorithm, the *Rayleigh quotient iteration* (RQI) method and its subroutine, its analysis and justification being beyond the scope of this book. The present algorithm can be useful for certain simple, stable eigenvalue problems, and does share some foundation with the elegant and effective but, alas, highly complicated QR eigenvalue method. The theory for both the RQI and QR methods is given in detail in S & Y (1978, Secs. 7.2.3 and 7.3).

The RQI method is an iterative method, and as such, requires the user to provide starting estimates. Let $\mathbf{x}^{(0)}$ be an initial guess of the eigenvector. (For theoretical reasons, it is well to take an initial guess that has a nonzero imaginary part, or the method has no hope of locating complex eigenvalues.) Assume that after k iterations, we have obtained an approximation $\mathbf{x}^{(k)}$ of the eigenvector. A RQI iteration has two steps:

1. Approximate the eigenvalue by the Rayleigh quotient:

$$\lambda^{(k)} = \frac{(\mathbf{x}^{(k)})^T \mathbf{A} \mathbf{x}^{(k)}}{(\mathbf{x}^{(k)})^T \mathbf{x}^{(k)}}. \tag{2.54}$$

2. Update eigenvector approximation and normalize. Compute the solution $\mathbf{q} = (q_1, \ldots, q_n)^T$ of

$$(\mathbf{A} - \lambda^{(k)} \mathbf{I}) \mathbf{q} = \mathbf{x}^{(k)} \tag{2.55}$$

and normalize, defining $\|\mathbf{q}\| = \Sigma_{i=1}^{n} |q_i|$, and define $\mathbf{x}^{(k+1)} = (x_1^{(k+1)}, \ldots , x_n^{(k+1)})^T$, where

$$x_i^{(k+1)} = \frac{q_i}{\|q\|} \qquad (1 \le i \le n).$$

When successive iterations $\mathbf{x}^{(k)}$ and $\mathbf{x}^{(k+1)}$ are within a prescribed tolerance, stop the process and accept the most recent estimates. Subroutine EIGEN (Table 2.25) implements the RQI method. It calls GAUS1 and requires that subroutine to have been appropriately modified for complex variables. In Table 2.25 we give these declaration modifications.

We have found the RQI method to be satisfactory for small to moderate-sized ($n = 20$) matrices, but the fundamental trouble is that when the successive approximations $\lambda^{(k)}$ of the eigenvalue λ are in fact getting close to λ, the matrix in (2.55) must become ill-conditioned. In fact, if $\lambda^{(k)}$ in (2.55) equals an eigenvalue, in view of (2.49) the matrix $\mathbf{A} - \lambda^{(k)}\mathbf{I}$ is singular. Another drawback to the RQI and related elementary techniques is that locating all the eigenvalues of a given matrix will either require a good deal of guesswork, or systematic matrix deflation, such as discussed in the preceding reference. In the computer study discussed in Example 2.26, we confront this problem by repeatedly calling EIGEN with randomly chosen initial eigenvector estimates until a complete set of eigenvalues are obtained.

The highly technical QR algorithm mentioned above overcomes both the instability problem and the problem of location of all the eigenvalues, and should be employed if we have a large (order greater than, say, 20) matrix. The eigenvalue subroutines in the IMSL[†] package are founded on the QR approach.

TABLE 2.25   Subroutine EIGEN for Eigenvalue Computation[a]

```
      SUBROUTINE EIGEN(N,A,EPS,EIGVEC,EIGVAL)
C
C     ***************************************************************
C     *  FUNCTION: THIS SUBROUTINE COMPUTES AN EIGENVALUE AND        *
C     *            EIGENVECTOR OF THE MATRIX A BY RAYLEIGH           *
C     *            QUOTIENT ITERATIONS                               *
C     *  USAGE:                                                      *
C     *        CALL SEQUENCE: CALL EIGEN(N,A,EPS,EIGVEC,EIGVAL)      *
C     *        EXTERNAL FUNCTIONS/SUBROUTINES:                       *
C     *                   SUBROUTINE GAUS1(N,1,ND,B,DELT)           *
C     *                   (MODIFIED FOR COMPLEX*16)                  *
C     *  PARAMETERS:                                                 *
C     *      INPUT:                                                  *
C     *          N=DIMENSION OF THE SQUARE MATRIX A                  *
C     *          A=N BY N MATRIX FOR WHICH THE EIGENVALUE AND        *
C     *            EIGENVECTOR IS TO BE COMPUTED. N MUST BE          *
C     *            LESS THEN OR EQUAL 50                             *
C     *          EPS=MINIMUM CHANGE TO COMPONENTS OF THE             *
C     *            EIGENVECTOR OR TO THE EIGENVALUE TO PROCEED       *
C     *            TO THE NEXT ITERATION                             *
C     *          EIGVEC=INITIAL GUESS AT THE VALUE OF THE EIGENVECTOR *
C     *      OUTPUT:                                                 *
C     *          EIGVEC=THE NORMALIZED EIGENVECTOR CORRESPONDING TO  *
C     *            EIGVAL                                            *
C     *          EIGVAL=THE COMPUTED EIGENVALUE                      *
C     ***************************************************************
C
```

†See the footnote on p. 85.

TABLE 2.25   (Continued)

```
        IMPLICIT COMPLEX*16 (A-H,O-Z)
        REAL EPS,ANORM,DELT
        DIMENSION A(N,N),EIGVEC(N),B(50,50)
        DELT=1.E-10
        EIGSAV=CMPLX(1.D+10,1.D+10)
        DO 100 WHILE (CDABS(EIGSAV-EIGVAL).GT.EPS)
C       *** UPDATE EIGVAL ***
        ANUM=CMPLX(0.D0,0.D0)
        DENOM=CMPLX(0.D0,0.D0)
        DO 60 I=1,N
           DENOM=DENOM+CONJG(EIGVEC(I))*EIGVEC(I)
           DO 50 J=1,N
              ANUM=ANUM+A(I,J)*CONJG(EIGVEC(I))*EIGVEC(J)
   50      CONTINUE
   60   CONTINUE
        EIGSAV=EIGVAL
        EIGVAL=ANUM/DENOM
C       *** CHECK FOR STOPPING CRITERIA ***
        IF(CDABS(EIGSAV-EIGVAL).GT.EPS) THEN
C       *** ASSEMBLE THE LINEAR EQUATIONS ***
           DO 20 I=1,N
              B(I,N+1)=EIGVEC(I)
              DO 10 J=1,N
                 B(I,J)=A(I,J)
                 IF(I.EQ.J) B(I,J)=B(I,J)-EIGVAL
   10         CONTINUE
   20      CONTINUE
C       *** SOLVE THE SYSTEM OF EQUATIONS ***
           CALL GAUS1(N,1,50,B,DELT)
C       *** NORMALIZE THE EIGENVECTORS ***
           ANORM=0.0
           DO 30 I=1,N
              ANORM=ANORM+CDABS(B(I,N+1))
   30      CONTINUE
           DO 40 I=1,N
              EIGVEC(I)=B(I,N+1)/ANORM
   40      CONTINUE
        ELSE
        ENDIF
  100 CONTINUE
        RETURN
        END
```

[a]Modifications Needed for GAUS1 are

1. Declaration statements

> IMPLICIT COMPLEX·16(A-H,O-Z)
> REAL DELT,U

2. Replace ABS function by CDABS, throughout.

━━━ **EXAMPLE 2.26** ━━━━━━━━━━━━━━━━━━━━━━━━━━━━

Here we find an eigenvalue/eigenvector pair for the matrix

$$\mathbf{A} = \begin{bmatrix} -4 & -3 & -7 \\ 2 & 3 & 2 \\ 4 & 2 & 7 \end{bmatrix}.$$

By means of the calling program in Table 2.26, we applied subroutine EIGEN to this matrix, to obtain the eigenvalue iterates displayed in Table 2.27. In a subsequent computation, the main program was modified to repeatedly obtain random initial eigenvector approximations (by calling the random number generator). Each such random starting eigenvector was passed to EIGEN and an eigenvalue/eigenvector pair was returned. After just a few repetitions, the complete set of eigenvalues, namely 1, 2, and 3, was uncovered, the processing time being negligible. Subroutine EIGEN and its calling program use double-precision complex variables to alleviate the ill-conditioning mentioned above. The variable declarations in GAUS1 must be modified accordingly, as shown in Table 2.25. We have rapidly and accurately solved eigenvalue problems of order 25 with randomly chosen coefficients by subroutine EIGEN.

TABLE 2.26   Program for Eigenvalue Computation

```
C       PROGRAM EIGENVAL
C
C       *****************************************************************
C       THIS PROGRAM DEMONSTRATES THE COMPUTATION OF EIGENVALUES
C       AND EIGENVECTORS
C       CALLS:      EIGEN,GAUS1(MODIFIED FOR COMPLEX*16)
C       OUTPUT:     EIGVAL=THE COMPUTED EIGENVALUE
C                   EIGVEC=THE CORRESPONDING EIGENVECTOR
C       *****************************************************************
C
        IMPLICIT COMPLEX*16(A-H,O-Z)
        REAL EPS,R1,R2
        DIMENSION A(3,3),X(3),Z(3)
        KSEED=12345
        N=3
C
C       *** CONSTRUCT THE TEST MATRIX AND GENERATE AN INITIAL     ***
C       *** EIGENVECTOR AT RANDOM                                 ***
C
        A(1,1)=CMPLX(-4.D0,0.D0)
        A(1,2)=CMPLX(-3.D0,0.D0)
        A(1,3)=CMPLX(-7.D0,0.D0)
        A(2,1)=CMPLX(2.D0,0.D0)
        A(2,2)=CMPLX(3.D0,0.D0)
        A(2,3)=CMPLX(2.D0,0.D0)
        A(3,1)=CMPLX(4.D0,0.D0)
        A(3,2)=CMPLX(2.D0,0.D0)
        A(3,3)=CMPLX(7.D0,0.D0)
        DO 10 I=1,N
           R1=RAN(KSEED)
           R2=RAN(KSEED)
           X(I)=CMPLX(R1,R2)
     10 CONTINUE
C
C       *** SUBROUTINE EIGEN WILL COMPUTE ONE EIGENVALUE AND THE  ***
C       *** NORMALIZED EIGENVECTOR                                ***
C
        EPS=.0001
        CALL EIGEN(N,A,EPS,X,Y)
        WRITE(10,*) Y
        WRITE(10,*)(X(I),I=1,N)
        STOP
        END
```

TABLE 2.27 Output of Eigenvalue Computation

Successive Eigenvalue Estimates from EIGEN
$(1.509799502841826, 1.146020421424286)$
$(1.509960413519013, 1.110282405927049)$
$(1.538221058711549, 0.2790532785529104)$
$(1.314871445299046, -0.2512895871666247)$
$(1.151647595028325, 0.1986352616137632)$
$(1.056218466137056, -3.6794216895795671E-02)$
$(0.9983627632762745, 4.4887362292788813E-03)$
$(1.000016738414568, 1.5167001284082388E-05)$
$(0.9999999999562700, -5.0627797487153684E-10)$

Output from EIGEN

Computed eigenvalue:

$(0.9999999999562700, -5.0627797487153684E-10)$

Computed eigenvector:

$(-0.3785400561340956, 0.3266610597361022)$
$(0.1892700278663577, -0.1633305300696822)$
$(0.1892700281334613, -0.1633305298005863)$

★2.7.3 Singular-Value Decomposition

Singular-value decomposition is now recognized to be a fundamental tool in analyzing and deriving numerical methods for linear algebra. Given an $m \times n$ real matrix $\mathbf{A}$, its *singular-value decomposition* is a representation

$$\mathbf{A} = \mathbf{U} \text{ diag } (\sigma_1, \sigma_2, \ldots, \sigma_p)\mathbf{V}^T,$$

where $\mathbf{U}$ and $\mathbf{V}$ are $m \times m$ and $n \times n$ orthogonal matrices (i.e., their inverses are their transposes), respectively, and $p = \min \{m, n\}$. The elements $\sigma_1, \sigma_2, \ldots, \sigma_p$ are presumed real and to satisfy

$$\sigma_1 \geq \sigma_2 \geq \cdots \geq \sigma_p \geq 0.$$

Golub and Van Loan (1983, Sec. 23) give numerical procedures for obtaining this decomposition. They also discuss applications to stability analysis and sensitivity. When $\mathbf{A}$ is positive definite (i.e., $\mathbf{A}^T = \mathbf{A}$ and $\mathbf{x}^T\mathbf{A}\mathbf{x} > 0$, for any nonzero vector $\mathbf{x}$), the σ_i's coincide with the eigenvalues of $\mathbf{A}$, and the columns of $\mathbf{V}$ constitute the eigenvectors, the ith column being the eigenvector associated with eigenvalue σ_i, $i = 1, 2, \ldots, p$.

2.8
SUPPLEMENTARY NOTES AND DISCUSSIONS

With the advent of digital computers, linear equations have become crucial and pervasive in all quantitative fields of science. An especially important need for their solution arose in the early days of digital computing, which coincided with the advent of thermonuclear devices. At one stage, deciding whether such devices would work at all or work too well depended on the solution of a large linear system resulting from discretization of a partial differential equation. In brief, there was a period (about 1950–1960) during which some of the very best scholars in computer science and mathematics devoted considerable effort to devising ingenious techniques for computational solution of linear equations. Sophisticated iterative methods related to those discussed in Section 2.6 were invented and analyzed during this period, as were "Monte Carlo" or probabilistic simulation techniques for linear equations. [For an introduction to the latter topic, the reader is referred to Yakowitz (1977), especially Chaps. 3 and 6.] Iterative and Monte Carlo methods initially attracted much interest and hope, and indeed these methods were well suited to the limited memory capacity of early electronic computers.

But at present, the fortunate state of affairs is that for small to moderate-sized linear systems ("moderate" currently being about 200 unknowns, and growing). Gauss elimination and its close cousin, LU decomposition, are clearly the methods of choice. We say "fortunately" because, in comparison to efficient iterative and Monte Carlo methods, their analysis and implementation is relatively simple. Even for larger systems, one often finds that special properties such as bandedness (discussed in Section 2.3.3) make variants of Gauss elimination competitive. However, "supercomputers" effectively employ parallel processing and vector structures, and for these machines, iterative methods may be more competitive.

Standard library codes for solving linear equations are invariably based on Gaussian elimination, or, more often its close cousin, LU decomposition (Section 2.5). As an important case in point, the several major IMSL routines for linear equations employ LU decomposition. They also incorporate equilibration and iterative refinement, which are heuristic features aimed at sharpening the calculations. Equilibration was discussed in Section 2.2.3. Problem 36 sketches the idea behind iterative refinement. Both equilibration and iterative refinement are analyzed in Golub and Van Loan (1983, Sec. 4.5).

In our exposition of pivoting and ill-conditioning, by example we have seen that instabilities can occur in small, innocuous linear systems such as those that arise in engineering and practical applications. We suggested that partial pivoting should be used as a manner of course and that an "instability detector" should be incorporated even if it is no more than an examination of the residual. If ill-conditioning is suspected, in our estimation the first line of defense should be double or multiple precision. In the past this was avoided because of fast memory constraints, but modern machines such as the VAX computer overcome this constraint to a large extent by storing parts of big arrays on disk. Because of quick "swapping" between fast (chip) memory and disk memory, these machines effectively handle huge arrays.

The domain in which iterative methods are currently thought to be superior on present-day standard computers includes solution of linear equations arising from discretization of partial differential equations. The application of iterative methods requires consideration of fairly delicate issues such as whether a given method will be convergent for the desired equation, and if several methods are convergent, which one is the best. Some iterative methods depend on a scaling parameter, the choice of which is somewhat at the user's discretion. In summary, our feeling is that if the direct methods we have discussed are not effective on a linear equation that you need to solve, you had better consult a numerical analyst or be prepared and willing to learn about some fairly deep aspects of numerical analysis. For further study and some basic references in iterative methods for linear equations, we refer the reader to S & Y (1978, Sec. 6.2).

In optional Section 2.7, we gave a rudimentary scheme and program for finding matrix eigenvalues and eigenvectors. The references in that section will lead the reader to more elegant procedures.

PROBLEMS

Section 2.2

1. Solve the following linear equations by (naive) Gauss elimination. Show your work. Check your solution by confirming that it does satisfy the equation.

(a) $x_1 + x_2 + x_3 = 6$

$x_1 - x_2 - x_3 = 6$

$2x_1 + x_2 + 7x_3 = 12.$

(b) $x_1 + 2x_2 + 3x_3 = 8$

$2x_1 + 6x_2 + 10x_3 = 28$

$-x_1 - 3x_2 - 6x_3 = 18.$

(c) $x_1 + 2x_2 + 3x_3 = 8$

$2x_1 + 4x_2 + 9x_3 = 8$

$4x_1 + 3x_2 + 2x_3 = 2.$

2. Use partial pivoting to perform elimination in Problem 1. Show your calculations.

3. Solve parts (a) through (c) of Problem 1 by total pivoting. Show your work.

4. Consider the linear equations $\mathbf{Ax} = \mathbf{b}$, with

$$a_{ij} = \left(\frac{i}{n}\right)^{j-1}, \quad b_i = \sum_{j=1}^{n} a_{ij}, \quad 1 \le i, j \le n,$$

and n a given positive integer. Use subroutine GAUSS (Table 2.3) to obtain the solution for $n = 3, 5, 7, 9, \ldots$, until one or more of the components of the computed solution x^* differ from their correct value (namely, $x_j = 1$, all j) by more than 0.5.

5. Modify subroutine Gauss so that it does
(a) No pivoting.
(b) Uses double precision and partial pivoting.
Then redo Problem 4, comparing performances.

★6. Modify subroutine GAUSS so that it does maximal pivoting, and redo Problem 4.

7. Assume that $\mathbf{U}$ is an upper triangular matrix, so that no elimination is needed for solving

$$\mathbf{Ux} = \mathbf{b}. \tag{2.56}$$

(a) Show that if for each i, the diagonal element $u_{ii} \neq 0$, back substitution uniquely determines the solution $\mathbf{x}$.

(b) Alternatively, show that if for some k, $u_{kk} = 0$, then either there is no solution or there is a family of solutions of the linear equation (2.56). What is the criterion that there be solutions?

★8. In analyzing the number of operations needed for Gaussian elimination, we used the fact that

$$1 + 2 + \cdots + n = \frac{n(n + 1)}{2}$$

and

$$1^2 + 2^2 + \cdots + n^2 = \frac{n(n + 1)(2n + 1)}{6}.$$

Prove these relations

(a) By finite induction.

(b) By adding the identities.

$(k + 1)^2 = k^2 + 2k + 1$ \qquad (for the top equation)

$(k + 1)^3 = k^3 + 3k^2 + 3k + 1$ \qquad (for the second equation)

for $k = 1, 2, \ldots, n$, and doing some moderately clever rearrangement.

9. Do Problem 4 with the same vector $\mathbf{b}$ but with coefficient matrix determined by

$$a_{ij} = \frac{1}{i + j - 1}, \qquad 1 \leq i, j \leq n.$$

Repeat the calculations without pivoting.

10. Do Problem 9 in double precision.

★11. Solve the linear equations below by hand calculations, showing your work. Give the general solutions and two particular solutions.

(a) $2x_1 + x_2 + x_3 + x_4 = 3$

$x_1 - x_2 + x_3 - x_4 = 0$

$3x_1 + 2x_3 = 3$

$x_1 + 2x_2 + 2x_4 = 3.$

(b) $x_1 + x_2 - x_3 - x_4 = 3$

$2x_1 + 3x_2 + x_3 + 2x_4 = 8$

$3x_1 + 4x_2 + x_4 = 11$

$x_1 + 2x_2 + 2x_3 + 3x_4 = 5.$

(c) $2x_1 + x_2 - x_3 = 4$

$x_1 + 2x_2 + 2x_3 = 2$

$x_1 - x_2 - 3x_3 = 2.$

Section 2.3

12. Find the inverses of the coefficient matrices in Problem 1. Use Gauss elimination, and show your work.

13. **(Continuation of Problem 12.)** From the results of Problem 12, solve the linear equations in Problem 1 according to the formula

$$\mathbf{x} = \mathbf{A}^{-1}\mathbf{b}.$$

Show your work.

14. Solve the matrix equation $\mathbf{AX} = \mathbf{B}$, by Gauss elimination, showing your work with $\mathbf{A}$ and $\mathbf{B}$ as specified.

(a) $\mathbf{A} = \begin{bmatrix} 1 & 1 & 1 \\ 1 & -1 & -1 \\ 2 & 1 & 7 \end{bmatrix}$, $\mathbf{B} = \begin{bmatrix} 3 & 6 \\ 3 & 6 \\ 6 & 12 \end{bmatrix}$.

(b) $\mathbf{A} = \begin{bmatrix} 1 & 2 & 3 \\ 2 & 6 & 10 \\ -1 & -3 & -6 \end{bmatrix}$, $\mathbf{B} = \begin{bmatrix} 4 & 6 \\ 14 & 20 \\ 9 & 12 \end{bmatrix}$.

(c) $\mathbf{A} = \begin{bmatrix} 1 & 2 & 3 \\ 2 & 4 & 9 \\ 4 & 3 & 2 \end{bmatrix}$, $\mathbf{B} = \begin{bmatrix} 4 & 8 \\ 4 & 8 \\ 1 & 2 \end{bmatrix}$.

15. (a) Solve the matrix equations of Problem 14 using the subroutine GAUSS.
    (b) **(Continuation of Problems 12 and 14.)** Solve the linear equations of Problem 14 by the relation

$$\mathbf{X} = \mathbf{A}^{-1}\mathbf{B},$$

using the inverses you obtained in Problem 12.

16. Use subroutine INVG (Table 2.13) to find the inverses of the matrices $\mathbf{A}$ and $\mathbf{B}$, with

(a) $a_{ij} = \left(\dfrac{i}{n}\right)^{j-1}$, $\quad 1 \le i,j \le n.$

(b) $a_{ij} = \dfrac{1}{i + j - 1}$, $\quad 1 \le i,j \le n.$

Take $n = 3, 5, 7, \ldots$, and for each n, check your result by calculating the product of your computed inverse, with the original matrix; it should be close to the identity matrix. Continue your experiment until the product is not close to the identity matrix.

17. Use subroutine INVG (Table 2.13) to find inverses of the matrices of Problem 1. Check to see that for each matrix $\mathbf{A}$, the defining relation $\mathbf{AA}^{-1} = \mathbf{I}$ is satisfied.

★18. Let $\mathbf{a}$ and $\mathbf{b}$ be column vectors of like order n. Show that if $\mathbf{A}$ and $(\mathbf{A} + \mathbf{ab}^T)$ are nonsingular matrices, then

$$(\mathbf{A} + \mathbf{ab}^T)^{-1} = \mathbf{A}^{-1} - \frac{\mathbf{A}^{-1}\mathbf{ab}^T\mathbf{A}^{-1}}{1 + \mathbf{b}^T\mathbf{A}^{-1}\mathbf{a}}.$$

★19.   Find the determinants of the coefficient matrices of Problem 1 by Gauss elimination and hand calculation. Show your work.

★20.   Find the determinants of the coefficient matrices of Problem 11 by Gauss elimination, showing your hand calculations.

★21.   Use subroutine DETC (Table 2.15) to find the determinants of the coefficient matrices of Problem 1. If you did Problem 19, compare the answers.

★22.   Solve the following band systems by Gauss elimination, showing your calculations.

(a) $2x_1 + 3x_2 \qquad\quad = 2$

$\quad\; x_1 + 2x_2 + \;\; x_3 = 2$

$\qquad\quad\; x_2 - \;\; x_3 = 2.$

(b) $x_1 + 2x_2 \qquad\qquad\qquad = 10$

$\quad\; x_1 - \;\; x_2 + \;\; x_3 \qquad\quad = -2$

$\qquad\qquad 2x_2 - \;\; x_3 + \;\; x_4 = \quad 8$

$\qquad\qquad\qquad\quad\; x_3 - \;\; x_4 = \quad 0.$

(c) $\;\; x_1 + \;\; x_2 \qquad\qquad\quad = 2$

$\quad 2x_1 + \;\; x_2 + \;\; x_3 \qquad\quad = 3$

$\qquad\qquad x_2 + \;\; x_3 - 3x_4 = 2$

$\qquad\qquad\qquad\; x_3 + \;\; x_4 = 0.$

★23.   Use subroutine BAND (Table 2.16) to solve the linear equations of Problem 22.

★24.   Modify subroutine BAND (Table 2.16) to invert the coefficient matrices of Problem 22.

★25.   Invert the matrices of Problem 22 by the Gauss elimination method, showing your hand calculations and preserving the band structure during the elimination process.

26.   A farmer has available three brands of nutrients which he intends to blend as feed for his livestock. Each brand has three qualities of interest to him: (1) price, (2) nutrition, and (3) shipping distance. He has constructed the following matrix:

Brands			
A	B	C	
100	90	50	Price/ton (dollars)
8	4	6	Nutrient/ton
6	2	5	Miles

and has decided that for his nutrient purchase, he will pay exactly $530. It must have a nutrition value of 38, and the distance to be shipped is 27 ton-miles. By what mixture of purchases can he satisfy these constraints?

Section 2.4

★27. Find the condition numbers of the coefficient matrices of Problem 1. Use the uniform norm. Show your work. (**HINT:** Use the results of Problem 12, if you did it.)

★28. Develop a subroutine to compute the norm of a square matrix, following the formula in Example 2.17. Use this subroutine and subroutine INVG (Table 2.13) to construct a program for finding condition numbers. Apply it to do Problem 27 automatically.

Section 2.5

★29. Let L_1 and L_2 be lower triangular matrices. Show that $L_1 L_2$ and L_1^{-1} are also lower triangular.

★30. Solve the linear equations of Problem 1 by Dolittle reduction. Show your hand calculations.

★31. Find the Cholesky decomposition of

$$\begin{bmatrix} 3 & -1 & 10 \\ -1 & 3 & 6 \\ 10 & 6 & 54 \end{bmatrix}.$$

Show your work.

★32. Modify the Dolittle subroutine COMPLU (Table 2.19) to do Cholesky decomposition. Test it by solving Example 2.22.

★33. Equations of the form

$$A^T A x = A^T b$$

arise naturally in least-squares problems, a focus of Chapter 6. Use Cholesky decomposition to solve this equation with A and b as in Problem 1.

Section 2.6

★34. Consider the circuit shown in the following figure:

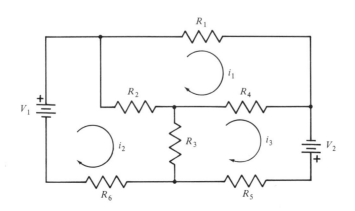

The associated equations relating current to the impressed voltages are

$$(R_1 + R_2 + R_4)i_1 - R_2 i_2 - R_4 i_3 = 0$$

$$-R_2 i_1 + (R_2 + R_3 + R_6)i_2 - R_3 i_3 = V_1$$

$$-R_4 i_1 - R_3 i_2 + (R_3 + R_4 + R_5)i_3 = V_2.$$

(a) Prove that for any arbitrary positive values for the R_i's, the system must have a unique solution.
(b) Show that this unique solution can be found by either Jacobi or Gauss–Seidel iterations.
(c) Solve the system for $R_1 = R_2 = R_3 = 1$, $R_4 = R_5 = R_6 = 2$, and $V_1 = V_2 = 1$ by Jacobi iterations. Stop iterations when two successive approximations agree to four figures.

★35. Do Problem 34, part (c), by Gauss–Siedel iterations.

★36. The principle of iterative refinement is to iterate on the residual. Thus if $\hat{x}$ is the computed solution to $\mathbf{Ax} = \mathbf{b}$, the residual is

$$\mathbf{r} = \mathbf{A}\hat{x} - b.$$

The solution is hopefully refined by the approximation

$$\tilde{x} = \hat{x} - \mathbf{u},$$

with $\mathbf{u}$ the solution of $\mathbf{Au} = \mathbf{r}$. Solve the system in Problem 4, comparing the computed solution with its correct value as stated in the problem, using the pure method, and then the method with one iterative refinement in each case by
(a) Gauss elimination (through subroutine GAUSS).
(b) LU decomposition (through subroutine COMPLU).

Section 2.7

★37. Prove that if $\mathbf{A}$ is singular, $\lambda = 0$ is an eigenvalue of $\mathbf{A}$.

★38. The eigenvalues of a matrix are the roots of the polynomial det $(\mathbf{A} - \lambda \mathbf{I})$. Use this fact to find the eigenvalues and eigenvectors of

$$\begin{bmatrix} 2 & -1 \\ 1 & 0 \end{bmatrix}.$$

Show your work.

★39. Find all the eigenvalues and associated eigenvectors of the matrix

$$\begin{bmatrix} 4 & 1 & 1 \\ 1 & 5 & 2 \\ 1 & 2 & 3 \end{bmatrix}.$$

CHAPTER 3

Interpolation

3.1
PRELIMINARIES

The two main practical tasks that motivate the methods of this chapter are (1) given some function $f(x)$ and an interval I, find a program that gives an adequate approximation to $f(x)$ for any x in I; and (2) given a collection of data points $(x_k, f(x_k))$, $k = 1, \ldots, n$, estimate the value of $f(x)$ at some domain point x not among the x_k's. These problems arise in many areas of science and engineering.

The activity of finding an approximating function that agrees with measurements at specific locations is called *interpolation*. The central aim of this chapter is to describe effective interpolation methods. These provide a direct solution of task (2), and are often suitable for task (1), above.

Application 3.1

Let us illustrate how need for interpolation might arise. Consider the projectile problem of Chapter 1, Application 1.1. In that example, we were concerned with the influence of initial condition measurement error on the trajectory. In this discussion the objective is to guess what the trajectory is, on the basis of a few instantaneous radar returns. Specifically, imagine that we have three range/height locations, (x_1, f_1), (x_2, f_2), (x_3, f_3). The task is to plot a proposed trajectory that is consistent with these points. We augment the earlier model to account for atmospheric drag, and furthermore assume that the initial location of the projectile is not known. It is a mathematical fact that without such information, knowledge of the complete trajectory cannot be recovered from only three data points.

A sensible elementary approach to the projectile graphing assignment is simply to construct a polynomial that passes through these data points. A motivation for this plan is that polynomial evaluation is free of truncation error.

The values (in meters) we presume given are

j	Position x_j	Height f_j
1	3030	2418
2	5835	3365
3	8293	2872

Since we have three data points, a polynomial with three coefficients would seem to be a reasonable approximator. These polynomials, which are called *quadratics*, will have the general form

$$p_2(x) = a_0 + a_1 x + a_2 x^2.$$

The interpolation conditions require that the graph of $p_2(x)$ pass through the points (x_j, f_j), $(j = 1, 2, 3)$. That is, for $j = 1, 2, 3$,

$$p_2(x_j) = f_j.$$

If we substitute the general quadratic form of $p_2(x)$ and data x_j, f_j, we obtain three equations for the three unknown constants a_0, a_1, a_2 as follows:

$$a_0 + a_1 \cdot 3030 + a_2 \cdot 3030^2 = 2418$$

$$a_0 + a_1 \cdot 5835 + a_2 \cdot 5835^2 = 3365$$

$$a_0 + a_1 \cdot 8293 + a_2 \cdot 8293^2 = 2872.$$

After solving these equations we get

$$a_0 = -418.36, \qquad a_1 = 1.2469, \qquad a_2 = -1.0257 \cdot 10^{-4}.$$

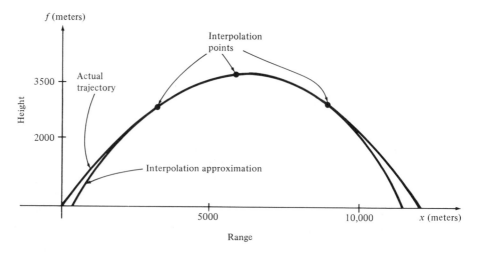

FIGURE 3.1 Trajectory and Its Interpolation Approximation

Thus

$$p_2(x) = -418.36 + 1.2469x - (1.0257 \cdot 10^{-4})x^2.$$

When plotted, we obtain the graph in Figure 3.1. Also shown in that figure is the actual solution to a projectile trajectory which accounts for air resistance. That is, the three points on which our polynomial estimation is constructed could have been points on the illustrated projectile path. Note that the approximation does not pass through the origin. This reflects the fact that the location of the cannon cannot be determined exactly by the measurements.

◇

Application 3.2

As a software task, suppose that you are to provide a routine for some particular function not in the library of the compiler at your disposal. (The Bessel and gamma functions and the Gaussian cumulative distribution function are relatively common functions that are seldom supplied.) You will recall from Chapter 1 that computers are capable only of arithmetical operations (addition, subtraction, multiplication, and division) and magnitude comparisons. Other functions, such as sin (x) and the ones just mentioned, cannot be computed exactly, even if there is no roundoff error. One must devise an approximation in terms of arithmetical operations. As a concrete illustration of polynomial approximation, for reasons given in a later section, for values of x near zero,

$$p_5(x) = x - \frac{x^3}{3!} + \frac{x^5}{5!}$$

is a good polynomial approximation of sin (x). For $x = 0.2$, $p_5(x) = 0.198669333$, which is correct to eight significant figures. The reader is invited to check this approximation against sin (x) at other x values.

◇

In addition to its importance for science and engineering tasks, the subject of interpolation plays a crucial role within the realm of numerical methods itself. For example, prominent methods for other numerical tasks such as integration (Chapter 4) and solution of nonlinear (Chapter 5) and differential equations (Chapter 7) are motivated by polynomial approximation. In particular, if we are assured that the polynomial $p(x)$ is close to a given function $f(x)$, it might rightly be suspected that for some interval $[a, b]$ of moderate length, $\int_a^b p(x) \, dx$ ought to be close to $\int_a^b f(x) \, dx$. The value of this insight is that polynomial integration is very simple.

We use polynomials as function approximators and as curves for data fitting, since they and their ratios are the only functions that can be reduced to elementary arithmetic. In particular, polynomial approximations lie at the heart of computer graphics. However, as we suggest in Section 6.4, other function classes, notably sinusoids, are useful alternatives in function approximation. The gist of the situation is that once computer methodology has been developed for approximation of members of some class (such as sinusoids) of functions, that class itself becomes available as a basis for approximation of yet more general function classes.

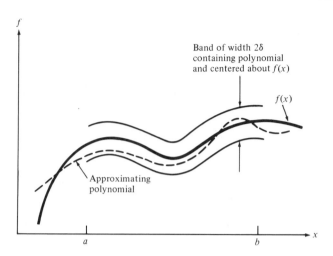

FIGURE 3.2 Illustration of the Weierstrass Theorem

It turns out that the class of polynomials is surprisingly powerful; one can feasibly approximate a great many common functions reasonably accurately over a limited domain. Examples supporting this claim will be offered, but also so will exceptions. There are theoretical reasons why we might hope for success with polynomials, the most noteworthy being the following statement.

> **Theorem.**　*Let $f(x)$ be any continuous function defined on a closed bounded interval $[a, b]$, and let δ be any positive number. Then there is a polynomial $p(x)$ such that for all $x \in [a, b]$,*
>
> $$|f(x) - p(x)| < \delta.$$

The proof of this theorem is found in many numerical analysis texts [e.g., S & Y, 1978, pp. 26–28].[†] Figure 3.2 illustrates this theorem. No matter how small a band you draw about the continuous function, there is some polynomial lying entirely inside this band.

As polynomials are fundamental to the methods of this chapter, discussion begins with an efficient scheme for their computer evaluation. Then use of polynomials as function approximation devices commences with a description of Taylor's series methods, which the reader has presumably encountered in calculus. Following that we describe polynomial and spline interpolation techniques.

3.2
HORNER'S RULE

A recurring task in this chapter and elsewhere is that of evaluating a given polynomial

$$p(x) = a_k x^k + a_{k-1} x^{k-1} + \cdots + a_0 \qquad (3.1)$$

[†]"S & Y" is an abbreviation used throughout this book to designate the intermediate-level book, Szidarovszky and Yakowitz, *Principles and Procedures of Numerical Analysis*, Plenum Publishing Corporation, N.Y., 1978.

at some specified value x. The coefficient a_k of the highest power in k is the *leading* coefficient, and k itself is the polynomial *degree*.

It is in the tradition of numerical analysis to seek efficient ways to evaluate frequently used formulas. If we thoughtlessly programmed the right side of (3.1) as it stands, with $x \times x$, $x \times x \times x$, ..., replacing x^2, x^3, and so on, then evaluation of $p(x)$ would require $k + (k - 1) + (k - 2) + \cdots + 1 = k(k + 1)/2$ multiplications and k additions. On the other hand, polynomial evaluation by Horner's rule requires only k additions and multiplications, k being the degree of the polynomial.

The idea behind Horner's rule is that of rewriting (3.1) as a "nested" formula,

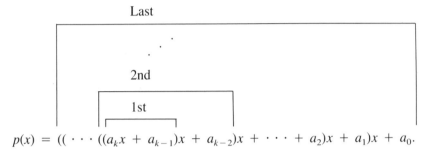

$$p(x) = ((\cdots ((a_k x + a_{k-1})x + a_{k-2})x + \cdots + a_2)x + a_1)x + a_0.$$

The convention is that the innermost expression $a_k x + a_{k-1}$ is to be calculated first. The resulting number constitutes a multiplicand for the expression at the next level. In this fashion, successive terms are computed as values for the lower levels (or inner parenthetical terms) become available. The number of levels equals the polynomial degree, k. By this procedure, only one addition and one multiplication is needed at each level. Although some improvement over Horner's rule is possible, it is known (Knuth, 1969, Sec. 4.6) that any general polynomial algorithm requires at least $k/2$ multiplications.

Horner's rule is implemented by construction of the sequence b_k, b_{k-1}, ..., b_0 from the coefficients a_k, a_{k-1}, ..., a_0 in the representation (3.1) according to

$$
\begin{aligned}
b_k &= a_k \\
b_{k-1} &= b_k x + a_{k-1} \\
&\vdots \\
b_j &= b_{j+1} x + a_j \\
&\vdots \\
b_1 &= b_2 x + a_1 \\
p(x) = b_0 &= b_1 x + a_0.
\end{aligned}
\tag{3.2}
$$

By this construct, $p(x) = b_0$.

──── **EXAMPLE 3.1** ────

Let us apply Horner's rule to evaluate the quadratic (second-degree polynomial)

$$p(x) = 3x^2 + x + 5$$

at $x = 6$. In the notation of (3.1), $k = 2$ and $a_2 = 3$, $a_1 = 1$, and $a_0 = 5$. So, according to (3.2),

$$b_2 = 3$$

$$b_1 = 3 \times 6 + 1 = 19$$

$$b_0 = 19 \times 6 + 5 = 119 = p(6).$$

Horner's rule entails performing the arithmetic operations as indicated by the following nested representation:

$$p(x) = (3x + 1)x + 5 = \overbrace{(b_2 x + 1)x}^{b_1} + 5.$$
$$\underbrace{\hspace{4cm}}_{b_0}$$

Subroutine HORNER for Horner's rule is given in Table 3.1. The arguments j for the coefficients $A(j)$ run from 1 to $k + 1$, instead of 0 to k because FORTRAN array variables must have positive indices. The role of b_j, in (3.2) is assumed by the variable P.

TABLE 3.1   Subroutine for Horner's Rule

```
      SUBROUTINE  HORNER(K,A,X,P)
C
C  ****************************************************************
C  *   FUNCTION: THIS SUBROUTINE COMPUTES THE VALUE OF A K-TH    *
C  *             DEGREE POLYNOMIAL P(X) AT A GIVEN INDEPENDENT   *
C  *             VALUE X USING THE HORNER'S RULE. THE K+1 BY 1   *
C  *             INPUT ARRAY A REPRESENTS THE POLYNOMIAL         *
C  *             ACCORDING TO:                                   *
C  *             P(X)=A(K+1)*X**K+A(K)*X**(K-1)+...+A(2)*X+A(1)  *
C  *   USAGE:                                                    *
C  *       CALL SEQUENCE: CALL HORNER(K,A,X,P)                   *
C  *   PARAMETERS:                                               *
C  *       INPUT:                                                *
C  *           K=POLYNOMIAL DEGREE                               *
C  *           A=(K+1) BY 1 ARRAY OF POLYNOMIAL COEFFICIENTS     *
C  *           X=GIVEN INDEPENDENT VALUE                         *
C  *       OUTPUT:                                               *
C  *           P=POLYNOMIAL VALUE P(X)                           *
C  ****************************************************************
C
      DIMENSION A(K+1)
C     *** INITIALIZATION ***
      P=A(K+1)
C     *** COMPUTE K-TH DEGREE POLYNOMIAL VALUE P(X) ***
      DO 1 I=K,1,-1
      P=P*X+A(I)
    1 CONTINUE
      RETURN
      END
```

3.3
TAYLOR'S POLYNOMIALS

Toward unifying the methodology of this chapter, Taylor's series ideas are now viewed from an unorthodox vantage point. Suppose that at some domain point x_0, we are given the values $f(x_0)$, $f'(x_0)$, $f^{(2)}(x_0)$, . . . , $f^{(n-1)}(x_0)$ of $f(x)$ and its first $n - 1$ derivatives. On the basis of these n numbers, we are to provide a computer-implementable approximation of $f(x)$. In keeping with our resolution to work with polynomials, it is natural to seek a minimal-degree polynomial that is consistent with these data. Our objective then is to find the polynomial $p_{n-1}(x)$ of degree less than n satisfying the n conditions

$$p_{n-1}(x_0) = f(x_0), \quad p'_{n-1}(x_0) = f'(x_0), \quad . . . , p^{(n-1)}_{n-1}(x_0) = f^{(n-1)}(x_0). \quad (3.3)$$

Before presenting the general formulation of polynomials satisfying these conditions, we examine some special cases.

Degree 0.   The simplest polynomial is the polynomial of degree 0, which is the constant function. That is,

$$p_0(x) = a_0.$$

It has only one parameter, a_0, so it can satisfy only one condition. Thus (3.3), with $n = 1$, would have us choose $a_0 = f(x_0)$, and we have

$$p_0(x) = f(x_0).$$

Degree 1.   Linear polynomials represent the next level of sophistication. Linear polynomials have the form

$$p_1(x) = a_0 + a_1x, \quad (3.4)$$

and their graphs are straight lines. Since they have two coefficients, they can fulfill two conditions, namely (3.3) for $n = 2$. In this case, (3.3) yields

$$p_1(x_0) = a_0 + a_1x_0 = f(x_0)$$

$$p'_1(x_0) = a_1 = f'(x_0).$$

The second equation gives immediately that $a_1 = f'(x_0)$ and substitution into the top equation yields that

$$a_0 = f(x_0) - f'(x_0)x_0.$$

That is, from (3.4),

$$p_1(x) = f(x_0) - f'(x_0)x_0 + f'(x_0)x.$$

Thus

$$p_1(x) = f(x_0) + f'(x_0)(x - x_0).$$

The Taylor polynomial $p_1(x)$ is, in fact, the tangent line at $x = x_0$.

Degree 2. As a final special case, a quadratic polynomial $p_2(x)$ is determined. In the quadratic case, $n = 3$, and (3.3) implies that $p_2(x_0) = f(x_0)$, $p_2'(x_0) = f'(x_0)$, and $p_2''(x_0) = f''(x_0)$. Since the general form of a quadratic polynomial is

$$p_2(x) = a_0 + a_1 x + a_2 x^2,$$

the conditions (3.3) determine the upper-triangular linear system

$$p_2(x_0) = a_0 + a_1 x_0 + a_2 x_0^2 = f(x_0)$$

$$p_2'(x_0) = \qquad a_1 + 2a_2 x_0 = f'(x_0)$$

$$p_2''(x_0) = \qquad\qquad 2a_2 = f''(x_0).$$

The last equation gives

$$a_2 = \frac{f''(x_0)}{2},$$

and from the second equation we conclude that

$$a_1 = f'(x_0) - 2 \cdot \frac{f''(x_0)}{2} \cdot x_0 = f'(x_0) - f''(x_0)x_0.$$

Finally, the first equation may be solved for a_0, to read

$$a_0 = f(x_0) - [f'(x_0) - f''(x_0)x_0]x_0 - \frac{f''(x_0)}{2} x_0^2$$

$$= f(x_0) - f'(x_0)x_0 + \frac{f''(x_0)}{2} x_0^2.$$

Consequently,

$$p_2(x) = \left[f(x_0) - f'(x_0)x_0 + \frac{f''(x_0)}{2} x_0^2 \right]$$

$$+ [f'(x_0) - f''(x_0)x_0]x + \frac{f''(x_0)}{2} x^2.$$

By rearranging the terms according to the factors $f(x_0)$, $f'(x_0)$, and $f''(x_0)$, we obtain

$$p_2(x) = f(x_0) + f'(x_0)(x - x_0) + f''(x_0) \frac{x_0^2 - 2x_0 x + x^2}{2}$$

$$= f(x_0) + f'(x_0)(x - x_0) + f''(x_0) \frac{(x - x_0)^2}{2}.$$

Figure 3.3 illustrates these three approximators.

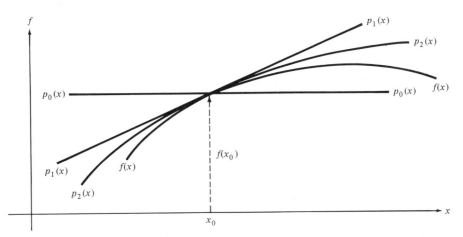

FIGURE 3.3 Approximation by Constant, Linear, and Quadratic Taylor's Polynomials

Observe now that $p_1(x)$ differs from $p_0(x)$ by way of the additional term $f'(x_0) \cdot (x - x_0)$, and $p_2(x)$ differs from $p_1(x)$ by the term

$$f''(x_0) \cdot \frac{(x - x_0)^2}{2}.$$

This insight is now extended.

General Degree.   Toward finding the general solution of the Taylor's polynomial satisfying condition (3.3), we introduce the polynomials $t_j(x)$, defined for $0 \le j \le n$, by

$$t_0(x) = 1, \quad t_1(x) = x - x_0,$$

$$t_2(x) = \frac{(x - x_0)^2}{2}, \quad \ldots, \quad t_j(x) = \frac{(x - x_0)^j}{j!}, \quad \ldots,$$

where $j! = j(j - 1)(j - 2) \cdot \ldots \cdot 3 \cdot 2 \cdot 1$. Since $t_0(x)$ is a constant,

$$t_0(x_0) = 1, \text{ and } t_0'(x_0) = t_0''(x_0) = \cdots = 0.$$

It is easy to see that

$$t_1(x_0) = 0, \qquad t_1'(x_0) = 1, \qquad t_1''(x_0) = t_1^{(3)}(x_0) = \cdots = 0,$$

since $t_1(x)$ has degree 1. Similarly, by differentiation, you may confirm that

$$t_2(x_0) = t_2'(x_0) = 0, \qquad t_2''(x_0) = 1, \qquad t_2^{(3)}(x_0) = t_2^{(4)}(x_0) = \cdots = 0.$$

In general, an obvious application of calculus shows that polynomials of the form

$$t_j(x) = \frac{(x - x_0)^j}{j!} \qquad (j = 0, 1, 2, \ldots)$$

satisfy the relation

$$t_j^{(k)}(x_0) = \begin{cases} 0 & \text{if } k \neq j \\ \dfrac{j!}{j!} = 1 & \text{if } k = j. \end{cases}$$

By using the functions $t_j(x)$ above, we may easily verify that the polynomial

$$p_{n-1}(x) = f(x_0)t_0(x) + f'(x_0)t_1(x) + \cdots + f^{(n-1)}(x_0)t_{n-1}(x) \quad (3.5)$$

with degree of most $n - 1$ satisfies the required "derivative matching" properties: For any $k = 0, 1, \ldots, n - 1$, we have

$$p_{n-1}^{(k)}(x_0) = f(x_0)t_0^{(k)}(x_0) + \cdots + f^{(j)}(x_0)t_j^{(k)}(x_0) + \cdots$$
$$+ f^{(n-1)}(x_0)t_{n-1}^{(k)}(x_0)$$
$$= 0 + 0 + \cdots + 0 + f^{(k)}(x_0)t_k^{(k)}(x_0) + 0 + \cdots + 0 + 0$$
$$= f^{(k)}(x_0) \cdot 1 = f^{(k)}(x_0),$$

because when $j \neq k$, $t_j^{(k)}(x_0)$ is equal to zero.

TABLE 3.2 Subroutine TAYLOR for Taylor's Polynomials

```
      SUBROUTINE TAYLOR(N,DF,X0,X,P)
C
C     ****************************************************************
C     * FUNCTION: THIS SUBROUTINE COMPUTES THE VALUE OF THE N-TH *
C     *           DEGREE TAYLOR'S POLYNOMIAL P(X)                *
C     *           GIVEN THE VALUE OF THE FUNCTION AND ITS FIRST  *
C     *           N DERIVATIVES AT A POINT X0                    *
C     * USAGE:                                                   *
C     *        CALL SEQUENCE:CALL TAYLOR(N,DF,X0,X,P)            *
C     * PARAMETERS:                                              *
C     *     INPUT:                                               *
C     *           N=DEGREE OF TAYLOR POLYNOMIAL                  *
C     *           DF=N+1 BY 1 ARRAY DF(J) IS (J-1)ST DERIVATIVE  *
C     *              OF F EVALUATED AT X0                        *
C     *           X=GIVEN INDEPENDENT VALUE                      *
C     *           X0=EXPANSION POINT                             *
C     *     OUTPUT:                                              *
C     *           P=TAYLOR POLYNOMIAL VALUE AT X                 *
C     ****************************************************************
C
      DIMENSION DF(N+1)
C     *** PROD=(X-X0)**(I-1) ***
      PROD=1.0
C     *** FACT= I FACTORIAL ***
      FACT=1.0
C     *** P ACCUMULATES THE TAYLOR POLYNOMIAL VALUE ***
      P=0.
      DO 10 I=1,N+1
         P=P+PROD*DF(I)/FACT
         PROD=PROD*(X-X0)
         FACT=FACT*I
   10 CONTINUE
      RETURN
      END
```

The polynomial $p_{n-1}(x)$ obtained through the constructs (3.5) is referred to as the *Taylor's polynomial*. It coincides with the first n terms of the Taylor's series expansion of $f(x)$ at x_0. One can summarize these developments to write the $(n-1)$st-degree Taylor's polynomial for $f(x)$ at x_0 as

$$p_{n-1}(x) = f(x_0) + \frac{f'(x_0)}{1!}(x - x_0) + \cdots + \frac{f^{(n-1)}(x_0)}{(n-1)!}(x - x_0)^{n-1}. \qquad (3.6)$$

It can be verified that the Taylor's polynomial is the only polynomial of degree less than n that satisfies (3.3). Note that (3.6) implies the recurrence relation

$$p_{n-1}(x) = p_{n-2}(x) + \frac{f^{(n-1)}(x_0)}{(n-1)!}(x - x_0)^{n-1}, \qquad (3.7)$$

for any n.

EXAMPLE 3.2

Let $f(x) = \sin(x)$ and $x_0 = 1$. Then (3.6) and (3.7) give

$$p_0(x) = f(x_0) = \sin(1)$$

$$p_1(x) = p_0(x_0) + f'(x_0)(x - x_0) = \sin(1) + \cos(1)(x - 1)$$

$$p_2(x) = p_1(x) + \tfrac{1}{2}f''(x_0)(x - x_0)^2$$

$$= \sin(1) + \cos(1)(x - 1) - \tfrac{1}{2}\sin(1)(x - 1)^2$$

and

$$p_3(x) = p_2(x) + \tfrac{1}{6}f^{(3)}(x_0)(x - x_0)^3$$

$$= \sin(1) + \cos(1)(x - 1) - \tfrac{1}{2}\sin(1)(x - 1)^2 - \tfrac{1}{6}\cos(1)(x - 1)^3.$$

When presented with derivative values (in array DF), subroutine TAYLOR (Table 3.2) computes (3.6). The subroutine makes use of the fact that the polynomials may be constructed recursively, according to relation (3.7).

EXAMPLE 3.3

Many numerical computations simply automate age-old formulas. The present study exemplifies this. Subroutine TAYLOR has the computer construct the Taylor's polynomial. We make use of this facility to redo the preceding example and obtain a table of the Taylor's polynomial approximation of $\sin(x)$. The driver program in Table 3.3 numerically evaluates such polynomials of degrees 1 through 3 at equally spaced values on the interval $0 \le x \le 2$, and compares them with the FORTRAN library functions of $\sin(x)$. The output is given in Table 3.4.

Figure 3.4 plots $p_1(x)$, $p_2(x)$, $p_3(x)$, and $\sin(x)$ on the interval $[0, 2]$. Note that $p_1(x)$ is the tangent line at $x_0 = 1$. Observe further that $p_3(x)$ gives credible

TABLE 3.3   Program for Taylor's Polynomial Example

```
C       PROGRAM TAYPOL
C
C       **************************************************************
C       COMPUTES TAYLOR POLYNOMIALS OF DEGREE 1 TO 3, FOR
C       SIN(X), ABOUT X0=1
C       CALLS:  TAYLOR
C       OUTPUT: X=THE VALUE OF THE INDEPENDENT VARIABLE
C               TRUE=THE VALUE OF SIN(X) AS COMPUTED BY THE
C                    FORTRAN LIBRARY FUNCTION SIN
C               P(K)=THE POLYNOMIAL APPROXIMATION AT X FOR DEGREE K
C               E(K)=THE ERROR IN APPROXIMATION AT X FOR EACH
C                    POLYNOMIAL
C       **************************************************************
C
        DIMENSION DF(4),P(3),E(3)
        PI=4*ATAN(1.)
        N=3
        X0=1.
C       *** COMPUTE THE DERIVATIVES                               ***
C       *** USES THAT COS(X0) = SIN(PI/2 + X(0)), ETC.            ***
        DO 10 I=1,N+1
            DF(I)=SIN(PI*(I-1)/2.+X0)
     10 CONTINUE
C
C       *** COMPUTES THE TRUE VALUES AT 10 EVENLY SPACED          ***
C       *** POINTS                                                ***
C
        DO 20 J=1,10
            X=J*.2
            TRUE=SIN(X)
C
C       *** SUBROUTINE TAYLOR COMPUTES THE K-TH DEGREE            ***
C       *** TAYLOR POLYNOMIAL THE ERROR IS THEN                   ***
C       *** COMPUTED AND ALL VALUES PRINTED                       ***
C
            DO 30 K=1,3
                CALL TAYLOR(K,DF,X0,X,F)
                P(K)=F
                E(K)=TRUE-P(K)
     30     CONTINUE
            WRITE(10,2)X,TRUE,P(1),E(1),P(2),E(2),P(3),E(3)
      2     FORMAT(1X,F3.1,1X,F10.6,3(1X,F10.6,1X,E12.3))
     20 CONTINUE
        STOP
        END
```

approximation to sin (x) over the interval $[0, 2]$. Your authors consider the accuracy of this simple approximation to be heartening. It can be seen that by taking advantage of the symmetry and periodicity of sin (x), its values for any x can be deduced from values in this interval.

TABLE 3.4   Application of Taylor's Formula

x	$\sin (x)$	$p_1(x)$	$\sin (x) - p_1(x)$	$p_2(x)$	$\sin (x) - p_2(x)$	$p_3(x)$	$\sin (x) - p_3(x)$
0.2	0.198669	0.409229	-0.211E+00	0.139958	0.587E-01	0.186064	0.126E-01
0.4	0.389418	0.517290	-0.128E+00	0.365825	0.236E-01	0.385276	0.414E-02
0.6	0.564642	0.625350	-0.607E-01	0.558032	0.661E-02	0.563796	0.847E-03
0.8	0.717356	0.733411	-0.161E-01	0.716581	0.775E-03	0.717301	0.546E-04
1.0	0.841471	0.841471	0.000E+00	0.841471	0.000E+00	0.841471	0.000E+00
1.2	0.932039	0.949531	-0.175E-01	0.932702	-0.663E-03	0.931982	0.575E-04
1.4	0.985450	1.057592	-0.721E-01	0.990274	-0.482E-02	0.984511	0.939E-03
1.6	0.999574	1.165652	-0.166E+00	1.014187	-0.146E-01	0.994737	0.484E-02
1.8	0.973848	1.273713	-0.300E+00	1.004442	-0.306E-01	0.958336	0.155E-01
2.0	0.909297	1.381773	-0.472E+00	0.961038	-0.517E-01	0.870987	0.383E-01

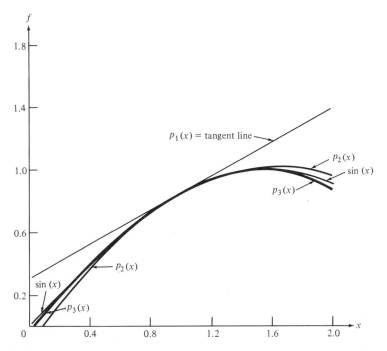

FIGURE 3.4   Taylor's Polynomial Approximation of sin (x)

Incidentally, nowadays, FORTRAN library routines can be relied on to compute intrinsic functions such as sin (x) to an accuracy commensurate with the computer roundoff error. In Problem 22, we suggest ways to use trigonometric identities to check the accuracy of sin (x) and other functions.

The remainder formula for Taylor's polynomials is often useful for finding absolute bounds for the truncation error of the Taylor's polynomial. If $f(x)$ is n times differentiable in any interval $[a, b]$ that contains x and x_0 and $p_{n-1}(x)$ is the $(n - 1)$st-degree Taylor's polynomial (3.6), then

$$f(x) - p_{n-1}(x) = \frac{f^{(n)}(\zeta)}{n!}(x - x_0)^n, \qquad (3.8)$$

where ζ is between x_0 and x. The term on the right side of (3.8) is called the *remainder term*.

EXAMPLE 3.4

As an application of the remainder term for Taylor's polynomials, consider again function $f(x) = \sin(x)$ with $x_0 = 1$. Now we will determine the smallest value of n such that the $(n - 1)$st-degree Taylor's polynomial of $f(x) = \sin(x)$ approximates $f(x)$ with an error not exceeding $\frac{1}{2} \cdot 10^{-6}$ for all $x \in [0, 2]$.

In this case $|f^{(n)}(\zeta)|$ is either $|\sin(\zeta)|$ or $|\cos(\zeta)|$; in either case,

$$|f^{(n)}(\zeta)| \leq 1 \qquad \text{and} \qquad |f(x) - p_{n-1}(x)| \leq \frac{|x - x_0|^n}{n!}.$$

Since for $x \in [0, 2]$, $|x - x_0| \leq 1$, the error of the Taylor's polynomial does not exceed $\frac{1}{2} \cdot 10^{-6}$, if n is chosen to satisfy

$$\frac{1}{n!} \cdot 1 \leq \frac{1}{2} \cdot 10^{-6}.$$

The minimal value n satisfying this inequality is $n = 10$; to confirm this, the reader may check that

$$\frac{1}{9!} > \frac{1}{2} \cdot 10^{-6} > \frac{1}{10!}.$$

By way of confirmation, we modified Program TAYPOL (Table 3.3) in an obvious manner and calculated that at $x = 1.8$, for example, the 10th degree Taylor's polynomial had an error of $1.2 \cdot 10^{-7}$.

∎

A drawback to the Taylor's polynomial approach is that it is not immediately applicable to the data-fitting task (2) described at the beginning of this chapter. Even for function approximation under the best of circumstances [i.e., when $f(x)$ is a known, sufficiently differentiable function], the Taylor's polynomial is typically awkward to implement because the expressions for higher derivatives are cumbersome.

The interpolation polynomial approach described in the following section does not require that the derivatives of $f(x)$ be known, or even exist. Moreover, its computer implementation is typically simple. Yet for "well-behaved" functions, the interpolation approach yields polynomial approximations of accuracy quite competitive with those of Taylor's series methods. A characteristic of the Taylor's polynomial is that it tends to be very accurate near x_0, but less accurate at a distance from x_0, whereas interpolation polynomials tend to "distribute" the error. The Taylor's series approach will be more important to us as an analytic device than as a computational technique.

3.4
POLYNOMIAL INTERPOLATION

3.4.1 Definition of Interpolation

Let $x_1, \ldots, x_n$ denote distinct real numbers and let $f_1, \ldots, f_n$ be arbitrary real numbers. The points (x_k, f_k), $k = 1, \ldots, n$, can be imagined to be data values to be connected by a curve. Any function $\hat{f}(x)$ satisfying the conditions

$$\hat{f}(x_k) = f_k \qquad (k = 1, 2, \ldots, n) \qquad (3.9)$$

is called an *interpolation function*. An interpolation function, then, is a curve that passes through the data points, as shown in Figure 3.5. In view of our computer orientation, we will be concerned with the case that $\hat{f}(x)$ is a polynomial.

Notice that the Taylor's polynomial was constructed from the consecutive de-

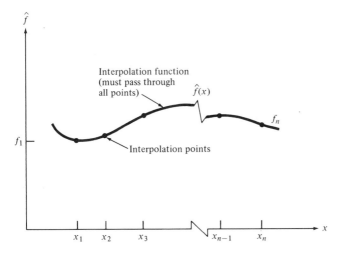

FIGURE 3.5 An Interpolation Function

rivatives $f(x_0)$, $f'(x_0)$, . . . , $f^{(n-1)}(x_0)$ of $f(x)$ at a specified point x_0, whereas the interpolation polynomial is to be determined by the function values $f(x_1)$, $f(x_2)$, . . . , $f(x_n)$ of $f(x)$ at specified domain points x_1, . . . , x_n. In both cases, n data values determine unique polynomials of degree less than n.

We state at the outset that in many situations, data interpolation is not recommended. Such situations include erratic functions and data with random components. Procedures in Chapter 6 should be considered in these contexts.

3.4.2 Lagrange Interpolation

In this section we introduce a method for constructing interpolation polynomials satisfying conditions (3.9). In Section 3.3 we learned that Taylor's polynomials are constructed to be consistent with derivative information. Lagrange interpolation polynomials are designed to be consistent with function-value information.

Degree 0. The polynomial of degree zero is the constant function

$$p_0(x) = a_0,$$

the graph of which is a horizontal line. Thus, as an interpolation function with $n = 1$, in (3.9), it is a horizontal line passing through the datum (x_1, f_1), as illustrated in Figure 3.6. Mathematically, we can express this curve as

$$p_0(x) = a_0 = f_1, \qquad \text{all } x.$$

Degree 1. The next most primitive polynomial is the linear (i.e., linear polynomial)

$$p_1(x) = a_0 + a_1 \cdot x.$$

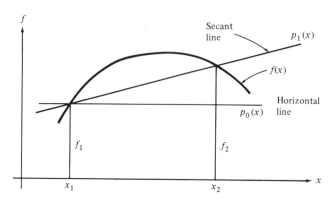

FIGURE 3.6 Illustration of Constant and Linear Interpolation

This first-degree polynomial has two coefficients and can interpolate the two points, (x_1, f_1) and (x_2, f_2), as Figure 3.6 illustrates. In view of (3.9) with $n = 2$, the interpolation condition is

$$p_1(x_1) = a_0 + a_1 \cdot x_1 = f_1$$

$$p_1(x_2) = a_0 + a_1 \cdot x_2 = f_2.$$

Solve for a_1 by subtracting the second equation from the first, and conclude that

$$a_1 = \frac{f_1 - f_2}{x_1 - x_2}.$$

Solve for a_0 by multiplying the top equation by x_2, the second by x_1, and subtracting the top from the bottom equation to confirm that

$$a_0 = \frac{x_2 f_1 - x_1 f_2}{x_2 - x_1}.$$

Thus the linear interpolation polynomial for the points (x_1, y_1) and (x_2, y_2) is

$$p_1(x) = \frac{x_2 f_1 - x_1 f_2}{x_2 - x_1} + x \cdot \frac{f_1 - f_2}{x_1 - x_2}.$$

The reader is invited to confirm that this formula really does interpolate: Check that $p_1(x_1) = f_1$, and $p_2(x_2) = f_2$. By rearranging this expression according to the functional values f_1 and f_2, we get

$$p_1(x) = f_1 \cdot \frac{x - x_2}{x_1 - x_2} + f_2 \cdot \frac{x - x_1}{x_2 - x_1}.$$

So

$$p_1(x) = f_1 \cdot l_1(x) + f_2 \cdot l_2(x)$$

with

$$l_1(x) = \frac{x - x_2}{x_1 - x_2} \quad \text{and} \quad l_2(x) = \frac{x - x_1}{x_2 - x_1}.$$

Then note the fundamental property that

$$l_1(x_1) = 1, \qquad l_1(x_2) = 0,$$

$$l_2(x_1) = 0, \qquad l_2(x_2) = 1.$$

This property lies at the heart of the Lagrange interpolation method for the general case, which is revealed next.

General Case. Suppose that for each j, $1 \leq j \leq n$, we can find an $(n - 1)$st-degree polynomial $l_j(x)$ such that for any k, $1 \leq j \leq n$,

$$l_j(x_k) = \begin{cases} 0 & \text{if } j \neq k \\ 1 & \text{if } j = k. \end{cases} \tag{3.10}$$

Then since the sum of polynomials of degree less than n is itself a polynomial of degree less than n,

$$p_{n-1}(x) = f_1 l_1(x) + f_2 l_2(x) + \cdots + f_n l_n(x)$$

is an interpolation polynomial of requisite degree. For observe that

$$p_{n-1}(x_j) = f_1 \cdot 0 + f_2 \cdot 0 + \cdots + f_{j-1} \cdot 0$$
$$+ f_j \cdot 1 + f_{j+1} \cdot 0 + \cdots + f_n \cdot 0 = f_j.$$

But the requisite polynomials $l_j(x)$ satisfying (3.10) are easy enough to construct. We consider the case $l_1(x)$ in detail. In light of (3.10), the distinct points $x_2, x_3, \ldots, x_n$ must be roots of $l_1(x)$. But this condition determines $l_1(x)$ up to a scalar multiple. For a standard factorization theorem of polynomial algebra states that if x_k is a root of any polynomial $g(x)$, then $(x - x_k)$ is a factor of $g(x)$. From this and (3.10) we conclude that $l_1(x)$ must have the factors $(x - x_2), (x - x_3), \ldots, (x - x_n)$. Since the degree must be less than n, these must be the only factors. Thus

$$l_1(x) = C(x - x_2) \cdots (x - x_n).$$

The remaining job is to find a scalar C so that $l_1(x)$ satisfies the remaining condition of (3.10), that $l_1(x_1) = 1$. But this is clearly achieved by setting

$$C = \frac{1}{(x_1 - x_2)(x_1 - x_3) \cdots (x_1 - x_n)}.$$

The other terms $l_j(x)$, $j > 1$, can be obtained by the same procedure. We have in this fashion constructed the *Lagrange interpolation polynomial* for the data (x_k, f_k), $k = 1, \ldots, n$. We summarize this construction as

$$p_{n-1}(x) = f_1 l_1(x) + f_2 l_2(x) + \cdots + f_n l_n(x),$$

where for $j = 1, 2, \ldots, n$,

$$l_j(x) = \frac{(x - x_1)(x - x_2) \cdots (x - x_{j-1})(x - x_{j+1}) \cdots (x - x_n)}{(x_j - x_1)(x_j - x_2) \cdots (x_j - x_{j-1})(x_j - x_{j+1}) \cdots (x_j - x_n)}. \tag{3.11}$$

Analogously to the Σ notation introduced in connection with Taylor's polynomial, the Π symbol allows concise representation of multiplication operations. For any numbers $y_1, \ldots, y_n$,

$$\prod_{k=1}^{n} y_k$$

denotes the product $y_1 \times y_2 \times \cdots \times y_n$, and the symbol

$$\prod_{\substack{k=1 \\ k \neq j}}^{n} y_k$$

denotes the product $y_1 \times y_2 \times \cdots \times y_{j-1} \times y_{j+1} \times \cdots \times y_n$. Thus we may now write the Lagrange factors in (3.11) as

$$l_j(x) = \left[\prod_{\substack{k=1 \\ k \neq j}}^{n} (x - x_k) \right] \Bigg/ \left[\prod_{\substack{k=1 \\ k \neq j}}^{n} (x_j - x_k) \right],$$

or even

$$l_j(x) = \prod_{\substack{k=1 \\ k \neq j}}^{n} \frac{x - x_k}{x_j - x_k}.$$

The reader should carefully note that the factors $l_j(x)$ *do not depend* on the function values, f_i. These values influence only $p_{n-1}(x)$ itself, as shown in (3.11).

EXAMPLE 3.5

A three-point Lagrange interpolation polynomial for $f(x) = \sin(x)$ is calculated in detail. We take the data given in Table 3.5.

TABLE 3.5   Data for Three-Point Interpolation Example

j	1	2	3
x_j	0	1	2
f_j	$\sin(0)$	$\sin(1)$	$\sin(2)$

Then by (3.11),

$$l_1(x) = \frac{(x - 1)(x - 2)}{(0 - 1)(0 - 2)} = \frac{(x - 1)(x - 2)}{2}$$

$$l_2(x) = \frac{(x - 0)(x - 2)}{(1 - 0)(1 - 2)} = -x(x - 2)$$

$$l_3(x) = \frac{(x - 0)(x - 1)}{(2 - 0)(2 - 1)} = \frac{x(x - 1)}{2}.$$

From (3.11) and the preceding equations,

$$p_2(x) = \sin (0) \frac{(x - 1)(x - 2)}{2} - \sin (1)x(x - 2) + \sin (2) \frac{x(x - 1)}{2}.$$

For $x = 1.5$, $p_2(1.5) \approx 0.9721$, and the correct value is $\sin (1.5) \approx 0.9975$. The relative error is about 2.6%. ∎

Next, our attention turns to automating the Lagrange polynomial construct. Subroutine LAGR for computing values of the Lagrange interpolation polynomial according to (3.11) is given in Table 3.6. The calling program passes the number

TABLE 3.6 Subroutine LAGR for Polynomial Interpolation

```
      SUBROUTINE LAGR(N,X,F,T,P)
C
C     ****************************************************************
C     *   FUNCTION: THIS SUBROUTINE COMPUTES THE LAGRANGE INTER-    *
C     *             POLATION POLYNOMIAL VALUE, GIVEN A SET OF N     *
C     *             DATA POINTS, AT A SPECIFIED VALUE T             *
C     *   USAGE:                                                     *
C     *        CALL SEQUENCE: CALL LAGR(N,X,F,T,P)                  *
C     *   PARAMETERS:                                                *
C     *        INPUT:                                                *
C     *             N=NUMBER OF DATA POINTS                          *
C     *             X=N BY 1 ARRAY OF INDEPENDENT DATA POINTS        *
C     *             F=N BY 1 ARRAY OF FUNCTIONAL VALUES              *
C     *             T=DESIRED POINT FOR INTERPOLATION                *
C     *        OUTPUT:                                               *
C     *             P=INTERPOLATION POLYNOMIAL VALUE AT T            *
C     ****************************************************************
C
      DIMENSION X(N),F(N)
C     *** INITIALIZATION ***
      P=0.0
C     *** COMPUTE LAGRANGIAN POLYNOMIAL VALUE P AT T ***
      DO 1 K=1,N
         FACTOR=1.0
C     *** COMPUTE LAGRANGIAN INTERPOLATION FACTORS ***
         DO 2 I=1,N
            IF (I.NE.K) THEN
               FACTOR=FACTOR*(T-X(I))/(X(K)-X(I))
            END IF
   2     CONTINUE
         P=P+FACTOR*F(K)
   1  CONTINUE
      RETURN
      END
```

N of points, arrays $X = (X(1), \ldots, X(N))$ and $F = (F(1), \ldots, F(N))$ of data values, and domain point T. The subroutine output variable P is the value $p(t)$ of the interpolation polynomial at $t = T$. The DO loop with label 2 computes the values $l_k(t)$, and they are stored as the variable FACTOR. The DO loop with label 1 multiplies these values by the functional values $F(K)$ and adds these products. The sum is returned as the variable P.

EXAMPLE 3.6

In Table 3.7 we have provided a calling program that utilizes subroutine LAGR (Table 3.6) to compute first-, second-, and third-degree Lagrange approximations to sin (x). These are denoted, respectively, by p_1, p_2, and p_3 in Table 3.8, which gives the results of evaluating these polynomials at 10 evenly spaced points on [0, 2].

In Figure 3.7, the first-, second-, and third-degree Lagrange interpolation polynomials have been plotted for comparison with sin (x) over the interval $I = [0, 2]$. For the two-point formula, only the endpoints are used, and this of course resulted in the secant line connecting the endpoints. The points in Table 3.5 served as data for the three-point formula, and the interpolation points x_1, x_2, x_3, and x_4 were 0, $\frac{2}{3}$, $\frac{4}{3}$, and 2, for the four-point (cubic) interpolation polynomial. In comparing Figure 3.7 to the corresponding Figure 3.4 of the Taylor's polynomial example, note that the latter tends to be more accurate near the middle of the interval, but the interpolation polynomial maintained good approximation toward the extremes. This illustrates developments discussed in the next section.

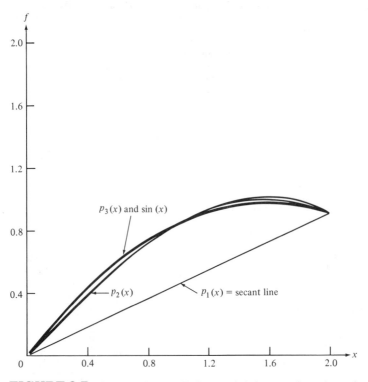

FIGURE 3.7   Interpolation Polynomial Approximation of sin (x)

TABLE 3.7   Program for Lagrange Polynomial Example

```
C       PROGRAM LAGRANGE
C
C       *****************************************************************
C       COMPUTES  LAGRANGE  INTERPOLATION POLYNOMIALS FOR THE
C       FUNCTION F(X)=SIN(X) AT 10 EQUALLY SPACED POINTS ON
C       THE INTERVAL [0,2]
C       CALLS: LAGR
C       OUTPUT: XD=DOMAIN POINTS FOR EVALUATION
C               TRUE=SIN(XD) AS COMPUTED BY THE LIBRARY FUNCTION
C               INTER(I)=VALUE OF THE INTERPOLATION POLYNOMIAL OF
C                         DEGREE (I)
C               ERR(I)= THE CORRESPONDING ERROR I=1,2,3
C       *****************************************************************
C
        REAL X(10),F(10),INTER(10),ERR(10)
        DO 10 N=1,10
          XD=N*0.2
          TRUE=SIN(XD)
          DO 20 I=1,3
            DO 30 J=1,I+1
C
C       *** COMPUTE THE DATA VALUES                                   ***
C
              X(J)=(J-1)*2./I
              F(J)=SIN(X(J))
   30       CONTINUE
C
C       *** SUBROUTINE LAGR COMPUTES THE INTERPOLATION VALUES         ***
C       *** AND ERR GIVES THE CORRESPONDING ERROR                    ***
C
            CALL LAGR(I+1,X,F,XD,P)
            ERR(I)=TRUE-P
            INTER(I)=P
   20     CONTINUE
          WRITE(10,2)XD,TRUE,(INTER(I),ERR(I),I=1,3)
    2     FORMAT(3X,F4.2,F10.6,3(3X,F10.6,3X,E12.3))
   10   CONTINUE
        STOP
        END
```

TABLE 3.8   Numerical Results of Example 3.6

x	$\sin(x)$	$p_1(x)$	$\sin(x) - p_1(x)$	$p_2(x)$	$\sin(x) - p_2(x)$	$p_3(x)$	$\sin(x) - p_3(x)$
0.20	0.198669	0.090930	0.108E+00	0.230186	-0.315E-01	0.204306	-0.564E-02
0.40	0.389418	0.181859	0.208E+00	0.429426	-0.400E-01	0.394319	-0.490E-02
0.60	0.564642	0.272789	0.292E+00	0.597720	-0.331E-01	0.565951	-0.131E-02
0.80	0.717356	0.363719	0.354E+00	0.735068	-0.177E-01	0.715113	0.224E-02
1.00	0.841471	0.454649	0.387E+00	0.841471	0.000E+00	0.837717	0.375E-02
1.20	0.932039	0.545578	0.386E+00	0.916928	0.151E-01	0.929676	0.236E-02
1.40	0.985450	0.636508	0.349E+00	0.961439	0.240E-01	0.986901	-0.145E-02
1.60	0.999574	0.727438	0.272E+00	0.975004	0.246E-01	1.005306	-0.573E-02
1.80	0.973848	0.818368	0.155E+00	0.957624	0.162E-01	0.980800	-0.695E-02
2.00	0.909297	0.909297	0.000E+00	0.909297	0.000E+00	0.909297	0.000E+00

Because of various constructions such as (3.11), and more to come, of "the" interpolation polynomial, it is reassuring to know that they are all different expressions for precisely the same function. That is, not only do the polynomials constructed by these various schemes all satisfy the requisite interpolation condition (3.9), but they also coincide for all other arguments x. To demonstrate this assertion, suppose that $p(x)$ and $q(x)$ are both interpolation polynomials of degree less than n for the same n data points. Then the polynomial

$$r(x) = p(x) - q(x)$$

must satisfy

$$r(x_k) = p(x_k) - q(x_k) = f_k - f_k = 0, \qquad 1 \le k \le n.$$

That is, $r(x)$ must have n distinct roots, although its degree is at most $n - 1$. But by the factorization property of polynomials, this is impossible unless $r(x)$ is the zero polynomial, in which case $p(x) = q(x)$, as we claimed.

If a Lagrange interpolation is to be evaluated at many different arguments x, it is worthwhile noting that we can calculate, once and for all, the terms

$$q_j = \frac{f_j}{\prod_{\substack{k=1 \\ k \ne j}}^{n} (x_j - x_k)}, \qquad 1 \le j \le n. \tag{3.12}$$

At each desired argument x, we compute

$$w_n(x) = \prod_{k=1}^{n} (x - x_k).$$

The Lagrange interpolation polynomial value $p_{n-1}(x)$ is then given by

$$p_{n-1}(x) = w_n(x)\left(\frac{q_1}{x - x_1} + \frac{q_2}{x - x_2} + \cdots + \frac{q_n}{x - x_n}\right), \tag{3.13}$$

which, as the reader may confirm, is algebraically identical to the defining equation (3.11). By this procedure, the main cost is the computation of the q_j terms, which together require $n(n - 2)$ multiplications, one division, and $n(n - 1)$ additions. But this need be done only once for each polynomial. Thereafter, (3.13) is evaluated at the cost of n multiplications and $2n - 1$ additions and n divisions. For purposes of simplicity, our subroutine LAGR did not follow this path, but evaluates (3.11) directly, at the cost of approximately n^2 multiplications per call. Our view is that for various reasons such as suggested in Section 3.4.4, the proper place of polynomial interpolation is instances in which the degree is 15 or less, and not a great many evaluations are to be made of any single polynomial.

It is useful to compare the Taylor's and interpolation polynomial constructs. They are similar in the sense that they determine minimal-degree polynomials which satisfy (or "collocate," as numerical analysts say) a finite set of function conditions. The difference is that in interpolation the information is function values at different points, and with Taylor's polynomials it is derivative information at a single point. In fact, it is feasible to construct hybrid polynomials that satisfy derivative conditions at several points, and such a plan sometimes serves a purpose. Problem 31 pursues this line.

3.4.3 Truncation Error of Interpolation Polynomials

In the spirit of (3.8) for Taylor's polynomial truncation error, the truncation error of the interpolation polynomial now occupies our attention. For this discussion it is presumed that $p_{n-1}(x)$ is the interpolation polynomial determined by the data (x_k, f_k), $k = 1, \ldots, n$, with $f_k = f(x_k)$ for some function $f(x)$.

Let $f(x)$ be n times differentiable on an interval $[a, b]$ that contains the points $x_1, \ldots, x_n$ and x. Then there exists a point $\zeta \in [a, b]$ such that

$$f(x) - p_{n-1}(x) = \frac{1}{n!} f^{(n)}(\zeta) w_n(x), \tag{3.14}$$

where $f^{(n)}(x)$ denotes the nth derivative of $f(x)$ and $w_n(x)$ is defined by

$$w_n(x) = (x - x_1)(x - x_2) \cdots (x - x_n). \tag{3.15}$$

Derivation of this error bound is given by S & Y (1978, pp. 31–32).

It is instructive to compare this truncation error formula with the remainder formula (3.8) for the error of the Taylor's polynomial approximation. It is clear that for x near x_0, Taylor's formula ought to be more accurate. But if $f^{(n)}(x)$ does not change appreciably on the interval of interest, and if the domain points x_k, $k = 1, \ldots, n$, are "evenly distributed," one would anticipate that for x closer to the extremes of $[a, b]$,

$$|w_n(x)| < |(x - x_0)^n|$$

and that Lagrange interpolation might well be more accurate. For example, if $f(x)$ happened to be an nth-degree polynomial, then $f^{(n)}(x)$ is a constant and our discussion would apply forcefully. In the next section we give a plan for choosing the points x_k, $1 \le k \le n$, in such a fashion as to make the maximum of $|w_n(x)|$ as small as possible.

───── **EXAMPLE 3.7** ─────────────────────────────

In Examples 3.2 and 3.5, the Taylor's and interpolation polynomials, respectively, were applied to the task of approximating $\sin(x)$ over the interval $[0, 2]$. Figure 3.8 shows the actual error, as a function of argument x, associated with the third-degree Taylor's and interpolation polynomial approximations. In keeping with our theoretical anticipations, the Taylor's polynomial error is relatively small near the expansion point $x_0 = 1$ and relatively large near the extremes of the interval.

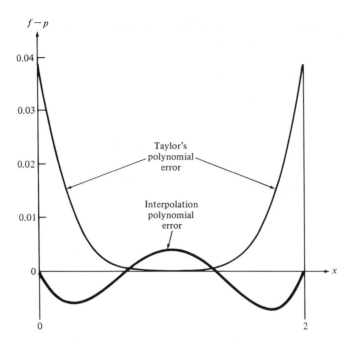

FIGURE 3.8   Comparison of Actual Error of Cubic Taylor's and Interpolation Polynomials of $f(x) = \sin(x)$

We remark on extrapolation. *Extrapolation* refers to evaluation of the interpolation polynomial outside the interval containing the data points x_k. It is to be noted that the term $w_n(x)$ in the error formula (3.14) can become very large for values x far away from the data. This prepares us for a well-known heuristic rule: Extrapolation is dangerous!

By way of illustration of this point, we repeated the Lagrange interpolation approximation experiment of Example 3.6. But here we evaluated x in the interval [1, 3], whereas the data all lie in the interval [0, 2]. The outcome of this experiment is summarized below for the cubic interpolation polynomial. It is evident that the error becomes much larger for points greater than 2. That is, the error grows drastically as we try to extrapolate the data.

x	$\sin(x)$	$p_3(x)$	$\sin(x) - p_3(x)$	
1.20	0.932039	0.929676	0.236E-02	Region of interpolation
1.40	0.985450	0.986901	-0.145E-02	
1.60	0.999574	1.005306	-0.573E-02	
1.80	0.973848	0.980800	-0.695E-02	
2.00	0.909297	0.909297	0.000E+00	
2.20	0.808496	0.786709	0.218E-01	
2.40	0.675463	0.608947	0.665E-01	
2.60	0.515501	0.371924	0.144E+00	Region of extrapolation
2.80	0.334988	0.071552	0.263E+00	
3.00	0.141120	-0.296257	0.437E+00	

3.4.4 Refinements and Limitations of Polynomial Interpolation

One might hope that if a function $f(x)$ is continuous and "well behaved" on a given finite interval $[a, b]$, then as the number of interpolation points x_k increases and becomes dense on that interval, the associated polynomial sequence $\{p_{n-1}(x)\}$ converges to $f(x)$ at each point x in $[a, b]$. This hope is dashed by Example 3.8. Here the x_k's are evenly spaced on $[-1, 1]$ and $f(x)$ is not only continuous but differentiable. Yet approximation actually gets worse as more points are used.

───── **EXAMPLE 3.8** ─────────────────────────────────────

Let $f(x) = 1/(1 + 25x^2)$, where $x \in [-1, 1]$. This function is called the *Runge function*. Figure 3.9 shows this function and its interpolation polynomials of degrees 10 and 20. It is known (Isaacson and Keller, 1966, pp. 275–278) that the sequence $\{p_{n-1}(x)\}$ of these interpolation polynomials with equally spaced interpolation points does not converge to $f(x)$ at any x in the intervals $[-1, -0.727]$ or $[0.727, 1]$. Note that the Runge function is fairly well represented by interpolation polynomials over the central 72.7% of the interval, but the approximation is very bad near the extremes.

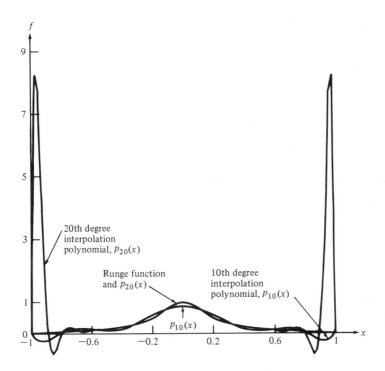

FIGURE 3.9   Interpolation Polynomial Approximation of the Runge Function

─── ■

The power of mathematical reasoning is most astonishing in cases in which it directs us to unintuitive conclusions. It would seem "reasonable" that equally spaced interpolation points x_k (i.e., $x_{k+1} - x_k$ the same for all k) ought to be best in the sense that they provide the most representative $f(x_k)$ samples. Thus it might

FIGURE 3.10   Distribution of Chebyshev Points

be expected that these ought to be the most logical points for constructing an interpolation polynomial. This line of reasoning is incorrect.

Let us recall from Section 3.4.3 that the truncation error for approximating an n-times differentiable function by an interpolation polynomial $p_{n-1}(x)$ with interpolation points $x_1, \ldots, x_n$ is

$$f(x) - p_{n-1}(x) = \frac{f^{(n)}(\zeta) w_n(x)}{n!}. \tag{3.16}$$

In (3.16), ζ is some number in the interval containing all interpolation points as well as x, and

$$w_n(x) = (x - x_1)(x - x_2) \cdots (x - x_n).$$

The term $f^{(n)}(\zeta)$ above is beyond our control. However, the term $w_n(x)$ offers possibilities if we are free to choose the interpolation points. A sensible ambition might then be to choose these points so that the maximum of $|w_n(x)|$ is as small as possible over the interval $[a, b]$ of interpolation. It turns out (S & Y, 1978, Sec. 2.2) that this ambition is realized by choosing the so-called Chebyshev points as the interpolation points. For the interval $[a, b]$, the *Chebyshev points* are defined to be

$$x_k = \frac{a + b}{2} + \frac{a - b}{2} \cos\left(\frac{2k - 1}{2n}\pi\right) \qquad (k = 1, \ldots, n). \tag{3.17}$$

In Figure 3.10 we have located the Chebyshev points for $n = 10$ on the interval $[-1, 1]$. Figure 3.11 compares $w_{10}(x)$ when x_k's are evenly spaced against $w_{10}(x)$ for x_k's the Chebyshev points.

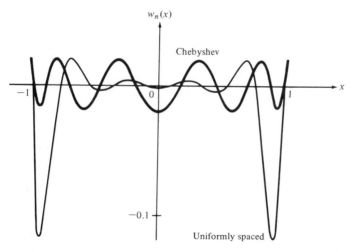

FIGURE 3.11   Comparison of $w_n(x)$ Functions

──────── **EXAMPLE 3.9** ───

By means of the simple calling program in Table 3.9 we have constructed the 31-point Chebyshev-interpolation polynomial for the Runge function (described in Example 3.8). In the output listing (Table 3.10), the interpolation error is tabulated at 20 evenly spaced values. We see that the Runge function is apparently under control.

TABLE 3.9   Interpolation of Runge Function Using Chebyshev Points

```
C       PROGRAM RUNGE
C
C       ****************************************************************
C       COMPUTES 30TH DEGREE INTERPOLATION POLYNOMIAL USING
C       CHEBYSHEV POINTS FOR THE RUNGE FUNCTION
C       CALLS:  LAGR
C       OUTPUT: T=THE VALUE OF THE INDEPENDENT VARIABLE
C               TRUE=THE FUNCTIONAL VALUE AT THE POINT T AS
C                    DETERMINED BY THE STATEMENT FUNCTION FF
C               P=THE VALUE OF THE INTERPOLATION POLYNOMIAL AT T
C               E=THE ERROR OF THE APPROXIMATION AT T
C       ****************************************************************
C
        DIMENSION X(40),F(40)
C
C       *** RUNGE FUNCTION STATEMENT                            ***
C
        FF(X)=1.0/(1.0+(5.0*X)**2)
C
C       *** COMPUTE VALUES AT CHEBYSHEV POINTS                  ***
C
        N=31
        PI=4.0*ATAN(1.0)
        DO 10 I=1,N
          X(I)=COS((2.0*I-1)*PI/(2.0*N))
          F(I)=FF(X(I))
     10 CONTINUE
C
C       *** SUBROUTINE LAGR WILL COMPUTE VALUE OF THE           ***
C       *** INTERPOLATION POLYNOMIAL AT T AND E GIVES THE ERROR ***
C
        DO 30 I=1,20
          T=-1.0+I*0.1
          CALL LAGR(N,X,F,T,P)
          TRUE=FF(T)
          E=TRUE-P
          WRITE(10,2)T,TRUE,P,E
      2   FORMAT(2X,F3.1,2X,E14.7,2X,E14.7,2X,E14.7)
     30 CONTINUE
        STOP
        END
```

TABLE 3.10   Output of Runge Function Interpolation

x	Runge Function	Approximation	Error
-.9	0.4705882E-01	0.4692032E-01	0.1385026E-03
-.8	0.5882353E-01	0.5837149E-01	0.4520416E-03
-.7	0.7547170E-01	0.7447892E-01	0.9927750E-03
-.6	0.9999998E-01	0.1011296E+00	-0.1129620E-02
-.5	0.1379310E+00	0.1372023E+00	0.7287264E-03
-.4	0.2000000E+00	0.2003204E+00	-0.3204048E-03
-.3	0.3076923E+00	0.3076517E+00	0.4056096E-04
-.2	0.5000001E+00	0.4999129E+00	0.8720160E-04
-.1	0.8000001E+00	0.8000615E+00	-0.6145239E-04

TABLE 3.10   (Continued)

x	Runge Function	Approximation	Error
0.0	0.1000000E+01	0.1000000E+01	-0.1192093E-06
0.1	0.8000000E+00	0.8000612E+00	-0.6127357E-04
0.2	0.4999999E+00	0.4999129E+00	0.8702278E-04
0.3	0.3076922E+00	0.3076518E+00	0.4041195E-04
0.4	0.2000000E+00	0.2003204E+00	-0.3203750E-03
0.5	0.1379310E+00	0.1372023E+00	0.7287711E-03
0.6	0.9999998E-01	0.1011297E+00	-0.1129672E-02
0.7	0.7547168E-01	0.7447891E-01	0.9927750E-03
0.8	0.5882351E-01	0.5837147E-01	0.4520416E-03
0.9	0.4705882E-01	0.4692034E-01	0.1384839E-03
1.0	0.3846154E-01	0.3764865E-01	0.8128881E-03

Have we mastered the approximation problem through interpolation using Chebyshev points? In some cases "yes" and in other cases "no." From de Boor (1978), for example, the following facts are known:

1. If (as in the case of the Runge function) $f(x)$ has a *continuous derivative* on $[a, b]$, then using Chebyshev points, for each x in $[a, b]$,

$$p_{n-1}(x) \to f(x), \qquad \text{as } n \to \infty.$$

2. No matter how interpolation points are chosen, there is some continuous function $f(x)$ for which $\{p_{n-1}(x)\}$ fails to converge for some value of x.
3. Even when $f(x)$ has a continuous derivative, adequate approximation may require an impossibly large n.

Point 3 is illustrated by our printout in Table 3.10, where a 30th-degree polynomial is scarcely accurate to three significant figures. In this regard we note that the degree must be over 1 million for $\sqrt{|x|}$ to be interpolated on $[-1, 1]$ to an accuracy of 10^{-3} (de Boor, 1978). Interpolation polynomials of degree 30 are on the borderline of the impractical, and degrees greater than 100 almost invariably lead to grievous roundoff effects.

Many alternative algorithms exist for constructing the interpolation and Taylor's polynomials. In view of Chapter 2, it is worthwhile noting that they can be found directly from solution of linear equations. We show the details in the interpolation case. Represent $p_{n-1}(x)$ in a conventional fashion as

$$p_{n-1}(x) = a_0 + a_1 x + \cdots + a_{n-1} x^{n-1} \qquad (3.18)$$

and recognize that the defining condition (3.9) for interpolation implies that $p_{n-1}(x)$ must satisfy the linear equation

$$\sum_{j=0}^{n-1} a_j x_i^j = f_i, \qquad 1 \le i \le n. \qquad (3.19)$$

One can write this in matrix form $\mathbf{Xa} = \mathbf{f}$, by defining

$$\mathbf{f} = (f_1, f_2, \ldots, f_{n-1})^T$$

$$\mathbf{a} = (a_0, a_1, \ldots, a_{n-1})^T$$

and

$$\mathbf{X} = \begin{pmatrix} 1 & x_1 & x_1^2 & \cdots & x_1^{n-1} \\ \vdots & \vdots & \vdots & & \vdots \\ 1 & x_n & x_n^2 & \cdots & x_n^{n-1} \end{pmatrix}.$$

Analogously, in the case of Taylor's polynomials, the "derivatives matching" condition implies that the $p_{n-1}(x)$ satisfy

$$\sum_{j=0}^{n-1} a_j x_0^j = f(x_0), \qquad i = 0$$

$$\sum_{j=i}^{n-1} j(j-1) \cdots (j-i+1) a_j x_0^{j-i} = f^{(i)}(x_0), \qquad 1 \le i \le n-1.$$

This has the same matrix form as before, but with coefficient vectors and matrix given, respectively, by

$$\mathbf{f} = (f(x_0), f'(x_0), \ldots, f^{n-1}(x_0))^T$$

$$\mathbf{a} = (a_0, a_1, \ldots, a_{n-1})^T$$

and

$$\mathbf{X} = \begin{pmatrix} 1 & x_0 & x_0^2 & \cdots & & x_0^{n-2} & x_0^{n-1} \\ 0 & 1 & 3x_0^2 & \cdots & & (n-2)x_0^{n-3} & (n-1)x_0^{n-2} \\ 0 & 0 & 2 & \cdots & & (n-2)(n-3)x_0^{n-4} & (n-1)(n-2)x_0^{n-3} \\ \vdots & \vdots & \vdots & \vdots\vdots\vdots & & \vdots & \vdots \\ 0 & 0 & 0 & \cdots & & 0 & (n-1)! \end{pmatrix}.$$

EXAMPLE 3.10

We redo the interpolation problem of Example 3.5 by the linear equation approach. The data for this problem are taken from Table 3.5, where 0, 1, and 2 were the abscissa values and sin (0), sin (1), and sin (2) were the corresponding function values. From (3.19), we obtain the linear equations

$$a_0 \qquad\qquad\qquad = \sin(0)$$

$$a_0 + a_1 + a_2 = \sin(1)$$

$$a_0 + 2a_1 + 4a_2 = \sin(2).$$

By a hand application of Gauss elimination, we find that $a_0 = 0$,

$$a_1 = \frac{4 \cdot \sin(1) - \sin(2)}{2} \qquad \text{and} \qquad a_2 = \frac{\sin(2) - 2 \cdot \sin(1)}{2}.$$

We checked that $p_2(x) = a_1 x + a_2 x^2$, with a_1, a_2 as above, gives the same value at $x = 1.5$ as that obtained in Example 3.5. ■

The ideas above for construction of Taylor's and interpolation polynomials through linear equations are simple and direct. However, they are seldom discussed in the literature. They do have drawbacks. We know from Section 2.2.5 that solution of a linear equation in n variables requires about $\frac{1}{3} n^3$ arithmetic operations, whereas the growth in effort by the Lagrange and Taylor's polynomial formulas is proportional to n^2. A more serious difficulty is that the linear systems associated with these equations tend to be ill-conditioned. [The matrix X for system (3.19) is a version of the notorious Vandermonde matrix of Example 2.8.] Nevertheless, the linear equation approach is to be respected for its incisiveness and universality. This theme will play an important role in Chapters 4 and 6.

As a final point, in view of developments in Chapter 1 on roundoff and sensitivity, one can anticipate that high-degree polynomials might tend to be ill-conditioned. Let

$$p(x) = \sum_{j=0}^{n} a_j x^j$$

and suppose that the degree n is very large. Then for very large j if $|x| > 1$, x^j has a very large magnitude, and some slight error (such as roundoff) in the coefficient a_j gets multiplied by this astronomical factor. On the other hand, if $|x| < 1$, the coefficients must tend to be extremely large to compensate for miniscule x. Here slight perturbations in x can cause huge deviations in polynomial values.

★3.4.5 The Newton Representation

From developments in Section 3.4.2, we know that all interpolation polynomials having degree not exceeding $n - 1$, n being the number of points to be interpolated, are identical to the Lagrange representation (3.11). But other representations sometimes serve useful purposes. For example, the *Newton representation* of the interpolating polynomial has the feature that it is easier to update—that is, to include an additional point (x_{n+1}, f_{n+1}). Also, if coded wisely, it requires only about half as many arithmetic operations per call as the Lagrange form and is less subject to deterioration due to roundoff effects.

The Newton representation of the interpolation polynomial for the data (x_k, f_k), $k = 1, \ldots, n$, is

$$
\begin{aligned}
p_{n-1}(x) = a_0 &+ a_1(x - x_1) + \cdots \\
&+ a_k(x - x_1)(x - x_2) \cdots (x - x_k) + \cdots \\
&+ a_{n-1}(x - x_1) \cdots (x - x_{n-1}).
\end{aligned}
\tag{3.20}
$$

where the coefficients $a_0, a_1, \ldots, a_{n-1}$ are determined so as to ensure that the data are interpolated [i.e., that $p_{n-1}(x_k) = f_k$]. The interpolation conditions at x_1 and x_2 require that

$$
\begin{aligned}
a_0 &= f_1 \\
a_1 &= \frac{f_2 - a_0}{x_2 - x_1},
\end{aligned}
\tag{3.21}
$$

and for $k = 2, \ldots, n - 1$,

$$a_k = \frac{f_{k+1} - a_0 - \sum_{l=1}^{k-1} a_l(x_{k+1} - x_1) \cdots (x_{k+1} - x_l)}{(x_{k+1} - x_1) \cdots (x_{k+1} - x_k)}. \qquad (3.22)$$

This formula, in conjunction with (3.21), provides a means of recursively computing the coefficients for the Newton representation (3.20). If one wishes to add an additional point (x_{n+1}, f_{n+1}) in order to obtain an nth-degree interpolation polynomial $p_n(x)$ for the pairs (x_k, f_k), $1 \le k \le n + 1$, then the coefficients $\bar{a}_k$ of p_n are identical to the coefficients a_k of p_{n-1}, for $k = 0, \ldots, n - 1$ and $\bar{a}_n$ is given by (3.22) with $k = n$. Thus in the Newton representation only one coefficient needs to be evaluated for updating, whereas by the Lagrange and linear equation constructs, in order to accommodate an additional data pair, the computations have to be redone in their entirety.

We now rewrite the Newton representation (3.20) using some traditional notation. For $k \ge 1$, define

$$f[x_k] = f_k$$

$$f[x_k, x_{k+1}] = \frac{f[x_{k+1}] - f[x_k]}{x_{k+1} - x_k}$$

$$f[x_k, x_{k+1}, x_{k+2}] = \frac{f[x_{k+1}, x_{k+2}] - f[x_k, x_{k+1}]}{x_{k+2} - x_k} \qquad (3.23)$$

$$\vdots$$

$$f[x_k, x_{k+1}, \ldots, x_i, x_{i+1}] = \frac{f[x_{k+1}, \ldots, x_{i+1}] - f[x_k, \ldots, x_i]}{x_{i+1} - x_k}$$

$$\vdots$$

These quantities are called *divided differences* and can be computed recursively by the equations above. Finite induction shows that the coefficients of the Newton representation satisfy the relations

$$a_0 = f[x_1]$$

$$a_1 = f[x_1, x_2] \qquad (3.24)$$

$$\vdots$$

$$a_{n-1} = f[x_1, x_2, \ldots, x_n].$$

Thus the Newton representation can be obtained through implementation of the above recursion. For $k = 1, \ldots, n$, define $f[x_k]$ to be equal to f_k. Then, for $k = 1, \ldots, n - 1$ compute the values of $f[x_k, x_{k+1}]$. Now, for $k = 1, \ldots, n - 2$ determine the quantities $f[x_k, x_{k+1}, x_{k+2}]$, and so on. Until the value of

$f[x_1, \ldots, x_n]$ is obtained. The *difference table* constructed from the interpolating points $x_1, \ldots, x_n$ and functional values $f_1, \ldots, f_n$ has the following form:

x_1	$f[x_1]$	$f[x_1, x_2]$	$\cdots$	$f[x_1, \ldots, x_{n-1}]$	$f[x_1, \ldots, x_n]$
x_2	$f[x_2]$	$f[x_2, x_3]$	$\cdots$	$f[x_2, \ldots, x_n]$	
x_3	$f[x_3]$	$f[x_3, x_4]$			
$\vdots$	$\vdots$	$\vdots$			
x_{n-2}	$f[x_{n-2}]$	$f[x_{n-2}, x_{n-1}]$	$f[x_{n-2}, x_{n-1}, x_n]$		
x_{n-1}	$f[x_{n-1}]$	$f[x_{n-1}, x_n]$			
x_n	$f[x_n]$				

The elements $f[x_1]$, $f[x_1, x_2]$, $\ldots$, $f[x_1, \ldots, x_n]$ of the top row are the coefficients $a_0, a_1, \ldots, a_{n-1}$ of the Newton representation (3.20).

------- **EXAMPLE 3.11** -------

Consider again the function $f(x) = \sin(x)$. The Newton representation of the interpolation polynomial with interpolating points $x_1 = 0$, $x_2 = 2$, and $x_3 = 1$ will be determined from the recursive relations (3.21)–(3.22). From (3.21),

$$a_0 = f_1 = f(x_1) = 0,$$

$$a_1 = \frac{f(x_2) - a_0}{x_2 - x_1} = \frac{\sin(2)}{2},$$

so the linear interpolating polynomial based on the points x_1 and x_2 is

$$p(x) = 0 + \frac{\sin(2)}{2} x.$$

To incorporate the additional interpolation point $x_3 = 1$ into the interpolation polynomial, in accordance with (3.22), we calculate that

$$a_2 = \frac{f(x_3) - a_0 - a_1(x_3 - x_1)}{(x_3 - x_1)(x_3 - x_2)}$$

$$= \frac{\sin(1) - 0 - a_1(1 - 0)}{(1 - 0)(1 - 2)}$$

$$= a_1 - \sin(1) = \frac{\sin(2)}{2} - \sin(1).$$

The reader may confirm that with these coefficients, (3.20) is a quadratic interpolation polynomial for $\sin(x)$ at x_1, x_2, and x_3, and because of the uniqueness of the interpolating polynomial, it must coincide with the quadratic Lagrange representation, the performance of which was investigated in Examples 3.5 and 3.10.

In terms of divided differences, these interpolation polynomials can be expressed as follows. Since

$$f[x_1] = f_1 = f(0) = 0$$

$$f[x_2] = f_2 = f(2) = \sin(2)$$

$$f[x_3] = f_3 = f(1) = \sin(1),$$

the recursion of the divided differences implies that

$$f[x_1, x_2] = f[0, 2] = \frac{\sin(2) - 0}{2 - 0} = \frac{\sin(2)}{2},$$

$$f[x_2, x_3] = f[2, 1] = \frac{\sin(1) - \sin(2)}{1 - 2} = \sin(2) - \sin(1),$$

and

$$f[x_1, x_2, x_3] = f[0, 2, 1] = \frac{\sin(2) - \sin(1) - \sin(2)/2}{1 - 0} = \frac{\sin(2)}{2} - \sin(1).$$

Thus the linear and quadratic interpolation polynomials are

$$p_1(x) = a_0 + a_1(x - x_1) = 0 + \frac{\sin(2)}{2} x$$

and

$$p_2(x) = a_0 + a_1(x - x_1) + a_2(x - x_1)(x - x_2)$$

$$= 0 + \frac{\sin(2)}{2} x + \left[\frac{\sin(2)}{2} - \sin(1) \right] x(x - 2).$$

■

3.5
SPLINE FUNCTIONS

3.5.1 Motivation for Piecewise Polynomial Methods

There are situations in which the performance of interpolation polynomials is found to be inferior to alternative techniques such as those discussed in this section and in Chapter 6. Specific situations for which splines, the subject of the present section, afford advantages over interpolation polynomials are

> *Situation 1.* The number n of data points to be interpolated is moderate to large (e.g., n is greater than 20).
> *Situation 2.* The data points are associated with some known or unknown function $f(x)$, the derivatives of which are large or do not exist.

Situation 3. The data points arise from a natural or "nonmathematical" source (e.g., the profile of an airplane fuselage or the boundary between two countries).

Roundoff error is a prime cause of difficulty when n is large. Using notation from Chapter 1, let f_k^*, $1 \le k \le n$, denote the data values actually used in computing the interpolation polynomial $p_{n-1}^*(x)$ and suppose the "correct" values to be f_k, with

$$|f_k - f_k^*| \le \delta, \tag{3.25}$$

where δ is an error bound. Then in the notation of (3.11) the difference of the Lagrange interpolation polynomials $p_{n-1}(x)$ and $p_{n-1}^*(x)$ based, respectively, on the data (x_k, f_k) and (x_k, f_k^*) can be bounded as follows:

$$|p_{n-1}(x) - p_{n-1}^*(x)| = \left| \sum_{k=1}^{n} f_k l_k(x) - \sum_{k=1}^{n} f_k^* l_k(x) \right|$$

$$= \left| \sum_{k=1}^{n} (f_k - f_k^*) l_k(x) \right|$$

$$\le \sum_{k=1}^{n} |f_k - f_k^*| \cdot |l_k(x)| \le \delta \sum_{k=1}^{n} |l_k(x)|.$$

The quantity on the right can increase dramatically with the number of data points. As the next example shows, even under the most favorable circumstances, roundoff error causes intolerable deterioration of high-degree interpolation polynomials. We thereby motivate situation 1 above.

EXAMPLE 3.12

The function $f(x) = \sin(x)$ is interpolated using evenly spaced domain points in the interval $[0, 1]$. This function is exceptionally suited to approximation by interpolation because the magnitudes of derivatives of any order are bounded by 1. From the printout (Table 3.11), which displays values of $\sin(x)$ and its Lagrange approximation at randomly chosen domain points in the unit interval, we see that the approximation is excellent for $n = 20$ but is a disaster for $n = 70$. This computational experiment will depend on the computer word length; this particular run used a VAX.

TABLE 3.11 Numerical Results of Example 3.12

	Argument x	sin (x)	Lagrange Interpolation $p_{n-1}(x)$
	0.1948200	0.1935899	0.1935901
	0.7324600	0.6687008	0.6687007
	0.6087400	0.5718342	0.5718342
	0.3225800	0.3170145	0.3170145
$n = 20$	0.1084500	0.1082375	0.1082376
	0.1884800	0.1873660	0.1873660
	0.6172300	0.5787785	0.5787784

TABLE 3.11   (Continued)

	Argument x	sin (x)	Lagrange Interpolation $p_{n-1}(x)$
	0.7132600	0.6543025	0.6543024
	0.6379100	0.5955178	0.5955178
	0.4875300	0.4684451	0.4684452
	0.1948200	0.1935899	0.1936576
	0.7324600	0.6687008	0.6687038
	0.6087400	0.5718342	0.5718339
	0.3225800	0.3170145	0.3170149
$n = 50$	0.1084500	0.1082375	0.1447353 ←
	0.1884800	0.1873660	0.1875511
	0.6172300	0.5787785	0.5787789
	0.7132600	0.6543025	0.6543033
	0.6379100	0.5955178	0.5955179
	0.4875300	0.4684451	0.4684451
	0.1948200	0.1935899	0.1949847
	0.7324600	0.6687008	0.6686892
	0.6087400	0.5718342	0.5718341
	0.3225800	0.3170145	0.3170152
$n = 70$	0.1084500	0.1082375	60.45348 ←
	0.1884800	0.1873660	0.1861881
	0.6172300	0.5787785	0.5787786
	0.7132600	0.6543025	0.6543000
	0.6379100	0.5955178	0.5955176
	0.4875300	0.4684451	0.4684451

De Boor (1978, p. 22) has offered a heuristic explanation as to why piecewise interpolation might provide relief with irregular curves (situations 2 and 3 at the start of this section):

> We stress the fact that polynomial interpolation at appropriately chosen points (e.g., the Chebyshev points) produces an approximation which, for all practical purposes, differs very little from the best possible approximant by polynomials of the same order. This allows us to illustrate the essential limitations of polynomial approximation: If the function to be approximated is badly behaved anywhere in the interval of approximation, then the approximation is poor everywhere. This global dependence on local properties can be avoided when using *piecewise* polynomial approximants.

During the past decade, piecewise polynomial approximations have become prominent both in theoretical studies and in applications. Instead of trying to approximate a function over the entire interval by one polynomial of high degree, one approximates the function by a piecewise polynomial function, where the degree of the polynomial "pieces" associated with each subinterval is small. A piecewise polynomial approximation is illustrated in Figure 3.12. Polynomial $s_1(x)$ approximates $f(x)$ on the interval $[x_1, x_2]$, $s_2(x)$ approximates $f(x)$ on $[x_2, x_3]$, and so on. Note in this graph that the piecewise polynomial displays jagged behavior

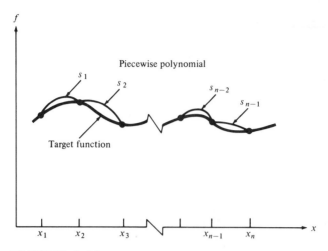

FIGURE 3.12   Piecewise Polynomial Interpolation

at the interpolation points. Splines, the subject discussed next, are piecewise polynomials that prevent such erratic profiles by imposing derivative constraints at the common boundary points of the polynomial pieces.

3.5.2 Definition of Splines

Spline functions are piecewise polynomials with derivatives constrained for the purpose of making the resulting function smooth at the node points x_i. Let $[a, b]$ be a finite interval containing the points $a = x_1 < x_2 < \cdots < x_n = b$. A *spline function* of degree m with interpolating points x_i, $i = 1, \ldots, n$, is a piecewise polynomial $s(x)$ satisfying the following properties:

1. $s(x)$ is $m - 1$ times differentiable at each point x_i, $1 \leq i \leq n$.
2. On each subinterval $[x_i, x_{i+1}]$ $(1 \leq i \leq n - 1)$, $s(x)$ is a polynomial of degree not exceeding m.

In words, according to property 2, a spline function (or, more simply, a spline) of degree m is a piecewise polynomial function whose "pieces" do not exceed degree m. Property 1 assures that the polynomial coefficients are constrained so that the derivatives, up to order $m - 1$, of adjacent polynomials agree at their common boundary point.

In Section 3.4 a polynomial was said to be an interpolation polynomial if it interpolates a specified data set. In the same spirit, a spline $s(x)$ is an *interpolation spline* for given points (x_i, f_i), $1 \leq i \leq n$, if for each i,

$$s(x_i) = f_i.$$

The interpolation splines of degree 1 are piecewise linear functions connecting the data points, as shown in Figure 3.13. On each subinterval $[x_i, x_{i+1}]$, $s(x)$ has the form

$$s(x) = s_i(x) = a_i + b_i(x - x_i),$$

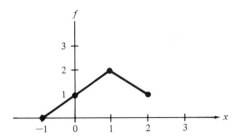

FIGURE 3.13 Spline Function of
Degree 1

which is a linear polynomial of $x - x_i$. (The coefficients a_i and b_i bear no relation
to the endpoints a and b of the approximation interval $[a, b]$.) The representation
of splines as polynomials in $x - x_i$ rather than x will lead to simpler formulas.
The coefficients a_i, b_i may vary with interval index i, but continuity (order 0
differentiability) at x_{i+1} requires that $s_{i+1}(x_{i+1}) = s_i(x_{i+1})$. That is, the coefficients must satisfy

$$a_{i+1} + b_{i+1}(x_{i+1} - x_{i+1}) = a_{i+1} = a_i + b_i(x_{i+1} - x_i), \qquad 1 \le i \le n - 2.$$

This implies that

$$b_i = \frac{a_{i+1} - a_i}{x_{i+1} - x_i}.$$

If the data values f_i are specified at each point x_i, "interpolation" requires that

$$f_i = s_i(x_i) = a_i + b_i(x_i - x_i) = a_i.$$

Thus each coefficient a_i equals the corresponding functional value f_i, and b_i equals
the slope connecting the neighboring data points (x_i, f_i) and (x_{i+1}, f_{i+1}).
   In summary, the linear interpolatory spline for data (x_i, f_i), $1 \le i \le n$, must
satisfy

$$\boxed{\begin{aligned} a_i &= f_i \\ b_i &= \frac{f_{i+1} - f_i}{x_{i+1} - x_i}, \qquad 1 \le i \le n - 1. \end{aligned}} \qquad (3.26)$$

To evaluate $s(x)$ at a point x, $x_1 \le x \le x_n$, find i such that $x_i \le x \le x_{i+1}$, and in
accordance with (3.26), set

$$s(x) = f_i + \frac{f_{i+1} - f_i}{x_{i+1} - x_i} (x - x_i).$$

━━━━ **EXAMPLE 3.13** ━━━━━━━━━━━━━━━━━━━━━━━━━━━━━━━━━━━━

Here we construct a linear interpolating spline for the following data set:

i	1	2	3	4
x_i	-1	0	1	2
f_i	0	1	2	1

Since we have just observed that $a_i = f_i$, we immediately conclude that

$$a_1 = 0, \quad a_2 = 1, \quad a_3 = 2, \quad a_4 = 1.$$

Then, using the formula

$$b_i = \frac{a_{i+1} - a_i}{x_{i+1} - x_i},$$

we calculate

$$b_1 = \frac{1 - 0}{1} = 1, \quad b_2 = \frac{2 - 1}{1} = 1, \quad b_3 = \frac{1 - 2}{1} = -1.$$

The resulting spline is the one depicted in Figure 3.13. ∎

As an application we mention that the popular numerical integration method known as the trapezoidal rule can be viewed as a method in which an interpolating spline function of degree 1 is integrated. We shall encounter this rule in Chapter 4.

The quadratic spline functions ($m = 2$) are piecewise quadratic polynomials, with continuous slopes at the interpolation points, as illustrated in Figure 3.14.

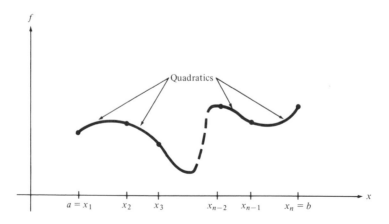

FIGURE 3.14   Spline Function of Degree 2

On subinterval $[x_i, x_{i+1}]$, the quadratic spline $s(x)$ must have the form

$$s_i(x) = a_i + b_i(x - x_i) + c_i(x - x_i)^2.$$

The interpolation property implies that for $i = 1, 2, \ldots, n - 1$,

$$s_i(x_i) = a_i + b_i(x_i - x_i) + c_i(x_i - x_i)^2$$

$$= a_i = f_i.$$

Furthermore, at $i = n$,

$$s_{n-1}(x_n) = a_{n-1} + b_{n-1}(x_n - x_{n-1}) + c_{n-1}(x_n - x_{n-1})^2$$

$$= f_n.$$

To be a quadratic spline, $s(x)$ must be continuous and have a first derivative at intermediate points x_i. Continuity requires that $s_{i+1}(x_{i+1}) = s_i(x_{i+1})$; that is, the coefficients satisfy

$$a_{i+1} + b_{i+1}(x_{i+1} - x_{i+1}) + c_{i+1}(x_{i+1} - x_{i+1})^2 = a_{i+1}$$

$$= a_i + b_i(x_{i+1} - x_i) + c_i(x_{i+1} - x_i)^2$$

and the existence of a derivative at x_{i+1} will require that $s'_{i+1}(x_{i+1}) = s'_i(x_{i+1})$. That is,

$$b_{i+1} + 2c_{i+1}(x_{i+1} - x_{i+1})$$

$$= b_{i+1} = b_i + 2c_i(x_{i+1} - x_i), \quad i = 1, 2, \ldots, n - 2.$$

Hence we have $3(n - 1) = 3n - 3$ unknowns and $(n - 1) + 1 + 2(n - 2) = 3n - 4$ equations; therefore, we have infinitely many solutions. The additional condition $c_1 = 0$ can be imposed to have a unique quadratic spline. By introducing the notation $h_i = x_{i+1} - x_i$ ($1 \le i \le n - 1$), the interpolation conditions can be rewritten as

$$a_i = f_i \quad (1 \le i \le n - 1)$$

$$a_{n-1} + b_{n-1}h_{n-1} + c_{n-1}h_{n-1}^2 = f_n.$$

The continuity of the spline function implies that

$$f_{i+1} = f_i + b_i h_i + c_i h_i^2 \quad (1 \le i \le n - 2),$$

and the differentiability of the spline function implies that

$$b_{i+1} = b_i + 2c_i h_i \quad (1 \le i \le n - 2).$$

By combining the last two equations, we conclude that the c_i's can be obtained recursively as

$$c_1 = 0$$

$$c_i = \frac{1}{h_i} \left(\frac{f_{i+1} - f_i}{h_i} - \frac{f_i - f_{i-1}}{h_{i-1}} + c_{i-1}h_{i-1} \right) \quad (2 \le i < n).$$

Furthermore,

$$b_i = \frac{f_{i+1} - f_i}{h_i} - c_i h_i \quad (1 \le i \le n - 1)$$

and

$$a_i = f_i \quad (1 \le i \le n - 1).$$

─────── **EXAMPLE 3.14** ───────

Here we investigate two piecewise quadratics to see if they are splines.

Case 1. Consider first the function

$$s(x) = \begin{cases} x^2 & \text{if } -1 \le x \le 0 \\ 2x^2 & \text{if } 0 < x \le 1 \\ x^2 + 1 & \text{if } 1 < x \le 2. \end{cases}$$

In this case $n = 4$, $x_1 = -1$, $x_2 = 0$, $x_3 = 1$, $x_4 = 2$,

$$s_1(x) = x^2, \qquad s_2 = 2x^2, \qquad s_3(x) = x^2 + 1.$$

This piecewise quadratic polynomial is continuous, since

$$s_1(x_2) = 0^2 = 0 = 2 \cdot 0^2 = s_2(x_2)$$

$$s_2(x_3) = 2 \cdot 1^2 = 2 = 1^2 + 1 = s_3(x_3).$$

Note that

$$s_1'(x_2) = 2 \cdot 0 = 0 = 4 \cdot 0 = s_2'(x_2);$$

that is, $s(x)$ is differentiable at x_2, but not at x_3, since

$$s_2'(x_3) = 4 \cdot 1 = 4 \ne 2 = 2 \cdot 1 = s_3'(x_3).$$

Thus this function is not a spline. The graph of $s(x)$ is shown in Figure 3.15.

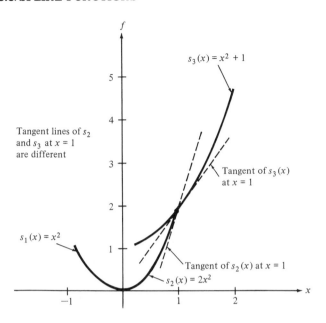

FIGURE 3.15 Graph of the Piecewise Quadratic Polynomial, Which Is Not a Quadratic Spline

Case 2. Consider next the function

$$s(x) = \begin{cases} x^2 & \text{if } -1 \le x \le 0 \\ 2x^2 & \text{if } 0 < x \le 1 \\ -2x^2 + 8x - 4 & \text{if } 1 < x \le 2. \end{cases}$$

The interpolation points and $s_1(x)$ and $s_2(x)$ are the same as in the Case 1. But in Case 2,

$$s_3(x) = -2x^2 + 8x - 4.$$

By examining the previous function we know that

$$s_1(x_2) = s_2(x_2), \qquad s_1'(x_2) = s_2'(x_2).$$

Simple calculation shows that this function is not only continuous at $x_3 = 1$, but also differentiable, since

$$s_2(x_3) = 2 \cdot 1^2 = 2 = -2 \cdot 1^2 + 8 \cdot 1 - 4 = s_3(x_3)$$

and

$$s_2'(x_3) = 4 \cdot 1 = 4 = -4 \cdot 1 + 8 = s_3'(x_3).$$

Each segment of $s(x)$ has degree 2, and thus $s(x)$ is a quadratic spline. This function is illustrated in Figure 3.16.

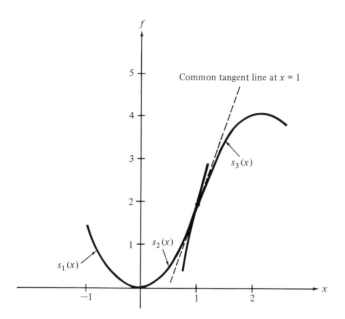

FIGURE 3.16   Graph of a Quadratic Spline

3.5.3   Cubic Splines

Cubic (degree 3) interpolating splines are the most common splines in the application literature. These splines are cubic (degree 3) polynomials on each subinterval, and at the boundary points, their first two derivatives must match the corresponding derivatives of the polynomials for adjacent intervals. Reasons for their popularity include their ability to interpolate data with curves that look smooth. Lower-degree splines do not "disguise" the data points well (see Figure 3.13 in this regard), and high-degree splines have the instabilities inherent in high-degree polynomials. Cubic splines appear to flow smoothly and indeed possess a minimum curvature property to be described in the next section. Let (x_1, f_1), (x_2, f_2), . . . , (x_n, f_n) be given data points. The aim of this section is to describe in detail the construction of a cubic interpolating spline for these points.

According to notation used in Section 3.5.2, on each subinterval $[x_i, x_{i+1}]$, a cubic spline $s(x)$ has the form

$$s_i(x) = a_i + b_i(x - x_i) + c_i(x - x_i)^2 + d_i(x - x_i)^3$$
$$(i = 1, 2, \ldots, n - 1), \tag{3.27}$$

where the coefficients a_i, b_i, c_i, d_i are to be determined from the definition of "cubic splines" and the interpolatory requirement.

Continuity and interpolation require that

$$s_i(x_{i+1}) = f_{i+1} = s_{i+1}(x_{i+1}),$$

so

$$a_i + b_i(x_{i+1} - x_i) + c_i(x_{i+1} - x_i)^2 + d_i(x_{i+1} - x_i)^3 = f_{i+1}$$

$$= a_{i+1} + b_{i+1}(x_{i+1} - x_{i+1}) + c_{i+1}(x_{i+1} - x_{i+1})^2 + d_{i+1}(x_{i+1} - x_{i+1})^3$$

$$= a_{i+1}. \tag{3.28}$$

By introducing the notation

$$h_i = x_{i+1} - x_i$$

for each $i = 1, 2, \ldots, n - 1$, relation (3.28) can be rewritten as

$$a_{i+1} = f_{i+1} = a_i + b_i h_i + c_i h_i^2 + d_i h_i^3. \tag{3.29}$$

Since cubic splines are twice differentiable at the nodes x_{i+1},

$$s_i'(x_{i+1}) = s_{i+1}'(x_{i+1}) \qquad \text{and} \qquad s_i''(x_{i+1}) = s_{i+1}''(x_{i+1}).$$

By using the expansion (3.27), these differentiability conditions may be written

$$b_i + 2c_i h_i + 3d_i h_i^2 = b_{i+1}, \ c_i + 3d_i h_i = c_{i+1}. \tag{3.30}$$

Solving for d_i in the second equation of (3.30) and substituting this value into (3.29) and the first equation of (3.30), we obtain the relations

$$a_{i+1} = a_i + b_i h_i + c_i h_i^2 + \frac{c_{i+1} - c_i}{3h_i} h_i^3$$

$$= a_i + b_i h_i + \frac{h_i^2}{3} (2c_i + c_{i+1}),$$

$$b_{i+1} = b_i + 2c_i h_i + 3 \frac{c_{i+1} - c_i}{3h_i} h_i^2 \tag{3.31}$$

$$= b_i + h_i(c_i + c_{i+1}).$$

The final relationship involving the coefficients is obtained by solving the first equation of (3.31) for b_i, to get

$$b_i = \frac{a_{i+1} - a_i}{h_i} - \frac{h_i}{3} (2c_i + c_{i+1}), \tag{3.32}$$

and after reducing the index by 1,

$$b_{i-1} = \frac{a_i - a_{i-1}}{h_{i-1}} - \frac{h_{i-1}}{3} (2c_{i-1} + c_i).$$

By substituting these values into the final equation of (3.31) with i replaced by $i - 1$, and using the fact (3.29) that for interpolation

$$a_i = f_i, \quad 1 \leq i \leq n - 1,$$

we have

$$h_{i-1}c_{i-1} + 2(h_{i-1} + h_i)c_i + h_ic_{i+1} = 3\frac{f_{i+1} - f_i}{h_i} - 3\frac{f_i - f_{i-1}}{h_{i-1}} \tag{3.33}$$

$$(i = 2, 3, \ldots, n - 2).$$

Once the coefficients c_i are found, the remaining coefficients are simply determined from (3.29) to (3.30) to be

$$a_i = f_i,$$

$$b_i = \frac{f_{i+1} - f_i}{h_i} - \frac{h_i}{3}(2c_i + c_{i+1}),$$

$$d_i = \frac{c_{i+1} - c_i}{3h_i}.$$

In (3.33), $c_1, c_2, \ldots, c_{n-1}$ are the unknowns. The number of equations (3.33) equals $n - 3$. Consequently, two more conditions are required to uniquely determine the c_i's. The conditions $s_1''(a) = s_{n-1}''(b) = 0$ are customarily introduced, and a unique cubic spline, the *natural spline*, is thereby determined. Observe that

$$s_1''(a) = 2c_1 + 6d_1(x_1 - x_1) = 2c_1, \qquad s_{n-1}''(b) = 2c_{n-1} + 6d_{n-1}h_{n-1}.$$

Thus

$$c_1 = 0, \qquad c_{n-1} + 3d_{n-1}h_{n-1} = 0$$

for natural splines.

The end conditions for c_1 and c_{n-1} are most conveniently imposed by defining the (extraneous) parameter $c_n = 0$; then (3.33) holds for $i = 2, 3, \ldots, n - 1$. In detail, (3.33) becomes

$$2(h_1 + h_2)c_2 + h_2c_3 \qquad\qquad = 3\frac{f_3 - f_2}{h_2} - 3\frac{f_2 - f_1}{h_1}$$

$$h_2c_2 + 2(h_2 + h_3)c_3 + h_3c_4 \qquad = 3\frac{f_4 - f_3}{h_3} - 3\frac{f_3 - f_2}{h_2}$$

$$\vdots \qquad\qquad\qquad\qquad\qquad\qquad\qquad \vdots$$

$$h_{n-3}c_{n-3} + 2(h_{n-3} + h_{n-2})c_{n-2} + h_{n-2}c_{n-1} = 3\frac{f_{n-1} - f_{n-2}}{h_{n-2}} - 3\frac{f_{n-2} - f_{n-3}}{h_{n-3}}$$

$$h_{n-2}c_{n-2} + 2(h_{n-2} + h_{n-1})c_{n-1} = 3\frac{f_n - f_{n-1}}{h_{n-1}} - 3\frac{f_{n-1} - f_{n-2}}{h_{n-2}},$$

$$\tag{3.34}$$

Here $h_i = x_{i+1} - x_i$, $i = 1, 2, \ldots, n - 1$.

In summary, the coefficients of cubic interpolation spline are determined by

$$h_{i-1}c_{i-1} + 2(h_{i-1} + h_i)c_i + h_i c_{i+1} = 3\frac{f_{i+1} - f_i}{h_i} - 3\frac{f_i - f_{i-1}}{h_{i-1}}$$

$$i = 2, 3, \ldots, n - 1,$$

$$a_i = f_i,$$

$$b_i = \frac{f_{i+1} - f_i}{h_i} - \frac{h_i}{3}(2c_i + c_{i+1}),$$

$$d_i = \frac{c_{i+1} - c_i}{3h_i},$$

(3.35)

EXAMPLE 3.15

Consider the $n = 3$ values

i	1	2	3
x_i	100	121	144
f_i	10	11	12

which are points from the square-root function. Since $n = 3$, $c_1 = c_3 = 0$, and there is only one unknown coefficient c_2. The value of c_2 can be obtained from the first equation of (3.34), which has the form

$$2(h_1 + h_2)c_2 = 3\frac{f_3 - f_2}{h_2} - 3\frac{f_2 - f_1}{h_1}.$$

Since $a_i = f_i$ $(i = 1, 2, 3)$,

$$a_1 = 10, \qquad a_2 = 11, \qquad a_3 = 12$$

and

$$h_1 = 121 - 100 = 21, \qquad h_2 = 144 - 121 = 23,$$

this equation is

$$88c_2 = -0.012422,$$

which implies that

$$c_2 = -0.000141.$$

Then the last two equations of (3.35) imply that

$$b_1 = \frac{f_2 - f_1}{h_1} - \frac{h_1}{3}(2c_1 + c_2) = 0.048607$$

$$b_2 = \frac{f_3 - f_2}{h_2} - \frac{h_2}{3}(2c_2 + c_3) = 0.045640$$

$$d_1 = \frac{c_2 - c_1}{3h_1} = -0.00000224$$

$$d_2 = \frac{c_3 - c_2}{3h_2} = -0.00000205.$$

When these values for a_i, b_i, c_i, and d_i are inserted into (3.27), one may construct the table of spline estimates given in Table 3.15.

For instance, the value $s(104)$ is found by noting that $100 < 104 < 121$, so 104 is in the domain of s_1, that is, the index $i = 1$. So

$$s_1(104) = a_1 + b_1(x - x_1) + c_1(x - x_1)^2 + d_1(x - x_1)^3.$$

Upon substitution of specific values as calculated above,

$$s(104) = 10 + 0.048607 \cdot (104 - 100) + 0 \cdot (104 - 100)^2$$
$$+ (-0.224) \cdot 10^{-5} \cdot (104 - 100)^3 = 10.19429.$$

Actually, to five places, $\sqrt{104} \simeq 10.198$. ∎

The computer program for solving the linear equations (3.35) and computing the coefficients a_i, b_i, and d_i is given by subroutine SPLN, shown in Table 3.12. Subroutine SPLE, given in Table 3.13, evaluates the spline function at any desired arguments, according to (3.27). It requires the coefficients a_i, b_i, c_i, d_i obtained by SPLN as input parameters. In subroutine SPLE, Horner's rule is used for evaluating the cubic polynomials on the right-hand side of (3.27).

TABLE 3.12   Subroutine SPLN for Evaluating Spline Coefficients

```
      SUBROUTINE  SPLN(N,X,F,A,B,C,D)
C
C     ****************************************************************
C     *     FUNCTION: THIS SUBROUTINE COMPUTES THE COEFFICIENTS FOR  *
C     *               A NATURAL CUBIC SPLINE                         *
C     *     USAGE:                                                   *
C     *          CALL SEQUENCE: CALL SPLN(N,X,F,A,B,C,D)             *
C     *          EXTERNAL FUNCTIONS/SUBROUTINES: SUBROUTINE GAUS1    *
C     *     PARAMETERS:                                              *
C     *          INPUT:                                              *
C     *               N=NUMBER OF DATA POINTS                        *
C     *                 (AT LEAST 3 AT MOST 101)                     *
C     *               X=N BY 1 ARRAY OF DOMAIN POINTS                *
C     *               F=N BY 1 ARRAY OF FUNCTIONAL VALUES            *
C     *          OUTPUT:                                             *
C     *               A,B,C,D=N BY 1 ARRAYS OF CUBIC SPLINE COEFFICIENTS *
C     ****************************************************************
C
      DIMENSION X(N),F(N),A(N),B(N),C(N),D(N),H(100),T(100,101),U(100)
C     *** INITIALIZATION ***
      DO 1 I=1,N-1
         H(I)=X(I+1)-X(I)
         U(I)=(F(I+1)-F(I))/H(I)
         A(I)=F(I)
    1 CONTINUE
```

TABLE 3.12   (Continued)

```
C       *** COMPUTE COEFFICIENTS OF THE LINEAR EQUATIONS ***
        DO 2 I=1,N-2
            DO 2 J=1,N-2
                T(I,J)=0.0
    2   CONTINUE
        DO 3 I=1,N-2
            T(I,I)=2.0*(H(I)+H(I+1))
    3   CONTINUE
        IF(N.GT.3) THEN
            DO 4 I=2,N-2
                T(I,I-1)=H(I)
                T(I-1,I)=H(I)
    4       CONTINUE
        END IF
        DO 5 I=1,N-2
            T(I,N-1)=3.0*(U(I+1)-U(I))
    5   CONTINUE
        N2=N-2
        M=1
        ND=100
        EPS=0.0000001
C       *** COMPUTE COEFFICIENTS C(I) USING GAUSSIAN ELIMINATION ***
        CALL GAUS1(N2,M,ND,T,EPS)
        DO 6 I=2,N-1
            C(I)=T(I-1,N-1)
    6   CONTINUE
        C(1)=0.0
        C(N)=0.0
        DO 7 I=1,N-1
            B(I)=U(I)-H(I)*(2.0*C(I)+C(I+1))/3.0
            D(I)=(C(I+1)-C(I))/(H(I)*3.0)
    7   CONTINUE
        RETURN
        END
```

TABLE 3.13   Subroutine SPLE for Evaluating Natural Spline Values

```
        SUBROUTINE SPLE(N,X,A,B,C,D,T,P)
C
C ******************************************************************
C *   FUNCTION: THIS SUBROUTINE COMPUTES THE VALUE OF A CUBIC     *
C *             SPLINE P(T) AT T   USING THE COEFFICIENTS         *
C *             A,B,C,D GENERATED BY THE SUBROUTINE SPLN          *
C *   USAGE:                                                      *
C *       CALL SEQUENCE: CALL SPLE(N,X,A,B,C,D,T,P)               *
C *       EXTERNAL FUNCTIONS/SUBROUTINES: SUBROUTINE SPLN         *
C *   PARAMETERS:                                                 *
C *       INPUT:                                                  *
C *           N=NUMBER OF DATA POINTS                             *
C *           X=N BY 1 ARRAY OF INDEPENDENT DATA POINTS           *
C *           A,B,C,D=N BY 1 ARRAY OF CUBIC SPLINE COEFFICIENTS   *
C *           U=GIVEN INDEPENDENT DATA VALUE                      *
C *       OUTPUT:                                                 *
C *           P=CUBIC SPLINE VALUE P(T)                           *
C ******************************************************************
C
        DIMENSION X(N),A(N),B(N),C(N),D(N)
C       *** DETERMINE SUBINTERVAL WHICH CONTAINS POINT T ***
        I=2
        DO WHILE(T.GT.X(I))
            I=I+1
        END DO
        I=I-1
C       *** COMPUTE CUBIC SPLINE VALUE AT P(T) ***
        T1=T-X(I)
        P=A(I)+T1*(B(I)+T1*(C(I)+D(I)*T1))
        RETURN
        END
```

━━━ **EXAMPLE 3.16** ━━━━━━━━━━━━━━━━━━━━━━━━━━━━━━━━━━━━━

By way of the calling program in Table 3.14, we have used the spline subroutines
SPLN and SPLE (Tables 3.12 and 3.13) to automate the construct of a table of
square-root values based on the data points of Example 3.15. The square-root
function and its spline approximation as determined by the driver program (Table
3.14) at evenly spaced points between 100 and 144 are presented in Table 3.15.

TABLE 3.14   Constructs a Spline for the Square-Root Function

```
C       PROGRAM CSPLIN
C
C       *****************************************************************
C       COMPUTES CUBIC SPLINE ESTIMATE OF F(X)=SQRT(X) AT X=100+4*I
C       I=0 TO 11
C       CALLS:   SPLN;SPLE;GAUS1
C       OUTPUT: X=THE VALUE OF THE INDEPENDENT VARIABLE
C               P=THE SPLINE FUNCTION EVALUATED AT X
C               TRUE=TRUE VALUE OF FUNCTION AS COMPUTED BY THE LIBRARY
C                    FUNCTION SQRT
C               ERR=THE CORRESPONDING ERROR (TRUE-P) AT X
C       *****************************************************************
C
        DIMENSION Y(3),F(3),A(3),B(3),C(3),D(3)
        N=3
        DATA (Y(I),I=1,3)/100.0,121.0,144.0/
        DATA (F(I),I=1,3)/10.0,11.0,12.0/
C
C       *** SUBROUTINE SPLN COMPUTES THE SPLINE COEFFICIENTS        ***
C
        CALL SPLN(N,Y,F,A,B,C,D)
        M=12
        H=4.0
        X=96.0
C
C       *** THIS LOOP GENERATES THE 12 VALUES OF X AND PRINTS       ***
C       *** THE SPECIFIED VALUES AT EACH POINT                     ***
C
        DO 8 I=1,M
          X=X+H
C
C       *** SUBROUTINE SPLE COMPUTES SPLINE APPROXIMATION AT X      ***
C
          CALL SPLE(N,Y,A,B,C,D,X,P)
          TRUE=SQRT(X)
          ERR=TRUE-P
          WRITE(10,9)X,P,TRUE,ERR
      9   FORMAT(18X,F5.1,3X,F8.5,3X,F8.5,3X,E9.2)
      8 CONTINUE
        STOP
        END
```

TABLE 3.15   Computations of Example 3.16

x	s(x)	$\sqrt{x}$	$\sqrt{x} - s(x)$
100.0	10.00000	10.00000	0.00E+00
104.0	10.19429	10.19804	0.38E-02
108.0	10.38771	10.39230	0.46E-02
112.0	10.57941	10.58300	0.36E-02
116.0	10.76854	10.77033	0.18E-02
120.0	10.95422	10.95445	0.23E-03
124.0	11.13571	11.13553	-0.18E-03
128.0	11.31328	11.31371	0.42E-03
132.0	11.48771	11.48913	0.14E-02
136.0	11.65978	11.66190	0.21E-02
140.0	11.83029	11.83216	0.19E-02
144.0	12.00000	12.00000	0.00E+00

Application 3.3 ─────────────────────────

Here we forcefully illustrate the utility of splines for interpolating nonmathematical curves (situation 3 at the beginning of this section). Our draftsman rendered the "generic" executive jet airplane profile that constitutes Figure 3.17 and picked off 20 position points along the top side of this profile. By means of the routines SPLN and SPLE (Tables 3.12 and 3.13), we plotted the spline associated with these data. This spline is shown in Figure 3.18, together with the positions of the original data used in the spline construction. When the routine LAGR (Table 3.6) was applied to the data points, the interpolation polynomial values were completely erratic.

In a similar vein, 32 positions were measured from the back of the polar bear sketched in Figure 3.19. They, together with the associated natural spline, are shown in Figure 3.20.

The thrust of this example is to show that splines are effective in economically "presenting" natural shapes to the computer. In computer graphics this approach is used for connecting data points for continuous curves. For simplicity and effectiveness, splines are nicely suited to such tasks.

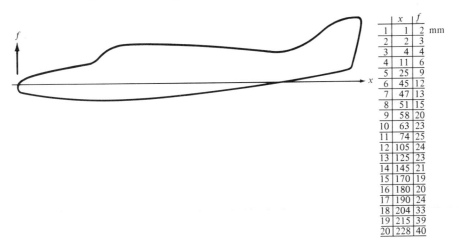

	x	f
1	1	2 mm
2	2	3
3	4	4
4	11	6
5	25	9
6	45	12
7	47	13
8	51	15
9	58	20
10	63	23
11	74	25
12	105	24
13	125	23
14	145	21
15	170	19
16	180	20
17	190	24
18	204	33
19	215	39
20	228	40

FIGURE 3.17   A Jet Plane

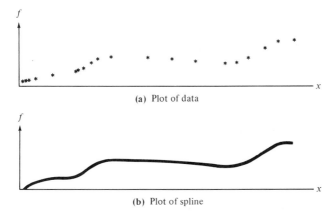

(a) Plot of data

(b) Plot of spline

FIGURE 3.18   Data and Spline of a Jet Plane

	x	f	
1	5	6	m
2	10	11	
3	15	14	
4	20	16	
5	25	18	
6	30	19	
7	35	18	
8	40	17.5	
9	45	17	
10	50	16	
11	55	16.5	
12	60	17.5	
13	65	18.5	
14	70	19	
15	75	18	
16	80	16.5	
17	85	15.5	
18	90	15.5	
19	95	16.5	
20	100	17	
21	105	18	
22	110	19	
23	115	20	
24	120	20	
25	125	19.5	
26	130	18.5	
27	135	17.5	
28	140	15	
29	145	12	
30	150	9	
31	155	3.5	
32	157	0	

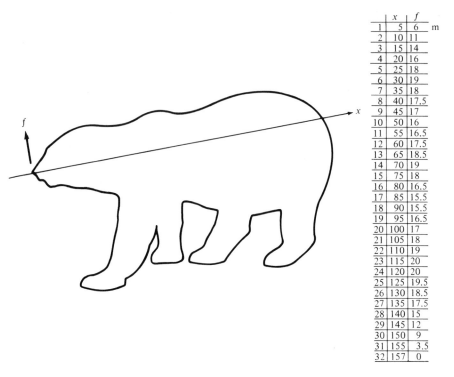

FIGURE 3.19   Polar Bear

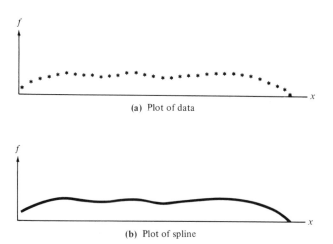

(a) Plot of data

(b) Plot of spline

FIGURE 3.20   Data and Spline of a Polar Bear

★3.5.4 Strengths and Limitations of Spline Interpolation

The term *spline* originally referred to a flexible strip that draftsmen use to draw smooth curves between given points. The procedure is to put the strip on its edge and adjust it so that it passes through the points. The draftsman then uses the resulting spline profile as the smooth interconnecting curve. Abstractly, one can say that the more twisted the spline profile, the higher its internal energy. In keeping with the minimal energy principle of physics, therefore, the spline adjusts its shape to become as smooth as possible, subject to its interpolating the desired points.

The mathematical cubic spline is known to retain this minimum strain energy property (e.g., de Boor, 1978, p. 66). A closely related property that seems to us even more interesting is that the cubic spline has minimal integrated squared second derivative among all twice differentiable curves passing through the data. We will prove this assertion, but first let us suggest its significance.

We ask the reader to refer back to Figure 3.9, showing the failure of interpolation polynomials on the Runge function. The failure is characterized by large excursions or "oscillations" of the polynomial between interpolation points. Such large excursions can occur only if the polynomial $p(x)$ has a large second derivative. It is amusing to see that we can substantiate this point by using the interpolation truncation error formula (3.14). For take $p_1(x)$ to be the linear interpolator $p_1(x) = f_1 l_1(x) + f_2 l_2(x)$, which connects the data point (x_1, f_1) with (x_2, f_2), as shown in Figure 3.21. Then by (3.14), with the interpolation polynomial $p(x)$ here playing the role of $f(x)$, we have

$$p(x) = p_1(x) + \tfrac{1}{2}p''(\zeta)(x - x_1)(x - x_2). \tag{3.36}$$

From (3.36) it is clear that $p(x)$ cannot deviate much from the line $p_1(x)$ unless its second derivative is large. In this sense one may say that failure of interpolation polynomials (or any other function, for that matter) manifests itself by large second

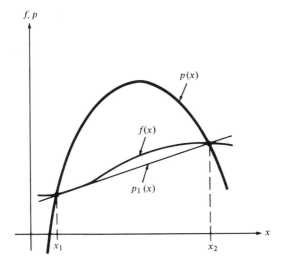

FIGURE 3.21 Large Interpolation Polynomial Deviation

derivatives. With this in mind, the following statement is interesting. It implies that a natural interpolation spline has an integrated squared second derivative which is as small as that of any other twice-differentiable interpolation function for the same data set.

> **Fact.** Let $s(x)$ be a natural cubic spline that interpolates the function $f(x)$ at the points $a = x_1 < \cdots < x_n = b$. Let $f''(x)$ be continuous on the interval $[a, b]$. Then

$$\int_a^b [s''(x)]^2 \, dx \leq \int_a^b [f''(x)]^2 \, dx. \qquad (3.37)$$

PROOF

Let $g(x) = f(x) - s(x)$; then

$$\int_a^b [f''(x)]^2 \, dx = \int_a^b [g''(x) + s''(x)]^2 \, dx = \int_a^b [g''(x)]^2 \, dx$$

$$+ \int_a^b [s''(x)]^2 \, dx + 2 \int_a^b [g''(x)s''(x)] \, dx. \qquad (3.38)$$

The last term is zero, since by integrating by parts and by dividing interval $[a, b]$ to the subintervals $[x_1, x_2], \ldots, [x_{n-1}, x_n]$, we get

$$\int_a^b s''(x)g''(x) \, dx = [s''(x)g'(x)] \Big|_a^b - \int_a^b s^{(3)}(x)g'(x) \, dx$$

$$= s''(b)g'(b) - s''(a)g'(a) - \sum_{k=2}^n \int_{x_{k-1}}^{x_k} s^{(3)}(x)g'(x) \, dx.$$

The constraint of natural splines implies that $s''(b) = s''(a) = 0$ and on each of the subintervals $[x_{k-1}, x_k]$, $s^{(3)}(x)$ is a constant, say C_k. Consequently,

$$\int_a^b s''(x)g''(x) \, dx = -\sum_{k=2}^n C_k \int_{x_{k-1}}^{x_k} g'(x) \, dx$$

$$= -\sum_{k=2}^n C_k[g(x_k) - g(x_{k-1})].$$

But this sum is zero because $s(x)$ interpolates, and thus the summands are each zero:

$$g(x_k) = f(x_k) - s(x_k) = 0, \qquad g(x_{k-1}) = f(x_{k-1}) - s(x_{k-1}) = 0.$$

Then (3.38) implies that

$$\int_a^b [f''(x)]^2 \, dx = \int_a^b [g''(x)]^2 \, dx + \int_a^b [s''(x)]^2 \, dx \geqq \int_a^b [s''(x)]^2 \, dx,$$

which completes the proof.

Experimentally, we have concluded that the spline approach does not fully resolve some approximation issues. To be a candidate for a computer library function, for example, we would anticipate that an algorithm ought to provide an answer with an accuracy of at least 7 to 10 significant decimals after very few arithmetic computations. Sometimes interpolation polynomials fill this need very nicely. We found that by using Chebyshev points, we could interpolate sin (x) on $[0, 1]$ to about 27 significant decimals with a 21st-order interpolation polynomial. The natural spline, using the same 21 data points, gave only about three places of accuracy, and even when we raised the number of data points n to 90, the interpolations were accurate to only about five significant places.

Our conclusion is that spline approximation is perfectly adequate if relative error on the order of 1% is acceptable. This is adequate for graphics. On the other hand, if library-function accuracy is required, alternative methods or piecewise polynomials more sophisticated than cubic splines will be needed, unless the intervals are small.

There are undeniably some loose ends to our attempted mastery of the function approximation problem. For example, it is known that there is no polynomial of degree less than 1 million, interpolating or otherwise, which approximates $\sqrt{|x|}$ to four significant places at all points on the interval $[-1, 1]$. In fact, experiments have convinced the authors that interpolation of this function on $[0, 1]$ by either splines or polynomials cannot feasibly be done accurately. Fortunately, we will see that by methods in Chapter 5 direct computation of $\sqrt{|x|}$ can be done quickly, accurately, and simply. One realm in which piecewise polynomials and splines appear to reign supreme is in approximation of "natural" and "nonmathematical" shapes.

3.6
SUPPLEMENTARY NOTES AND DISCUSSIONS

We have considered three basic techniques—Taylor's polynomials, interpolation polynomials, and splines—for approximating functions and "smooth" data. The background developments for Taylor's and interpolation polynomials will serve us well in describing numerical methods for other problem areas. Of these three procedures, Taylor's polynomials have been the least widely used in actual numerical computation (but most widely used in mathematical analysis of numerical algorithms). Our first thought was that the lack of enthusiasm stemmed from the requirement of higher derivatives in (3.6). Higher derivatives of functions other than polynomials are typically at least a nuisance to obtain, and frequently a rich source of error because of calculus mistakes.

Using numerical differentiation ideas such as those offered in Chapter 4, one can in many cases obtain adequate approximations to Taylor's polynomials. Moreover, algebraic computer languages (e.g., MACSYMA and MU-MATH), which automate differentiation, are becoming increasingly available. Another drawback then comes to the fore. In contrast to interpolation polynomials, Taylor's polynomial approximation tends to be much more accurate than needed in the vicinity of the expansion point x_0, and defective for large values of $|x - x_0|$. Interpolation error, while also tending to be larger near the endpoints of the interpolation interval, does spread the error out more evenly (particularly if Chebyshev interpolation points are used). In Example 3.9 (see Figure 3.11), this more even distribution of approximation error is clearly in evidence.

For "smooth" functions, interpolation polynomials are adequate for many needs. When the curve or data set has more erratic features, piecewise polynomial approximation and splines have some appealing advantages. Whereas our discussion centered on natural cubic splines, we notify the reader that in recent years, the tendency has been to keep all options open and choose the piecewise polynomial approach most suited to the application at hand. For instance, in interpolating solutions of differential equations, some investigators have found the higher-derivative requirement of the "spline" definition to be overly constricting. Even within the domain of cubic interpolation splines, "natural" splines such as we and most other numerical methods authors propose are known to have certain technical deficiencies. Nevertheless, they do guarantee convergence to any continuous limiting function, as the number of node points x_i become dense, a property that we have noted is not shared by interpolating polynomials.

The techniques given in this chapter are adequate for obtaining computer approximations of common functions, and for transcribing "natural" curves, such as demand/sales curves or transistor operating characteristic curves, into a computer-manageable form. Also, they are useful for computer graphics displays.

We hasten to point out, however, that program functions, such as in computer libraries or commercial packages, employ much more sophisticated principles than can be related at the level of this textbook. The subject of computer approximation of functions is a lively and sophisticated research area. Algorithms employing advanced theory have greater accuracy, for a given computational effort, than the prototypical techniques related here. On the other hand, the advanced methods are, for the most part, an outgrowth of principles presented in this chapter and Chapter 6.

The methods of the present chapter presume that interpolation is truly a sensible activity for the given data. In some cases, interpolation is not the best procedure. Most notably if significant error in the function values f_i is thought to be present, or if the data arise from observations of a random phenomenon, the curve-fitting methods of Chapter 6 should be considered. In curve fitting we do not insist that the approximating function interpolate (pass through the data). Rather we seek a

TABLE 3.16   Match of Interpolation Problem Characteristics and Methods

Function Characteristics	*Suggested Method*[a]
Few Data Points (<20)	
Derivatives not large	I, S
Large derivatives	S
User can choose data locations x_i, function fairly smooth	IC
Many Data Points	
Data due to "natural" (i.e., nonmathematical) origin	S
Function smooth, regular	IL
Large errors or random origins for data	Go to Chapter 6

[a]I, interpolation polynomials; IC, interpolation polynomial using Chebyshev points; S, splines; IL, interpolation polynomial using only a moderate number of local (neighboring) points [i.e., if you wish to approximate at x, construct $p_{n-1}(x)$ on basis of n data pairs (x_i, f_i) such that the x_i's are as close to x as possible].

polynomial of specified degree which, according to some measure, is as close as possible to the data points. In Table 3.16 we have summarized the appropriate problem domains for various techniques.

PROBLEMS

Section 3.2

1. Use Horner's rule to evaluate

$$p(x) = 3x^5 - x^4 + 3x^3 - 2x^2 + x + 1$$

at $x = 2$. Show your work.

2. Define $p(x) = a_k x^k + a_{k-1}x^{k-1} + \cdots + a_1 x + a_0$. Let $b_1, b_2, \ldots, b_k$ be determined by applying Horner's rule to evaluate $p(x)$ at $x = x_0$. Show that in the notation of (3.2), the polynomial

$$q(x) = b_k x^{k-1} + b_{k-1}x^{k-2} + \cdots + b_2 x + b_1$$

satisfies the relation

$$p(x) = q(x)(x - x_0) + b_0.$$

Thus $q(x)$ is the quotient polynomial $p(x)/(x - x_0)$ and b_0 is the remainder. [**HINT:** Equate the coefficients of like powers of x and see that (3.2) is recovered.]

3. **(a)** Give a Horner-type algorithm for finding the coefficients of the polynomial

$$h(x) = p(x - x_0)$$

in terms of the coefficients of $p(x)$.
(b) Write a subroutine to do this conversion.

4. Give an algorithm for finding the coefficients of the polynomial

$$h(x) = \frac{d}{dx} p(x)$$

in terms of the coefficients of $p(x)$.

★5. Find a recursive relation for the error bound of the computed value of

$$p(x) = a_0 + a_1 x + \cdots + a_k x^k$$

using approximations x^* and a_i^* if Horner's rule is applied, and $\delta(a_i^*) = \delta$, $i = 0, \ldots, k$, and $\delta(x^*) = \hat{\delta}$ are bounds for coefficient and argument errors.

★6. Assume that the integer N, in terms of its binary coefficients, is

$$N = a_k 2^k + a_{k-1}2^{k-1} + \cdots + a_0$$

(a_j either 0 or 1) and that x is a positive real number. Show that if we define

$$y_0 = x, \quad y_1 = x^2, \quad y_2 = x^{2^2}, \ldots, y_k = x^{2^k},$$

and calculate them by the recursion $y_0 = x$, $y_{i+1} = y_i^2$, $i > 0$, then

$$x^N = \Pi y_j,$$

where the product is taken over all j for which $a_j = 1$. For large N, this requires far fewer multiplications than evaluation of

$$\underbrace{x \cdot x \cdot \ldots \cdot x.}_{N \text{ times}}$$

Compare the number of multiplication operations of the two methods.

Section 3.3

7. Verify the polynomial multiplication formula

$$p(x)q(x) = a_0b_0 + (a_0b_1 + a_1b_0)x + \cdots$$
$$+ (a_0b_{m+k} + a_1b_{m+k-1} + \cdots + a_{m+k-1}b_1 + a_{m+k}b_0)x^{m+k},$$

where $p(x) = a_0 + a_1x + \cdots + a_kx^k$, $q(x) = b_0 + b_1x + \cdots + b_mx^m$. Take $a_j = 0, j > k, b_j = 0, j > m$.

8. **(Continuation of Problem 7.)** Apply the preceding formula to evaluation of the fourth-degree Taylor's polynomial of

$$h(x) = \sin(x)\cos(x).$$

Check your answer by the identity $\sin(x)\cos(x) = \sin(2x)/2$.

9. Find the formula for the Taylor's polynomial of $\sqrt{x}$ about $x_0 = 1$. Explain why the expansion cannot be taken at 0. Evaluate the approximation, and its error, at $x = 0.1$, for degrees $n = 3$ and 5.

10. Confirm the Taylor's polynomial approximation

$$1 + x + x^2 + \cdots + x^n \approx \frac{1}{1-x}$$

for any x satisfying, $0 < |x| < 1$. [Obtain this relation by taking the Taylor's expansion of $f(x) = 1/(1-x)$, $x_0 = 0$.]

11. Use the relation in Problem 10 to approximate w/z by addition, subtraction, and multiplication only (not division), for any real w and real z, $0 < z < 2$.

12. Find the linear, quadratic, and cubic Taylor's polynomials for the following functions, expanded about the points indicated:

(a) $\sin(2x)$, $x_0 = 0, \quad \dfrac{\pi}{4}$.

(b) sqrt (x), $x_0 = 1$.
(c) $\exp(x^2)$, $x_0 = 0$.

(d) $\dfrac{1}{1-x}$, $x_0 = 0$.

(e) sqrt $(x + 2)$, $x_0 = 0$.

Use a computer to calculate these approximating polynomials at points $x_0 \pm j/10$, $j = 1, 2, \ldots, 9$, and compare with the corresponding FORTRAN or Pascal library functions at these values in the cubic case.

13. Find the formulas for the nth-degree Taylor polynomials, at $x_0 = 0$, for the following:
   (a) $e^{2x} + \sin x$.
   (b) $\dfrac{e^x + e^{-x}}{2}$.
   (c) $\dfrac{e^x - e^{-x}}{2}$.
   (d) $\sin(x) + \cos(x)$.
   (e) $\ln(1 + x)$.
   (f) $(1 + x)^{\alpha}$.
   (g) $\dfrac{1}{1 - x}$.
   (h) $\dfrac{1}{1 + x}$.

14. Bound the error of approximating $\sin x$ by

$$ x - \frac{x^3}{3!} + \frac{x^5}{5!}, $$

   for any x in $[0, 1]$.

15. Approximate $\exp(x)$ by the nth-degree Taylor's polynomial

$$ p_n(x) = 1 + \frac{x}{1!} + \frac{x^2}{2!} + \cdots + \frac{x^n}{n!}. $$

   If $R_n(x)$ denotes the actual error of this approximation at x, for $0 < x < 1$:
   (a) Prove that $|R_n| < e/(n + 1)!$.
   (b) Bound the number of terms needed to assure that, in this range, the approximation is accurate to seven significant places.

16. The values of $\cos(0.5)$ and $\exp(0.5)$ are to be computed by Taylor's series approximation about $x_0 = 0$. Use the Taylor's series remainder formula to determine the number n of terms needed to assure that the approximation is accurate to five significant digits.
   (a) Show your calculation of n.
   (b) Actually make the Taylor's approximation and find the error against the library functions of your computer at these points.

17. Sometimes the Taylor's series method has a good deal of truncation error unless a great many terms are used. To illustrate this point, find the Taylor's series expansion of $\ln(1 + x)$ about $x_0 = 0$. Use this expansion to evaluate $\ln(0.1)$ for $n = 5, 10, 15,$ and 20. What is the error?

18. Use Taylor's polynomials to evaluate $\sin(0.5)$ to four significant figures. How many terms are needed, in theory, to get the required accuracy? Show your analysis.

Section 3.4

19. Find the constant, linear, and quadratic interpolating polynomials for $f(x) = x^3$ using interpolating points $x_1 = 0$, $x_2 = 1$, $x_3 = -1$. Thus form the constant

polynomial $p_0(x)$ from x_1 and $f(x_1)$, $p_2(x)$ from the first two points, and so on. Explain why $p_1(x) = p_2(x)$. What happens if, instead, $x_2 = 2$?

20.   With respect to the functions listed below, compare the errors at the test points $i/11$, $i = 1, 2, \ldots, 11$. Use the following approximation methods.
   (1) Fourth-degree Taylor's polynomial about $x_0 = 0.5$.
   (2) Lagrange interpolation with data points $x_1 = 0$, $x_2 = 0.25$, $x_3 = 0.5$, $x_4 = 0.75$, and $x_5 = 1.0$.
   (3) Five-point Chebyshev interpolation (for the interval $[0, 1]$).
      (a) $\sin (3x)$.
      (b) e^{2x}.
      (c) $\sqrt{x + 1}$.
      (d) $\dfrac{1}{1 + x^2}$.
      (e) x^{10}.
      (f) $\ln (1 + x)$.

21.   Find the Lagrange interpolating polynomial for the following data set:

x	-3	-1	0	1	3
f	3	1	0	1	3

22.   Indirectly check the accuracy of your computer's library functions by seeing how well the following identities hold at values $x_j = \pi j/20$ $(j = 1, 2, \ldots, 9)$.
   (a) $\cos (2x) = \cos^2 (x) - \sin^2 x$.
   (b) $\tan \dfrac{x}{2} = \sqrt{\dfrac{1 - \cos (x)}{1 + \cos (x)}}$.
   (c) $1 = \sin^2 (x) + \cos^2 (x)$.
   (d) $e^x \cdot e^x = e^{2x}$.
   (e) $\ln (e^{3x}) = 3x$.
   (f) $\sqrt{x} \cdot \sqrt{x^3} = x^2$.

   [**HINT:** For obtaining π, it is useful to use $\pi = 4 \tan^{-1} (1.0)$.]

★23.   Prove that for any interpolatory points $x_1, x_2, \ldots, x_n$, and for *any* real number x,

$$\sum_{i=1}^{n} l_i(x) = 1,$$

where the l_i's are the Lagrange factor polynomials defined by (3.11). Generalize, to show that

$$\sum_{i=1}^{n} l_i(x)x_i^j = x^j, \text{ all } x, \text{ and } j = 1, 2, \ldots, n - 1.$$

24.   Suppose that a projectile has an initial velocity of 20 m/s and the gravitation constant is $g = 9.81$ m/s^2. Then as a function of angle θ, and ignoring the effects of friction, the maximum height the projectile will reach is given by

$$h(\theta) = \frac{200 \sin^2 (\theta)}{g}, \qquad 0 < \theta < \frac{\pi}{2}.$$

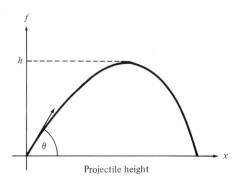

Projectile height

Approximate this function by an interpolation polynomial evaluated at the points $\pi j/10$, $j = 0, 1, 2, 3, 4, 5$. By computer evaluate the polynomial thus constructed at the angles $q_i = \pi i/201$, $i = 1, 2, \ldots, 100$, and print out the maximum absolute error

$$\max_{1 \le i \le 100} |h(\theta_i) - p(\theta_i)|$$

at these test points.

25. Interpolate $f(x) = \sin(\pi x/2)$ on the basis of the points $x_0 = -1$, $x_1 = 0$, and $x_2 = 1$. Explain the dangers of interpolation without consideration of the origins of the data.

26. The function

$$f(t) = 10 \sin(1.2 + 0.75t)$$

is a solution to a simple harmonic oscillator equation. For $N = 5, 10, 15$, use a computer to find an interpolation polynomial p_{N-1} using the points

$$t_j = \frac{j-1}{N-1}, \qquad j = 1, 2, \ldots, N.$$

(a) Check the accuracy of the approximation according to the criterion

$$\max_{1 \le k \le 101} \left| f\left(\frac{k}{101}\right) - p_{N-1}\left(\frac{k}{101}\right) \right|.$$

(b) Try to extrapolate by evaluating the foregoing maximum over the range $101 < k < 150$.

27. (a) Find the interpolating polynomial of appropriate degree for the data

x	-2	-1	0	1	2
f	-9	-1	1	3	11

by the Lagrange method; show your work.
(b) Use the linear equation formula (3.19), and the GAUSS subroutine to find the coefficients of the interpolator in the form (3.18).

28. Interpolate

$$f(x) = \sin(\pi x)$$

on the basis of the points $x_1 = 0$, $x_2 = \frac{1}{2}$, and $x_3 = 1$. What is the maximum error in $[0, 1]$ according to the criterion of Problem 26? What is the bound for the error according to the error formula (3.14)? [**HINT:** Use calculus ideas for finding extrema of $w_3(x)$.]

29. Interpolation methods are handy in the many cases in which values of indefinite integrals are needed. Often, one has to resort to relative tedious computer methods (such as in Chapter 4) to evaluate integrals. Once several of these values become known, one can obtain other values by interpolation. In essence, we get an approximation of the indefinite integral by evaluating several definite integrals and interpolating.

   As a case in point, often error of a physical measurement is thought to be normal (or, synonymously, Gaussian). That is,

$$\Phi(x) = \text{Prob [measurement} - \text{true value} \leq x]$$

$$= \frac{1}{\sigma} \int_{-\infty}^{x} g\left(\frac{y}{\sigma}\right) dy,$$

where σ is some fixed positive scalar and

$$g(y) = \frac{1}{\sqrt{2\pi}} \exp\left(\frac{-y^2}{2}\right).$$

The integral is known not to have a closed-form representation in terms of standard FORTRAN or Pascal library functions. Below we have given a chart for several values of $\Phi(x)$.

(a) Approximate $\Phi(0.15)$ by Lagrange interpolation applied to these data. [It turns out that to the accuracy shown, the exact value is $\Phi(0.15) = 0.5596$.]

x	$\Phi(x)$
0	0.5
0.1	0.5398
0.2	0.5793
0.3	0.6179

(b) Use the fact that $\Phi(-x) = 1 - \Phi(x)$ to extend the table above to negative arguments:

x	$\Phi(x)$
−0.1	0.4602
−0.2	0.4207
−0.3	0.3021

Now approximate $\Phi(x)$ by a sixth-degree interpolation polynomial and evaluate $\Phi(0.15)$.

30. Evaluation of interpolation functions outside the interval determined by the data points is called *extrapolation*. In the figure below, estimation of $f(x)$ for $x < x_1$, or $x > x_n$ would constitute extrapolation.

(a) Explain, as well as you can, pitfalls of extrapolation. Your explanation should incorporate references to error formulas of interpolation polynomials.

(b) Extrapolate experimentally. Form the fourth-degree interpolation polynomial for $f(x) = \log(x)$, using the data at values $x = 0, \frac{1}{4}, \frac{1}{2}, \frac{3}{4}, 2$. Compute $p_3(x)$ at $x = 2.1, 2.5, 3, 5, 10$ (which lie outside the interpolation interval), and compare to $\log(x)$ at these points.

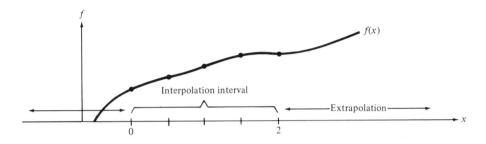

★31.   It turns out that Taylor's and Lagrange polynomials can profitably be viewed within a unified framework wherein one seeks a polynomial to satisfy derivative conditions at several points. Construct a cubic polynomial $p_3(x)$ such that

$$p_3(x_j) = f(x_j)$$

$$p_3(x_j) = f'(x_j), \qquad j = 1, 2.$$

Approximate $\sin(x)$ by $p_3(x)$ using $x_1 = 0$, $x_2 = \pi/4$.

32.   Consider the function

$$f(x) = \cos\left(\frac{\pi x}{2}\right).$$

For various N, specify the interpolating points to be

$$x_k = \frac{k-1}{N-1}, \qquad k = 1, 2, \ldots, N.$$

Check the accuracy according to the criterion

$$\text{MAXERROR}(N) = \max_{1 \le i \le 500} \left| f\left(\frac{i}{501}\right) - P\left(\frac{i}{501}\right) \right|.$$

Take $N = 5, 10, 15, \ldots$, and $1 \le i \le 500$. Notice that $\text{MAXERROR}(N)$ first decreases and then increases. Tabulate your findings and explain why accuracy deteriorates.

★33.   If $f(z)$ is a real function, its (functional) inverse is a function $g(x)$ such that $f(g(x)) = x$. For example, $\ln(x)$ is the inverse if $\exp(x)$, since $\exp(\ln(x)) = x$. It is possible to get the interpolation polynomial of inverse functions directly from the function itself: Let $f_i = f(x_i)$. Then reverse the roles of x_i and f_i in the defining equation for the interpolation polynomial

$$p(y) = \sum_{i=1}^{n} x_i \prod_{j \ne i} \frac{y - f_j}{f_i - f_j}.$$

Apply this idea to the data

i	x_i	$f_i = \exp(x_i)$
1	0.5	1.648721
2	0.75	2.117000
3	1.00	2.718281
4	1.25	3.490343

to get the cubic interpolation function for $\ln(y)$. Check the interpolator at $y = 2.5$. [$\ln(2.5) \approx 0.9162907$.]

Section 3.5

34. Solve Problem 24 by cubic splines.

35. Solve Problem 25 by cubic splines.

36. Solve Problem 26 by cubic splines

37. Solve Problem 27 by cubic splines.

38. Solve Problem 29 by cubic splines.

39. Decide which of the following piecewise polynomials are splines. Show your calculations.

(a) $f(x) = \begin{cases} 2x, & -1 \le x \le 0 \\ 3x, & 0 \le x \le 1 \\ x + 2, & 1 \le x \le 2. \end{cases}$

(b) $f(x = \begin{cases} x + 1, & -1 \le x \le 0 \\ 2x + 1, & 0 \le x \le 1 \\ x + 2, & 1 \le x \le 2. \end{cases}$

(c) $f(x) = \begin{cases} x^2, & -1 \le x \le 0 \\ 2x, & 0 \le x \le 1 \\ x^2 + 1, & 1 \le x \le 2. \end{cases}$

40. For the data points

x	−3	−2	−1	0	1	2
f	1	0	1	0	1	0

by hand calculation:

(a) Find the linear interpolation spline.

(b) Find the quadratic interpolation spline.

(c) Formulate the linear equations for the cubic spline for these data and write a program to solve by use of subroutine GAUSS.

41. Perform the tasks of Problem 40, but with respect to the data set

x	0	1	2	3	4
f	2	1	0	1	2

42. Find the values of the coefficients a and b such that

(a) $f(x) = \begin{cases} ax^3 + x, & -1 \le x \le 0 \\ x^3 + bx, & 0 \le x \le 1 \end{cases}$

and

(b) $f(x) = \begin{cases} x^3 + ax, & -1 \le x \le 0 \\ bx^3 + x, & 0 \le x \le 1 \end{cases}$

are cubic splines.

43. Obtain a magazine or book picture of a reasonably smooth object (e.g., an automobile, a mountain, the border between states) and measure positions of points similarly to Application 3.3. Approximate the profile by cubic splines, through application of subroutines SPLN and SPLE.

CHAPTER 4

Numerical Differentiation and Integration

4.1
PRELIMINARIES

A need for numerical differentiation and integration techniques arises quite extensively and regularly in engineering, physics, and other quantitative sciences.

For an illustration of very elementary situations in which numerical differentiation or integration problems arise, we turn to beginning physics. Suppose that we wish to check the law of gravitation and can measure the vertical position of a falling apple at certain closely spaced time points. Then to check that

$$v(t) = g \cdot t,$$

g being the gravitational constant and t being the time that the apple has been falling, we need to estimate the downward velocity $v(t)$ from the position points, $x(t_i)$, $i = 1, 2, \ldots$. A crude derivative formula was mentioned in Chapter 1, Example 1.2, namely,

$$v(t_i) \simeq \frac{x(t_{i+1}) - x(t_i)}{t_{i+1} - t_i}.$$

Analysis of this formula and presentation of more accurate rules will be the first order of business in this chapter.

It is also known from physics that the energy E required to move a body from a position x_1 to a position x_2 along a straight line is given by

$$E = \int_{x_1}^{x_2} F(x) \, dx,$$

where $F(x)$ is the reactive force. Such a formula would be relevant to estimating the explosive charge needed to give a cannon a prescribed range, or equivalently,

177

the fuel needed to put a satellite into a given orbit. In both cases the retarding forces are viscous atmospheric friction and gravitational attraction. Methods of this chapter are the proper means of evaluating the energy E when a mathematical expression for the indefinite integral is not available, or when $F(x)$ is known only at certain discrete points, perhaps by measurement.

Numerical differentiation formulas characteristically seek to estimate the derivative $f'(x)$ of a function at a specified point x_0 through functional values $f(x_j)$ at points x_j near x_0. These formulas are central to several prominent optimization methods, as well as to ordinary differential equations and to the solution of all types of partial differential equations.

Furthermore, numerical integration is very important in the study of probabilistic models. We remark that probabilistic models are playing an increasingly important role in all areas of engineering. Even the most elementary analysis of probabilistic systems leads to integrals that admit no closed-form representation in terms of the common library functions. In this context we mention that $\exp(-x^2)$, $\exp(-x)x^{\alpha-1}$, and $x^{\alpha}(1-x)^{\beta}$, (α, β positive and real), are integrands encountered with three of the most popular random variables in probability theory. None of these functions have indefinite integrals expressible in terms of the usual FORTRAN library functions.

The interpolation methods of Chapter 3 provide the foundation for numerical differentiation and integration. The basic idea that serves very effectively is the following: Given a function $f(x)$ to be differentiated or integrated, approximate $f(x)$ by an interpolation polynomial $p(x)$. Then differentiate or integrate $p(x)$. Differentiation and integration of polynomials are arithmetic operations, ready for immediate computer implementation.

We conclude this introduction by giving some standard notation that will serve us throughout this book. A function $g(h)$ is said to be $O(h)$ (read "big oh of h") when h tends to 0 if there are positive numbers C and D such that whenever $|h| \leq D$, then $|g(h)| \leq C|h|$. Under this circumstance, we sometimes write $g(h) = O(h)$. For example, $\sin(h)$ is $O(h)$ because $|\sin(h)| \leq |h|$ for every number h. More generally, for q positive, $g(h)$ is $O(h^q)$ at $h = 0$ if there exist numbers C and D such that whenever $|h| \leq D$,

$$|g(h)| \leq C|h^q|.$$

For instance, $\cos(h) - 1$ is $O(h^2)$ at $h = 0$, since the examination of its Taylor's series expansion reveals that $|\cos(h) - 1| \leq \frac{1}{2}|h|^2$ when $|h| \leq 1$. Similarly, $\sin(h) - h$ is $O(h^3)$. It is customary to express statements such as these in the form

$$\cos(h) = 1 + O(h^2)$$
$$\sin(h) = h + O(h^3)$$

and

$$\cos(\pi + h) = -1 + O(h^2).$$

Often $O(h^q)$ will refer to the truncation error of some approximating formula. In this context one says that the *order* of the error is q. Usually, the higher the order of truncation error, the more accurate the rule.

The notation $O(h^q)$ is intimately related to Taylor's series expansions. Note that if $p_{n-1}(x)$ is the $(n-1)$st-degree Taylor's polynomial of an n-times continuously differentiable function $f(x)$, then in view of the remainder formula (3.8) $g(h) = f(x_0 + h) - p_{n-1}(x_0 + h)$ is $O(h^n)$. One may write

$$f(x) = p_{n-1}(x) + O((x - x_0)^n).$$

4.2
INTERPOLATORY DIFFERENTIATION

The most elementary situation is as illustrated in Figure 4.1: One has a function $f(x)$ defined on a domain $[x_0, x_1]$ and constructs the linear interpolating polynomial

$$p_1(x) = f(x_0) \cdot \frac{x - x_1}{x_0 - x_1} + f(x_1) \cdot \frac{x - x_0}{x_1 - x_0}. \qquad (4.1)$$

In keeping with conventional notation of numerical differentiation, interpolating points are here denoted by x_0 and x_1. Upon differentiating both sides of (4.1) and substituting h for $(x_1 - x_0)$, we have

$$p_1'(x) = f(x_0) \cdot \frac{1}{-h} + f(x_0 + h) \cdot \frac{1}{h} = \frac{f(x_0 + h) - f(x_0)}{h}.$$

By accepting the secant slope as the approximation of the derivative of the original function, we obtain the two-point formula

$$f'(x_0) \approx \frac{f(x_0 + h) - f(x_0)}{h}. \qquad (4.2)$$

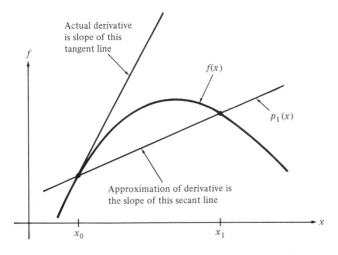

FIGURE 4.1   Derivative Approximation

Application 4.1

Attention turns again to the ballistics problem of earlier applications. Here the intention is to make estimates of the horizontal projectile velocity at various times. One can imagine that positions x_i are known at a few evenly spaced times t_i, perhaps on the basis of radar returns. The velocity estimates can be useful in turn for estimating frictional viscosity of air. Viscosity is known to depend on altitude, temperature, and other atmospheric conditions. Viscosity estimates can, in turn, be used for calculation of aiming corrections. Alternatively, such estimates might aid in projectile design.

We return to the model discussed in Application 3.1 for numerical values. The third and fourth columns of Table 4.1 give, respectively, exact position and velocity values at various times, these values coming from numerical solution of the ballistics equation of that example. The final column is composed of numerical estimates of the velocity; they are obtained directly from the simple two-point formula (4.2). The estimated and exact derivatives are compared in Figure 4.2.

TABLE 4.1. Ballistic Velocity and Its Estimate

j	Time, t_j	Distance, x_j	True Velocity, $v(x_j)$	Estimated Velocity, $v_j = \dfrac{x_{j+1} - x_j}{t_{j+1} - t_j}$
1	0.4500E+01	0.1242E+04	0.2692E+03	0.2619E+03
2	0.9500E+01	0.2551E+04	0.2548E+03	0.2479E+03
3	0.1450E+02	0.3791E+04	0.2411E+03	0.2346E+03
4	0.1950E+02	0.4964E+04	0.2282E+03	0.2221E+03
5	0.2450E+02	0.6074E+04	0.2160E+03	0.2102E+03
6	0.2950E+02	0.7125E+04	0.2045E+03	0.1989E+03
7	0.3450E+02	0.8120E+04	0.1935E+03	0.1883E+03
8	0.3950E+02	0.9062E+04	0.1832E+03	0.1782E+03
9	0.4450E+02	0.9953E+04	0.1734E+03	0.1687E+03

The error of the derivative approximation can, in principle, be bounded by differentiating the error formula for Lagrange interpolation. Assuming that all derivatives to be mentioned exist, from (3.14), we have

$$f(x) - p_1(x) = \tfrac{1}{2} \cdot f''(\xi(x)) \cdot (x - x_0)(x - x_1).$$

So

$$f'(x) - p_1'(x) = \tfrac{1}{2} \cdot [f^{(3)}(\xi(x)) \cdot \xi'(x)(x - x_0)(x - x_1)$$
$$+ f''(\xi(x))(x - x_1) + f''(\xi(x))(x - x_0)].$$

Only the second term is nonzero when $x = x_0$, and therefore

$$f'(x_0) = \frac{f(x_0 + h) - f(x_0)}{h} - \tfrac{1}{2} f''(\xi(x_0)) \cdot h. \qquad (4.3)$$

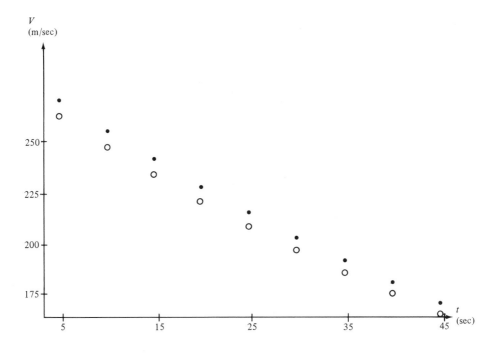

● = True velocity
O = Estimated velocity

FIGURE 4.2   Comparison of Actual and Computed Velocities

Thus the error is proportional to h; that is,

$$f'(x_0) = \frac{f(x_0 + h) - f(x_0)}{h} + O(h).$$

If $h \ll 1$, then evidently $h^2 \ll h$, so a formula with $O(h^2)$ error might be more desirable. Such a formula can be achieved by approximating $f(x)$ by a quadratic, instead of a linear, Lagrange interpolator. We presume that we have three equidistant interpolation points x_0, $x_{-1} = x_0 - h$, $x_1 = x_0 + h$, and we wish to approximate the derivative of $f(x)$ at x_0. The interpolation polynomial is

$$p_2(x) = f(x_{-1}) \cdot \frac{(x - x_0)(x - x_1)}{(x_{-1} - x_0)(x_{-1} - x_1)} + f(x_0) \cdot \frac{(x - x_{-1})(x - x_1)}{(x_0 - x_{-1})(x_0 - x_1)}$$

$$+ f(x_1) \cdot \frac{(x - x_{-1})(x - x_0)}{(x_1 - x_{-1})(x_1 - x_0)}. \quad (4.4)$$

After differentiating $p_2(x)$ with respect to x, we have

$$p_2'(x) = f(x_{-1}) \cdot \frac{(x - x_1) + (x - x_0)}{2h^2} + f(x_0) \cdot \frac{(x - x_1) + (x - x_{-1})}{-h^2}$$

$$+ f(x_1) \cdot \frac{(x - x_0) + (x - x_{-1})}{2h^2}. \quad (4.5)$$

By substituting $x = x_0$ and accepting the derivative $p_2'(x_0)$ as the approximation of $f'(x)$, we obtain the three-point formula

$$f'(x_0) \approx \frac{f(x_0 + h) - f(x_0 - h)}{2h}.$$

(4.6)

The quadratic approximation error as given by (3.14) is

$$f(x) - p_2(x) = \tfrac{1}{6} f^{(3)}(\xi(x))(x - x_0)(x - x_{-1})(x - x_1),$$

(4.7)

so in the manner that (4.3) was obtained, one confirms that

$$f'(x_0) = \frac{f(x_0 + h) - f(x_0 - h)}{2h} - \frac{h^2}{6} f^{(3)}(\xi(x_0)).$$

That is, the error is proportional to h^2. In summary,

$$f'(x_0) = \frac{f(x_0 + h) - f(x_0 - h)}{2h} + O(h^2).$$

(4.8)

The distinction between the two- and three-point formulas is illustrated in Figure 4.3.

Upon differentiating the interpolating polynomial $p_2(x)$ in (4.4) twice, we obtain the corresponding approximating formula for the second derivative:

$$f''(x_0) \approx \frac{f(x_0 + h) - 2f(x_0) + f(x_0 - h)}{h^2}.$$

(4.9)

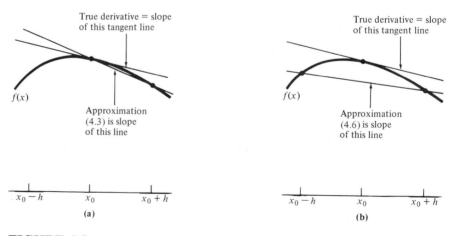

FIGURE 4.3 Numerical Approximation of a First Derivative

To confirm this, differentiate (4.5) and note that

$$\left[\frac{(x - x_1) + (x - x_0)}{2h^2} \right]' = \frac{2}{2h^2} = \frac{1}{h^2},$$

$$\left[\frac{(x - x_1) + (x - x_{-1})}{-h^2} \right]' = \frac{2}{-h^2} = \frac{-2}{h^2},$$

and

$$\left[\frac{(x - x_0) + (x - x_{-1})}{2h^2} \right]' = \frac{2}{2h^2} = \frac{1}{h^2}.$$

To analyze the error, double differentiation of formula (4.7) and some analysis yields the error formula

$$f''(x_0) = \frac{f(x_0 + h) - 2f(x_0) + f(x_0 - h)}{h^2} + O(h^2). \qquad (4.10)$$

Generalizations are to be found in Isaacson and Keller (1966, Chap. 6).

───── **EXAMPLE 4.1** ─────

Some values of $f(x) = e^x$ are given in Table 4.2, for $h = 0.1$, along with a list of derivative approximations and the associated errors of (4.2), (4.6), and (4.9) at $x_0 = 0$.

TABLE 4.2   A Derivative Approximation

j	x_j	e^x
-1	-0.1	0.904837
0	0.0	1.000000
1	0.1	1.105172

Error[a]

(a) Exact value: $f'(0) = 1.000000$
    Approximation by (4.2):
    $$\frac{f(x_1) - f(x_0)}{h} = \frac{1.105172 - 1.00000}{0.1}$$

    $$= 1.05172 \qquad\qquad -0.05172$$

    Approximation by (4.6):
    $$\frac{f(x_1) - f(x_{-1})}{2h} = \frac{1.105172 - 0.904837}{0.2}$$

    $$= 1.001675 \qquad\qquad -0.00168$$

(b) Exact value: $f''(0) = 1.000000$
    Approximation by (4.9):
    $$\frac{f(x_1) + f(x_{-1}) - 2f(x_0)}{h^2} = \frac{1.105172 + 0.904837 - 2.0}{0.01}$$

    $$= \frac{0.010009}{0.01} = 1.0009 \qquad\qquad -0.0009$$

[a]Error = exact value − approximation.

Application 4.2 ───────────────────────────────────────

In the introduction to this chapter, we mentioned that numerical differentiation formulas are useful for finding the velocity of a moving body on the basis of position observations at discrete times. By way of the example of a moving body, suppose that the following data had been collected:

i	1	2	3	4	5
Time, t_i	0.99	1.00	1.01	1.02	1.03
Position, $x(t_i)$	4.807	4.905	5.004	5.103	5.204

Then by using the three-point formula where possible and the two-point formula otherwise, we obtain the following velocity estimates:

$$v(0.99) = \frac{x(1.00) - x(0.99)}{1.00 - 0.99} = \frac{0.098}{0.01} = 9.80 \quad (\text{m/s})$$

$$v(1.00) = \frac{x(1.01) - x(0.99)}{1.01 - 0.99} = \frac{0.197}{0.02} = 9.85 \quad (\text{m/s})$$

$$v(1.01) = \frac{x(1.02) - x(1.00)}{1.02 - 1.00} = \frac{0.198}{0.02} = 9.9 \quad (\text{m/s})$$

$$v(1.02) = \frac{x(1.03) - x(1.01)}{1.03 - 1.01} = \frac{0.200}{0.02} = 10 \quad (\text{m/s})$$

and finally,

$$v(1.03) = \frac{x(1.02) - x(1.03)}{1.02 - 1.03} = \frac{-0.101}{-0.01} = 10.1 \quad (\text{m/s}).$$

Actually, the preceding data were obtained from the exact formula

$$x(t_i) = \tfrac{1}{2} g \cdot t_i^2.$$

The velocity values and approximations are

i	1	2	3	4	5
Time, t_i	0.99	1.00	1.01	1.02	1.03
Computed velocity	9.8	9.85	9.9	10.0	10.1
Theoretical velocity	9.71	9.81	9.91	10.01	10.10

For a comparison we listed the theoretical velocity values according to the formula

$$v(t_i) = g \cdot t_i.$$

Some popular numerical differentiation formulas for evenly spaced interpolation points are given in Table 4.3. At first glance, the three-point approximation

TABLE 4.3   Some Popular Derivative Approximations

First derivative approximations
  Three-point
$$f'(x) = \frac{f(x + h) - f(x - h)}{2h} + O(h^2)$$

  Four-point
$$f'(x) = \frac{-f(x + 2h) + 6f(x + h) - 3f(x) - 2f(x - h)}{6h} + O(h^3)$$

  Five-point
$$f'(x) = \frac{-2f(x + 2h) + 16f(x + h) - 16f(x - h) + 2f(x - 2h)}{24h} + O(h^4)$$

Second derivative approximations
  Three-point
$$f''(x) = \frac{f(x + h) - 2f(x) + f(x - h)}{h^2} + O(h^2)$$

  Four-point
  Coincides with three-point formula
  Five-point
$$f''(x) = \frac{-f(x + 2h) + 16f(x + h) - 30f(x) + 16f(x - h) - f(x - 2h)}{12h^2}$$
$$+ O(h^4)$$

[handwritten: NUM, INT = @SUM (B... +B3) = TOTAL area.]

for $f'(x)$ might seem a misnomer, since only two values are used. Actually, it gives highest order among all formulas using the three data points $f(x - h)$, $f(x)$, and $f(x + h)$.

Application 4.3

Let us return to the ballistics problem. The theoretical law relating viscous friction coefficient D to velocity change $x''(t)$ is

$$x''(t) = -Dx'(t).$$

From the following position values taken from Table 4.1

t_j (s)	$x(t_j)$ (km)
4.5	1.242
9.5	2.551
14.5	3.791

[handwritten: $h\left[\dfrac{f(A2) - f(A1)}{2}\right]$ = area under ~ +B3 - B2 = SLOPE ÷A3 - A1]

we approximate

$$x'(t_1) \approx \frac{x_2 - x_0}{t_2 - t_0} = 0.255$$

$$x''(t_1) \approx \frac{x_2 - 2x_1 + x_0}{(t_1 - t_0)^2} = -0.00274$$

[handwritten: $f''(x) =$]

from formulas (4.6) and (4.9), respectively. Putting these approximations into the formula

$$D \approx \frac{-x''(t_1)}{x'(t_1)},$$

we get the approximation that $D = 0.0108$. In fact, the exact value used in the ballistics model was 0.0110. This example illustrates an important engineering activity, *systems identification*. Identification is the science of finding model parameters from data.

$\Diamond$

In contrast to integration, discussed in the next section, numerical differentiation is notoriously sensitive to the effects of roundoff and data error. Let us refer to inexactness of function values as roundoff error, since it may well stem from floating-point representation approximation. To illustrate this point, assume that we use the approximation (4.2). That is,

$$f'(x_0) \approx \frac{f(x_0 + h) - f(x_0)}{h} = \frac{f_1 - f_0}{h}.$$

Let $\bar{f}_0$ and $\bar{f}_1$ be known approximations to the exact unknown values $f_0 = f(x_0)$ and $f_1 = f(x_0 + h)$, respectively, and assume that we have a bound δ so that

$$|f_0 - \bar{f}_0| \leq \delta \qquad \text{and} \qquad |f_1 - \bar{f}_1| \leq \delta.$$

Then $f'(x_0)$ is approximated by

$$\frac{\bar{f}_1 - \bar{f}_0}{h}.$$

The error can be bounded as follows:

$$\left| f'(x_0) - \frac{\bar{f}_1 - \bar{f}_0}{h} \right| \leq \left| f'(x_0) - \frac{f_1 - f_0}{h} \right| + \left| \frac{f_1 - f_0}{h} - \frac{\bar{f}_1 - \bar{f}_0}{h} \right|$$

$$\leq \frac{M_2 h}{2} + \frac{1}{h}(|f_1 - \bar{f}_1| + |f_0 - \bar{f}_0|) \leq \frac{M_2 h}{2} + \frac{2\delta}{h},$$

where the error formula of (4.2) gives us the bound

$$M_2 = \max_{x_0 \leq t \leq x_0 + h} |f''(t)|.$$

We have used

$$|f_1 - \bar{f}_1| + |f_0 - \bar{f}_0| \leq 2\delta.$$

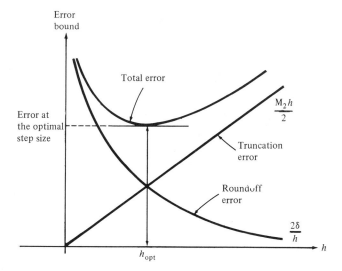

FIGURE 4.4 Error Bound, as a Function of Step Size

Thus the total absolute error satisfies

$$\left| f'(x_0) - \frac{\bar{f}_1 - \bar{f}_0}{h} \right| \leq \frac{M_2 h}{2} + \frac{2\delta}{h}. \tag{4.11}$$

Observe that for larger values of h the truncation term $M_2 h/2$ dominates. If the magnitude of h is small, the roundoff error term $2\delta/h$ exerts overriding influence. This observation implies that judgment must be exercised in choosing the step size h. The effect of a crude approximation of the derivative arising from too large a step size must be balanced against the effect of dividing functional errors by a positive power of the step size. This reasoning applies to all the differentiation formulas mentioned in this section. In our case the minimum of the function $M_2 h/2 + 2\delta/h$ gives the optimal step. The shape of this function is shown in Figure 4.4.

────── **EXAMPLE 4.2** ──────

By means of the program listed in Table 4.4, we have used the three-point formula of Table 4.3 to estimate the derivative of exp (x) at $x = 0$. Notice in the printout that as the step size h decreases, the approximation first becomes better, and then deteriorates; from (4.11), such behavior should be anticipated. The sources of error here are those due to computer word roundoff and inaccuracy in the library function for exp (x). These errors are machine dependent, of course. Our computation was performed by a VAX. Notice that even at the best step size h, the relative error is about 1000 times larger than machine epsilon.

TABLE 4.4   Program for Derivative Computation

```
C       PROGRAM DERIVATIVE
C
C
C       ****************************************************************
C       CALCULATES DERIVATIVE OF F(X)=EXP(X) AT X=0 BY THREE POINT
C       RULE USING 10 DIFFERENT STEP SIZES
C       OUTPUT: H=STEP SIZE
C               DERIV=DERIVATIVE ESTIMATED USING THREE POINT RULE
C               ERROR=THE DIFFERENCE BETWEEN THE TRUE VALUE OF THE
C                     DERIVATIVE AND THE APPROXIMATION
C       ****************************************************************
C
C       *** STATEMENT FUNCTION FOR CALCULATING COMPONENTS OF    ***
C       *** APPROXIMATION                                       ***
C
C       F(X)=EXP(X)
C
C       *** THIS LOOP ITERATES THE STEP SIZE H AND COMPUTES     ***
C       *** THE CORRESPONDING DERIVATIVE APPROXIMATION          ***
C
        DO 1 N=1,10
           H=0.1**N
           DERIV=(F(H)-F(-H))/(2.0*H)
           ERROR=1.0-DERIV
           WRITE(10,*)H,DERIV,ERROR
      1 CONTINUE
        STOP
        END
```

An important phenomenon is exemplified in the error column of Table 4.5. From (4.8), the error, in theory, is proportional to h^2, since $f^{(3)}$ is smooth. This tells us that if we use two step sizes, h_1 and h_2, where $h_2 = h_1/10$, the associated errors err (h_1) and err (h_2) ought to be related by

$$\text{err }(h_2) \approx \text{err }(h_1) \left(\frac{h_2}{h_1}\right)^2 = \frac{\text{err }(h_1)}{100}.$$

Examination of the error column in Table 4.5 reveals that this relation is satisfied very nicely in the first two rows in which truncation error is the limiting factor. The important fact here is that our truncation error formulas do give accurate indications of what to expect in practical situations.

Now that we have a more mature understanding of finite difference approximations, the reader may be interested in turning back to Figure 1.2, where he or

TABLE 4.5   Printout for Derivative Computation

h	Estimate $f(0)$	Error	
0.1000	1.001668	-1.6676188E-03	
1.0000E-02	1.000017	-1.6808510E-05	Truncation error
1.0000E-03	1.000017	-1.6927719E-05	dominates
1.0000E-04	1.000166	-1.6582012E-04	
1.0000E-05	1.001358	-1.3579130E-03	
1.0000E-06	0.9834764	1.6523600E-02	Roundoff error
1.0000E-07	1.192093	-0.1920927	dominates
1.0000E-08	0.0000000E+00	1.000000	
1.0000E-09	0.0000000E+00	1.000000	
1.0000E-10	0.0000000E+00	1.000000	

TABLE 4.6   Derivative Printout for Inaccurate Function Values

h	Estimate of $f'(0)$	Error
0.1000000	1.001631	-1.6306639E-03
1.0000001E-02	0.9994476	5.5235624E-04
1.0000000E-03	1.002491	-2.4905205E-03
1.0000001E-04	0.8606910	0.1393090
1.0000002E-05	1.245737	-0.2457368
1.0000002E-06	-2.712011	3.712011
1.0000002E-07	-379.9796	380.9796
1.0000003E-08	77.48602	-76.48602
1.0000003E-09	-7927.416	7928.416
1.0000004E-10	218152.9	-218151.9

she will see that the log-log plot associated with the error of approximation (4.2) has a slope of approximately 45° when truncation error dominates. This is confirmation that the error order of that formula is $O(h)$.

In our next computational experiment we replaced the declared function of the program in Table 4.4 by

$$F(X) = EXP(X) + 0.0001 * (RAN(KSEED) - 0.5),$$

which effectively adds a little random error to the function values. The expression "RAN(KSEED)" calls the VAX random number routine to generate values between 0 and 1. The function values are still correct to three or four significant figures. But from the listing in Table 4.6 we see that even this miniscule noise devastates our derivative approximations.   ∎

4.3
INTERPOLATORY QUADRATURE

Suppose that you had the task of guessing the value of an integral $\int_a^b f(x)\,dx$ entirely on the basis of a single value $f(x_1)$ at a domain point x_1 of your choosing. A logical idea would be to choose x_1 to be in the middle of the integration domain $[a, b]$, and to guess that the area under $f(x)$ is approximated by the rectangle shown in Figure 4.5. In fact, theory will confirm that in an important sense, this rule is optimal among all simple rules using only a single point of information.

One can view this plan within the Lagrange interpolation context: Approximate $f(x)$ by the simplest interpolation polynomial $p_0(x)$, and integrate the approximation over the domain. In the above one-point rule, $p_0(x)$ is the constant polynomial

$$p_0(x) = f(x_1)$$

based on one single datum $(x_1, f(x_1))$, where $x_1 = (b + a)/2$ is the midpoint of the integration domain. The approximation, then, is

$$\int_a^b f(x)\,dx \approx \int_a^b p_0(x)\,dx = \int_a^b f(x_1)\,dx = f(x_1)\int_a^b dx = (b - a)f(x_1),$$

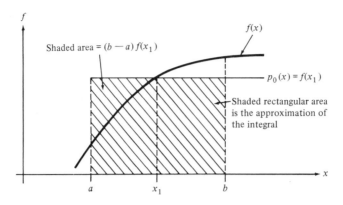

FIGURE 4.5   One-Point Quadrature Formula

which is called the *simple midpoint formula*.

To follow this interpolation idea a step further, one could hope to achieve increased accuracy by taking a linear interpolation, with interpolating points $x_1 = a$ and $x_2 = b$, that is,

$$p_1(x) = f(a) \frac{x - b}{a - b} + f(b) \frac{x - a}{b - a},$$

to achieve the approximation (see Figure 4.6)

$$\int_a^b f(x)\, dx \approx \int_a^b p_1(x)\, dx = \frac{f(a) + f(b)}{2}(b - a).$$

Here the region under the graph of $p_1(x)$ is a trapezoid with parallel sides of lengths $f(a)$ and $f(b)$, and width $b - a$. The area of the trapezoid, which is $((f(a) + f(b))/2)(b - a)$, serves as an integral approximation. This approximation is called the *simple trapezoidal formula*.

In fact, this elementary line of thinking has led us to the most fundamental and important family of numerical integration rules, the interpolatory quadrature family. We now explore this family systematically. Generally, in interpolatory quad-

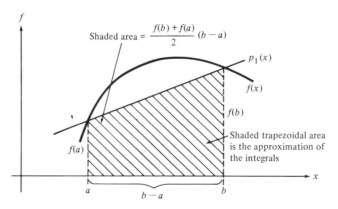

FIGURE 4.6   Two-Point Quadrature Formula

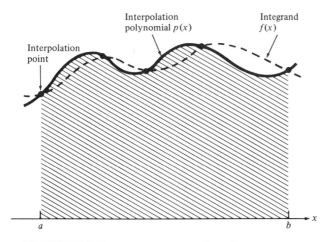

FIGURE 4.7 Interpolatory Quadrature

rature, one uses an interpolation polynomial $p(x)$ to approximate the intergrand $f(x)$ over the domain $[a, b]$ of integration. Then the desired integral

$$\int_a^b f(x)\, dx$$

is approximated by the easily computed value of the integral

$$\int_a^b p(x)\, dx$$

of the interpolation polynomial. In Figure 4.7 we illustrate the principle of interpolatory quadrature. The desired integral is the area under $f(x)$, and its interpolatory quadrature approximation is the crosshatched area under the interpolation polynomial.

Assume that we wish to approximate the integral of $f(x)$ over a finite interval $[a, b]$. Let $x_1, \ldots, x_n$ be distinct points and define $p(x)$ to be the interpolation polynomial for $f(x_i)$, $1 \le i \le n$. Then (3.14) implies that

$$\int_a^b f(x)\, dx = \int_a^b p(x)\, dx + \int_a^b \frac{f^{(n)}(\zeta(x))}{n!}\, w_n(x)\, dx. \qquad (4.12)$$

The first term of the right-hand side can be viewed as a computational approximation of the integral and the second term gives the truncation error of this approximation.

By using the Lagrangian representation (3.11) for the interpolation polynomial, we have

$$\int_a^b p(x)\, dx = \int_a^b \sum_{k=1}^n f(x_k) l_k(x)\, dx = \sum_{k=1}^n f(x_k) \int_a^b l_k(x)\, dx.$$

Thus *interpolatory-type* integration rules have the form

$$\int_a^b f(x)\, dx \approx \sum_{k=1}^n f(x_k) A_k, \tag{4.13}$$

with

$$A_k = \int_a^b l_k(x)\, dx, \qquad 1 \le k \le n. \tag{4.14}$$

The coefficients A_k depend only on the choice of the interpolating points x_k, $1 \le k \le n$, and the domain $[a, b]$ of integration. Regardless of the rationale for choosing the A_k's, any numerical integration rule of the form (4.13) is known as a *quadrature formula*. Essentially all integration formulas are of this type. The numbers x_k are called *quadrature points*. The values A_k are called *quadrature weights*. If the interpolating points $a = x_1 < x_2 < \cdots < x_n = b$ are equally spaced, (4.13) is called a *Newton–Cotes formula*. Newton–Cotes formulas are a popular class of interpolatory rules, but Gauss interpolatory quadrature (Section 4.6), with its more scientific selection of quadrature points, has many advantages, as we will see.

──────── **EXAMPLE 4.3** ──

Let $[a, b] = [-1, 1]$, $n = 3$, $x_1 = -1$, $x_2 = 0$, and $x_3 = 1$. Then

$$l_1(x) = \frac{(x - 0)(x - 1)}{(-1 - 0)(-1 - 1)} = \frac{1}{2}(x^2 - x)$$

$$l_2(x) = \frac{(x + 1)(x - 1)}{(0 + 1)(0 - 1)} = -x^2 + 1$$

$$l_3(x) = \frac{(x + 1)(x - 0)}{(1 + 1)(1 - 0)} = \frac{1}{2}(x^2 + x),$$

which implies that

$$A_1 = \int_{-1}^1 \tfrac{1}{2}(x^2 - x)\, dx = \tfrac{1}{3}$$

$$A_2 = \int_{-1}^1 (-x^2 + 1)\, dx = \tfrac{4}{3}$$

$$A_3 = \int_{-1}^1 \tfrac{1}{2}(x^2 + x)\, dx = \tfrac{1}{3}.$$

Thus we have derived the integration formula

$$\int_{-1}^1 f(x)\, dx \approx \tfrac{1}{3}f(-1) + \tfrac{4}{3}f(0) + \tfrac{1}{3}f(1).$$

As an example, this formula is applied to approximate the integral $\int_{-1}^{1} e^x \, dx$. The formula gives the estimate

$$\frac{e^{-1} + 4e^0 + e^{+1}}{3} \approx 2.362.$$

To three decimal places the exact value equals 2.350. ∎

A more algorithmic way to find interpolatory quadrature weights is through a linear equation construct. If $p(x)$ is a polynomial of degree $n - 1$ or less, then $p(x)$ is its own interpolation polynomial and quadrature is exact. Consequently,

$$\int_a^b f(x) \, dx = \int_a^b p(x) \, dx = \sum_{k=1}^{n} p(x_k) A_k. \tag{4.15}$$

By choosing $p_j(x) = x^j$ ($j = 0, 1, \ldots, n - 1$), this relation gives a system of linear equations for the unknown interpolatory quadrature weights $A_1, \ldots, A_n$:

$$
\begin{aligned}
A_1 x_1^0 + A_2 x_2^0 + \cdots + A_n x_n^0 &= \int_a^b x^0 \, dx = b - a \\[2mm]
A_1 x_1^1 + A_2 x_2^1 + \cdots + A_n x_n^1 &= \int_a^b x^1 \, dx = \frac{b^2 - a^2}{2} \\[2mm]
&\quad \cdot \quad \cdot \quad \cdot \quad \cdot \quad \cdot \\[2mm]
A_1 x_1^{n-1} + A_2 x_2^{n-1} + \cdots + A_n x_n^{n-1} &= \int_a^b x^{n-1} \, dx = \frac{b^n - a^n}{n}.
\end{aligned}
\tag{4.16}
$$

If the points $x_1, \ldots, x_n$ are distinct, the linear system of equations (4.16) has a unique solution (Bellman, 1970, p. 193).

EXAMPLE 4.4

From the linear equation approach, we reconstruct the coefficients obtained in Example 4.3, where $a = -1$, $b = 1$, and $x_1 = -1$, $x_2 = 0$, $x_3 = 1$. Equations (4.16) take the values

$$A_1 + A_2 + A_3 = 2$$

$$-A_1 \qquad\quad + A_3 = 0$$

$$A_1 \qquad\quad + A_3 = \tfrac{2}{3}.$$

From a simple Gauss elimination calculation, one finds that the solution is $A_1 = A_3 = \tfrac{1}{3}$ and $A_2 = \tfrac{4}{3}$. This yields the numerical integration formula

$$\int_{-1}^{1} f(x) \, dx \approx \tfrac{1}{3}f(-1) + \tfrac{4}{3}f(0) + \tfrac{1}{3}f(1).$$

This coincides with the formula obtained in Example 4.3, as it must. ∎

TABLE 4.7   Subroutine COEFF for Interpolatory Quadrature Weights

```
      SUBROUTINE COEFF(N,X,A,B,AA)
C
C     ***************************************************************
C     *   FUNCTION: THIS SUBROUTINE COMPUTES THE QUADRATURE          *
C     *             WEIGHTS FOR INTERPOLATORY QUADRATURE OVER        *
C     *             THE INTERVAL [A,B]                               *
C     *   USAGE:                                                     *
C     *         CALL SEQUENCE: CALL COEFF(N,X,A,B,AA)                *
C     *         EXTERNAL FUNCTIONS/SUBROUTINES:                      *
C     *                       SUBROUTINE GAUS1(N,M,ND,T,EPS)         *
C     *   PARAMETERS:                                                *
C     *      INPUT:                                                  *
C     *            N=NUMBER OF QUADRATURE POINTS (NOT LESS THAN 2,   *
C     *               NOT MORE THAN 30)                              *
C     *            X=N BY 1 ARRAY OF QUADRATURE POINTS               *
C     *            A=INTERVAL LEFT ENDPOINT                          *
C     *            B=INTERVAL RIGHT ENDPOINT                         *
C     *      OUTPUT:                                                 *
C     *            AA=N BY 1 ARRAY OF QUADRATURE WEIGHTS             *
C     ***************************************************************
C
      DIMENSION X(N),AA(N),T(30,31)
C
C     *** INITIALIZATION ***
C
      U=B
      V=A
C
C     *** ASSEMBLE SYSTEM MATRIX ***
      DO 1 J=1,N
        T(1,J)=1.0
    1 CONTINUE
      T(1,N+1)=U-V
      DO 2 I=2,N
        DO 3 J=1,N
          T(I,J)=T(I-1,J)*X(J)
    3   CONTINUE
        U=U*B
        V=V*A
        T(I,N+1)=(U-V)/I
    2 CONTINUE
C     *** COMPUTE QUAD. WTS. BY GAUSSIAN ELIMINATION ***
      M=1
      ND=30
      EPS=0.000001
      CALL GAUS1(N,M,ND,T,EPS)
      DO 4 I=1,N
        AA(I)=T(I,N+1)
    4 CONTINUE
      RETURN
      END
```

Subroutine COEFF (Table 4.7), using the linear equation representation (4.16), constructs the interpolatory quadrature weights for any given set of points and for any domain [a, b] of integration. It requires the external subroutine GAUS1 (Table 2.6) to find the solution of a system of linear equations.

EXAMPLE 4.5

Table 4.8 gives a simple driver program that redoes Example 4.3 by calling COEFF to obtain quadrature weights, and then applies these to the quadrature formula to obtain the three-point Newton–Cotes approximation of

$$\int_{-1}^{1} \exp(x)\,dx.$$

TABLE 4.8   Driver Program for Interpolatory Quadrature

```
C     PROGRAM INTEXP
C
C     ****************************************************************
C     THIS PROGRAM SOLVES THE PROBLEM OF APPROXIMATING THE INTEGRAL
C     OF EXP(X) OVER [-1,1] BY INTERPOLATORY QUADRATURE
C     CALLS:  SUBROUTINE COEFF
C     OUTPUT: ESTIMATE OF THE INTEGRAL
C     ****************************************************************
C
      DIMENSION X(10), AA(10)

C     *** DECLARE THE INTEGRAND                                  ***

      F(X) = EXP(X)


C     *** N IS NUMBER OF QUADRATURE POINTS                       ***

      N = 3

C     *** INTEGRATE FROM A TO B                                  ***

      A = -1.0
      B = 1.0

C     *** ASSIGN THE INTERPOLATION POINTS                        ***

      DO J = 1,N
         X(J) = A + (J-1)*(B-A)/(N-1)
      ENDDO

C     *** CALL COEFF TO GET QUADRATURE WEIGHTS                   ***

      CALL COEFF(N,X,A,B,AA)

C
C     *** COMPUTE AND ADD THE SUCCESSIVE SUMMANDS OF THE         ***
C     *** QUADRATURE FORMULA TO GET THE ESTIMATE OF THE          ***
C     *** INTEGERAL AND WRITE ITS VALUE                          ***
C
      VAL = 0.0
      DO 1 J = 1,N
         VAL = VAL + F(X(J))*AA(J)
1     CONTINUE
      WRITE(10,*) VAL
      END
```

Other Newton–Cotes approximations obtained from this program are also tabulated below.

Newton–Cotes

n	Estimate	Error	
3	2.362054	-0.12E-01	
4	2.355648	-0.52E-02	
5	2.350471	-0.69E-04	
6	2.350441	-0.39E-04	Limited by
7	2.350403	-0.48E-06	Roundoff

Application 4.4

Recently, the possible influence of changing weather patterns on the Antarctic ice cap has been in the news. Your authors have participated in ice mass modeling efforts. One activity is to infer the steady-state shape of an ice mass, given assumptions about temperature and accumulation (snow and melt) and other boundary effects. As an oversimplified example (Figure 4.8) of such a study, assume that annual accumulation rate ACC (h) as a function of altitude h is known, and that the height $h(r)$ as a function of radius r (in tens of kilometers) must satisfy a certain given relationship. Then in order that the shape be unchanging with time, it is obviously necessary that the net accumulation be zero. That is, the evaporation (which tends to be accentuated at lower altitudes h) must counterbalance the deposits at higher altitudes. Mathematically, this requirement may be stated as

$$I(R) = \int_0^R ACC\ (h(r))\ dr = 0. \tag{4.17}$$

This "conservation of mass" condition may be used to determine the extent R of the cap. As a simple illustration of this, and as a test of our quadrature skills, presume that

$$ACC\ (h) = h - 0.5$$

and that the profile of the cap must follow the rule

$$h(r) = \cos\ (r^2).$$

Then (4.17) becomes

$$I(R) = \int_0^R \cos\ (r^2)\ dr - 0.5R.$$

This indefinite integral is known not to have a representation in terms of elementary functions. We called on the preceding interpolatory quadrature driver (Table

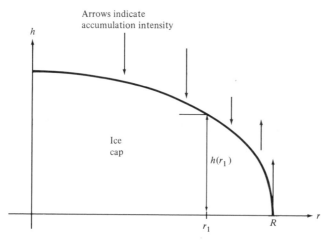

FIGURE 4.8   Idealized Ice Cap

TABLE 4.9
Computed Net
Accumulations

R	$I(R)$
0.2	0.111E+00
0.4	0.199E+00
0.6	0.292E+00
0.8	0.368E+00
1.0	0.405E+00
1.2	0.374E+00
1.4	0.250E+00
1.6	0.252E-01
1.8	-0.266E+00
2.0	-0.541E+00

4.8) to provide values of this integral at various points R. We simply substituted COS $(X**2) - 0.5$ as the declared function $F(X)$, set A to 0, and read out values for various upper limits B. By this means, and using $N = 7$ points, we obtained Table 4.9. As a check that truncation error is not serious, the calculations were repeated for $N = 14$ points. The values agreed with the seven-point run to four significant digits.

From the table, we may infer that to the extent that this model is trustworthy, the radius R of a stable ice cap is about $1.6 \cdot 10^4$ m.

◇

4.4
COMPOUND QUADRATURE FORMULAS

4.4.1   Midpoint, Trapezoidal, Simpson's, and Related Rules

In Section 3.4.4 and elsewhere in Chapter 3, we observed that polynomial interpolation is, in some instances, surprisingly difficult. Approximations for some continuous functions can get worse, rather than better, as more data points are used. Other functions can require impossibly high-degree polynomials for reasonable accuracy, no matter which interpolation points are chosen. The use of even moderately high degree polynomials can engender instabilities from roundoff error. Unfortunately, as one might anticipate, these effects carry over to interpolatory-type quadrature rules offered in the preceding section: Newton–Cotes truncation error need not go to zero as the number n of points increases. Even for rules having as few as 10 points, computation of weights A_k can be numerically unstable.

In the case of interpolation, to some extent we were able to bypass these difficulties by resorting to piecewise polynomials such as splines. Several of the most popular quadrature rules can be motivated by the viewpoint that they integrate piecewise interpolation polynomials. One advantage of these "compound" quadrature formulas, as they are called, is that they always converge to the integral as more points are used (S & Y, 1978, Sec. 3.2).

EXAMPLE 4.6

At the outset of Section 4.3, when allowed two function points for integration, we chose to use them to obtain a linear interpolation polynomial. A sensible

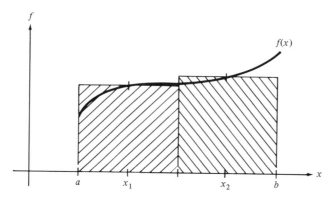

FIGURE 4.9   Compounding of Two Midpoint Steps

alternative might have simply been to subdivide the domain of integration into two intervals, and to apply the simple midpoint formula (as in Figure 4.5) to each interval separately. This idea, illustrated in Figure 4.9, has merit and is consistent with the plan followed in Chapter 3 of avoiding pitfalls of high-degree interpolation by piecewise low-degree polynomial interpolation.

The general formulation of compound quadrature formulas can be given as follows. Let N be an integer greater than 1, $[a, b]$ be the interval of integration, and assume that we have a numerical integration formula available. Then the associated compound formula requires that the interval $[a, b]$ be divided into N subintervals, usually of equal lengths, and has us apply our integration formula over each of the subintervals. Specifically, N being the number of subintervals, let

$$a = z_0 < z_1 < \cdots < z_{N-1} < z_N = b$$

denote the partition points, and then observe that

$$\int_a^b f(x)\, dx = \int_{z_0}^{z_1} f(x)\, dx + \int_{z_1}^{z_2} f(x)\, dx + \cdots + \int_{z_{N-1}}^{z_N} f(x)\, dx.$$

The *compound quadrature formula* requires that for each k, $0 \leq k < N$, we apply the given integration rule to estimate

$$\int_{z_k}^{z_{k+1}} f(x)\, dx$$

on each of the subintervals $[z_k, z_{k+1}]$ and then sum these estimates. In Figure 4.10 we suggest how points of the given quadrature formula are distributed into each subinterval to obtain the quadrature points of the associated compound formula.

The advantage of this procedure is that, as we will see, we can get fairly accurate estimates of the integral without having to solve a formidable linear equation for the coefficients. A disadvantage is that often we can achieve greater

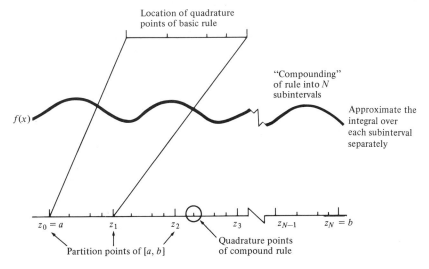

Location of quadrature
points of basic rule

"Compounding"
of rule into N
subintervals

$f(x)$

Approximate the
integral over
each subinterval
separately

$z_0 = a$ z_1 z_2 z_3 z_{N-1} $z_N = b$

Partition points of $[a, b]$

Quadrature points
of compound rule

FIGURE 4.10   Compounding of a Basic Quadrature Formula

accuracy by a single high-order interpolatory rule, for a given set of function values, than by a compound formula using this same set of values. This will be shown in Example 4.11.

We now reveal the most common of the compound rules. They are obtained by compounding the simplest possible interpolatory-type formulas. The original interpolatory integration formulas, such as the simple midpoint and simple trapezoidal formulas, result from selecting $N = 1$. Assume that the interval $[a, b]$ is divided into N equal subintervals by points $a = z_0 < z_1 < \cdots < z_{N-1} < z_N = b$. Consider now one of the subintervals, say $[z_k, z_{k+1}]$.

The simplest compound formula can be obtained if we take all subintervals to have the same length h and select the single interpolation point

$$x_{k+1} = \frac{z_k + z_{k+1}}{2}$$

from each subinterval $[z_k, z_{k+1}]$. Then on the kth interval, $f(x)$ is approximated by the constant interpolation polynomial $p_0(x) = f(x_{k+1})$ based on this interpolating point. Then we obtain the one-point interpolatory-type formula

$$\int_{z_k}^{z_{k+1}} f(x) \, dx \approx \int_{z_k}^{z_{k+1}} f(x_{k+1}) \, dx = hf(x_{k+1}) \qquad (4.18)$$

for $k = 0, 1, \ldots, N - 1$, and $h = z_{k+1} - z_k$. (For $N = 2$, this coincides with the heuristic rule offered in Example 4.6 and illustrated in Figure 4.9.) Adding the integral approximations over all subintervals, we obtain the compound formula approximation

$$m_N = h[f(x_1) + f(x_2) + \cdots + f(x_N)]$$

$$\text{for } h = \frac{b - a}{N}, \; x_k = a + (k - \tfrac{1}{2})h, \; k = 1, 2, \ldots, N. \qquad (4.19)$$

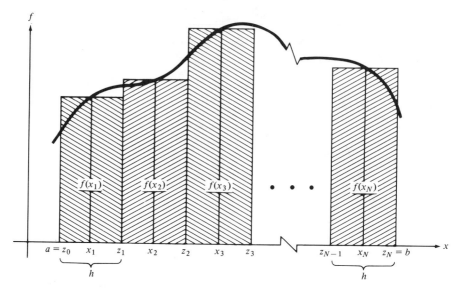

FIGURE 4.11   The Midpoint Formula

This is known as the *midpoint formula*, a graphical interpretation of which is given in Figure 4.11. This generalizes the construction shown in Figure 4.9 to N subintervals instead of two.

──── **EXAMPLE 4.7** ──

We apply the midpoint formula to the integral

$$\int_{-1}^{1} e^x \, dx.$$

Select $N = 2$. Then $h = 1$, and the subintervals are $[-1, 0]$ and $[0, 1]$ with midpoints $x_1 = -0.5$ and $x_2 = 0.5$. Hence

$$m_2 = 1 \cdot (e^{-0.5} + e^{0.5}) \approx 1 \cdot (0.6065 + 1.6487) = 2.2552.$$

Next select $N = 4$. Then $h = 0.5$; the subintervals are $[-1, -0.5]$, $[-0.5, 0]$, $[0, 0.5]$, and $[0.5, 1]$; and therefore the midpoints are $x_1 = -0.75$, $x_2 = -0.25$, $x_3 = 0.25$, and $x_4 = 0.75$. Consequently,

$$m_4 = 0.5(e^{-0.75} + e^{-0.25} + e^{0.25} + e^{0.75})$$

$$\approx 0.5 \cdot (0.4724 + 0.7788 + 1.2840 + 2.1170)$$

$$= 0.5 \cdot 4.6522 \approx 2.3261.$$

As a comparison we mention that the true value of the integral to five correct significant figures equals 2.3504. Note that m_4 is a considerably better approximation of the integral than m_2, but much worse than the four-point Newton–Cotes value $NC_4 = 2.3556$, in Example 4.5, based on the same function data.   ∎

Alternatively, by using the subinterval endpoints $x_k = z_k$, $x_{k+1} = z_{k+1}$ as interpolating points and by constructing a linear interpolation polynomial $p_1(x)$, as in Figure 4.6, we get the functional approximation

$$f(x) \approx p_1(x) = \frac{x - x_{k+1}}{x_k - x_{k+1}} f(x_k) + \frac{x - x_k}{x_{k+1} - x_k} f(x_{k+1}),$$

which leads to the two-point interpolatory-type formula

$$\int_{z_k}^{z_{k+1}} f(x) \, dx \approx f(x_k) \int_{z_k}^{z_{k+1}} \frac{x - x_{k+1}}{-h} \, dx + f(x_{k+1}) \int_{z_k}^{z_{k+1}} \frac{x - x_k}{h} \, dx$$

$$= \frac{h}{2} \left(f(x_k) + f(x_{k+1}) \right). \tag{4.20}$$

Adding the integrals (4.20) over all subintervals, we obtain the compound formula approximations of $\int_a^b f(x) \, dx$ given by

$$t_N = h[\tfrac{1}{2}f(x_0) + f(x_1) + f(x_2) + \cdots + f(x_{N-1}) + \tfrac{1}{2}f(x_N)]$$

$$\text{for } h = \frac{b - a}{N}, \ x_k = a + kh, \ k = 0, 1, \ldots, N. \tag{4.21}$$

This is called the *trapezoidal rule*.

The rule is graphed in Figure 4.12. By comparing Figures 4.10 and 4.12 the reader will see the compounding idea clearly.

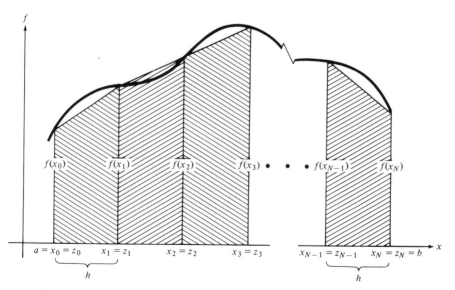

FIGURE 4.12 The Trapezoidal Rule

EXAMPLE 4.8

We apply the trapezoidal rule to integrate

$$\int_{-1}^{1} e^x \, dx,$$

the integral in Example 4.3. The approximation t_2, according to (4.21), with x_0, x_1, and x_2 being -1, 0, and 1, respectively, is

$$1 \cdot (\tfrac{1}{2} e^{-1} + e^0 + \tfrac{1}{2} e^1) \approx 2.54.$$

To three places, the correct value is 2.35.

The trapezoidal rule t_4 gives

$$t_4 = 0.5 \cdot (\tfrac{1}{2} \cdot e^{-1} + e^{-0.5} + e^0 + e^{0.5} + \tfrac{1}{2} \cdot e^1)$$

$$\approx 0.5 \cdot (\tfrac{1}{2} \cdot 0.3679 + 0.6065 + 1. + 1.6487 + \tfrac{1}{2} \cdot 2.7183)$$

$$\approx 2.399.$$

As exemplified here, the trapezoidal rule has approximately the same accuracy as the midpoint formula and is less accurate than Newton–Cotes formulas (Example 4.5), using the same data. ∎

TABLE 4.10   Subroutine TRAP for the Trapezoidal Rule

```
      SUBROUTINE TRAP(A,B,N,E)

C
C     ****************************************************************
C     *   FUNCTION: APPROXIMATES THE INTEGRAL OF F(X) OVER THE      *
C     *             INTERVAL [A,B] BY THE TRAPEZOIDAL RULE          *
C     *   USAGE:                                                    *
C     *        CALL SEQUENCE: CALL TRAP(A,B,N,E)                    *
C     *        EXTERNAL FUNCTIONS/SUBROUTINES: FUNCTION F(X)        *
C     *   PARAMETERS:                                               *
C     *        INPUT:                                               *
C     *             A=INTERVAL LEFT ENDPOINT                        *
C     *             B=INTERVAL RIGHT ENDPOINT                       *
C     *             N=NUMBER OF SUBINTERVALS                        *
C     *        OUTPUT:                                              *
C     *             E=ESTIMATE OF THE INTEGRAL                      *
C     ****************************************************************
C
C     *** INITIALIZATION ***
      H=(B-A)/N
      E=(F(A)+F(B))/2.0
      IF (N.GT.1) THEN
C     *** THE TRAPEZOIDAL FORMULA ***
         X=A
         DO 1 I=1,N-1
            X=X+H
            E=E+F(X)
    1    CONTINUE
      END IF
      E=E*H
      RETURN
      END
```

The trapezoidal rule can be viewed as an integral of the linear spline (or broken-line or piecewise linear function) which interpolates the data $(x_k, f(x_k))$, $k = 0$, . . . , N. Many textbooks, for example, Davis and Rabinowitz (1975), use the notation t_N and refer to t_N as the N-point trapezoidal rule, although strictly speaking, it uses $N + 1$ quadrature points. The midpoint formula m_N uses exactly N points.

The graphical representations of the midpoint formula and the trapezoidal rule were given in Figures 4.11 and 4.12. The approximating value m_N of the integral is given by the sum of the areas of rectangles shown in Figure 4.11, and similarly the trapezoidal rule t_N is the total area of the trapezoids in Figure 4.12.

Subroutine TRAP for computing the trapezoidal rule t_N is given in Table 4.10.

───────── **EXAMPLE 4.9** ───

By means of the FORTRAN program shown in Table 4.11, the value of the 10-point trapezoidal rule applied to approximating

$$\int_0^{10} 10 \sin (1 - 0.1x)\, dx$$

is found. The output of this computation is presented in Table 4.12.

TABLE 4.11   Program for Example 4.9

```
C       PROGRAM TRAPEZOID
C
C       ****************************************************************
C       CALCULATES THE INTEGRAL OF F(X)=10*SIN(1-0.1*X) OVER [0,10]
C       BY THE TRAPEZOIDAL RULE
C       CALLS: TRAP
C       OUTPUT: TRUE=TRUE VALUE OF THE INTEGRAL AS CALCULATED USING
C                    LIBRARY FUNCTION COS
C               EST=ESTIMATED VALUE CALCULATED BY THE TRAPEZOID RULE
C               ERROR=TRUE-EST
C       ****************************************************************
C
        A=0.
        B=10.
        N=10
        TRUE=100.*(1-COS(1.0))
C
C       *** SUBROUTINE TRAP ESTIMATES THE INTEGRAL BY TRAPEZOIDAL   ***
C       *** RULE                                                    ***
C
        CALL TRAP(A,B,N,EST)
        ERROR=TRUE-EST
        WRITE(10,*)TRUE,EST,ERROR
        STOP
        END
C
C       *** SUBROUTINE FUNCTION F(X) COMPUTES THE INTEGRAND         ***
C
        FUNCTION F(X)
        F=10.*SIN(1.-0.1*X)
        RETURN
        END
```

TABLE 4.12   Output of Example 4.9

True	10-Point Trapezoidal	Error
45.96977	45.93146	3.8314819E-02

--■

Consider again one subinterval $[z_k, z_{k+1}]$, and approximate the function $f(x)$ by a quadratic interpolation polynomial based on the endpoints and the midpoint of this subinterval. Then, by recalling Example 4.3 and introducing the new variable

$$z = \frac{2x - (z_{k+1} + z_k)}{z_{k+1} - z_k},$$

we get the approximation

$$\int_{z_k}^{z_{k+1}} f(x)\, dx \approx \frac{h}{3}\left[f(z_k) + 4f\left(\frac{z_k + z_{k+1}}{2}\right) + f(z_{k+1}) \right],$$

where now $h = \frac{1}{2}(z_{k+1} - z_k)$. The quadrature points $x_0, x_1, \ldots, x_M$ are related to the compounding interval endpoints $z_0, z_1, \ldots, z_N$ by $M = 2N$ and

$$x_0 = z_0, \ x_1 = \frac{z_0 + z_1}{2}, \ x_2 = z_1,$$

$$x_3 = \frac{z_1 + z_2}{2}, \ \ldots, \ x_{M-2} = z_{N-1},$$

$$x_{M-1} = \frac{z_{N-1} + z_N}{2}, \ x_M = z_N.$$

In terms of these quadrature points and after adding the quadratures over each subinterval, we have

$$
\begin{aligned}
s_M = \frac{h}{3}\,[f(x_0) &+ 4f(x_1) + 2f(x_2) + 4f(x_3) + \cdots + 2f(x_{M-2}) \\
&+ 4f(x_{M-1}) + f(x_M)],
\end{aligned}
$$

(4.22)

where $h = \dfrac{b - a}{M}$, and for $k = 0, 1, \ldots, M$, $x_k = a + kh$.

Formula (4.22) is known as *Simpson's rule*. In words, it can be described as follows: Select an *even* positive integer M, and compute the step size as

$$h = \frac{b - a}{M}$$

and as usual, set $x_k = a + kh$. Except for $f(x_0)$ and $f(x_M)$, $f(x_k)$ gets weighted by 4 if the index k is odd and 2 if k is even. The (weighted) terms are then added to $f(x_0)$ and $f(x_M)$ and scaled by $h/3$ to get s_M.

—————— **EXAMPLE 4.10** ——————

In the case of the integral

$$\int_{-1}^{1} e^x \, dx,$$

the integration formula that was derived in Example 4.3 coincides with Simpson's rule s_2. Using the points of Example 4.8, we have

$$s_4 = \frac{0.5}{3} \cdot (e^{-1} + 4 \cdot e^{-0.5} + 2 \cdot e^0 + 4 \cdot e^{0.5} + e^1)$$

$$\approx \frac{0.5}{3} \cdot (0.36788 + 4 \cdot 0.60653 + 2 \cdot 1.0 + 4 \cdot 1.64872 + 2.71828)$$

$$= 2.35119.$$

To five significant figures, the true value is 2.3504. Thus s_4 is much more accurate than t_4 or m_4. There are theoretical reasons for expecting this; they will be mentioned in Sections 4.4.2 and 4.5.1.

◼

Subroutine SIMP for Simpson's rule is given in Table 4.13, where the calling parameter M is defined as above. The graphical representation of Simpson's rule

TABLE 4.13   Subroutine SIMP for Simpson's Rule

```
      SUBROUTINE SIMP(A,B,M,E)
C
C     ***************************************************************
C     *   FUNCTION: APPROXIMATES THE INTEGRAL OF F(X) OVER THE      *
C     *             INTERVAL [A,B] BY SIMPSON'S RULE                *
C     *   USAGE:                                                    *
C     *       CALL SEQUENCE: CALL SIMP(A,B,M,E)                     *
C     *       EXTERNAL FUNCTIONS/SUBROUTINES: FUNCTION F(X)         *
C     *   PARAMETERS:                                               *
C     *       INPUT:                                                *
C     *           A=INTERVAL LEFT ENDPOINT                          *
C     *           B=INTERVAL RIGHT ENDPOINT                         *
C     *           M=NUMBER OF POINTS OF SIMPSON RULE                *
C     *           (M IS POSITIVE EVEN INTEGER-SEE TEXT)             *
C     *       OUTPUT:                                               *
C     *           E=ESTIMATE OF THE INTEGRAL                        *
C     ***************************************************************
C
C     *** INITIALIZATION ***
      E=F(A)+F(B)
      H=(B-A)/M
      X=A-H
C     *** COMPUTE THE SUM OF ODD INDEX TERMS ***
      DO 1 I=1,M-1,2
          X=X+2.0*H
          E=E+4.0*F(X)
    1 CONTINUE
C     *** COMPUTE THE SUM OF EVEN INDEX TERMS ***
      X=A
      DO 2 I=2,M-2,2
          X=X+2.0*H
          E=E+2.0*F(X)
    2 CONTINUE
      E=E*H/3.0
      RETURN
      END
```

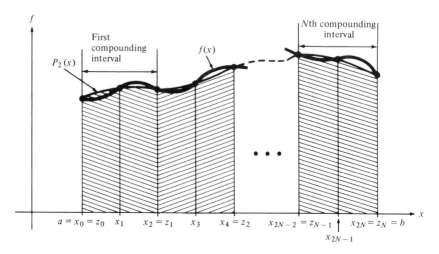

FIGURE 4.13   Graphical Representation of Simpson's Rule

is given in Figure 4.13. For $k = 0, 2, \ldots, 2N - 2$, consider the interpolating points x_k, x_{k+1}, x_{k+2}, the corresponding functional values $f(x_k), f(x_{k+1}), f(x_{k+2})$, and the quadratic interpolating polynomial $p_2(x)$ based on these data. Then the integral of $f(x)$ over the interval $[x_k, x_{k+2}]$ is approximated by the area under this quadratic interpolation polynomial, and the integral $\int_a^b f(x)\, dx$ is approximated by summing the areas under these quadratic polynomials, for $k = 0, 2, \ldots, 2N - 2$. The integral approximation is the crosshatched area shown in the figure.

Simpson's rule can be viewed as the integral of a continuous piecewise quadratic interpolation function. The quadratic pieces are the second-degree polynomials that interpolate the data $(x_k, f(x_k))$, $(x_{k+1}, f(x_{k+1}))$, and $(x_{k+2}, f(x_{k+2}))$, $k = 0, 2, \ldots, M - 2$, where $M = 2N$. The resultant piecewise polynomial is not, technically speaking, a quadratic spline because the first derivatives need not exist at the points z_k.

A simple computer example is reported next.

──────── **EXAMPLE 4.11** ──

The integral

$$\int_0^{10} 10 \sin (1 - 0.1x)\, dx$$

in Example 4.9 was computed by Simpson's rule, with $M = 2N = 10$. Subroutine SIMP given in Table 4.13 was applied to get the approximation

$$s_{10} = 45.96979,$$

which is much closer to the true value of 45.96977 than the value obtained by the trapezoidal rule t_{10}. Note that both t_{10} and s_{10} used the same quadrature points and function values. As stated in the optional section to follow, theory tells us that the error of the trapezoidal and midpoint rules is $O(h^2)$, whereas for Simpson's rule, the error is $O(h^4)$.   ∎

**TABLE 4.14 Accuracies of
Several Rules**

	Error
Trapezoidal	$-4.9 \cdot 10^{-2}$
Simpson	$-7.9 \cdot 10^{-3}$
Newton–Cotes	$-6.9 \cdot 10^{-5}$

A theme in our discussion of quadrature rules is that by applying different quadrature weights A_k, some rules achieve remarkable improvement of accuracy over others which use the very same points x_k and function values $f(x_k)$. In particular, for

$$\int_{-1}^{1} \exp(x) \, dx,$$

we obtained the performances that are listed in Table 4.14 by different weightings of $\exp(-1)$, $\exp(-0.5)$, $\exp(0)$, $\exp(0.5)$, and $\exp(1)$.

The relative performance levels above are typical. A tribute to mathematical analysis is that it leads one to understand and anticipate this variation. Intuition alone does not suffice for guessing how best to use functional data to estimate integrals. It is to be admitted that although among rules using equally spaced data, Newton–Cotes quadrature is by far the best, when the number of points is about 10 or larger, the system matrix (4.16) for determining Newton–Cotes weights becomes so ill-conditioned that the method becomes unsatisfactory. A principal reason is that this system matrix for determining interpolatory weights coincides with the notorious Vandermonde matrix, the instability of which was demonstrated in Example 2.19.

In the section that follows we explore some issues of compound-formula error analysis.

★4.4.2 Error Analysis of Compound Formulas

The truncation error of the trapezoidal rule will be derived in detail. Other compound formulas can be examined similarly (Davis and Rabinowitz, 1975, Sec. 2.4). They all spring from the idea of integrating (3.14).

From the error formula for linear interpolating polynomials [equation (3.14) with $n = 2$] we have

$$f(x) - p_1(x) = \frac{f''(\zeta(x))}{2!} (x - x_k)(x - x_{k+1}),$$

where $p_1(x)$ is the linear interpolation polynomial based on the abscissas x_k, x_{k+1}. Then formally

$$\int_{x_k}^{x_{k+1}} f(x) \, dx - \int_{x_k}^{x_{k+1}} p_1(x) \, dx = \int_{xk}^{x_{k+1}} \frac{f''(\zeta(x))}{2} (x - x_k)(x - x_{k+1}) \, dx.$$

The second term of the left-hand side is given in (4.20), and by substituting the variable $t = (x - x_k)/h$ into the integral, we get

$$\int_{x_k}^{x_{k+1}} f(x)\, dx - \frac{h}{2}(f(x_k) + f(x_{k+1})) = \int_0^1 \frac{h^3 f''(\zeta(t))}{2} t(t - 1)\, dt. \quad (4.23)$$

Since $t(t - 1)$ has no roots in the open interval $(0, 1)$, the mean-value theorem for integral calculus [equation (B.19) of Appendix B] implies that the right-hand side is equal to

$$\frac{h^3 f''(\eta_k)}{2} \int_0^1 t(t - 1)\, dt = -\frac{h^3 f''(\eta_k)}{12}, \quad (4.24)$$

where $\eta_k \in (x_k, x_{k+1})$. After adding (4.23) for $k = 0, 1, \ldots, N - 1$ and using (4.24), the intermediate-value theorem (Appendix B, property 21) for derivatives applied to $f''(x)$ implies that

$$\int_a^b f(x)\, dx = t_N - \sum_{k=0}^{N-1} \frac{h^3 f''(\eta_k)}{12} = t_N - \frac{h^3 N}{12} \frac{1}{N} \sum_{k=0}^{N-1} f''(\eta_k)$$

$$= t_N - \frac{h^3 N f \cdot (\eta)}{12},$$

where $\eta \in (a, b)$. Since $h = (b - a)/N$, we conclude that the error of the trapezoidal formula can be rewritten as

$$\int_a^b f(x)\, dx - t_N = -\frac{(b - a)h^2 f''(\eta)}{12} \quad (4.25)$$

and the absolute value of the truncation error can be bounded by:

$$\boxed{\left| \int_a^b f(x)\, dx - t_N \right| \leq \frac{M_2(b - a)h^2}{12},} \quad (4.26)$$

where M_2 is selected so that

$$|f''(x)| \leq M_2$$

for all $x \in (a, b)$.

We emphasize that the bound (4.26) accounts only for truncation error. For N large (above 1000, say), and computer word length short, roundoff error can cause further degradation.

EXAMPLE 4.12

We bound the error of the integral computed in Example 4.9. Since $N = 10$, $a = 0$, $b = 10$, $h = 1.0$, and

$$f(x) = 10 \sin(1 - 0.1x),$$

we have

$$f'(x) = -\cos(1 - 0.1x)$$

and

$$f''(x) = -0.1 \sin(1 - 0.1x).$$

Thus $M_2 = 0.1$, and the truncation error can be bounded by

$$\frac{M_2(b - a)h^2}{12} = \frac{1}{12} = 0.08383. \ldots$$

To five significant decimals, the exact value of the integral is 45,970, and in Example 4.9 we have seen that the actual error is 0.039.

Formula (4.26) can be used to find the number N of subintervals needed to assure six-decimal-place accuracy. In this case the error will not exceed $\frac{1}{2} \times 10^{-6}$ if the value of N satisfies

$$\frac{M_2(b - a)^3}{12N^2} \le \frac{1}{2} \cdot 10^{-6},$$

which follows from the fact that $h = (b - a)/N$. That is,

$$\frac{10^2}{12N^2} \le \frac{1}{2} \cdot 10^{-6}.$$

Solving for N, we calculate

$$N \ge \left(\frac{10^2 \cdot 10^6 \cdot 2}{12}\right)^{1/2} = \frac{10^4}{\sqrt{6}} \approx 4082.48,$$

which implies that $N = 4083$ is satisfactory. In fact, by applying subroutine TRAP (Table 4.10), with $N = 4083$ to the integration problem above, the authors found the actual error to be about $-2.3 \cdot 10^{-7}$. The calculations were done on a VAX computer in double precision. In single precision, roundoff error is the limiting factor, and the error is about $-9 \cdot 10^{-7}$. ∎

Table 4.15 summarizes the specific Newton–Cotes integration rules and associated errors of methods in Section 4.3, and we have included a few other popular Newton–Cotes formulas. These and other rules may be found in Abramowitz and Stegun (1965, pp. 885–887). Table 4.16 similarly recapitulates popular compound formulas and associated errors.

TABLE 4.15   Some Popular Interpolatory-Type Formulas and Their Errors

Name	Step size $h > 0$, $x_{k+1} = x_k + h$, $f_k = f(x_k)$, ζ a point in the domain of integration
Simple trapezoidal rule	$$\int_{x_0}^{x_1} f(x)\,dx \approx \frac{h}{2}(f_0 + f_1)$$ $$\text{error} = -\frac{h^3}{12} f''(\zeta)$$
Simple Simpson's rule	$$\int_{x_0}^{x_2} f(x)\,dx \approx \frac{h}{3}(f_0 + 4f_1 + f_2)$$ $$\text{error} = -\frac{h^5}{90} f^{(4)}(\zeta)$$
Simple Simpson's $\frac{3}{8}$ rule	$$\int_{x_0}^{x_3} f(x)\,dx \approx \frac{3h}{8}(f_0 + 3f_1 + 3f_2 + f_3)$$ $$\text{error} = -\frac{3h^5}{80} f^{(4)}(\zeta)$$
Simple Bode's rule	$$\int_{x_0}^{x_4} f(x)\,dx \approx \frac{2h}{45}(7f_0 + 32f_1 + 12f_2 + 32f_3 + 7f_4)$$ $$\text{error} = -\frac{8h^7}{945} f^{(6)}(\zeta)$$

$\int_{0}^{1} f(x)dx = @SUM(C3..C101)$

TABLE 4.16   Some Popular Compound Formulas and Their Errors

Name	Step size $h = \dfrac{b-a}{N}$, $x_{k+1} = x_k + h$, $f_k = f(x_k)$, ζ a point in the domain of integration
Trapezoidal rule	$$\int_a^b f(x)\,dx \approx h\left(\frac{f_0}{2} + f_1 + \cdots + f_{N-1} + \frac{f_N}{2}\right) = t_N$$ $$\text{error} = -\frac{(b-a)h^2}{12} f''(\zeta)$$
Modified trapezoidal rule	$$\int_a^b f(x)\,dx \approx h\left(\frac{f_0}{2} + f_1 + \cdots + f_{N-1} + \frac{f_N}{2}\right)$$ $$+ \frac{h}{24}(f_{-1} + f_1 + f_{N-1} - f_{N+1})$$ $$\text{error} = -\frac{11(b-a)h^4}{720} f^{(4)}(\zeta)$$
Simpson's rule	$$\int_a^b f(x)\,dx \approx \frac{h}{3}[f_0 + 4f_1 + 2f_2 + 4f_3 + \cdots$$ $$+ 2f_{M-2} + 4f_{M-1} + f_M] = s_M$$ $$\text{error} = -\frac{(b-a)h^4}{180} f^{(4)}(\zeta)\left(h = \frac{b-a}{M}\right)$$

──────── **EXAMPLE 4.13** ────────────────────────

Here we compare the performances of Simpson's rule with that of the New-ton–Cotes formula using the very same data values (x_k, f_k), $k = 1, \ldots, n$. By means of the program and function subroutine listed in Table 4.17, we applied subroutines SIMP and COEFF to evaluate the "usual" integral

$$\int_0^{10} 10 \sin (1 - 0.1x) \, dx. \qquad \text{EC\$3.. would} \atop \text{make this}$$

For reasons to be noted in a moment, these computations were done in double precision.

From the output, summarized in Table 4.18, we see that in the case of three points, the Newton–Cotes and Simpson's rules give exactly the same value. This is because the corresponding Simpson's rule *is* the three-point Newton–Cotes formula. As the number of points increases, the Newton–Cotes formula becomes much more accurate than Simpson's rule, but after the 11-point formula, its per-formance starts deteriorating until by 21 points, the answer is quite erroneous. The cause of deterioration is not the Newton–Cotes method itself, but the fact that as the number of points increases the solution of the linear equation (4.16) tends to become subject to extreme errors as a result of roundoff, even in double pre-cision. A reason why we can confidently ascribe blame to the linear equation, rather than instabilities in polynomial approximation, is that error in the solution of polynomial approximation of $\sin (x)$ is quite stable and accurate. The basis of this assertion is that interpolation error formula (3.14) predicts small error [all derivatives of $\sin (x)$ have absolute value not exceeding 1], and the experiment in Example 3.12 exhibits great accuracy at 20 points. Small error in interpolation polynomial approximation implies small error in interpolatory quadrature. Ill-conditioned linear equations were discussed further in Chapter 2. Observe that the error of the 11-point Newton–Cotes rule is less than that of the 201-point Simpson estimate.

A questionable aspect of Newton–Cotes quadrature is the choice of quadrature points. We know from Section 3.4.4 that evenly spaced interpolatory points, in theory and in our experiment, lead to less accurate interpolation than use of Chebyshev points. It is therefore natural to speculate that interpolatory quadrature with Chebyshev points might be more accurate than Newton–Cotes quadrature. In fact, we altered the program in Table 4.17 by declaring (but using double-precision notation, of course) that

$$x_k = \frac{a + b}{2} + \frac{a - b}{2} \cos \left(\frac{2k - 1}{2n} \pi \right),$$

as defined in (3.17).

From Table 4.19 we see that some improvement of accuracy and stability over the Newton–Cotes points has been obtained. But much more impressive improve-ment will be realized in Section 4.6, where Gauss quadrature is revealed. Gauss quadrature makes a systematic science of quadrature point selection.

TABLE 4.17   Program to Compare Compound Simpson's and Newton–Cotes Integration

```
C       PROGRAM COMPARISON
C
C       *************************************************************
C       COMPARES NEWTON-COTES AND SIMPSON'S RULE ON THE
C       INTEGRAL OF F(X)=10*SIN(1-0.1*X) OVER [0.,10.]
C       CALLS:COEFF,GAUS1,SIMP(MODIFIED FOR DOUBLE PRECISION)
C       OUTPUT: NN(I)=NUMBER OF POINTS
C               TRUE=TRUE INTEGRAL OF F(X)
C               S=NEWTON-COTES INTEGRAL ESTIMATE OF F(X)
C               ERRS=NEWTON-COTES ERROR
C               E=SIMPSON'S INTEGRAL ESTIMATE OF F(X)
C               ERRE=SIMPSON'S ERROR
C       *************************************************************
C
        IMPLICIT DOUBLE PRECISION(A-H,O-Z)
        DIMENSION X(250),AA(250),NN(20)
        DATA (NN(I),I=1,9)/3,5,7,9,11,13,15,19,21/
        V=1.0D0
        A=0.0D0
        B=10.0D0
        TRUE=100.0D0*(1.0D0-DCOS(V))
C
C       *** ITERATES ON THE NUMBER OF POINTS                        ***
C
        DO 6 I=1,9
           H=(B-A)/(NN(I)-1)
           X(1)=A
           DO 3 J=2,NN(I)
              X(J)=X(J-1)+H
3       CONTINUE
C
C       *** SUBROUTINE COEFF COMPUTES INTEGRATION COEFFICIENTS ***
C       *** OF NEWTON-COTES METHOD                             ***
C
        CALL COEFF(NN(I),X,A,B,AA)
        S=0.0D0
        DO 4 J=1,NN(I)
C
C       *** COMPUTES INTEGRAL BY NEWTON-COTES RULE                  ***
C
           S=S+AA(J)*F(X(J))
4       CONTINUE
        ERRS=TRUE-S
C
C       *** SUBROUTINE SIMP COMPUTES INTEGRAL BY SIMPSON'S RULE***
C
        CALL SIMP(A,B,NN(I)-1,E)
        ERRE=TRUE-E
        WRITE(10,7)NN(I),ERRS,ERRE
7       FORMAT(10X,I2,2(3X,F17.10))
6    CONTINUE
     STOP
     END
C
C       *** SUBROUTINE FUNCTION F COMPUTES THE FUNCTIONAL         ***
C       *** VALUES AT THE POINT X                                ***
C
        REAL*8 FUNCTION F(X)
        IMPLICIT DOUBLE PRECISION(A-H,O-Z)
        V=1.0D0-0.1D0*X
        F=10.0D0*DSIN(V)
        RETURN
        END
```

TABLE 4.18   Error Comparison for Example 4.13

Number of Points	Error, Newton–Cotes	Error, Simpson
3	-0.0164495739	-0.0164495739
5	0.0000245534	-0.0010050795
7	-0.0000000304	-0.0001977119
9	-0.0000000003	-0.0000624667
11	0.0000000000	-0.0000255692
13	-0.0000000021	-0.0000123263
15	0.0000017216	-0.0000066520
19	0.0590227117	-0.0000024337
21	27.1303181091	-0.0000015966
31		-0.0000003153
91		-0.0000000039
151		-0.0000000005
201		-0.0000000002

TABLE 4.19   Interpolatory Quadrature with Chebyshev Points

Number of Points	Error or Interpolatory Quadrature Using Chebyshev Points
5	0.00000305634
7	-0.00000000160
9	0.00000000000
11	0.00000000100
13	-0.00000000272
15	0.00000001234
19	-0.00042770685
21	-0.01569321089
23	0.10685271142

The practical significance of truncation error analysis may be assessed from Table 4.18. From Table 4.16 we know that the error of Simpson's rule is proportional to h^4. So if $h_2 = h_1/2$, for instance, the errors err (h_1) and err (h_2) ought to be related by

$$\text{err } (h_2) \cong \text{err } (h_1) \left(\frac{h_2}{h_1}\right)^4 = \frac{\text{err } (h_1)}{16},$$

assuming that $f^{(4)}(x)$ changes slowly. For the number of points 5 and 9, the ratio of step sizes equals $\frac{1}{2}$, and the ratio of errors is in fact, very close to $\frac{1}{16}$. Similarly, the reader can check that for 11 and 21 points, the ratio of errors is again very close to $\frac{1}{16}$.

The essence of the situation is that Newton–Cotes integration, if done carefully, can be appreciably more accurate than the Simpson method, but because of the instability of the associated system of linear equations for a large number of points, care must be exercised. In this regard it is useful to note from examination of (4.16) that the solution of the system of linear equations does not depend on the integrand. So before accepting an answer concerning an unknown integral, we can check the Newton–Cotes coefficients computed by COEFF by applying them to integrals having known values.

Let us examine the effect of roundoff errors of the functional values. Assume that instead of the true values $f(x_k)$, only their approximations $\bar{f}_k$ are known, and that for all values of k, we have an absolute error bound δ. That is,

$$|f(x_k) - \bar{f}_k| \leq \delta. \tag{4.27}$$

Then the roundoff error of the trapezoidal rule can be bounded as follows:

$$|h[\tfrac{1}{2}f(x_0) + f(x_1) + \cdots + f(x_{N-1}) + \tfrac{1}{2}f(x_N)] - h(\tfrac{1}{2}\bar{f}_0 + \bar{f}_1 + \cdots + \bar{f}_{N-1} + \tfrac{1}{2}\bar{f}_N)|$$
$$\leq h[\tfrac{1}{2}|f(x_0) - \bar{f}_0| + |f(x_1) - \bar{f}_1| + \cdots + |f(x_{N-1}) - \bar{f}_{N-1}|$$
$$+ \tfrac{1}{2}|f(x_N) - \bar{f}_N|] \leq hN\,\delta = (b - a)\,\delta.$$

The bound $(b - a)\,\delta$ is valid for all compound and interpolatory quadrature formulas having no negative coefficients. For any such rule (this includes trapezoidal, midpoint, and Simpson's rules),

$$\left| I_N(\bar{f}) - \int_a^b f(x)\,dx \right| \leq O(h^p) + (b - a)\,\delta,$$

where p is the order of the error and $I_N(\bar{f})$ is the value of the numerical integration formula computed using imperfect functional values $\bar{f}_k$, and $O(h^p)$ is a bound for the error of the integration formula when the correct functional values are used. From its definition,

$$O(h^p) \to 0 \qquad \text{as} \qquad h \to 0.$$

So, ignoring roundoff effects, no harm is done (except perhaps some wasted computational expense) if a very small step size h is used. By contrast, we saw in Section 4.2 that in numerical differentiation formulas, the step size shows up in the denominator of the term representing the effect of functional error. As the step size decreases, therefore, the error of the computed derivative can become arbitrarily large. (If h is so small that an enormously large N is needed, smearing can occur. This effect motivates Problem 24.)

4.5
EXTRAPOLATION AND ROMBERG INTEGRATION

Richardson extrapolation, described in the optional section that follows, is a powerful but subtle concept serving as the foundation for Romberg quadrature and other numerical methods. The section after that, on the implementation of the popular and efficient Romberg quadrature method, may be read independently.

★4.5.1   Richardson's Extrapolation and Corrected Formulas

The notion of Richardson's extrapolation will be described in the context of "correcting" the compound trapezoidal formula t_N given by (4.21). As in the preceding section, we wish to approximate $\int_a^b f(x)\,dx$. Let $h = (b - a)/N$ and assume that

$f(x)$ is a function with a Taylor's series representation valid over the interval $[a, b]$. Then (S & Y 1978, Sec. 3.2.4) there exist constants $c_2, c_4, \ldots$, which depend on $f(x)$, the interval $[a, b]$, but not on N or h, such that

$$\int_a^b f(x) \, dx - t_N = c_2 h^2 + c_4 h^4 + c_6 h^6 + \cdots. \tag{4.28}$$

For some N, let h be $(b - a)/N$, and then note that if N is doubled, the step size becomes $h/2$, and therefore

$$\int_a^b f(x) \, dx - t_{2N} = c_2 \frac{h^2}{4} + c_4 \frac{h^4}{16} + c_6 \frac{h^6}{64} + \cdots. \tag{4.29}$$

By subtracting the multiple 4 of this equation from (4.28) with step size h, we get the relation

$$-3 \int_a^b f(x) \, dx + 4t_{2N} - t_N = c_4(1 - \tfrac{1}{4})h^4 + c_6(1 - \tfrac{1}{16})h^6 + \cdots, \tag{4.30}$$

which implies that

$$\int_a^b f(x) \, dx - \tfrac{1}{3}(4t_{2N} - t_N) = d_4 h^4 + d_6 h^6 + \cdots, \tag{4.31}$$

where $d_4, d_6, \ldots$, are also independent of h or N.

The quadrature formula

$$\tilde{t}_{2N} = \tfrac{1}{3}(4t_{2N} - t_N) \tag{4.32}$$

is called the *corrected* trapezoidal formula. It has the characteristic that its truncation error is, in view of (4.31), $O(h^4)$ instead of merely $O(h^2)$, the order of the "uncorrected" trapezoidal formula. In turns out that the corrected trapezoidal formula coincides with the Simpson rule, as may be verified by simple algebra. So at this stage we have only a new idea, not a new formula. The idea of adding together two formulas dependent on h so as to remove the lowest term in the power series expansion of the truncation error is known as *Richardson's extrapolation*. Its repeated application to remove successively higher terms in the truncation error expansion of the trapezoidal formula leads us to the Romberg integration method of the following section. Let us proceed one more step along this pathway. Noting that $\tilde{t}_{2N}$ defined by (4.32) is really the Simpson formula s_{2N}, as in (4.31), we obtain

$$\int_a^b f(x) \, dx - s_{2N} = d_4 h^4 + d_6 h^6 + \cdots,$$

where the coefficients $d_4, d_6, \ldots$ are independent of N and h. And as in the first extrapolation, a judicious sum of s_N and s_{2N} can rid us of the h^4 term. Specifically, the Richardson correction of the Simpson formula gives us the representation

$$\int_a^b f(x) \, dx = \tfrac{1}{15}(16s_{2N} - s_N) + O(h^6). \tag{4.33}$$

The corrected Simpson rule is

$$\tilde{s}_{2N} = \tfrac{1}{15}(16s_{2N} - s_N),$$

which is known as *Bode's rule*. From (4.33), its truncation error is $O(h^6)$, whereas the uncorrected rule (4.31) was $O(h^4)$. As seen in the next example, increasing the order of the truncation error can have dramatic practical significance.

──────── **EXAMPLE 4.14** ──

We apply the corrected Simpson's formula immediately above, with $N = 2$, to our familiar integral

$$\int_0^{10} 10 \sin (1 - 0.1x) \, dx.$$

In our computations using subroutine SIMP, in double precision, we found the following:

Formula	Estimate	Error
s_2	45.9862	0.016450
s_4	45.9707	0.001005
$\tilde{s}_4 = \tfrac{1}{15}(16s_4 - s_2)$	45.969769	0.000022

The improvement in accuracy achieved by Richardson extrapolation is remarkable. This idea is fundamental to the integration procedure in the next section. ∎

4.5.2 Romberg Integration

The error of the trapezoidal rule (4.21) is known to satisfy

$$\int_a^b f(x) \, dx - t_N = c_2 h^2 + c_4 h^4 + \cdots. \tag{4.34}$$

Here $h = (b - a)/N$ and the constants $c_2, c_4, \ldots$ do not depend on N. We have used this observation and Richardson extrapolation to construct the Simpson method as the corrected trapezoidal rule, wherein the h^2 term in the error is eliminated. Repeated use of this idea, eliminating successively the h^2, h^4, h^6, $\ldots$ terms in the truncation error, leads to *Romberg integration*. The method can be described as follows.

First define the numbers

$$T_{0,k} = t_{2^k} \quad (k = 0, 1, 2, \ldots, M), \tag{4.35}$$

where M is a given positive integer and t_{2^k} is the 2^k-point trapezoidal rule. The successive values of $T_{0,k}$ can be found efficiently from the recursion

$$T_{0,k} = \frac{T_{0,k-1}}{2} + h_k[f(a + h_k) + f(a + 3h_k) + f(a + 5h_k) + \cdots$$
$$+ f(a + (2^k - 1)h_k)],$$
(4.36)

where $h_k = (b - a)/2^k$. Then, for $l = 1, 2, \ldots, M$, recursively obtain

$$T_{l,k} = \frac{1}{4^l - 1} (4^l T_{l-1,k} - T_{l-1,k-1}) \qquad (k = l, l + 1, \ldots, M).$$
(4.37)

The value T_{MM} is the Romberg approximation of the integral.

━━━━━ **EXAMPLE 4.15** ━━━━━

We compute the Romberg approximation T_{22} for $\int_{-1}^{1} e^x \, dx$. First, from (4.35) and the definition of the trapezoid rule, we get

$$T_{00} = t_{2^0} = t_1 = \frac{h}{2} (f_1 + f_0).$$

Set $a = -1$, $b = 1$, and $h_0 = (b - a)/2^0 = 2$. Then calculate

$$T_{00} = 2 \cdot (\tfrac{1}{2} \exp(-1) + \tfrac{1}{2} \exp(1)) = 3.086161.$$

Now by (4.36), obtain

$$T_{01} = \frac{T_{00}}{2} + h_1 f(a + h_1),$$

where $h_1 = (b - a)/2^1 = 1$, $a + h_1 = 0$. Thus

$$T_{01} = \frac{T_{00}}{2} + 1 \cdot e^0 = 2.543081$$

and with $k = 2$, $h_2 = (b - a)/2^2 = \tfrac{1}{2}$. So

$$T_{02} = \frac{T_{01}}{2} + h_2[f(a + h_2) + f(a + 3h_2)]$$
$$= \frac{T_{01}}{2} + \frac{1}{2} (e^{-1/2} + e^{1/2})$$
$$= 2.399166.$$

Now apply (4.37) to find

$$T_{11} = \tfrac{1}{3}(4T_{01} - T_{00}) = 2.362054$$

and

$$T_{12} = \tfrac{1}{3}(4T_{02} - T_{01}) = 2.351195.$$

Finally, again use the relation (4.37) with $l = 2$, to obtain

$$T_{22} = \tfrac{1}{15}(16T_{12} - T_{11}) = 2.350471.$$

Hence the Romberg estimate is $T_{22} = 2.350471$. For comparison, note that the exact value of the integral is

$$\int_{-1}^{1} e^x \, dx = e^1 - e^{-1} = 2.350402$$

to the accuracy shown.

■

In practice, it is convenient to compute the array $\{T_{l,k}\}$ column by column in the order indicated by Figure 4.14. The tails of the arrows pointing to a term show that quantities needed for the calculation of that term.

An adaptive stopping criterion in Romberg integration can be derived as follows. From relation (4.28) we conclude that

$$r_k = \frac{I - T_{0,k+1}}{I - T_{0,k}} \approx \frac{1}{4},$$

where I is the exact value of the integral. The Romberg iterations can stop whenever

$$|T_{k+1,k+1} - T_{0,k+1}| > \tfrac{1}{2}|T_{k+1,k+1} - T_{0,k}|$$

with the idea in mind that if $T_{k+1,k+1}$ is close to I, roundoff error in evaluating $f(x)$ is becoming a limiting factor.

Table 4.20 gives a listing of subroutine ROMB, which performs Romberg integration. The array **T** gives the values of $T_{l,k}$ $l \le k \le M$. The value of $T_{M,M}$ is returned to the main program by the calling parameter E.

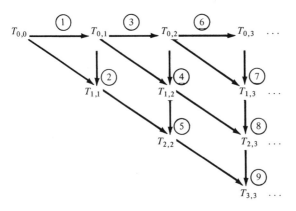

FIGURE 4.14 Order of Computations for Romberg Integration

TABLE 4.20   Subroutine ROMB for Romberg Integration

```
      SUBROUTINE ROMB(A,B,M,E)
C
C     ****************************************************************
C     *   FUNCTION: APPROXIMATES THE INTEGRAL OF F(X) OVER THE       *
C     *             INTERVAL [A,B] BY THE ROMBERG METHOD             *
C     *   USAGE:                                                     *
C     *       CALL SEQUENCE: CALL ROMB(A,B,M,E)                      *
C     *       EXTERNAL FUNCTIONS/SUBROUTINES: FUNCTION F(X)          *
C     *   PARAMETERS:                                                *
C     *       INPUT:                                                 *
C     *           A=INTERVAL LEFT ENDPOINT                           *
C     *           B=INTERVAL RIGHT ENDPOINT                          *
C     *           M=NUMBER OF ITERATIVE STEPS                        *
C     *             (NOT GREATER THAN 100)                           *
C     *       OUTPUT:                                                *
C     *           E=ESTIMATE OF THE INTEGRAL                         *
C     ****************************************************************
C
      DIMENSION T(101,101)
C     *** INITIALIZATION ***
      K=1
      H=B-A
      T(1,1)=(F(A)+F(B))/2.0*H
      DO 1 I=2,M+1
C     *** COMPUTE THE TRAPEZOIDAL TERM ***
        K=2*K
        H=H/2.0
        X=A-H
        E=0.0
        T(1,I)=T(1,I-1)/2.0
        DO 2 J=1,K-1,2
          X=X+2.0*H
          E=E+F(X)
    2   CONTINUE
C     *** RICHARDSON EXTRAPOLATION ***
        T(1,I)=T(1,I)+E*H
        LA=1
        DO 3 J=2,I
          LA=LA*4
          T(J,I)=(LA*T(J-1,I)-T(J-1,I-1))/(LA-1)
    3   CONTINUE
    1 CONTINUE
      E=T(M+1,M+1)
      RETURN
      END
```

──────── **EXAMPLE 4.16** ────────

The Romberg subroutine was called upon to evaluate the integral

$$\int_0^{10} 10 \sin (1 - 0.1x) \, dx,$$

which has served us in earlier examples. The number of extrapolations was set to $M = 5$. To the number of places shown, 45,96977 is the correct answer. From the printout shown in Table 4.21, one sees that the values of $T_{l,k}$ tend to increase in accuracy quite dramatically with increase in l, in accordance with the discussion that immediately follows this example.

TABLE 4.21   Romberg Integration Terms $T_{l,k}$

		0	1	2	3	4	5
					k		
	0	42.07355	45.00806	45.73010	45.90990	45.95481	45.96603
	1	0.00000	45.98623	45.97078	45.96984	45.96978	45.96978
1	2	0.00000	0.00000	45.96975	45.96978	45.96978	45.96978
	3	0.00000	0.00000	0.00000	45.96978	45.96978	45.96978
	4	0.00000	0.00000	0.00000	0.00000	45.96978	45.96978
	5	0.00000	0.00000	0.00000	0.00000	0.00000	45.96978

Let us examine the error of Romberg integration. Construction (4.35) implies that $T_{0,k}$ is a trapezoidal rule. Results in the preceding subsection imply that $T_{1,k}$ is a Simpson's formula and $T_{2,k}$ is Bode's rule. Repeated application of the Richardson extrapolation technique and finite induction implies that for some array of constants $\{\gamma_{l,k}\}$,

$$\int_a^b f(x)\,dx - T_{l,k} = \sum_{j=l+1}^\infty \gamma_{l,j}\left(\frac{b-a}{2^k}\right)^{2j}, \tag{4.38}$$

a formula derived in S & Y, Sec. 3.2.5.

The effectiveness of Romberg integration, in terms of its order of error, simplicity, and stability, is quite remarkable. The accuracy cannot readily be seen from the limited number of digits displayed in Table 4.21, but in fact, the error of $T_{2,3}$ is 2.45×10^{-5}; $T_{3,3}$, -9.6×10^{-9}; and $T_{4,4}$, 99.5×10^{-13}. $T_{2,2}$ is a Newton–Cotes rule, and the error of $T_{3,3}$ is only about a factor of 30 greater than the (nine-point) Newton–Cotes rule using exactly the same data as reported in Table 4.18. Linear equation instabilities, which plague the Newton–Cotes procedure, are not a factor with Romberg formulas. Moreover, it is known (Davis and Rabinowitz, 1975, Chap. 6) that in the absence of roundoff, as M grows, $T_{M,M}$ converges to the exact integral for any (Riemann) integrable function. On the other hand, Newton–Cotes quadrature may diverge as the number of points increases, for some continuous integrands. However, interpolatory integration is not to be discarded. The supreme integration rule, in terms of accuracy and stability, Gaussian quadrature, is an interpolatory rule. This method occupies the following section.

Application 4.5

Modern digital feedback and hydraulic systems are making it increasingly practical to design suspension systems of automobiles and other vehicles to follow any desired rule. For example, the designer can effectively choose any nonlinear spring force law $F(x)$ that seems reasonable. With reference to Figure 4.15, the energy absorbed by a spring after it has been compressed a distance x_L is, according to basic physics,

$$\int_0^{x_L} F(x)\,dx.$$

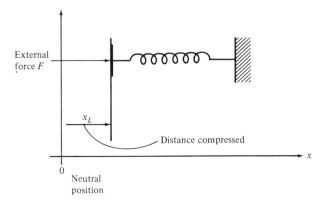

FIGURE 4.15   Spring Compression

Suppose a spring has been designed so that the reactive force is

$$F(x) = 20 \sin \left(\frac{x^2}{100} \right) \qquad \text{newtons.}$$

The question to be answered is: How much energy is absorbed in a 5-cm compression? The work between points $a = 0$ and $b = 5$, then, is given by

$$\int_0^5 20 \sin \left(\frac{x^2}{100} \right) dx \qquad \text{N} \cdot \text{cm.}$$

This integral does not have a closed-form representation in terms of the common functions. We resort, therefore, to numerical methods. Our plan is to use Romberg quadrature to achieve high accuracy and relative stability, without recourse to tables or sophistication. We let the Romberg parameter M in subroutine ROMB (Table 4.20) vary between 2 and 5, and if the associated estimates lie close to each other, we take that as a sign that the truncation error is correspondingly small. For so few points, one would not anticipate roundoff to be a problem.

For $M = 3$, 4, and 5, the computed integral "held steady" at 8.2962048 $N \cdot$ cm. We accept this as our approximation of the work.

$\diamondsuit$

4.6
GAUSS QUADRATURE

In Section 4.3 we saw that for any choice of interpolating points $x_1, \ldots, x_n$, the interpolatory-type integration formula (4.15) gives the true value of the integral when $f(x)$ is a polynomial of degree not exceeding $n - 1$. We will see that by choosing $x_1, \ldots, x_n$ wisely, the degree of polynomials that can be integrated exactly by an n-point rule is more than doubled, going from $n - 1$ to $2n - 1$. We assume that the interval for integration is $[-1, 1]$. Later we will discuss how to transform any finite interval of integration to $[-1, 1]$.

In (4.16), the interpolating points were assumed to be given and the values $A_1, \ldots, A_n$ were unknowns. If we are also allowed to select the interpolating points, the number of unknowns in (4.16) is equal to $2n$, since the interpolating points are also variables. Consequently, we can add on more equations to (4.16) in order to have the same number of variables (i.e., $A_1, \ldots, A_n, x_1, \ldots, x_n$) and equations. These additional equations are determined by the condition that the numerical integration formulas should give the exact value of the integral for polynomials of as high a degree as possible. This idea leads us to the set of $2n$ equations:

$$A_1 x_1^0 + A_2 x_2^0 + \cdots + A_n x_n^0 = \int_{-1}^{1} 1 \, dx = (+1) - (-1) = 2$$

$$A_1 x_1^1 + A_2 x_2^1 + \cdots + A_n x_n^1 = \int_{-1}^{1} x \, dx = \frac{(+1)^2 - (-1)^2}{2} = 0$$

$$\cdots \cdots$$

$$A_1 x_1^k + A_2 x_2^k + \cdots + A_n x_n^k = \frac{(+1)^{k+1} - (-1)^{k+1}}{k + 1}$$

$$= \begin{cases} 0 & \text{if } k \text{ is odd} \\ \\ \dfrac{2}{k + 1} & \text{if } k \text{ is even} \end{cases} \tag{4.39}$$

$$\cdots \cdots$$

$$A_1 x_1^{2n-1} + A_2 x_2^{2n-1} + \cdots + A_n x_n^{2n-1} = \frac{(+1)^{2n} - (-1)^{2n}}{2n} = 0.$$

Notice how this generalizes (4.16), with $a = -1$ and $b = 1$. Relation (4.39) is a system of $2n$ equations, and (4.16) is a system of n equations. In (4.39), the x_j's as well as the A_j's are regarded as variables, whereas in (4.16), only the A_j's are to be found.

For any $n = 1, 2, \ldots$, this system (4.39) of nonlinear equations has a unique solution satisfying $-1 < x_k < 1$, and $A_k > 0$ ($1 \leq k \leq n$) (Davis and Rabinowitz, 1975, Sec. 2.7). The interpolatory-type quadrature formula

$$\int_{-1}^{1} f(x) \, dx \approx A_1 f(x_1) + A_2 f(x_2) + \cdots + A_n f(x_n), \tag{4.40}$$

having the coefficients A_k and interpolating points x_k ($1 \leq k \leq n$) which satisfy (4.39), is called *Gauss quadrature*.

───── **EXAMPLE 4.17** ─────────────────────────────

For $n = 1$, equations (4.39) have the form

$$A_1 x_1^0 = A_1 = 2$$

$$A_1 x_1^1 = A_1 x_1 = 0,$$

which implies that $A_1 = 2$ and $x_1 = 0$. The one-point Gaussian formula, then, is

$$\int_{-1}^{1} f(x)\, dx = 2f(0).$$

This coincides with the simple midpoint formula discussed in Section 4.3. For $n = 2$, equations (4.39) have the form

$$A_1 x_1^0 + A_2 x_2^0 = 2$$

$$A_1 x_1 + A_2 x_2 = 0 \qquad\qquad (4.41)$$

$$A_1 x_1^2 + A_2 x_2^2 = \tfrac{2}{3}$$

$$A_1 x_1^3 + A_2 x_2^3 = 0.$$

The reader can check by substitution that the solution is

$$x_1 = -\frac{\sqrt{3}}{3}, \qquad x_2 = \frac{\sqrt{3}}{3}, \qquad A_1 = A_2 = 1.$$

Thus we have the Gauss quadrature formula for $n = 2$, namely

$$\int_{-1}^{1} f(x)\, dx \approx f\left(-\frac{\sqrt{3}}{3}\right) + f\left(\frac{\sqrt{3}}{3}\right).$$

Application of this two-point rule to our familiar integral

$$\int_{-1}^{1} \exp(x)\, dx$$

yields the estimate 2.3426. This is more accurate than the three-point Newton–Cotes rule, and almost as accurate as the five-point ($M = 4$) Simpson formula, in this case. ∎

One can derive the solution of (4.41) from a tedious algebraic hand calculation, but for three or more points, one must bring in more sophisticated analytic tools and a digital computer. We will point the interested reader toward concepts and source material on determination of Gauss quadrature points at the close of this section. A computational method is given as Application 5.3 in Chapter 5.

In Figure 4.16 we have compared the areas associated with the two-point trapezoidal and Gauss rules. One sees that with its centered data points, the Gauss rule does have some capacity to account for changing slopes.

The points and weights of several Gauss-quadrature formulas are given in Table 4.22. A more extensive table, with values stated to 20 significant decimal places, is given as Table 25.4 of Abramowitz and Stegun (1965). The use of Table 4.22 is as follows: Pick any number n of points, and then, for $i = 1, 2, \ldots, n$,

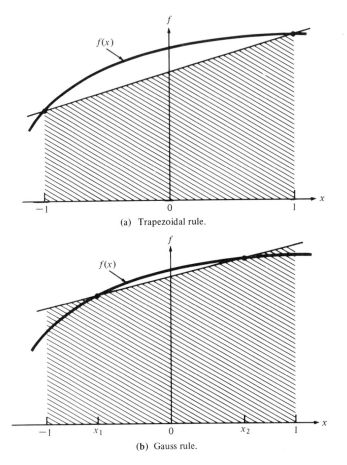

(a) Trapezoidal rule.

(b) Gauss rule.

FIGURE 4.16 Comparison of 2-point Gauss and Trapezoidal Rules

repeat the following step. If $i \leq n/2 + \frac{1}{2}$, A_i and x_i are tabulated. If $i > n/2 + \frac{1}{2}$, then select $A_i = A_{n+1-i}$ and $x_i = -x_{n+1-i}$, where A_{n+1-i} and x_{n+1-i} are tabulated. As an example, take $n = 5$. Then $i \leq \frac{5}{2} + \frac{1}{2} = 3.0$ is satisfied for $i = 1, 2,$ and 3, and from the table you see that $x_1, x_2, x_3, A_1, A_2, A_3$ are tabulated. If $i = 4$, then $n + 1 - i = 6 - 4 = 2$, and if $i = 5$, then $n + 1 - i = 1$. Consequently, to the accuracy shown,

$$A_4 = A_2 \approx 0.4786, \qquad A_5 = A_1 \approx 0.2369, \qquad A_3 \approx 0.5689$$

and

$$x_4 = -x_2 \approx 0.5385, \qquad x_5 = -x_1 \approx 0.9062, \qquad x_3 = 0.0000.$$

In brief, the five-point Gauss rule is, to four significant places,

$$GA_5 = 0.2369 \cdot (f(-0.9062) + f(0.9062))$$
$$+ 0.4786 \cdot (f(-0.5385) + f(0.5385)) + 0.5689 \cdot f(0).$$

TABLE 4.22 Gauss Quadrature Weights and Coefficients

Number, n, of Points	Gauss Quadrature Weights, A_j			
	A_1	A_2	A_3	A_4
1	2.0000000000000000			
2	1.0000000000000000			
3	0.5555555555555555	0.8888888888888888		
4	0.3478548451374538	0.6521451548625461		
5	0.2369268850561890	0.4786286704993664	0.5688888888888888	
6	0.1713244923791703	0.3607615730481386	0.4679139345726910	
7	0.1294849661688696	0.2797053914892766	0.3818300505051189	0.4179591836734693

Number, n, of Points	Gauss Quadrature Points, x_j			
	x_1	x_2	x_3	x_4
1	0.0000000000000000			
2	-0.5773502691896257			
3	-0.7745966692414833	0.0000000000000000		
4	-0.8611363115940525	-0.3399810435848562		
5	-0.9061798459386639	-0.5384693101056830	0.0000000000000000	
6	-0.9324695142031520	-0.6612093864662645	-0.2386191860831969	
7	-0.9491079123427585	-0.7415311855993944	-0.4058451513773971	0.0000000000000000

We applied this rule, using the full accuracy of Table 4.22, to

$$\int_{-1}^{1} \exp(x)\, dx$$

and obtained the approximation

$$GA_5 = 2.350403.$$

This is accurate to the limit of the single-precision variables used for the calculation on a VAX computer. It is instructive to compare the accuracy to entries in Table 4.14, which listed results from other five-point rules applied to this integral. The error of the five-point Gauss rule is less than a percent of the Newton–Cotes error, and the trapezoidal rule gave only two-place accuracy.

The computer subroutine GAQU for Gauss quadrature is given in Table 4.23. The Gaussian quadrature weights A_k and quadrature points x_k of Table 4.22 are presumed to be in the user's file area, in a file named GAUSS.DAT. Gauss quadrature is so very accurate that there is little need to tabulate beyond seven points, as given.

So far in our discussion and tabulation of Gauss quadrature points, we have been limited to the integration domain $[-1, 1]$. There is a classical trick from calculus by which any finite interval of integration can be transformed to any other interval. By using this device (which is embedded in the routine GAQU), one can make $[-1, 1]$ serve all domains.

TABLE 4.23   Subroutine GAQU for Gauss Quadrature

```
      SUBROUTINE GAQU(A,B,N,E)
C
C     ****************************************************************
C     *  FUNCTION: THIS SUBROUTINE COMPUTES THE AREA (INTEGRAL)      *
C     *            UNDER THE CURVE F(X) OVER THE INTERVAL [A,B]      *
C     *            USING GAUSSIAN QUADRATURE                         *
C     *  USAGE:                                                      *
C     *      CALL SEQUENCE: CALL GAQU(A,B,N,E)                       *
C     *      EXTERNAL FUNCTIONS/SUBROUTINES: FUNCTION F(X)           *
C     *      EXTERNAL DATA FILES:GAUSS.DAT                           *
C     *  PARAMETERS:                                                 *
C     *      INPUT:                                                  *
C     *          A=INTERVAL LEFT ENDPOINT                            *
C     *          B=INTERVAL RIGHT ENDPOINT                           *
C     *          N=NUMBER OF INTERPOLATING POINTS                    *
C     *          (NOT GREATER THAN 7)                                *
C     *          E=VALUE OF THE INTEGRAL                             *
C     ****************************************************************
C
      DIMENSION X(10),AA(10)
C
C     *** OBTAIN THE QUADRATURE POINTS AND QUADRATURE ***
C     *** WEIGHTS FOR GAUSS QUADRATURE                ***
C
      OPEN(UNIT=10,FILE='GAUSS.DAT',STATUS='OLD')

      DO I = 1,N-1
        READ(10,*)DUMMY
      ENDDO
      READ(10,*)(AA(I),I=1,(N+1)/2)
      DO I =1,6
        READ(10,*)DUMMY
      ENDDO
      READ(10,*)(X(I),I=1,(N+1)/2)

      CLOSE(10)

C     *** INITIALIZATION ***
      E=0.0
      V=(B-A)/2.0
      W=(A+B)/2.0
C     *** COMPUTE GAUSSIAN QUADRATURE FACTORS ***
      DO 1 I=1,(N+1)/2
        X1=V*X(I)+W
        XX1=-V*X(I)+W
        IF(X1.EQ.XX1)THEN
          E=E+F(X1)*AA(I)
        ELSE
          E=E+(F(X1)+F(XX1))*AA(I)
        ENDIF
    1 CONTINUE
      E=V*E
      RETURN
      END
```

Toward deriving this transformation method, consider the integral

$$I = \int_a^b f(x)\ dx.$$

By substituting the variable

$$t = \alpha x + \beta,$$

we have that

$$I = \int_{\alpha a + \beta}^{\alpha b + \beta} f\left(\frac{t - \beta}{\alpha}\right) \cdot \frac{1}{\alpha} \, dt,$$

since from the defining equation of t, we conclude that

$$x = \frac{t - \beta}{\alpha}$$

and

$$\frac{dx}{dt} = \frac{1}{\alpha} \qquad \text{or} \qquad dx = \frac{1}{\alpha} \, dt.$$

The coefficients α and β should be selected so that the integration domain of the transformed integral is the interval $[-1, 1]$. That is,

$$\alpha a + \beta = -1$$
$$\alpha b + \beta = 1.$$

These equations imply that

$$\alpha = \frac{-2}{a - b} \qquad \text{and} \qquad \beta = \frac{a + b}{a - b}.$$

Hence after rearrangement of terms,

$$I = \int_{-1}^{1} \frac{b - a}{2} f\left(\frac{b - a}{2} t + \frac{b + a}{2}\right) dt.$$

Consequently, if the quadrature points and weights for the integration domain $[-1, 1]$ are (x_k, A_k), $k = 1, 2, \ldots, n$, then

$$\boxed{\int_a^b f(x) \, dx \approx \frac{b - a}{2} \sum_{k=1}^{n} A_k f\left(\frac{b - a}{2} x_k + \frac{b + a}{2}\right).} \qquad (4.42)$$

This simple technique for conversion of integration domains to a fixed interval $[-1, 1]$ makes quadrature point and weight tables such as Table 4.22 and handbook tables (e.g., Abramowitz and Stegun, 1965, Chap. 25) universally applicable.

──────── **EXAMPLE 4.18** ──

The task here is to approximate $\int_{2.0}^{2.5} e^t \, dt$ by using three-point Guass quadrature and Table 4.22. In the notation of (4.42), $a = 2.0$, $b = 2.5$, so

$$\frac{b - a}{2} = \frac{0.5}{2} = 0.25, \qquad \frac{b + a}{2} = \frac{4.5}{2} = 2.25.$$

According to Table 4.22, the Gauss quadrature rule with three points for the interval $[-1, 1]$ is

$$\int_{-1}^{1} f(x)\, dx \approx A_1 f(x_1) + A_2 f(x_2) + A_3 f(x_3)$$

with $A_1 = A_3 \approx 0.555556$, $A_2 \approx 0.888889$, and $x_1 = -x_3 \approx -0.774597$, $x_2 \approx 0.000000$. Hence, by (4.42),

$$\int_{2.0}^{2.5} e^t\, dt = 0.25\,\{0.555556 \cdot \exp\,[0.25(-0.774597) + 2.25]$$

$$+\ 0.888889 \cdot \exp\,[0.25(0.000000) + 2.25]$$

$$+\ 0.555556 \cdot \exp\,[0.25(0.774597) + 2.25]\}$$

$$=\ 0.25\,\{0.888889 \cdot \exp\,(2.25)$$

$$+\ 0.555556 \cdot [\exp\,(0.25 \cdot 0.774597 + 2.25)$$

$$+\ \exp\,(-0.25 \cdot 0.774597 + 2.25)]\}$$

$$=\ 4.793440.$$

The correct value of the integral, to the accuracy shown, is 4.793438.

EXAMPLE 4.19

By way of comparison with earlier quadrature examples, we computed the approximating values of the integral

$$\int_{0}^{10} 10 \sin\,(1 - 0.1x)\, dx$$

using Gauss quadrature rules with two, three, and five points. Gauss quadrature is at its best when, as in this case, the function is smooth (i.e., f has many derivatives and the magnitudes of these derivatives do not grow quickly with increasing order). From Table 4.24 we see how phenomenal the performance of Gauss quadrature can be. Since the answer is about 45.969759, with but two points, the approximation is correct to four significant decimal places, and with but three points, the estimate is correct to seven figures.

TABLE 4.24 Comparison of Accuracy for Different Quadrature Rules

Number of Points	Quadrature Errors					
	Midpoint	Trapezoidal	Simpson	Romberg	Newton–Cotes	Gauss
2	$-4.8 \cdot 10^{-1}$	3.9	[a]	[a]	3.9	$1.1 \cdot 10^{-2}$
3	$-2.1 \cdot 10^{-1}$	$9.6 \cdot 10^{-1}$	$1.6 \cdot 10^{-2}$	[a]	$1.6 \cdot 10^{-2}$	$-2.4 \cdot 10^{-5}$
5	$-7.7 \cdot 10^{-2}$	$2.4 \cdot 10^{-1}$	$-1.0 \cdot 10^{-3}$	$-2.4 \cdot 10^{-5}$	$-2.4 \cdot 10^{-5}$	$-1.9 \cdot 10^{-11}$

[a]There is no n-point rule of this type.

It can be proven (see S & Y, 1978, pp. 93–94) that for continuous functions the Gauss quadrature formulas converge to the exact value of the integral as $n \rightarrow \infty$. If $f(x)$ is $2n$-times differentiable, the error term of Gauss quadrature is given by

$$\int_{-1}^{1} f(x) \, dx - \sum_{i=1}^{n} A_i f(x_i) = \frac{(n!)^4 2^{2n+1} f^{(2n)}(\eta)}{((2n)!)^3 (2n+1)}, \qquad (4.43)$$

where $\eta \in (-1, 1)$.

From the preceding discussion and example, we have evidence concerning the impressive power of Gauss quadrature. Without question, when the integrand possesses derivatives of all orders, Gauss quadrature stands supreme in its accuracy for a given number of interpolation points. Moreover, in comparison to Newton–Cotes rules, Gauss rules have reduced sensitivity to smearing (Section 1.4.2) because the coefficients A_k are positive.

A drawback to the Gaussian quadrature approach, however, is that the points and coefficients must be entered or computed. Finding the Gauss points x_k is a relatively difficult task. But once these points are made known, one can easily find the weights by the approach (and use of subroutine COEFF) in Section 4.3, since Gauss quadrature is a particular interpolatory quadrature. The difficulty in solving (4.39) lies in the fact that it is a nonlinear system of equations. A standard method (e.g., S & Y, 1978, Sec. 3.2.3) involves showing that the Gauss points are roots of a certain polynomial (the Legendre polynomial) the coefficients of which are fairly easy to find. Once the coefficients are known, polynomial root-finding methods such as to be presented in Chapter 5 can locate the points. Application 5.3 employs this idea to produce the quadrature points of Table 4.22.

★4.7
IMPROPER INTEGRALS

In the preceding sections we have assumed that the interval $[a, b]$ of integration is finite and the integrand remains bounded. In many applications we need to compute integrals for which at least one of these assumptions fails. In such cases the integral is said to be *improper*, and its calculation needs special consideration. We discuss two cases here: (1) The interval is finite but $f(x)$ is unbounded, and (2) the interval is infinite.

Case 1. Consider the integral

$$\int_{0}^{1} \frac{\cos(x)}{\sqrt{x}} \, dx,$$

for which the integrand is infinite at $x = 0$. If δ is a small positive number, the integral

$$\int_{\delta}^{1} \frac{\cos(x)}{\sqrt{x}} \, dx$$

gives a good approximation of the original integral. Observe that in the interval $[\delta, 1]$ the integrand is continuous. Consequently, the value of this approximating integral can in principle be computed by the use of the methods discussed earlier in this chapter. We can also bound the error introduced by this truncation:

$$0 < \int_0^1 \frac{\cos (x)}{\sqrt{x}} \, dx - \int_\delta^1 \frac{\cos (x)}{\sqrt{x}} \, dx = \int_0^\delta \frac{\cos (x)}{\sqrt{x}} \, dx < \int_0^\delta \frac{1}{\sqrt{x}} \, dx = [2\sqrt{x}]_0^\delta$$

$$= 2\sqrt{\delta}.$$

It happens, however, that at this stage the integration problem is far from being solved. For example, if one blithely sets δ to 10^{-3} and applies Simpson's rule s_{20} (which under "normal" circumstances, ought to be pretty accurate), the integral estimate turns out to be 18; we have similarly that $s_{50} = 8.3$. As we will see below, the correct integral value, to six places, is 1.80905.

The difficulty stems from the fact that whereas the integrand is, in fact, continuous on the interval $[10^{-3}, 1]$ it undergoes a large variation in values near the lower end of the interval. The more erratic the integrand, the less reliable the numerical approximation. For erratic behavior is associated with large fluctuations in derivatives, and error bounds such as in Table 4.16 are similarly large.

There are often clever ways to overcome the effects of integrand singularities, but, of course, inventiveness will be required, and each problem has to be handled on its own terms. For the problem at hand, a substitution of variables is effective. Let $t = \sqrt{x}$. Then $x = t^2$; consequently, $dx = 2t \, dt$, and

$$\int_0^1 \frac{\cos (x)}{\sqrt{x}} \, dx = \int_0^1 \frac{\cos (t^2)}{t} 2t \, dt = \int_0^1 2 \cos (t^2) \, dt.$$

Now the integrand $2 \cos (t^2)$ is well behaved in every respect. When Simpson's rule s_{20} is applied to the equivalent integrand over the interval $[0, 1]$, the approximation of the integral is 1.809048, which is correct to six significant places.

For many unbounded integrands, the use of Taylor's series methods can be warmly endorsed as a means of getting rid of singularities such as $1/\sqrt{x}$. In our example we have

$$\int_0^1 \frac{\cos (x)}{\sqrt{x}} \, dx = \int_0^1 \frac{1}{\sqrt{x}} \left(1 - \frac{x^2}{2!} + \frac{x^4}{4!} - \frac{x^6}{6!} + \cdots \right) dx$$

$$= \int_0^1 \left(\frac{1}{\sqrt{x}} - \frac{x^{3/2}}{2!} + \frac{x^{7/2}}{4!} - \frac{x^{11/2}}{6!} + \cdots \right) dx$$

$$= \left[2\sqrt{x} - \frac{2}{5} \cdot \frac{x^{5/2}}{2!} + \frac{2}{9} \cdot \frac{x^{9/2}}{4!} - \frac{2}{13} \cdot \frac{x^{13/2}}{6!} + \cdots \right]_0^1$$

$$= 2 - \frac{2}{5 \cdot 2!} + \frac{2}{9 \cdot 4!} - \frac{2}{13 \cdot 6!} + \cdots .$$

The four terms explicitly shown above add to 1.809046, and this Taylor's series is alternating and decreasing in magnitude, so that the error is bounded by the magnitude of the first truncated term, which is $2/(17 \cdot 8!)$, or less than 10^{-5}.

Case 2. Sometimes a wise substitution of variables can be used to change an improper integral into a well-behaved proper one. By introducing the transformation $t = 1/x$, the improper integral

$$\int_1^\infty \frac{\cos (1/x^2)}{x^2} \, dx$$

becomes the proper integral

$$\int_0^1 \cos (t^2) \, dt.$$

We now turn our attention to an approach more in the tradition of numerical analysis than calculus. The interpolatory quadrature approach in Section 4.3 can be extended to infinite domains of integration by the artifice of introducing a "weighting" function $w(x)$ which diminishes for large $|x|$ fast enough to assure that for any $k \geq 0$,

$$\int_a^b |w(x)x^k| \, dx < \infty.$$

Then following the linear equation representation (4.16), for quadrature points x_j, $1 \leq j \leq n$, one computes quadrature coefficients A_j so that if $p(x)$ is a polynomial of degree less than n, then $\int_a^b w(x)p(x) \, dx$ is integrated exactly. This condition is enforced by choosing the A_j's to satisfy the linear system of equations:

$$
\begin{aligned}
A_1 x_1^0 + A_2 x_2^0 + \cdots + A_n x_n^0 &= \int_a^b w(x)x^0 \, dx \\[2mm]
A_1 x_1^1 + A_2 x_2^1 + \cdots + A_n x_n^1 &= \int_a^b w(x)x^1 \, dx \\[2mm]
\cdot \quad \cdot \quad \cdot \quad \cdot & \\[2mm]
A_1 x_1^{n-1} + A_2 x_2^{n-1} + \cdots + A_n x_n^{n-1} &= \int_a^b w(x)x^{n-1} \, dx.
\end{aligned}
\qquad (4.44)
$$

As in interpolatory quadrature generally, the linear equation (4.44) is subject to numerical instabilities for n larger than about 10.

To use (4.44), rewrite the integrand as $f(x) = w(x)g(x)$, and then the quadrature approximant is

$$\int_a^b f(x) \, dx \approx \sum_{k=1}^n A_k g(x_k).$$

For evaluation of

$$\int_0^1 \frac{\cos (x)}{\sqrt{x}} \, dx$$

we can set $w(x) = 1/\sqrt{x}$ and let cos (x) play the role of $g(x)$. Then one could find the weights, at any given points $x_1, \ldots, x_n$, by solving the linear equation

$$A_1 x_1^0 + A_2 x_2^0 + \cdots + A_n x_n^0 = \int_0^1 \frac{1}{\sqrt{x}} x^0 \, dx = 2$$

$$A_1 x_1^1 + A_2 x_2^1 + \cdots + A_n x_n^1 = \int_0^1 \frac{1}{\sqrt{x}} x^1 \, dx = \frac{2}{3}$$

$$\vdots \qquad\qquad \vdots$$

$$A_1 x_1^{n-1} + A_2 x_2^{n-1} + \cdots + A_n x_n^{n-1} = \int_0^1 \frac{1}{\sqrt{x}} x^{n-1} \, dx = \frac{2}{2n-1} \ .$$

An advantage of this interpolatory type of approach is that it does not require construction of a Taylor's series and it is applicable to any integral. We explore this in the example to follow.

EXAMPLE 4.20

By means of the calling program listed in Table 4.25, we constructed a five-point quadrature rule for integrating $\int_0^\infty w(x)g(x) \, dx$, with $w(x) = e^{-x}$. The points x_i in

TABLE 4.25 Interpolatory Quadrature for an Infinite Domain of Integration

```
C      PROGRAM INFDOM
C
C      ****************************************************************
C      THIS PROGRAM IMPLEMENTS INTERPOLATORY INTEGRATION OF SIN(X)
C      OVER THE POSITIVE REALS, WITH THE WEIGHT FUNCTION EXP(-X)
C      CALLS:   GAUS1(MODIFIED FOR DOUBLE PRECISION)
C      OUTPUT: NUMBER OF QUADRATURE POINTS AND CORRESPONDING ESTIMATE
C              OF THE INTEGRAL
C      ****************************************************************
C
       IMPLICIT DOUBLE PRECISION (A-H,O-Z)
       DIMENSION A(100,101),X(100)

C      *** DECLARE THE INTEGRAND                                    ***

       F(X) = DSIN(X)
C
C      *** FOR N-NUMBER OF QUADRATURE POINTS PERFORM THE            ***
C      *** INTERPOLATORY QUADRATURE APPROXIMATION                   ***
C
       DO 5 N = 5,15

          EST=0.
          H=.1
          FACT=1.

C
C      *** THE QUADRATURE POINTS AND THE VALUES FOR THE             ***
C      *** RIGHT-HAND SIDE OF OUR SYSTEM OF EQUATIONS               ***
C      *** ARE COMPUTED. WHEN COMPUTING THE RIGHT HAND              ***
C      *** SIDE OF THE   SYSTEM WE HAVE USED THE FACT THAT          ***
C      *** THE INTEGRAL OF EXP(-X)*(X**N) FROM ZERO TO              ***
C      *** INFINITY IS EQUAL TO N!                                  ***
C
```

TABLE 4.25   (Continued)

```
            DO 1 J=1,N
               A(J,N+1)=FACT
               FACT=FACT*J
               X(J)=H*J*J
1           CONTINUE

C
C       *** VALUES FOR THE LEFT HAND SIDE OF OUR SYSTEM OF         ***
C       *** EQUATIONS ARE COMPUTED                                 ***
C
            DO 2 J=1,N
               DO 12 I=1,N
                  A(I,J)=X(J)**(I-1)
12          CONTINUE
2           CONTINUE

C
C       *** SUBROUTINE GAUS1 WILL SOLVE THE SYSTEM OF EQUATIONS    ***
C       *** THE SOLUTION IS RETURNED IN THE LAST COLUMN OF A       ***
C
            EPS=1.E-10
            CALL GAUS1(N,1,100,A,EPS)
C
C       *** SUCCESSIVE SUMMANDS (QUDRATURE WEIGHT TIMES THE        ***
C       *** FUNCTION VALUE AT EACH QUADRATURE POINT) ARE           ***
C       *** COMPUTED AND ADDED TO GET OUR APPROXIMATION            ***
C
            DO 3 J=1,N
               EST=EST+A(J,N+1)*F(X(J))
3           CONTINUE
            WRITE(10,'(I5,G15.7)')N,EST
5           CONTINUE
            STOP
            END
```

(4.44) were taken to be $x_i = 0.1 \cdot i^2$ ($i = 1, 2, \ldots, 5$), and on the right-hand side of the linear equations we used the fact that

$$\int_0^\infty w(x)x^n \, dx = \int_0^\infty e^{-x}x^n \, dx = n!.$$

The program applies this rule to the integral

$$I = \int_0^\infty e^{-x} \sin (x) \, dx.$$

It can be recognized that this integral is the Laplace transformation of sin (x), evaluated at 1; this turns out to be $I = 0.5$. In Table 4.26 we give the estimates produced by the preceding program.

We will mention that accuracy for this interpolatory quadrature approach depends critically on the choice of points x_i. A bad choice is evidenced by wildly oscillating weights A_j.

The Gauss principle (Section 4.6) for optimal location of quadrature points may be extended in an obvious manner to weighted quadrature for improper integrals (Davis and Rabinowitz, 1975, Chap. 3). When this is done for the preceding example, the three-point rule gives the estimate 0.496 and for four points, 0.5048.

TABLE 4.26   Interpolatory Quadrature Estimates for an Improper Integral

Number of Points N	Estimate of I
5	0.5679169
6	0.5840291
7	0.4403196
8	0.5076003
9	0.5078841
10	0.4953857
11	0.5010254
12	0.5000069
13	0.4999375
14	0.5000222
15	0.4999942

★4.8
ON-LINE ERROR ESTIMATION AND ADAPTIVE QUADRATURE

★4.8.1   Estimation and Control of Error

In Section 4.4.2 we gave a technique for bounding and controlling integration error. That technique required that a derivative bound be available. Often, such bounds are difficult to find, and in many cases, they lead to pessimistic error estimates. Here we sidestep the derivative estimation problem and get error estimates and control strategies that are often quite accurate, as in an example to follow.

Suppose that one has in mind some specific integration problem of the form

$$I = \int_a^b f(x) \, dx. \tag{4.45}$$

Let $I(h)$ denote its numerical approximation obtained by some compound integration formula, with h the common lengths of the subintervals. That is, $h = (b - a)/N$, N being the number of "compoundings." Assume that the order of error of the rule is k. From the considerations that led to the error formulas in Table 4.16, one may conclude that, provided $f(x)$ is $k + 1$ times continuously differentiable, for some constant C, the error of the integral approximation is given by

$$I(h) - I = Ch^k + O(h^{k+1}). \tag{4.46}$$

In other words, as step size h becomes small, the dominant portion of the error is Ch^k. In this section we explain how the representation (4.46) can be employed to get a good approximation of the error. This can be useful information in itself, and it can also be a vital input to a procedure for error control, so as to obtain a final integral estimate that falls within a prescribed tolerance bound.

The idea we will explore is very closely related to Richardson's extrapolation (Section 4.5.1) and Romberg integration (Section 4.5.2). The latter techniques were motivated by the obvious idea that, since we can estimate what the error is, we can use it to get a more accurate answer. Let us see in detail how the error can be approximated.

Let h_1 and h_2 be two distinct step sizes. Then from (4.46), and ignoring the $O(h^{k+1})$ term, we can estimate C by

$$I(h_1) - I(h_2) \approx C(h_1^k - h_2^k). \qquad (4.47)$$

Solve for C, and insert h_1 in place of h in (4.46) to get that the integration error for step size h_1, for example, is

$$\boxed{I(h_1) - I \approx \frac{I(h_1) - I(h_2)}{1 - (h_2/h_1)^k}} \cdot \qquad (4.48)$$

―――― **EXAMPLE 4.21** ――――――――――――――――――――――――――――

Here we estimate the error of Simpson's rule with $[a, b]$ divided into four intervals $[M = 4$, in the notation of (4.22)]. In terms of the preceding discussion, we set $h_1 = (b - a)/2$ and $h_2 = (b - a)/4$. The integral studied is our usual one:

$$10 \int_0^{10} \sin (1. - 0.1x) \, dx$$

and the error estimate provided by (4.48), with $k = 4$, in accordance with Table 4.16, was computed to be 0.001005. The exact error of Simpson's rule using h_1 is 0.00103. When you consider that the integral value itself is on the order of 45, you must appreciate that the guess provided by our technique is not bad. ∎

An automatic *error control routine* for integration is a program for which the user specifies the integrand $f(x)$, the domain $[a, b]$ of integration, and a positive number ε. The program is expected to provide an estimate $I(h)$ of the exact integral I satisfying

$$|I(h) - I| < \varepsilon.$$

The formulas (4.46) and (4.48) can serve as a basis for construction of an error control routine. For in view of (4.47), one may approximate C by

$$C \approx \frac{I(h_1) - I(h_2)}{h_1^k - h_2^k} \cdot$$

Then from (4.46), and neglecting the $O(h^{k+1})$ term, one can conclude that if h_0 is defined as

$$\boxed{h_0 = \left| \frac{\varepsilon(h_1^k - h_2^k)}{I(h_1) - I(h_2)} \right|^{1/k}}, \qquad (4.49)$$

then for any $h < h_0$, the condition

$$|I(h) - I| < \varepsilon$$

should be satisfied.

──────── **EXAMPLE 4.22** ───────────────────────────────────────

Suppose that by means of Simpson's rule we wish to approximate our "usual" integral

$$I = 10 \int_0^{10} \sin (1. - 0.1x) \, dx$$

to five significant decimal places. Then we set $\epsilon = 5 \cdot 10^{-6}$. With h_1 and h_2 as in Example 4.21, by (4.49) one calculates h_0 to be 0.66. Since $b - a$ is 10, the smallest even positive integer M for which $(b - a)/M < h_0$ is $M = 16$. Take M in subroutine SIMP (Table 4.13) to be 16 and the actual error, when the calculations are performed on the VAX in double precision, turns out to be $3.9 \cdot 10^{-6}$.

─── ■

The reader should bear in mind that there are some critical assumptions that must be in force before the error estimate (4.48) can be trusted, and in many applications, these conditions are difficult to check. First, the integrand $f(x)$ must be $k + 1$ times continuously differentiable, and second, the step size h must be sufficiently small that the $O(h^{k+1})$ term in (4.46) really is negligible. Davis and Rabinowitz (1975, Chap. 6) give amusing examples of innocent-looking integration problems in which automatic error control routines mistakenly announce very faulty answers as being within a prescribed tolerance region.

★4.8.2 Adaptive Quadrature

We saw in Section 4.8.1 that on-line error estimation is possible in numerical integration. This capability can be used in an alternative way to the one sketched above. The alternative has some appeal if the integrand is well behaved in some portions of the domain and fluctuates drastically in others. For the function illustrated in Figure 4.17, for example, one would think it reasonable to select quad-

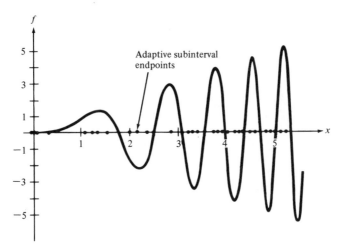

FIGURE 4.17 Integrand and ASIMP Quadrature Points

rature points more densely in the right-hand portion of the interval than in the left. Methods we have discussed up to this point do not allow for such function-dependent flexibility.

However, in Section 4.8.1 we established techniques for obtaining, for any x and positive h:

1. A quadrature estimate $I_x(h)$ of

$$I(x, x + h) = \int_x^{x+h} f(x)\, dx.$$

2. An estimate $E_x(h)$ of the truncation error

$$\left| I(x, x + h) - I_x(h) \right|.$$

With these constructs it is not difficult to "adaptively" allocate quadrature points so that they will typically be dense where the integrand $f(x)$ is erratic and sparse where it is smooth. Moreover, the adaptive technique can meanwhile attempt to keep the total quadrature error within a prescribed bound, which we will designate as TOL (for "tolerance").

The following general idea is representative of a family of rules referred to collectively as *adaptive quadrature*. Assume an integrand $f(x)$; an interval $[a, b]$ of integration; a quadrature rule giving an estimate $I_x(h)$ and error approximation $E_x(h)$, as in constructs 1 and 2 above, and that a positive number TOL is specified. Initialize by setting $x = a$, SUM $= 0$, and taking some small but positive number for h. Then proceed recursively as follows:

A. Compute $I_x(h)$ and $E_x(h)$.
B. If $E_x(h) \geq h * \text{TOL}/(b - a)$, reduce h and go to step A.
C. Otherwise, set SUM $=$ SUM $+ I(x, x + h)$, and $x = x + h$, and if $x < b$, increase the step size h and return to step A.

By this procedure, if $E_x(h)$ really does bound the error, then by summing over accepted quadrature points x,

$$\left| I(a, b) - \text{SUM} \right| \leq \sum_x \left| I(x, x + h) - I_x(h) \right| \leq \sum_x E_x(h)$$

$$< \sum_x \frac{h\ \text{TOL}}{b - a} = \text{TOL}. \tag{4.50}$$

We may anticipate that satisfaction of the condition $E_x(h) < h\ \text{TOL}/(b - a)$ will require h to be relatively small where $f(x)$ is fluctuating dramatically.

In Table 4.27, we present subroutine ASIMP, which applies the Simpson formula (4.22), via subroutine SIMP, to realize the quadrature rule $I_x(h)$. The estimate (4.48), with $h_2 = h_1/2$, is employed as $E_x(h)$. In the case of the Simpson rule, from Table 4.16, we have that $k = 4$. If the condition in step B fails, h is reduced by a factor of 10, and otherwise, h is set to three times its former value.

TABLE 4.27   Subroutine ASIMP for Adaptive Quadrature

```
        SUBROUTINE ASIMP(A,B,M,TOL,SUM)
C
C   ****************************************************************
C   *   FUNCTION: THIS SUBROUTINE COMPUTES THE ESTIMATE OF THE     *
C   *             INTEGRAL OF THE FUNCTION F(X) USING THE          *
C   *             ADAPTIVE SIMPSON'S METHOD                        *
C   *   USAGE:                                                     *
C   *         CALL SEQUENCE: CALL ASIMP(A,B,M,TOL,SUM)             *
C   *         EXTERNAL FUNCTIONS/SUBROUTINES:                      *
C   *                        SUBROUTINE SIMP(A,B,M,E)              *
C   *   PARAMETERS:                                                *
C   *       INPUT:                                                 *
C   *            A=INTERVAL LEFT ENDPOINT                          *
C   *            B=INTERVAL RIGHT ENDPOINT                         *
C   *            M=MAXIMUM NUMBER OF ITERATIONS                    *
C   *          TOL=TOLERANCE                                       *
C   *       OUTPUT:                                                *
C   *            SUM=ESTIMATE OF THE INTEGRAL                      *
C   ****************************************************************
C
C       *** INITIALIZATION ***
        H=.10E-02
        N1=4
        X=A
        N2=8
        SUM=0.0
C       *** COMPUTE SOLUTION ITERATIVELY ***
        DO WHILE(X.LT.B)
           N=N+1
           CALL SIMP(X,X+H,N1,E1)
           CALL SIMP(X,X+H,N2,E2)
           CORR=(16.0*E2-E1)/15.0
           ERR=CORR-E1
C       *** TEST IF THE NUMBER OF ITERATIONS EXCEEDED ***
           IF(N.GT.M) THEN
              WRITE(6,1)
    1         FORMAT(1X,'PROGRAM STOPPED TOO MANY ITERATIONS')
              STOP
           END IF
C       *** TEST STEP SIZE ***
           IF(ABS(ERR).LT.TOL*H) THEN
              X=X+H
              H=3.0*H
              SUM=SUM+E2
              WRITE(3,2) X
    2         FORMAT(33X,1PE14.7)
           ELSE
              H=H/10.0
           END IF
        END DO
        X=X-H/3.0
        SUM=SUM-E2
        H=B-X
        CALL SIMP(X,X+H,N2,E2)
        SUM=SUM+E2
        RETURN
        END
```

━━━━━ **EXAMPLE 4.23** ━━

The subroutine ASIMP was used to approximate $\int_a^b x \sin (x^2)\, dx$. TOL was set to 10^{-3} and $a = 0$, $b = 3\sqrt{\pi}$. By substitution of variables, with $t = x^2$, one may confirm that the true value is exactly 1. In the printout (Table 4.28), we have given the values of x at which acceptance (passage to step C in the adaptive quadrature algorithm) occurred. One confirms from this printout that initially the quadrature points are dense and then, toward the end of the integration interval,

TABLE 4.28 Partition Points of Adaptive Quadrature Subintervals

Accepted x Values
1.0000000E-03
4.0000002E-03
1.3000001E-02
4.0000003E-02
1.2100001E-01
3.6400005E-01
1.0930002E+00
1.3117002E+00
1.3773103E+00
1.5741403E+00
2.1646304E+00
2.3417773E+00
2.8732183E+00
3.0326507E+00
3.0804803E+00
3.2239695E+00
3.2670162E+00
3.3961563E+00
3.7835770E+00
3.8998032E+00
3.9346709E+00
4.0392747E+00
4.0706558E+00
4.1647992E+00
4.1930423E+00
4.2777710E+00
4.5319576E+00
4.6082134E+00
4.8369813E+00
4.9056115E+00
5.1115026E+00
5.1732702E+00
5.3585725E+00

Computed value of the integral = 1.0000324

they again become dense. To begin with, h was set to a relatively small number (10^{-3}) to try to ensure that the h^k term in the truncation error expansion dominates. The algorithm comes to recognize that h is small because the estimated error is far below the tolerance threshold. Thus h is allowed to increase. Later, as the integrand becomes more oscillatory, the subinterval length must and does become smaller. In subinterval [1, 2], where the integrand is smooth and the step size has adaptively been increased, there are only four steps. As the integrand becomes increasingly ragged, the steps get smaller. There are three, eight, and nine integration subintervals in [2, 3], [3, 4], and [4, 5], respectively. Figure 4.17 displays the integrand as well as the interval steps accepted by ASIMP.

■

   The adaptive quadrature subroutine ASIMP is intended for illustrative purposes only. It lacks the efficiency and truncation-error-sensing safeguards of professional library-quality programs.
   The design of adaptive quadrature algorithms is as much an art as it is a science. Because of their heuristics and intricacies, their analysis in terms of precise convergence statements is difficult. For every such adaptive algorithm, there exists some perverse integrand that misleads it and forces the algorithm to be satisfied

with a highly erroneous estimate. Nevertheless, for many applications, these adaptive techniques are quite satisfactory, and their use is becoming increasingly popular. The IMSL† library has an adaptive quadrature routine, DCADRE, which is built around the Romberg integration technique.

4.9
SUPPLEMENTARY NOTES AND DISCUSSIONS

We saw that standard numerical differentiation formulas and their error bounds can be derived directly from either the Taylor's or interpolation polynomial approaches. It was noted that numerical differentiation tended to be unstable in the sense that as the step size h between successive domain points decreases, error resulting from roundoff and inexact measurement can become overwhelmingly large. Such a phenomenon does not occur for any compound rule, or for Romberg or Gauss quadrature or any other interpolatory system for which the weights are all nonnegative.

The popular quadrature formulas were derived by integrating interpolation polynomials or piecewise polynomials. The most popular compound formulas, the trapezoidal, midpoint, and Simpson rules, were described and their error formulas were given. At this point we caution the reader that these particular popular formulas are holdovers from the age of hand calculation. They are simple to understand and easy to implement. But if the integrand is "smooth," one can obtain a more accurate estimate of the integral by using Gaussian or Romberg quadrature. We noted a danger arising from high-order Newton–Cotes rules: The linear equations for the quadrature weights tend to be sensitive to roundoff error. There are further drawbacks we did not mention.

Heuristically speaking, for integrands that possess several derivatives (we need not calculate what they are), much more information is contained in the data points (x_1, f_1), (x_2, f_2), . . . , (x_n, f_n) than is extracted by the popular compound formulas. Romberg's method does effectively achieve a high order of accuracy. The mechanism for this success was explained through the principle of Richardson's extrapolation.

TABLE 4.29   Match of Integration Problem Characteristics and Methods

Integrand Characteristic	Method[a]
Few Data Points (< 10)	
Points evenly spaced, accuracy not as critical, as simplicity, or no computer available	M, S, T
Points equally spaced, accuracy critical	RO, NC
Points may be chosen at discretion of user	G
Points irregularly spaced but fixed	I
Many Data Points (≥ 10)	
Simplicity above all	S, T, M
Accuracy important	High order G, RO

[a]G, Gauss quadrature; I, interpolatory rule; M, midpoint rule; NC, Newton–Cotes; RO, Romberg integration; S, Simpson's rule; T, trapezoidal formula.

† IMSL is the acronym of the International Mathematical and Statistical Libraries, Inc., NBC Building, 7500 Bellaire Boulevard, Houston, TX 77031.

If we are constrained to use an n-point quadrature rule, but the quadrature points $x_1, \ldots, x_n$ can be placed at our discretion, then from a certain reasonable point of view, Gauss quadrature constitutes the best possible integration method. Our derivation of quadrature domain points and weights is, pedagogically, as simple as any we know of. But from a numerical standpoint, more sophisticated techniques (some of which are described in S & Y, 1978, Sec 3.2.3) are available.

In Table 4.29, which is meant to be suggestive rather than canonical, we have tried to indicate the appropriate domains for various techniques studied in this chapter.

PROBLEMS

Section 4.1
1. Find the order q in $O(h^q)$ for the following functions:
    (a) $\sin(h)$.
    (b) $e^h - \cos(h)$.
    (c) $e^h - e^{-h} - 2h$.
    (d) $e^{h^2} - 1$.
    (e) $\dfrac{1}{1 + h} + \dfrac{1}{1 - h} - 2$.

    (**HINT:** Taylor's series expansion about 0 provides a systematic approach to this problem.)

2. Find the order q in $O((x - x_0)^q)$ of the following functions at the points indicated.
    (a) $\sin(x)$, $x_0 = \pi$.
    (b) $\dfrac{x - 1}{x + 1}$, $x_0 = 1$.

Section 4.2
★3. Derive the error term of the three-point second-derivative approximation (as in Table 4.3).

4. Taylor's polynomials can be used in place of Lagrange polynomials for deriving numerical differentiation formulas. For example, the expansion with remainder
$$f(x_0 + h) = f(x_0) + f'(x_0)h + \tfrac{1}{2}f''(\xi)h^2$$
implies, after rearrangement, that
$$f'(x_0) = \frac{f(x_0 + h) - f(x_0)}{h} + O(h),$$
which is formula (4.2). Derive the three-point formula of Table 4.3 by this Taylor's polynomial approach.

5. Two values of the standard normal distribution function $\Phi(x)$ are tabulated below:

x	$\Phi(x)$
0	0.5
0.1	0.5398
0.2	0.5793

Estimate $\Phi'(0)$ as accurately as you can:

(a) By using the tabulated data.

(b) By using the fact that $\Phi(-x) = 1 - \Phi(x)$, conclude that $\Phi(-0.1) = 0.4602$ and $\phi(-0.2) = 0.4207$.

Compare the estimates in parts (a) and (b) to the exact answer, which is $1/\sqrt{2\pi} = 0.3989422$, to the accuracy shown.

6. Apply the two-, three-, and four-point formulas of Table 4.3 to estimate derivatives of the following functions at $x_0 = 0$. Use step sizes $h = 10^{-j}$, $j = 1, 2, \ldots, 10$. Find the actual error by comparison with the analytic derivatives. Indicate ranges in which the truncation error of your computed derivative estimates exceeds roundoff.

(a) $\cos (x)$.

(b) $x^3 + x^2 + x + 1$.

(c) $\exp (x) \cdot \sin (x)$.

(d) $\ln (1 + x^2)$.

7. Use the three-point rules for $f'(x)$ and $f''(x)$ to obtain estimates of the first and second derivatives of the functions listed below at the points

$$x_i = \frac{i - 1}{100}, \qquad 1 \le i \le 101.$$

(a) $\cos (x)$.

(b) $x^3 + x^2 + x + 1$.

(c) $\exp (x) \sin (x)$.

(d) $\ln (1 + x^2)$.

Use $h = \frac{1}{100}$ and accompany the estimate with the correct derivative values.

Section 4.3

8. Find which of the following quadrature formulas are of the interpolatory type. Show your analysis.

(a) $\int_{-1}^{1} f(x)\, dx \approx \frac{3}{4}f(-1) + \frac{5}{4}f(1)$.

(b) $\int_{-1}^{1} f(x)\, dx \approx f(-1) + f(1)$.

(c) $\int_{0}^{4} f(x)\, dx \approx \frac{2}{3}f(0) + \frac{8}{3}f(2) + \frac{2}{3}f(4)$.

9. Derive an interpolatory rule for the domain $[0, 1]$ using the quadrature points $x_1 = 0$, $x_2 = \frac{2}{3}$, $x_3 = 1$. Apply it to integrating $f(x) = x^2$, x^3, and x^4. Tabulate the errors. Show your work. Explain why this rule is exact for one case but not for the others.

★10. Suppose that one has data $f(x_1)$, $f(x_2)$, and $f'(x_1)$. Using these data, make a quadrature rule that is exact for all quadratic polynomials with respect to $\int_{a}^{b} f(x)\, dx$.

11. In theory there is no need to insist that quadrature points be in the domain of integration. With the help of subroutine COEFF (Table 4.7), obtain the (Newton–Cotes) interpolatory quadrature formula for the domain $[0, 1]$ on the basis of the points

$$x_1 = -1, \qquad x_2 = -\tfrac{1}{2}, \qquad x_3 = 0, \qquad x_4 = \tfrac{1}{2}, \qquad x_5 = 1.$$

12. **(Continuation of Problem 11.)** Apply the rule in Problem 11 to the following integrands, to obtain estimates of

$$\int_0^1 f(x) \, dx$$

with $f(x)$ given by
(a) x^3.
(b) $\sin (x)$.
(c) $\exp (x)$.
Use the computer. Give the error in each case. Obtain the solutions using also the "more natural" points $x_1 = 0$, $x_2 = \frac{1}{4}$, $x_3 = \frac{1}{2}$, $x_4 = \frac{3}{4}$, and $x_5 = 1$, and compare with correct integrals.

Section 4.4

13. Approximate the integral

$$\int_0^2 x \exp (x) \, dx$$

by t_1, t_2, t_4, s_2, and s_4. Either do your work by hand calculation or write a self-contained program. Do *not* use TRAP, SIMP, or any other "package."

14. Approximate the integral

$$\int_0^2 \frac{x - 1}{x + 1} \, dx$$

by t_4 and s_4. (The correct value is approximately -0.1972.)

15. Approximate the integral

$$\int_0^1 \sin (\pi x) \, dx$$

by
(a) t_{10}, t_{20}, t_{50}.
(b) s_{10}, s_{20}, s_{50}.

Give the error in each case.

16. Approximate the integrals
(a) $\int_{\pi/2}^\pi \frac{\sin (x)}{x} \, dx$. $h = \pi/20$
(b) $\int_0^2 \frac{\sin (x)}{x} \, dx$ [take $\sin (x)/x$ at $x = 0$ to be 1]. $h = \frac{1}{5}$
(c) $\int_0^1 e^{x^2} \, dx$ $h = \frac{1}{10}$
    by use of
    (1) t_{10} and s_{10}.
    (2) t_j and s_j, $j = 20, 30, 40$, and 50.

17. Since the derivative of $\tan^{-1}(x) = 1/(1 + x^2)$, application of quadrature to the integral

$$\int_0^1 \frac{4}{1 + x^2} \, dx$$

serves as a way of approximating π by arithmetic operations alone, since $\pi/4 =$ $\tan^{-1}(1)$. Check the approximation by the formulas indicated:

(a) t_{10}, t_{20}, t_{50}.

(b) s_{10}, s_{20}, s_{50}.

18. The *RC* circuit shown responds to an input voltage according to a convolution

$$y(t) = \int_0^t \exp\left(\frac{t - v}{b}\right) u(v)\, dv \qquad \text{with } b = 1.$$

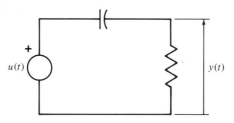

Find the output voltage at time 1 if the input $u(t) = 0$, $t < 0$, and at time $t > 0$ is

(a) $\exp(-t^2)$.

(b) $\sin(t^{1/2})$.

Use a method of your choosing, but present some argument and analysis to justify that your answer is correct to three significant places.

19. Energy gained in riding a frictionless bicycle down a "Gaussian" hill is, at horizontal position x, as shown, given by

$$E(x) = \int_0^x 9.8 \cdot M \frac{\exp\left[-(x')^2/2\right]}{\sqrt{2\pi}}\, dx'.$$

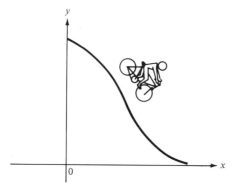

At position x, as a response to conversion from potential to kinetic energy, the velocity is $(2E/M)^{1/2}$. How fast is a rider going after he or she has traveled to $x = 1$ and $x = 2$? Assume that the rider does not pedal.

20. The initial position of a particle is $x(0) = 0$, and it is known to obey the velocity law

$$v(t) = \frac{\sin(t)}{(t + 1)^2 \exp(t)}.$$

Find the position $x(1)$ by evaluating $\int_0^1 v(t)\, dt$ according to the following quadratures:

(a) The trapezoidal rules t_6, t_{10}, t_{20}.
(b) Simpson's rules s_6, s_{10}, s_{20}.

21. The current through a resistor under transient decay from charged capacitors in a certain nonlinear circuit is known to satisfy

$$i(t) = \int_0^t t' \exp(-t') \, dt' \qquad \text{coulombs/s.}$$

It is known that the energy dissipated over a time interval $[0, T]$ is

$$E(t) = R \int_0^t i(t')^2 \, dt'.$$

Find how much energy a resistor of $R = 100 \, \Omega$ dissipates by unit time ($t = 1$). Use t_j and s_j, $j = 10$, 20, and 50, and compare.

22. Approximate the integral

$$\int_0^1 \sin(\pi x) \, dx$$

by hand calculations, using the following quadrature rules. Show your work.
(a) The trapezoidal rules t_2, t_4, and t_6.
(b) Simpson's rules s_4 and s_6.
Note that s_n and t_n use the same data. Compare their accuracy.

23. Compute the integral

$$\int_0^1 (e^{x^2} - 1) \, dx \qquad \text{and} \qquad \int_1^2 (e^{x^2} - 1) \, dx$$

by
(a) Trapezoidal rules t_{10}, t_{20}, t_{50}.
(b) Simpson's rules s_{10}, s_{20}, s_{50}.

24. Davis and Rabinowitz (1975) use the term "overcomputation" to refer to the situation in which one has so many quadrature points that because of roundoff error, the estimate is less accurate than it would be had fewer points been used. The following program, run on a VAX, and printout provide an illustration of this phenomenon.

```
A=0.0
B=2.0
TRUE=EXP(2.0)-1.0
DO 1 K=4,20
    N=2**K
    CALL TRAP(A,B,N,EST)
    ERROR=TRUE-EST
    TYPE *,ERROR,EST,N
1 CONTINUE
STOP
END

FUNCTION F(X)
F=EXP(X)
RETURN
END
```

Actual Quadrature Errors	Estimate	Number, N, of Points
−8.3174706E−03	6.397374	16
−2.0799637E−03	6.391136	32
−5.1975250E−04	6.389576	64
−1.2922287E−04	6.389185	128
−3.0994415E−05	6.389087	256
−8.1062317E−06	6.389064	512
−3.8146973E−06	6.389060	1024
−2.3841858E−06	6.389059	2048
−9.5367432E−07	6.389057	4096
0.0000000	6.389056	8192
6.6757202E−06	6.389050	16384
−1.4305115E−06	6.389058	32768
4.2915344E−06	6.389052	65536
1.7166138E−05	6.389039	131072
3.1948090E−05	6.389024	262144
8.4400177E−05	6.388972	524288

Exhibit this effect on your computer. Run the program and then use a different compound rule. Finally, use a different integrand. Explain whether you would anticipate the effect to be more or less pronounced if the basic compound rule is of higher order than the trapezoidal rule used here.

25. Assume that the value of the integral

$$\int_{-1}^{1} e^{x^2} \, dx$$

has to be determined within an error bound of $\frac{1}{2} \cdot 10^{-6}$. Determine the number of subintervals required for the trapezoidal rule to assure this accuracy. (This function does not have a closed-form indefinite integral.)

26. Approximate the integral

$$\int_{0}^{2} x \exp(x) \, dx$$

by Romberg integration with
(a) $M = 3$, and by hand calculation.
(b) $M = 5$, and by use of routine ROMB (Table 4.20).

(**Remark:** The true integral is $e^2 + 1 = 8.38905699$.)

27. By computer, use Romberg integration to approximate

$$\int_{0}^{1} \sin(\pi x) \, dx.$$

Increase M until the last two estimates differ by less than $0.5 \cdot 10^{-3}$.

28. The force as a function of distance x between two unit charges of opposite sign is, in a normalized system of units,

$$F(x) = \frac{1}{x^2}$$

and the energy required to separate them by an incremental distance dx, accounting for inefficiency of converting rule to work, is modeled by

$$dE(x) = F(x) \left| \ln \left(F(x) \right) \right| dx.$$

Compute by 5- and 10-point Romberg integration and by calculus the energy required to separate the particles, initially 1 unit apart, to a distance of 2 units.

29. Imagine that an engineer is to test a bar composed of high-quality metal as to its energy absorbtion as a function of strain. It is presumed that the engineer will use a highly accurate instrument. The absorbed energy and thermal dissipation is given by

$$E(x) = \int_0^x F(x') \, dx'$$

as a function of applied force $F(x')$ at distension length x'. The question is: If measurements of $F(x_j)$ at certain levels x_j have been made, is it worthwhile using a Newton–Cotes rule to estimate $E(x)$, or is nothing to be gained over merely using the midpoint rule? Argue your case in terms of developments in this chapter and your common sense. Your answer should relate to the number of measurements.

30. Compute the integral

$$\int_0^{10} \exp \left(\frac{-1}{1 + x^2} \right) dx$$

by Romberg integration with $M = 3, 5, 10,$ and 15.

31. Suppose that a borehole has been sunk into an ore deposit, and at various depths y_j a core sample has been extracted and assayed for percentage of mineral content. Let $Q(y)$ denote the percentage content of mineral. The mining engineer would like to know the content of the stratum through which the core samples were taken. The exact quantity he seeks is

$$\text{quality} = \frac{1}{D} \int_0^D Q(y) \, dy.$$

It can be anticipated that there is some error in the assay and in the representation of the sample itself. The question is: Would you recommend using a seven-point Newton–Cotes rule, or would it be just as sensible to use the midpoint rule to estimate quality, as just defined, from the samples? Defend your advice in terms of developments in this chapter.

Section 4.6
32. We have remarked that Gauss quadrature is, in fact, an interpolatory-type rule. For $n = 2, 3, 4,$ and 5, calculate the weights A_j for Gaussian quadrature from knowledge of the quadrature points x_j (Table 4.22) and use of subroutine COEFF. Verify that these computed weights are those of Table 4.22, up to limits determined by roundoff error.

33. Approximate the integral

$$\int_0^2 x \exp(x)\, dx$$

with n-point rules, $n = 1, 3, 5, 7$, by
(a) Gauss quadrature.
(b) The trapezoidal rule.
Show the error in each case.

34. Approximate the integral

$$\int_0^{10} \exp\left(\frac{-1}{1 + x^2}\right) dx$$

by Gauss quadrature, with $n = 1, 3, 5$, and 7.

35. In view of our findings in Section 3.4.4 that Chebyshev points [defined in (3.17)] provide more accurate interpolation polynomial approximation than do equally spaced points, an appealing idea is to chose Chebyshev points as quadrature points. It turns out that this is indeed a sensible path, as we avoid the pain of finding the optimal (Gauss) quadrature points, since Cheybshev points are simple to compute, yet it is indeed true that Cheybyshev-point quadrature tends to be more accurate than Newton–Cotes rules of like order. Furthermore, unlike Newton–Cotes, Chebyshev-point interpolatory quadrature is guaranteed to have vanishingly small truncation error as the number of points increases. By use of subroutines COEFF and GAQU, compare the accuracy of Newton–Cotes, Chebyshev-interpolatory, and Gauss quadrature of orders $n = 3, 4, 5$, and 6 on the following integrals:

(a) $\int_0^1 \frac{4}{1 + x^2}\, dx.$

(b) $\int_{-1}^1 \pi \frac{1}{(1 + x^2)^2}\, dx.$

Section 4.7

★36. Compute the values of the following improper integrals to three significant digits by modifying the program of Table 4.25. Experiment with location and number of quadrature points. Give a justification for your answer, with some sort of error assessment.

(a) $\int_0^\infty \frac{x}{1 + x^4}\, dx.$

(b) $\int_{-\infty}^\infty x^2 e^{-x^2}\, dx.$

(c) $\int_0^1 \frac{e^x}{\sqrt[3]{x}}\, dx.$

Use ideas in Section 4.7.

★37. Compute the following improper integrals.

(a) $\int_0^\infty x e^{-x}\, dx.$

(b) $\int_1^\infty \frac{x + 1}{x^4}\, dx.$

by any scheme of your choosing.

CHAPTER 5

Nonlinear Equations

5.1 PRELIMINARIES

The concern of this chapter is equations of the form

$$f(x) = 0, \qquad (5.1)$$

where x and $f(x)$ are real, complex, or vector valued.

Our task will be to find a value or values of the independent variable x or vector $\mathbf{x}$ that satisfies nonlinear equation (5.1). Such values are technically known as *roots* of the equation (5.1) or *zeros* of the function $f(x)$. On the other hand, in accordance with common usage, we will sometimes speak of roots of a function, when we really mean zeros. If $f(x)$ is linear [i.e., $f(\mathbf{x}) = \mathbf{Ax} - \mathbf{b}$, for some matrix $\mathbf{A}$ and vector $\mathbf{b}$], the methods discussed in Chapter 2 are more appropriate for solving the equation.

Application 5.1

It can readily be confirmed from elementary circuit theory that for the loop shown in Figure 5.1, the voltage $v(t)$ across the capacitor, as a function of time, satisfies

$$v(t) = 1 - 2 \cdot \exp(-t) + 1 \cdot \exp(-2t).$$

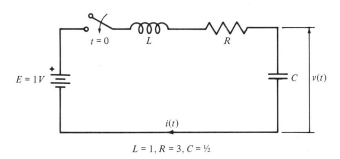

$$L = 1, R = 3, C = \tfrac{1}{2}$$

FIGURE 5.1 Simple *RLC* Loop

249

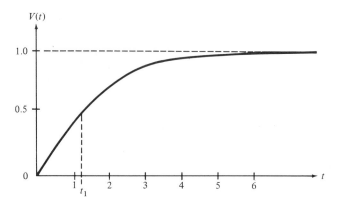

FIGURE 5.2   Capacitor Voltage Curve

The question of when the voltage rises to half its final value is one that demands numerical methods: There is no closed-form solution in terms of elementary functions. Yet by any of the techniques to be offered in this chapter, one may compute the solution t_1 such that

$$v(t_1) - 0.5 = 0.$$

It turns out that $t_1 = 1.227947$ s, to the accuracy shown. These relations are illustrated in Figure 5.2.

Nonlinear equation techniques are standard fare in computer library and calculator implementations of functional inverses. For example, once some technique (perhaps such as described in Chapter 3) has been found for computing $\sin(x)$, methods to be described here provide a convenient way to evaluate $\sin^{-1}(y)$ by solving the equation $f(x) = \sin(x) - y = 0$. In this regard it is informative to note that the path of finding a polynomial approximation to $\sin^{-1}(y)$ itself is not practical. Hart et al. (1968, p. 51) mention that to get a polynomial approximation with error less than 10^{-8} on $[-1, 1]$, one would need a polynomial of degree at least 10,000, no matter how the polynomial is constructed.

In discussing techniques for linear equations (Chapter 2), we drew the distinction between direct methods (e.g., Gauss elimination), which require only a predetermined number of operations, and iterative methods (e.g., the Jacobi method), which for $k = 1, 2, \ldots$ iteratively construct x_k on the basis of x_{k-1}, and possibly earlier values, until some stopping condition is met. Whereas in the case of linear equations, iterative methods are merely an option, in the case of nonlinear equations, they are mandatory. Developments in mathematics imply that direct methods for nonlinear equations do not exist except for certain restrictive cases.

5.2
THE GRAPHICAL APPROACH

We have mentioned that all prominent nonlinear equation methods are iterative. The user must supply the initial "guess," x_0, of the root location. Whether or not the successive iterates x_1, x_2, . . . , converge will, in many cases, depend on the initial guess being in the "vicinity" of a root. Ideas offered in the present section are useful for choosing a sensible initial guess.

An adequate approximation for a root can often be found by strictly graphical (hand calculator and plotting paper) techniques. Such graphical techniques amount to simply calculating a few functional values and perhaps interpolating between arguments for which the function "straddles" zero. In fact, before the computer age, this was the standard approach in many instances. By strategically choosing successive "sample" points, one could indeed get very accurate answers. Now, with computers so readily available, once we resolve to use a strategy, for the sake of convenience and avoidance of error, the strategy should be encoded and run. The "computer methods" offered in this chapter predate the computer age— in fact, they predate the twentieth century. But they are still appropriate for commonplace problems and the obvious gateway to recent techniques.

We offer a brief discussion of graphical methods without strategy. A first step is to seek a finite "search" interval that we can count on to contain a root. In the special case of polynomial equations, many theoretical results relating roots to coefficients are available. Below we give one sample of such a result and then provide an example of its use. In the case of polynomial equations, all roots can readily be localized into a disk in the complex plane. Define the polynomial representation

$$f(x) = a_n x^n + a_{n-1} x^{n-1} + \cdots + a_0. \tag{5.2}$$

Then all (real or complex) roots x^* of $f(x)$ satisfy the inequality

$$|x^*| \leq 1 + \frac{1}{|a_n|} \max \{|a_0|, |a_1|, \ldots, |a_{n-1}|\}, \tag{5.3}$$

where the "max" operation denotes the maximum of the absolute values $|a_0|$, $|a_1|$, . . . , $|a_{n-1}|$. This and other expressions relating polynomial coefficients to roots are given by Wilf (1960).

━━━━━ **EXAMPLE 5.1** ━━━━━

Consider the polynomial

$$f(x) = x^3 - 3x^2 - x + 9.$$

In our case $n = 3$, $a_0 = 9$, $a_1 = -1$, $a_2 = -3$, and $a_3 = 1$. Then by (5.3), all roots x^* of $f(x)$ must satisfy the relation

$$|x^*| \leq 1 + \max \{9, 1, 3\} = 10.$$

Thus the real roots lie within the interval $[-10, 10]$. Table 5.1 gives the values of $f(x)$ between -10 and $+10$ at integer arguments. From this, and the fact that polynomials are continuous, we see that the interval $[-2, -1]$ contains a root. In Figure 5.3 we have plotted 11 evenly spaced points in this interval.

TABLE 5.1   Values of $f(x)$

x	$f(x)$	x	$f(x)$	x	$f(x)$
-10	-1281	-3	-42	4	21
-9	-954	-2	-9	5	54
-8	-687	-1	6	6	111
-7	-474	0	9	7	198
-6	-309	1	6	8	321
-5	-186	2	3	9	486
-4	-99	3	6	10	699

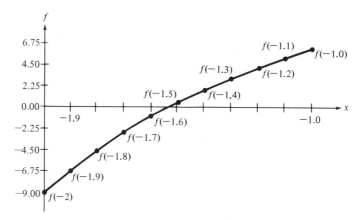

FIGURE 5.3   Plot of Function Points for Graphical Approach

It would take luck to see that to three significant places, $x^* = -1.52$. Greater accuracy requires a graph with greater resolution. The graphical approach is infeasible here if we require that the relative error of the root be less than 0.01. We should push ahead to the purely algorithmic methods described in the following sections. ■

5.3
THE BISECTION METHOD

Assume that the real function $f(x)$ is continuous on the interval $[a, b]$ and that $f(a)$ and $f(b)$ have different signs. Then there is at least one root of $f(x)$ between a and b.

Let $x_L = a$, $x_R = b$, and define x_M to be the midpoint of $[a, b]$; that is, $x_M = (x_L + x_R)/2$. Thus view L, R, and M as abbreviations for "left," "right," and "middle." If $f(x_M) = 0$, we are done. Otherwise, either $f(x_L)f(x_M) < 0$ or $f(x_M)f(x_R) < 0$. In other words, either $f(x_L)$ and $f(x_M)$, or $f(x_M)$ and $f(x_R)$ have different signs. In the first case, interval (x_L, x_M) contains a root, and in the second case, a root is in (x_M, x_R). Observe that by the bisection step, we can locate a root of $f(x)$ within an interval of length $(b - a)/2$, which is the half of the length of the original interval. By repeating the foregoing step successively with $[x_L, x_M]$

or $[x_M, x_R]$ now playing the role of $[a, b]$, we may locate a root of $f(x)$ in an interval half again as small. The general step of the algorithm is given as follows. Assume that x_L and x_R, $x_L < x_R$, satisfying $f(x_L)f(x_R) < 0$, are available from the preceding step. Then

Let

$$x_M = \frac{x_L + x_R}{2}$$

If $f(x_M)f(x_L) < 0$, set   (5.4)

$$x_R = x_M;$$

otherwise, set

$$x_L = x_M.$$

In Figure 5.4 we illustrate this single bisection step.

For purposes of discussing a succession of bisection steps, we resubscript so that $x_0 = x_L$ and $x_1 = x_R$, and x_2, x_3, and x_4 are the successive x_M values. This

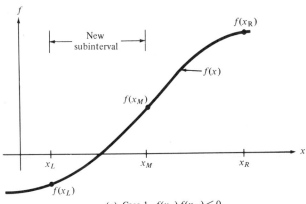

(a) Case 1. $f(x_L)f(x_M) < 0$.

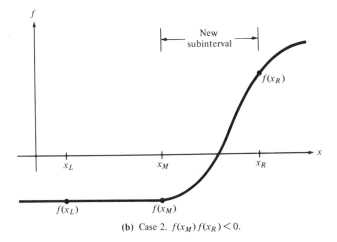

(b) Case 2. $f(x_M)f(x_R) < 0$.

FIGURE 5.4   One Bisection Step

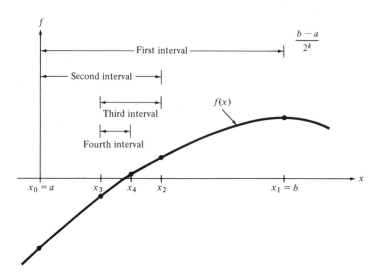

FIGURE 5.5   Successive Bisection Steps

process, illustrated in Figure 5.5, is called the *bisection method*. After K bisection steps, the root is localized within an interval of length

$$\frac{b - a}{2^K}.$$

───── **EXAMPLE 5.2** ─────────────────────────────────────

From Example 5.1 we know that the function

$$f(x) = x^3 - 3x^2 - x + 9$$

has a root in the interval $(-2, -1)$. Thus we take $a = -2$ and $b = -1$, or in the notation of (5.4), $x_L = -2$, $x_R = -1$, and $x_M = (-2 - 1)/2 = -\frac{3}{2}$.

$$f(x_L) = f(-2) = -8 - 12 + 2 + 9 < 0$$

$$f(x_M) = f\left(-\frac{3}{2}\right) = \frac{-27 - 27 \cdot 2 + 3 \cdot 4 + 9 \cdot 8}{8}$$

$$= \frac{3}{8} > 0.$$

Since $f(x_L)f(x_M) < 0$, the root must be in $[-2, -\frac{3}{2}]$, and for the next bisection step,

$$x_L = -2 \quad \text{and} \quad x_R = -\frac{3}{2}.$$

In the reduced interval $[-2, -\frac{3}{2}]$, the midpoint is

$$x_M = \frac{-2 - \frac{3}{2}}{2} = -\frac{7}{4} = -1.75,$$

and furthermore we have seen that

$$f(x_L) = f(-2) < 0.$$

So a simple calculation shows that

$$f(x_M) = \frac{-343}{64} - 3\frac{49}{16} + \frac{7}{4} + 9 \approx -3.7969 < 0.$$

Thus

$$f(x_L)f(x_M) > 0,$$

and consequently, the next reduced interval has endpoints

$$x_L = -\frac{7}{4} \quad \text{and} \quad x_R = -\frac{3}{2}.$$

Table 5.2 provides subroutine BISE for implementing the bisection method. The calling parameter EPS must be larger than the product of the root magnitude and machine epsilon (this product being a bound for the error of approximating the root by a machine word), or else roundoff error may prevent program termination. The user is expected to supply a function subprogram giving the function whose zero is sought. The example that follows gives details on calling BISE. The routine uses the fact that the value of $f(x_L)$ need never be updated, since only the sign matters.

TABLE 5.2   Subroutine BISE for the Bisection Method

```
      SUBROUTINE BISE(A,B,X,EPS)
C
C     ***********************************************************
C     *   FUNCTION: THIS SUBROUTINE APPROXIMATES THE ROOT       *
C     *             OF F(X)=0 OVER THE INTERVAL [A,B] USING THE  *
C     *             BISECTION METHOD                             *
C     *   USAGE:                                                 *
C     *        CALL SEQUENCE: CALL BISE(A,B,X,EPS)               *
C     *        EXTERNAL FUNCTIONS/SUBROUTINES: FUNCTION F(X)     *
C     *   PARAMETERS:                                            *
C     *        INPUT:                                            *
C     *            A=INTERVAL LEFT ENDPOINT                      *
C     *            B=INTERVAL RIGHT ENDPOINT                     *
C     *          EPS=ERROR BOUND                                 *
C     *        OUTPUT:                                           *
C     *            X=BISECTION APPROXIMATION OF THE ROOT         *
C     ***********************************************************
C
      XL=A
      XR=B
      FL=F(XL)
      XM=XR
      DO WHILE(ABS(XM-XL).GE.EPS)
          IF(FL*F(XM).LT.0.0) THEN
              XR=XM
          ELSE
              XL=XM
          END IF
          XM=(XL+XR)/2.0
      END DO
      X=XM
      RETURN
      END
```

━━━ **EXAMPLE 5.3** ━━━

TABLE 5.3   Program for Bisection Example

```
C       PROGRAM BISECT
C
C       ****************************************************************
C       THIS PROGRAM ILLUSTRATES THE BISECTION METHOD BY FINDING
C       A ROOT OF THE FUNCTION F(X)=X**3-3*X**2-X+9 IN THE INTERVAL
C       [-2.,-1.]
C       CALLS:   BISE (MODIFIED FOR DOUBLE PRECISION)
C       OUTPUT(FROM FUNCTION F):
C                X=VALUE OF X AT CURRENT ITERATION
C                F=FUNCTIONAL VALUE AT X
C       ****************************************************************
C
        IMPLICIT DOUBLE PRECISION(A-H,O-Z)
        A=-2.0D0
        B=-1.0D0
        EPS=0.5D-6
C
C       *** SUBROUTINE BISE WILL USE FUNCTION F (BELOW) TO FIND   ***
C       *** A ROOT IN THIS INTERVAL                               ***
C
        CALL BISE(A,B,X,EPS)
        STOP
        END
C
C       *** FUNCTION F IS CALLED BY BISE TO CALCULATE FUNCTIONAL  ***
C       *** VALUES FOR THE PASSED POINT X                         ***
C
        FUNCTION F(X)
        IMPLICIT DOUBLE PRECISION(A-H,O-Z)
        F=X**3-3.0D0*X**2-X+9.0D0
        WRITE(10,1)X,F
   1    FORMAT(22X,D16.7,4X,D16.7)
        RETURN
        END
```

TABLE 5.4   Successive Bisection Iterates

k	x_k	$f(x_k)$	Number of Correct Significant Decimals in x_k
0	-0.2000000D+01	-0.9000000D+01	0
1	-0.1000000D+01	0.6000000D+01	1
2	-0.1500000D+01	0.3750000D+02	2
3	-0.1750000D+01	-0.3796875D+01	1
4	-0.1625000D+01	-0.1587891D+01	1
5	-0.1562500D+01	-0.5764160D+00	2
6	-0.1531250D+01	-0.9329224D-01	2
7	-0.1515625D+01	0.1426964D+00	2
8	-0.1523438D+01	0.2516413D-01	3
9	-0.1527344D+01	-0.3394836D-01	3
10	-0.1525391D+01	-0.4363216D-02	4
11	-0.1524414D+01	0.1040768D-01	3
12	-0.1524902D+01	0.3024037D-02	4
13	-0.1525146D+01	-0.6691384D-03	5
14	-0.1525024D+01	0.1177562D-02	5
15	-0.1525085D+01	0.2542400D-03	6
16	-0.1525116D+01	-0.2074421D-03	5
17	-0.1525101D+01	0.2340073D-04	6
18	-0.1525108D+01	-0.9202025D-04	6
19	-0.1525105D+01	-0.3430965D-04	6
20	-0.1525103D+01	-0.5454435D-05	6
21	-0.1525102D+01	0.8973153D-05	7

A computer program that uses BISE to repeat and continue the steps of Example 5.2 is given in Table 5.3, and successive values of x_k and $f(x_k)$ ($k \geq 0$) are given in Table 5.4. Double precision was used in this driver program, and several to follow, for more exacting answers. Of course, BISE was accordingly modified for double precision by inserting the declaration, "IMPLICIT DOUBLE PRECISION (A$-$H, O$-$Z)." ∎

If we regard the most recently computed midpoint x_k as an approximation of the root, then from discussion at the beginning of this subsection, one may say that the approximation error is "about" halved at each bisection iteration. Another way of viewing this is to say that the approximation x_k picks up approximately a significant bit at each iteration, or one significant decimal place in three or four iterations, since $2^{-3} > \frac{1}{10} > 2^{-4}$. One can see this phenomenon exhibited clearly in Table 5.4. After every three to four iterations, the x_k value becomes one significant decimal closer to the final entry.

In Figure 5.6 we have plotted successive bisection midpoints x_k and values $f_k = f(x_k)$. It is instructive to compare the way the bisection method quickly concentrates about the root, with the corresponding Figure 5.3 for the "graphical" approach. Accuracy indicated in Table 5.4 is infeasible by graphical means.

5.4
THE SECANT METHOD

Let x_0 and x_1 be two real numbers. In contrast to the bisection method, we do not insist that $x_0 < x_1$ or that $f(x_0)$ and $f(x_1)$ have different signs. Let us approximate the function $f(x)$ by a linear interpolating polynomial with interpolating points x_0 and x_1. From the Lagrange representation (Section 3.4.2)

$$l_0(x) = \frac{x - x_1}{x_0 - x_1} \quad \text{and} \quad l_1(x) = \frac{x - x_0}{x_1 - x_0}, \tag{5.5}$$

so

$$p(x) = f(x_0) \frac{x - x_1}{x_0 - x_1} + f(x_1) \frac{x - x_0}{x_1 - x_0}. \tag{5.6}$$

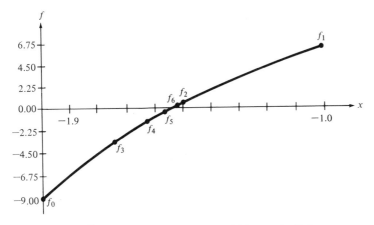

FIGURE 5.6   Bisection Iteration of Example 5.3

The line $p(x)$ is the secant line for $f(x)$ at x_0 and x_1. The *secant method* has us obtain a new approximation x_2 of the root by solving the linear equation $p(x) = 0$. Toward deriving an explicit formula for the next secant point, multiply both sides of the equation

$$f(x_0) \frac{x - x_1}{x_0 - x_1} + f(x_1) \frac{x - x_0}{x_1 - x_0} = 0$$

by $(x_1 - x_0)$, to get

$$-f(x_0)(x - x_1) + f(x_1)(x - x_0) = 0.$$

Upon rearrangement, the equation above becomes

$$x[f(x_1) - f(x_0)] + [f(x_0)x_1 - f(x_1)x_0] = 0.$$

Consequently,

$$x = \frac{f(x_1)x_0 - f(x_0)x_1}{f(x_1) - f(x_0)}.$$

By adding and subtracting $f(x_1)x_1$ in the numerator, the equation above may be reworked into a more conventional formula

$$x = \frac{f(x_1)x_0 - f(x_1)x_1 + f(x_1)x_1 - f(x_0)x_1}{f(x_1) - f(x_0)}$$

$$= \frac{[f(x_1) - f(x_0)]x_1 - f(x_1)(x_1 - x_0)}{f(x_1) - f(x_0)}$$

$$= x_1 - \frac{f(x_1)(x_1 - x_0)}{f(x_1) - f(x_0)}.$$

If this root is selected as the next approximation x_2, then

$$x_2 = x_1 - \frac{f(x_1)(x_1 - x_0)}{f(x_1) - f(x_0)}.$$

One step of the secant method is shown in Figure 5.7. We see in this figure that x_2 is the x-intercept of the secant line connecting $(x_0, f(x_0))$ with $(x_1, f(x_1))$. This secant line itself is the linear polynomial $p(x)$ given by (5.6).

By repeating this procedure, and letting x_1 and x_2 play the the roles of x_0 and x_1, we have

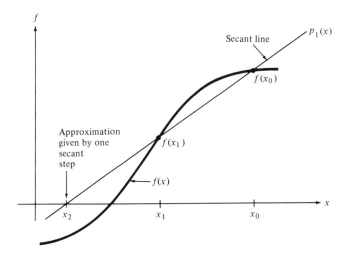

FIGURE 5.7   One Secant Step

$$x_3 = x_2 - \frac{f(x_2)(x_2 - x_1)}{f(x_2) - f(x_1)},$$

and so on. The general secant method step is

$$x_{k+1} = x_k - \frac{f(x_k)(x_k - x_{k-1})}{f(x_k) - f(x_{k-1})} \qquad (k \geq 1). \tag{5.7}$$

Note that the value of the new root approximation depends on the previous *two* approximations and corresponding functional values. The successive steps of the secant method are illustrated in Figure 5.8. The computer subroutine SECA for the secant method is given in Table 5.5.

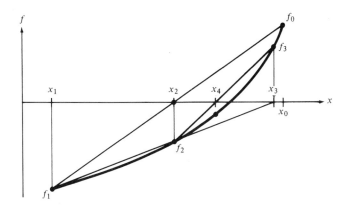

FIGURE 5.8   The Secant Method

TABLE 5.5   Subroutine SECA for the Secant Method

```
        SUBROUTINE SECA(A,B,X,EPS)
C
C       ****************************************************************
C       *    FUNCTION: THIS SUBROUTINE COMPUTES THE APPROXIMATE ROOT   *
C       *              OF F(X)=0 USING THE SECANT METHOD               *
C       *    USAGE:                                                    *
C       *        CALL SEQUENCE: CALL SECA(A,B,X,EPS)                   *
C       *        EXTERNAL FUNCTIONS/SUBROUTINES: FUNCTION F(X)         *
C       *    PARAMETERS:                                               *
C       *        INPUT:                                                *
C       *            A=INITIAL APPROXIMATION X(0)                      *
C       *            B=INITIAL APPROXIMATION X(1)                      *
C       *            EPS=ERROR BOUND                                   *
C       *        OUTPUT:                                               *
C       *            X=SECANT APPROXIMATION OF THE ROOT                *
C       ****************************************************************
C
C       ***   INITIALIZATION   ***
C
        X = B
        XOLD = A
        FX=F(X)
        FOLD=F(XOLD)
C
C       *** COMPUTE APPROXIMATE ROOT ITERATIVELY   ***
C
        DO WHILE(ABS(X-XOLD).GT.EPS)
          SAVE=X
          X=X-FX*(X-XOLD)/(FX-FOLD)
          FOLD=FX
          FX=F(X)
          XOLD=SAVE
        END DO
        RETURN
        END
```

── **EXAMPLE 5.4** ──────

Here the secant method is applied to the function $f(x) = x^3 - 3x^2 - x + 9$ of Example 5.2. Again we take $x_0 = -2$ and $x_1 = -1$. Thus according to (5.7) with $k = 1$, we calculate that

$$f(x_0) = f(-2) = -9, \qquad f(x_1) = f(-1) = 6,$$

and

$$x_2 = -1 - \frac{6[-1 - (-2)]}{6 - (-9)} = -1 - \frac{6}{15} = -1.4.$$

A calculation shows that $f(-1.4) = 1.776$. The next secant point, then, is

$$x_3 = -1.4 - \frac{f(-1.4)(-1.4 + 1)}{f(-1.4) - f(-1)}$$

$$= -1.4 - \frac{1.776\,(-0.4)}{1.776 - 6.0} = -1.56818.$$

───── **EXAMPLE 5.5** ───

The calculations of Example 5.4 are now automated. Through the driver program in Table 5.6, we avail ourselves of subroutine SECA (Table 5.5), which was first modified for double precision. The results are listed in Table 5.7. The root approximations are presented only to eight digits, but the last column shows the accuracy of the stored numbers. Successive secant points are displayed in Figure 5.9.

TABLE 5.6   Program for Secant Example

```
C      PROGRAM SECANT
C
C      ***************************************************************
C      THIS PROGRAM ILLUSTRATES THE SECANT METHOD BY FINDING
C      A ROOT OF THE FUNCTION F(X)=X**3-3*X**2-X+9
C      STARTING AT X0=-2, X1=-1.
C      CALLS:   SECA (MODIFIED FOR DOUBLE PRECISION)
C      OUTPUT(FROM FUNCTION F):
C               X=VALUE OF X AT CURRENT ITERATION
C               F=FUNCTIONAL VALUE AT X
C      ***************************************************************
C
       IMPLICIT DOUBLE PRECISION(A-H,O-Z)
       A=-2.0D0
       B=-1.0D0
       EPS=0.5D-6
C
C      *** SUBROUTINE SECA WILL FIND A ROOT IN THIS INTERVAL    ***
C
       CALL SECA(A,B,X,EPS)
       STOP
       END
C
C      *** FUNCTION F IS CALLED BY SECA. THIS IS THE FUNCTION TO ***
C      *** BE ZEROED                                            ***
C
       FUNCTION F(X)
       IMPLICIT DOUBLE PRECISION(A-H,O-Z)
       F=X**3-3.0D0*X**2-X+9.0D0
       WRITE(10,1)X,F
     1 FORMAT(22X,D16.8,4X,D16.8)
       RETURN
       END
```

TABLE 5.7   Successive Secant Iterations

k	x_k	$f(x_k)$	Number of Correct Significant Decimals in x_k
0	$-.20000000E+01$	$-.90000000E+01$	0
1	$-.10000000E+01$	$.60000000E+01$	1
2	$-.14000000E+01$	$.17760000E+01$	1
3	$-.15681818E+01$	$-.66586448E+00$	2
4	$-.15223208E+01$	$.42019874E-01$	3
5	$-.15250431E+01$	$.89434209E-03$	4
6	$-.15251023E+01$	$-.12469362E-05$	8
7	$-.15251023E+01$	$.36914471E-10$	12

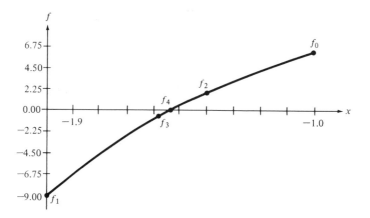

FIGURE 5.9   Secant Iterations of Example 5.5

It is known (S & Y, 1978, Sec. 5.1.3) that in a neighborhood of a root of a smooth function, the secant method converges far faster than the bisection rule. Recall that successive estimates obtained by the latter gain a new significant decimal every three iterations. Successive iterates of the secant method, close to the solution, increase the number of correct significant decimals by about 50%. The more rapid convergence of the secant method on our test problem is evident in Table 5.7, compared with Table 5.4. Much fewer steps were used to obtain the same accuracy, and in the last step the number of correct decimal places jumps from 8 to 12. On the other hand, provided that one can find points on either side of a root, the bisection method is fail-safe: As long as the magnitude $|f(x_k)|$ is large enough that the computer can correctly distinguish the sign, the bisection method always converges. The secant method may diverge unless the starting points are sufficiently close to the root, as shown in Example 5.6.

EXAMPLE 5.6

Here we see a case in which successive approximations x_k actually get farther from the root. If we do so much as multiply the polynomial of preceding examples by exp (x), thus obtaining

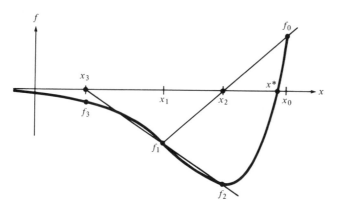

FIGURE 5.10   Function Demonstrating Secant Divergence

$$f(x) = (x^3 - 3x^2 - x + 9) \exp(x),$$

then the roots are unchanged. But the secant method, starting with $x_0 = -1$, $x_1 = -2$, diverges. A glance at the graph of $f(x)$ (Figure 5.10) suggests why: Once consecutive points are located to the left of the hump, the algorithm will thereafter "think" that the root is to the left because the secant line connecting the most recent pair of estimates x_{k-1} and x_k has negative slope and intersects the axis to the left of these points. Locations of the first four secant function points are shown in Figure 5.10.   ■

Application 5.2

At the beginning of this chapter we mentioned an application to finding the rise time to half of the full voltage of an *RLC* circuit. The reader may easily compute the answer to this problem by modifying the function subprogram in Table 5.6 so that

$$F = 0.5 - 2 * \text{EXP}(-X) + \text{EXP}(-2 * X)$$

and in the driver, taking A = 0, B = 1, to start the secant iterations.

A slightly more challenging problem is that of finding the first return to 0 of the response of the *LR* circuit shown in Figure 5.11. In this case the governing nonlinear equation has infinitely many positive solutions. Assume that $R = 20$ Ω, $L = 4$ henrys, and the voltage, as a function of the time t, is $V(t) = 100\sqrt{2} \sin (5t)$ for $t \geq 0$, and $V(t) = 0$ for $t < 0$. If we assume that $i(0) = 0$, the current can be expressed as

$$i(t) = 5e^{-5t} \sin \left(\frac{\pi}{4} \right) + 5 \sin \left(5t - \frac{\pi}{4} \right).$$

In order to compute the earliest positive time at which the current is zero, we must solve the nonlinear equation

$$i(t) = 5e^{-5t} \sin \left(\frac{\pi}{4} \right) + 5 \sin \left(5t - \frac{\pi}{4} \right) = 0. \tag{5.8}$$

One aspect of this problem which requires a little thought is that if one locates a root of (5.8), it might not be obvious that it is the *least* positive root. Whereas analytic means of assuring conditions for the least root are available from intermediate analysis, we take the more pragmatic route of examining computer-gen-

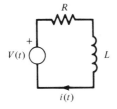

R

$V(t)$

L

$i(t)$

FIGURE 5.11   Electric Circuit

erated point plots of the function. Two graphs are given in Figure 5.12. The first is based on 30 function values, and the second, on 60. One reason for making two graphs is that if they resemble one another, we have some heuristic assurance that we are using enough values, and the graph has no narrow lobes sweeping through the axis which escaped the resolution of the earlier graph.

From these graphs we see that the minimum positive root seems to be between 0.5 and 1.0. Using these two points as starting values for the secant method, the trivial calling program listed in Table 5.8 generates the successive secant estimates shown in Table 5.9. The sequence limit

$$t^* = 0.7881466$$

does lie in the region which the graphs indicate contains a minimum root, and at this point, the function value $i(t^*) \approx 1.1 \cdot 10^{-7}$.

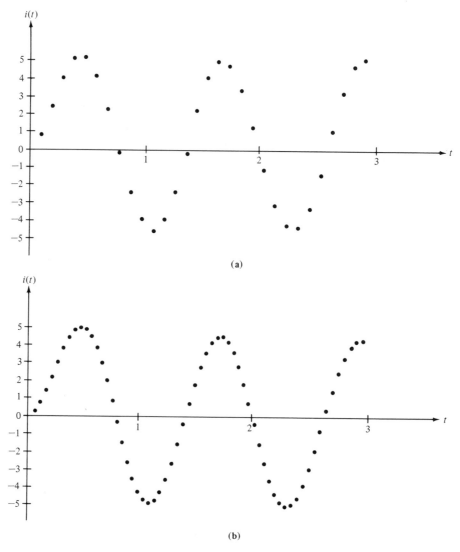

(a)

(b)

FIGURE 5.12   Graphs for Application 5.2

TABLE 5.8   Program for Circuit Application

```
C       PROGRAM ZEROCROSS
C
C       ******************************************************************
C       THIS PROGRAM COMPUTES THE TIME UNTIL THE  CURRENT IN THE R-L
C       CIRCUIT (FIGURE 5-11) BECOMES ZERO FOR THE FIRST TIME
C       (APPLICATION 5.2).   THIS IS DONE BY USING THE SECANT METHOD
C       TO FIND THE ZERO IN THE INTERVAL [0.5,1.0] OF THE FUNCTION
C       F(T)=5(SIN(PI/4)EXP(-5T)+SIN(5T-PI/4)) .
C       CALLS:   SECA
C       OUTPUT: T= THE APPROXIMATION TO THE ZERO OF F(T) IN [0.5,1.0]
C       OUTPUT(FROM FUNCTION F):
C                   X=VALUE OF X AT CURRENT ITERATION
C                   F=FUNCTION VALUE ( F(X) ) AT X
C       ******************************************************************
C
        T0=0.5
        T1=1.0
        EPS=1.E-7
C
C       *** SUBROUTINE SECA WILL FIND A ROOT OF F(X)                  ***
C       *** USING THE TWO INITIAL POINTS T0 AND T1                    ***
C
        CALL SECA(T0,T1,T,EPS)
        WRITE (10,*)'THE SOLUTION IS ',T
        STOP
        END
C
C       *** FUNCTION F IS CALLED BY SECA. THIS IS THE FUNCTION        ***
C       *** WHOSE ZERO IS SOUGHT                                      ***
C
        FUNCTION F(X)
        PI=4*ATAN(1.0)
        F=5*(EXP(-5*X)*SIN(PI/4.0)+SIN(5*X-PI/4.0))
        WRITE(10,1)X,F
  1     FORMAT(10X,E16.8,4X,E16.8)
        RETURN
        END
```

TABLE 5.9   Output for Circuit Application

j	Time, t_j	Current $i(t_j)$
1	0.10000000E+01	-0.43693848E+01
2	0.50000000E+00	0.52386036E+01
3	0.77261710E+00	0.39356664E+00
4	0.79140592E+00	-0.82572050E-01
5	0.78814757E+00	-0.24060719E-04
6	0.78814662E+00	0.11175871E-06
7	0.78814662E+00	0.11175871E-06

◇

★Application 5.3

This application is to another numerical computations task, the determination of the Gauss quadrature points x_i, $1 \le i \le n$. As discussed in Section 4.6, this task is the difficult part of setting up Gauss quadrature formulas. For Gauss quadrature is a particular type of interpolatory quadrature, and once the points are found, a simple application of subroutine COEFF (Table 4.7) gives the weights A_i.

We refer the reader to S & Y (Sec. 3.2.3), or Davis and Rabinowitz (1975) for greater detail, for the rationale of the formulas to be used. The gist of the theory behind the computational method is that the Gaussian quadrature points are the roots of the polynomial $P_n(x)$ determined, for any value x, by the recurrence

$$P_0(x) = 1, \qquad P_1(x) = x,$$

and for $j = 2, 3, \ldots, j - 1$,

$$P_j(x) = \left(\frac{j-1}{j}\right) [xP_{j-1}(x) - P_{j-2}(x)] + xP_{j-1}(x). \qquad (5.9)$$

The theory tells us further that all roots of $P_n(x)$, for any n, must be in the interval $[-1, 1]$. Moreover, they are symmetric: If x^* is a root, so is $-x^*$. Thus it suffices to locate only negative roots. While the recursion (5.9) may seem a bit awkward to write, it is easy to program. Table 5.10 gives a simple driver for SECA which produced the 16-significant-place Gauss points offered in Table 5.11. These values were checked against a published table; they are correct. The driver is a trivial modification of the one for Example 5.6; we provided the function subprogram with a loop giving (5.9). Note that the driver uses double-precision variables (SECA must correspondingly be changed for double precision). To construct a quadrature formula, the secant starting points must be varied to uncover all the roots. Davis and Rabinowitz (1975, p. 89) give a formula that is useful in this regard. A good approximation $\psi(k, n)$ to the kth point of an n-point Gaussian rule is

$$\psi(k, n) = \cos(\theta(k, n)),$$

where

$$\theta(k, n) = \frac{4k - 1}{4n + 2}\pi + \frac{n - 1}{8n^3}\cot\left(\frac{4k - 1}{4n + 2}\pi\right).$$

Each of the n roots of $P_n(x)$ are uncovered by Program Gausspoint (Table 5.10), which for each k, $1 \le k \le n$, sets initial points A and B to be

$$A = \psi(k, n) - \frac{1}{4n + 2}$$

$$B = \psi(k, n) + \frac{1}{4n + 2}.$$

TABLE 5.10 Program for Gauss Points

```
C       PROGRAM GAUSSPOINT
C
C       **********************************************************************
C       THIS PROGRAM COMPUTES THE GAUSS QUADRATURE POINTS FOR A
C       N-POINT RULE ON THE INTERVAL [-1,1] BY USING THE SECANT
C       METHOD TO FIND THE NEGATIVE ROOTS OF THE N-TH DEGREE
C       LEGENDRE POLYNOMIAL (N=2,3,4,...,7)
C       CALLS:    SECA (MODIFIED FOR DOUBLE PRECISION)
C       OUTPUT:   GAUSS QUADRATURE POINTS
C       **********************************************************************
C
```

TABLE 5.10   (Continued)

```
          IMPLICIT DOUBLE PRECISION(A-H,O-Z)
          COMMON N
          PI=4*DATAN(1.0D0)
          MAXN=7
C
C     *** COMPUTE THE GAUSS POINTS FOR THE N-POINT RULE , WHERE   ***
C     *** N = 2,3,...,MAXN                                        ***
C
          DO 1 N=2,MAXN
             WRITE(10,3)N
     3       FORMAT(/,'   NO OF QUAD. PTS',I5)
             K=1
             DEN=DFLOAT(4*N+2)
C
C     *** FIND THE K-TH  (K=1,2,..,INT((N+1)/2) ) NEGATIVE ROOT   ***
C     *** OF THE N-TH DEGREE LEGENDRE POLYNOMIAL   PSI IS AN       ***
C     *** APPROXIMATION TO THE K-TH NEGATIVE ROOT OF THE N-TH      ***
C     *** DEGREE LEGENDRE POLYNOMIAL     1/DEN IS ADDED AND        ***
C     *** SUBTRACTED FROM PSI TO OBTAIN AN INTERVAL [A,B] IN       ***
C     *** WHICH A NEGATIVE ROOT OF THE LEGENDRE POLYNOMIAL LIES    ***
C     *** (PSI IS THE APPROXIMATION TO THIS ROOT) THE SECANT       ***
C     *** METHOD IS STARTED WITH THE INITIAL POINTS A AND B TO     ***
C     *** FIND THIS ROOT                                          ***
C
          DO WHILE (K .LE. (N+1)/2)
             THETA = (4*K-1)/DEN*PI
             THETA = THETA +((N-1)/DFLOAT(8*N**3))*
     1          DTAN(DEN/(DFLOAT(4*K -1)*PI))
             PSI=-DCOS(THETA)
             A=PSI- 1/DEN
             B=PSI+1/DEN
             EPS=0.5D-10
C
C     ***     SUBROUTINE SECA WILL FIND A ROOT OF F(X)             ***
C     ***     ITERATIVELY USING THE INITIAL POINTS A AND B         ***
C
             CALL SECA(A,B,X,EPS)
             WRITE (10,2),K,X
     2       FORMAT(22X,I3,10X,D26.18)
             K=K+1
          ENDDO
     1    CONTINUE
          STOP
          END
C
C     *** SUBROUTINE SECA FINDS A ZERO OF THE FUNCTION F   HERE    ***
C     *** F IS THE N-TH DEGREE LEGENDRE POLYNOMIAL AND IT IS       ***
C     *** COMPUTED ITERATIVELY BY FORMULAE (5.9)                   ***
C
          FUNCTION F(X)
          IMPLICIT DOUBLE PRECISION(A-H,O-Z)
          COMMON N
          POLD=1.0D0
          P=X
          DO J = 2,N
             F=((J-1)/DFLOAT(J))*(X*P-POLD)+X*P
             POLD=P
             P=F
          END DO
          RETURN
          END
```

TABLE 5.11   Gauss Points in $[-1, 0]$

			VALUES
NO OF QUAD. PTS	2		
		1	-0.577350269189625759D+00
NO OF QUAD. PTS	3		
		1	-0.774596669241483377D+00
		2	-0.646952716980803992D-25
NO OF QUAD. PTS	4		
		1	-0.861136311594052559D+00
		2	-0.339981043584856264D+00
NO OF QUAD. PTS	5		
		1	-0.906179845938663991D+00
		2	-0.538469310105683094D+00
		3	-0.176726536444400222D-25
NO OF QUAD. PTS	6		
		1	-0.932469514203152022D+00
		2	-0.661209386466264523D+00
		3	-0.238619186083196908D+00
NO OF QUAD. PTS	7		
		1	-0.949107912342758514D+00
		2	-0.741531185599394446D+00
		3	-0.405845151377397163D+00
		4	-0.392073730656158130D-26

$\diamond$

5.5
NEWTON'S METHOD

The secant method has us choose the successive point as the zero of the linear interpolation polynomial based on the two most recent points. Newton's method, analogously, has us choose the successive point as the zero to the linear Taylor's polynomial, the expansion being about the current point. Whereas two points, x_0 and x_1, were needed to "start" the secant iterations, only one point, x_0, determines the Newton iterations.

Let us denote the linear Taylor's polynomial of $f(x)$ about x_0 by

$$p(x) = f(x_0) + f'(x_0)(x - x_0).$$

Then the new approximation x_1 of the root is the solution of the linear equation $p(x) = 0$. This implies that

$$x_1 = x_0 - \frac{f(x_0)}{f'(x_0)} \, .$$

The linear Taylor's polynomial is the tangent line at x_0. A single Newton's step is illustrated in Figure 5.13. The successor x_1 is the x-intercept of this tangent line.

By repeating this procedure, a sequence $\{x_k\}$ is determined by the recursive rule

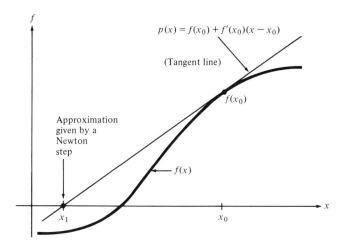

FIGURE 5.13   One Step of Newton's Method

$$x_{k+1} = x_k - \frac{f(x_k)}{f'(x_k)} . \qquad (5.10)$$

This method (5.10) is called *Newton's method* (or, alternatively, the *Newton–Raphson method*).

──────── **EXAMPLE 5.7** ──

Newton's method is now applied to our familiar polynomial equation

$$f(x) = x^3 - 3x^2 - x + 9 = 0.$$

Let the initial approximation be given by $x_0 = -2$. Then, according to (5.10) with $k = 0$ and $f'(x) = 3x^2 - 6x - 1$,

$$x_1 = x_0 - \frac{f(x_0)}{f'(x_0)} = -2 - \frac{-9}{23} = -1.608696.$$

Since $f(x_1) \approx -1.31816$ and $f'(x_1) \approx 16.41588$, the next Newton iterate is

$$x_2 = -1.608696 + 0.080298 = -1.528398.$$

    The computer subroutine NEIT for Newton's method is given in Table 5.12. It requires the user to supply function subprograms F(X) and DF(X) for $f(x)$ and $f'(x)$, respectively.

TABLE 5.12   Subroutine NEIT for Newton's Method

```
          SUBROUTINE NEIT(X0,X,EPS)
C
C    **************************************************************
C    *   FUNCTION: THE SUBROUTINE APPROXIMATES THE ROOT OF       *
C    *              F(X)=0 GIVEN THE INITIAL POINT X0 AND THE     *
C    *              DERIVATIVE FUNCTION DF(X) USING THE NEWTON    *
C    *              METHOD                                        *
C    *   USAGE:                                                   *
C    *       CALL SEQUENCE: CALL NEIT(X0,X,EPS)                   *
C    *       EXTERNAL FUNCTIONS/SUBROUTINES: FUNCTION F(X)        *
C    *                                       FUNCTION DF(X)       *
C    *   PARAMETERS:                                              *
C    *       INPUT:                                               *
C    *            X0=INITIAL ROOT APPROXIMATION                   *
C    *            EPS=ERROR BOUND                                 *
C    *       OUTPUT:                                              *
C    *            X=NEWTON APPROXIMATION OF THE ROOT              *
C    **************************************************************
C
C       *** INITIALIZATION ***
          X=X0-(F(X0)/DF(X0))
C       *** COMPUTE APPROXIMATE ROOT ITERATIVELY ***
          DO WHILE(ABS(X-X0).GT.EPS)
              X0=X
              X=X0-(F(X0)/DF(X0))
          END DO
          RETURN
          END
```

EXAMPLE 5.8

The successive Newton iterations for the problem in Example 5.7 are obtained according to the program in Table 5.13 and are given in Table 5.14. The faster convergence of Newton's method compared to the secant method is obvious. For purposes of comparison with Figures 5.6 and 5.9, the Newton iterations are plotted in Figure 5.14.

TABLE 5.13   Program for Illustration of Newton's Method

```
C       PROGRAM NEWTON
C
C       **************************************************************
C       THIS PROGRAM ILLUSTRATES THE NEWTONS METHOD ON THE FUNCTION
C       F(X)=X**3-3*X**2-X+9 STARTING AT X=-2.0
C       CALLS:   NEIT (MODIFIED FOR DOUBLE PRECISION)
C       OUTPUT(FROM FUNCTION F):
C                 X=VALUE OF X AT CURRENT ITERATION
C                 F=FUNCTIONAL VALUE AT X
C       **************************************************************
C
        IMPLICIT DOUBLE PRECISION(A-H,O-Z)
        X0=-2.0D0
        EPS=0.5D-6
C
C       *** SUBROUTINE NEIT IS USED TO FIND A ROOT STARTING WITH   ***
C       *** THE INITIAL GUESS X0                                   ***
C
```

TABLE 5.13   (Continued)

```
          CALL NEIT(X0,X,EPS)
          STOP
          END
C
C      *** FUNCTION F IS CALLED BY NEIT TO CALCULATE FUNCTIONAL   ***
C      *** VALUES FOR THE PASSED POINT X                          ***
C
          FUNCTION F(X)
          IMPLICIT DOUBLE PRECISION(A-H,O-Z)
          F=X**3-3.0D0*X**2-X+9.0D0
          WRITE(10,1)X,F
        1 FORMAT(22X,D16.7,4X,D16.7)
          RETURN
          END
C
C      *** FUNCTION DF(X) IS CALLED BY NEIT TO CALCULATE THE      ***
C      *** DERIVATIVE AT X                                        ***
C
          FUNCTION DF(X)
          IMPLICIT DOUBLE PRECISION(A-H,O-Z)
          DF=3.0D0*X**2-6.0D0*X-1.0D0
          RETURN
          END
```

TABLE 5.14   Successive Newton Iterates

k	x_k	$f(x_k)$	Number of Correct Significant Decimals in x_k
0	-0.2000000D+01	-0.9000000D+01	1
1	-0.1608696D+01	-0.1318156D+01	1
2	-0.1528398D+01	-0.4994256D-01	3
3	-0.1525108D+01	-0.8208588D-04	6
4	-0.1525102D+01	-0.2230209D-09	11

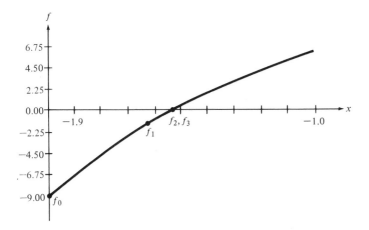

FIGURE 5.14   Newton Iterations for Example 5.8

In the following optional section (Section 5.6) we give theoretical reasons why Newton's method converges even faster than the bisection and secant methods. In the neighborhood of a root of a smooth function, the number of correct significant figures approximately doubles at each Newton iteration. This phenomenon is exhibited in Table 5.14. (Not all the correct digits of x_4 are shown.) Because of its typical efficiency, Newton's method is popular when the derivative of $f(x)$ is available. The price paid for the increased convergence rate of Newton's method over the bisection and secant methods is that it requires two function calls [$f(x_k)$ and its derivative, $f'(x_k)$] per iteration rather than one.

The derivative requirement of Newton's method can be sidestepped through suitable numerical differentiation techniques given in Section 4.2. By making the step size h in the derivative formula decrease proportionally to $|f(x_k)|$, one can preserve the rapid convergence property of Newton's method (Dennis and Schnabel, 1983). Note that if the derivative $f'(x)$ is approximated by

$$\frac{f(x_k) - f(x_{k-1})}{x_k - x_{k-1}},$$

the secant method is obtained. [But in the secant case, the step size h is proportional to $f(x_{k-1})$ rather than $f(x_k)$.]

──────── **EXAMPLE 5.9** ────────────────────────────

Let us examine how square roots may be extracted by elementary arithmetical operations alone through use of Newton's method. It is evident that $\sqrt{A}$ is the positive root of the equation

$$f(x) = x^2 - A = 0.$$

The, from (5.10), Newton's method chooses

$$x_{k+1} = x_k - \frac{f(x_k)}{f'(x_k)} = x_k - \frac{x_k^2 - A}{2x_k} = \frac{1}{2}\left(x_k + \frac{A}{x_k}\right). \qquad (5.11)$$

For example, if $A = x_0 = 5$, then

$$x_1 = \tfrac{1}{2}(5 + 1) = 3$$

$$x_2 = \tfrac{1}{2}(3 + \tfrac{5}{3}) = \tfrac{7}{3}$$

and continuing, we get the list below. The estimate x_5 of $\sqrt{5}$ is correct in all digits displayed:

$$x_3 = 2.238095238$$

$$x_4 = 2.236068896$$

$$x_5 = 2.236067977.$$

This example is particularly significant because we observed in Chapter 3 that the square-root function has no accurate low-degree polynomial approximators.

Other roots $\sqrt[n]{A}$ can be obtained arithmetically by this procedure, by finding the root of $f(x) = x^n - A = 0$. Then the Newton method gives the following generalization of (5.11):

$$x_{k+1} = x_k - \frac{x_k^n - A}{nx_k^{n-1}} = \frac{1}{n}\left[(n - 1)x_k + \frac{A}{x_k^{n-1}}\right]. \qquad (5.12)$$

∎

──── **EXAMPLE 5.10** ────────────────────────────────

The bothersome function of Example 5.6 can cause divergence of Newton as well as secant iterations. Here we illustrate a different type of difficulty. Take

$$f(x) = 1 - 2 \exp(-|x|).$$

The function is shown in Figure 5.15. It has no derivative at 0, but this could be trivially corrected. The real problem is that at a distance from the root, the slope is so close to 0 that the next Newton iteration seriously overshoots and ends up even farther from the roots. This, in turn, results in even a worse gyration in the opposite direction at the next iteration. If Newton iterations are started at $x_0 = 2.5$, then as shown in Figure 5.15, Newton iterates oscillate about the origin with ever-increasing amplitude until overflow results. On the other hand, if $0 < x_0 < x^*$, rapid convergence will be observed.

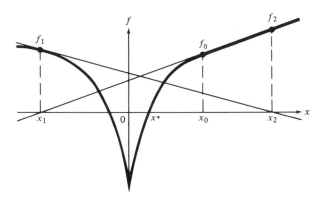

FIGURE 5.15 Function Demonstrating Newton Divergence

∎

★5.6
CONVERGENCE AND ERROR PROPERTIES OF THE BISECTION, SECANT, AND NEWTON'S METHODS

Let x^* denote the root of the equation $f(x) = 0$, where $f(x)$ is a real-valued function. After k bisection steps, the root is located inside an interval of length $(b - a)/2^k$. Consequently, either endpoint approximates the root within the error bound $(b - a)/2^k$.

In applying the secant or the Newton method, a sequence $x_0, x_1, x_2, \ldots$ is computed. It is known (e.g., S & Y, 1978, Secs. 5.1.3 and 5.1.4) that if $f''(x)$ exists and is bounded and furthermore if $f'(x)$ differs from zero in the neighborhood of the root x^*, then for the starting point x_0 sufficiently close to x^*, both of these methods are convergent and there exist constants C and r such that

$$|x_{k+1} - x^*| \leq C|x_k - x^*|^r. \tag{5.13}$$

In the case of the secant method $r = (1 + \sqrt{5})/2 \approx 1.615$, and for Newton's method $r = 2$. The exponent r is known as the *convergence rate*.

It is not difficult to confirm that methods having larger r ultimately have smaller error, no matter what C is. Thus, all things being equal, we would like to achieve as large a convergence rate r as possible without entailing excessive additional computational cost or numerical instability.

The Newton and secant methods were motivated by approximating the function $f(x)$ by linear polynomials (Taylor's and interpolation polynomials, respectively) and choosing the successive estimate to be the root of the linear polynomial. This suggests that one could perhaps get a faster convergence rate by increasing the degree of the approximating polynomial, thereby getting a better "fit" to $f(x)$. The Taylor expansion avenue does generalize. If we approximate $f(x)$ by a Taylor's polynomial of degree D, for well-behaved $f(x)$, the rate of convergence will be $D + 1$. (Thus Newton's method is the special case that $D = 1$.) However, this avenue has not become popular. Recall from Chapters 3 and 4 that Taylor's expansions have not led to convenient numerical schemes because of the bother of evaluating higher derivatives. Moreover, other troubles arise from Taylor's polynomial approximations. For example, one must solve the polynomial nonlinear equation problem in order to find the roots of the approximating Taylor's polynomial. Then the question arises as to which of the roots should then be selected as the next approximation. To summarize, the secant and Newton's methods, despite their age and simplicity, are still the methods of choice for routine nonlinear equation problems.

5.7
POLYNOMIAL ROOTS

5.7.1 Background Information

Because of their pervasive role in science and mathematics, polynomial equations, that is, equations of the form

$$f(z) = a_n z^n + a_{n-1} z^{n-1} + \cdots + a_0 = 0, \tag{5.14}$$

warrant special attention. The coefficients a_k ($0 \leq k \leq n$) may be either real or complex numbers. For such polynomials, the roots can be either real or complex. (Recall that a polynomial with real coefficients may have complex roots. In particular, the imaginary number $i = \sqrt{-1}$ is defined as a root of the real polynomial $z^2 + 1$.) In this section we use z, rather than x, to denote the independent variable. This is to emphasize that here we presume polynomials to be evaluated on the set of complex, rather than real, numbers.

The bisection method is not applicable to finding complex roots, because the implementation of the method requires ordering the values of $f(x)$, which must therefore be real. It is known (e.g., Ortega and Rheinboldt, 1970) that the Newton and secant methods are convergent if the roots $r_1, r_2, \ldots, r_n$ are simple (i.e., all different). Because derivatives of polynomials are easy to obtain, and because of its fast convergence rate and stable behavior (e.g., Ralston and Rabinowitz, 1978, Sec. 8.6) near repeated roots, Newton's method is appropriate for polynomial equations.

We will use the following facts (see Herstein, 1964, Chap. 5) regarding the roots of the nth-degree polynomial (5.14) with real or complex coefficients:

1. There are n (not necessarily distinct) real or complex roots.
2. If n is odd and all coefficients are real, there is at least one real root.
3. If all coefficients are real and complex roots exist, they occur in conjugate pairs.
4. If $z*$ is a root of (5.14), then necessarily

$$f(z) = (z - z*)g(z), \tag{5.15}$$

where $g(z)$ is a polynomial of degee $n - 1$.

This last fact can be utilized for reducing the degree of a polynomial, as successive roots are computed, by *synthetic division*. Specifically, let

$$f(z) = \sum_{j=0}^{n} a_j z^j \quad \text{and} \quad g(z) = \sum_{j=0}^{n-1} b_j z^j$$

be related as in property 4. Then

$$\begin{aligned} f(z) &= a_n z^n + a_{n-1} z^{n-1} + \cdots + a_1 z + a_0 \\ &= (z - z*)(b_{n-1} z^{n-1} + b_{n-2} z^{n-2} + \cdots + b_0). \end{aligned} \tag{5.16}$$

By equating coefficients of like powers of z in (5.16), we can solve for the b_j's. Thus, collecting the coefficients of z^i, $i = n, n - 1, \ldots, 1$, we conclude that

$$a_i = b_{i-1} - z* b_i$$

or

$$\boxed{b_{i-1} = a_i + z* b_i, \quad i = n, n - 1, \ldots, 1.} \tag{5.17}$$

In (5.17) we define $b_n = 0$ and recursively use that formula to get $b_{n-1}, b_{n-2}, \ldots, b_0$. The activity of obtaining lower-degree factor polynomials $g(z)$ is referred to as polynomial *deflation*.

―――― **EXAMPLE 5.11** ――――

Observe that $z* = 2$ is a root of the polynomial equation

$$f(z) = z^4 - 2z^3 + 3z^2 - 7z + 2 = 0.$$

In the nomenclature of (5.16) and (5.17), $n = 4$, and

$$a_4 = 1, a_3 = -2, a_2 = 3, a_1 = -7, \text{ and } a_0 = 2.$$

From (5.17),

$$b_4 = 0$$

$$b_3 = a_4 + 2 \cdot 0 = 1$$

$$b_2 = a_3 + 2 \cdot 1 = 0$$

$$b_1 = a_2 + 2 \cdot 0 = 3$$

$$b_0 = a_1 + 2 \cdot 3 = -1.$$

The factor polynomial $g(z)$ is, then, $z^3 + 3z - 1$. One may check that $g(z)$ really is a factor by multiplying $(z - 2)$ by $(z^3 + 3z - 1)$ to recover the original polynomial $f(z)$.

■

5.7.2 Polynomial Roots by Newton's Method

In FORTRAN, complex arithmetic may be undertaken simply by declaring variables of interest to be complex. Recall that Newton's method for finding a root z^* of $f(z)$ is determined by the recursive equation

$$z_{k+1} = z_k - \frac{f(z_k)}{f'(z_k)}.$$

If $f(z)$ is a polynomial, it is clear that its derivative $f'(z)$ exists and is easy to evaluate. In the polynomial case, the root z^* may be a complex number. We must therefore presume that the approximations z_k and perhaps the coefficients of the polynomial $f(z)$ are complex. Even if we start with a polynomial having real coefficients, after synthetic division by a linear polynomial $(z - z^*)$, with z^* complex, the "deflated" polynomial will have complex coefficients.

The reader may confirm that if $f(z)$ has real coefficients and the imaginary part of z_0 is zero, successive Newton iterates will thereafter be constrained to be real and therefore cannot possibly locate complex roots. Thus the initial estimate should be complex.

The subroutine NTPOL given in Table 5.15 will attempt to locate all roots of a given polynomial having real or complex coefficients. It proceeds by successively applying Newton's method and polynomial deflation to obtain polynomials of lower and lower degree. In this routine, Horner's rule (Section 3.2) is used for evaluating $f(z)$ and its derivative. The program makes use of the observation that (5.17) for the coefficients of the deflated polynomial is identical to the intermediate terms b_i in the formula (3.2) for Horner's method. In specifying the coefficients $(A(1), \ldots, A(N + 1))$ to the subroutine NTPOL, it is presumed that $f(z)$ is represented according to

$$F(Z) = A(N + 1)Z^N + \cdots + A(2)Z + A(1).$$

**TABLE 5.15   Subroutine NTPOL for Newton
Polynomial Root Computation**

```
          SUBROUTINE NTPOL(N,A,ROOT,EPS)
C
C     ****************************************x*****************
C     *   FUNCTION: THIS SUBROUTINE COMPUTES ALL ROOTS FOR THE   *
C     *              POLYNOMIAL                                   *
C     *                  F(Z)=A(1)+A(2)*Z+...+A(N+1)*Z**N         *
C     *              USING NEWTON'S METHOD                        *
C     *   USAGE:                                                  *
C     *        CALL SEQUENCE: CALL NTPOL(N,A,ROOT,EPS)            *
C     *   PARAMETERS:                                             *
C     *        INPUT:                                             *
C     *            N=DEGREE OF THE COMPLEX POLYNOMIAL             *
C     *            A=N+1 BY 1 ARRAY OF COMPLEX POLYNOMIAL         *
C     *              COEFFICIENTS                                 *
C     *          EPS=ERROR BOUND                                 *
C     *        OUTPUT:                                           *
C     *          ROOT=N BY 1 ARRAY OF COMPLEX ROOT APPROXIMATIONS *
C     ****************************************************************
C
          IMPLICIT COMPLEX(A-H,O-Z)
          REAL EPS
          DIMENSION A(N+1),B(100),ROOT(N)
C     *** COMPUTE POLYNOMIAL ROOT ***
          ZSTAR=(1.0,1.0)
          DO WHILE(N.GT.1)
             X=ZSTAR+2.0*EPS
             DO WHILE(CABS(X-ZSTAR).GE.EPS)
                ZSTAR=X
C     *** COMPUTE U=F(ZSTAR) AND ITS DERIVATIVE ***
C     *** V=DF(ZSTAR) BY HORNERS RULE           ***
                DO 1 I=N+1,1,-1
                   U=ZSTAR*U+A(I)
                   IF(I.NE.1) THEN
                      V=ZSTAR*V+A(I)*(I-1)
                   END IF
    1           CONTINUE
                X=ZSTAR-U/V
                U=(0.0,0.0)
                V=(0.0,0.0)
             END DO
             ZSTAR=X
             ROOT(N)=ZSTAR
C     *** DEFLATE POLYNOMIAL BY DIVISION (Z-ZSTAR) ***
             N=N-1
             DO 2 I=N+1,1,-1
                B(I)=A(I+1)+ZSTAR*B(I+1)
    2        CONTINUE
             DO 3 I=1,N+1
                A(I)=B(I)
                B(I)=0.
    3        CONTINUE
             IF(ABS(AIMAG(ZSTAR)).GT.EPS) THEN
                ZSTAR=CONJG(ZSTAR)
             ELSE
                ZSTAR=(1.0,1.0)
             END IF
          END DO
          ROOT(1)=-A(1)/A(2)
          RETURN
          END
```

Note that this differs from polynomial representations such as (5.14) used earlier in this chapter. This modified representation is needed because in FORTRAN, array arguments must be positive. If the subroutine is called according to the main program statement

$$\text{CALL NTPOL(N,A,ROOT,EPS)},$$

it is to be interpreted that N is the degree of the polynomial and arrays A and ROOT must be declared complex in the calling program and dimensioned appropriately. We will illustrate the use of subroutine NTPOL in the example to follow. The N roots of $f(z)$ will be returned in the array ROOT.

—— **EXAMPLE 5.12** ——————————————————————————————

The complex Newton's method and subroutine NTPOL (Table 5.15) for Newton extraction of polynomial roots and deflation will be applied to the function

$$f(z) = z^3 - 3z^2 - z + 9,$$

which has been subject of earlier examples. Let the initial approximation of the root be selected as $z = 1 + i$. Then

$$f(z_0) = (1 + i)^3 - 3(1 + i)^2 - (1 + i) + 9$$

$$= 1 + 3i - 3 - i - 3 - 6i + 3 - 1 - i + 9 = 6 - 5i$$

$$f'(z_0) = 3(1 + i)^2 - 6(1 + i) - 1$$

$$= 3 + 6i - 3 - 6 - 6i - 1 = -7,$$

so the first Newton step gives the approximating root:

$$z_1 = z_0 - \frac{f(z_0)}{f'(z_0)} = 1 + i - \frac{6 - 5i}{-7}$$

$$= \frac{13}{7} + \frac{2}{7} i \approx 1.857142 + 0.285714i.$$

Further Newton iterates can be obtained analogously by replacing z_0 by z_1 and by repeating the calculation above. The computer program directing the entire iteration method is given in Table 5.16, together with the output of the calculation (Table 5.17). We see that the computation uncovered the real root obtained by previous methods as well as a complex conjugate pair of roots. Thus the roots of $f(z)$ are as follows:

$$z_1^* = -1.5251020$$

$$z_2^* = 2.2625510 - 0.8843676i$$

$$z_3^* = 2.2625510 + 0.8843676i.$$

By evaluating $f(z)$ at these points, we may confirm that, indeed, they are roots.

TABLE 5.16   Program for Root Extraction

```
C       PROGRAM COMPLEX
C
C       ****************************************************************
C       THIS PROGRAM ILLUSTRATES NEWTONS METHOD IN THE COMPLEX CASE
C       BY FINDING ALL ROOTS OF THE FUNCTION F(Z)=Z**3-3*Z**2-Z+9
C       CALLS:    NTPOL
C       OUTPUT:
C                 ROOT(I)=ROOTS OF THE FUNCTION I=1,2,3
C       ****************************************************************
C
        COMPLEX A(4),ROOT(3)
        EPS=1.E-6
        N=3
        A(1)=9.
        A(2)=-1.
        A(3)=-3.
        A(4)=1.
C
C       *** SUBROUTINE NTPOL WILL CALCULATE THE ROOTS              ***
C
        CALL NTPOL(N,A,ROOT,EPS)
        WRITE(10,*)(ROOT(I),I=1,3)
        STOP
        END
```

TABLE 5.17   Output of Computation

Polynomial Roots
(-1.525102,-5.9604645E-08) (2.262551,-0.8843675) (2.262551,0.8843676)

Some authors (e.g., Ralston and Rabinowitz, 1978, Sec. 8.13) solemnly warn about problems arising because of ill-conditioning in the polynomial equation problem. By this, they mean that either slight changes in the coefficients or round-off errors in the computations can result in large shifts of computed roots. A famous polynomial subject to this effect is the polynomial having as its roots the integers -1 to -20. Our impression is that with polynomials of degree 10 or less, ill-conditioning is not usually a difficulty, and the methods of this section are adequate. For higher-degree polynomials, precaution is advisable. Deflation can be undertaken more accurately if it is done in order of increasing root magnitudes. A procedure known as *purification* achieves this as follows:

1. Use some root extraction procedure such as NTPOL to get approximations $z_1, \ldots, z_n$ of the roots.
2. Reindex so that $|z_1| \le |z_2| \le \cdots \le |z_n|$.
3. Run the procedure again, using z_1 as the starting point in NTPOL, and after each deflation, take the next largest z_j as initial approximation.

The IMSL mathematical library uses the Jenkins–Traub technique (Ralston and Rabinowitz, 1978, pp. 383–391), which can be viewed as a Newton method applied to a rational function (ratio of polynomials) approximation of the given polynomial.

In Section 5.2 we discussed root localization. In the case of polynomials, there exist methods (S & Y, 1978, Sec. 5.2.2), which, for any given polynomial $p(z)$ of degree n and positive number ε, provide estimates z_i, $1 \le i \le n$, such that if z^* is a root of $p(z)$, then for some j, $|z_j - z^*| < \varepsilon$. These localization methods accomplish the task within a predetermined number of computer operations, the number depending on the polynomial coefficients and the error tolerance bound ε. The computations proceed by first bounding the roots into some finite disk in the plane, by (5.3), for example. Then this disk is subdivided into a finite collection of regions having dimensions less than ε, and each of these regions is checked for interior roots. It turns out that in comparison to iterative methods, these localization methods are cumbersome to program and require excessive running time. In particular, the number of regions to be checked grows as the square of $1/\varepsilon$.

★5.7.3   Bairstow's Method

In FORTRAN it is sensible and convenient to locate roots of polynomials by performing Newton's method in complex arithmetic. On the other hand, some popular programming languages (e.g., BASIC and Pascal) do not supply complex arithmetic. Moreover, a weakness to the approach of using Newton's method in complex arithmetic, as proposed in the preceding section, is that on many computers, this limits us to single-precision computation. In some cases the root location is extremely sensitive to polynomial coefficient values and avoidance of roundoff is essential. Bairstow's method, in essence, provides the capability of using Newton's method in real arithmetic to locate complex polynomial roots. This enables the FORTRAN user to employ multiple precision and thereby greatly increase the accuracy of the computations. In addition, since all variables are real, Bairstow's method can easily be coded in Pascal or BASIC. Bairstow's method avoids requiring complex arithmetic for polynomials with real coefficients because it obtains quadratic rather than linear factors; these quadratics also have real coefficients. Of course, one can alternatively sidestep complex arithmetic by doing real arithmetic on the real and imaginary parts of each number of Newton's method. Indeed, this is what the computer itself ultimately does. Through this device, the technique for the preceding section may be implemented, but the coding is complicated.

Assume now that all coefficients of $f(z)$ are real. Then, as we have noted, if a complex number $\alpha + i\beta$ is a root of $f(z)$, its complex conjugate, $\alpha - i\beta$, is also a root. As a consequence, the real quadratic

$$h(z) = [z - (\alpha + i\beta)][z - (\alpha - i\beta)] = z^2 - 2\alpha z + (\alpha^2 + \beta^2) \quad (5.18)$$

must be a factor of $f(z)$.

Bairstow's method obtains real quadratic factors of real polynomials. All the complex roots of $f(z)$ are necessarily among the roots of the quadratic factors.

Let $h(z) = z^2 - pz - q$, where p and q are coefficients to be determined. In order that the notation of our discussion of Bairstow's method conform with the standard literature, we will index the coefficients of polynomials in reverse order to preceding sections. Thus we write

$$f(z) = a_0 z^n + a_1 z^{n-1} + \cdots + a_{n-1}z + a_n. \quad (5.19)$$

According to polynomial factorization theory (e.g., Herstein, 1964, Chap. 5), regardless of p and q, we may always find coefficients $b_0, b_1, \ldots, b_n$, so that

$$f(z) = a_0 z^n + a_1 z^{n-1} + \cdots + a_n$$

$$= (z^2 - pz - q)(b_0 z^{n-2} + b_1 z^{n-3} + \cdots + b_{n-2}) \qquad (5.20)$$

$$+ b_{n-1}(z - p) + b_n.$$

This equation has the form

$$f(z) = h(z)g(z) + r(z),$$

$r(z) = b_{n-1}(z - p) + b_n$ being the *remainder polynomial*. (The remainder polynomial is written as a linear polynomial of the difference $z - p$ in order to obtain more convenient formulas later.) The object in Bairstow's method is to calculate coefficients p and q of $h(z)$ so that $r(z) = 0$; that is, so that $h(z)$ is a factor of $f(z)$. Toward this end, we need to represent the coefficients b_i in (5.20) in terms of the coefficients a_i of $f(z)$ and p and q. The coefficients b_i ($i \geq 0$) are determined by matching the coefficients of various powers of z on the left- and right-hand sides of (5.20), which implies that

$$a_0 = b_0$$

$$a_1 = b_1 - pb_0$$

$$a_2 = b_2 - pb_1 - qb_0$$

$$\vdots$$

$$a_{n-1} = b_{n-1} - pb_{n-2} - qb_{n-3}$$

$$a_n = b_n - pb_{n-1} - qb_{n-2}.$$

After some elementary algebraic manipulations, the preceding equation yields an explicit formula for the coefficients b_i:

$$
\boxed{
\begin{aligned}
b_0 &= a_0 \\[4pt]
b_1 &= a_1 + pb_0 \\[4pt]
b_2 &= a_2 + pb_1 + qb_0 \\[4pt]
&\ \vdots \\[4pt]
b_{n-1} &= a_{n-1} + pb_{n-2} + qb_{n-3} \\[4pt]
b_n &= a_n + pb_{n-1} + qb_{n-2}.
\end{aligned}
}
\qquad (5.21)
$$

In view of (5.20), one can verify that $h(z)$ factors $f(z)$ if and only if

$$\boxed{b_{n-1} = b_{n-1}(p, q) = 0 \quad \text{and} \quad b_n = b_n(p, q) = 0.} \qquad (5.22)$$

This is a system of two nonlinear equations in the two variables p and q. It can be solved by the multivariable Newton's method to be discussed in Section 5.8. If this is done, the algorithm is called *Bairstow's method*.

As we shall see in the next section, the application of the multivariable Newton's method computes sequences of pairs $\{(p_i, q_i)\}$ which, under suitable conditions, converge to the exact solution of (5.22). The multivariable Newton's method requires the first partial derivatives of $b_{n-1}(p, q)$ and $b_n(p, q)$. As derived in Johnson and Riess (1977, pp. 150–151), these derivatives may be obtained by simple recursive relations. Starting from initial values $c_{-2} = c_{-1} = 0$, define the sequence $\{c_i\}$ by the following relations:

$$c_i = b_i + pc_{i-1} + qc_{i-2}, \quad i = 0, 1, \ldots, n - 1;$$

that is, let

$$c_0 = b_0$$

$$c_1 = b_1 + pc_0$$

$$c_2 = b_2 + pc_1 + qc_0 \tag{5.23}$$

$$\vdots$$

$$c_{n-1} = b_{n-1} + pc_{n-2} + qc_{n-3}.$$

Then the first partial derivatives are given by

$$\frac{\partial b_{n-1}(p, q)}{\partial q} = c_{n-3}, \qquad \frac{\partial b_n(p, q)}{\partial p} = c_{n-1},$$

$$\frac{\partial b_{n-1}(p, q)}{\partial p} = \frac{\partial b_n(p, q)}{\partial q} = c_{n-2}. \tag{5.24}$$

─────── **EXAMPLE 5.13** ───────

In the case of our usual polynomial $f(z) = z^3 - 3z^2 - z + 9$, $n = 3$ and (5.21) takes the specific values

$$b_0 = 1$$

$$b_1 = -3 + p$$

$$b_2 = -1 + p(p - 3) + q = p^2 - 3p + q - 1$$

$$b_3 = 9 + p(p^2 - 3p + q - 1) + q(p - 3)$$

$$= p^3 - 3p^2 + 2pq - p - 3q + 9.$$

In accordance with (5.23), the terms c_i are

$$c_0 = 1$$

$$c_1 = (-3 + p) + p = 2p - 3$$

$$c_2 = (p^2 - 3p + q - 1) + p(2p - 3) + q = 3p^2 - 6p + 2q - 1.$$

Now we see that for our example, the system of nonlinear equations (5.22) becomes

$$b_2(p, q) = p^2 - 3p + q - 1 = 0$$

and

$$b_3(p, q) = p^3 - 3p^2 + 2pq - p - 3q + 9 = 0.$$

We may simplify the foregoing expression of $b_3(p, q)$ by noting that $b_2 = b_{n-1}(p, q)$ must be 0. Then, from (5.21), and ignoring the pb_{n-1} addend in b_n, we have $b_3(p, q) = a_3 + qb_1 = 9 + q(p - 3)$. Then the partial derivatives of $b_2(p, q)$ and $b_3(p, q)$ can be obtained by relations (5.24) to get

$$\frac{\partial b_2}{\partial q} = c_0 = 1, \qquad \frac{\partial b_2}{\partial p} = \frac{\partial b_3}{\partial q} = c_1 = 2p - 3,$$

$$\frac{\partial b_3}{\partial p} = c_2 = 3p^2 - 6p + 2q - 1.$$

In Example 5.14 we shall see that the solution of (5.22) is

$$p \approx 4.525102255, \qquad q \approx -5.901243652,$$

from which we can conclude that

$$z_1^*, z_2^* \approx 2.262551128 \pm i0.88436759756,$$

since z_1^* and z_2^* are the roots of the quadratic $z^2 - pz - q$. ∎

★5.8
SYSTEMS OF NONLINEAR EQUATIONS

Attention now focuses on simultaneous nonlinear equations. Such equations can be expressed by

$$f_i(x_1, \ldots , x_n) = 0 \qquad (i = 1, 2, \ldots , n), \qquad (5.25)$$

where the f_i's represent real-valued functions. A *root* is any vector $\mathbf{x}^* = (x_1^*, \ldots , x_n^*)$ of real numbers for which (5.25) is satisfied simultaneously for all i. The multivariable generalization of the Newton's method, which is introduced next, is one of the most popular and effective techniques for solving nonlinear equations.

The single-variable Newton's method—as we have seen—can be interpreted as follows. If an approximation x_k of the root is given, $f(x)$ is approximated by the linear Taylor's polynomial

$$p(x) = f(x_k) + f'(x_k)(x - x_k), \qquad (5.26)$$

and the next approximation x_{k+1} is defined to be the root of this linear approximating function. This idea can be generalized to the multivariable case in the following way. Let $\mathbf{x}^{(k)} = (x_1^{(k)}, \ldots, x_n^{(k)})$ be an approximation of the root. Then the univariate linear approximating polynomial (5.26) is replaced by its multivariable counterpart,

$$p_i(x_1, \ldots, x_n) = f_i(x_1^{(k)}, \ldots, x_n^{(k)})$$

$$+ \sum_{j=1}^{n} \frac{\partial f_i(x_1^{(k)}, \ldots, x_n^{(k)})}{\partial x_j} (x_j - x_j^{(k)}) \qquad (i = 1, \ldots, n).$$

The next approximation $\mathbf{x}^{(k+1)}$ is defined to be the solution of the corresponding linear equations:

$$p_i(x_1, \ldots, x_n) = 0 \qquad (i = 1, \ldots, n). \tag{5.27}$$

The multivariable Newton's algorithm becomes more transparent through introduction of matrix notation. The higher-dimensional generalization of a derivative $f'(x)$ is the *Jacobian matrix* $\mathbf{J}(\mathbf{x})$, the (i, j)th element of which is defined to be

$$J_{ij}(\mathbf{x}) = \frac{\partial}{\partial x_j} f_i(x_1, x_2, \ldots, x_n).$$

Define $\mathbf{J}^{(k)} = \mathbf{J}(\mathbf{x}^{(k)})$ to be the Jacobian matrix of $(f_1(\mathbf{x}), \ldots, f_n(\mathbf{x}))$, evaluated at the kth iteration estimate $\mathbf{x}^{(k)}$, and introduce the vector

$$\mathbf{f}^{(k)} = \begin{bmatrix} f_1(\mathbf{x}^{(k)}) \\ \vdots \\ f_n(\mathbf{x}^{(k)}) \end{bmatrix}.$$

Then the *multivariable Newton method* is expressible, analogously to its real counterpart, (5.10), as

$$\boxed{\mathbf{x}^{(k+1)} = \mathbf{x}^{(k)} - (\mathbf{J}^{(k)})^{-1}\mathbf{f}^{(k)}.} \tag{5.28}$$

Of course, for computational reasons offered in Chapter 2, evaluation of the inverse matrix is not as efficient as solution of the equivalent linear equation

$$\mathbf{J}^{(k)}(\mathbf{x}^{(k+1)} - \mathbf{x}^{(k)}) = -\mathbf{f}^{(k)}$$

by Gauss elimination methods. Under certain smoothness assumptions concerning the second partial derivatives of the f_i's, the successive estimates can be shown to have the same convergence rate as in the real case. That is, if $(x_1^*, \ldots, x_n^*)$ is the exact root, then for some constant C and all i, $1 \le i \le n$,

$$|x_i^{(k+1)} - x_i^*| \le C|x_i^{(k)} - x_i^*|^2, \qquad k = 1, 2, \ldots.$$

TABLE 5.18   Subroutine MVNE for the Multivariable Newton Method

```
          SUBROUTINE MVNE(N,X0,X,EPS)
C
C       ****************************************************************
C       *   FUNCTION: THIS SUBROUTINE COMPUTES THE ROOT VECTOR        *
C       *             OF A SYSTEM OF EQUATIONS F(I,X)=0 I=1,...,N      *
C       *             USING THE MULTIVARIATE NEWTON METHOD            *
C       *   USAGE:                                                     *
C       *        CALL SEQUENCE: CALL MVNE(N,X0,X,EPS)                  *
C       *        EXTERNAL FUNCTIONS/SUBROUTINES:                       *
C       *                        FUNCTION F(I,X)                       *
C       *                        FUNCTION DF(I,J,X0)                   *
C       *                        SUBROUTINE GAUS1(N,M,ND,A,DELT)       *
C       *   PARAMETERS:                                                *
C       *        INPUT:                                                *
C       *           N=NUMBER OF SIMULTANEOUS LINEAR EQUATIONS(LESS     *
C       *              THEN 30)                                        *
C       *           X0=N BY 1 ARRAY OF INITIAL APPROXIMATE ROOT        *
C       *              VECTOR VALUES                                   *
C       *           EPS=ERROR BOUND (TOLERANCE)                        *
C       *        OUTPUT:                                               *
C       *           X=N BY 1 ARRAY OF APPROXIMATE ROOTS                *
C       ****************************************************************
C
          DIMENSION X0(N),X(N),A(30,31)
C       *** INITIALIZATION ***
          K=1
C       *** COMPUTE VECTOR X AS THE ROOT ***
          DO 5 WHILE(K.LE.N)
             DO 1 I=1,N
                DO 2 J=1,N
                   A(I,J)=DF(I,J,X0)
     2          CONTINUE
                A(I,N+1)=-F(I,X0)
     1       CONTINUE
C       *** PERFORM GAUSSIAN ELIMINATION ***
             M=1
             ND=30
             DELT=0.000001
             CALL GAUS1(N,M,ND,A,DELT)
             DO 3 I=1,N
                X(I)=X0(I)+A(I,N+1)
     3       CONTINUE
C       *** IF SOLUTION CHANGE IS SMALL, STOP ***
             K=1
             DO WHILE(ABS(X(K)-X0(K)).LT.EPS.AND.K.LE.N)
                K=K+1
             END DO
             IF(K.LE.N) THEN
                DO 4 I=1,N
                   X0(I)=X(I)
     4          CONTINUE
             END IF
     5    CONTINUE
          RETURN
          END
```

A precise statement and proof of this assertion is given, for example by S & Y (1978, Sec. 5.3.1). Subroutine MVNE, which implements the multivariable Newton's method, constitutes Table 5.18. It presumes that the user provides program subfunctions $F(I, X)$, and $DF(I, J, X)$, which returns the values $f_i(\mathbf{x})$ and $J_{ij}(\mathbf{x})$, if $I = i, J = j$, and $X = \mathbf{x}$.

──────── **EXAMPLE 5.14** ────────────────────────────────

In Example 5.13 we have seen that the application of the Bairstow's method for solving the polynomial equation

$$f(z) = z^3 - 3z^2 - z + 9 = 0$$

requires the solution of the nonlinear equations

$$b_2(p, q) = -1 - 3p + p^2 + q = 0$$
$$b_3(p, q) = 9 - 3q + pq = 0.$$

The elements of the Jacobian matrix were found to be

$$\frac{\partial b_2(p, q)}{\partial p} = 2p - 3, \qquad \frac{\partial b_2(p, q)}{\delta q} = 1$$

$$\frac{\partial b_3(p, q)}{\partial p} = q, \qquad \frac{\partial b_3(p, q)}{\partial q} = -3 + p.$$

Then

$$\mathbf{J}^{(k)} = \begin{bmatrix} 2p^{(k)} - 3 & 1 \\ q^{(k)} & -3 + p^{(k)} \end{bmatrix}$$

and

$$\mathbf{f}^{(k)} = \begin{bmatrix} -1 - 3p^{(k)} + (p^{(k)})^2 + q^{(k)} \\ 9 - 3q^{(k)} + p^{(k)}q^{(k)} \end{bmatrix}.$$

Let us start the application of the multivariable Newton's method with the initial approximates $p^{(0)} = 2$, $q^{(0)} = -3$. Then the corresponding Jacobian matrix $\mathbf{J}^{(0)}$ and vector $\mathbf{f}^{(0)}$ are as follows:

$$\mathbf{J}^{(0)} = \begin{bmatrix} 2 \cdot 2 - 3 & 1 \\ -3 & -3 + 2 \end{bmatrix} = \begin{bmatrix} 1 & 1 \\ -3 & -1 \end{bmatrix}$$

$$\mathbf{f}^{(0)} = \begin{bmatrix} -1 - 3 \cdot 2 + 2^2 + (-3) \\ 9 - 3 \cdot (-3) + 2 \cdot (-3) \end{bmatrix} = \begin{bmatrix} -6 \\ 12 \end{bmatrix}.$$

Since in this case

$$\mathbf{x}^{(0)} = \begin{bmatrix} p^{(0)} \\ q^{(0)} \end{bmatrix} = \begin{bmatrix} 2 \\ -3 \end{bmatrix},$$

one step of the multivariable Newton's method (5.28) requires solution of the linear equation

$$\mathbf{J}^{(0)}(\mathbf{x}^{(1)} - \mathbf{x}^{(0)}) = -\mathbf{f}^{(0)};$$

or in the notation of (5.28),

$$\mathbf{x}^{(1)} = \mathbf{x}^{(0)} - (\mathbf{J}^{(0)})^{-1}\mathbf{f}^{(0)}.$$

In our case we obtain the equation

$$\begin{bmatrix} 1 & 1 \\ -3 & -1 \end{bmatrix}\begin{bmatrix} p^{(1)} - 2 \\ q^{(1)} + 3 \end{bmatrix} = \begin{bmatrix} 6 \\ -12 \end{bmatrix},$$

which has the unique solution $p^{(1)} = 5$, $q^{(1)} = 0$. The step above is then repeated by replacing $p^{(0)}$, $q^{(0)}$ by $p^{(1)}$, $q^{(1)}$, respectively. Successive Newton iterates and the corresponding functional values are displayed in Table 5.19. The roots associated with the quadratic factor were computed by solving the quadratic equation

$$z^2 - pz - q = 0,$$

with p and q as in the last entry of Table 5.19, by the quadratic formula

$$z_1, z_2 = \frac{p \pm \sqrt{p^2 + 4q}}{2}.$$

By this means we conclude that the complex roots are

$$2.262551128 \pm i0.8843675975.$$

This agrees with our computation in Section 5.7.2.

TABLE 5.19   Application of the Multivariable Newton Method

$p^{(k)}$	$q^{(k)}$	$b_2(p^{(k)}, q^{(k)})$	$b_3(p^{(k)}, q^{(k)})$
2.000000	-3.000000	-6.000000	12.00000
5.000000	0.0000000E+00	9.000000	9.000000
4.357143	-4.500000	0.4132643	2.892857
4.547431	-6.000624	3.6211491E-02	-0.2855511
4.525296	-5.901927	4.9066544E-04	-2.1858215E-03
4.525102	-5.901244	-1.4305115E-06	1.9073486E-06

5.9
SUPPLEMENTARY NOTES AND DISCUSSIONS

The techniques offered in this chapter for solving nonlinear equations (5.1) for $f(x)$ a real function are usually effective and simple to implement. For such functions, prior reflection (through graphics) on the general shape of $f(x)$ is often rewarding: It is helpful to have some idea how many (if any) roots exist, and their approximate locations on the real line. Such "localization" is useful, within limits. But once we have some confidence that the computation does not suffer from pathological problems such as shown in Examples 5.6 and 5.10, it is well to implement some nonlinear equation algorithm and be done with the job. A safety feature is that in the vast majority of cases either successive iterations will not be

TABLE 5.20   Match of Nonlinear Equation Problem Characteristics and Methods

Nonlinear Equation Characteristics	Method*
Real Function f(x) in (5.1)	
Points a, b, $a < b$, and root known to be in $[a, b]$; $f(x)$ not expensive to evaluate	B, S
Same as above, but speed of convergence a concern	N, S
No points a, b bracketing roots are known	N, S
Same as above, but derivative not available, or expensive to evaluate	S
f(x) a Polynomial	
Complex computer arithmetic available, roundoff not troublesome	CN
Complex arithmetic not available, or accuracy important	BA, perhaps in double precision; CN, in double precision
Multivariable Function f(x)	
Derivatives available	MN
Derivatives unavailable, or MN does not converge	Assistance or further study needed

*B, bisection; BA, Bairstow; CN, complex Newton; MN, multivariable Newton; N, Newton; S, secant.

converging at all, or they will be converging to the correct answer. We often find that programmable calculators (especially those programmable in BASIC) are adequate and convenient for solving real nonlinear equations, using any of the methods described in this chapter.

On the other hand, the subject of nonlinear equations, like several other areas of numerical analysis, becomes murky when the problem involves functions $f(x)$ of several variables. To begin with, there is no evident multivariable version of the bisection method, and the task of localizing roots and inferring the nature of the function from a manageable number of evaluations becomes complicated or even hopeless, especially in light of the fact that graphs are not readily available to guide the intuition. Whereas the secant method has several multivariable interpretations, the extension of Newton's method as described in Section 5.5 is unambiguous in light of the Taylor's series motivation. We will assert that many convergence properties of both the Newton's methods and standard extensions of the secant method remain valid in a suitable multivariable interpretation, but their justification requires much heavier mathematical machinery than is needed in the univariate case. The reader is referred to S & Y (1978, Chaps. 4 and 5) for further analytical developments and references to the advanced literature on nonlinear equations of several variables.

There are strong links between nonlinear equation problems and function optimization. As a simple but instructive example, recall from calculus that an interior point x^* is a local maximum or minimum point of a differentiable function $f(x)$ only if it is a root of $f'(x)$. Thus the task of finding the optimum of a function $f(x)$ defined on an interval $[a, b]$ can be rephrased as the problem of finding all the roots of $f'(x)$ on that interval. Then the optimum point can be found by comparing the values of $f(x)$ at all these points and endpoints of the interval. Conversely, it is sometimes useful to recognize that $\mathbf{x}^* = (x_1^*, \ldots, x_n^*)$ is a solution of the system of nonlinear equations

$$f_i(x_1, \ldots, x_n) = 0 \qquad (1 \leq i \leq n)$$

if and only if the function

$$F(\mathbf{x}) = f_1^2(\mathbf{x}) + \cdots + f_n^2(\mathbf{x})$$

has minimal value at $\mathbf{x} = \mathbf{x}^*$, and that value is zero.

In Table 5.20 we have tried to relate nonlinear equation problem characteristics to what we regard as the most appropriate of the methods of the present chapter for those characteristics.

PROBLEMS

Section 5.2

1. Find the intervals on which the polynomial

$$p(x) = x^3 - 6x^2 + 9x - 5$$

is monotonically increasing. Sketch the graph of this function.

2. Find a finite interval that contains at least one real root of the polynomial $p(x)$ in Problem 1. [**HINT:** Use relation (5.3).]

3. Find an interval of at most unit length that you can assure contains a root of $p(x) = x^3 - 6x^2 + 9x - 5$. [**HINT:** A computer or programmable calculator can be useful here.)

4. Give graphical evidence that the following functions have infinitely many real roots, and locate the smallest positive root of each of them within an interval of unit length.
    (a) $x \cdot \tan x - 1$.
    (b) $\sin (2x) - \sin (x)$.
    (c) $\sin (3x) - \sin (x)$.
    (d) $x \cdot \sin (x) - 1$.
    (e) $\ln (x) - \tan (x)$.

5. Show mathematically (i.e., not graphically) that the function

$$f(x) = x \sin (x) - 1$$

has a unique root in the interval $(1, \pi/2)$.

6. Show mathematically (i.e., not graphically) that the function

$$f(x) = x \tan (x) - 1$$

has a unique root in the interval $(0, 1)$.

7. Show that the equation

$$\exp(x) - 3x = 0$$

has two real roots, and that they lie in the intervals $(0, 1)$ and $(1, 2)$.

8. Show that any root $x*$ of the polynomial

$$p(x) = x^6 + 3x^4 - x^3 + 2x^2 - 6x + 4$$

satisfies $|x| \leq 7$. Show further that if $x*$ is real, then $0 < x* \leq 7$. [**HINT:** The bound (5.3) is not good enough here. Think about the function.]

9. Localize the roots of the following equations into intervals of unit length. (**HINT:** A computer can help here.)
    (a) $x^2 - \sqrt{x} = 2$.
    (b) $x - e^x = -2$.
    (c) $\ln(x) + \sqrt{x} = 2$.
    (d) $2x = e^{-x}$.
    (e) $e^x - 5x = 0$.

★10. Show that if $x*$ is a zero of

$$p(x) = a_n x^n + a_{n-1} x^{n-1} + \cdots + a_1 x + a_0,$$

then

    (a) $|x*| \leq 1 + \dfrac{1}{|a_n|} \max \{|a_0|; \ldots; |a_{n-1}|\}$.

    (b) $|x*| \leq \max \left\{ 1, \dfrac{1}{|a_n|} (|a_0| + \cdots + |a_{n-1}|) \right\}$.

Section 5.3
11. Confirm that the polynomial

$$p(x) = x^3 - 6x^2 + 9x - 5$$

has a zero in the interval $(4, 5)$. Then perform two iterations by the bisection method. Show your hand calculations.

12. Find the zero of $p(x)$ in Problem 11 to three significant places using the bisection method and starting from the interval $(4, 5)$. Use a computer. Give an analysis to verify the accuracy.

13. Imagine that $x_L - x_R = 0.5$. What is the minimum number of bisection steps needed to assure that afterward, the approximation error of x_M is less than 10^{-10}? Do not use your computer; use your head.

14. The functions below have roots in the intervals which are specified on their right sides. Compute the roots of these functions to an assured three significant figures by use of the bisection method.
    (a) $x \cdot \tan(x) - 1$, $(0, 1)$.
    (b) $\sin(2x) - \sin(x)$, $(0.7, 1.7)$.

(c) $\sin (3x) - \sin (x)$,   (0.5, 1.5).
(d) $x \cdot \sin (x) - 1$,   (1, 2).
(e) $\ln (x) - \tan (x)$,   (3.8, 4.8).

15. The functions below have roots in the intervals which are specified on their right sides. Compute the roots of these functions in each of the intervals to an assured three significant figures by use of the bisection method.
(a) $e^x - 3x$,   (0, 1) and (1, 2).
(b) $x^2 - \sqrt{x} - 2$,   (1, 2).
(c) $x - e^x + 2$,   (-2, -1) and (1, 2).
(d) $\ln (x) + \sqrt{x} - 2$,   (1, 2).
(e) $2x - e^{-x}$,   (0, 1).
(f) $e^x - 5x$,   (0, 1) and (2, 3).

16. Approximate the value of π by solving

(a) $\tan \left(\dfrac{x}{4}\right) - 1 = 0.$

(b) $\sin \left(\dfrac{x}{4}\right) - \cos \left(\dfrac{x}{4}\right) = 0.$

Use the bisection method to determine the roots to five significant figures. Do these figures agree with $\pi = 3.14159265$?

17. Apply the bisection method to determine the roots of the following equations to three significant decimal figures.
(a) $x^4 - 2x^3 - x - 3 = 0$,   (2, 3).
(b) $x^5 - x - 0.46 = 0$,   (1, 2).
(c) $x^5 + x + 1 = 0$,   (-1, 0).
(d) $x^5 - 3x^2 - 100 = 0$,   (2, 3).

★18. Consider the "trisection" method. Divide $[a, b]$ into three equal parts. If $f(a)f(b) < 0$, at least one of the subintervals must have a solution. Redefine $[a, b]$ to be the endpoints of that subinterval, and again subdivide into three equal subintervals, and continue.
(a) Modify the subroutine BISE (Table 5.2) to trisect. Apply it to Problem 12.
(b) Give the number of iterations required to assure that a final endpoint of the trisection iterations approximates the root with error no greater than ε, as a function of the initial interval length and a given error tolerance ε. Compare this with the number of bisection iterations needed and the number of function calls required by each of the two methods.

Section 5.4
19. Solve Problem 11 by the secant method. Show your hand calculations. Use the endpoints as initial approximations. Does it matter which endpoint you assign to x_0 and x_1 in the secant iterations?

20. Do Problem 12 by the secant method.

21. Determine the roots of the functions given in Problem 14 by the secant method. Use the given interval endpoints to start the algorithm.

22. Determine the roots of the functions of Problem 15 using the secant method. Use the interval endpoints as initial values.

23. Do Problem 16 by the secant method. Pick your own starting points.

24. Do Problem 17 by the secant method, with interval endpoints as starting points.

25. Find the value of $\sqrt{2}$ to five decimal figures by the secant method. Check your answer by squaring it. (**HINT:** Solve $x^2 - 2 = 0$.)

Section 5.5

26. Solve Problem 11 by the Newton method. Start at $x_0 = 4.0$. Show your hand calculations for two iterations.

27. Solve Problem 12 by Newton's method using the computer. Iterate until two successive estimates agree to within $10 \cdot$ machine epsilon.

28. Determine the roots of the functions in Problem 14 by using Newton's method. Start at the left endpoints of the intervals given.

29. Determine the roots of the functions in Problem 15 by Newton's method. Start at the left endpoints of the intervals given.

30. Do Problem 16 by Newton's method. Choose your own starting points.

31. Do Problem 17 by Newton's method. Begin with the left endpoints as initial estimates.

32. Find the square roots of m, $m = 2, 3, \ldots , 10$, by Newton's method. Do this by solving $x^2 - m = 0$, and take as starting points, $m/2$. Use a computer and do 10 iterations in each case, and check to see if the square of the estimate minus m is close to zero.

33. The shaded area A in the figure depends on radius r and angle α (in radians) according to

$$A = \frac{r^2}{2} [\alpha - \sin (\alpha)].$$

Suppose that the area is known to be 2 and $r = 1.25$. Find the value of α.

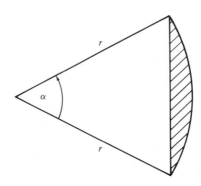

34. Kepler's equation relates the angle (in radians) ϕ of a planet, as shown in the figure, to time t by

$$\phi - e \sin (\phi) = a \cdot (t - t_0),$$

where t_0 is the time of the start of the most recent cycle. For $a = 0.5$, $t = 1.0$, $t_0 = 0$, and $e = 0.4$, find the angle ϕ. First find a sensible initial approximation by the graphical approach, and then begin Newton iterations.

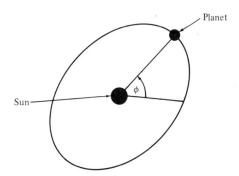

35. Consider the circuit shown and imagine that as a response to heat dissipation, the resistor R changes its value according to

$$R(i) = 100 + 10\sqrt{i}.$$

From elementary physics or circuit theory, the current i satisfies

$$V = R(i) \cdot i.$$

For the circuit shown, find the current.

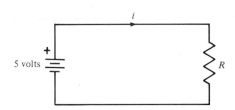

Section 5.6

★36. Assume that

$$|f''(x)| \leq M, \qquad |f'(x)| \geq m > 0$$

in an open interval containing a root x^* of $f(x)$. Prove that for $\{x_j\}$ a sequence of points in this interval obtained by application of Newton's method, and for

$$\varepsilon_k = \frac{M}{2m} |x_k - x^*|,$$

we have

$$\varepsilon_k \leq \varepsilon_{k-1}^2$$

Section 5.7

37. **(a)** Let $p(z)$ denote a polynomial with real coefficients. Prove that if z is a root with a nonzero imaginary part, its complex conjugate z^* is a root of $p(z)$.

(b) One can confirm by substitution that $z_1 = 1 - i$ is a root of the polynomial

$$p(z) = z^4 - 2z^3 + 4z^2 - 4z + 4.$$

From this and the information in part (a), find all the roots of the polynomial.

38. A corporate unit is trying to decide whether to purchase a large number of micro-computers or, alternatively, a mainframe to handle its processing needs. Let W denote the average central processing work per hour required by the corporate unit. Roughly speaking, $MC(W)$, the cost of satisfying processing demand W by microcomputer, grows linearly with W; this reflects that you simply buy enough micros to satisfy the demand; twice the demand implies twice the number of computers. Thus we argue that in units of $10,000,

$$MC(W) = W.$$

A mainframe has a large fixed purchase and maintenance cost, and (assuming that it really is a powerful computer and can handle any foreseeable work load) the cost grows only slightly with demand W, say

$$MFC(W) = 100 + \log (W + 1),$$

in units of $10,000. Find the workload W^* at which the mainframe cost equals that of the flock of micros. Use any procedure of your choice.

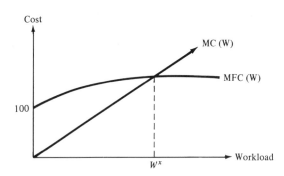

39. Use subroutine NTPOL (Table 5.15) to find the roots of the polynomial

$$p(z) = z^4 - 2z^3 + 4z^2 - 4z + 4.$$

Substitute these roots into the polynomial to assure that in each case, the value is close to zero.

★40. Use Bairstow's method to locate the roots of

$$p(z) = z^4 - 2z^3 + 4z^2 - 4z + 4.$$

All roots of this polynomial have nonzero imaginary parts.

Section 5.8

★**41.** Find the solution of the system of nonlinear equations

$$x^2 + y^2 = 4$$
$$x^2 - y^2 = 1$$

by use of the bivariable Newton's method. Take as starting value the pair $(x_0, y_0) = (2.3, 1.7)$.

★**42.** Solve the nonlinear system of equations

$$x - \exp(y) = 1$$
$$xy = 1$$

by first sketching the curves and then using the apparent intersection as the initial point for application of subroutine MVNE (Table 5.18).

★**43.** The "predator–prey" population model is intended to describe the interaction of a prey population X and a predator population Y. This model is discussed in more detail in Section 7.5, but details are not required for presentation of the problem here. By the appended terms "$+1$" and "-0.2" at the right of the equations, the standard model has been adapted to reflect a constant rate of addition of prey to the stock (perhaps trout from a trout farm), and a constant rate of deletion of predators (e.g., through beaver trapping). Thus we have

$$\frac{dX}{dt} = X - 0.2X^2 - 0.05XY + 1$$

$$\frac{dY}{dt} = -0.2Y + 0.5XY - 0.2.$$

The question you are to answer is: What is the equilibrium population? That is, for what values X and Y of predator and prey is the population exactly constant? The population growth dX/dt and dY/dt are exactly 0 at "equilibrium" when the right sides of the equations above are 0. Thus what is the equilibrium population for this particular model?

★**44.** Solve the nonlinear equation

$$x^3 - y = 0$$
$$x^2 + y^3 = 1,$$

using first a graphical method and then Newton iterations with starting point based on where the curves seem to intersect. Do one iteration by hand calculation, showing your work. Then call upon subroutine MVNE (Table 5.18). Confirm that when you substitute your computed roots into these equations, you get zero, to machine accuracy.

CHAPTER 6

Function Approximation and Data Fitting

6.1
PRELIMINARIES

The motivation and foundations for function approximation and data fitting stem from considerations introduced in Chapter 3. Specifically, one desires a computer-amenable approximation for a given function $f(x)$, or for fitting a curve to given data points. As in Chapter 3, our focus will be on use of polynomials as the computer-amenable approximating functions. In the closing sections, however, trigonometric Fourier methods and rational functions will be introduced. Chapter 3 restricted interest to interpolation; the functions we constructed were required to pass through the data. In "approximation" we drop the interpolation restriction.

Let us now distinguish between the interpolation problems studied in Chapter 3 and the class of tasks for which the methods of the present chapter are intended. First, interpolation is appropriate only if the data are believed to consist of accurate values from a well-behaved function. For example, if the graph of the data points resembles Figure 6.1, then interpolation is sensible. Such a set of data, which almost calls out to be connected by a smooth curve, might represent radiation intensity from a radioactive source, measured at equally spaced times. Moreover, the interpolation polynomial for these data ought to give a very good estimate of the radiation intensity that would have been found if an observation had been taken at time point t not among the data values.

Still, as we saw in the Runge example (see Example 3.8), even when the data are from a fairly smooth and regular curve, polynomial interpolation methods are not always adequate. Although spline techniques can be expected to handle some of these situations, splines are nevertheless sometimes bothersome to use, in comparison to polynomials, especially when evaluation speed and minimal programming and memory requirements are of prime consideration.

Some data sets arise from phenomena having random components or other unpredictable mechanisms. In Figure 6.2 we have plotted test scores of the math-

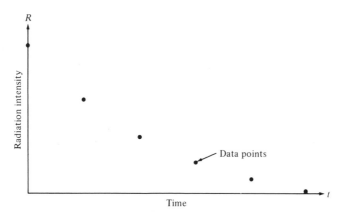

FIGURE 6.1   Data Well-Suited to Interpolation

ematics section of the Scholastic Aptitude Test as reported in U.S. Bureau of Census (1984, p. 158). Although these points do seem to contain trend information, interpolation of these points by the Lagrange polynomial (via subroutine LAGR, Table 3.6) resulted in the meaningless plot of Figure 6.3.

The approximation methods of this chapter are suited to finding a polynomial of relatively low degree (thus assuring "smoothness") which "fits" these data in the sense that the curve passes as closely as possible to the data points, subject to the constraint that the polynomial degree not exceed a specified number m.

Outside the realm of interpolatory methods such as those discussed in Chapter 3, the three most popular techniques for function approximation are

1. Least-squares polynomials.
2. Fourier methods.
3. Rational functions.

These methods are described in terms of measures of "fit." Let (x_1, f_1), (x_2, f_2), . . . , (x_n, f_n) denote the data pairs to be approximated, and let m be the desired maximal degree of the polynomial approximation. Then the *least-squares poly-*

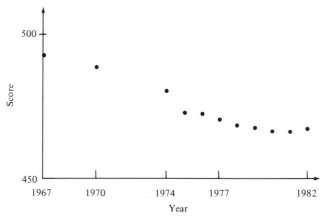

FIGURE 6.2   Plot of SAT Scores

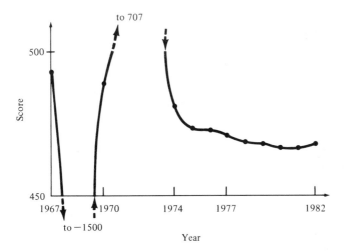

FIGURE 6.3 Polynomial Interpolation of SAT Test Scores

nomial for the data is any polynomial of degree m or less that minimizes the criterion

$$Q(f, p) = \sum_{i=1}^{n} [f_i - p(x_i)]^2 \qquad (6.1)$$

over all polynomials $p(x)$ of degree m or less (Figure 6.4). Thus the least-squares polynomial minimizes the sum of the squares of the approximation errors at the data points. Fourier methods provide a more stable computation of the least-squares polynomial and also serve as motivation for trigonometric polynomials. The least-squares approach can be extended to rational functions. Rational approximations are used in practice where efficiency and high accuracy are required.

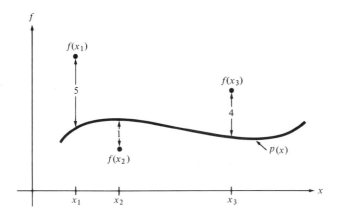

Least squares criterion:
$$Q(f, p) = [f(x_1) - p(x_1)]^2 + [f(x_2) - p(x_2)]^2 + [f(x_3) - p(x_3)]^2$$
$$= 5^2 + 1^2 + 4^2 = 42$$

FIGURE 6.4 Illustration of the Least-Squares Criterion

6.2
LEAST-SQUARES APPROXIMATION

6.2.1   Construction of Least-Squares Polynomials

Let $x_1, \ldots, x_n$ be distinct domain points and let $f_1, \ldots, f_n$ be the corresponding values. Suppose that we wish to approximate these data by a polynomial $p(x)$ of degree not exceeding m. If $m = n - 1$, the unique interpolating polynomial provides perfect "fit" to the data. But if $m < n - 1$, typically no interpolation polynomial of degree m exists. In such cases we seek a polynomial of degree m that is "closest," in some sense, to the given data set. In the method of least squares, the discrepancy of the data points $(x_1, f_1), (x_2, f_2), \ldots, (x_n, f_n)$ and approximating polynomial $p(x)$ is measured by the sum of the squared residuals:

$$Q(f, p) = \sum_{i=1}^{n} [f_i - p(x_i)]^2.$$

Under the least-squares principle, this quantity $Q(f, p)$ has to be minimized, the minimization being over the coefficients $a_0, a_1, \ldots, a_m$ of the polynomial $p(x) = a_0 + a_1x + \cdots + a_mx^m$. A positive integer in having been chosen, the polynomial $p(x)$ minimizing $Q(f, p)$ over all polynomials p of degree m or less is called the *least-squares polynomial* of degree m. Toward seeing the principle behind the general method, let us study the simplest case.

Assume first that $m = 0$. That is, the least-squares constant polynomial is to be determined. The only parameter to be chosen is a_0. In this case

$$Q(f, p) = \sum_{i=1}^{n} (f_i - a_0)^2 = \sum_{i=1}^{n} (f_i^2 - 2f_ia_0 + a_0^2)$$

$$= na_0^2 - 2a_0 \left(\sum_{i=1}^{n} f_i \right) + \sum_{i=1}^{n} f_i^2,$$

(6.2)

which is a quadratic function of a_0. Since the coefficient of a_0^2 is positive, there is a minimum point of this parabola that can be obtained by differentiation with respect to a_0. Thus the optimum point is the root of the equation

$$\frac{d}{da_0} Q(f, p) = 2na_0 - 2\sum_{i=1}^{n} f_i = 0.$$

That is,

$$a_0 = \frac{1}{n} \sum_{i=1}^{n} f_i.$$

(6.3).

The zero-degree least-squares polynomial (illustrated in Figure 6.5) is, then, the constant polynomial which for every x equals the average of the function values $f_1, f_2, \ldots, f_n$.

We turn to the general case, in which the degree is any given nonnegative integer $m < n - 1$. To minimize the quantity $Q(f, p)$, view the objective function $Q(f, p)$ as an explicit function of the unknown coefficients $a_0, a_1, \ldots, a_m$. Since

$$p(x) = a_0 + a_1x + a_2x^2 + \cdots + a_mx^m = \sum_{k=0}^{m} a_kx^k,$$

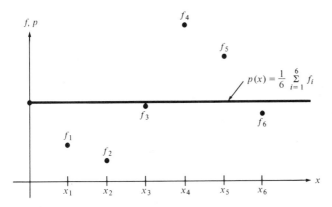

FIGURE 6.5 Approximation by the Least-Squares Constant Polynomial

we have

$$Q(f, p) = \sum_{i=1}^{n} \left(f_i - \sum_{k=0}^{m} a_k x_i^k \right)^2. \tag{6.4}$$

By taking the partial derivatives (Appendix B, Section B4) of this function with respect to the unknown coefficients a_j ($j = 0, 1, \ldots, m$), we get the necessary conditions (Kaplan, 1952, Sec. 2-15) for minimizing $Q(f, p)$:

$$\frac{\partial}{\partial a_j} Q(f, p) = -2 \sum_{i=1}^{n} \left(f_i - \sum_{k=0}^{m} a_k x_i^k \right) x_i^j = 0 \qquad (0 \leq j \leq m). \tag{6.5}$$

After some obvious algebra, the above can be represented as the linear system

$$\boxed{\sum_{k=0}^{m} \left(\sum_{i=1}^{n} x_i^{k+j} \right) a_k = \sum_{i=1}^{n} f_i x_i^j \qquad (0 \leq j \leq m).} \tag{6.6}$$

.

which are called *normal equations*. It is known (S & Y, 1978) that the normal equations have a unique solution $a_0, a_1, \ldots, a_m$, which indeed are the coefficients of the least-squares polynomial.

Since (6.6) comprise a system of linear algebraic equations, if it is sufficiently well-conditioned, this system can be efficiently solved by the Gaussian elimination method, discussed in Chapter 2.

────────── **EXAMPLE 6.1** ──────────

Let $n = 5$ and suppose that the data points are specified by

$$x_1 = -2, \quad x_2 = -1, \quad x_3 = 0, \quad x_4 = 1, \quad x_5 = 2$$

$$f_1 = 0, \quad f_2 = 1, \quad f_3 = 2, \quad f_4 = 1, \quad f_5 = 0.$$

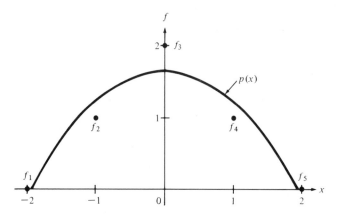

FIGURE 6.6   Data Points and Quadratic Least-
Squares Approximation for Example 6.1

A graph of these points (Figure 6.6) suggests that a quadratic ($m = 2$) approximation should be attempted. Toward constructing the normal equations (6.6), we
first compute the coefficients:

$$\sum_{i=1}^{5} x_i^0 = 5, \ \sum_{i=1}^{5} x_i^1 = 0, \ \sum_{i=1}^{5} x_i^2 = 10, \ \sum_{i=1}^{5} x_i^3 = 0,$$

$$\sum_{i=1}^{5} x_i^4 = 34, \ \sum_{i=1}^{5} x_i^0 f_i = 4, \ \sum_{i=1}^{5} x_i^1 f_i = 0, \ \sum_{i=1}^{5} x_i^2 f_i = 2,$$

which implies that the system of normal equations is as follows:

$$\text{(for } j = 0) \qquad 5a_0 + 0a_1 + 10a_2 = 4$$
$$\text{(for } j = 1) \qquad 0a_0 + 10a_1 + 0a_2 = 0$$
$$\text{(for } j = 2) \qquad 10a_0 + 0a_1 + 34a_2 = 2.$$

The solution to these equations is

$$a_0 = \tfrac{58}{35}, \qquad a_1 = 0, \qquad a_2 = -\tfrac{3}{7},$$

and the corresponding least-squares polynomial is

$$p(x) = -\tfrac{3}{7}x^2 + \tfrac{58}{35}.$$

The curve shown in Figure 6.6 is actually this polynomial.

■

To introduce the matrix representation of the least-squares method, let us adopt
the following definitions:

$$\mathbf{X} = \begin{bmatrix} 1 & x_1 & \cdots & x_1^m \\ 1 & x_2 & \cdots & x_2^m \\ \cdots & \cdots & \cdots & \cdots \\ 1 & x_n & \cdots & x_n^m \end{bmatrix}, \quad \mathbf{a} = \begin{bmatrix} a_0 \\ a_1 \\ \vdots \\ a_m \end{bmatrix}, \quad \mathbf{f} = \begin{bmatrix} f_1 \\ f_2 \\ \vdots \\ f_n \end{bmatrix}. \tag{6.7}$$

With this notation, the normal equations (6.6) can be expressed compactly as

$$(\mathbf{X}^T\mathbf{X})\mathbf{a} = \mathbf{X}^T\mathbf{f}, \tag{6.8}$$

where superscript T denotes ''transpose'' as defined by property 7 of Appendix A. By using property 18 of Appendix A, from (6.8) we obtain

$$\boxed{\mathbf{a} = (\mathbf{X}^T\mathbf{X})^{-1}\mathbf{X}^T\mathbf{f}.} \tag{6.9}$$

From discussions in Chapter 2 we recognize, however, that solution of the linear equation (6.8) is more efficient than matrix inversion and a matrix-vector multiplication as suggested by (6.9).

From the form of (6.8) we may explain why equations (6.6) are called ''normal equations.'' Observe first that (6.8) can be rewritten as

$$\mathbf{x}^{(j)}(\mathbf{X}\mathbf{a} - \mathbf{f}) = 0 \qquad (0 \le j \le m) \tag{6.10}$$

where the rows of matrix $\mathbf{X}^T$ are

$$\mathbf{x}^{(j)} = (x_1^j, x_2^j, \ldots, x_n^j) \qquad (j = 0, 1, \ldots, m),$$

and the vector $\mathbf{r} = \mathbf{X}\mathbf{a} - \mathbf{f}$ equals the residual error vector $(p(x_1) - f_1, p(x_2) - f_2, \ldots, p(x_n) - f_n)^T$. With this notation (6.10) implies that the row vectors $\mathbf{x}^{(j)}$ are perpendicular, in other words, *normal*, to the residual error vector $\mathbf{r}$. That is,

$$\mathbf{x}^{(j)}\mathbf{r} = 0, \qquad 0 \le j \le m.$$

──────── **EXAMPLE 6.2** ────────

In the case of Example 6.1,

$$\mathbf{X} = \begin{bmatrix} 1 & -2 & 4 \\ 1 & -1 & 1 \\ 1 & 0 & 0 \\ 1 & 1 & 1 \\ 1 & 2 & 4 \end{bmatrix}, \quad \mathbf{a} = \begin{bmatrix} a_0 \\ a_1 \\ a_2 \end{bmatrix}, \quad \mathbf{f} = \begin{bmatrix} 0 \\ 1 \\ 2 \\ 1 \\ 0 \end{bmatrix}.$$

Then

$$\mathbf{X}^T\mathbf{X} = \begin{bmatrix} 1 & 1 & 1 & 1 & 1 \\ -2 & -1 & 0 & 1 & 2 \\ 4 & 1 & 0 & 1 & 4 \end{bmatrix} \begin{bmatrix} 1 & -2 & 4 \\ 1 & -1 & 1 \\ 1 & 0 & 0 \\ 1 & 1 & 1 \\ 1 & 2 & 4 \end{bmatrix} = \begin{bmatrix} 5 & 0 & 10 \\ 0 & 10 & 0 \\ 10 & 0 & 34 \end{bmatrix}$$

and

$$\mathbf{X}^T\mathbf{f} = \begin{bmatrix} 1 & 1 & 1 & 1 & 1 \\ -2 & -1 & 0 & 1 & 2 \\ 4 & 1 & 0 & 1 & 4 \end{bmatrix} \begin{bmatrix} 0 \\ 1 \\ 2 \\ 1 \\ 0 \end{bmatrix} = \begin{bmatrix} 4 \\ 0 \\ 2 \end{bmatrix}.$$

Consequently, (6.8) has the form

$$\begin{bmatrix} 5 & 0 & 10 \\ 0 & 10 & 0 \\ 10 & 0 & 34 \end{bmatrix} \begin{bmatrix} a_0 \\ a_1 \\ a_2 \end{bmatrix} = \begin{bmatrix} 4 \\ 0 \\ 2 \end{bmatrix},$$

which coincides with the normal equations obtained in Example 6.1. One easily calculates from the least-squares polynomial constructed in that example that the residual

$$\mathbf{r} = \begin{bmatrix} 0.057 \\ -0.2285 \\ 0.343 \\ -0.2285 \\ 0.057 \end{bmatrix}$$

and confirms that this vector indeed is normal to the rows $\mathbf{x}^{(j)}$ of $\mathbf{X}$. ∎

Table 6.1 presents a listing of the subroutine LSQM for least-squares polynomial approximation. The subroutine compiles the normal equations from the data and calls on GAUS1 (Table 2.6) to provide the solution, which is available as an output array C. The numbers in this array are related to the least-squares polynomial coefficients by $a_k = C(K + 1)$. The structure of subroutine LSQM is as follows. DO loops with labels 1 and 2 compute the right-hand side of the first normal equation ($j = 0$). The DO loop with label 3 computes the right-hand sides

TABLE 6.1   Subroutine LSQM for the Least-Squares Method

```
        SUBROUTINE LSQM(N,M,X,F,C)
C
C       ****************************************************************
C       *   FUNCTION: THIS SUBROUTINE COMPUTES THE COEFFICIENTS OF   *
C       *             THE LEAST-SQUARES POLYNOMIAL                   *
C       *             P(X)=C(1)+C(2)*X+...+C(M+1)*X**M               *
C       *             FOR A SET OF FUNCTIONAL VALUES F AND DOMAIN    *
C       *             POINTS X                                       *
C       *   USAGE:                                                   *
C       *         CALL SEQUENCE: CALL LSQM(N,M,X,F,C)                *
C       *         EXTERNAL FUNCTIONS/SUBROUTINES:                    *
C       *                        SUBROUTINE GAUS1                    *
C       *   PARAMETERS:                                              *
C       *         INPUT:                                             *
C       *             N=NUMBER OF POINTS (NOT GREATER THAN 1000)     *
C       *             M=POLYNOMIAL DEGREE (LESS THAN 30)             *
C       *             X=N BY 1 ARRAY OF DOMAIN POINTS                *
C       *             F=N BY 1 ARRAY OF FUNCTION VALUES              *
C       *         OUTPUT:                                            *
C       *             C=M+1 BY 1 ARRAY OF COEFFICIENTS FOR THE       *
C       *             LEAST-SQUARES POLYNOMIAL                       *
C       ****************************************************************
C
        DIMENSION X(N),F(N),C(M+1),POWX(1000),FX(1000)
        DIMENSION XX(30,31),SUMPOW(100)
C       *** INITIALIZATION ***
        DO 1 I=1,N
            POWX(I)=1.0
            FX(I)=F(I)
      1 CONTINUE
C
C       *** THE FIRST M+1 COLUMNS OF XX IS EQUAL TO X    ***
C       *** TRANSPOSE TIMES X, WHERE X IS AS IN (6.7)    ***
C       *** THE LAST COLUMN (M+2-TH) OF XX IS EQUAL TO   ***
C       *** THE RIGHT HAND SIDE OF THE NORMAL EQUATIONS  ***
C       *** (6.8)                                        ***
C       *** FX(J) IS F(J)( X(J)**(I-1) )                 ***
C       *** POWX(J) IS X(J)**(I-1)                       ***
C       *** SUMPOW(I) IS SUM OVER J OF POWX(J)           ***
C
C
C       *** COMPUTE THE RIGHT HAND SIDE OF THE FIRST     ***
C       *** NORMAL EQUATION                              ***
C
        XX(1,M+2)=0.0
        DO 2 I=1,N
            XX(1,M+2)=XX(1,M+2)+F(I)
      2 CONTINUE
C
C       *** COMPUTE THE RIGHT HAND SIDE OF THE OTHER     ***
C       *** NORMAL EQUATIONS   ALSO, COMPUTE THE SUMS    ***
C       *** ( OVER J ) OF X(J)**(I-1) FOR I=1,...,M+1    ***
C
        SUMPOW(1)=N
        DO 3 I=2,M+1
            SUMPOW(I)=0.0
            XX(I,M+2)=0.0
            DO 3 J=1,N
                POWX(J)=POWX(J)*X(J)
                FX(J)=FX(J)*X(J)
                SUMPOW(I)=SUMPOW(I)+POWX(J)
                XX(I,M+2)=XX(I,M+2)+FX(J)
      3 CONTINUE
C
C       *** COMPUTE THE SUMS( OVER J) OF X(J)**(I-1) FOR           ***
C       *** I=M+2,...,2(M+1) AND STORE IN SUMPOW(I)  NOTE THAT     ***
```

(continued)

TABLE 6.1   (Continued)

```
C     *** AT THIS POINT POWX(J) IS EQUAL TO X(J)**M AND THE    ***
C     *** SUMS X(J)**(I-1) FOR I=1,...,M+1 HAVE BEEN STORED    ***
C     *** IN SUMPOW(I)                                         ***
C
      DO 4 I=M+2,2*(M+1)
         SUMPOW(I)=0.0
         DO 4 J=1,N
            POWX(J)=POWX(J)*X(J)
            SUMPOW(I)=SUMPOW(I)+POWX(J)
    4 CONTINUE
C
C     *** SET UP THE FIRST M+1 COLUMNS OF THE XX MATRIX    THE  ***
C     *** LAST COLUMN (M+2-TH) OF XX HAS ALREADY BEEN SET UP    ***
C     *** ALL ELEMENTS OF THE FIRST M+1 COLUMNS OF XX HAVE BEEN ***
C     *** COMPUTED AND STORED IN THE ARRAY SUMPOW              ***
C
      DO 5 I=1,M+1
         DO 5 J=1,M+1
            XX(I,J)=SUMPOW(I+J-1)
    5 CONTINUE
C     *** PERFORM GAUSSIAN ELIMINATION ***
      N1=M+1
      M1=1
      ND=30
C     *** USER MAY WANT TO RESET EPS ***
      EPS=0.000001
      CALL GAUS1(N1,M1,ND,XX,EPS)
C     *** THE SOLUTION IS PLACED IN THE ARRAY C ***
      DO 6 I=1,M+1
         C(I)=XX(I,M+2)
    6 CONTINUE
      RETURN
      END
```

of all other normal equations. DO loop with label 4 computes the sums $s_j = \sum_{i=1}^{n} x_i^j$ and DO loop with label 5 accumulates these sums as the coefficients of the normal equations. The matrix $\mathbf{X}^T\mathbf{X}$ of (6.8) is stored as the principal $(m + 1) \times (m + 1)$ submatrix of XX in the program. The last column of the XX array is $\mathbf{X}^T\mathbf{f}$, as in (6.8). The solution of the normal equations is then obtained by Gaussian elimination (through subroutine GAUS1), and the DO loop with label 6 produces the output array C from the solution. Example 6.5 in Section 6.2.2 includes a calling program (Table 6.2) that uses LSQM.

The linear approximating polynomials obtained by the use of the least-squares method are sometimes called *linear regression functions*. In this particular case, $m = 1$, and the normal equations have the special form

$$a_0 n + a_1 \sum_{i=1}^{n} x_i = \sum_{i=1}^{n} f_i$$

$$a_0 \sum_{i=1}^{n} x_i + a_1 \sum_{i=1}^{n} x_i^2 = \sum_{i=1}^{n} x_i f_i.$$

One may verify that the solution coefficients a_0 and a_1 of the linear regression function $p(x) = a_0 + a_1 x$ are given by the equations

$$a_1 = \frac{\overline{xf} - (\bar{x})(\bar{f})}{\overline{x^2} - (\bar{x})^2} \tag{6.11}$$

$$a_0 = \bar{f} - a_1 \bar{x}, \tag{6.12}$$

where

$$\bar{x} = \frac{1}{n} \sum_{i=1}^{n} x_i, \quad \overline{x^2} = \frac{1}{n} \sum_{i=1}^{n} x_i^2, \quad \bar{f} = \frac{1}{n} \sum_{i=1}^{n} f_i, \quad \overline{xf} = \frac{1}{n} \sum_{i=1}^{n} x_i f_i. \tag{6.13}$$

EXAMPLE 6.3

The foregoing procedure for linear regression functions is exemplified. Here we take $n = 4$,

$$x_1 = 0, \quad x_2 = 1, \quad x_3 = 2, \quad x_4 = 3,$$

$$f_1 = 0, \quad f_2 = 2, \quad f_3 = 1, \quad f_4 = 2.$$

Then the average values defined in (6.13) are

$$\bar{x} = \tfrac{1}{4}(0 + 1 + 2 + 3) = \tfrac{6}{4} = 1.5$$

$$\overline{x^2} = \tfrac{1}{4}(0 + 1 + 4 + 9) = \tfrac{14}{4} = 3.5$$

$$\bar{f} = \tfrac{1}{4}(0 + 2 + 1 + 2) = \tfrac{5}{4} = 1.25$$

$$\overline{xf} = \tfrac{1}{4}(0 \cdot 0 + 1 \cdot 2 + 2 \cdot 1 + 3 \cdot 2) = \tfrac{10}{4} = 2.5.$$

Thus (6.11) and (6.12) imply that

$$a_1 = \frac{2.5 - 1.5 \cdot 1.25}{3.5 - 1.5^2} = 0.5$$

$$a_0 = 1.25 - 0.5 \cdot 1.5 = 0.5.$$

Consequently, the linear least-squares polynomial is

$$p(x) = 0.5 + 0.5x.$$

Figure 6.7 shows the data points and the approximating linear polynomial.

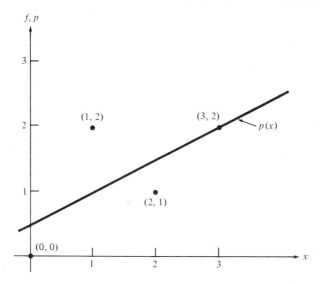

FIGURE 6.7   Data and Approximating Polynomial of Example 6.3

With respect to least-squares approximation, an important procedural issue is the selection of m, the approximation polynomial degree. Unfortunately, only in certain very specialized statistical settings is there a definitive theory for this issue. In some instances, visual inspection of a graph of the data can be useful. For example, the points in Figure 6.6 suggested a quadratic approximation. With respect to the data set illustrated in Figure 6.2, one would anticipate that a constant ($m = 0$) is not as sensible as a line ($m = 1$) with negative slope. Ralston and Rabinowitz (1978, Sec. 6.3-2) offer some statistically motivated selection procedures based on increasing m until the squared residual error

$$Q(f, p) = \sum_{i=1}^{n} [f_i - p_m(x_i)]^2$$

of approximation by $p_m(x)$, the mth-degree least-squares polynomial, does not decrease "sufficiently" with further increase in m.

6.2.2 Practical Considerations and Case Studies

In this section we put previous methodology into action. Low-degree least-squares polynomials are constructed from various data sets. The least-squares approach, and data smoothing in general, raises some procedural concerns, some of which are encountered even in the simple studies here.

──────── **EXAMPLE 6.4** ────────────────────────────────────

This study illustrates the least-squares polynomial application to curve fitting of the scattered data shown in Figure 6.8. Figure 6.9 reproduces these data points, which serve as input for the subroutine LSQM (Table 6.1), and the resulting least-squares polynomial approximations $p_0(x)$, $p_1(x)$, and $p_8(x)$ of degrees 0, 1, and 8.

Visually, the constant polynomial $p_0(x)$ does not seem well centered with respect to the data. This illustrates *underfitting*. On the other hand, the degree 8 approximation is so erratic as to give rise to the suspicion that it is trying to fit the random irregularities of the data. Such a situation is referred to as *overfitting*. The data were, in fact, generated by adding scaled random numbers to the exponentially decaying curve shown in Figure 6.10.

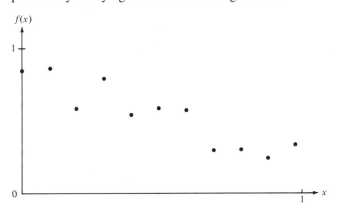

FIGURE 6.8 A Data Set

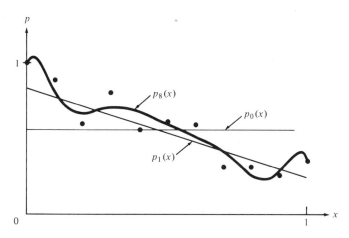

FIGURE 6.9 Least-Squares Fitting of Scattered Data

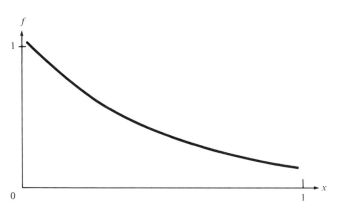

FIGURE 6.10 Underlying Function for Example 6.4

EXAMPLE 6.5

In this case study the least-squares method has been applied to the problem (studied also in Examples 3.3 and 3.6) of finding an approximating polynomial for sin (x), over the interval $I = [0, 2]$. For this example 50 data points are used, and domain points x_i $(1 \leq i \leq 50)$ are evenly spaced along the interval I. The calling program and the output for this experiment are presented in Tables 6.2 and 6.3. The values of the least-squares polynomial are compared with those of sin (x) at 10 points evenly spaced between 0 and 2. The subscript m of $p_m(x)$ in Table 6.3 indicates the degree m of the least-squares approximating polynomial. In Figure 6.11 the graphs of these approximating polynomials are plotted against the "target" function sin (x). The reader may wish to compare this figure with Figures 3.4 and 3.7, which approximate the same target function by Taylor's and interpolation polynomials, respectively. In comparing these figures, we see that the linear approximation $p_1(x)$ by least squares seems much better positioned than the linear Taylor's and Lagrange approximations. The approximation errors listed in Table 6.3 are similarly, almost without exception, less than their Taylor's and Lagrange counterparts listed in Tables 3.4 and 3.8.

TABLE 6.2   Program for Example 6.5

```
C       PROGRAM LSQUARE
C
C       ****************************************************************
C       THIS PROGRAM FINDS LEAST-SQUARES POLYNOMIALS FOR SIN(X) ON
C       THE INTERVAL [0,2]. THE DATA CONSIST OF VALUES SIN(2.*J/50.)
C       FOR J=1,...,50
C       CALLS:    LSQM,GAUS1
C       OUTPUT:
C                 X=VALUE OF X
C                 TRUE=VALUE OF SIN(X)
C                 P=POLYNOMIAL APPROXIMATION AT X
C                 DIFF=DIFFERENCE (TRUE-P) FOR EACH X
C       ****************************************************************
C
        DIMENSION X1(50),F(50),C(6)
        N=50
        Y=0.
        H=2./50.
C
C       *** CONSTRUCT DATA X1 AND SIN(X1) FOR THE APPROXIMATION    ***
C
        DO 10 J=1,N
          Y=Y+H
          X1(J)=Y
          F(J)=SIN(X1(J))
     10 CONTINUE
C
C       *** M IS THE DEGREE OF THE LEAST-SQUARES POLYNOMIAL        ***
C
        DO 40 M=1,3
          WRITE(10,1)
      1   FORMAT(////)
C
C       *** SUBROUTINE LSQM WILL CALCULATE THE M-TH DEGREE LEAST   ***
C       *** SQUARES POLYNOMIAL COEFFICIENTS                        ***
C
          CALL LSQM(N,M,X1,F,C)
C
C       *** NEXT COMPUTE THE VALUE OF THE POLYNOMIAL AT 10 EQUALLY***
C       *** SPACED POINTS AND COMPARE THESE VALUES WITH SIN(X) AT ***
C       *** THESE POINTS                                          ***
C
          X=0.
          DO 30 I=1,10
            X=X+.2
            P=0.
            DO 20 K=1,M+1
              K1=K-1
              T=C(K)*X**K1
              P=P+T
     20     CONTINUE
            TRUE=SIN(X)
            DIFF=TRUE-P
            WRITE(10,*) X,TRUE,P,DIFF
     30   CONTINUE
     40 CONTINUE
        STOP
        END
```

TABLE 6.3 Application of Least-Squares Polynomials

x	sin (x)	$p_1(x)$	sin (x) $- p_1(x)$	$p_2(x)$	sin (x) $- p_2(x)$	$p_3(x)$	sin (x) $- p_3(x)$
0.2	0.1986693	0.3292865	-0.1306172	0.1947901	3.8792044E-03	0.1997269	-1.0576099E-03
0.4	0.3894183	0.4238683	-3.4449995E-02	0.4035662	-1.4147878E-02	0.3925681	-3.1497478E-03
0.6	0.5646425	0.5184502	4.6192288E-02	0.5806217	-1.5979230E-02	0.5659643	-1.3218522E-03
0.8	0.7173561	0.6130320	0.1043240	0.7259566	-8.6005330E-03	0.7159558	1.4002919E-03
1.0	0.8414710	0.7076139	0.1338571	0.8395711	1.8998981E-03	0.8385826	2.8883815E-03
1.2	0.9320391	0.8021957	0.1298434	0.9214648	1.0574281E-02	0.9298849	2.1541715E-03
1.4	0.9854497	0.8967776	8.8672161E-02	0.9716381	1.3811588E-02	0.9859029	-4.5317411E-04
1.6	0.9995736	0.9913595	8.2141161E-03	0.9900907	9.4828606E-03	1.002676	-3.1028986E-03
1.8	0.9738476	1.085941	-0.1120937	0.9768227	-2.9751658E-03	0.9762460	-2.3984313E-03
2.0	0.9092973	1.180523	-0.2712259	0.9318342	-2.2536874E-02	0.9026516	6.6457391E-03

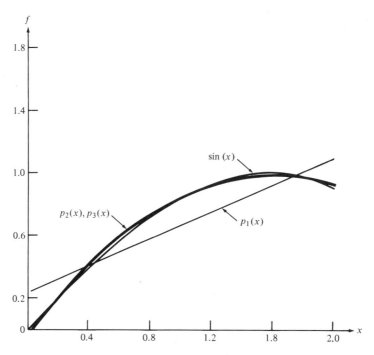

FIGURE 6.11   Least-Squares Approximation Graph

Application 6.1

Mathematics Scholastic Aptitude Test scores are thought to be good indicators of the proportion of entering freshmen nationwide who are qualified for serious programs in computer science, engineering, mathematics, physics, and other quantitative disciplines. With this in mind, we have used least-squares polynomials, as constructed by subroutine LSQM (Table 6.1), to examine the SAT score data of Figure 6.2 in the hope of discovering some sort of trend and thereby a suggestion as to what may be expected in the future.

Unfortunately, the graphs (Figure 6.12) of polynomials of varying degree m give different suggestions. The linear ($m = 1$) least-squares polynomial shows a depressing monotonic decline, but this polynomial has a very limited structure and is incapable of detecting changes in "trend." Polynomials of degrees $m = 2$ through 4 seem to suggest that a leveling off has occurred and a rise in average SAT scores may be anticipated. The cases $m = 3$ and 4 are optimistic in this regard.

Of course, the difficulty now is selecting which of the graphs to believe. Here strict scientific methodology is not available, and personal judgment must be exercised; all the graphs fit the data fairly closely. the authors' inclination is to accept the middle graphs and say only that the decline in scores seems to be leveling off. There is some statistical thinking (e.g., Savage, 1954) which bears on how to draw conclusions from statistical evidence. On a less profound but more amusing level, the reader may be interested in *How to Lie with Statistics* by Huff (1954). (We mention parenthetically that in our initial calculations, the

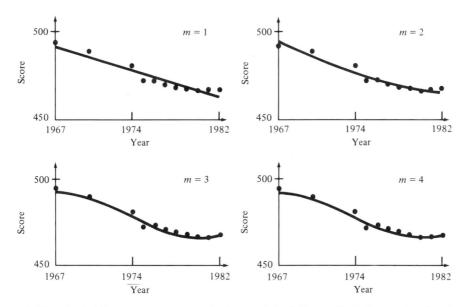

FIGURE 6.12   Least-Squares Polynomial Fitting of Mathematics SAT Scores

fourth-degree polynomial did not come close to the data. We quickly recognized that this was due to numerical instabilities which are discussed in Section 6.2.4. When the calculations were redone in double precision we obtained the graph shown.)

$\diamondsuit$

★6.2.3 Linear and Nonlinear Least-Squares Problems

The problem of finding the polynomial $p(x) = a_0 + a_1 x + \cdots + a_m x^m$ that minimizes the squared error criterion $Q(f, p) = \sum_{i=1}^{n} [f_i - p(x_i)]^2$ is said to be a *linear* least-squares problem because $p(x)$ is, in the terminology of algebra, a linear function in the unknown coefficients $a_0, a_1, \ldots, a_m$.

It is sometimes useful to observe that if other "basis" functions $\varphi_0(x), \varphi_1(x), \ldots, \varphi_m(x)$ are substituted for $1, x, \ldots, x^m$ in the least-squares approach, the methods and results of the preceding section apply with very little modification. Assume that a least-squares approximation of the form

$$p(x) = a_0\varphi_0(x) + a_1\varphi_1(x) + \cdots + a_m\varphi_m(x)$$

is desired. Then the matrix $\mathbf{X}$ of (6.7) and (6.9) is replaced by the matrix

$$\mathbf{\Phi} = \begin{bmatrix} \varphi_0(x_1) & \varphi_1(x_1) & \cdots & \varphi_m(x_1) \\ \varphi_0(x_2) & \varphi_1(x_2) & \cdots & \varphi_m(x_2) \\ \vdots & \vdots & & \vdots \\ \varphi_0(x_n) & \varphi_1(x_n) & \cdots & \varphi_m(x_n) \end{bmatrix}. \tag{6.14}$$

The normal equations for the problem of finding the coefficients $a_0, a_1, \ldots, a_m$ to minimize

$$Q(f, \varphi) = \sum_{i=1}^{n} \left[f_i - \sum_{j=0}^{m} a_j \varphi_j(x_i) \right]^2$$

lead [in the notation of (6.7) and (6.14)] to the normal equations (in matrix form)

$$(\Phi^T \Phi)\mathbf{a} = \Phi^T \mathbf{f}. \tag{6.15}$$

The vector $\mathbf{a}$ of least-squares coefficients can be represented explicitly as

$$\boxed{\mathbf{a} = (\Phi^T \Phi)^{-1} \Phi^T \mathbf{f}.} \tag{6.16}$$

Here $\mathbf{a} = (a_0, a_1, \ldots, a_m)^T$ and $\mathbf{f} = (f_1, \ldots, f_n)^T$ again.

Linear least-squares problems using basis functions other than polynomials arise in approximation of periodic and diurnal data such as traffic intensity or height of tides, where sinusoidal $\varphi_j(x)$ are sensible, or in approximating radioactivity after a nuclear event, in which for physical reasons it would be natural to use negative exponential functions $\varphi_j(x) = \exp(-c_j x)$ as "basis" functions. In Section 6.3 we will find that even when we desire a polynomial least-squares approximation, for reasons of numerical stability, it is useful to consider a polynomial basis $\varphi_0(x)$, $\varphi_1(x), \ldots, \varphi_m(x)$ other than $1, x, \ldots, x^m$.

The vector $\mathbf{a}$ can be viewed as a parameter that determines an approximating function according to the rule

$$\varphi_\mathbf{a}(x) = \sum_{j=0}^{m} a_j \varphi_j(x).$$

A *nonlinear* least-squares problem arises when the approximating function $\varphi_\mathbf{a}(x)$ does not depend linearly on $\mathbf{a}$. For example, consider the parameter pair $\mathbf{a} = (a_1, a_2)$ and the approximating function

$$\varphi_{(a_1,a_2)}(x) = a_1 \exp(a_2 x), \qquad -\infty < a_1, a_2 < \infty. \tag{6.17}$$

Such a family of approximating functions is appropriate if for physical reasons the values $f_j = f(x_j)$ are known to be points on a solution curve of the linear differential equation

$$\frac{d}{dx} f(x) = \alpha f(x) \tag{6.18}$$

with coefficient α and the initial condition unknown. In this case, a nonlinear least-squares problem occurs if we wish to "identify" the initial condition $a_1 = f(0)$ and the differential equation parameter $a_2 = \alpha$ by finding the parameter vector $\mathbf{a} = (a_1, a_2)$ giving the least-squares fit to the data $(x_1, f_1), (x_2, f_2), \ldots, (x_n, f_n)$. That is, we solve for unknowns a_1 and a_2 which minimize

$$Q(f, \mathbf{a}) = \sum_{i=1}^{n} [f_i - a_1 \exp (a_2 x_i)]^2. \tag{6.19}$$

[In the identification theory literature, it is typically presumed that the observation values f_i are not exactly equal to the solution values of (6.18) but are corrupted by measurement error.] The resulting nonlinear normal equations for (6.19), obtained by taking first partial derivatives with respect to the parameters a_1 and a_2, respectively, are

$$\sum_{i=1}^{n} \{[f_i - a_1 \exp (a_2 x_i)] \exp (a_2 x_i)\} = 0$$
$$\tag{6.20}$$
$$\sum_{i=1}^{n} \{[f_i - a_1 \exp (a_2 x_i)]a_1 x_i \exp (a_2 x_i)\} = 0.$$

The multivariable nonlinear equation technique given in Section 5.8 may be employed to find the root of (6.20).

──────── **EXAMPLE 6.6** ────────────────────────────────────

Here we illustrate implementation of the nonlinear least-squares identification technique discussed above. The procedure is to obtain data points (x_i, f_i) of the function (6.17) with known parameters a_1 and a_2, and then see how well the least-squares technique can identify these known parameters from the data. The parameters were selected to be

$$a_1 = 1 = f(0) \quad \text{and} \quad a_2 = \alpha = -0.25,$$

respectively. Thus $f(x) = \exp (-0.25x)$. The data consisted of the points (x_i, f_i), with $x_i = 0.4(i - 1)$ and, of course, $f_i = f(x_i)$, $1 \le i \le 20$. The data points are plotted in Figure 6.13. The multivariable Newton's method (subroutine MVNE in Section 5.8) was used for solving the normal equations (6.20), and the listing of our implementation is given in Table 6.4. The array DAT contains the values f_i, and the function subprogram F is used in the sense of the MVNE comment lines. Otherwise, we have followed the notation in the discussion above. The

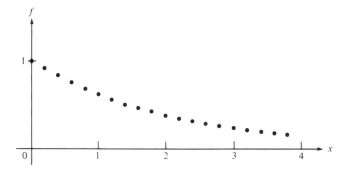

FIGURE 6.13 Noiseless Data for Nonlinear Least-Squares Identification

TABLE 6.4 Listing of Nonlinear Least-Squares Systems Identification Program

```
C       PROGRAM NONLINLS
C
C       ****************************************************************
C       THIS PROGRAM GENERATES A SET OF 20 DATA POINTS USING THE
C       FUNCTIONAL VALUES EXP(-.25X) FOR X=0,.4,.8,...,7.6
C       THESE DATA ARE USED IN THE FUNCTIONS F AND DF TO DETERMINE THE
C       NORMAL EQUATIONS FOR THE NON-LINEAR LEAST-SQUARES PROBLEM
C       OF THE FORM A0(1)*EXP(A0(2)*X)
C       CALLS:  MVNE,GAUS1
C       OUTPUT(PRINTED FROM SUBROUTINE MVNE):
C               A(0)=SUCCESSIVE NEWTON APPROXIMATIONS OF THE FIRST
C                    LEAST-SQUARES COEFFICIENT ABOVE
C               A(1)=SUCCESSIVE NEWTON APPROXIMATIONS OF THE SECOND
C                    LEAST-SQUARES COEFFICIENT ABOVE
C       ****************************************************************
C
        COMMON DAT(20),X(20),NT
        DIMENSION A0(2),A(2)
C
C       *** SPECIFY INPUT PARAMETERS FOR MVNE                       ***
C
        N=2
        DATA (A0(I),I=1,2)/1.5,-0.4/
        EPS=1.E-04
C
C       *** GENERATE THE DATA TO BE FIT                             ***
C
        DO 10 I=1,20
           X(I)=.4*(I-1)
           DAT(I)=EXP(-.25*X(I))
     10 CONTINUE
        NT=20
C
C       *** SUBROUTINE MVNE WILL PERFORM NEWTONS METHOD USING       ***
C       *** THE SUBROUTINES F AND DF BELOW                          ***
C
        CALL MVNE(N,A0,A,EPS)
        STOP
        END


        FUNCTION F(K,A)
C
C       *** THIS FUNCTION IS CALLED BY SUBROUTINE MVNE TO           ***
C       *** CALCULATE FUNCTION VALUES NEEDED FOR NEWTONS METHOD     ***
C
        DIMENSION A(2)
        COMMON DAT(20),X(20),NT
        S=0.
        IF(K.EQ.1) THEN
           DO 10 I=1,NT
              S=S+(DAT(I)-A(1)*EXP(A(2)*X(I)))*EXP(A(2)*X(I))
     10    CONTINUE
           A1=S
        ELSE
           DO 20 I=1,NT
              S=S+(DAT(I)-A(1)*EXP(A(2)*X(I)))*A(1)*X(I)*EXP(A(2)*X(I))
     20    CONTINUE
           A2=S
        END IF
        F=S
        RETURN
        END


        FUNCTION DF(K1,K2,A)
C
```

TABLE 6.4 (Continued)

```
C     *** THIS FUNCTION IS CALLED BY SUBROUTINE MVNE TO        ***
C     *** CALCULATE DERIVATIVE VALUES NEEDED FOR NEWTONS METHOD ***
C
      DIMENSION A(2)
      COMMON DAT(20),X(20),NT
      S=0.
      IF(K1.EQ.1) THEN
         IF(K2.EQ.1) THEN
            DO 10 I=1,NT
               S=S-EXP(2*A(2)*X(I))
10          CONTINUE
         ELSE
            DO 20 I=1,NT
               Q=(DAT(I)-A(1)*EXP(A(2)*X(I)))*X(I)*EXP(A(2)*X(I))
               Q=Q-X(I)*A(1)*EXP(2*A(2)*X(I))
               S=S+Q
20          CONTINUE
         END IF
      ELSE IF(K1.EQ.2) THEN
         IF(K2.EQ.1) THEN
            DO 30 I=1,NT
               Q=(DAT(I)-A(1)*EXP(A(2)*X(I)))*X(I)*EXP(A(2)*X(I))
               Q=Q-X(I)*A(1)*EXP(2*A(2)*X(I))
               S=S+Q
30          CONTINUE
         ELSE
            DO 40 I=1,NT
               Q=(X(I)**2)*
     1            (EXP(A(2)*X(I))*(DAT(I)-A(1)*EXP(A(2)*X(I))))*A(1)
               Q=Q-EXP(2*A(2)*X(I))*(A(1)*X(I))**2
               S=S+Q
40          CONTINUE
         END IF
      END IF
      DF=S
      RETURN
      END
```

initial parameter estimates were taken as $a_1 = 1.5$ and $a_2 = -0.4$, and the successive MVNE iterates are displayed in Table 6.5. The parameters were recovered perfectly.

In a second computation, we "stimulated" measurement error by using the computer random number generator to corrupt the function values f_i. The noisy data are displayed in Figure 6.14. The least-squares estimates provided by our program on this data set are given in Table 6.6.

TABLE 6.5 Nonlinear Least-Squares Identification with Noiseless Measurement

a_1	a_2
1.500000	-0.4000000
0.8643785	-0.2130418
0.9845823	-0.2429858
0.9998832	-0.2499678
1.000000	-0.2500000

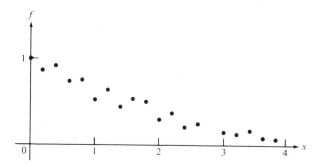

FIGURE 6.14 Noisy Data for Nonlinear Least-
Squares Identification

**TABLE 6.6 Nonlinear
Least-Squares Identification
with Measurement Error**

a_1	a_2
1.500000	-0.4000000
0.9087929	-0.2279210
1.011362	-0.2633236
1.016372	-0.2651989
1.016384	-0.2652051

6.2.4 Ill-Conditioning in Least-Squares Methods

Let us return our attention to the least-squares polynomial approximation problem
determined by (6.1). Practitioners find that when the degree of the approximating
polynomial is moderate (say 8) to large, solution of the normal equations (6.8)
for the polynomial coefficients often leads to seriously erroneous answers. The
heart of the problem is that the matrix $\mathbf{S} = \mathbf{X}^T\mathbf{X}$, with $\mathbf{X}$ defined by (6.7), tends
to be ill-conditioned in the sense discussed in Section 2.4. As a consequence, the
computed solution of the linear equation (6.8) tends to differ substantially from
its exact solution.

   To demonstrate that ill-conditioning can arise in very natural least-squares settings, consider the case in which the x_i values are evenly spaced along the unit
interval. Thus let

$$x_i = \frac{i}{n}, \qquad 1 \le i \le n.$$

Regardless of $\mathbf{X}$, from (6.7), we see that if $\mathbf{S} = \mathbf{X}^T\mathbf{X}$, and s_{kj} is the (k, j) coordinate
of $\mathbf{S}$ and x_{kj} the (k, j) coordinate of $\mathbf{X}$, then

$$s_{kj} = \sum_{i=1}^{n} x_{ik}x_{ij} = \sum_{i=1}^{n} (x_i^{k-1})(x_i^{j-1}) = \sum_{i=1}^{n} x_i^{k+j-2}. \qquad (6.21)$$

For $x_i = i/n$, we readily calculate that

$$s_{kj} = n \sum_{i=1}^{n} \left(\frac{i}{n}\right)^{k+j-2} \frac{1}{n} \approx n \int_{0}^{1} t^{k+j-2} \, dt = \frac{n}{k+j-1} \, . \tag{6.22}$$

We have used the fact that

$$\sum_{i=1}^{n} \left(\frac{i}{n}\right)^{k+j-2} \frac{1}{n} \tag{6.23}$$

is a Riemann sum approximation for the integral

$$\int_{0}^{1} t^{k+j-2} \, dt = \frac{1}{k+j-1} \, .$$

From (6.22) one readily concludes that $\mathbf{H} \approx (1/n)\mathbf{S}$, where $\mathbf{H}$ is the notoriously unstable nth-order Hilbert segment matrix the (k, j) coordinate of which equals $1/(k+j-1)$. The ill-conditioning of $\mathbf{H}$, for moderate order n, was established in Problem 9 of Chapter 2.

EXAMPLE 6.7

Here we exemplify normal equation ill-conditioning by making a simple modification of the computation in Example 6.5 of least-squares polynomial approximation of the sine function. Specifically, the only change we made was to define the degree m of the least-squares polynomial to be an input variable in the program listed in Table 6.2, and to modify the program and subroutines for double precision to increase the accuracy. For $m = 9$ the errors at the 10 output points were on the order of 10^{-9}. No matter how high the degree, the average error did not fall below 10^{-11}, whereas in double precision, an accuracy of 10^{-16} ought to be achievable. The conclusion is that on the computer we used for this experiment (a VAX), by the conventional equation (6.8), it is impossible to get an accuracy of 12 significant decimals in the least-squares approximation of sin (x), $0 \le x \le 2$, using 50 equally spaced data points on this interval. If m is less than 10, then the degree is not high enough to obtain such accuracy, and if m is 10 or larger, the accuracy deteriorates as a result of $\mathbf{S} = \mathbf{X}^T\mathbf{X}$ being ill-conditioned. To some extent, the limits of accuracy depend on the computer used.

A standard way of alleviating the least-squares ill-conditioning problem is to make use of a different polynomial basis $\varphi_0(x)$, $\varphi_1(x)$, . . . , $\varphi_m(x)$. As stated in Section 6.2.3, for any set of basis polynomials,

$$\varphi_0(x), \ \varphi_1(x), \ . \ . \ . \ , \ \varphi_m(x),$$

we may define the matrix $\mathbf{\Phi}$ as in (6.14) with (i, j) coordinate

$$\varphi_{ij} = \varphi_j(x_i), \qquad 1 \le i \le n, \quad 0 \le j \le m,$$

and solve the normal equations $(\boldsymbol{\Phi}^T\boldsymbol{\Phi})\mathbf{a} = \boldsymbol{\Phi}^T\mathbf{f}$ to obtain the coefficient vector $\mathbf{a} = (a_0, a_1, \ldots, a_m)^T$. Then $p(x) = \sum_{j=0}^m a_j\varphi_j(x)$ is the least-squares polynomial. The value of this insight is that one can find basis functions for which $\mathbf{S} = \boldsymbol{\Phi}^T\boldsymbol{\Phi}$ is well-conditioned. In Section 6.3 we will see how "orthogonal" polynomials can serve to achieve well-conditioned least-squares equations. In that section we return to the sine function approximation problem that stymied us in the preceding example. Through the use of orthogonal polynomials, we will be able to achieve a least-squares polynomial approximation of the sine function having an accuracy commensurate with the double-precision computer word length (about 16 significant decimal places) of the VAX.

★6.2.5 Links Between the Least-Squares Theory and Statistics

In this section we assume that the reader has completed introductory course work in probability and statistics.

The idea behind polynomial approximation is that the coefficients $a_0, a_1, \ldots, a_m$ are to be chosen so that the polynomial $p(x)$ "fits" the data $(x_1, f_1), (x_2, f_2), \ldots, (x_n, f_n)$ in the sense that

$$p(x_i) = a_0 + a_1 x_i + \cdots + a_m x_i^m \approx f_i, \qquad 1 \le i \le n.$$

In statistical theory, we give more structure to the "fitting" problem by writing the system of equations

$$f_i = a_0 + a_1 x_i + \cdots + a_m x_i^m + e_i, \qquad 1 \le i \le n,$$

where the e_i's are regarded as random variables representing measurement error. In fact, analogous to this polynomial case, we enlarge the scope of possible "models" and representations by the more general formulation

$$f_i = a_0 x_{i0} + a_1 x_{i1} + \cdots + a_m x_{im} + e_i, \qquad 1 \le i \le n, \qquad (6.24)$$

where $x_{i0}, x_{i1}, \ldots, x_{im}$, and f_i, $1 \le i \le n$, are the given data. In the polynomial case, $x_{ij} = x_i^j$, and in the particular case of (6.14), $x_{ij} = \varphi_j(x_i)$. By introducing the matrix notation

$$\mathbf{X} = \begin{bmatrix} x_{10} & x_{11} & \cdots & x_{1m} \\ x_{20} & x_{21} & \cdots & x_{2m} \\ \vdots & \vdots & & \vdots \\ x_{n0} & x_{n1} & \cdots & x_{nm} \end{bmatrix}, \quad \mathbf{a} = \begin{bmatrix} a_0 \\ a_1 \\ \vdots \\ a_m \end{bmatrix}, \quad \mathbf{e} = \begin{bmatrix} e_1 \\ e_2 \\ \vdots \\ e_n \end{bmatrix}$$

equations (6.24) can be rewritten

$$\mathbf{f} = \mathbf{Xa} + \mathbf{e}. \qquad (6.25)$$

In this equation, the vector $\mathbf{f} = (f_1, \ldots, f_n)^T$ and the matrix $\mathbf{X}$ are to be regarded as observed data, and the parameter vector $\mathbf{a} = (a_0, a_1, \ldots, a_m)^T$ is an unknown to be determined. In the terminology of statistics, (6.25) is the *general linear model* if the e_j's are presumed independent normal random variables with zero mean and a common variance σ^2. From developments in Section 6.2.1, we may readily confirm that the vector $\hat{\mathbf{a}}$ which minimizes the least-squares criterion

$$Q(\mathbf{f}, \mathbf{a}) = \sum_{i=1}^{n} \left(f_i - \sum_{j=0}^{m} a_j x_{ij} \right)^2 \qquad (6.26)$$

is determined by the normal equation

$$\boxed{\hat{\mathbf{a}} = (\mathbf{X}^T\mathbf{X})^{-1}\mathbf{X}^T\mathbf{f}.} \qquad (6.27)$$

The components of vector $\hat{\mathbf{a}}$ are viewed as estimates of the unknown parameters a_j $(0 \le j \le m)$ in (6.25). The statistical properties of these estimates will be examined next.

Let E denote expectation with respect to the variables e_i and $\mathbf{0}$ the column vector of zeros. Then one calculates that

$$E[\hat{\mathbf{a}}] = E[(\mathbf{X}^T\mathbf{X})^{-1}\mathbf{X}^T\mathbf{f}] = (\mathbf{X}^T\mathbf{X})^{-1}\mathbf{X}^T E[\mathbf{f}] \qquad (6.28)$$
$$= (\mathbf{X}^T\mathbf{X})^{-1}\mathbf{X}^T E[\mathbf{X}\mathbf{a} + \mathbf{e}] = (\mathbf{X}^T\mathbf{X})^{-1}\mathbf{X}^T\mathbf{X}\mathbf{a} + (\mathbf{X}^T\mathbf{X})^{-1}\mathbf{X}^T\mathbf{0} = \mathbf{a}.$$

Thus the expected value of the estimator equals the value to be estimated. In statistical terms we say that estimator $\hat{\mathbf{a}}$ is *unbiased*. A famous result of statistics (the Gauss–Markov theorem) states that $\hat{\mathbf{a}}$, as determined by (6.27), is also the minimum variance estimator for $\mathbf{a}$, among all unbiased linear functions of the vector $\mathbf{f}$. That is, if $\mathbf{M}$ is any $(m + 1) \times n$-order matrix and the estimator as given in the linear form $\mathbf{M}\mathbf{f}$ is such that

$$E[\mathbf{M}\mathbf{f}] = \mathbf{a}, \qquad (6.29)$$

the expected sum of the squared differences of the components of the unknown parameter $\mathbf{a}$ and the estimator is minimal for $\mathbf{M} = (\mathbf{X}^T\mathbf{X})^{-1}\mathbf{X}^T$. That is, for arbitrary matrix $\mathbf{M}$ satisfying (6.29),

$$E[(\mathbf{a} - \mathbf{M}\mathbf{f})^T(\mathbf{a} - \mathbf{M}\mathbf{f})] \ge E[(\mathbf{a} - \hat{\mathbf{a}})^T(\mathbf{a} - \hat{\mathbf{a}})].$$

We refer the reader to Bickel and Doksum (1977, Chap. 7) for a proof and for supplementary information. The Gauss–Markov theorem is true regardless of the law governing the independent variables e_i, provided only that their means are all zero and that they have a common variance σ^2. If, in addition, the e_i's are normally distributed, it is known that $\hat{\mathbf{a}}$ is also the maximum-likelihood estimator of the parameter.

From (6.27) and the definition (6.25) of "general linear model," we may verify that

$$E[(\mathbf{a} - \hat{\mathbf{a}})(\mathbf{a} - \hat{\mathbf{a}})^T] = \sigma^2(\mathbf{X}^T\mathbf{X})^{-1},$$

and by summing up the diagonal elements on both sides, we find that the expected sum of the squared error is

$$E\left[\sum_{j=0}^{m} (a_j - \hat{a}_j)^2\right] = \sigma^2 \text{ trace } [(\mathbf{X}^T\mathbf{X})^{-1}],$$

where the trace of a square matrix is defined to be the sum of the diagonal elements.

Instability, discussed in the preceding section in connection with least-squares polynomials, plagues computation of the minimum-variance estimator as well. The orthogonal polynomial remedy to be presented in Section 6.3 is not applicable to the more general linear model (6.24). A methodology based on "singular-value decompositions" (mentioned in Section 2.7.3) is the state-of-the-art technique. Forsythe et al. (1977) devote Chapter 9 to this topic. Lawson and Hanson (1974) contains advanced topics on these and related matters.

★6.3
STABILIZATION OF LEAST-SQUARES APPROXIMATIONS BY ORTHOGONAL POLYNOMIALS

Orthogonal function methods are a powerful safeguard against the least-squares instability phenomenon discussed in Section 6.2.4. Additionally, they have served well in a myriad of other pursuits in pure and applied mathematics, especially in differential equation theory, stochastic processes, communication and control, and probability theory. Our focus in this section will be on stable least-squares procedures.

Orthogonal functions are defined in terms of "inner products." Let $X = \{x_1, \ldots, x_n\}$ be first a finite set of points, and let functions $f(x)$ and $g(x)$ be defined on X. Then the (discrete) *inner product* of functions $f(x)$ and $g(x)$ is defined to be

$$(f, g) = \sum_{k=1}^{n} f(x_k)g(x_k). \tag{6.30}$$

Alternatively, if X is any (finite or infinite) interval on the real line, then the (continuous) *inner product* is

$$(f, g) = \int_X f(x)g(x)\,dx. \tag{6.31}$$

Functions $f(x)$ and $g(x)$ are said to be *orthogonal* with respect to a given inner product if $(f, g) = 0$. Any finite or infinite sequence of functions $\varphi_0(x)$, $\varphi_1(x)$, . . . is called an *orthogonal system* if and only if for all i and j,

$$(\varphi_i, \varphi_j) = 0 \quad (i \neq j) \quad \text{and} \quad (\varphi_i, \varphi_i) \neq 0. \tag{6.32}$$

Let us now specialize to an orthogonal function system, $\varphi_0(x)$, $\varphi_1(x)$, . . . , $\varphi_m(x)$ of polynomials with subscript i indicating the degree of $\varphi_i(x)$, and the leading coefficient of $\varphi_i(x)$ (i.e., the coefficient of x^i) being 1. For any particular inner product, such a system is unique and is known (Ralston and Rabinowitz, 1978, Sec. 6.4) to satisfy the *three-term recurrence relation*

$$\varphi_i(x) = (x - b_i)\varphi_{i-1}(x) - c_i\varphi_{i-2}(x), \tag{6.33}$$

where

$$b_i = \frac{(x\varphi_{i-1}, \varphi_{i-1})}{(\varphi_{i-1}, \varphi_{i-1})} \qquad (i = 1, 2, \ldots) \tag{6.34}$$

and

$$c_i = \frac{(x\varphi_{i-1}, \varphi_{i-2})}{(\varphi_{i-2}, \varphi_{i-2})} \qquad (i = 2, 3, \ldots) \tag{6.35}$$

with $c_1 = 0$. Construction proceeds by defining the initial terms to be $\varphi_0 = 1$ and $\varphi_{-1} = 0$. The recursion (6.33)–(6.35) is highly useful for computing the entire orthogonal polynomial system and for the implementation of orthogonal polynomial approximation.

Let us now demonstrate that orthogonal polynomials can effectively alleviate the instability of least-squares polynomial approximation observed in Section 6.2.4. Let $\varphi_0(x), \varphi_1(x), \ldots, \varphi_m(x)$ be the system of orthogonal polynomials for the discrete inner product associated with the given set $\{x_1, \ldots, x_n\}$ of points. Then the least-squares polynomial approximation for the data (x_1, f_1), (x_2, f_2), $\ldots, (x_n, f_n)$ bears the representation

$$p_m(x) = \sum_{j=0}^{m} a_j\varphi_j(x), \tag{6.36}$$

where, in view of (6.16),

$$\mathbf{a} = (\mathbf{\Phi}^T\mathbf{\Phi})^{-1}\mathbf{\Phi}^T\mathbf{f} \tag{6.37}$$

and according to (6.14),

$$\mathbf{\Phi} = \begin{bmatrix} \varphi_0(x_1) & \varphi_1(x_1) & \cdots & \varphi_m(x_1) \\ \varphi_0(x_2) & \varphi_1(x_2) & \cdots & \varphi_m(x_2) \\ \vdots & \vdots & & \vdots \\ \varphi_0(x_n) & \varphi_1(x_n) & \cdots & \varphi_m(x_n) \end{bmatrix}, \quad \mathbf{f} = \begin{bmatrix} f_1 \\ f_2 \\ \vdots \\ f_n \end{bmatrix}, \quad \mathbf{a} = \begin{bmatrix} a_0 \\ a_1 \\ \vdots \\ a_m \end{bmatrix}. \tag{6.38}$$

The main property of orthogonal polynomials that overcomes the ill-conditioning is that $\mathbf{S} = \mathbf{\Phi}^T\mathbf{\Phi}$ here is a diagonal matrix, for the (i, j) coordinate s_{ij} of matrix $\mathbf{S}$ is given by

$$s_{ij} = \sum_{k=1}^{n} \varphi_i(x_k)\varphi_j(x_k) = (\varphi_i, \varphi_j) = 0, \qquad \text{for } i \neq j. \tag{6.39}$$

The inversion of a diagonal matrix is trivial; it is the diagonal matrix the diagonal coordinates of which are the reciprocals of the corresponding diagonal elements in the original matrix. That is,

$$(\mathbf{\Phi}^T\mathbf{\Phi})^{-1} = \begin{bmatrix} \dfrac{1}{(\varphi_0, \varphi_0)} & 0 & \cdots & 0 \\[2ex] 0 & \dfrac{1}{(\varphi_1, \varphi_1)} & \cdots & 0 \\[2ex] \vdots & \vdots & & \vdots \\[2ex] 0 & 0 & \cdots & \dfrac{1}{(\varphi_m, \varphi_m)} \end{bmatrix} \qquad (6.40)$$

and from (6.40) we easily compute the coefficients a_j in (6.37) to be

$$a_j = \frac{(f, \varphi_j)}{(\varphi_j, \varphi_j)} \qquad (j = 0, 1, \ldots, m). \qquad (6.41)$$

If for each j, the jth column of $\mathbf{\Phi}$ is scaled by $1/\sqrt{(\phi_j, \phi_j)}$, and the resulting matrix is designated by $\hat{\mathbf{\Phi}}$, then (6.39) implies that

$$\hat{\mathbf{\Phi}}^T\hat{\mathbf{\Phi}} = \mathbf{I}.$$

Matrices $\hat{\mathbf{\Phi}}$ satisfying this condition are said to be *orthogonal*.

In summary, through the orthogonal polynomial approach we have avoided the numerical solution of simultaneous linear equations altogether, and obtained the coefficients a_j in closed form.

──── **EXAMPLE 6.8** ────

The least-squares problem that was the subject of Example 6.1 will now be solved by orthogonal polynomials. In this case $x_1 = -2$, $x_2 = -1$, $x_3 = 0$, $x_4 = 1$, and $x_5 = 2$. We start the procedure by initializing $\varphi_{-1} = 0$, $\varphi_0 = 1$. Then $\varphi_1(x)$ can be obtained from (6.33), where

$$b_1 = \frac{(x\varphi_0, \varphi_0)}{(\varphi_0, \varphi_0)}, \qquad c_1 = 0.$$

To obtain the inner products in the numerator and denominator, note that the values of function φ_0 are all 1's at the points x_i and the values of $x\varphi_0(x) = x$ are

$$-2, -1, 0, 1, 2.$$

Thus

$$(x\varphi_0, \varphi_0) = (x, 1) = (-2) \cdot 1 + (-1) \cdot 1 + 0 \cdot 1 + 1 \cdot 1 + 2 \cdot 1 = 0$$

$$(\varphi_0, \varphi_0) = (1, 1) = 1 \cdot 1 + 1 \cdot 1 + 1 \cdot 1 + 1 \cdot 1 + 1 \cdot 1 = 5.$$

Consequently, $b_1 = 0$ and

$$\varphi_1(x) = (x - 0)\varphi_0(x) - 0 \cdot 0 = x.$$

One similarly gets

$$b_2 = \frac{(x\varphi_1, \varphi_1)}{(\varphi_1, \varphi_1)} = 0, \qquad c_2 = \frac{(x\varphi_1, \varphi_0)}{(\varphi_0, \varphi_0)} = 2,$$

since

$$(x\varphi_1, \varphi_1) = (x^2, x) = 4 \cdot (-2) + 1 \cdot (-1) + 0 \cdot 0 + 1 \cdot 1 + 4 \cdot 2 = 0,$$

$$(\varphi_1, \varphi_1) = (x, x) = (-2) \cdot (-2) + (-1) \cdot (-1) + 0 \cdot 0 + 1 \cdot 1 + 2 \cdot 2$$

$$= 10,$$

$$(x\varphi_1, \varphi_0) = (x^2, 1) = 4 \cdot 1 + 1 \cdot 1 + 0 \cdot 1 + 1 \cdot 1 + 4 \cdot 1 = 10.$$

Thus

$$\varphi_2(x) = (x - b_2)\varphi_1(x) - c_2\varphi_0(x) = (x - 0) \cdot x - 2 \cdot 1 = x^2 - 2.$$

The quadratic least-squares polynomial can then be determined by using (6.41) and (6.36) with $m = 2$. In our case the values of $f(x)$ at the data points x_i are

$$0, \ 1, \ 2, \ 1, \ 0,$$

respectively, which imply that

$$(f, \varphi_0) = 0 \cdot 1 + 1 \cdot 1 + 2 \cdot 1 + 1 \cdot 1 + 0 \cdot 1 = 4$$

$$(f, \varphi_1) = 0 \cdot (-2) + 1 \cdot (-1) + 2 \cdot 0 + 1 \cdot 1 + 0 \cdot 2 = 0$$

$$(f, \varphi_2) = 0 \cdot 2 + 1 \cdot (-1) + 2 \cdot (-2) + 1 \cdot (-1) + 0 \cdot 2 = -6.$$

Furthermore,

$$(\varphi_2, \varphi_2) = 2 \cdot 2 + (-1) \cdot (-1) + (-2) \cdot (-2) + (-1) \cdot (-1)$$
$$+ 2 \cdot 2 = 14,$$

since

$$\varphi_2(x_1) = x_1^2 - 2 = (-2)^2 - 2 = 2, \qquad \varphi_2(x_2) = (-1)^2 - 2 = -1,$$

$$\varphi_2(x_3) = 0^2 - 2 = -2, \qquad \varphi_2(x_4) = 1^2 - 2 = -1,$$

$$\varphi_2(x_5) = 2^2 - 2 = 2.$$

Then, from (6.41), we conclude that

$$a_0 = \frac{(f, \varphi_0)}{(\varphi_0, \varphi_0)} = \frac{4}{5}, \qquad a_1 = \frac{(f, \varphi_1)}{(\varphi_1, \varphi_1)} = 0, \qquad a_2 = \frac{(f, \varphi_2)}{(\varphi_2, \varphi_2)} = -\frac{3}{7},$$

that is,

$$p_2(x) = a_0\varphi_0(x) + a_1\varphi_1(x) + a_2\varphi_2(x)$$

$$= \tfrac{4}{5} \cdot 1 + 0 \cdot x - \tfrac{3}{7} \cdot (x^2 - 2) = -\tfrac{3}{7}x^2 + \tfrac{58}{35},$$

which coincides with the result obtained in Example 6.1.

The gist of the situation is that although the correct least-squares solution must be the same in both cases, the orthogonal polynomial method is less subject to roundoff error. This advantage can be appreciated only when more demanding problems, such as in the example to follow, are tackled. ∎

Subroutine ORTH (Table 6.7) finds the least-squares polynomial approximation $p_m(x)$ for any given data set (x_1, f_1), (x_2, f_2), . . . , (x_n, f_n) and any specified degree m. In this code we have made use of a property that if $\varphi_0(x)$, $\varphi_1(x)$, . . . is an orthogonal system of polynomials, and $p_0(x)$, $p_1(x)$, . . . the least-squares approximations of degrees indicated by the subscripts, then

$$p_{j+1}(x) = a_{j+1}\varphi_{j+1}(x) + p_j(x), \tag{6.42}$$

which is a simple consequence of (6.41) and (6.36). Through this recursion, the least-squares approximators at specified points in the ORTH array T are computed as the successive orthogonal polynomials are constructed. If for some reason the user wants the coefficients a_j in (6.36), they can be obtained by printing out values of the variable COE every time it is updated. The structure of subroutine ORTH is as follows. DO loops with labels 1 and 2 do the initialization. The DO loop with label 3 computes the least-squares polynomials $p_k(x)$ $(k = 1, 2, \ldots, m)$, and for each value of k, the DO loop with label 4 computes the inner products

TABLE 6.7   Subroutine ORTH for Orthogonal Least-Squares Approximation

```
        SUBROUTINE ORTH(N,M,NT,X,F,T,Y)
C
C   ****************************************************************
C   *    FUNCTION: THIS SUBROUTINE COMPUTES THE LEAST- SQUARES     *
C   *              POLYNOMIAL VALUES Y ON A SET T OF DOMAIN        *
C   *              POINTS FOR THE DATA PAIRS (X,F) BY THE USE OF   *
C   *              AN ORTHOGONAL POLYNOMIAL BASIS                  *
C   *    USAGE:                                                    *
C   *        CALL SEQUENCE: CALL ORTH(N,M,NT,X,F,T,Y)             *
C   *    PARAMETERS:                                               *
C   *        INPUT:                                                *
C   *            N=NUMBER OF DATA POINTS                           *
C   *            M=DEGREE OF THE LEAST SQUARES POLYNOMIAL          *
C   *            NT=NUMBER OF LEAST SQUARES POLYNOMIAL             *
C   *            EVALUATIONS                                       *
C   *            X=N BY 1 ARRAY OF INDEPENDENT DATA VALUES         *
C   *            F=N BY 1 ARRAY OF DEPENDENT FUNCTIONAL VALUES     *
C   *            T=NT BY 1 ARRAY OF POINTS FOR LEAST-SQUARES       *
C   *            EVALUATION                                        *
C   *        OUTPUT:                                               *
C   *            Y=NT BY 1 ARRAY OF VALUES OF LEAST-SQUARES        *
C   *            POLYNOMIALS                                       *
C   ****************************************************************
```

TABLE 6.7   (Continued)

```
C
      DIMENSION X(N),F(N),P(100),PO(100),Y(NT),PT(100),PTO(100),T(NT)
C     *** INITIALIZATION ***
      S1=0.0
      COE=0.0
      BE=0.
      DO 1 I=1,N
         P(I)=1.0
         PO(I)=0.
         S1=S1+X(I)
         COE=COE+F(I)
    1 CONTINUE
      COE=COE/N
      DO 2 I=1,NT
         PT(I)=1.0
         PTO(I)=0.
         Y(I)=COE
    2 CONTINUE
      AL=S1/FLOAT(N)
C     *** START ITERATIONS ***
      DO 3 K=1,M
         S1=0.0
         S2=0.0
         S3=0.0
         S4=0.0
         S5=0.0
C     *** SET S1=(XPK,PK),S2=(PK,PK),S3=(XPK,PK-1)  ***
C     ***     SET S4=(FKPK,PK),S5=(PK-1,PK-1)        ***
         DO 4 I=1,N
            W=(X(I)-AL)*P(I)-BE*PO(I)
            S1=S1+X(I)*W**2
            S2=S2+W**2
            S3=S3+X(I)*W*P(I)
            S4=S4+F(I)*W
            S5=S5+P(I)**2
            PO(I)=P(I)
            P(I)=W
    4    CONTINUE
C     *** UPDATE LEAST-SQUARES ESTIMATE Y=P(T) ON VALUES T ***
         COE=S4/S2
         DO 5 I=1,NT
            W=(T(I)-AL)*PT(I)-BE*PTO(I)
            Y(I)=COE*W+Y(I)
            PTO(I)=PT(I)
            PT(I)=W
    5    CONTINUE
         AL=S1/S2
         BE=S3/S5
    3 CONTINUE
      RETURN
      END
```

needed in using (6.34) and (6.35), and then DO loop with label 5 evaluates these relations.

───── **EXAMPLE 6.9** ─────

We reconsider Example 6.7, in which we found it impossible to achieve 12-significant-decimal-place accuracy in approximating the sine function on the interval [0, 2], using the conventional least-squares representation (6.9). By means of the calling program in Table 6.8, we applied subroutine ORTH in double precision, using the same 50 data and 10 readout points as in the earlier example. For degrees $m = 0$ through 3, the results were identical to those in Table 6.3.

TABLE 6.8   Computes Orthogonal Least-Squares Approximation of sin (x)

```
C       PROGRAM ORTHPOLY
C
C       **************************************************************
C       THIS PROGRAM FINDS HIGH DEGREE ORTHOGONAL POLYNOMIAL
C       APPROXIMATIONS FOR SIN(X) ON THE INTERVAL [0,2].
C       THE DATA CONSIST OF VALUES SIN(2*J/50), J=1,...,50
C       CALLS:    ORTH (MODIFIED FOR DOUBLE PRECISION)
C       OUTPUT:
C                 X(I)=VALUE OF X AT CURRENT ITERATION
C                 TRUE=VALUE OF SIN(X)
C                 P(I)=POLYNOMIAL APPROXIMATION AT X
C                 DIFF=DIFFERENCE (TRUE-P) FOR EACH X
C       **************************************************************
C
        IMPLICIT DOUBLE PRECISION (A-H,O-Z)
        DIMENSION X(10),XX(50),F(50),P(10)
        N=50
        NT=10
C
C       *** CONSTRUCT DATA ARRAYS XX AND SIN(XX) FOR FOR USE IN THE   ***
C       *** APPROXIMATION. THE POLYNOMIAL IS TO BE EVALUATED AT       ***
C       *** POINTS IN THE ARRAY X                                     ***
C
        DO 10 J=1,N
           XX(J)=.04D0*J
           F(J)=DSIN(XX(J))
     10 CONTINUE
        DO 20 I=1,10
           X(I)=I*.2D0
     20 CONTINUE
C
C       *** M IS THE DEGREE OF THE POLYNOMIAL REQUESTED               ***
C
        DO 40 M=1,25
           WRITE(10,1)
      1    FORMAT(////)
C
C       *** SUBROUTINE ORTH WILL CALCULATE THE M-TH DEGREE LEAST      ***
C       *** SQUARES POLYNOMIAL USING ORTHOGONAL POLYNOMIALS           ***
C       *** RETURNING POLYNOMIAL VALUES P FOR EACH OF THE NT          ***
C       *** POINTS SPECIFIED IN X                                     ***
C
           CALL ORTH(N,M,NT,XX,F,X,P)
C
C       *** NEXT COMPARE THE VALUE OF THE POLYNOMIAL AT 10 EQUALLY    ***
C       *** SPACED POINTS WITH THE VALUES OF SIN(X) AT THESE          ***
C       *** POINTS                                                    ***
C
           DO 30 I=1,10
              TRUE=DSIN(X(I))
              DIFF=TRUE-P(I)
              WRITE(10,25) X(I),TRUE,P(I),DIFF
     25       FORMAT(5X,F8.2,5X,D15.5,3X,D15.5,3X,D15.5)
     30    CONTINUE
     40 CONTINUE
        STOP
        END
```

As we increased m, the accuracy increased, the error being about 10^{-11} for $m = 10$, and decreasing to about 10^{-16} for $m = 14$. This is the approximate limit of the double-precision accuracy of the computer used, and for higher-degree m, the error did not decrease further, but neither did it increase. Seventeen-significant-figure accuracy was observed for $m = 25$, the highest degree that we attempted. The printout for $m = 15$ is displayed in Table 6.9.

**TABLE 6.9 Errors of
Fifteenth-Degree
Orthogonal Least-
Squares Polynomial
Approximation**

x	Error, $\sin(x) - p_{15}(x)$
0.2	-0.69389D-17
0.4	0.34694D-15
0.6	-0.30531D-15
0.8	0.99920D-15
1.0	-0.15127D-14
1.2	-0.37470D-15
1.4	0.41633D-15
1.6	-0.11102D-15
1.8	-0.55511D-16
2.0	-0.55511D-16

★6.4
FOURIER ANALYSIS

★6.4.1 Fourier Series

The orthogonal polynomial approach to the least-squares approximation problem is a particular example of *Fourier analysis*. The general framework of Fourier analysis is now sketched.

First, define generalized versions of the inner products (6.30) and (6.31) as follows:

$$(f, g) = \sum_{k=1}^{n} f(x_k)g(x_k)w(x_k) \tag{6.43}$$

and

$$(f, g) = \int_X f(x)g(x)w(x) \, dx, \tag{6.44}$$

where $w(x) > 0$. Consider a finite or infinite system $\varphi_0(x)$, $\varphi_1(x)$, . . . of real orthogonal functions [i.e., a system satisfying (6.32)] and a function $f(x)$ for which (f, f) is finite. Then the series

$$f_m(x) = \sum_{j=0}^{m} \frac{(f, \varphi_j)}{(\varphi_j, \varphi_j)} \varphi_j(x), \tag{6.45}$$

with m either finite or infinite, is called the (generalized) *Fourier series* of $f(x)$. The ratios $\beta_j = (f, \varphi_j)/(\varphi_j, \varphi_j)$ are termed *Fourier coefficients*. In this terminology, then, (6.36) and (6.41) imply that the orthogonal polynomial representation of the least-squares polynomial is a special Fourier series with the discrete inner product and $w(x) = 1$. More generally, in the discrete inner product case, the Fourier series minimizes the sum

$$\sum_{i=1}^{n}\left[f(x_i) - \sum_{j=0}^{m} a_j\varphi_j(x_i)\right]^2 w(x_i) \tag{6.46}$$

over all possible choices of coefficients a_j, (Apostol, 1957, Sec. 15.5). An analogous statement holds with respect to minimizing the integral

$$\int_X \left[f(x) - \sum_{j=0}^{m} a_j\varphi_j(x)\right]^2 w(x)\, dx$$

in the case of the "continuous" inner products (6.44).

The best-known Fourier series is that determined by the inner product (6.44) with $w(x) = 1$ and the integration being over the interval $(-\pi, \pi)$. The orthogonal sequence is $\frac{1}{2}$, sin (x), cos (x), sin $(2x)$, cos $(2x)$, . . . , sin (mx), cos (mx), ... The expression "trigonometric series" or, for finite series, "trigonometric polynomials" refers to this setting, which has played a prominent role in pure and applied mathematics, engineering, and physics since the nineteenth century. Such series also lead to major computational methods for linear systems, time series, signal processing, and in their extension to two-dimensional domains, for digital image processing.

EXAMPLE 6.10

Let us construct a trigonometric Fourier series of the "square-wave" function

$$f(x) = \begin{cases} -1 & \text{if } -\pi < x < 0 \\ 1 & \text{if } 0 < x < \pi. \end{cases}$$

For this orthogonal system, the Fourier representation (6.45) takes on the specific form

$$\frac{a_0}{2} + \sum_{k=1}^{\infty} [a_k \cos (kx) + b_k \sin (kx)],$$

where

$$a_k = \frac{1}{\pi}\int_{-\pi}^{\pi} f(x) \cos (kx)\, dx \qquad (k = 0, 1, 2, \ldots)$$

and

$$b_k = \frac{1}{\pi}\int_{-\pi}^{\pi} f(x) \sin (kx)\, dx \qquad (k = 1, 2, 3, \ldots).$$

[Here we used that (sin (mx), sin (mx)) = (cos (mx), cos (mx)) = π, if $m \neq 0$.] This special Fourier series is often called the *continuous Fourier transformation*, in contrast to the discrete Fourier transformation discussed in the next section.

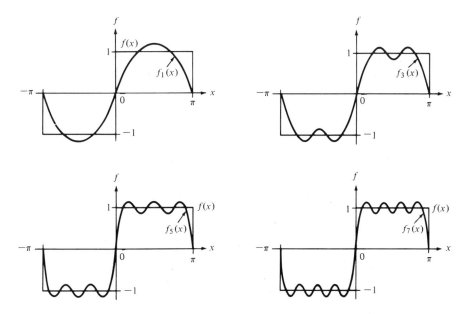

FIGURE 6.15   Fourier Series Approximation of the Square-Wave Function

For our particular square-wave function, the Fourier coefficients are

$$a_k = \frac{1}{\pi} \left\{ -\int_{-\pi}^{0} \cos (kx) \, dx + \int_{0}^{\pi} \cos (kx) \, dx \right\} = 0$$

and

$$b_k = \frac{1}{\pi} \left\{ -\int_{-\pi}^{0} \sin (kx) \, dx + \int_{0}^{\pi} \sin (kx) \, dx \right\} = \frac{2}{\pi k} [1 - (-1)^k]$$

$$= \begin{cases} 0 & \text{if } k \text{ even} \\ \dfrac{4}{\pi k} & \text{if } k \text{ odd.} \end{cases}$$

In summary, for odd m, the mth-order trigonometric polynomial of $f(x)$ is

$$f_m(x) = \frac{4}{\pi} \sin (x) + \frac{4}{3\pi} \sin (3x) + \cdots + \frac{4}{m\pi} \sin (mx).$$

It is known (Apostol, 1957) that $f_m(x) \to f(x)$ for $m \to \infty$, except at x values that are multiples of π. In Figure 6.15 we compare $f_1(x)$, $f_3(x)$, $f_5(x)$, and $f_7(x)$ with $f(x)$. A curiosity is that since $f(x) = 1$,

$$\frac{\pi}{4} = \sin (x) + \frac{\sin (3x)}{3} + \frac{\sin (5x)}{5} + \cdots \qquad (0 < x < \pi).$$

★6.4.2 Discrete Fourier Transforms

The trigonometric Fourier series representation of finite data sets has attracted attention in recent years because it is relatively inexpensive to compute. The representation now discussed is called the *discrete Fourier transform*. We describe its use as an approximation method for functions defined on the unit interval [0, 1].

This transform has as a basis the compex-valued orthogonal functions of the form

$$\varphi_k(x) = \exp(i2\pi kx) = \cos(2\pi kx) + i\sin(2\pi kx)$$
$$(k = 0, 1, -1, 2, -2, \ldots). \tag{6.47}$$

Here, as before, i is $\sqrt{-1}$. These orthogonal functions are closely allied to the trigonometric polynomials in the preceding section. Specifically, for any integer k,

$$\cos(2\pi kx) = \frac{1}{2}[\varphi_k(x) + \varphi_{-k}(x)]$$

and   (6.48)

$$\sin(2\pi kx) = \frac{1}{2i}[\varphi_k(x) - \varphi_{-k}(x)].$$

One could thereby avoid complex functions by using the trigonometric functions $\sin(2\pi kx)$ and $\cos(2\pi kx)$ in this section, but this would lead to more complicated expressions.

The inner product by which orthogonality and the Fourier coefficients are defined in the discrete Fourier transform is a generalization of (6.43) to the complex case. In this section, N being a given positive integer, the points x_j are determined by

$$x_j = \frac{j}{N}, \qquad 0 \le j \le N - 1. \tag{6.49}$$

That is, the x_j's comprise a uniformly spaced grid on the unit interval. With respect to N and these points x_j, the discrete Fourier transform of two complex-valued functions $f(x)$ and $g(x)$ is based on the discrete inner product

$$(f, g) = \sum_{j=0}^{N-1} f(x_j)\overline{g}(x_j), \tag{6.50}$$

where the overbar denotes the complex conjugate of $g(x_j)$. This generalizes the relation defined in (6.30) for real functions.

The discrete Fourier transform depends on noting that the $\varphi_k(x)$'s in (6.47) are orthogonal with respect to the inner product (6.50). Toward showing this assertion, first recall that for any complex number r other than $1 + i \cdot 0$, the sum of the initial part of a geometric series satisfies the relation

$$\sum_{k=0}^{N-1} r^k = \frac{1 - r^N}{1 - r}. \tag{6.51}$$

From this we see that for $0 \le k,\ m \le N - 1,\ k \ne m$,

$$(\varphi_k,\ \varphi_m) = \sum_{j=0}^{N-1} \exp\ (i2\pi k x_j)\ \exp\ (-i2\pi m x_j) = \sum_{j=0}^{N-1} \exp\ (i2\pi(k - m)/N)^j.$$

If we select $r = \exp\ (i2\pi(k - m)/N)$, then by using (6.51) we get that

$$(\varphi_k,\ \varphi_m) = \frac{1 - \exp\ (i2\pi(k - m))}{1 - \exp\ (i2\pi(k - m)/N)}. \tag{6.52}$$

Thus the functions $\varphi_k(x) = \exp\ (i2\pi k x),\ 0 \le k \le N - 1$ constitute an orthogonal set with respect to the inner product (6.50), since from (6.47), the numerator is readily seen to be zero. Also, it is a simple matter to confirm that for every k, $(\varphi_k,\ \varphi_k) = N$.

We now turn attention to discrete Fourier transforms as approximators and interpolators for a function $f(x)$ defined on the unit interval. Let S be a finite set of integers. In view of (6.45) and the orthogonality of the φ_k's just established, the trigonometric polynomial

$$\boxed{p(x) = \sum_{k \in S} \beta_k \exp\ (i2\pi k x)} \tag{6.53}$$

is a Fourier series for $f(x)$, with respect to $\varphi_k,\ k \in S$, if

$$\beta_k = \frac{(f,\ \varphi_k)}{(\varphi_k,\ \varphi_k)} = \frac{(f,\ \varphi_k)}{N}, \tag{6.54}$$

or, what is the same thing,

$$\boxed{\beta_k = \frac{1}{N} \sum_{j=0}^{N-1} f\left(\frac{j}{N}\right) \exp\left(\frac{-i2\pi k j}{N}\right),\qquad k \in S.} \tag{6.55}$$

Incidentally, the nomenclature "trigonometric polynomial" is more transparent here than in the preceding section. For if $S = \{0, 1, \ldots, N - 1\}$, then in view of (6.53),

$$p(x) = \sum_{k=0}^{N-1} \beta_k[\exp\ (i2\pi x)]^k = \hat{p}(z), \tag{6.56}$$

where $\hat{p}(z) = \sum_{k=0}^{N-1} \beta_k z^k$, and in (6.56) the variable

$$z = \exp\ (i2\pi x) = \cos\ (2\pi x) + i \sin\ (2\pi x).$$

In summary, the discrete Fourier representation of the data $f(j/N),\ 0 \le j \le N - 1$, is the trigonometric polynomial $p(x)$ defined by (6.53), where the coefficients are calculated according to (6.55).

Some elementary observations about the discrete Fourier transform include:

1. Whenever $(k - m)$ is not a multiple of N, as a consequence of (6.52) the inner product (ϕ_k, ϕ_m) is 0. Let S be any set of N integers, no two of which differ by a multiple of N. Then $\{\phi_k, k \in S\}$ constitutes an orthogonal basis. The Fourier coefficients with respect to this basis yield a trigonometric polynomial as defined in (6.53) that interpolates $f(x)$ at every $x_j = j/N$, $0 \le j \le N - 1$.

2. If S has fewer than N numbers, $p(x)$ gives that approximation of $f(x)$ which minimizes the least-squares criterion,

$$Q(f, p) = \sum_{k=0}^{N-1} |f(k/N) - p(k/N)|^2 = (f - p, f - p)$$

over all possible complex linear combinations of $\varphi_j(x)$, $j \in S$.

By fact 1, many different sets S yield bases for interpolating $f(x)$; at values x other than interpolation points, trigonometric polynomials depend very strongly on which such basis was selected. It is obvious that when $|k|$ is large, the basis function

$$\exp(i2\pi kx) = \cos(2\pi kx) + i \sin(2\pi kx)$$

is much more oscillatory than when k is near 0. For this reason, for even N it is usually wise to select

$$S = \left\{ -\left(\frac{N}{2}\right), \ldots -1, 0, 1, \ldots, \left(\frac{N}{2}\right) - 1 \right\}$$

and for odd N, and $[\cdot]$ denoting "integer part,"

$$S = \left\{ -\left[\frac{N}{2}\right], \ldots, -1, 0, 1, \ldots, \left[\frac{N}{2}\right] \right\}.$$

This is, in fact, the set used by our discrete Fourier transform code. It constructs trigonometric polynomials that not only interpolate, but also give fairly accurate approximations at other points. Stoer and Bulirsch (1980, Sec. 2.3) mention this fact and offer analysis of sensitivity to roundoff.

In Table 6.10 we offer subroutine SFT, which constructs the discrete Fourier transform associated with a selected *odd* number N and an interval $[A, B]$ of approximation. The subroutine returns the value $p(x)$ as the calling parameter P, where x is the argument specified in the calling parameter X. The variable $N2$ takes the value $[N/2]$ in SFT. Using this notation and following item 1 and the discussion, we find that the orthogonal basis is taken to be $\phi_j(x)$, $-N2 \le j \le N2$. Because, in FORTRAN, array indices must be positive, the value BETA (J) actually is the coefficient of $\phi_{-N2-1+j}$.

The acronym SFT stands for "slow Fourier transform," in contrast to a faster discrete Fourier transformation algorithm to be described after the next example.

The discrete Fourier transform can be regarded as a Riemann sum approximation of the continuous Fourier transformation to be discussed in Example 6.12.

TABLE 6.10   Subroutine SFT for Discrete Fourier Transform

```
      SUBROUTINE SFT(N,A,B,F,X,P)
C
C     ***********************************************************************
C     *    FUNCTION: THIS SUBROUTINE COMPUTES AND EVALUATES THE           *
C     *              DISCRETE FOURIER TRANSFORM OF A GIVEN DATA ARRAY     *
C     *    USAGE:                                                          *
C     *         CALL SEQUENCE: CALL SFT(N,A,B,F,X,P)                       *
C     *    PARAMETERS:                                                     *
C     *         INPUT:                                                     *
C     *              N=NUMBER OF DATA POINTS                               *
C     *              A=LEFT ENDPOINT OF THE INTERVAL OF INTERPOLATION      *
C     *              B=RIGHT ENDPOINT OF THE INTERVAL OF INTERPOLATION     *
C     *              F=N BY 1 ARRAY OF FUNCTIONAL VALUES                   *
C     *              X=THE REAL ARGUEMENT AT WHICH THE TRIGONOMETRIC       *
C     *                POLYNOMIAL IS TO BE EVALUATED                       *
C     *         OUTPUT:                                                    *
C     *              P=THE TRIGONOMETRIC POLYNOMIAL VALUE AT X             *
C     ***********************************************************************
C
      IMPLICIT COMPLEX(A-H,O-Z)
      REAL A,B,T,PI,X,FLAG,FLOATN
      DIMENSION F(N),BETA(100)
C     *** INITIALIZATION ***
C     ***    PI=3.141..    ***
C     ***    EYE=SQRT(-1)  ***
      PI=4.*ATAN(1.)
      N2=N/2
      EYE=(0.,1.0)
      CONS=2.*PI*EYE/(B-A)
      FLOATN=FLOAT(N)
      CONS2=(B-A)/FLOATN
C
C     *** NOTE: FLAG IS ASSUMED TO BE INITIALIZED TO ZERO BY    ***
C     ***       THE COMPUTER (AS IN VAX FORTRAN)    IT ASSURES  ***
C     ***       THAT IN THE CASE OF MULTIPLE CALLS TO THE       ***
C     ***       SUBROUTINE TO EVALUATE THE SAME FOURIER         ***
C     ***       POLYNOMIAL AT DIFFERENT POINTS, THE FOURIER     ***
C     ***       COEFFICIENTS ARE COMPUTED ONLY ONCE             ***
C
      IF(FLAG.GT.1.)GOTO 10
C     *** COMPUTE FOURIER COEFFICIENTS BETA ***
      FLAG=5.0
      DO 10 J=1,N
         BETA(J)=(0.,0.)
         DO 10 K=1,N
            X1=A+(K-1)*CONS2
            BETA(J)=BETA(J)+F(K)*CEXP(-CONS*(-N2+J-1)*X1)/FLOATN
   10 CONTINUE
C     *** EVALUATE THE TRIGONOMETRIC POLYNOMIAL AT X ***
      P=(0.,0.)
      DO 20 J=1,N
         P=P+BETA(J)*CEXP(CONS*X*(-N2+J-1))
   20 CONTINUE
      RETURN
      END
```

The point is that the discrete Fourier transform is directly computer implementable, whereas we still face methodological problems and truncation error in performing the integration required by the continuous Fourier transformation. As the number N increases, the discrete Fourier transformation with S as above should in theory converge to the continuous Fourier transformation if $f(x)$ is continuous and round-off effects are negligible.

―― **EXAMPLE 6.11** ――――――――――――――――――――――

TABLE 6.11 **Program for Discrete Fourier Approximation Example**

```
C       PROGRAM DISFOUR
C
C       ****************************************************************
C       THIS PROGRAM COMPUTES THE DISCRETE FOURIER TRANSFORM OF A SQUARE
C       WAVE FUNCTION DEFINED ON THE INTERVAL [0,10]
C       CALLS:   SFT
C       OUTPUT:
C               X=VALUE OF X AT CURRENT ITERATION
C               P=VALUE OF POLYNOMIAL APPROXIMATION AT X
C       ****************************************************************
C
        COMPLEX F(11),P
        N=11
C
C       *** FIRST COMPUTE THE FUNCTIONAL VALUES TO DEFINE THE      ***
C       *** SQUARE WAVE                                            ***
C
        F(1)=0.
        DO 10 J=2,6
          F(J)=1.0
          F(5+J)=-1.0
     10 CONTINUE
C
C       *** NEXT CALCULATE THE POLYNOMIAL APPROXIMATION P(X) FOR   ***
C       *** VALUES OF X RANGING FROM 0 TO 2                        ***
C
        A=0.
        B=10.
        X=0.
        DO 20 J=1,100
C
C       *** SUBROUTINE SFT WILL COMPUTE THE DISCRETE FOURIER       ***
C       *** TRANSFORM                                             ***
C
        CALL SFT(N,A,B,F,X,P)
        X=X+10./101.
        WRITE(10,30) X,REAL(P)
     30     FORMAT(5X,F20.12,5X,F20.12)
     20 CONTINUE
        STOP
        END
```

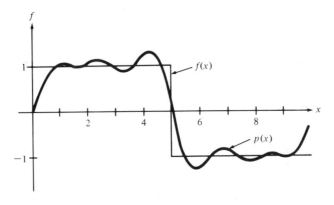

FIGURE 6.16 Discrete 11-Point Fourier Approximation to the Square Wave

Here we find the discrete Fourier transform of the square-wave function. In Example 6.10 we have already found and plotted its continuous Fourier representation. In the present example, we took N, the number of points to be interpolated, to be 11. The calling program for our calculation is listed in Table 6.11. Figure 6.16 is a plot of the output values. This should be compared with the plot of $f_5(x)$ in Figure 6.15. These two graphs depend on exactly the same basis functions; the only difference is that the former uses the continuous inner product (6.44), and the latter, the discrete approximation (6.50) of that inner product. In our actual computation, we put a flag in the subroutine SFT so that the coefficients BETA(J) were computed only once.

∎

The simple routine SFT has a wide range of capabilities. Below, $N2 = [N/2]$.

Forward Transformation. One can calculate the discrete Fourier transformation (6.55) of any desired sequence $\{F(k)\}$ as follows:

A. Declare the sequence as the array F in the driver "DISFOUR," and then
B. Read out the discrete Fourier transform array BETA from SFT.

The coefficients β_k [$=$ BETA($N2$) $+ K + 1$] also represent a useful approximation of the values of the continuous exponential Fourier transformation

$$\beta_k \approx b_k = \int_a^b \exp\left(-k\omega_0 x\right)F(x)\,dx \qquad (6.57)$$

with

$$\omega_0 = \frac{2\pi}{b - a}.$$

Inverse Transformation. One reverses the preceding steps to achieve an inverse discrete Fourier transform (6.53):

A. Assign values to the Fourier coefficients BETA, in SFT. [Remember that BETA(K) is the Fourier coefficient for $\phi_{-N2-1+k}(x)$.] Then
B. Read off inverse values from calls to SFT, as the values of $P(x)$, in DISFOUR. That is,

$$F(k) = P\left(A + \frac{2k}{B - A}\right), \qquad 1 \le k \le N,$$

A and B being the interval parameters in DISFOUR.

This inverse discrete transform serves as an approximation for the continuous inverse Fourier transformation

$$F(x) = \frac{1}{b - a} \sum_{k=-\infty}^{\infty} \exp\left(ik\omega_0 x\right)b_k.$$

By numerical Fourier analysis as above, one can obtain series not tabulated in handbooks, or which fail to exist in closed form. Moreover, one can experiment and to some extent, automate, Fourier analysis. We suggest a small step in this direction in the application to follow.

Application 6.2

The principal uses of Fourier series in the applications literature are for solving linear differential equations (or equivalently, "filter analysis") and for smoothing, and prediction in time series (sometimes referred to as "spectral analysis"). The filtering activity is more straightforward and serves as the subject of this application.

Consider the *RL* circuit shown in Figure 6.17. From elementary considerations, it is known that the current $i(t)$ responds to an impressed voltage $v(t)$ according to the differential equation

$$\frac{d}{dt} i(t) = -\frac{R}{L} i(t) + \frac{1}{L} v(t). \tag{6.58}$$

Fourier transforms allow us to convert this into an algebraic relation. The properties needed are as follows:

1. If $\{X(k)\}$ are the Fourier coefficients for a periodic function $x(t)$ [as determined by (6.53)], then $\{(ik\omega_0)X(k)\}$ is the Fourier series for $dx(t)/dt$.
2. The Fourier transform is additive. The kth coefficient of the discrete Fourier transform of $[f(t) + g(t)]$ is the sum of the kth coefficient of $f(t)$ and the kth coefficient of $g(t)$.

Property 1 can be verified by integration by parts and property 2 is a direct consequence of the definition and the linearity property of integration itself.

Now letting $\{I(k)\}$ and $\{V(k)\}$ denote the Fourier sequences of $i(t)$ and $v(t)$, respectively, we see that these properties and (6.58) imply that

$$ik\omega_0 I(k) = -\frac{R}{L} I(k) + \frac{1}{L} V(k),$$

or

$$I(k) = \frac{1/R}{1 + ik\omega_0(L/R)} V(k), \qquad \text{for all } k.$$

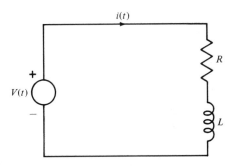

FIGURE 6.17   Illustration of an *RL* Circuit

For convenience, we write this as

$$I(k) = H(k\omega_0)V(k), \tag{6.59}$$

where

$$H(\omega) = \frac{C}{1 + i\omega\tau} \tag{6.60}$$

with

$$C = \frac{1}{R} \quad \text{and} \quad \tau = \frac{L}{R}. \tag{6.61}$$

In this context, the function $H(k\omega_0)$ is spoken of as being a *filter* or, alternatively, a *transfer function*. The latter terminology is clearly appreciated if one regards $I(k)$ as being the output to the input $V(k)$. Then (6.59) yields that the transfer function

$$H(k\omega_0) = \frac{I(k)}{V(k)},$$

which is the ratio of the output to the input.

For our computational experiment, imagine that the voltage impressed on the circuit in Figure 6.17 is a square wave, as in the preceding example. Instead of solving the differential equation (6.58), we find the associated output simply by multiplying each Fourier coefficient in the array BETA by the associated transfer function value. This is effected in the subroutine FILTER (Table 6.12), which is a simple modification of the subroutine SFT. The transfer function is declared immediately below the dimension statements, and the transfer function weighting (6.59) takes place in the DO loop labeled 13. We have achieved accuracy by setting the number of Fourier terms N to 101, but otherwise, our driver program CIRCUIT is the same as DISFOUR (Table 6.11), by which we generated the transform of a square wave.

Figure 6.18 shows a plot of several cycles of the input function $V(t)$, after it has been transformed to a Fourier series according to (6.55) and then inverse-transformed back to the time domain, according to (6.53). It appears to be a fine fascimile of the original function. Next, the first graph of Figure 6.19 shows the inverse transform after the Fourier coefficient weighting according to (6.60). The parameter was taken to be $\tau = 10$.

We checked our solution by comparing it to one obtained using a numerical differential equation method (to be revealed in Section 7.3) directly on (6.58). The results were indistinguishable.

It is convenient to experiment with filter shaping by trying different parameters in the transfer function. By increasing the time constant to $\tau = 40$, we obtained the second graph in Figure 6.19. The effect of increasing the time constant is to make the response more sluggish; this is apparent in the solution.

As a final experiment, we converted $H(\omega)$ in (6.60) to a "low-pass" filter by declaring that

$$H(\omega) = \begin{cases} 1 & |\omega| \le 10 \text{ rad/s} \\ 0 & \text{otherwise.} \end{cases}$$

TABLE 6.12   FORTRAN Program for Fourier Series Application

```
          SUBROUTINE FILTER(N,A,B,F,X,P)
C
C      ****************************************************************
C      *    FUNCTION: THIS SUBROUTINE COMPUTES THE VALUE OF A FILTERED    *
C      *              (BY SOME GIVEN FILTER) DISCRETE FOURIER TRANSFORM   *
C      *              OF A GIVEN DATA ARRAY AT A PRESCRIBED POINT         *
C      *    USAGE:                                                        *
C      *         CALL SEQUENCE: CALL FILTER(N,A,B,F,X,P)                  *
C      *    PARAMETERS:                                                   *
C      *         INPUT:                                                   *
C      *         H(W)=THE FILTER TO BE USED (DECLARED AS A COMPLEX        *
C      *              FUNCTION BELOW THE DIMENSION STATEMENT)             *
C      *              N=NUMBER OF DATA POINTS (PRESUMED ODD)              *
C      *              A=LEFT ENDPOINT OF THE INTERVAL OF INTERPOLATION    *
C      *              B=RIGHT ENDPOINT OF THE INTERVAL OF INTERPOLATION   *
C      *              F=N BY 1 ARRAY OF FUNCTIONAL VALUES                 *
C      *              X=THE POINT AT WHICH THE FILTERED FOURIER           *
C      *                POLYNOMIAL IS TO BE EVALUATED                     *
C      *         OUTPUT:                                                  *
C      *              P=THE VALUE OF THE FILTERED FOURIER POLYNOMIAL      *
C      *                AT X                                              *
C      ****************************************************************
C
          IMPLICIT COMPLEX(A-H,O-Z)
          REAL A,B,T,PI,X,FLAG,BAND,FLOATN
          DIMENSION F(N),BETA(1000)
C      *** PRESCRIBE THE FILTER (TRANSFER FUNCTION) ****
          H(W) = 1/(1 + EYE*W*TAU)
C
C      *** INITIALIZATION ***
C      ***     PI=3.141..    ***
C      ***     EYE=SQRT(-1)  ***
C
          PI=4.*ATAN(1.)
          EYE=(0.,1.0)
          N2=N/2
          TAU=10.0
          CONS=2.*PI*EYE/(B-A)
          FLOATN=FLOAT(N)
          CONS2=(B-A)/FLOATN
C
C      *** NOTE: FLAG IS ASSUMED TO BE INITIALIZED TO ZERO BY      ***
C      ***       THE COMPUTER (AS IN VAX FORTRAN)   IT ASSURES     ***
C      ***       THAT IN THE CASE OF MULTIPLE CALLS TO THE         ***
C      ***       SUBROUTINE TO EVALUATE THE SAME FOURIER           ***
C      ***       POLYNOMIAL AT DIFFERENT POINTS, THE FOURIER       ***
C      ***       COEFFICIENTS ARE COMPUTED ONLY ONCE               ***
C
          IF(FLAG.GT.1.0) GOTO 14
C      *** COMPUTE SFT FOURIER COEFFICIENTS BETA ***
          FLAG=5.0
          DO 10 J=1,N
             BETA(J)=(0.,0.)
             DO 11 K=1,N
                X1=A+(K-1)*CONS2
                BETA(J)=BETA(J)+F(K)*CEXP(-CONS*(-N2+J-1)*X1)/FLOATN
    11       CONTINUE
    10    CONTINUE
C      *** FILTER THE COEFFICIENTS BETA OF THE FOURIER POLYNOMIAL ***
    13    DO 14 J=1,N
             ARG=2*PI*(-N2+J-1)/FLOATN
             BAND = 1.0
             BETA(J)=H(ARG)*BETA(J)
    14    CONTINUE
C      *** EVALUATE THE FILTERED POLYNOMIAL AT X ***
          P=(0.,0.)
          DO 20 J=1,N
          P=P+BETA(J)*CEXP(CONS*X*(-N2+J-1))
    20 CONTINUE
       RETURN
       END
```

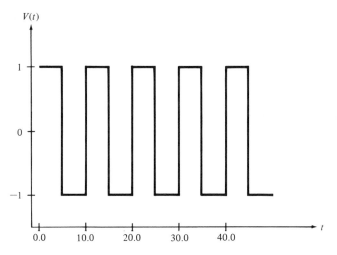

FIGURE 6.18   Graph of Trigonometric Polynomial of Input Wave

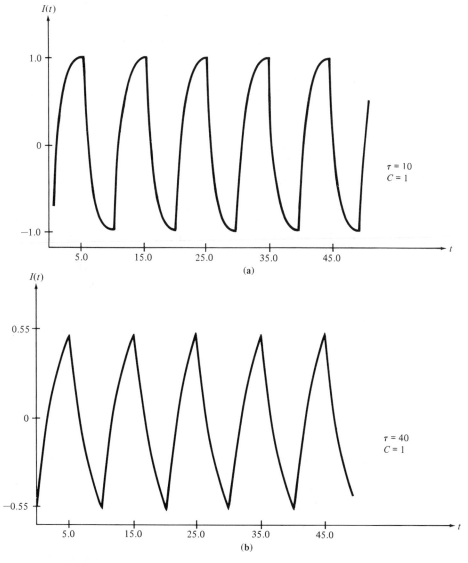

(a)

(b)

FIGURE 6.19   Graph of Trigonometric Polynomial of Filtered Wave **341**

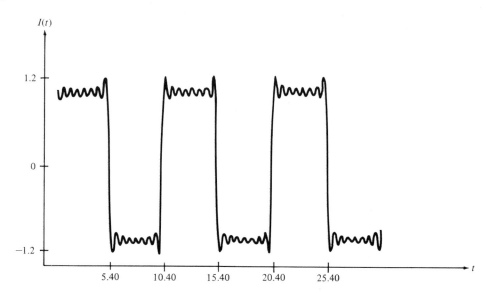

FIGURE 6.20   Effect of Bandlimiting a Square Wave

The resultant reshaping of the square wave shown in Figure 6.20 is a phenomenon well known to communication theorists: The curve loses its sharp corners and fast rises. It is a troublesome phenomenon because it is a source of intersymbol interference and "equivocation" in binary information transmission.

★6.4.3   Fast Fourier Transforms

For some while it was thought that determination of the coefficients of the N-point discrete Fourier transform required in the order of N^2 operations: N multiplications and $(N - 1)$ additions for each value of β_j, and repeated for each of the j values. It was therefore considered a major breakthrough when in the mid-1960's, Cooley, Tukey, Sande, and others found a trick by which operations grow as $N \log (N)$, as N increases. The schemes that compute the discrete Fourier transformation with this efficiency are commonly referred to as *fast Fourier transforms*. Since for large N, $\log (N) << N$, fast Fourier transforms have much computational appeal. The reader should bear firmly in mind, however, that the fast Fourier transform is a fast way for getting the discrete Fourier transformation; it is not a different transformation and in fact, a fast Fourier transform should end up giving exactly the same answers as our subroutine SFT; it just gets them quicker.

   We describe in detail the Cooley–Tukey fast Fourier transformation. Other methods have similar motivation and depend in some manner on factorization of N. Here we assume that N is a power of 2; that is, for some integer n, $N = 2^n$. Our interpolation index set will be $S = \{0, 1, \ldots, N - 1\}$, and the interpolation points are $x_j = j/N$, $0 \leq j \leq N - 1$.

   The Cooley–Tukey form of the fast Fourier transform is a recursive method. At the initial stage $m = 0$ it starts with N polynomials $p_0^{(0)}(x)$, $p_1^{(0)}(x)$, . . . , $p_{N-1}^{(0)}(x)$. Each has zero degree and interpolates the target function $f(x)$ at one point. At each stage $m \geq 0$ we define $M = 2^m$ and $R = N/M$ for the number of the interpolating points and number of polynomials. Thus at the initial stage

$M = 1, R = N$. At each new stage the number R of polynomials becomes halved, the number of nodes M at which the polynomials interpolate is doubled, and the degree of the polynomials increases by 2^m. At stage $m = 1$, $M = 2$ and $R = N/2$. Thus we have $N/2$ quadratic polynomials. Each of them interpolates function $f(x)$ at two points. By repeating this process until the nth stage, the number of polynomials becomes $N/2^n = 1$, it has degree $\sum_{m=0}^{n-1} 2^m = 2^n - 1 = N - 1$, and interpolates at $2^n = N$ points. Thus the final polynomial $p_0^{(n)}(x)$ is the desired interpolator.

The updating formula of the polynomials $p_j^{(m)}(x)$ ($j = 0, 1, \ldots, M - 1$) is based on the following simple observation. Assume that somehow we have constructed polynomials $q(x)$ and $r(x)$ which for some even positive integer M satisfy

$$q\left(\frac{2j}{M}\right) = f\left(\frac{2j}{M}\right)$$

$$r\left(\frac{2j}{M}\right) = f\left(\frac{2j+1}{M}\right) \qquad (0 \le j \le M/2 - 1); \tag{6.62}$$

then, evidently,

$$p(x) = \frac{1 + \exp(i\pi xM)}{2} q(x) + \frac{1 - \exp(i\pi xM)}{2} r\left(x - \frac{1}{M}\right) \tag{6.63}$$

interpolates $f(j/M)$, $0 \le j \le M - 1$. This is because $\exp(i\pi(j/M)M)$ is $+1$ or -1 according to whether j is even or odd. Armed with this formula, we begin at stage $m = 0$ by constructing N constant polynomials,

$$p_j^{(0)}(x) = f\left(\frac{j}{N}\right) \qquad (0 \le j \le N - 1) \tag{6.64}$$

and then apply (6.63) step by step, with increasing index m. Recall that n was defined so that $2^n = N$, and that at stage m,

$$M = 2^m \qquad \text{and} \qquad R = 2^{n-m}. \tag{6.65}$$

Assume inductively that for some nonnegative integer m, we have R polynomials $p_j^{(m)}(x)$, which for each j, $0 \le j \le R$, satisy the M-point interpolatory properties

$$p_j^{(m)}\left(\frac{k}{M}\right) = f\left(\frac{j}{N} + \frac{k}{M}\right) \qquad (0 \le k \le M - 1). \tag{6.66}$$

Clearly, this relation holds for the constant polynomials $p_j^{(0)}(x)$ in (6.64), since $m = 0$, $M = 1$, $R = 2^n = N$, and $k = 0$. For m, R, M, and $p_j^{(m)}(x)$, $0 \le j \le R - 1$ as in (6.65) and (6.66), define a successor set of polynomials by

$$p_j^{(m+1)}(x) = \frac{1 + \exp(i2\pi xM)}{2} p_j^{(m)}(x)$$

$$+ \frac{1 - \exp(i2\pi xM)}{2} p_{j+(R/2)}^{(m)}\left(x - \frac{1}{2M}\right). \tag{6.67}$$

These new polynomials satisfy relations (6.66) with m replaced by $m + 1$, and therefore with M replaced by $2M$. For if k is even, then set $k' = k/2$ and from (6.66) and (6.67), calculate that

$$p_j^{(m+1)}\left(\frac{k}{2M}\right) = p_j^{(m+1)}\left(\frac{2k'}{2M}\right) = p_j^{(m)}\left(\frac{2k'}{2M}\right)$$

$$= p_j^{(m)}\left(\frac{k'}{M}\right) = f\left(\frac{j}{N} + \frac{k'}{M}\right) = f\left(\frac{j}{N} + \frac{2k'}{2M}\right).$$

Alternatively, if k is odd, we define $k' = (k - 1)/2$. Then

$$p_j^{(m+1)}\left(\frac{2k' + 1}{2M}\right) = p_{j+(R/2)}^{(m)}\left(\frac{2k'}{2M}\right)$$

$$= p_{j+(R/2)}^{(m)}\left(\frac{k'}{M}\right) = f\left(\frac{j + (R/2)}{N} + \frac{k'}{M}\right)$$

$$= f\left(\frac{j}{N} + \frac{R}{2N} + \frac{2k'}{2M}\right) = f\left(\frac{j}{N} + \frac{2k' + 1}{2M}\right),$$

where we have used $R/N = 1/M$. Thus (6.66) holds for $m + 1$ and by induction for all m, $0 \le m \le n$. The recursion terminates at stage $m = n$ with a single polynomial $p_0^{(n)}(x)$, which, in view of (6.66) and using the fact that here, $M = N$, satisfies the complete interpolation requirement

$$p_0^{(n)}\left(\frac{k}{N}\right) = f\left(\frac{k}{N}\right) \qquad (0 \le k < N).$$

The construct can be described entirely in terms of the Fourier coefficients $\beta_{jk}^{(m)}$ of $p_j^{(m)}(x)$. From (6.67) we can conclude that

$$
\boxed{
\begin{aligned}
2\beta_{jk}^{(m+1)} &= \beta_{jk}^{(m)} + \beta_{j+(R/2),k}^{(m)} \exp\left(-i\pi\left(\frac{j}{2M}\right)\right) \\[2mm]
2\beta_{j,M+k}^{(m+1)} &= \beta_{jk}^{(m)} - \beta_{j+(R/2),k}^{(m)} \exp\left(-i\pi\left(\frac{j}{2M}\right)\right) \qquad (0 \le k < M).
\end{aligned}
}
\tag{6.68}
$$

The process begins by observing that the only coefficient of each polynomial $p_j^{(0)}(x)$ is

$$\boxed{\beta_{j,0}^{(0)} = f\left(\frac{j}{N}\right).}$$

Let us assess the computational effort of the fast Fourier transform. At each stage m there are $R = 2^{n-m}$ polynomials $p_j^{(m)}(x)$, each having 2^m Fourier coefficients $\beta_{jk}^{(m)}$. For each such coefficient one addition and one multiplication are required in (6.68). Therefore, at stage m, there are $3 \cdot 2^n$ operations, and there are n stages. Thus the grand total is $3n \cdot 2^n = 3nN$ operations. But $n = \log_2(N)$, so this is how we conclude that with the fast Fourier transform, the processing effort grows proportionally to $N \log (N)$.

──────── **EXAMPLE 6.12** ──────────────────────────────

Suppose that $N = 4 = 2^2$, so that $n = 2$. We wish to interpolate a function $f(x)$ such that $f(j/4) = j$, $0 \leq j \leq 3$. The construction begins by defining $m = 0$, and $\beta_{j,0}^{(0)} = j$, $0 \leq j < R = 2^{2-0} = 4$. Now apply (6.68),

$$\beta_{0,0}^{(1)} = \tfrac{1}{2}(\beta_{0,0}^{(0)} + \beta_{2,0}^{(0)}) = 1$$

$$\beta_{0,1}^{(1)} = \tfrac{1}{2}(\beta_{0,0}^{(0)} - \beta_{2,0}^{(0)}) = -1$$

$$\beta_{1,0}^{(1)} = \tfrac{1}{2}(\beta_{1,0}^{(0)} + \beta_{3,0}^{(0)}) = 2$$

$$\beta_{1,1}^{(1)} = \tfrac{1}{2}(\beta_{1,0}^{(0)} - \beta_{3,0}^{(0)}) = -1.$$

Finally, for the $m = 2$ terms, after updating, $R = 1$, $M = 2$, and

$$\beta_{0,0}^{(2)} = \frac{1}{2}(\beta_{0,0}^{(1)} + \beta_{1,0}^{(1)}) = \frac{3}{2}$$

$$\beta_{0,1}^{(2)} = \frac{1}{2}\left[\beta_{0,1}^{(1)} + \beta_{1,1}^{(1)} \exp\left(-\frac{2\pi i}{4}\right)\right] = \frac{1}{2}\left[-1 - \exp\left(-\frac{2\pi i}{4}\right)\right]$$

$$\beta_{0,2}^{(2)} = \frac{1}{2}(\beta_{0,0}^{(1)} - \beta_{1,0}^{(1)}) = -\frac{1}{2}$$

and

$$\beta_{0,3}^{(2)} = \frac{1}{2}\left[\beta_{0,1}^{(1)} - \beta_{1,1}^{(1)} \exp\left(-\frac{2\pi i}{4}\right)\right] = \frac{1}{2}\left[-1 + \exp\left(-\frac{2\pi i}{4}\right)\right].$$

As one may verify, trigonometric polynomial with these coefficients does interpolate $f(x)$ at 0, $\tfrac{1}{4}$, $\tfrac{1}{2}$, and $\tfrac{3}{4}$.

━━━ ■

We refer the reader to Bloomfield (1976, pp. 75–76) for FORTRAN code for a fast Fourier transform. Also, this reference has much supplementary information and contains studies of specific data sets. Stoer and Bulirsch (1980, Sec. 2.3) describe several other such transforms. The IMSL routine FFTCC also computes fast Fourier transforms.

Unless the reader is wishing to interpolate more than 100 points, or is designing an algorithm that will be used repeatedly, he or she will probably find the SFT subroutine (Table 6.10) satisfactory for discrete Fourier series interpolation.

★6.5
APPROXIMATION BY RATIONAL FUNCTIONS

After polynomial and Fourier series, the rational functions are the third-most important class of approximation functions. A function $r(x)$ is a *rational function* if it can be written as the ratio of two polynomials

$$r(x) = \frac{a_0 + a_1 x + \cdots + a_n x^n}{b_0 + b_1 x + \cdots + b_m x^m}. \tag{6.69}$$

We will speak of $r(x)$ in (6.69) as being a rational function of degree (n, m). There are $m + n + 1$ free parameters, since multiplication of numerator and denominator by a scalar leaves $r(x)$ unchanged, and therefore we can fix the value of any nonzero coefficient as unity. For purposes of this section, we will make the convention that $b_0 = 1$, but mention that this is a restriction if one needs a "pole" at the origin. In the following developments, we let $a(x)$ and $b(x)$ denote the numerator and denominator polynomials, respectively, of $r(x)$. That is, $r(x) = a(x)/b(x)$.

Rational functions tend to be particularly favorable in cases in which the function to be approximated, when viewed as a complex function, has singularities not too far from the approximation domain. The device favoring rational functions here is that the roots of the denominator can "model" the singularity.

Interpolation by rational functions of specified degree (n, m) converts to a linear equation task. That is, the problem of finding $r(x)$ of degree (n, m) so that

$$r(x_i) = \frac{a(x_i)}{b(x_i)} = f_i \qquad (1 \le i \le m + n + 1) \qquad (6.70)$$

requires finding the solution of the equations

$$a_0 + a_1 x_i + \cdots + a_n x_i^n$$
$$= f_i(1 + b_1 x_i + \cdots + b_m x_i^m) \qquad (1 \le i \le n + m + 1)$$

in terms of the variables a_j and b_k, $0 \le j \le n$, $1 \le k \le m$.

We have written this system so that it is obviously obtained from the condition

$$a(x_i) = f_i b(x_i) \qquad (1 \le i \le n + m + 1),$$

but you will recognize that we can next move all the terms in the variable b_j over to the left-hand side and a more standard form of the linear equation appears:

$$a_0 + x_i a_1 + \cdots + x_i^n a_n - (f_i x_i) b_1 - \cdots - (f_i x_i^m) b_m = f_i$$
$$(1 \le i \le n + m + 1). \qquad (6.71)$$

This system always has a solution (Stoer and Bulirsch, 1980, Sec. 2.2) but under certain (physically unlikely) circumstances, it might not satisfy the interpolation condition (6.70). In Problem 29 we meet such a case.

─────── **EXAMPLE 6.13** ───────

As an illustration of the procedure described above, consider the interpolation points $x_1 = -1$, $x_2 = 0$, $x_3 = 1$, and corresponding functional values $f_1 = 1$, $f_2 = 2$, $f_3 = -1$. Since three points are given, rational interpolating functions are determined for $n + m + 1 = 3$. Specially for degree $(1, 1)$, equations (6.71) have the form

$$a_0 + (-1) \cdot a_1 - (-1) \cdot b_1 = 1$$
$$a_0 + \quad 0 \cdot a_1 - \quad 0 \cdot b_1 = 2$$
$$a_0 + \quad 1 \cdot a_1 - (-1) \cdot b_1 = -1,$$

and the solution is

$$a_0 = 2, \qquad a_1 = -1, \qquad b_1 = -2.$$

Hence the interpolating rational function of degree $(1, 1)$ is

$$r(x) = \frac{2 - x}{1 - 2x}.$$

Simple substitution shows that this function really interpolates the given data.

The interpolation condition $n + m + 1 = 3$ is satisfied in two more cases: degrees $(0, 2)$ and $(2, 0)$. In the first case, equations (6.71) read

$$a_0 - (-1) \cdot b_1 - \quad 1 \cdot b_2 = \quad 1$$

$$a_0 - \quad 0 \cdot b_1 - \quad 0 \cdot b_2 = \quad 2$$

$$a_0 - (-1) \cdot b_1 - (-1) \cdot b_2 = -1,$$

and the solution is

$$a_0 = 2, \qquad b_1 = -2, \qquad b_2 = -1.$$

With these values we have

$$r(x) = \frac{2}{1 - 2x - x^2}. \tag{6.72}$$

In the second case, equations (6.71) are

$$a_0 + (-1) \cdot a_1 + 1 \cdot a_2 = \quad 1$$

$$a_0 + \quad 0 \cdot a_1 + 0 \cdot a_2 = \quad 2$$

$$a_0 + \quad 1 \cdot a_1 + 1 \cdot a_2 = -1,$$

and the solution is

$$a_0 = 2, \qquad a_1 = -1, \qquad a_2 = -2.$$

Hence

$$r(x) = 2 - x - 2x^2. \tag{6.73}$$

It is easy to verify that functions (6.72) and (6.73) both interpolate the given data.

Note that the last two cases (i.e., when $n = 0$ or $m = 0$) can be solved by using Lagrange interpolation on the basis of abscissas x_1, x_2, x_3, and functional values $1/f_1, 1/f_2, 1/f_3$, and f_1, f_2, f_3, respectively.

In practical applications, selection of the most appropriate degree (n, m) requires intuition and a prior knowledge of the analytic properties of the function to be approximated.

Point interpolation is only one setting for approximation by rational functions. In Example 6.14, to follow, we explore least-squares approximation. A third rational function construct generalizes Taylor's polynomials, to require that at some point $x = x_0$,

$$\frac{d^j}{dx^j} r(x) = \frac{d^j}{dx^j} f(x) \qquad (0 \leq j \leq m + n). \qquad (6.74)$$

In many cases, least-squares approximation is safer than interpolation when the choice of data pairs is at your discretion.

───── **EXAMPLE 6.14** ───

To stay within the scope of methods offered in this chapter, we apply the least-squares criterion in a very simple setting. Given a function $f(x)$ and a set x_1, $x_2, \ldots, x_N$ of test points, we seek a rational function

$$r(x; a_0, a_1, b_1) = \frac{a_0 + a_1 x}{1 + b_1 x},$$

which minimizes the squared error criterion

$$J(a_0, a_1, b_1) = \sum_{i=1}^{n} [f(x_i) - r(x_i; a_0, a_1, b_1)]^2.$$

To simplify the nonlinear optimization problem, we observe that for any given parameter b_1, the problem of finding the best a_0 and a_1 is a (linear) polynomial regression problem. We let

$$H(b_1) = \min_{a_0, a_1} J(a_0, a_1, b_1)$$

and use the secant rule to find the critical point $b_1^* = b_1$ for which

$$\frac{d}{db_1} H(b_1) = 0.$$

Program RATFUN in Table 6.13 implements this plan. We applied this program to approximate ["atan," or "arctan," or "tan^{-1}"] atan (x), $0 \leq x \leq 50$. Its performance is very respectable. Table 6.14 compares this performance with the squared error of polynomial interpolation of varying degrees, using Chebyshev points (Section 3.4.4), which typically does about as well as polynomial approximation can do. It would be fair to compare $r(x)$ with the quadratic least-squares

TABLE 6.13   Computer Program for Example 6.14

```
C       PROGRAM RATFUN
C
C       ***************************************************************
C       THIS PROGRAM COMPUTES THE BEST (IN THE LEAST-SQUARES SENSE)
C       RATIONAL APPROXIMATION R(X) OF THE FORM
C       R(X)=(A0+A1.X)/(1+B1.X) TO THE FUNCTION ATAN(X) BASED ON A
C       UNIFORM GRID OF POINTS ON [0,50]  THIS IS DONE BY FIRST
C       SOLVING , FOR A GIVEN B1, A LINEAR LEAST-SQUARES PROBLEM TO
C       FIND THE BEST A0 AND A1 AND THEN USING THE SECANT METHOD TO
C       OBTAIN THE BEST B1 BY MINIMIZING THE SUM OF SQUARED ERROR
C       (ATAN(X)-R(X))**2 WITH THE BEST VALUES OF A1 AND A2
C       SUBSTITUTED IN R(X)
C       CALLS:   SECA,GAUS1
C       OUTPUT: SUM=THE SUM OF SQUARED ERROR OVER THE GRID OF POINTS
C               WITH THE BEST VALUES FOUND SUBSTITUTED FOR A0,A1
C               AND B1 IN R(X)
C       ***************************************************************
C
        COMMON Y(100),X(100),EST(100),SUM
C       *** DECLARE THE FUNCTION TO BE APPROXIMATED           ***
        FF(X) = ATAN(X)
C
C       *** EVALUATE AND STORE THE FUNCTION VALUES AT THE     ***
C       *** UNIFORM GRID POINTS AND ALSO STORE THE GRID POINTS ***
C
        DO 1 J = 1,50
           X(J)=J
           Y(J)=FF(X(J))
      1    CONTINUE
C       *** START THE SECANT METHOD WITH 0 AND 1 AS INITIAL POINTS ***
        X1 = 0.0
        X2 = 1.0
        EPS = 1.0E-5
        CALL SECA(X1,X2,B1,EPS)
        WRITE(10,*)'SUM OF SQ.ERROR = ',SUM
        END


C
C       *** PRESCRIBE THE FUNCTION F(B1) (=dH(B1)/dB1  EX. 6.14),  ***
C       *** THE ZERO OF WHICH IS SOUGHT BY SUBROUTINE SECA        ***
C
        FUNCTION F(B1)
        COMMON Y(100),X(100),EST(100),SUM
        DIMENSION A(2,3)
C
C       *** DECLARE FUNCTIONS FUN1 AND FUN2   THEY ARE USED TO SET ***
C       *** UP THE SYSTEM OF LINEAR EQUATIONS WHICH DETERMINE A0   ***
C       *** AND A1                                                 ***
C
        FUN1(X)=1.0/(1.0+B1*X)
        FUN2(X)=X/(1.0+B1*X)
C
C       *** INITIALIZE THE COEFFICIENTS AND THE RIGHT HAND SIDE    ***
C       *** OF THE SYSTEM OF LINEAR EQUATIONS WHICH SPECIFIES THE  ***
C       *** BEST A0 AND A1 FOR A GIVEN VALUE OF B1                 ***
C
        A(1,1) = 0.0
        A(1,2) = 0.0
        A(2,2) = 0.0
        A(1,3) = 0.0
        A(2,3) = 0.0
C
C       *** COMPUTE THE COEFFICIENTS AND THE RIGHT HAND SIDE OF    ***
C       *** THE SYSTEM OF LINEAR EQUATIONS WHICH SPECIFIES A0 AND  ***
C       *** A1 AND SOLVE THIS SYSTEM BY CALLING GAUS1              ***
C       *** THE SOLUTION WILL BE IN A(1,3) AND A(2,3)              ***
```

(continued)

TABLE 6.13 (Continued)

```
C

      DO 1 J = 1,50
        A(1,1) = A(1,1) + FUN1(X(J))**2
        A(1,2) = A(1,2) + FUN1(X(J))*FUN2(X(J))
        A(2,2) = A(2,2) + FUN2(X(J))**2
        A(1,3) = A(1,3) + Y(J)*FUN1(X(J))
        A(2,3) = A(2,3) + Y(J)*FUN2(X(J))
    1 CONTINUE
      A(2,1) = A(1,2)
      EPS = 1.0E-5
      CALL GAUSS(2,1,A,EPS)
      A0 = A(1,3)
      A1 = A(2,3)
C
C     *** SUBSTITUTE THE VALUES A0 AND A1 IN R(X) AND COMPUTE    ***
C     *** THE SUM OF SQUARED ERRORS (ATAN(X)-R(X))**2 OVER       ***
C     *** THE SET OF UNIFORM GRID POINTS AND STORE IN SUM        ***
C     *** THE VALUE OF H(B1) AT THE GIVEN POINT B1 (EX. 6.14)    ***
C     *** IS EQUAL TO THE ABOVE SUM   F IS SET EQUAL TO THE      ***
C     *** DERIVATIVE OF H(B1) AT THE POINT B1                    ***
C
      DERIV=0.0
      SUM = 0.0
      DO 2 J=1, 50
        EST(J)=A0*FUN1(X(J))+ A1*FUN2(X(J))
        TEMP= Y(J)-EST(J)
        SUM = SUM + (Y(J)-EST(J))**2
        DERIV = DERIV + (Y(J)-EST(J))*EST(J)*FUN2(X(J))
    2 CONTINUE
      F = DERIV
      END
```

polynomial, since they both have the same number of free parameters and require about the same number of floating-point operations to evaluate.

Finally, we remark that criteria other than least-squares are sometimes used. Let $x_1, x_2, \ldots, x_n$ denote the node points and $f_1, f_2, \ldots, f_n$ be given function

TABLE 6.14   Results for Example 6.14

Approximation by:	Sum of Squared Error
Rational function of degree (1, 1)	$1.6 \cdot 10^{-4}$
4-Point Chebyshev interpolation	0.20
10-Point Chebyshev interpolation	$1.83 \cdot 10^{-2}$
15-Point Chebyshev interpolation	$1.7 \cdot 10^{-4}$

values. If p is a class of functions to be used for approximation, then in uniform approximation the maximum error

$$\max_{1 \le i \le n} |p(x_i) - f_i|$$

is minimized over p. It can be proven (see S & Y, 1978, Sec. 2.2) that this maximum error criterion induces a linear programming problem, and computers are very effective here.

6.6
SUPPLEMENTARY NOTES AND DISCUSSIONS

In this chapter we resumed a path initiated in Chapter 3, namely, the quest for computer-amenable representations of functions that are given only at a finite set of data. In that chapter there were some loose ends and here we attended to some of these. In particular, if there are a great many data points, polynomial interpolation is not suitable since under the best of curcumstances, it tends to be unstable for high degree (say 20). Spline interpolation does not suffer this defect, but even after the spline function coefficients have been computed for a given data set, spline evaluation requires more programming, memory, and running time than polynomials. Therefore, splines are not suitable for use as library functions, for example. Moreover, interpolation is unsatisfactory when the data are irregular, indicating a random or highly oscillatory character in the data.

The methods of least squares and rational approximation, which are the central topics of this chapter, do overcome these difficulties to a large extent. However, they too can exhibit drawbacks and numerical instabilities. We saw that in its most simplistic form, least-squares approximation tends to result in ill-conditioned linear equation problems, and consequent numerical instability, when the degree of the approximating polynomial is moderate to large. We drew connections between the least-squares approximation problem and the general linear model in statistics. (Statisticians, too, are aware of instabilities associated with the least-squares approach, this instability being referred to by them as "collinearity.") The orthogonal polynomial approach for overcoming this instability was described and implemented in our routine ORTH. This approach is taken by the IMSL least-squares approximation routine RLFOTH.

The orthogonal polynomial scheme for achieving stability in least-squares approximation was viewed as a particular example of the Fourier approach. Fourier methods play an important role in communication theory and time-series analysis, and two-dimensional versions are central to many of the techniques in the fast-growing discipline of digital image analysis and enhancement. By presentation of Fourier trigonometric polynomials and a version of fast Fourier transforms, we hope to provide the reader with a foundation for understanding recent computational developments in these areas.

Rational approximation displays many of the advantages of the least-squares approach, but its implementation requires a program for solving nonlinear equations. Such programs are available in many computer centers. For determining interpolating rational functions of given degree, the solution of a system of linear equations is required.

PROBLEMS

Section 6.2

1. Find the constant and linear least-squares polynomials based on the following data sets:

(a)

x_i	-2	-1	0	1
f_i	6	3	2	2

(b)

x_i	-1	0	1	2
f_i	1	1	3	5

(c)

x_i	-1	0	1	2
f_i	0	1	3	6

Do by hand calculation and show your work.

2. **(a)** Approximate the functions below by linear, quadratic, and cubic least-squares polynomials in the inverval $[0, 1]$, based on the given data points: $x_1 = 0$, $x_2 = 0.25$, $x_3 = 0.5$, $x_4 = 0.75$, $x_5 = 1.0$.
   (1) $\sin(3x)$.
   (2) e^{2x}.
   (3) $\sqrt{x + 1}$.
   (4) $\dfrac{1}{1 + x^2}$.
   (5) x^{10}.
   (6) $\ln(1 + x)$.
   Use a computer. Give the error at the test points $t_i = i/11$, $i = 1, 2, \ldots,$ 10.
   (b) By way of comparison, do this problem using Lagrange interpolation [by calling subroutine LAGR (Table 3.6)].

3. Ideally, a projectile fired at angle θ with an initial velocity of V_0 meters/second rises to a height given by

$$h(\theta) = (V_0)^2 \, \frac{\sin^2(\theta)}{2g}.$$

The accompanying figure illustrates this situation. However, this formula is not easily applicable because V_0 is difficult to measure accurately and the ideal formula does not account for friction and atmospheric resistance. Following are three tables, one giving exact values for the altitude equation, and the next two giving noisy values. Toward appreciating a central benefit of the least-squares approach, approximate the trajectory in each case with:
   (a) Cubic splines, obtained from use of subroutines SPLE and SPLN (Tables 3.12 and 3.13).
   (b) Lagrange interpolation [through use of LAGR (Table 3.6)].
   (c) The least-squares approach (LSQM, Table 6.1).

There is no "right answer" to this problem. But one can see by viewing plots of the interpolated data that with increasing noise, the methods of Chapter 3 become less and less sensible. Plot the values given by the various approximators at angles $j \cdot \pi/40, j = 1, \ldots, 20$.

Data Set 1

θ	$h(\theta)$
0.1428	2.2110
0.2856	18.5552
0.4284	29.7024
0.5712	68.7458
0.7140	88.1653
0.8568	112.2261
0.9996	128.9043
1.1424	152.4128
1.2852	180.6135
1.4280	210.0712

Data Set 2

θ	$h(\theta)$
0.1428	4.0507
0.2856	15.8746
0.4284	34.5139
0.5712	58.4585
0.7140	85.7685
0.8568	114.2315
0.9996	141.5415
1.1424	165.4861
1.2852	184.1254
1.4280	195.9493

Data Set 3

θ	$h(\theta)$
0.1428	14.4756
0.2856	7.3384
0.4284	59.4973
0.5712	66.1519
0.7140	88.6189
0.8568	101.2210
0.9996	156.6157
1.1424	164.0392
1.2852	245.8884
1.4280	248.2409

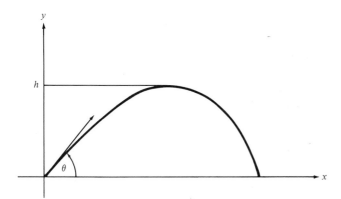

4. Vibrations, being periodic functions, are usually well described by sinusioids. Suppose that some vibration is described by

$$f(t) = 10 \sin (1.2 + 0.75t).$$

For $N = 5$, select the points $t_k = (k - 1)/(N - 1)$, $k = 1, 2, \ldots, N$, as observation times, and find the least-squares polynomials of degrees $m = 1, 2$, and 3. Compare the mean-squared errors

$$\frac{1}{101} \sum_{k=0}^{100} \left[f\left(\frac{k}{101}\right) - p_m\left(\frac{k}{101}\right) \right]^2$$

of these various approximators. Repeat for $N = 5$, 10, and 15. Note that raising the number of sample points beyond a certain range does not lead to a significant increase in accuracy. For effective approximation, the degrees and data sets need to be increased together. There is no definitive theory on how to do this; experimentation is in order.

5. Suppose that

$$f(t) = t^4.$$

For $N = 5$, select the points $t_k = (k - 1)/(N - 1)$, $k = 1, 2, \ldots, N$, as observation times, and find the least-squares polynomials of degrees $m = 1, 2$, and 3. Compare the mean-squared errors

$$\frac{1}{101} \sum_{k=1}^{100} \left[f\left(\frac{k}{101}\right) - p_m\left(\frac{k}{101}\right) \right]^2$$

of these various approximators. Repeat for $N = 10$, 20, and 50.

6. The following data were obtained by observing noisy values of the line

$$f^*(x_i) = x_i + n_i,$$

the noise n_i being uniformly distributed on the interval $(-0.2, 0.2)$. Use a computer to obtain the third-degree least-squares polynomial approximation of these data. Also compute the spline and Lagrange interpolators (use the subroutines in Tables 3.6, 3.12, and 3.13). Make plots or graphs of $f^*(x)$ and its three approximators. Comment on the performance characteristics.

x_i	$f^*(x_i)$
0.0621	0.0072
0.1293	0.2079
0.1582	0.1831
0.1957	0.1861
0.2113	0.2058
0.3997	0.4547
0.5106	0.4260
0.5398	0.6085
0.7727	0.8504
0.8083	0.8049

7. On the basis of the values of cos (x) at points $x_i = 0, 0.1, 0.2, 0.3, 0.4$, and 0.5, find the cubic least-squares polynomial and evaluate it at $x = 0.25$. Compare this with the true value cos $(0.25) = 0.9689124$.

8. Find the parameters a and b satisfying the least-squares condition according to the models indicated and the data values given.

(a) $y = a + bx^2$ (0, 0), (1, 1), (2, 5).

(b) $y = a \cdot \sin (x) + b \cdot \sin (2x)$ $(0, 0)$, $\left(\dfrac{\pi}{4}, 1\right)$, $\left(\dfrac{\pi}{2}, 0\right)$.

(c) $y = ax + be^x$ (0, 0), (1, 2), (2, 4).

9. It is possible, and sometimes even sensible, to use least-squares codes to perform interpolation.
    (a) Describe how to find the interpolation polynomial using LSQM on N data points.
    (b) Compare the number of arithmetic floating-point operations needed to evaluate the approximators at $2N$ different "test" points, by
        (1) The driver in Table 3.7 in conjunction with LAGR.
        (2) The driver in Table 6.2 in conjunction with LSQM.
    (c) Under what circumstances is use of LSQM competitive with LAGR for interpolation?

★10. (a) Find the quadratic least-squares polynomial of the function $f(x) = |x|$ with respect to the inner product (6.31) over the interval $[-1, 1]$. That is, find a, b, and c to minimize the function

$$Q(a, b, c) = \int_{-1}^{1} (|x| - a - bx - cx^2)^2 \, dx.$$

Show your work.
    (b) Since $|x|$ is symmetric about 0, odd-order coefficients must be 0. Thus use the approximation polynomial $p(x) = a + cx^2$. Explain why the same result is obtained.

11. **(Continuation of Problem 10.)** Find estimates a, b, and c as above, but instead, use the criterion

$$\sum_{i=1}^{100} (|x_i| - a - bx_i - cx_i^2)^2 \qquad \text{with } x_i = \frac{2i - 99}{101}.$$

Compare the values obtained this way with values obtained analytically in Problem 10 at $x = 0.1, 0.2, 0.5$, and 1.0.

12. Let $f(x)$ be a function that is symmetric about $x = 0$, and suppose that the design points x_i are also symmetrically placed; that is, if x_i is a design point, then for some k,

$$x_k = -x_i.$$

Show that in this case, the linear least-squares polynomial is a constant function, and that in the quadratic least-squares approximation $a_0 + a_1 x + a_2 x^2$, the value a_1 will be 0.

13. Compare the Hilbert segment matrix of order n and the matrix S as in equation (6.21). Thus for $n = 5$ and 10, print out

$$h_{ij} - \frac{1}{n} s_{ij}, \qquad \text{all even values of } i \text{ and } j.$$

Here $h_{ij} = 1/(1 + i + j)$.

14. The following data are taken from the *Statistical Abstract of the United States, 1984*, published by the U.S. Department of Commerce Bureau of the Census (p. 99).

Year	1960	1965	1970	1974	1975	1976	1977	1978	1979	1980
Total Aliens Naturalized (thousands)	119.4	104.3	110.4	131.7	141.5	142.5	159.9	173.5	164.2	157.9

In the spirit of Application 6.1, examine these data using least-squares approximations of various orders. Try to offer an interpretation of the data. Is it suggesting a trend?

15. A common use of the least-squares idea is in inferring physical constants from actual measurements.

(a) It is thought that Hooke's law

$$F(x) = kx$$

gives a good approximation of the contraction force of a spring that has been stretched by an amount x (meters). How would you use the least-squares approach to estimate k from a set of measurements (x_i, F_i), $i = 1, 2, \ldots, n$?

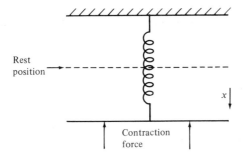

(b) It is postulated in physics that the time required for a radioactive atom to decay is random and exponentially distributed. The implication is that if at time 0, you have $N(0)$ radioactive particles, at time t you will have

$$N(t) = N(0) \exp(-rt)$$

particles left, r being a physical constant associated with the particular particle type. A Geiger counter, through count intensity, makes imperfect estimates $Y(t_i)$ of $N(t_i)$ at times t_i, $i = 1, 2, \ldots, n$. Imagine that for some constant C, $Y(t_i) = CN(t_i) + N_i$, where N_i is measurement noise. Show how to use the least-squares idea to guess the constant r:

(i) Assuming that $CN(0)$ is known.
(ii) Assuming that $CN(0)$ is unknown.

16. Let Φ be as in (6.14), or, in fact, any square matrix. Show that

$$\Phi^T \Phi$$

is symmetric and nonnegative definite. By *nonnegative definite*, we mean that for any vector $\mathbf{u}$ of appropriate length,

$$\mathbf{u}^T \Phi^T \Phi \mathbf{u} \geq 0.$$

★Section 6.3

★17. Find the linear and quadratic orthogonal polynomials $\phi_1(x)$ and $\phi_2(x)$ if $\phi_0(x) = 1$, all x, and

(a) $n = 4$, $x_1 = -2$, $x_2 = -1$, $x_3 = 0$, $x_4 = 1$.
(b) $n = 4$, $x_1 = -1$, $x_2 = 0$, $x_3 = 1$, $x_4 = 2$.
(c) $T = [-1, 1]$ and $w(x) = 1$.
Show your calculations.

★18. Find the constant and linear least-squares polynomials for the data values

(a)

x_i	-2	-1	0	1
f_i	6	3	2	2

(b)

x_i	-1	0	1	2
f_i	1	1	3	5

(c)

x_i	-1	0	1	2
f_i	0	1	3	6

★19. Do Problem 10, but replace x and x^2 by the polynomials obtained by doing Problem 17c.

★20. Use subroutine ORTH to redo Example 6.9. Try to find the most accurate polynomial approximations by LSQM and ORTH for the approximation problem in that example, using your computer. Work in double precision, if available.

★21. Redo Example 6.5, but increase the polynomial degree m, and find the limits beyond which the estimated values become inaccurate or the LSQM becomes unstable. Then apply subroutine ORTH to the same problem and see if it has improved results.

★Section 6.4

★22. Confirm that the functions 1, sin (kx), cos (kx), $k = 1, 2, \ldots$, as in Example 6.10 are really orthogonal, as claimed.

★23. Find the trigonometric series for the function

$$f(x) = (x - [x])^2,$$

where $[x]$ means the "integer part of x." For this problem, take as inner product (6.44) with X the unit interval $[0, 1]$.

★24. One can give a matrix interpretation of the discrete Fourier transform method. Analogously to (6.38) define

$$\Phi = \{\exp{(i2\pi x_j k)}\}_{j,k=0}^N$$

and then show that if Φ^H is the matrix obtained by taking the complex conjugates of the elements in Φ^T, then

$$\Phi^H\Phi = N\mathbf{I}.$$

In terms of Φ, express the forward and inverse discrete Fourier transforms as linear operations on the vectors $\mathbf{F} = (F_0, F_1, \ldots, F_{N-1})^T$ and $\boldsymbol{\beta} = (\beta_0, \beta_1, \ldots, \beta_{N-1})^T$.

★**25.** Find the coefficients of the discrete Fourier transformation of the function $f(x)$ in Problem 23. Evaluate the function and the inverse transform at the points $t_i = i/101$, $i = 1, 2, \ldots, 100$. Take $N = 20, 100,$ and 200. Print the approximation error in each case at the test points t_i above.

★**26.** Apply the filters

(a) $H(\omega) = \dfrac{\omega + 1}{\omega^2 + 5\omega + 6}$,

(b) $H(\omega) = \dfrac{1}{\omega^2 + 0.2\omega + 5}$,

in place of the filter in Application 6.2.

★**27.** As suggested in Application 6.2, the solution of any (constant-coefficient) linear differential equation with periodic forcing function can be found by filtering the coefficients of the discrete Fourier transform of the forcing function. The spring/mass/damper system depicted below leads to the differential equation

$$y'' + y' + y = u(t).$$

If $u(t)$ is the sawtooth wave, $u(t) = t - [t]$ ($[t]$ = integer part of t), find the trajectory $y(t)$. Make a plot. [**HINT:** The easiest way might be to use subroutine FILTER (Table 6.12).]

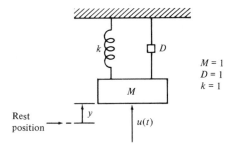

★**28.** Find the coefficients of the discrete Fourier transform of

$$f(x) = (x - [x])^2.$$

Compare with the coefficients obtained in Problem 23, for $n = 5$.

★**Section 6.5**

★**29.** Find the rational interpolating function of the form

$$r(x) = \frac{a_0 + a_1 x}{1 + b_1 x + b_2 x^2}$$

for the data points as given in Problem 1.

★**30.** Redo Problem 2, but take as the approximating function the rational function of the form

$$r(x) = \frac{a_0 + a_1 x + a_2 x^2}{1 + b_1 x + b_2 x^2}.$$

CHAPTER 7

Ordinary Differential Equations

7.1
PRELIMINARIES

Many models of physics, engineering, economics, and essentially every other quantitative science fall within the category of differential equations. That is, the evolutionary behavior of certain quantities satisfies some equation that depends not only on the quantities themselves, but also on their derivatives. For example, the law governing the velocity $v(t)$ of an unforced sliding mass subject only to viscous frictional effects and Newton's second law of motion is postulated to be

$$m \frac{d}{dt} v(t) = -Dv(t), \tag{7.1}$$

m being the mass of the object and D the damping coefficient. By substitution one may verify that the function

$$v(t) = C \exp\left(-\frac{D}{m} t\right) \tag{7.2}$$

satisfies (7.1), since

$$m \frac{d}{dt} v(t) = -mC \frac{D}{m} \exp\left(-\frac{D}{m} t\right) = -Dv(t).$$

If the velocity at time $t = 0$ is known to be v_0, we must have that $C = v_0$ in order for (7.2) to be numerically consistent with this initial information. In this context, v_0 is an initial condition, and the parameter C in the solution (7.2) of the differential equation (7.1) allows us a means of incorporating this initial condition.

In this chapter we offer numerical methods for solving ordinary differential equations. We study two central problems in the computational theory for ordinary differential equations: initial- and boundary-value problems.

359

Initial-value problems are differential equation problems in which information about the solution is given at a single time point. This information determines the solution parameters. The damping problem above is an example of an initial-value problem inasmuch as the "initial value" $v(0) = v_0$ is sufficient to determine the only solution parameter, C, in (7.2).

Boundary-value problems, by contrast, provide solution information at two or more time points. For example, if instead of specifying above that $v(0) = v_0$ we had known that $v(0) + v(1) = 1.0$, then we would have had an example of a boundary-value problem. In this case we could have solved for C by noting that

$$v(0) + v(1) = C + C \exp\left(-\frac{D}{m}\right) = 1.0.$$

The major thrust of our studies is directed at initial-value problems. In Section 7.7 we examine ways to recast boundary-value problems as initial-value problems.

7.2
THE MOST ELEMENTARY METHODS
AND THEIR LIMITATIONS

The *initial value problem* of an ordinary first-order differential equation has the form

$$y'(x) = f(x, y(x)), \qquad y(x_0) = y_0, \tag{7.3}$$

where x is a scalar variable, $y(x)$ and $f(x, y)$ are real-valued functions, and y_0 is a given real number. The reason this equation is called *first* order is that only the unknown function and its *first* derivative are included in the equation. In (7.3) and in what follows, $y'(x)$ represents $dy(x)/dx$. The second derivative is denoted by $y''(x)$, and in general the kth derivative, by $y^{(k)}(x)$. The solution of equation (7.3) will be determined on a finite interval $[x_0, b]$ starting with the initial point x_0. It is the tradition of differential equation literature to freely write f in place of $f(x, y)$, y for $y(x)$, $y^{(k)}$ for $y^{(k)}(x)$, and so on. We will also use this simplifying notation.

7.2.1 The Taylor's Series Method

Taylor's series, introduced in Chapter 3, lead to methods for solving (7.3). The motivation for Taylor's series as a tool for solving ordinary differential equations is that the derivatives of the solution function are sometimes easily found from the differential equation itself. We begin by applying the Taylor's series procedure in a particularly simple setting.

──────── **EXAMPLE 7.1** ────────────────────────────────────

Consider the differential equation

$$y' = x^2 + y^2, \qquad y(0) = 0.$$

By substituting $x = 0$, we get

$$y'(0) = 0^2 + y(0)^2 = 0^2 + 0^2 = 0.$$

By differentiating both sides of the differential equation in accordance with the chain rule (Appendix B, property 36), we find the relation

$$y'' = 2x + 2yy'.$$

So

$$y''(0) = 2 \cdot 0 + 2 \cdot y(0) \cdot y'(0) = 0.$$

After further differentiation, we find that

$$y^{(3)} = 2 + 2y'y' + 2yy'',$$

which implies that

$$y^{(3)}(0) = 2 + 2 \cdot 0 \cdot 0 + 2 \cdot 0 \cdot 0 = 2.$$

Continuing this process, we obtain the relations

$$y^{(4)} = 2y''y' + 2y'y'' + 2y'y'' + 2yy^{(3)}$$
$$= 6y'y'' + 2yy^{(3)}$$
$$y^{(5)} = 6y''y'' + 6y'y^{(3)} + 2y'y^{(3)} + 2yy^{(4)}$$
$$= 6(y'')^2 + 8y'y^{(3)} + 2yy^{(4)},$$

which imply

$$y^{(4)}(0) = 6 \cdot 0 \cdot 0 + 2 \cdot 0 \cdot 2 = 0$$
$$y^{(5)}(0) = 6 \cdot 0^2 + 8 \cdot 0 \cdot 2 + 2 \cdot 0 \cdot 0 = 0.$$

With these derivatives in hand, in view of (3.6) with "y" replacing "f," we see that the fifth-degree Taylor's polynomial approximation of the solution function is given by

$$y(x) \approx \frac{2x^3}{3!} = \frac{x^3}{3}.$$

At $x = 0.5$ and $x = 1.0$, this approximation gives, respectively, 0.04166 and 0.3333, whereas to the accuracy shown, the correct answers are $y(0.5) = 0.04179$ and $y(1.0) = 0.3502$. ∎

The methodology illustrated in the example above can be extended. In the following discussions we assume that all derivatives mentioned do exist. The derivatives of the solution can be determined recursively by the use of the chain rule of elementary calculus (Appendix B, property 36). In the representations below, subscripts indicate that partial derivatives have been taken with respect to the displayed variables. For instance,

$$f_x(x, y) = \frac{\partial}{\partial x} f(x, y), \qquad f_y(x, y) = \frac{\partial}{\partial y} f(x, y), \qquad f_{xx}(x, y) = \frac{\partial^2}{\partial x^2} f(x, y),$$

and so on. Then from (7.3), $y'(x) = f(x, y(x))$ and by successive differentiation, we recursively construct the relations

$$
\begin{aligned}
y'(x) &= f(x, y(x)) \\
y''(x) &= f_x(x, y(x)) + f_y(x, y(x))y'(x) \\
y^{(3)}(x) &= f_{xx}(x, y(x)) + 2f_{xy}(x, y(x))y'(x) + f_{yy}(x, y(x))y'(x)^2 \\
&\quad + f_y(x, y(x))y''(x)
\end{aligned}
\qquad (7.4)
$$

$$\vdots \qquad \vdots$$

Using the expressions above, evaluated at $x = x_0$ and $y = y_0$, the approximation of $y(x)$ can be computed from the Taylor's polynomial

$$y(x) \approx y(x_0) + \frac{y'(x_0)}{1!}(x - x_0) + \cdots + \frac{y^{(m)}(x_0)}{m!}(x - x_0)^m. \qquad (7.5)$$

The error of this approximation is $O((x - x_0)^{m+1})$, in the notation of Section 4.1.

If $|x - x_0|$ is large, the error of the approximation (7.5) can also become large, and consequently the accuracy of this method in an interval $[x_0, b]$ of moderate length is often found to be unsatisfactory. Accuracy can be improved through a modification in which Taylor's expansions are successively computed along a grid $x_0, x_1, x_2, \ldots$ of increasing x values. By this device, $|x - x_j|$ need never be large. Let step size $h = (b - x_0)/N$, where $N > 1$ is a given positive integer, and $[x_0, b]$ be the solution interval. Define the grid points

$$x_j = x_0 + jh \qquad (j = 0, 1, 2, \ldots, N).$$

Then between grid points x_j and x_{j+1} the solution can be approximated by

$$y(x) \approx y(x_j) + \frac{y'(x_j)}{1!}(x - x_j) + \cdots + \frac{y^{(m)}(x_j)}{m!}(x - x_j)^m.$$

On the basis of this approximation the following algorithm is offered for solving the initial-value problem by ''marching'' along the x-axis from x_0: For x between x_0 and x_1, apply this Taylor polynomial with $j = 0$ to approximate $y(x)$, where the derivatives are computed by using (7.4). For $x = x_1$, in particular, we calculate the approximation

$$y_1 = y_0 + \frac{y_0'}{1!} h + \cdots + \frac{y_0^{(m)}}{m!} h^m$$

of $y(x_1)$. Here $y_0', \ldots, y_0^{(m)}$ denote the derivative values $y'(x_0), \ldots, y^{(m)}(x_0)$. If x is between x_1 and x_2, the solution function is approximated by the Taylor polynomial with $j = 1$. For $j = 1$, use (7.4) with $y = y_1$, as computed above, and $x = x_1$. Then between x_1 and x_2 approximate the solution $y(x)$ by

$$y(x) \approx y_1 + \frac{y_1'}{1!} (x - x_1) + \cdots + \frac{y_1^{(m)}}{m!} (x - x_1)^m.$$

In particular, at $x = x_2$, the approximation of $y(x_2)$ is given by

$$y_2 = y_1 + \frac{y_1'}{1!} h + \cdots + \frac{y_1^{(m)}}{m!} h^m.$$

If we continue in this fashion, the solution can be extended to the further subintervals $[x_j, x_{j+1}]$, $j = 2, \ldots, N - 1$, by the relation

$$y(x) \approx y_j + \frac{y_j'}{1!} (x - x_j) + \cdots + \frac{y_j^{(m)}}{m!} (x - x_j)^m.$$

Then the approximation of $y(x_{j+1})$ is

$$y_{j+1} = y_j + \frac{y_j'}{1!} h + \cdots + \frac{y_j^{(m)}}{m!} h^m, \tag{7.6}$$

where the derivatives $y_j^{(k)}$ are determined by (7.4) evaluated at $x = x_j$, $y = y_j$. This formula can be used recursively to construct piecewise polynomial approximations of the solution. We thereby create separate Taylor's polynomial for each subinterval $[x_j, x_{j+1}]$. In applications one often seeks a table of grid points $x_0, x_1, x_2, \ldots$ and corresponding solution values $y_0, y_1, y_2, \ldots$. These values can be computed recursively by using (7.6), with y_j obtained in the previous step, and the approximating derivative values $y_j', \ldots, y_j^{(m)}$ are computed according to (7.4), at $x = x_j$ and $y = y_j$.

EXAMPLE 7.2

The equation

$$y' = x^2 + y^2, \qquad y(0) = 0$$

of Example 7.1 was solved by the recursive method (7.6), in the interval $[0, 1]$. We chose $N = 10$, so $x_j = (0.1)j$ ($j = 0, 1, \ldots, 10$). Table 7.1 compares the values of the solution obtained by applying the Taylor's series methods (7.4) and (7.6) with $m = 3$ to the above differential equation.

The improvement in accuracy with increasing x obtained by the recursions is obvious in this case.

TABLE 7.1   Computations of Examples 7.1 and 7.2

x_j	$y(x_j) = \frac{1}{3}x_j^3$ [Method (7.5)]	y_j Obtained by Recursion (7.6)	Exact Value of $y(x_j)$
0.0	0.000000	0.000000	0.000000
0.1	0.000333	0.000333	0.000333
0.2	0.002667	0.002667	0.002667
0.3	0.009000	0.009003	0.009003
0.4	0.021333	0.021357	0.021359
0.5	0.041667	0.041784	0.041791
0.6	0.072000	0.072433	0.072448
0.7	0.114333	0.115630	0.115660
0.8	0.170667	0.174025	0.174080
0.9	0.243000	0.250810	0.250907
1.0	0.333333	0.350064	0.350232

■

Another Taylor's series approach is outlined in Problem 2 at the end of the chapter. Since the higher-order derivatives of $y(x)$ can seldom be determined conveniently [because in most cases the recursive equations (7.4) become very complicated], the Taylor's series approach is not presently competitive with the techniques to follow, but it does provide insight into their construction.

7.2.2 Euler's Method

Consider the Taylor series method (7.6) with $m = 1$. This gives the recursive relation

$$y_{j+1} = y_j + hy_j',$$

where the approximating derivative value y_j' is obtained from the first equation of (7.4), with $y(x_j)$ replaced by y_j. That is, this recursion can be rewritten as

$$\boxed{y_{j+1} = y_j + hf(x_j, y_j).} \tag{7.7}$$

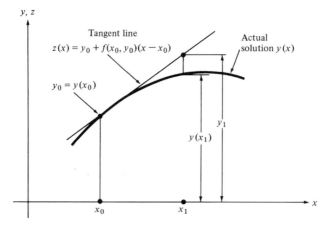

FIGURE 7.1   Euler's Method

Equation (7.7) recursively provides estimates y_1, y_2, y_3, . . . of $y(x_1)$, $y(x_2)$, $y(x_3)$, . . . , starting from the initial condition $y_0 = y(x_0)$. This particular successive Taylor's series formula is called *Euler's method*. Observe that no differentiation is required by (7.7).

A geometric interpretation of Euler's method is shown in Figure 7.1, in which one step at $j = 0$ is illustrated. Consider the linear function

$$z(x) = y_0 + y'(x_0)(x - x_0) = y_0 + f(x_0, y_0)(x - x_0),$$

which is the tangent line at $x = x_0$ of that solution of the differential equation which passes through the point (x_0, y_0). Then y_1 is the value of $z(x)$ at $x = x_1$. For larger values of j, the approximation y_{j+1} is the value at x_{j+1} of the tangent line of that solution curve which passes through the preceding point (x_j, y_j).

Subroutine EULER, given in Table 7.2, allows us to implement Euler's method by simply specifying the domain $[x_0, b]$ on which the solution is desired, the initial value y_0, the number N of Euler's steps, and the function $f(x, y)$. This function may be specified as a function subprogram. The initial values x_0 and y_0 are transmitted to the subroutine as the numbers $X(1)$ and $Y(1)$ in the arrays X and Y. The calling parameter N and the step size in (7.7) are, of course, related by

$$h = \frac{b - x_0}{N}.$$

Whereas Euler's method is attractive for its simplicity and ease of implementation, when accuracy counts, other methods employing greater sophistication are

TABLE 7.2   Subroutine for Euler's Method

```
          SUBROUTINE EULER(X,Y,N,B)
C
C     ****************************************************************
C     *   FUNCTION: THIS SUBROUTINE COMPUTES THE SOLUTION OF THE     *
C     *            FIRST ORDER DIFFERENTIAL EQUATION Y'=F(X,Y)       *
C     *            OVER THE INTERVAL [X(1),B] USING EULER'S METHOD*
C     *   USAGE:                                                     *
C     *        CALL SEQUENCE: CALL EULER(X,Y,N,B)                    *
C     *        EXTERNAL FUNCTIONS/SUBROUTINES: FUNCTION F(X,Y)       *
C     *   PARAMETERS:                                                *
C     *        INPUT:                                                *
C     *            N=NUMBER OF STEPS                                 *
C     *            X(1)=INITIAL IDEPENDENT VARIABLE VALUE            *
C     *            B=SOLUTION INTERVAL ENDPOINT (LAST X VALUE)       *
C     *            Y(1)=INITIAL DEPENDENT VARIABLE VALUE             *
C     *        OUTPUT:                                               *
C     *            X=N+1 BY 1 ARRAY OF INDEPENDENT VARIABLE VALUES   *
C     *            Y=N+1 BY 1 ARRAY OF DEPENDENT VARIABLE SOLUTION   *
C     *            VALUES                                            *
C     ****************************************************************
C
          DIMENSION X(N+1),Y(N+1)
C         *** INITIALIZATION ***
          H=(B-X(1))/N
C         *** RECURSIVELY COMPUTE THE SOLUTION VALUES ***
          DO 1 I=2,N+1
             X(I)=X(I-1)+H
C            *** EULER'S STEP ***
             Y(I)=Y(I-1)+H*F(X(I-1),Y(I-1))
        1 CONTINUE
          RETURN
          END
```

vastly more efficient. Theoretical and computational evidence supporting this
claim is offered in the sections to follow.

EXAMPLE 7.3

We have applied Euler's method to the differential equation

$$y' = x^2 + y^2, \qquad y(0) = 0,$$

of the previous examples with $N = 10$ and $h = 0.1$ again.

The initial condition implies that $x_0 = 0$ and $y_0 = 0$. Then from the recursion
(7.7) with $j = 0$ we conclude that at $x_1 = 0.1$ the solution approximation is

$$y_1 = y_0 + hf(x_0, y_0) = y_0 + 0.1(x_0^2 + y_0^2) = 0,$$

and with $j = 1$ we get the value

$$y_2 = y_1 + hf(x_1, y_1) = y_1 + 0.1(x_1^2 + y_1^2) = 0 + 0.1(0.01 + 0) = 0.001.$$

Continuing this calculation yields the values reported in Table 7.4. A calling
program for these computations is given in Table 7.3. The function $f(x, y)$ is

TABLE 7.3   Illustration of Euler's Method

```
C       PROGRAM EMETH
C
C       ******************************************************************
C       THIS PROGRAM SOLVES THE DIFFERENTIAL EQUATION Y'=X**2+Y**2
C       WITH THE INITIAL CONDITION Y(0.)=0. THE SOLUTION IS OBTAINED
C       AT 11 POINTS OVER THE INTERVAL [0,1] USING EULERS METHOD
C       CALLS:    EULER
C       OUTPUT:
C                 X(I)=VALUE OF X FOR I=1,11
C                 Y(I)=APPROXIMATED VALUE OF Y AT X(I)
C       ******************************************************************
C
        DIMENSION X(11),Y(11)
C
C       *** INITIALIZE                                              ***
C
        X(1)=0.
        Y(1)=0.
        B=1.
        N=10
C
C       *** SUBROUTINE EULER WILL APPROXIMATE THE SOLUTION          ***
C       *** RETURNING N+1 VALUES IN ARRAYS X AND Y                  ***
C
        CALL EULER(X,Y,N,B)
        WRITE(10,1)(X(I),Y(I),I=1,N+1)
      1 FORMAT(5X,F4.1,5X,F10.6)
        STOP
        END
C
C       *** FUNCTION F SPECIFIES THE DIFFERENTIAL EQUATION. IT IS   ***
C       *** CALLED BY SUBROUTINE EULER                              ***
C
        FUNCTION F(X,Y)
        F=X**2+Y**2
        RETURN
        END
```

TABLE 7.4 Output of Euler's Computation

x_j	y_j	Exact Value, $y(x_j)$
0.0	0.000000	0.000000
0.1	0.000000	0.000333
0.2	0.001000	0.002667
0.3	0.005000	0.009003
0.4	0.014003	0.021359
0.5	0.030022	0.041791
0.6	0.055112	0.072448
0.7	0.091416	0.115660
0.8	0.141252	0.174080
0.9	0.207247	0.250907
1.0	0.292542	0.350232

specified by means of a function subprogram, and the step size h is taken to be 0.1. That is, $N = 10$ is selected. We remark that when we took $h = 10^{-4}$ (i.e., $N = 10,000$), the computed Euler estimate (in double precision) of $y(1)$ was 0.3501692. This answer is correct to only four significant decimal places. ∎

★7.2.3 Foundations for More Accurate Methods

Plan 1. The linear Taylor's polynomial (7.6) is the basis for Euler's method. The main advantages of Euler's method over the higher-order Taylor's methods of Section 7.2.1 are: (1) no differentiation is required, and (2) its computer implementation is simple. A weakness of Euler's method is that larger truncation error can be anticipated. Because of this weakness, Euler's method is seldom used for serious computational tasks.

It is possible to construct approximation polynomials that coincide, up to a higher order, with the Taylor's polynomial, but which nevertheless do not require derivative information and the complicated formulas (7.4). The basic trick is that functional values at different values of x can be made to "substitute" for derivative information. The two prominent categories of numerical differential equation methods, the Runge–Kutta and the Adams rules, are based on different exploitations of this idea. We illustrate these exploitations now by deriving some simple formulas that are far more accurate than Euler's method. Then in Sections 7.3 and 7.4, the general principles are abstracted.

Consider the Taylor's series method (7.6) with $m = 2$:

$$y_{j+1} = y_j + \frac{y_j'}{1!} h + \frac{y_j''}{2!} h^2. \tag{7.8}$$

On the right-hand side, y_j' can be approximated by

$$y_j' \approx y'(x_j) = f(x_j, y(x_j)) \approx f(x_j, y_j).$$

Let h^* be a small step (not necessarily equal to h), and approximate y_j'' by the numerical differentiation formula (4.2) of Chapter 4 to obtain

$$y_j'' \approx y''(x_j) \approx \frac{y'(x_j + h^*) - y'(x_j)}{h^*}$$

$$= \frac{f(x_j + h^*, y(x_j + h^*)) - f(x_j, y(x_j))}{h^*}$$

$$\approx \frac{f(x_j + h^*, y(x_j) + h^*y'(x_j)) - f(x_j, y(x_j))}{h^*}$$ (7.9)

$$\approx \frac{f(x_j + h^*, y_j + h^*f(x_j, y_j)) - f(x_j, y_j)}{h^*}.$$

If we choose $h^* = \lambda h$ (λ being a constant), then by substituting this approximation into (7.8) we get the following relation:

$$y_{j+1} = y_j + h\left[\left(1 - \frac{1}{2\lambda}\right)f(x_j, y_j) + \frac{1}{2\lambda}f(x_j + \lambda h, y_j + \lambda h f(x_j, y_j))\right].$$ (7.10)

In order to simplify this lengthy equation, we introduce the following notation:

$$
\boxed{
\begin{aligned}
k_1 &= f(x_j, y_j) \\[4pt]
k_2 &= f(x_j + \lambda h, y_j + \lambda h k_1) \\[4pt]
\alpha_1 &= 1 - \frac{1}{2\lambda}, \qquad \alpha_2 = \frac{1}{2\lambda}.
\end{aligned}
}
$$ (7.11)

Then (7.10) can be rewritten,

$$\boxed{y_{j+1} = y_j + h(\alpha_1 k_1 + \alpha_2 k_2).}$$ (7.12)

This formulation is at the heart of Runge–Kutta-type methods. In the section to follow we will see that Heun's method is the special case of (7.11)–(7.12) in which $\lambda = \frac{2}{3}$. When applied to the test problem of Example 7.3, Heun's method calculates $y(1) \approx 0.349640$, whereas the true value is $y(1) = 0.350232$. Euler's method with $h = 0.1$, in Example 7.3, calculated $y(1) \approx 0.292542$. To be fair to Euler's method, it requires only 10 calls to the function $f(x, y)$, whereas Heun's method requires 20. At $h = 0.05$, Euler's method also makes 20 calls, and gives the approximation $y(1) \approx 0.3202117$, which still has about 50 times the error of Heun's method.

Plan 2. Consider again the Taylor's series representation (7.8), and approximate the derivatives y_j' and y_j'' as follows:

$$y_j' \approx y'(x_j) = f(x_j, y(x_j)) \approx f(x_j, y_j),$$

and by using the Chapter 4 derivative approximation (4.2), with h replaced by $-h$, we write

$$y''_j = \frac{y'(x_j) - y'(x_j - h)}{h} = \frac{y'(x_j) - y'(x_{j-1})}{h}$$

$$= \frac{f(x_j, y(x_j)) - f(x_{j-1}, y(x_{j-1}))}{h}$$

$$\approx \frac{f(x_j, y_j) - f(x_{j-1}, y_{j-1})}{h}.$$

Substituting these estimates into (7.8) gives the recursion

$$y_{j+1} = y_j + h[\tfrac{3}{2}f(x_j, y_j) - \tfrac{1}{2}f(x_{j-1}, y_{j-1})]. \tag{7.13}$$

By introducing the notation

$$f_{j-1} = f(x_{j-1}, y_{j-1}), \qquad f_j = f(x_j, y_j)$$

$$\beta_2 = -\tfrac{1}{2}, \qquad \beta_1 = \tfrac{3}{2},$$

recursion (7.13) can be rewritten as

$$\boxed{y_{j+1} = y_j + h(\beta_1 f_j + \beta_2 f_{j-1}).} \tag{7.14}$$

This idea generalizes to give the Adams methods, the subject of Section 7.4. In fact, (7.14) is the simplest Adams–Bashforth formula. This formula, with step size $h = 0.1$, computes $y(1) = 0.33873$ for the problem in Example 7.3. This is also more accurate than the Euler's method approximation.

7.3
RUNGE–KUTTA METHODS

7.3.1 Runge–Kutta Formulas

Recall from Section 7.2.1 that the recursive Taylor's series approach, while seemingly sufficiently accurate, was hampered by the inconvenience of requiring higher-order derivatives of the function $f(x, y)$. The Runge–Kutta method succeeds in approximating the Taylor's polynomial, without taking derivatives. The idea behind the technique was outlined in Section 7.2.3: Various exploratory steps are taken from the current location $x = x_j$ and solution estimate $y = y_j$, and the function $f(x, y)$ is evaluated at these nearby locations. These estimates are combined in such a fashion that the sum must agree with the Taylor's expansion of the solution, up to a certain power in step size h.

The (explicit) *Runge–Kutta* method for numerical solution of differential equations has us compute the approximating solution values $y_1, y_2, \ldots$ on a grid $x_1 = x_0 + h, x_2 = x_0 + 2h, \ldots$ starting from the initial condition $y_0 = y(x_0)$.

The successor estimate y_{j+1} is computed recursively from y_j $(j = 0, 1, \ldots)$ by the formula

$$y_{j+1} = y_j + h\left(\sum_{i=1}^{t} \alpha_i k_i\right), \tag{7.15}$$

where the terms k_i are computed recursively according to

$$k_1 = f(x_j, y_j), \tag{7.16}$$

and for $i = 2, \ldots, t$,

$$k_i = f\left(x_j + h\mu_i, y_j + h\left(\sum_{m=1}^{i-1} \lambda_{im} k_m\right)\right). \tag{7.17}$$

In (7.15), (7.16), and (7.17), α_i, μ_i and λ_{im}, $1 \le m \le i - 1$, $1 \le i \le t$, are parameters to be chosen to make the method as accurate as possible. The integer t in (7.15) determines the number of *stages* of the rule. Further motivation of the Runge–Kutta method and detailed analysis of the selection of the parameters for certain cases will be related in the section to follow. For now, let us simply note that the Runge–Kutta formula (7.15) allows us to obtain a Taylor's polynomial approximation of the solution $y(x)$ about x_j, and evaluated at x_{j+1}, without having to find derivatives. At this point, since (7.15) and (7.17) are a bit complicated, we offer some well-known examples of Runge–Kutta formulas and investigate their performance on our standard test problem.

───── **EXAMPLE 7.4** ─────────────────────────────────────

For one-stage rules ($t = 1$), in view of (7.15) and (7.17), the Runge–Kutta method necessarily takes the form

$$y_{j+1} = y_j + h\alpha_1 f(x_j, y_j).$$

It will be seen in the section to follow that for small h, the truncation error is minimized by taking $\alpha_1 = 1$. Therefore, the one-stage Runge–Kutta formula coincides with Euler's method, the performance of which was examined in Example 7.3.

───── **EXAMPLE 7.5** ─────────────────────────────────────

The *corrected Euler's formula* is a two-stage ($t = 2$) rule. If we define

$$\begin{aligned} k_1 &= f(x_j, y_j) \\ k_2 &= f\left(x_j + \frac{h}{2}, y_j + \frac{h}{2}k_1\right), \end{aligned} \tag{7.18}$$

TABLE 7.5 Output for the Corrected Euler's Computation

x_j	y_j	Exact Value $y(x_j)$
0.0	0.000000	0.000000
0.1	0.000250	0 000333
0.2	0.002500	0.002667
0.3	0.008752	0.009003
0.4	0.021020	0.021359
0.5	0.041354	0.041791
0.6	0.071895	0.072448
0.7	0.114958	0.115660
0.8	0.173171	0.174080
0.9	0.249692	0.250907
1.0	0.348545	0.350232

then the method is determined by the recursion

$$\boxed{y_{j+1} = y_j + hk_2.}$$ (7.19)

This is a Runge–Kutta method with $t = 2$ and

$$\alpha_1 = 0, \quad \alpha_2 = 1, \quad \mu_2 = \tfrac{1}{2}, \quad \lambda_{21} = \tfrac{1}{2}.$$

If we apply the corrected Euler's formula with $h = 0.1$ to our test equation

$$y' = x^2 + y^2, \qquad y(0) = 0,$$

for $j = 0$, our calculation proceeds as follows:

$$k_1 = x_0^2 + y_0^2 = 0^2 + 0^2 = 0$$

$$k_2 = \left(0 + \frac{0.1}{2}\right)^2 + \left(0 + \frac{0.1}{2} \cdot 0\right)^2 = 0.00250.$$

Consequently,

$$y_1 = y_0 + hk_2 = 0 + 0.1 \cdot 0.00250 = 0.000250.$$

Updating x_j and y_j and continuing this recursion, we obtain the results given in Table 7.5. ∎

EXAMPLE 7.6

The *Heun method* is a popular two-stage ($t = 2$) rule. It is determined by the parameters

$$\alpha_1 = \tfrac{1}{4}, \qquad \alpha_2 = \tfrac{3}{4}$$

$$\mu_2 = \tfrac{2}{3}, \qquad \lambda_{21} = \tfrac{2}{3}.$$

TABLE 7.6   Computational Example for Heun's Method

x_j	y_j	Exact Value, $y(x_j)$
0.0	0.000000	0.000000
0.1	0.000333	0 000333
0.2	0.002667	0.002667
0.3	0.009002	0.009003
0.4	0.021355	0.021359
0.5	0.041776	0.041791
0.6	0.072411	0.072448
0.7	0.115577	0.115660
0.8	0.173913	0.174080
0.9	0.250586	0.250907
1.0	0.349640	0.350232

Thus in the Heun method,

$$
\begin{aligned}
k_1 &= f(x_j, y_j) \\
k_2 &= f(x_j + \tfrac{2}{3}h, y_j + \tfrac{2}{3}hk_1) \\
&\text{and} \\
y_{j+1} &= y_j + h(\tfrac{1}{4}k_1 + \tfrac{3}{4}k_2).
\end{aligned}
\tag{7.20}
$$

Consider again the differential equation

$$ y' = x^2 + y^2, \qquad y(0) = 0, $$

and let $h = 0.1$. Then for $j = 0$,

$$ k_1 = 0^2 + 0^2 = 0, $$

$$ k_2 = (0 + \tfrac{2}{3} \cdot 0.1)^2 + 0^2 = 0.004444 $$

$$ y_1 = 0 + 0.1(\tfrac{1}{4} \cdot 0 + \tfrac{3}{4} \cdot 0.004444) = 0.000333. $$

Table 7.6 gives a listing of further solution values obtained by the Heun method.

∎

EXAMPLE 7.7

The most popular four-stage ($t = 4$) Runge–Kutta method is the *classical Runge–Kutta formula*, which is determined by the relations

$$
\begin{aligned}
k_1 &= f(x_j, y_j) \\
k_2 &= f(x_j + \tfrac{1}{2}h, y_j + \tfrac{1}{2}hk_1) \\
k_3 &= f(x_j + \tfrac{1}{2}h, y_j + \tfrac{1}{2}hk_2) \\
k_4 &= f(x_j + h, y_j + hk_3) \\
y_{j+1} &= y_j + \frac{h}{6}(k_1 + 2k_2 + 2k_3 + k_4).
\end{aligned}
\tag{7.21}
$$

In applying this method to our test equation

$$y' = x^2 + y^2, \qquad y(0) = 0$$

with $h = 0.1$ and $j = 0$, we get the values

$$k_1 = 0^2 + 0^2 = 0$$

$$k_2 = \left(0 + \frac{0.1}{2}\right)^2 + \left(0 + \frac{0.1}{2} \cdot 0\right)^2 = 0.0025$$

$$k_3 = \left(0 + \frac{0.1}{2}\right)^2 + \left(0 + \frac{0.1}{2} \cdot 0.0025\right)^2 \approx 0.002500$$

$$k_4 = (0 + 0.1)^2 + (0 + 0.1 \cdot 0.002500)^2 \approx 0.010000.$$

TABLE 7.7   Subroutine for the Classical Runge–Kutta Method

```
      SUBROUTINE RUKU(X,Y,N,B)
C
C  *******************************************************
C  *   FUNCTION: THIS SUBROUTINE COMPUTES THE SOLUTION OF A  *
C  *             DIFFERENTIAL EQUATION Y'=F(X,Y) OVER        *
C  *             THE INTERVAL [X(1),B] USING THE CLASSICAL   *
C  *             4-TH ORDER RUNGE-KUTTA METHOD               *
C  *   USAGE:                                                *
C  *         CALL SEQUENCE: CALL RUKU(X,Y,N,B)               *
C  *         EXTERNAL FUNCTIONS/SUBROUTINES: FUNCTION F(U,V) *
C  *   PARAMETERS:                                           *
C  *       INPUT:                                            *
C  *         X(1)=INDEPENDENT VARIABLE INITIAL VALUE         *
C  *         Y(1)=DEPENDENT VARIABLE INITIAL VALUE           *
C  *            N=NUMBER OF STEPS                             *
C  *            B=SOLUTION INTERVAL ENDPOINT (LAST X VALUE)  *
C  *       OUTPUT:                                           *
C  *            X=N+1 BY 1 ARRAY OF INDEPENDENT VARIABLE      *
C  *              VALUES                                     *
C  *            Y=N+1 BY 1 ARRAY OF DEPENDENT VARIABLE        *
C  *              SOLUTION VALUES                            *
C  *******************************************************
C
      DIMENSION X(N+1),Y(N+1)
      H=(B-X(1))/N
C     *** TJ IS AS K(J) IN THE TEXT ***
      DO 1 I=2,N+1
        X(I)=X(I-1)+H
        U=X(I-1)
        V=Y(I-1)
        T1=F(U,V)
        U=U+0.5*H
        V=V+0.5*H*T1
        T2=F(U,V)
        V=Y(I-1)+0.5*H*T2
        T3=F(U,V)
        U=U+0.5*H
        V=Y(I-1)+H*T3
        T4=F(U,V)
        Y(I)=Y(I-1)+H*(T1+2.0*T2+2.0*T3+T4)/6.0
    1 CONTINUE
      RETURN
      END
```

TABLE 7.8   Program Illustrating the Classical Runge–Kutta Method

```
C     PROGRAM RKMETH
C
C     ****************************************************************
C     THIS PROGRAM WILL SET UP AND SOLVE THE DIFFERENTIAL EQUATION
C     Y'=X**2+Y**2 WITH THE INITIAL CONDITION Y(0.)=0.
C     THE SOLUTION IS OBTAINED AT 11 GRID POINTS IN THE INTERVAL
C     [0,1] USING THE CLASSICAL RUNGE-KUTTA METHOD
C     CALLS:   RUKU
C     OUTPUT:
C              X(I)=VALUE OF X FOR I=1,11
C              Y(I)=APPROXIMATED VALUE OF Y AT X(I)
C     ****************************************************************
C
      DIMENSION X(11),Y(11)
C
C     *** FIRST, THE INITIAL CONDITION AND ENDPOINT ARE ESTABLISHED***
C
      X(1)=0.
      Y(1)=0.
      B=1.
      N=10
      N1=N+1
C
C     *** SUBROUTINE RUKU WILL APPROXIMATE THE SOLUTION         ***
C     *** RETURNING N1 VALUES IN ARRAYS X AND Y                 ***
C
      CALL RUKU(X,Y,N,B)
      WRITE(10,1)(X(I),Y(I),I=1,N1)
    1 FORMAT(5X,F4.1,5X,F10.6)
      STOP
      END
C
C     *** FUNCTION F SPECIFIES THE DIFFERENTIAL EQUATION. IT IS ***
C     *** CALLED BY SUBROUTINE RUKU                             ***
C
      FUNCTION F(X,Y)
      F=X**2+Y**2
      RETURN
      END
```

Consequently,

$$y_1 = 0 + \frac{0.1}{6}(0 + 0.005000 + 0.005000 + 0.010000)$$
$$\approx 0.000333.$$

TABLE 7.9   Output for Example 7.7

x_j	Classical Runge–Kutta, y_j	Exact Value, $y(x_j)$
0.0	0.000000	0.000000
0.1	0.000333	0 000333
0.2	0.002667	0.002667
0.3	0.009003	0.009003
0.4	0.021359	0.021359
0.5	0.041791	0.041791
0.6	0.072448	0.072448
0.7	0.115660	0.115660
0.8	0.174081	0.174080
0.9	0.250908	0.250907
1.0	0.350234	0.350232

The subroutine RUKU for this method is listed in Table 7.7. This subroutine is called by the program listed in Table 7.8, which applies the classical Runge–Kutta method to our test problem. The numerical results are presented in Table 7.9. ∎

Application 7.1

Assume that $N(t)$ denotes population size of wild rabbits, say, in an isolated area at time t. By "isolated" we mean that migration does not occur. Further, we presume that the population is relatively large so that whereas, strictly speaking, $N(t)$ is integer, nevertheless, to nearsighted eyes, a plot would look continuous. So with this argument, $N(t)$ will be viewed as a continuous function. For an animal such as a rabbit, it is reasonable to assume that if food is plentiful, the population increase depends only on the reproductive capacity of the population. On the other hand, if the population becomes too large, lack of food becomes a factor, and the rate of increase declines or even becomes negative because malnutrition enhances susceptibility to diseases and reduces reproductive capacity.

An elementary model quantifying these effects (e.g., Haberman, 1977, Sec. 34) is based on a differential equation of the form

$$N' = R(N)N.$$

The function $R(N)$ is called the population *growth rate*. The most elementary model assumes that $R(N) = R$, a constant, and the solution is the exponential growth function,

$$N(t) = N(t_0) \exp [R(t - t_0)].$$

Here $N(t_0)$ is the population at initial time t_0.

This model implies that the population increases ever more rapidly and without bound. This seems unreasonable, and the next level of complexity is the postulation that $R(N)$ is a line with negative slope. The root of this line (sketched in Figure 7.2) would be a point at which the derivative is zero, that is, a point at which the population remains constant. This point $N_C = a/b$ is sometimes spoken

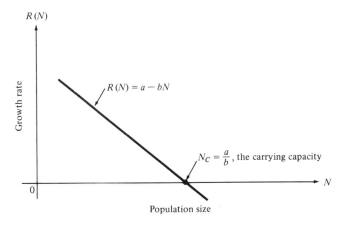

FIGURE 7.2 Linear Growth Rate Function

of appropriately as the "carrying capacity" of the population. The implication, then, is that the population grows according to the differential equation

$$N' = (a - bN)N.$$

This model is known as the *logistic* equation. For $N \ll N_C$, the population does grow nearly exponentially, since $R(N) \approx a$ is nearly constant. As N increases the derivative converges to 0, and the population tends to the constant, $N_C = a/b$. If somehow N were larger than the carrying capacity, then the growth rate would be negative and the population would decline toward the carrying capacity.

Suppose that at time 0, there are $N(0) = 500$ rabbits, and $a = 1.0$ and $b = 10^{-3}$. We wish to know how many rabbits there will be at time $t = 1$. Our plan will be to apply the classical Runge–Kutta rule [equation (7.21)] by means of subroutine RUKU (Table 7.7). Now the key question, of course, is: What size should step size h be? An intuitive answer is, small enough that if we halve the step size from h to $h/2$, the solution does not change much. (In Section 7.8, more sophisticated notations for step-size choice are offered.) Our computation plan began by starting with $h = 1$ and successively solving the population equation with $h = 1, \frac{1}{2}, \frac{1}{4}, \ldots$ until to five places, the computed approximation of $N(1)$ remained unchanged from the last run. Our findings are summarized as follows:

Step Size, h	Population at $t = 1$, $N(1)$
1	730.9103
1/2	731.0474
1/4	731.0579
1/8	731.0585
1/16	731.0586

Intuitively, from the regularity of these numbers, we feel confident that to six or seven significant digits, the exact solution is 731.0586. It turns out (Haberman, 1977) that the logistics equation has an analytic solution which agrees with our computed solution to the accuracy shown. ◇

★7.3.2 Parameter Selection for Runge–Kutta Formulas

Later in this section we give some rationale for selection of the number t of stages. For now, assume that t has already been chosen. Attention focuses on choice of the parameters α_i, μ_i, and λ_{im} in (7.15) and (7.17) for our fixed number t.

The central principle of the Runge–Kutta approach is that the parameters should be chosen so that a power series expansion in h of the right side of (7.15) agrees with the Taylor's series expansion of $y(x_j + h)$ for as high a power of h as possible. Let $y(x)$ denote the solution of the differential equation $y' = f(x, y)$, which passes through the point (x_j, y_j). Let us represent the heady expression on the right side of (7.15) by $g(x_j, y_j, h)$, where we have presumably accounted for the dependence of the k_i's on h through (7.17). Then

$$y_{j+1} = y_j + hg(x_j, y_j, h).$$

As we have mentioned above, the idea behind the Runge–Kutta approach is to choose the parameters so that for as large an integer p as possible, the pth-degree Taylor's polynomial in h of the solution $y(x_{j+1}) = y(x_j + h)$ coincides with the Taylor's polynomial of $y_j + hg(x_j, y_j, h)$. That is, we choose parameters so that for maximial p,

$$\sum_{q=0}^{p} \frac{y^{(q)}(x_j)}{q!} h^q = y_j + h \sum_{q=0}^{p-1} \frac{\dfrac{d^q}{dh^q} g(x_j, y_j, h)}{q!} h^q. \tag{7.22}$$

Equating coefficients of the qth power of h in (7.22) and placing derivatives of $g(x_j, y_j, h)$ with those of the defining expression (7.15), we obtain the criterion for determining the Runge–Kutta parameters: namely, for $q = 0$ we get the relation, $y(x_j) = y_j$, and for $q = 1, 2, \ldots, p$,

$$y^{(q)}(x_j) = q \left. \frac{d^{q-1}}{dh^{q-1}} \left[\sum_{i=1}^{t} \alpha_i f\left(x_j + h\mu_i, y_j + h \sum_{m=1}^{i-1} \lambda_{im} k_m \right) \right] \right|_{h=0}. \tag{7.23}$$

The parameter design criterion has us choose parameters α_i, μ_i, and λ_{im} so that (7.23) holds for as large an integer p as possible over all sufficiently many times differentiable functions $y(x)$ and $f(x, y)$, with $y'(x)$ and $f(x, y)$ related by $y' = f(x, y)$. Observe that (7.16) implies that in (7.23), $\mu_1 = 0$. As we will see in the example to follow, the procedure involves expressing $y^{(q)}(x_j)$ explicitly in terms of $f(x_j, y_j)$ and its derivatives, through (7.4), and then equating like coefficients of these derivatives.

The criterion (7.23) appears formidable, and indeed for moderate to large values of t, its detailed implementation is messy. But the next pair of examples will help to illustrate that the idea behind the use of (7.23) for constructing Runge–Kutta parameters is straightforward, if tedious.

The criterion (7.23) is appealing in the following sense: For any method of type (7.15) not satisfying (7.23), we may anticipate that there is some Runge–Kutta formula with the same number t of stages which is ultimately more accurate as h gets smaller.

EXAMPLE 7.8

Let $t = 1$. Then in view of (7.15), the only parameter to be selected is α_1. From (7.23), with $q = 1$, we have

$$y'(x_j) = \alpha_1 f(x_j, y_j).$$

But necessarily, $y'(x_j) = f(x_j, y_j)$, so to satisfy (7.23), with $q = 1$, we must set $\alpha_1 = 1$. Thus the one-stage Runge–Kutta rule coincides with the Euler method. ∎

EXAMPLE 7.9

Let $t = 2$. Then

$$y_{j+1} = y_j + h[\alpha_1 f(x_j, y_j) + \alpha_2 f(x_j + h\mu_2, y_j + h\lambda_{21} f(x_j, y_j))].$$

From (7.23), with $q = 1$, we have

$$y'(x_j) = f(x_j, y_j) = (\alpha_1 + \alpha_2)f(x_j, y_j). \tag{7.24}$$

For $q = 2$, and by use of the chain rule (Appendix B, property 36) as in (7.4),

$$
\begin{aligned}
y''(x_j) &= f_x(x_j, y_j) + f_y(x_j, y_j)f(x_j, y_j) \\
&= 2\alpha_2[\mu_2 f_x(x_j, y_j) + \lambda_{21} f_y(x_j, y_j)f(x_j, y_j)].
\end{aligned}
\tag{7.25}
$$

In the above, subscripts of f denote partial derivatives with respect to the indicated variable. Equations (7.24) and (7.25) must hold for every possible $f(x_j, y_j)$, $f_x(x_j, y_j)$, and $f_y(x_j, y_j)$. So, for example, from (7.24) we must have $\alpha_1 + \alpha_2 = 1$. By equating like coefficients of $f_x(x_j, y_j)$ in (7.25), we have that $2\alpha_2\mu_2 = 1$, and from the coefficients of $f_y(x_j, y_j)f(x_j, y_j)$, we see that $2\alpha_2\lambda_{21} = 1$. Collecting these relations, we may assert that every two-stage Runge–Kutta formula satisfies

$$
\boxed{
\begin{aligned}
\alpha_1 + \alpha_2 &= 1 \\[4pt]
2\alpha_2\mu_2 &= 1 \\[4pt]
2\alpha_2\lambda_{21} &= 1.
\end{aligned}
}
\tag{7.26}
$$

The two-stage Heun method (see Example 7.6) with $\alpha_1 = \frac{1}{4}$, $\alpha_2 = \frac{3}{4}$, $\mu_2 = \frac{2}{3}$, and $\lambda_{21} = \frac{2}{3}$ satisfies these conditions, as does the corrected Euler method, with parameters $\alpha_1 = 0$, $\alpha_2 = 1$, $\mu_2 = \frac{1}{2}$, and $\lambda_{21} = \frac{1}{2}$. Since there are more unknowns than equations, system (7.26) has infinitely many solutions. Thus there are infinitely many two-stage rules satisfying (7.23) for $p = 2$. One may confirm that for $p = 3$ in (7.23) there are more conditions than unknowns. Consequently, no parameter set for a two-stage rule satisfies (7.23) for $p = 3$. ∎

In the introductory section of Chapter 4 we said that a function $g(h)$ was $O(h^q)$ if for some positive number C,

$$|g(h)| \leq C|h|^q$$

whenever $|h|$ is small enough. We say that a Runge–Kutta method is of order p if after one step of size h, and with $y_0 = y(x_0)$,

$$|y_1 - y(x_1)| = |y_1 - y(x_0 + h)| = O(h^{p+1}).$$

If two power series in h agree through the pth power, their difference is $O(h^{p+1})$, as the reader may check. Therefore, if a Runge–Kutta rule satisfies (7.23) for a certain number p, it is pth order. By construction, the single-stage rule (Euler's method) is first order, and the two-stage rules given in Examples 7.5 and 7.6 are second order. The classical four-stage Runge–Kutta rule is known to be fourth order. Above four stages, the order is less than the number of stages. Up to 11 stage rules, the relation between the order and number of stages (see Butcher, 1964) is as summarized in Table 7.10.

To illustrate forcefully that the order of a Runge–Kutta method has practical merit, we mention a result (derived in Henrici, 1962, for example) that for a

TABLE 7.10   Attainable Runge–Kutta Method Order p as Function of Number of Stages t

Number of Stages, t	1	2	3	4	5	6	7	8	9	10	11
Attainable Order, p	1	2	3	4	4	5	6	6	7	8	9

differential equation having a solution on a finite interval $[x_0, b]$, and for the sequence $y_0, y_1, y_2, \ldots$ determined by a pth-order Runge–Kutta method, and $y(x)$ the solution of (7.3),

$$\max_{0 \le k \le N} |y(x_0 + kh) - y_k| = O(h^p), \qquad (7.27)$$

where $x_0 + Nh = b$. This result can be interpreted as follows. In one step the error of the approximating solution is $O(h^{p+1})$, but these errors are accumulating during the entire calculation. Inequality (7.27) guarantees that the accumulated error is $O(h^p)$. We may summarize by saying that the order of the accumulated error equals the order of the method.

──── **EXAMPLE 7.10** ──

We used subroutine RUKU (Table 7.7) with various step sizes h on our test equation

$$y' = x^2 + y^2, \qquad y(0) = 0,$$

to indicate a consequence of (7.27) that $|y(1) - y_{N(h)}| = O(h^4)$, where $N(h) = 1/h$, 4 being the order of the classical Runge–Kutta method, as mentioned. By undertaking our calculations in double precision, Table 7.11 was compiled. In the rightmost column we see that the error, when divided by h^4, tends to a constant as h decreases.

In theory, for any differential equation with a "smooth" solution, as the step size h becomes smaller, the higher the value of p in (7.23) is, the more accurate the Runge–Kutta solution approximation will be. Experience will confirm that for a fixed step size, higher-order Runge–Kutta rules do enhance the accuracy of the computation. For instance, in comparing Examples 7.3, 7.5, and 7.7, we see that by successively increasing t from 1 to 2, and then to 4, the estimates of $y(1)$ have increased in accuracy from one significant place to five, without much change in programming or computational effort. Computation of the solution of the differ-

TABLE 7.11   Illustration of Order of Error for the Classical Runge–Kutta Method

h	Error	Error$/h^4$
0.500000	-0.5550E-03	-0.008881
0.250000	-0.5745E-04	-0.014707
0.125000	-0.4449E-05	-0.018225
0.062500	-0.3070E-06	-0.020120
0.031250	-0.2005E-07	-0.021025
0.015625	-0.1214E-08	-0.020367

ential equation in our examples to five-place accuracy by Euler's method would require on the order of 1000-fold increase in computational effort over that required by Table 7.9.

∎

In practice, specialists prefer Runge–Kutta methods with stage numbers between 4 and 6. These families of Runge–Kutta methods provide sufficient accuracy for well-behaved problems. In order for a great number of stages (say 10 or higher) to be advantageous, we would have to use large step size h; but for large step sizes, the Taylor's polynomial approximations motivating the Runge–Kutta method become unreliable.

7.4
ADAMS AND LINEAR MULTISTEP METHODS

Runge–Kutta methods are referred to as *single-step methods* because, as is readily seen by inspection of (7.15), y_{j+1} depends on y_j, but not on "steps" $y_{j-1}, y_{j-2}, \ldots$, further back in the past. The methods to be considered next are *multistep methods*: y_{j+1} will depend on at least one of the past values $y_{j-1}, y_{j-2}, \ldots$. Assume again that the solution of the initial-value problem (7.3) is to be calculated at node points in an interval $[x_0, b]$. Define step size h by $h = (b - x_0)/N$, where $N > 1$ is a given integer. As in the case of the single-step methods, the solution will be approximated at the set of node points $x_j = x_0 + jh$ ($j = 0, 1, 2, \ldots, N$). Assume that the approximations $y_0, y_1, \ldots, y_j$ of $y(x_0), y(x_1), \ldots, y(x_j)$ are already available. Then the subsequent value y_{j+1} can be calculated recursively according to the *linear multistep method*, which has the general form

$$ y_{j+1} = -\sum_{m=1}^{i} \alpha_m y_{j+1-m} + h \sum_{m=0}^{i} \beta_m f_{j+1-m}, \qquad (7.28) $$

where

$$ f_{j+1-m} = f(x_{j+1-m}, y_{j+1-m}). $$

The integer i and the coefficients α_m and β_m are the parameters of the method. The rule (7.28) is explicit only if $\beta_0 = 0$. Otherwise, the function value $f_{j+1} = f(x_{j+1}, y_{j+1})$ appears on the right-hand side. This depends on the unknown value y_{j+1}. In such a case (the "implicit" case), a nonlinear equation must be solved for y_{j+1}.

The literature of multistep mehods concentrates on a certain subfamily, the *Adams methods*. These methods are characterized by the constraints that

$$ \alpha_1 = -1 \text{ and } \alpha_m = 0, \qquad \text{for } m > 1. \qquad (7.29) $$

The Adams method coefficients β_m are chosen so that the truncation error $y(x_j + h) - y_{j+1}$ is of as high an order as possible in step size h. We defer details to (S & Y, 1978, Sec. 8.1.4). But a procedure is outlined in Problem 16.

One reason for specialization in Adams methods is that outside this class, the linear multistep algorithms are often found to be unstable, in the sense that the

TABLE 7.12   Coefficients for Adams–Bashforth Formulas

Number of Steps, i	β_1	β_2	β_3	β_4	β_5
2	$\dfrac{3}{2}$	$-\dfrac{1}{2}$			
3	$\dfrac{23}{12}$	$-\dfrac{16}{12}$	$\dfrac{5}{12}$		
4	$\dfrac{55}{24}$	$-\dfrac{59}{24}$	$\dfrac{37}{24}$	$-\dfrac{9}{24}$	
5	$\dfrac{1901}{720}$	$-\dfrac{2774}{720}$	$\dfrac{2616}{720}$	$-\dfrac{1276}{720}$	$\dfrac{251}{720}$

TABLE 7.13   Subroutine for the Third-Order Adams–Bashforth Method

```
      SUBROUTINE ADAMS(X,Y,N,B)
C
C     ********************************************************
C     *   FUNCTION: THIS SUBROUTINE COMPUTES THE SOLUTION OF A   *
C     *             DIFFERENTIAL EQUATION OVER THE INTERVAL      *
C     *             [X(1),B] USING THE DEFINING FUNCTION F(U,V)  *
C     *             AND THE EXPLICIT 3-STEP ADAMS-BASHFORTH      *
C     *             METHOD                                       *
C     *   USAGE:                                                 *
C     *       CALL SEQUENCE: CALL ADAMS(X,Y,N,B)                 *
C     *       EXTERNAL FUNCTIONS/SUBROUTINES: FUNCTION F(U,V)    *
C     *   PARAMETERS:                                            *
C     *       INPUT:                                             *
C     *           N=NUMBER OF ITERATIONS (<1000)                *
C     *       X(1),X(2),X(3)                                     *
C     *           =INDEPENDENT VARIABLE INITIAL VALUES           *
C     *           B=SOLUTION INTERVAL ENDPOINT (LAST X VALUE)    *
C     *       Y(1),Y(2),Y(3)                                     *
C     *           =DEPENDENT VARIABLE INITIAL SOLUTION VALUES    *
C     *       OUTPUT:                                            *
C     *           X=N+1 BY 1 ARRAY OF INDEPENDENT VARIABLE       *
C     *             VALUES                                       *
C     *           Y=N+1 BY 1 ARRAY OF DEPENDENT VARIABLE         *
C     *             SOLUTION VALUES                              *
C     ********************************************************
C
      DIMENSION X(N+1),Y(N+1),T(1001)
C     *** INITIALIZATION ***
      H=(B-X(1))/N
      DO 1 I=1,3
         U=X(I)
         V=Y(I)
         T(I)=F(U,V)
    1 CONTINUE
C     *** COMPUTE ITERATIVE SOLUTION ***
      DO 2 I=4,N+1
         X(I)=X(I-1)+H
         Y(I)=Y(I-1)+H*(23.0*T(I-1)-16.0*T(I-2)+5.0*T(I-3))/12.0
         U=X(I)
         V=Y(I)
         T(I)=F(U,V)
    2 CONTINUE
      RETURN
      END
```

error increases exponentially as it propagates with increasing j in (7.28). But even among stable linear multistep rules, the Adams methods have certain attractive theoretical features with respect to error attenuation. Another reason for their popularity is that the implementation of the Adams methods is particularly easy.

In view of the constraint (7.29), Adams methods are characterized by the formula

$$y_{j+1} = y_j + h \sum_{m=0}^{i} \beta_m f_{j+1-m}. \qquad (7.30)$$

In the case that β_0 in (7.30) is constrained to be zero, we have what are known as the *Adams–Bashforth* methods. These methods have the feature that they are explicit in the sense that the right side of (7.30) will not depend on the unknown y_{j+1}. The coefficients of the first several Adams–Bashforth formulas are given in Table 7.12, and subroutine ADAMS for implementing the three-step Adams–Bashforth formula is provided by Table 7.13.

─────── **EXAMPLE 7.11** ───

By the use of the three-step Adams–Bashforth formula, we solve our standard test equation

$$y' = x^2 + y^2, \qquad y(0) = 0.$$

From Table 7.12 we see that the formula to be used has the form

$$y_{j+1} = y_j + h \left(\frac{23}{12} f_j - \frac{16}{12} f_{j-1} + \frac{5}{12} f_{j-2} \right).$$

We first illustrate the use of this formula for $h = 0.1$ and $j = 2$ (since this is the smallest value of j for which the method can be applied). The values y_1 and y_2 are taken as the values obtained in the classical Runge–Kutta computation (Example 7.7). Thus to start the computation, we have the values

$$y_0 = 0, \qquad y_1 = 0.000333, \qquad y_2 = 0.002667.$$

Then

$$f_0 = x_0^2 + y_0^2 = 0^2 + 0^2 = 0$$
$$f_1 = x_1^2 + y_1^2 = (0.1)^2 + (0.000333)^2 \approx 0.010000$$
$$f_2 = x_2^2 + y_2^2 = (0.2)^2 + (0.002667)^2 \approx 0.040007,$$

and consequently,

$$y_3 = 0.002667 + 0.1 \left(\frac{23}{12} \cdot 0.040007 - \frac{16}{12} \cdot 0.010000 + \frac{5}{12} \cdot 0 \right)$$

$$\approx 0.009002.$$

We have performed the complete calculations by means of the calling program listed in Table 7.14, for obtaining the values $y_3, y_4, \ldots, y_{10}$ of the solution. The results are reported in Table 7.15.

TABLE 7.14 Program to Exemplify the Adams Method

```
C     PROGRAM ABMETH
C
C     *****************************************************************
C     THIS PROGRAM WILL SET UP AND SOLVE NUMERICALLY THE DIFFERENTIAL
C     EQUATION Y'=X**2+Y**2 WITH THE INITIAL CONDITION Y(0.)=0.
C     THE SOLUTION IS OBTAINED AT 11 POINTS OVER THE INTERVAL [0,1]
C     USING THE THREE STEP ADAMS-BASHFORTH METHOD
C     CALLS:    ADAMS
C     OUTPUT:
C               X(I)=VALUE OF X FOR I=1,11
C               Y(I)=APPROXIMATED VALUE OF Y AT X(I)
C     *****************************************************************
C
      DIMENSION X(11),Y(11)
C
C     *** FIRST, THE INITIAL VALUES AND ENDPOINT ARE DEFINED       ***
C
      H=.1
      X(1)=0.
      X(2)=H
      X(3)=2*H
      Y(1)=0.
      Y(2)=.000333
      Y(3)=.002667
      B=1.
      N=10
C
C     *** SUBROUTINE ADAMS WILL APPROXIMATE THE SOLUTION          ***
C     *** RETURNING 11 VALUES IN ARRAYS X AND Y                   ***
C
      CALL ADAMS(X,Y,N,B)
      WRITE(10,1)(X(I),Y(I),I=1,11)
    1 FORMAT(5X,F4.1,5X,F10.6)
      STOP
      END
C
C     *** FUNCTION F SPECIFIES THE DIFFERENTIAL EQUATION. IT IS    ***
C     *** CALLED BY SUBROUTINE ADAMS                              ***
C
      FUNCTION F(X,Y)
      F=X**2+Y**2
      RETURN
      END
```

TABLE 7.15   Output for Adams–Bashforth Example

x_j	y_j	Exact Value, $y(x_j)$
0.0	0.000000	0.000000
0.1	0.000333	0 000333
0.2	0.002667	0.002667
0.3	0.009002	0.009003
0.4	0.021350	0.021359
0.5	0.041760	0.041791
0.6	0.072370	0.072448
0.7	0.115494	0.115660
0.8	0.173758	0.174080
0.9	0.250318	0.250907
1.0	0.349191	0.350232

TABLE 7.16   Coefficients for Adams–Moulton Formulas

Number of Steps, i	β_0	β_1	β_2	β_3	β_4
1	$\dfrac{1}{2}$	$\dfrac{1}{2}$	0	0	0
2	$\dfrac{5}{12}$	$\dfrac{8}{12}$	$-\dfrac{1}{12}$	0	0
3	$\dfrac{9}{24}$	$\dfrac{19}{24}$	$-\dfrac{5}{24}$	$\dfrac{1}{24}$	0
4	$\dfrac{251}{720}$	$\dfrac{646}{720}$	$-\dfrac{264}{720}$	$\dfrac{106}{720}$	$-\dfrac{19}{720}$

When in (7.30), $\beta_0 \neq 0$, the right-hand side depends on the unknown value of y_{j+1} [since $f_{j+1} = f(x_{j+1}, y_{j+1})$], and we have an *implicit* Adams formula. This class of Adams formulas is known as the *Adams–Moulton method*. Of course, such implicit equations entail solving a nonlinear equation problem for y_{j+1}. Nevertheless, for certain types of differential equations (notably what are known as "stiff" differential equations), the Adams–Moulton class has certain theoretical and practical appeal in comparison to Adams–Bashforth formulas. For that reason, they are useful despite the technical complications arising from their being implicit. The coefficients of the first few Adams–Moulton formulas are summarized in Table 7.16.

A common procedure for implementing an Adams–Moulton method is to use it conjunctively with an Adams–Bashforth formula of like number of steps, as follows. Assume that values $y_j, \ldots, y_{j+1-i}$ have already been obtained. Let y_{j+1}^I denote a "predictor" of y_{j+1} obtained from the (explicit) Adams–Bashforth formula. Then define f_{j+1}^I to be $f(x_{j+1}, y_{j+1}^I)$ and construct the "corrected" y_{j+1}^{II} according to the Adams–Moulton formula, but with f_{j+1}^I replacing f_{j+1} in (7.30). Some authors recommend continuing the "correction" process by computing f_{j+1}^{II} from y_{j+1}^{II}, and substituting this new corrector f_{j+1}^{II} into the Adams–Moulton formula and continuing such iterations until magnitudes of successive corrections are less than some chosen threshold. Other authors argue that refinement of corrections is not computationally tenable. Regardless of whether subsequent correction iterations are used, conjunctive application of Adams–Bashforth and Adams–Moulton methods are known as *predictor–corrector methods*.

7.5
SIMULTANEOUS AND HIGHER-ORDER DIFFERENTIAL EQUATIONS

In many applications we are required to solve a system of several first-order differential equations with several unknown functions. The initial value problems of such equations may be expressed as

$$y_1'(x) = f_1(x, y_1(x), \ldots, y_n(x)), \qquad y_1(x_0) = y_{10}$$

$$y_2'(x) = f_2(x, y_1(x), \ldots, y_n(x)), \qquad y_2(x_0) = y_{20} \qquad (7.31)$$

$$\vdots \qquad\qquad \vdots \qquad\qquad\qquad \vdots$$

$$y_n'(x) = f_n(x, y_1(x), \ldots, y_n(x)), \qquad y_n(x_0) = y_{n0}.$$

It is convenient to write this system in a vector form by introducing the notation

$$\mathbf{y}(x) = (y_1(x), \ldots, y_n(x))^T, \quad \mathbf{f}(x, \mathbf{y}(x)) = (f_1(x, \mathbf{y}(x)), \ldots, f_n(x, \mathbf{y}(x))^T$$

and

$$\mathbf{y}_0 = (y_{10}, \ldots, y_{n0})^T.$$

In this notation (7.31) becomes

$$\boxed{\mathbf{y}'(x) = \mathbf{f}(x, \mathbf{y}(x)), \qquad \mathbf{y}(x_0) = \mathbf{y}_0.} \qquad (7.32)$$

The point of this section is that our earlier Runge–Kutta and linear multistep methods can readily be applied to solve simultaneous first-order differential equations.

Before exploring details of the solution of (7.32), we first present a standard device for converting higher-order differential equations into first-order simultaneous equations. This extends the domain of application of the techniques to be described. The initial value problem of a kth-order differential equation has the form

$$\boxed{\begin{aligned} y^{(k)}(x) &= f(x, y(x), y'(x), \ldots, y^{(k-1)}(x)), \\ y^{(j)}(x_0) &= y_0^{(j)} \qquad (0 \leq j \leq k - 1) \end{aligned}} \qquad (7.33)$$

relating the kth-order derivative of $y(x)$ to derivatives of lower order. Here y and f are real-valued functions of the indicated variables, and $y_0^{(j)}$ $(0 \leq j \leq k - 1)$ are given numbers: Equation (7.33) can be reduced to a simultaneous system of first-order equations by introducing the new variables

$$y_1(x) = y(x), \quad y_2(x) = y'(x), \ldots, y_k(x) = y^{(k-1)}(x).$$

For then, (7.33) can be written as

$$\begin{aligned} y_1'(x) &= y_2(x), & y_1(x_0) &= y_0^{(0)} \\ y_2'(x) &= y_3(x), & y_2(x_0) &= y_0^{(1)} \\ & \cdots & & \cdots \\ y_{k-1}'(x) &= y_k(x), & y_{k-1}(x_0) &= y_0^{(k-2)} \\ y_k'(x) &= f(x, y_1(x), \ldots, y_k(x)), & y_k(x_0) &= y_0^{(k-1)}. \end{aligned} \qquad (7.34)$$

That is, in this case, (7.34) has the structure (7.32), where

$$\mathbf{y}(x) = \begin{bmatrix} y_1(x) \\ \vdots \\ y_{k-1}(x) \\ y_k(x) \end{bmatrix}, \qquad \mathbf{y}_0 = \begin{bmatrix} y_0^{(0)} \\ \vdots \\ y_0^{(k-2)} \\ y_0^{(k-1)} \end{bmatrix}$$

and

$$\mathbf{f}(x, \mathbf{y}(x)) = \begin{bmatrix} y_2(x) \\ \vdots \\ y_k(x) \\ f(x, \mathbf{y}(x)) \end{bmatrix}.$$

─────── **EXAMPLE 7.12** ───────────────────────────────────────

Consider the second-order differential equation

$$y''(x) = y(x)y'(x) + x^2 + 1$$

with initial conditions

$$y(0) = y'(0) = 0.$$

Then by introducing the new variables

$$y_1(x) = y(x), \qquad y_2(x) = y'(x)$$

we get

$$
\begin{aligned}
y_1'(x) &= y_2(x) & y_1(0) &= 0 \\
y_2'(x) &= y_1(x)y_2(x) + x^2 + 1 & y_2(0) &= 0,
\end{aligned}
\tag{7.35}
$$

which is an initial-value problem for a system of two first-order differential equations with two unknown functions, $y_1(x)$ and $y_2(x)$.
■

Although there are numerical methods specifically devoted to the simultaneous differential equation problem, it turns out that the obvious vector generalizations of the univariate techniques described earlier in this chapter are usually adequate and effective. If the reader will inspect the Runge–Kutta- and Adams-type formulas, he or she will see that they continue to have meaning if the variables y and the derivative functions $f(x, y)$ are presumed to be vector valued. Thus with this understanding, our methodology for single differential equations is directly applicable.

The subroutine MRUKU listed in Table 7.17 is an obvious multivariable gen-

TABLE 7.17   Subroutine MRUKU for Multivariate Runge–Kutta Method

```
      SUBROUTINE MRUKU(X,Y,N,B,M)
C
C     **************************************************************
C     *  FUNCTION: THIS SUBROUTINE COMPUTES THE SOLUTION TO A SET*
C     *            OF SIMULTANEOUS DIFFERENTIAL EQUATIONS OVER    *
C     *            THE INTERVAL [X(1),B] GIVEN THE J-TH COORDIN-  *
C     *            ATE OF THE DEFINING FUNCTION F(U,V,J) AND      *
C     *            USING THE 4-TH ORDER RUNGE-KUTTA METHOD        *
C     *  USAGE:                                                   *
C     *       CALL SEQUENCE: CALL MRUKU(X,Y,N,B,M)               *
C     *       EXTERNAL FUNCTIONS/SUBROUTINES: FUNCTION F(U,V,J)   *
C     *  PARAMETERS:                                              *
C     *       INPUT:                                              *
C     *            M=NUMBER OF DIFFERENTIAL EQUATIONS             *
C     *            (MAXIMUM OF 100)                               *
C     *         X(1)=INDEPENDENT VARIABLE INITIAL VALUE           *
C     *         Y(1,1),Y(2,1),...,Y(M,1)                          *
C     *            =DEPENDENT VARIABLE INITIAL VALUES             *
C     *            B=SOLUTION INTERVAL ENDPOINT (LAST X VALUE)    *
C     *            N=NUMBER OF MRUKU STEPS                        *
C     *       OUTPUT:                                             *
C     *            X=N+1 BY 1 ARRAY OF INDEPENDENT VARIABLE       *
C     *            VALUES                                         *
C     *            Y=M BY N+1 ARRAY OF DEPENDENT VARIABLE SOLU-   *
C     *            TION VALUES (EACH ARRAY ROW IS THE SOLUTION    *
C     *            FOR ONE OF THE M DIFFERENTIAL EQUATIONS)       *
C     **************************************************************
C
      DIMENSION X(N+1),Y(M,N+1),V(100),T(100,4)
      H=(B-X(1))/N
      DO 1 I=2,N+1
        X(I)=X(I-1)+H
        U=X(I-1)
        DO 2 J=1,M
          V(J)=Y(J,I-1)
 2      CONTINUE
        DO 3 J=1,M
          T(J,1)=F(U,V,J)
 3      CONTINUE
        U=U+0.5*H
        DO 4 J=1,M
          V(J)=V(J)+0.5*H*T(J,1)
 4      CONTINUE
        DO 5 J=1,M
          T(J,2)=F(U,V,J)
 5      CONTINUE
        DO 6 J=1,M
          V(J)=Y(J,I-1)+0.5*H*T(J,2)
 6      CONTINUE
        DO 7 J=1,M
          T(J,3)=F(U,V,J)
 7      CONTINUE
        U=U+0.5*H
        DO 8 J=1,M
          V(J)=Y(J,I-1)+H*T(J,3)
 8      CONTINUE
        DO 9 J=1,M
          T(J,4)=F(U,V,J)
 9      CONTINUE
        DO 10 J=1,M
          Y(J,I)=Y(J,I-1)+H*(T(J,1)+2.0*T(J,2)+2.0*T(J,3)+T(J,4))/6.0
 10     CONTINUE
 1    CONTINUE
      RETURN
      END
```

eralization of the classical Runge–Kutta rule RUKU (Table 7.7). The number of simultaneous equations is entered as calling parameter M, and the derivative function $\mathbf{f}(x, \mathbf{y})$ in (7.32) is presumed supplied by an external function program F(X.Y.J), where Y is an array of dimension M, and J denotes the index of the coordinate of $\mathbf{f}(x, \mathbf{y})$ to be obtained at that evaluation.

Application 7.2

The two dimensional "predator–prey" model

$$y_1' = \gamma_1 y_1 - \gamma_2 y_1 y_2 \tag{7.36}$$

$$y_2' = -\gamma_3 y_2 + \gamma_4 y_1 y_2 \tag{7.37}$$

has appeared prominently in recent texts on mathematical modeling and numerical methods for differential equations. Here $y_1(t)$ represents the prey and $y_2(t)$ the

TABLE 7.18 Calling Program for Example 7.13

```
C       PROGRAM MRKMETH
C
C       ********************************************************************
C       THIS PROGRAM WILL SET UP AND SOLVE NUMERICALLY THE PAIR OF
C       DIFFERENTIAL EQUATIONS Y1'=.25*Y1-.01*Y1*Y2 AND Y2'=-Y2+.01*Y1*Y2
C       WITH THE INITIAL CONDITION Y1(0.)=80., Y2(0.)=30.
C       THE SOLUTION IS OBTAINED AT 25 POINTS OVER THE INTERVAL [0,80]
C       USING MULTIVARIATE 4-TH ORDER RUNGE-KUTTA METHOD
C       CALLS:    MRUKU
C       OUTPUT:
C                 X(I)=VALUE OF X FOR I=1,25
C                 Y(J,I)=APPROXIMATED VALUE OF Y1 AND Y2 AT X(I)
C       ********************************************************************
C
        DIMENSION X(26),Y(2,26)
C
C       *** FIRST, THE INITIAL CONDITION AND ENDPOINT ARE ESTABLISHED ***
C
        Y(1,1)=80.
        Y(2,1)=30.
        X(1)=0.
        B=80.
        N=25
C
C       *** SUBROUTINE MRUKU WILL APPROXIMATE THE SOLUTION         ***
C       *** RETURNING N+1 VALUES IN ARRAYS X AND Y                ***
C
        CALL MRUKU(X,Y,N,B,2)
        WRITE(10,1)(X(I),Y(1,I),Y(2,I),I=1,N+1)
      1 FORMAT(5X,F4.1,5X,F10.6,5X,F10.6)
        STOP
        END
C
C       *** FUNCTION F SPECIFIES THE DIFFERENTIAL EQUATION. IT IS  ***
C       *** CALLED BY SUBROUTINE MRUKU                            ***
C
        FUNCTION F(X,Y,M)
        DIMENSION Y(2)
        IF(M.EQ.1) THEN
            F=.25*Y(1)-.01*Y(1)*Y(2)
        ELSE
            F=-Y(2)+.01*Y(1)*Y(2)
        ENDIF
        RETURN
        END
```

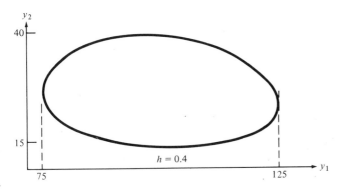

FIGURE 7.3 Computed Two-Dimensional Predator–Prey Trajectory with $h = 0.4$

predator, and the first term on the right in (7.36) tells us that the population growth
per unit time is proportional to the prey population, and the second, that the
decrease rate (per unit time) is proportional to the product of the population of
prey and predator. The right side of (7.37) implies that the predator growth is
negatively proportional to the predator population (presumably reflecting compe-
tition) and is positively proportional to the product of the two populations. The
prey population influences the growth rate of the predators by way of nutrient.

From the computational standpoint, an interesting aspect of the predator-prey
equation is that its solution is known (e.g., Haberman, 1977, Sec. 48) to be
periodic. That is, for some positive number T, and all t,

$$y_j(t + T) = y_j(t), \qquad j = 1, 2.$$

If one plots the points $(y_1(t), y_2(t))$ in the $y_1 - y_2$-plane, the solution curve must
therefore be closed. An inadequate numerical solution will manifest itself by
producing "phase-plane" $y_1 - y_2$ curves that do not close on themselves.

By means of the calling program listed in Table 7.18, we have utilized MRUKU
to produce phase-plane plots. Following Ortega and Poole (1981), we have chosen
as parameters and initial condition, the numbers

$$\gamma_1 = 0.25, \qquad \gamma_2 = 0.01, \qquad \gamma_3 = 1.0$$

$$\gamma_4 = 0.01, \qquad y_1(0) = 80, \qquad y_2(0) = 30.$$

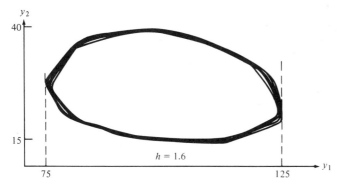

FIGURE 7.4 Computed Two-Dimensional Predator–Prey Trajectory with $h = 1.6$

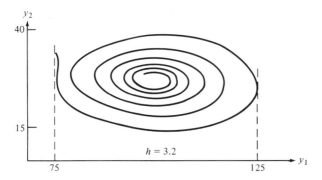

FIGURE   7.5   Computed   Two-Dimensional Predator–Prey Trajectory with $h = 3.2$

In Figures 7.3 to 7.5, the (connected) plots of the solution points are presented for various step sizes h. The time interval was taken as $[0, 80]$ (i.e., $b = 80$). Through these plots we see the deterioration of performance as the step size increases. To the accuracy of the plotter resolution, Figure 7.3 is correct: Six successive cycles are essentially coincident in the phase plane.   ◇

★7.6
NUMERICAL METHODS FOR TRANSFER FUNCTIONS AND BLOCK DIAGRAMS

Classical engineering methodology, especially system design, is steeped in (time-invariant) linear differential equation models. For this class, in principle, analytic solutions are available. The ease of obtaining such solutions, however, evaporates quickly as the complexity of the linear model increases. Thus practicing engineers find themselves seeking computational solutions.

A conventional way to prescribe a linear system is through a block diagram. Such a diagram usually appears as a collection of blocks and summing junctions, interconnected by directed paths, typically scaled. A simple instance of a block diagram is given in Figure 7.6.

We refer the reader to Luenberger (1979, p. 293) for background, but will later give enough explanation that background reading is not really needed for our purposes. Within each block one typically finds a proper rational function (i.e., the ratio of two polynomials), most often in the variable s, as a reminder that the function represented is actually the Laplace transform of an impulse response.

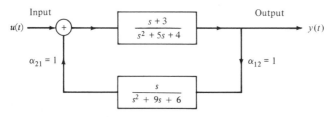

FIGURE 7.6   Simple Block Diagram

The rational function, usually called a *transfer function* or *filter*, as in Application 6.2, determines a differential equation relating the output to the input. Specifically,

$$H(s) = \frac{\sum_{i=0}^{m} b_i s^{m-i}}{\sum_{j=0}^{n} a_j s^{n-j}}, \qquad m < n, \tag{7.38}$$

can be viewed as a code to designate that the output $y(t)$ is related to the input $u(t)$ according to

$$\sum_{j=0}^{n} a_j y^{(n-j)}(t) = \sum_{i=0}^{m} b_i u^{(m-i)}(t), \tag{7.39}$$

with the convention that $a_0 = 1$. As usual, the superscript "(k)" denotes "kth derivative of."

Since our numerical methodology is constrained to first-order differential equations, the first step is to convert (7.39) to a system of equations. One such system, based on principles of Section 7.5, is given, for example, in Brogan (1985, Chap. 9). It is written

$$\frac{d}{dt} \begin{bmatrix} x_1 \\ x_2 \\ \vdots \\ x_{n-1} \\ x_n \end{bmatrix} = \begin{bmatrix} 0 & 1 & 0 & \cdots & 0 & 0 \\ 0 & 0 & 1 & \cdots & 0 & 0 \\ \vdots & \vdots & \vdots & & \vdots & \vdots \\ 0 & 0 & 0 & \cdots & 0 & 1 \\ -a_n & -a_{n-1} & -a_{n-2} & \cdots & -a_2 & -a_1 \end{bmatrix} \begin{bmatrix} x_1 \\ x_2 \\ \vdots \\ x_{n-1} \\ x_n \end{bmatrix} + \begin{bmatrix} 0 \\ 0 \\ \vdots \\ 0 \\ 1 \end{bmatrix} u,$$

$$y = b_1 x_m + b_2 x_{m-1} + \cdots + b_m x_1. \tag{7.40}$$

Here the a_i's and b_j's are as in (7.39). This is a *state-space representation* of the system having transfer function $H(s)$ as in (7.38). More generally, state-space representations take the form

$$\begin{aligned} \dot{x} &= Ax + bu \\ y &= c^T x \end{aligned} \tag{7.41}$$

for some square matrix A and column and row vectors b and c^T all of order n. Thus (7.41) is determined by the parameters (A, b, c). The vector $x(t)$ is referred to as the *state*, and the real-valued functions $u(t)$ and $y(t)$ are the input and output, respectively. To compute the output of a linear system specified in the state-space form (7.41), for any given input function $u(t)$, one applies MRUKU with the function determined by

$$F(t, x, j) = \sum_{k=1}^{n} a_{jk} x_k + b_j u(t). \tag{7.42}$$

TABLE 7.19   Program to Solve Systems in State-Space Form

```
C       PROGRAM STATEREP
C
C       *****************************************************************
C       THIS PROGRAM WILL SET UP AND SOLVE NUMERICALLY (BY THE
C       MULTIVARIATE 4-TH ORDER RUNGE-KUTTA METHOD) THE STATE
C       SPACE MODEL OF THE FORM:
C          D/DT X = AX + BU
C          Y = (C TRANSPOSE)X
C       WHERE A IS A  N BY N MATRIX AND B AND C ARE COLUMN VECTORS
C       AND U = U(T) IS A REAL FUNCTION
C       CALLS:  MRUKU
C       OUTPUT:
C               T(I)=VALUES OF T (TIME)
C               X(I,J)=APPROXIMATED VALUE OF I-TH STATE COORDINATE
C                 AT TIME T(J)
C       *****************************************************************
C
        DIMENSION T(101),X(2,101),Y(101),C(2)
C
C       *** ASSIGN VALUES TO DIMENSION, INITIAL STATE AND TIME      ***
C       *** INTERVAL, WHERE N = DIMENSION, FINTIM = FINAL TIME,     ***
C       *** NUMSTP = NUMBER OF MUTILVARIATE RUNGE-KUTTA STEPS       ***
C
        N = 2
C       *** SPECIFY THE INITITIAL STATE                            ***
        X(1,1)=0.0
        X(2,1)=0.0
C
C       *** SPECIFY C.  A AND B ARE SPECIFIED IN THE FUNCTION      ***
C       *** SUBPROGRAM F(T,X,J)                                    ***
C
        C(1)=2.0
        FINTIM=10.
        NUMSTP=100
C
C       *** SUBROUTINE MRUKU WILL APPROXIMATE THE SOLUTION         ***
C       *** RETURNING NUMSTP+1 VALUES IN ARRAYS T AND X            ***
C
        CALL MRUKU(T,X,NUMSTP,FINTIM,N)
C       *** COMPUTE OUTPUT Y = (C TRANSPOSE)X                      ***
        DO 2 J1 = 1,NUMSTP
          Y(J1) = 0.0
          DO 3 J2 = 1, N
            Y(J1) = Y(J1)+C(J2)*X(J2,J1)
      3   CONTINUE
          WRITE(10,1)(T(J1),Y(J1))
      2 CONTINUE
      1 FORMAT(5X,E15.6,5X,E15.6)
        STOP
        END
C
C       *** FUNCTION F SPECIFIES THE DIFFERENTIAL EQUATION   IT IS ***
C       *** CALLED BY SUBROUTINE MRUKU                             ***
C
        FUNCTION F(T,X,J)
        DIMENSION X(2),A(2),B(2)
        A(1) = -3.0
        A(2) = -2.0
        B(2) = 1.0
        U = 1.0
        IF(J.EQ.1) THEN
            F=X(2)
        ELSE
            F=A(1)*X(2) + A(2)*X(1)+ B(2)*U
        ENDIF
        RETURN
        END
```

The state vector values for $\mathbf{x}(t_i)$ computed by MRUKU are multiplied by $\mathbf{c}^T$ to obtain the outputs, $y(t_i)$. Table 7.19 presents a FORTRAN program implementing the methodology above, with F(T, X, J) as needed for the example below. ∎

─────── **EXAMPLE 7.13** ──────────────────────────────────────

We consider a simple *RLC* loop (studied previously in Application 5.1) shown in Figure 7.7. Assume that the charges on the capacitor and the current are initially 0. Then from Kirchhoff's loop law, we have

$$v''(t) + \frac{R}{L} v'(t) + \frac{1}{LC} v(t) = \frac{1}{LC} u(t). \qquad (7.43)$$

Thus in the notation of (7.39),

$$a_0 = 1, \qquad a_1 = \frac{R}{L}, \qquad a_2 = \frac{1}{LC}, \qquad b_2 = \frac{1}{LC}.$$

For the circuit element values shown in the figure and for $u(t)$ the unit step function [i.e., $u(t) = 0$, $t < 0$, $u(t) = 1$, $t > 0$], we follow (7.40) in writing

$$\mathbf{A} = \begin{bmatrix} 0 & 1 \\ -\dfrac{1}{LC} & -\dfrac{R}{L} \end{bmatrix}, \qquad \mathbf{c}^T = \left(\frac{1}{LC}, 0 \right), \qquad \mathbf{b} = \begin{pmatrix} 0 \\ 1 \end{pmatrix} \qquad (7.44)$$

or

$$\mathbf{A} = \begin{bmatrix} 0 & 1 \\ -2 & -3 \end{bmatrix}, \qquad \mathbf{c}^T = (2, 0), \qquad \mathbf{b} = \begin{pmatrix} 0 \\ 1 \end{pmatrix} \qquad (7.45)$$

The program of Table 7.18 solves this circuit problem. The capacitor voltage $\mathbf{c}^T\mathbf{x}(t)$ is plotted in Figure 7.8. It coincides with the analytic solution mentioned in Application 5.1.

Returning to the block diagram setting, we first convert every transfer function

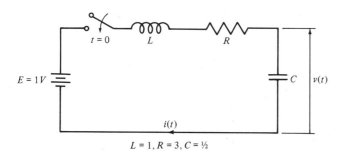

FIGURE 7.7 Simple *RLC* Loop

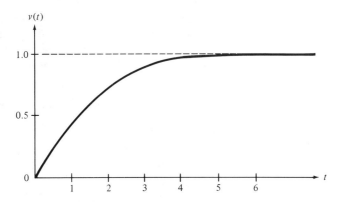

FIGURE 7.8 Capacitor Voltage Curve

to a state-space form. Then if, as in the case shown in Figure 7.6, the blocks take output from other blocks as part of their input, one augments the system matrix to include the relevant states from other blocks. Specifically, suppose that the output $y_2(t)$ of block 2 is among the inputs of the summing junction for block 1 having state-space parameters $(\mathbf{A}_1, \mathbf{b}_1, \mathbf{c}_1)$. Presume that the signal is scaled (i.e., amplified) by α_{21} by that connection. Let $(\mathbf{A}_2, \mathbf{b}_2, \mathbf{c}_2)$ denote the parameters for this other block. Then the state-space equation can be made to reflect this input by recognizing that the state x_1 must satisfy

$$
\begin{aligned}
\frac{d}{dt} \mathbf{x}_1 &= \mathbf{A}_1 \mathbf{x}_1(t) + \mathbf{b}_1(u(t) + \alpha_{21} y_2(t) + \text{other inputs}) \\
&= \mathbf{A}_1 \mathbf{x}_1(t) + \mathbf{b}_1(u(t) + \alpha_{21} \mathbf{c}_2^T \mathbf{x}_2(t) + \text{other inputs}) \qquad (7.46) \\
&= \mathbf{A}_1 \mathbf{x}_1(t) + \alpha_{21} \mathbf{b}_1 \mathbf{c}_2^T \mathbf{x}_2(t) + \mathbf{b}_1(u(t) + \text{other inputs}).
\end{aligned}
$$

From these considerations, one concludes that the overall system of k blocks must have the composite-state space representation

$$
\mathbf{A}_{\text{big}} = \begin{bmatrix} \mathbf{A}_{11} & \mathbf{A}_{12} & \cdots & \mathbf{A}_{1k} \\ \vdots & \vdots & & \vdots \\ \mathbf{A}_{k1} & \mathbf{A}_{k2} & \cdots & \mathbf{A}_{kk} \end{bmatrix},
$$

where

$$
\mathbf{A}_{ij} = \begin{cases} \mathbf{A}_i + \alpha_{ii} \mathbf{b}_i \mathbf{c}_j^T & \text{if } i = j \\ \alpha_{ji} \mathbf{b}_i \mathbf{c}_j^T & \text{if } i \neq j. \end{cases} \qquad (7.47)
$$

Furthermore,

$$
\mathbf{b}_{\text{big}} = \begin{pmatrix} \mathbf{b}_1 \theta_1 \\ \vdots \\ \mathbf{b}_k \theta_k \end{pmatrix}, \qquad \mathbf{c}_{\text{big}}^T = (\psi_1 \mathbf{c}_1^T, \ldots, \psi_k \mathbf{c}_k^T).
$$

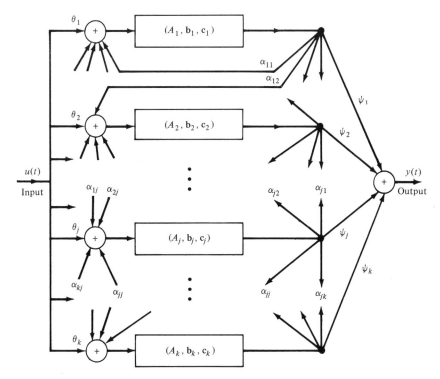

FIGURE 7.9 Schematic of a System of Subsystems: α_{ij}, Θ_i, y_j, $1 \leq i, j \leq k$ are scalars

Note that $(\mathbf{A}_i, \mathbf{b}_i, \mathbf{c}_i)$ denotes the state-space parameters for block i, and θ_i's and ψ_j's are output scalars, as shown in Figure 7.9.

If there is no signal transfer from block j to block i, then α_{ji} is taken to be zero, and if no input appears at block j, then $\theta_j = 0$. Similarly, $\psi_i = 0$ if block i does not contribute to the output. Some relatively obvious generalizations of the scheme above can account for a multitude of inputs to the overall system, and obviously the outputs can be similarly generalized. Both of these generalities are accomplished by using matrices, rather than vectors, for $\mathbf{b}_{\text{big}}$ and $\mathbf{c}_{\text{big}}$. In any case, once $\mathbf{A}_{\text{big}}$, $\mathbf{b}_{\text{big}}$, $\mathbf{c}_{\text{big}}$ have been constructed, the system is ready for solution by the program STATEREP (Table 7.19).

As an example, consider again the case of Figure 7.6, with transfer functions given by

$$H_1(s) = \frac{s + 3}{s^2 + 5s + 4}, \qquad H_2(s) = \frac{s}{s^2 + 9s + 6}.$$

The state-space representation of block 1 is, according to (7.40), achieved by

$$\mathbf{A}_1 = \begin{bmatrix} 0 & 1 \\ -4 & -5 \end{bmatrix}, \qquad \mathbf{b}_1 = \begin{pmatrix} 0 \\ 1 \end{pmatrix}, \qquad \mathbf{c}_1^T = (3, 1),$$

and for block 2, by

$$\mathbf{A}_2 = \begin{bmatrix} 0 & 1 \\ -6 & -9 \end{bmatrix}, \qquad \mathbf{b}_2 = \begin{pmatrix} 0 \\ 1 \end{pmatrix}, \qquad \mathbf{c}_2^T = (0, 1).$$

By using relations (7.47) with $\theta_1 = 1$, $\theta_2 = 0$, $\psi_1 = 1$, $\psi_2 = 0$, $\alpha_{12} = \alpha_{21} = 1$, one sees that the overall system matrix is

$$\mathbf{A}_{\text{big}} = \begin{bmatrix} 0 & 1 & 0 & 0 \\ -4 & -5 & 0 & 1 \\ 0 & 0 & 0 & 1 \\ 3 & 1 & -6 & -9 \end{bmatrix}, \quad \mathbf{b}_{\text{big}} = (0, 1, 0, 0)^T, \quad \mathbf{c}_{\text{big}}^T = (3, 1, 0, 0).$$

★7.7
TWO-POINT BOUNDARY-VALUE PROBLEMS

Let a and b $(a < b)$ be given numbers and $g(u, v)$ a given real- or vector-valued function of two variables. Two-point boundary-value problems of first-order differential equations require the solution of the differential equation

$$y' = f(x, y) \tag{7.48}$$

subject to a two-point boundary condition, usually expressible as

$$g(y(a), y(b)) = 0, \tag{7.49}$$

the numbers a and b being the "two points." Here f, g, and y can be either real or vector valued.

Many two-point boundary-value problem studies concentrate on real second-order differential equations, which are equations of the form

$$y'' = f(x, y, y'). \tag{7.50}$$

Such equations can, of course, be converted into a system of the form (7.48) by the procedure at the beginning of Section 7.5. On the other hand, the exposition of techniques is sometimes a bit clearer in the real-variable case. We will follow the latter path in the discussion of the linear equation case (Section 7.7.1), but in Section 7.7.2, reduction to first-order equations is undertaken.

Typically, (7.49), as well as (7.48), is a system of equations. A common instance of (7.49) requires that $y(a) = A$ and $y(b) = B$, A and B being given constants. This can be phrased as a vector-valued function by

$$g(y(a), y(b)) = \begin{bmatrix} y(a) - A \\ y(b) - B \end{bmatrix} = \begin{bmatrix} 0 \\ 0 \end{bmatrix}. \tag{7.51}$$

If the boundary conditions are specified as $f(a) = A$, $f'(b) = B$, this can be rewritten as

$$g(y(a), y'(b)) = \begin{bmatrix} y(a) - A \\ y'(b) - B \end{bmatrix} = \begin{bmatrix} 0 \\ 0 \end{bmatrix}. \tag{7.52}$$

—————— **EXAMPLE 7.14** ——————

Take the points $a = 0$ and $b = 1$. Our test differential equation

$$y' = x^2 + y^2$$

leads to a two-point boundary-value problem if the condition

$$g(y(0), y(1)) = y(0) + y(1) - 1 = 0$$

is imposed. Solution of this problem will exemplify the "shooting method" discussed in Section 7.7.2.   ■

★7.7.1   Linear Two-Point Boundary-Value Problems

If the differential equation and the boundary conditions are linear in $y(t)$ and its derivatives, the problem may be converted to an initial-value problem and solved relatively conveniently by the technique introduced in Sections 7.3 and 7.5. We illustrate this conversion in the second-order case (7.50) with condition (7.51). In the linear case, the problem takes the form

$$y'' + p(x)y' + q(x)y = r(x), \qquad y(a) = A, \quad y(b) = B, \qquad (7.53)$$

where the functions $p(x)$, $q(x)$, and $r(x)$ are assumed to be continuous on the interval $[a, b]$. The reduction to initial-value problems proceeds in two stages.
   First, solve the homogeneous initial-value problem

$$u'' + p(x)u' + q(x)u = 0, \qquad u(a) = 0, \quad u'(a) = 1, \qquad (7.54)$$

and then solve the inhomogeneous problem

$$z'' + p(x)z' + q(x)z = r(x), \qquad z(a) = A, \quad z'(a) = 0. \qquad (7.55)$$

Let $u(x)$ and $z(x)$ denote the solutions of the initial-value problems (7.54) and (7.55), respectively. As we shall verify, a suitable linear combination of functions $u(x)$ and $z(x)$ gives the solution of the original boundary-value problem.
   Consider the function

$$y(x) = \alpha u(x) + z(x), \qquad (7.56)$$

where the number α is to be determined. Regardless of α, the function $y(x)$ satisfies the differential equation (7.53), since by substitution we have

$$\begin{aligned}
y'' + p(x)y' + q(x)y &= (\alpha u'' + z'') + p(x)(\alpha u' + z') + q(x)(\alpha u + z) \\
&= \alpha[u'' + p(x)u' + q(x)u] + [z'' + p(x)z' + q(x)z] \\
&= \alpha \cdot 0 + r(x) = r(x).
\end{aligned}$$

The boundary condition $y(a) = A$ is also satisfied, since

$$y(a) = \alpha u(a) + z(a) = \alpha \cdot 0 + A = A.$$

Coefficient α will now be determined so that $y(x)$ satisfies the remaining boundary condition $y(b) = B$. By substitution we obtain

$$y(b) = \alpha u(b) + z(b),$$

which equals B if and only if

$$\alpha = \frac{B - z(b)}{u(b)}.$$

Thus the function

$$y(x) = z(x) + \frac{B - z(b)}{u(b)} u(x) \qquad\qquad (7.57)$$

is the solution of the original boundary-value problem.

EXAMPLE 7.15

Consider the boundary-value problem

$$y'' - 3y' + 2y = 2, \qquad y(0) = 1, \quad y(1) = 4.$$

In this case the initial-value problem (7.54) has the form

$$u'' - 3u' + 2u = 0, \qquad u(0) = 0, \quad u'(0) = 1,$$

which has a unique solution

$$u(x) = e^{2x} - e^x.$$

The initial-value problem (7.55) can be written as

$$z'' - 3z' + 2z = 2, \qquad z(0) = 1, \quad z'(0) = 0,$$

and

$$z(x) = 1$$

is the only solution. Since

$$u(b) = u(1) = e^2 - e \text{ and } z(b) = 1,$$

(7.57) implies that the function

$$y(x) = 1 + \frac{4 - 1}{e^2 - e} \cdot (e^{2x} - e^x) = 1 + \frac{3(e^{2x} - e^x)}{e^2 - e}$$

gives the solution of the original boundary-value problem.

★7.7.2 The Shooting Method for Nonlinear Two-Point Boundary-Value Problems

If either the differential equation or the boundary condition is nonlinear in y, we have a nonlinear two-point boundary-value problem. Consider first the first-order representation (7.48). If the value of $y(a)$ were known, it would give a complete initial condition through the differential equation (7.48), and under the usual regularity conditions, it uniquely determines $y(b)$. In the shooting method, we regard $y(a)$ as a variable and seek to determine the value of $y(a)$ that satisfies the two-point boundary condition

$$F(y(a)) = g(y(a), y(b)) = 0. \qquad (7.58)$$

The rationale here is that $y(b)$ is a uniquely determined function (through the differential equation) of $y(a)$. We remark that in the second-order case (7.50), the initial condition is the vector $\mathbf{y}(a) = (y(a), y'(a))^T$, and in this case, in the shooting method, we seek the root of $F(y(a), y'(a))$. The shooting method is not really a "method" in the sense that it leaves unspecified how we are supposed to solve the resulting nonlinear equation.

The nomenclature "shooting" can be motivated by the ballistics problem illustrated in Figure 7.10. Here we have a cannon located at position a on the x-axis, and a target at $x = b$. If an artillery shell with known initial velocity is subject only to Newton's law of motion and viscous damping, then its trajectory $y(x)$ satisfies a second-order differential equation of the form (7.50). The natural boundary condition is that the height $y(x)$ of the shell should be 0 at a and b, or $y(a) = y(b) = 0$. Under the shooting method, one adjusts $y'(a) = \tan(\theta)$ until $y(b) = 0$.

Toward solving (7.58), one may employ techniques of Chapter 5. If, as in the ballistics problem, the initial condition allows only one free variable z (which in our case represents the value of $y'(a)$), then (7.58) has the form

$$F(z) = 0.$$

The secant method leads, in this case, to the iteration scheme

$$z_{k+1} = z_k - F(z_k) \frac{z_k - z_{k-1}}{F(z_k) - F(z_{k-1})}, \qquad (7.59)$$

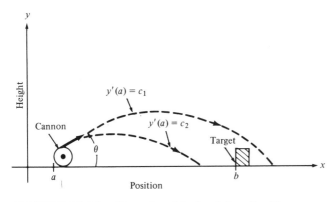

FIGURE 7.10 Shooting Method Application

where z_0 and z_1 are two initial numbers to be specified or guessed. Then in this case, the shooting method can be implemented by conjunctive use of the subroutine SECA (Table 5.5) for secant iterations on successive initial conditions, and the classical Runge–Kutta routine RUKU (Table 7.7) to calculate the requisite terminal condition $y(b)$ needed to evaluate $F(z)$.

─────── **EXAMPLE 7.16** ───────

We illustrate the shooting method implementation using secant iterations to update the initial condition and Runge–Kutta computation of the terminal state. Consider Example 7.14, which we restate:

TABLE 7.20   Program Implementing the Shooting Method

```
C        PROGRAM SMETH
C
C        ****************************************************************
C        THIS PROGRAM WILL SET UP AND SOLVE NUMERICALLY THE DIFFERENTIAL
C        EQUATION Y'=X**2+Y**2 WITH THE BOUNDARY CONDITION Y(0.)+Y(1.)=1.
C        THE SOLUTION IS OBTAINED USING THE SHOOTING METHOD.
C        SUBROUTINE SECA IS USED TO UPDATE THE INITIAL CONDITIONS
C        AND RUKU WILL CALCULATE THE TERMINAL STATE AT EACH ITERATION
C        CALLS:   SECA (MODIFIED AS DESCRIBED IN THE TEXT),RUKU
C        OUTPUT:
C                  X(I)=VALUE OF X FOR I=1,21
C                  Y(I)=APPROXIMATED VALUE OF Y AT X(I)
C        ****************************************************************
C
C        *** FIRST, ASSIGN STARTING PARAMETERS FOR SUBROUTINE SECA    ***
C
         Z0=0.
         Z1=.1
         EPS=1.E-5
C
C        *** SUBROUTINE SECA WILL UPDATE INITIAL CONDITIONS          ***
C        *** UNTIL THE BOUNDARY CONDITIONS ARE SATISFIED             ***
C
         CALL SECA(Z0,Z1,XX,EPS)
         STOP
         END
C
C        *** FUNCTION Y1 WILL SOLVE THE INITIAL VALUE PROBLEM USING   ***
C        *** SUBROUTINE RUKU AND THE INITIAL CONDITION PASSED BY SECA ***
C
         FUNCTION Y1(C)
         DIMENSION X(21),Y(21)
C
C        *** SET UP INITIAL CONDITIONS                               ***
C
         X(1)=0.
         Y(1)=C
         CALL RUKU(X,Y,20,1.0)
         Y1=1-(C+Y(21))
         WRITE(10,1) C,Y(21),Y1
       1 FORMAT(5X,3(F10.6,5X))
         RETURN
         END
C
C        *** FUNCTION F SPECIFIES THE DIFFERENTIAL EQUATION. IT IS   ***
C        *** CALLED BY SUBROUTINE RUKU                               ***
C
         FUNCTION F(X,Y)
         F=X**2+Y**2
         RETURN
         END
```

**TABLE 7.21   Results of Shooting
Method Iteration**

j	$y(0) = z_j$	$y(1)$	$F(z_j)$
0	0.100000	0.482560	0.417440
1	0.000000	0.350232	0.649768
2	0.279677	0.817244	-0.096922
3	0.245821	0.741406	0.012774
4	0.249763	0.749868	0.000369
5	0.249880	0.750121	-0.000002
6	0.249880	0.750120	0.000000

$$y' = x^2 + y^2, \qquad y(0) + y(1) = 1. \tag{7.60}$$

By means of the calling program listed in Table 7.20, we have obtained initial-state iterations (Table 7.21) which do indeed converge to a solution of (7.60). The starting parameters z_0 and z_1 for the routine SECA were selected as 0.0 and 0.1, respectively. We call the reader's attention to our redefining the external function for SECA·as FUNCTION Y1(X), instead of FUNCTION F(X), as described in the SECA comment lines. The reason for this modification, which must be accounted for in the two instructions at which SECA calls for F(X), is that RUKU also requires an external function designated by F, and this refers to the derivative function $f(x, y)$ of the differential equation, not the boundary condition. ∎

★7.8
ADAPTIVE STEP-SIZE SELECTION AND ERROR CONTROL

Up to this point we have not discussed how the step size h of the preceding methods is to be chosen. Obviously, there is a trade-off to be made: If the step size is too small, then computer time is needlessly wasted and accumulation of arithmetic roundoff errors can become a hazard. A large step size invites large truncation error associated with higher-order terms neglected in the construction of the methods. We examine principles for step-size selection. For simplicity, our developments will be concerned only with Runge–Kutta rules.

Techniques for automatic step-size selection are based on estimating the local error at each step and then choosing the step size to keep this estimated error within some tolerance bound. Thus step-size selection hinges on estimation of the *local error*, which at the jth step is defined to be

$$\hat{y}(x_{j+1}) - y_{j+1}.$$

Here y_{j+1} is, of course, the computed approximation of $y(x_{j+1})$, and $\hat{y}(x_{j+1})$ we define to be the exact value at x_{j+1} of the differential equation solution that passes through the previous point (x_j, y_j). That is, $\hat{y}(x)$ solves the initial-value problem

$$\hat{y}' = f(x, \hat{y}), \qquad \hat{y}(x_j) = y_j.$$

In contrast to local errors, the *global error* at x_{j+1} is defined to be

$$y(x_{j+1}) - y_{j+1},$$

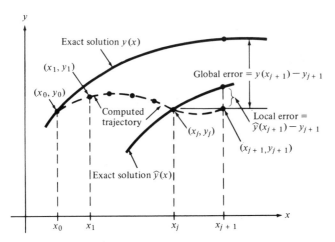

FIGURE 7.11   Relationship Between $y(x)$, $\hat{y}(x)$,
Local and Global Errors

where $y(x)$ is the exact solution of the original initial-value problem (7.3). Figure
7.11 illustrates the relationships between $y(x)$, $\hat{y}(x)$, and local and global errors.
Intuitively, the local error is the additional truncation error arising from inexact
solution at a given step. The global error gives the accumulated total error propagating from the entire sequence of steps.

Assume that some Runge–Kutta procedure has been selected. We let y_0, y_1,
y_2, . . . denote the computed solution values at the arguments x_0, x_1, x_2, ...
The local error estimation techniques at each stage apply a higher-order technique
to compute an additional approximation, say z_{j+1}, of $y(x_{j+1})$. Since a higher-order
technique is used, if the solution is "well behaved" and the step size h is small
enough that neglected terms really are negligible, then one may anticipate that the

TABLE 7.22   Runge–Kutta–Fehlberg Formula

$$k_1 = f(x_j, y_j)$$

$$k_2 = f\left(x_j + \frac{1}{4}h, y_j + \frac{1}{4}hk_1\right)$$

$$k_3 = f\left(x_j + \frac{3}{8}h, y_j + h\left(\frac{3}{32}k_1 + \frac{9}{32}k_2\right)\right)$$

$$k_4 = f\left(x_j + \frac{12}{13}h, y_j + h\left(\frac{1932}{2197}k_1 - \frac{7200}{2197}k_2 + \frac{7296}{2197}k_3\right)\right)$$

$$k_5 = f\left(x_j + h, y_j + h\left(\frac{439}{216}k_1 - 8k_2 + \frac{3680}{513}k_3 - \frac{845}{4104}k_4\right)\right)$$

$$k_6 = f\left(x_j + \frac{1}{2}h, y_j + h\left(-\frac{8}{27}k_1 + 2k_2 - \frac{3544}{2565}k_3 + \frac{1859}{4104}k_4 - \frac{11}{40}k_5\right)\right)$$

$$y_{j+1} = y_j + h\left(\frac{25}{216}k_1 + \frac{1408}{2565}k_3 + \frac{2197}{4104}k_4 - \frac{1}{5}k_5\right)$$

$$z_{j+1} = y_j + h\left(\frac{16}{135}k_1 + \frac{6656}{12825}k_3 + \frac{28561}{56430}k_4 - \frac{9}{50}k_5 + \frac{2}{55}k_6\right)$$

local error of the higher-order method is much less than that of the selected Runge–Kutta procedure. That is,

$$|\hat{y}(x_{j+1}) - z_{j+1}| << |\hat{y}(x_{j+1}) - y_{j+1}|. \tag{7.61}$$

If the approximation above indeed holds, then

$$z_{j+1} - y_{j+1} \simeq \hat{y}(x_{j+1}) - y_{j+1}, \tag{7.62}$$

and we take $z_{j+1} - y_{j+1}$ as the estimate of local error.

TABLE 7.23   Subroutine RKF for the Runge–Kutta–Fehlberg Formula

```
      SUBROUTINE RKF(XI,YI,H,YOUT,ZOUT)
C
C *****************************************************************
C *   FUNCTION: A CALL TO THIS SUBROUTINE COMPUTES ONE STEP OF*
C *             THE SOLUTION AND A GUESS OF THE ERROR FOR A    *
C *             DIFFERENTIAL EQUATION Y'=F(X,Y) WITH INITIAL   *
C *             VALUES XI, YI. THIS SOLUTION IS OBTAINED       *
C *             USING A 4-TH ORDER RUNGE-KUTTA FEHLBERG STEP   *
C *             METHOD IMBEDDED IN A 5-TH ORDER STEP SOLUTION  *
C *   USAGE:                                                   *
C *        CALL SEQUENCE: CALL RKF(XI,YI,H,YOUT,ZOUT)          *
C *        EXTERNAL FUNCTIONS/SUBROUTINES: FUNCTION F(U,V)     *
C *   PARAMETERS:                                              *
C *        INPUT:                                              *
C *            XI=INDEPENDENT VARIABLE INITIAL VALUE           *
C *            YI=DEPENDENT VARIABLE INITIAL VALUE             *
C *            H=INTERVAL STEP SIZE                            *
C *        OUTPUT:                                             *
C *            YOUT=4-TH ORDER SOLUTION ESTIMATE              *
C *            ZOUT=5-TH ORDER SOLUTION ESTIMATE              *
C *                 (ZOUT-YOUT=LOCAL ERROR ESTIMATE)          *
C *****************************************************************
C
      REAL K1,K2,K3,K4,K5,K6
      K1=F(XI,YI)
      U=XI+0.25*H
      V=YI+0.25*H*K1
      K2=F(U,V)
      U=XI+(3./8.)*H
      V=YI+H*((3./32.)*K1+(9./32.)*K2)
      K3=F(U,V)
      U=XI+H*(12./13.)
      V=YI+(H/2197.)*(1932.*K1-7200.*K2+7296.*K3)
      K4=F(U,V)
      U=XI+H
      V=YI+H*((439./216.)*K1-8.*K2+(3680./513.)*K3-
     1(845./4104.)*K4)
      K5=F(U,V)
      U=XI+0.5*H
      V=-(8./27.)*K1+2.*K2-(3544./2565.)*K3+
     1(1859./4104.)*K4-(11./40.)*K5
      V=YI+H*V
      K6=F(U,V)
      YOUT=(25./216.)*K1+(1408./2565.)*K3+
     1(2197./4104.)*K4-K5/5.
      YOUT=YI+H*YOUT
      ZOUT=(16./135.)*K1+(6656./12825.)*K3+
     1(28561./56430.)*K4-(9./50.)*K5
      ZOUT=ZOUT+(2./55.)*K6
      ZOUT=YI+H*ZOUT
      RETURN
      END
```

TABLE 7.24   Subroutine ARUKU for the Adaptive Runge–Kutta Method

```
          SUBROUTINE ARUKU(X,Y,B,M,TOL)
C
C         ***************************************************************
C         *  FUNCTION: THIS SUBROUTINE COMPUTES THE SOLUTION OF A        *
C         *            DIFFERENTIAL EQUATION BY ADAPTIVELY CHOOSING      *
C         *            THE STEP SIZE TO LIMIT THE LOCAL ERROR EST-       *
C         *            IMATE WITHIN A GIVEN TOLERANCE. A 4-TH ORDER      *
C         *            RUNGE-KUTTA FEHLBERG METHOD IS USED               *
C         *  USAGE:                                                      *
C         *      CALL SEQUENCE: CALL ARUKU(X,Y,B,M,TOL)                  *
C         *      EXTERNAL FUNCTIONS/SUBROUTINES:                         *
C         *                     SUBROUTINE RKF(XI,YI,H,YOUT,ZOUT)        *
C         *  PARAMETERS:                                                 *
C         *      INPUT:                                                  *
C         *      X(1)=INDEPENDENT VARIABLE INITIAL VALUE                 *
C         *      Y(1)=DEPENDENT VARIABLE INITIAL VALUE                   *
C         *         B=SOLUTION INTERVAL ENDPOINT (LAST X VALUE)          *
C         *         M=MAXIMUM NUMBER OF ITERATIONS                       *
C         *      OUTPUT:                                                 *
C         *         X=M BY 1 ARRAY OF INDEPENDENT VARIABLE VALUES        *
C         *         Y=M BY 1 ARRAY OF DEPENDENT VARIABLE SOLUTION        *
C         *           VALUES                                            *
C         ***************************************************************
C
          DIMENSION X(M),Y(M)
C         *** INITIALIZATION ***
          H=.10E-02
          I=1
          N=0
C         *** COMPUTE SOLUTION ITERATIVELY ***
          DO WHILE(X(I).LT.B+H)
              N=N+1
              CALL RKF(X(I),Y(I),H,YOUT,ZOUT)
              ERR=ZOUT-YOUT
C         *** TEST IF THE NUMBER OF ITERATIONS EXCEEDED ***
              IF(N.GT.M) THEN
                  WRITE(6,1)
    1             FORMAT(1X,'PROGRAM STOPPED TOO MANY ITERATIONS')
                  STOP
              END IF
C         *** TEST STEP SIZE ***
              IF(ABS(ERR).LT.TOL) THEN
                  I=I+1
                  X(I)=X(I-1)+H
                  H=3.0*H
                  Y(I)=ZOUT
              ELSE
                  H=H/10.0
              END IF
          END DO
          M=I
          H=B-X(I)
          X(M)=X(I)+H
          CALL RKF(X(I),Y(I),H,Y(M),ZOUT)
          RETURN
          END
```

Of course, computation of z_{j+1} is typically more expensive than that of y_{j+1} itself, since z_{j+1} must be more accurate. Here, as in other walks of life, information must be paid for. A popular idea toward making this expense as small as possible has been offered by Fehlberg (1964). For a given order, say $p + 1$, the corresponding member of the Fehlberg family computes z_{j+1} with a minimum number of function calls, according to the limitations in Table 7.10, and then provides the pth-order estimate y_{j+1} without any additional function calls. A particularly popular Fehlberg rule is given in Table 7.22, which gives a fifth-order estimate z_{j+1} for a fourth-order rule y_{j+1}.

Subroutine RKF (Table 7.23) implements a single step of this Runge–Kutta–Fehlberg formula, outputting y_{j+1} and z_{j+1} as the parameters YOUT and ZOUT. In view of (7.62), the difference of these values provides a local error estimate. Subroutine ARUKU (Table 7.24) utilizes RKF to update the step size as the computation progresses. If the absolute value of ZOUT-YOUT is less than the user-specified value TOL (for tolerance), the value ZOUT is accepted for y_{j+1}, and a larger step size (by a factor of 3) is chosen for the next step. Otherwise, h is reduced by a factor of 10, and the computation is repeated from the same condition x_j and y_j. Strictly speaking, YOUT, rather than ZOUT, should be chosen for y_{j+1}, but since in principle the higher-order estimate ZOUT should be more accurate, and since it is available, we adopt the pragmatic viewpoint that it should be used. The reader will note that ARUKU is an obvious modification of subroutine ASIMP for adaptive quadrature (Section 4.8.2).

We serve notice that the code ARUKU is intended only to illustrate the principles of automatic error control. It is inefficient and does not have the safeguards of a professional differential equation program package. More will be said about this matter after the following computational example.

──── **EXAMPLE 7.17** ────────────────────────────────────

By means of the calling program given in Table 7.25, the automatic step-size routine ARUKU is called on to solve the differential equation

$$y' = y, \qquad y(0) = 1 \qquad (7.63)$$

over the interval $[0, 1]$. We chose this over our "usual" differential equation because in the present case it is easy to compute the exact local error $\hat{y}(x_{j+1}) - y_{j+1}$ and thereby see how well the RKF error estimator is doing. Specifically, the solution of (7.63) that passes through points (x_j, y_j) is

$$\hat{y}(x) = y_j \exp (x - x_j),$$

and if h is the current step size, then the exact local error is given by

$$y_j \exp (h) - \text{YOUT}.$$

The bound TOL was set to 10^{-4}. In addition to converting the subroutines and program functions to double precision, a print statement was added to ARUKU to obtain output (Table 7.26) giving the estimated and actual local error and other information. The first line of Table 7.26 corresponds to the starting step-size value of $h = 0.001$. Since the computed local error ($-0.278\text{E}-16$) is less than TOL $= 10^{-4}$, in the next step h is multiplied by 3. Since the local error remains again under 10^{-4}, h is multiplied again by 3, and so on. The consecutive increased values of h, from 0.001 to 0.729, can be found in the first seven lines of the table. In the seventh line, the computed local error becomes greater than 10^{-4} (actually it equals $-0.276\text{E}-3$). Consequently, we divide h by 10 and repeat the step. In this case the new value of h becomes $0.729\text{E}-1$, and the new value of x becomes $0.3640000 + 0.072900 = 0.436900$. Along this path, we obtain the further lines of Table 7.26. The computed estimate of $y(1)$ is 2.7182811. Note

TABLE 7.25   Calling Program for the Subroutine ARUKU

```
C       PROGRAM RKFMETH
C
C       ****************************************************************
C       THIS PROGRAM WILL SET UP AND SOLVE NUMERICALLY THE DIFFERENTIAL
C       EQUATION Y'=Y WITH THE INITIAL CONDITION Y(0.)=1.
C       THE SOLUTION IS OBTAINED USING THE AUTOMATIC STEPSIZE ROUTINE
C       USING 4-TH ORDER RUNGE-KUTTA FEHLBERG-METHOD
C       CALLS:    ARUKU,RKF (BOTH MODIFIED FOR DOUBLE PRECISION)
C       OUTPUT:
C                 X(I)=VALUE OF X FOR I=1,...  (MAX=50)
C                 Y(I)=APPROXIMATED VALUE OF Y AT X(I)
C       ****************************************************************
C
        IMPLICIT DOUBLE PRECISION(A-H,O-Z)
        DIMENSION X(50),Y(50)
C
C       *** FIRST, THE INITIAL CONDITION AND ENDPOINT ARE ESTABLISHED***
C       *** THE MAXIMUM NUMBER OF ITERATIONS IS SET TO 50            ***
C
        X(1)=0.D0
        Y(1)=1.D0
        B=1.D0
        MAX=50
        TOL=1.D-4
C
C       *** SUBROUTINE ARUKU WILL APPROXIMATE THE SOLUTION          ***
C       *** RETURNING AT MOST 50 VALUES IN ARRAYS X AND Y           ***
C
        CALL ARUKU(X,Y,B,MAX,TOL)
        WRITE(10,*)(X(I),Y(I),I=1,50)
        STOP
        END
C
C       *** FUNCTION F SPECIFIES THE DIFFERENTIAL EQUATION. IT IS   ***
C       *** CALLED BY SUBROUTINE RKF                                ***
C
        FUNCTION F(X,Y)
        IMPLICIT DOUBLE PRECISION(A-H,O-Z)
        F=Y
        RETURN
        END
```

TABLE 7.26   Computation Using ARUKU

x_j	y_j	h	Computed Local Error	Actual Local Error
0.0000000	1.0000000	0.001	-0.278D-16	-0.278D-16
0.0010000	1.0010005	0.003	-0.305D-15	-0.305D-15
0.0040000	1.0040080	0.009	-0.757D-13	-0.753D-13
0.0130000	1.0130849	0.027	-0.184D-10	-0.181D-10
0.0400000	1.0408108	0.081	-0.451D-08	-0.424D-08
0.1210000	1.1286249	0.243	-0.111D-05	-0.892D-06
0.3640000	1.4390740	0.729	-0.276D-03	-0.455D-04
0.3640000	1.4390740	0.073	-0.369D-08	-0.350D-08
0.4369000	1.5479010	0.219	-0.911D-06	-0.750D-06
0.6556000	1.9262975	0.656	-0.226D-03	-0.651D-04
0.6556000	1.9262975	0.066	-0.293D-08	-0.279D-08
0.7212100	2.0569201	0.197	-0.722D-06	-0.608D-06
0.9180400	2.5043763	0.590	-0.179D-03	-0.696D-04
0.9180400	2.5043763	0.059	-0.225D-08	-0.216D-08
0.9770890	2.6567105	0.177	-0.555D-06	-0.477D-06
1.0000000	2.7182811	0.023	-0.555D-06	-0.477D-06

that to the accuracy shown, the exact value of $y(1)$ is 2.7182818. We see that in this case, the Runge–Kutta–Fehlberg technique is successful in giving "ballpark" error estimates. As is to be expected, the smaller the step size h, the better the estimate. The computation required 16 calls to RKF, of which 13 were accepted for new y_j values.

$\blacksquare$

We emphasize again that routine ARUKU is intended for illustrative use only. It does not have sophistication and safeguards one would expect of a professional program package. A popular package, the code RKF45 by Shampine and Watts, is presented in Forsythe et al. (1977, Chap. 6). This algorithm, like ours, is based on the formula given in Table 7.22, but it has much more stringent tests for step-size adjustment and initialization. It also includes provision for approximating the "optimal" step size—the largest step that does not lead to violation of the local error bound. The price paid for the greater sophistication is that the code occupies 14 pages of fairly small print.

7.9
SUPPLEMENTARY NOTES AND DISCUSSIONS

Numerical solution of differential equations can, in some respects, be regarded as a generalization of numerical integration, or quadrature, discussed in Chapter 4. For example, if $f(x, y)$ in (7.3) really depends only on x, that is, if $f(x, y) = f(x)$, then the initial-value problem has the form $y'(x) = f(x)$, $y(x_0) = y_0$ and the solution is

$$y(x) = y(x_0) + \int_{x_0}^{x} f(x)\,dx.$$

For such functions, some of the differential equation methods coincide with standard quadrature formulas. For example, the corrected Euler's method presented in Example 7.5 specializes to the midpoint rule.

Another similarity between the major integration and differential equation solution methods are that they tend to provide evidence of the value of mathematical analysis. Sophisticated but unintuitive methods are far more accurate than commonsense approaches. For example, in integration, common sense would seem to suggest that the best one could do with n points is to uniformly sample and average the functional values over the domain of integration. This should result in something like the midpoint or trapezoidal rule. But, for well-behaved functions, Gaussian quadrature, the points and weights of which it is fair to say are unlikely to be guessed by anyone, is typically more accurate by many orders of magnitude. Similarly, in this chapter we saw that Runge–Kutta rules, about which we have no heuristic explanation to offer except in terms of Taylor's expansions and numerical differentiation, are much more successful, for a given computational effort, than the intuitively obvious Euler's method.

It is a mathematical fact that the values of x_j and y_j uniquely determine the solution values at x greater than x_j. With this fact in mind, without allusion to interpolation polynomials, it is hard to explain why Adams methods should successfully use earlier information (x_{j-1}, y_{j-1}), (x_{j-2}, y_{j-2}), . . . from the more distant past. It is in this sense that we assert that the demonstrated success of

Gauss quadrature, Runge–Kutta, and linear multistep methods are a tribute to the value of series expansions in particular and mathematical analysis in general.

In the examples of this chapter we were able to obtain fairly accurate answers to our test differential equation problem, without great programming effort or expenditure of running time. In fact, hand-held programmable calculators often suffice for textbook-sized problems. As further evidence of the manageability of initial-value problems for ordinary differential equations, we mention that there are a number of good computer packages available. For example, the IMSL library, resident at many computer centers, has three packages, one using a Runge–Kutta method, another based on linear-multistep techniques, and a third based on an approach not studied here. These and other sophisticated codes provide inexpensive, reliable answers to well-behaved initial-value differential equation problems. Such packages have error control features that incorporate adaptive step-size selection in order to maintain an error tolerance specified by the user.

Two classes of numerical differential equation problems require considerable sophistication. The first of these is the nonlinear two-point boundary problem. By "nonlinear" we mean that $f(x, y)$ in (7.3) cannot be expressed in the special form

$$f(x, y(x)) = g_1(x)y(x) + g_2(x). \tag{7.64}$$

By "two-point" we mean constraints such as those discussed in Section 7.7. For such problems readers are advised to seek professional help or continue their studies in numerical methods. The other important class of truculent problems is initial-value differential equations that are "stiff." The notion of "stiff" is somewhat imprecise, but it embodies the idea that the solution has various components, some of which change much more rapidly than others. Quite often, it is hard to tell in advance whether a given differential equation is stiff. Among the methods discussed in this chapter, implicit Adams formulas have the most attractive theoretical features for stiff systems. But implicit Runge–Kutta formulas (which we have not discussed) are also of value in this context. The IMSL library program DGEAR has a stiff differential equation option based on the Adams multistep approach. Recent editions of IMSL also contain two-point boundary-value problem codes, one based on the shooting method; the other, for linear problems, uses difference equation techniques. The basic idea of difference equation methods can be found in S & Y (1978, Sec. 8.2.3).

PROBLEMS

Section 7.2

1. Approximate the solutions of the following initial-value problems by the cubic Taylor's polynomials of the solution about the initial point $x_0 = 0$. Show your hand calculations.

(a) $y' = xy, \quad y(0) = 1 \qquad [y(x) = e^{x^2/2}]$.
(b) $y' = x^3 + y, \quad y(0) = 2 \qquad [y(x) = 8e^x - 6 - 6x - 3x^2 - x^3]$.
(c) $y' = y \cdot \sin(x), \quad y(0) = 1 \qquad [y(x) = e^{-\cos(x)+1}]$.
(d) $y' = x + xy, \quad y(0) = 1 \qquad [y(x) = 2e^{x^2/2} - 1]$.

The exact analytic solutions are given in the brackets.

★**2.** Another way to use Taylor's expansions to solve differential equations is to develop relations between coefficients of the Taylor's series of the solution. For example, consider the equation

$$y' = \alpha y, \qquad y(0) = 1.$$

Represent the solution as

$$y(x) = \sum_{i=0}^{\infty} a_i x^i,$$

and recognize that $y'(x) = \sum_{i=1}^{\infty} i a_i x^{i-1}$. The differential equation then reads

$$\sum_{i=1}^{\infty} i a_i x^{i-1} = \alpha \sum_{i=1}^{\infty} a_i x^i.$$

Now use the fact that two series (i.e., the left- and right-hand sides above) are equal if and only if coefficients of like powers of x are equal. So equating x^0 terms yields $\alpha a_0 = a_1$. But also $y(0) = a_0 = 1$. So $a_1 = \alpha$. From x^1, $2a_2 = \alpha a_1$, and $a_2 = \alpha^2/2$. From x^2, $3a_3 = \alpha a_2$ and $a_3 = \alpha^3/3!$. Continuing, we have

$$a_j = \frac{1}{j} \frac{\alpha^j}{(j-1)!} = \frac{\alpha^j}{j!}.$$

Thus

$$y(x) = \sum_{j=0}^{\infty} \frac{\alpha^j x^j}{j!} = \exp(\alpha x).$$

Apply this approach to the differential equations in Problem 1.

3. Do two recursive Taylor steps by hand calculations, with $h = 0.1$, toward finding the solutions of the differential equations listed below. Take degrees 0 and 1.

(a) $y' = \dfrac{(x + 1)y}{x}$, $\quad y(1) = 1 \quad$ $[y(x) = xe^{x-1}]$

(b) $y' = -y \cos(x)$, $\quad y(0) = 1 \quad$ $[y(x) = e^{-\sin(x)}]$

4. Solve the differential equations listed in Problem 1 by the Euler method. Take $h = 0.1$ and do two steps by hand calculation, showing your work. Then take eight more steps by use of subroutine EULER (Table 7.2). Print out your computed values at each step, and the error as calculated with respect to the analytic solution given in brackets on the right, in each case.

5. The voltage across the capacitor in the RC circuit is governed by the differential equation

$$v'(t) = 1 - v(t), \qquad v(0) = 0.$$

Use Euler's method with $h = 0.1$, and then 0.01, to plot the solution at times $j/10, j = 1, 2, \ldots, 10$.

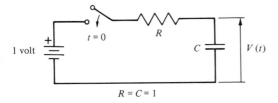

$R = C = 1$

6.   As explained in Application 7.1, a famous model (the logistics equation) for population size P, as a function of time, is given by

$$\frac{d}{dt}P(t) = aP(t)[b - P(t)].$$

The idea is that if the population is relatively small, the growth rate is maximal, being limited only by reproductive capacity. As the population rises, resources become a limitation, and the growth rate approaches 0 as population P converges to b. Solve this equation, with $a = 0.001$, $b = 1000$, and $P(0) = 5$, using Euler's method, up to time 10. Take $h = 0.1$, and then 0.01, and graph the solution values at $t_j = j/10$, $1 \le j \le 100$. (Use EULER, Table 7.2.)

7.   With differential equation methods at our disposal, we are in a position to examine and experiment with the projectile problem which has served as applications at several points in this book. For example, in the vertical direction, the acceleration V' is the negative of the gravity constant and a term due to friction. Mathematically, for viscous air resistance, the vertical velocity satisfies

$$V' = -aV - g.$$

Take $V(0)$ to be 200 m/s, $g = 9.8$ m/s^2, and use Euler's method (Table 7.2) with $h = 0.001$ to find out how long the shot takes to reach its maximum height [i.e., when $V(t) = 0$] assuming
(a) $a = 0$ (no friction).
(b) $a = 0.01$ (light friction).
(c) $a = 0.10$ (considerable resistence).

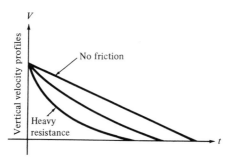

8.   Apply stepwise Taylor's approximations as in (7.6), with degrees $m = 0, 1, 2, 3$, to the differential equation

$$y' = 2y, \qquad y(0) = 1.0.$$

Use a computer, take $h = 0.1$, and print the error between y_j and the analytic solution at the computation points $x_j = j/10$, $j = 1, \ldots, 20$. [The analytic solution is $y(x) = \exp(2x)$.]

★9.   Solve the differential equations in Problem 1 by Heun's method [equations (7.11) and (7.12) with $\lambda = \frac{2}{3}$]. Take $h = (0.1)^k$, $k = 1, 2, 3$. Compare the computed with the exact solution.

Section 7.3

10. Apply the classical Runge–Kutta formula (by use of subroutine RUKU, Table 7.7) to the differential equation of Problem 8. Take the same step size and test points. If you did Problem 8, compare the results.

11. Apply the corrected Euler's formula (7.18) to the differential equations in Problem 1. Take $h = 0.1$ and perform two steps by hand calculation, showing your work.

12. Apply the classical Runge–Kutta formula (using RUKU, Table 7.7) to the differential equations in Problem 1, over the interval $[0, 1]$. Try the step sizes $h = (0.1)^k$, $k = 1, 2, 3$. Observe the error (in comparison to the given analytic function values) at the test points $x = 0.1, 0.2, \ldots, 1.0$.

13. Apply subroutine RUKU (Table 7.7) to the RC model in Problem 5. Use the test points given there, and compare with the analytic solution, which is $V(t) = 1 - \exp(-t)$. Experiment with different step sizes h.

★14. Find a two-step Runge–Kutta rule in which $\alpha_1 = \frac{2}{3}$. Is it unique? [**HINT:**Apply relations (7.26).]

Section 7.4

★15. Solve Problem 1 by use of the three-step Adams–Bashforth formulas (see Table 7.12) over the interval $[0, 1]$. Obtain starting points by application of RUKU (Table 7.7). Take $h = (0.1)^k$, $k = 1, 2$, and 3. Compare your computed solutions with the exact solutions given there.

★16. Whereas we noted that the coefficients β_m in the Adams methods (7.30) are defined so as to give a maximal-order truncation error, it turns out that this can be achieved by integrating the interpolation polynomial for the data $\{(x_{j+1-m}, f_{j+1-m})\}$. Specifically, after integrating the differential equation

$$y'(x) = f(x, y(x))$$

we conclude that

$$y(x_{j+1}) = y(x_j) + \int_{x_j}^{x_{j+1}} f(x, y(x)) \, dx.$$

Let $p(x) = \sum_{m=1}^{i} f_{j+1-m} l_m(x)$ be the interpolation polynomial for $f(x, y(x))$, based on the values at (x_{j+1-m}, f_{j+1-m}), $1 \le m \le i$. Thus

$$l_m(x) = \prod_{\substack{v=1 \\ v \ne m}}^{i} \frac{x - x_v}{x_m - x_v}.$$

Then the interpolatory quadrature formula for $\int_{x_j}^{x_{j+1}} f(x, y(x)) \, dx$ is, in view of Section 4.3, given by $\sum_{m=1}^{i} h\beta_m f_{j+1-m}$, where

$$h\beta_m = \int_{x_j}^{x_{j+1}} l_m(x) \, dx.$$

Use this insight to verify the Adams–Bashforth coefficients for $i = 2$ in Table 7.12.

Section 7.5

17. Solve the following simultaneous differential equations by use of MRUKU (Table 7.17). Take $h = 0.1$ and print out values at $x_i = i/10$, $i = 1, 2, \ldots, 10$.

    (a) $y_1' = x + y_1 + y_2,$ $y_1(0) = 0$
        $y_2' = x^2 + y_1 y_2,$ $y_2(0) = 1.$

    (b) $y_1' = y_1 y_2^2 - x - y_1,$ $y_1(0) = 2$
        $y_2' = x^2 + x y_1 y_2,$ $y_2(0) = 1.$

    (c) $y_1' = y_1 + y_2 + y_3 x,$ $y_1(0) = 0$
        $y_2' = y_1 - y_2^2 + x^2,$ $y_2(0) = 1$
        $y_3' = 2 y_1 y_2 y_3,$ $y_3(0) = 2.$

18. Convert the higher-order differential equations below to simultaneous first-order problems, and solve by use of MRUKU.

    (a) Vanderpol's equation for a nonlinear self-sustained oscillation

    $$y'' = 0.1 \left(\frac{y' - (y')^3}{3} \right) - y, \qquad y(0) = y'(0) = 1.$$

    (b) If r is the distance of a planet from the sun, and $u = 1/r$, then under suitable units of measure

    $$u''(\theta) = \frac{m}{h^2} - u(\theta),$$

    where h is the angular momentum and m is the planet mass. Set $m/h = 1$, and solve. (**HINT:** In both parts the solution should be periodic. Solve for the interval $[0, 20]$ to confirm this and calculate the period.)

19. To show your mastery of the principle behind this section, in the spirit of MRUKU, make a vector generalization of subroutine EULER (Table 7.2) and call it MEULER. Use it to solve part (a) of Problem 17. Obtain a solution and compare it with one obtained through application of MRUKU.

20. Redo the predator–prey study (Application 7.2) experimenting with parameters and step sizes. Plot the predator and prey as a function of time, as well as in phase-plane form as in Figure 7.4. What is the period of the time curve? How does it change if γ_1, in (7.36), is changed to 0.5? Does the period depend on initial conditions?

★21. Linear constant-coefficient homogeneous differential equations are equations of the form

    $$a_0 y^{(n)} + a_1 y^{(n-1)} + \cdots + a_n y = 0,$$

    $$y(0) = y_0, \quad y'(0) = y_0', \quad \ldots, \quad y^{(n-1)}(0) = y_0^{(n-1)}.$$

    Associate with this equation the polynomial

    $$P(z) = a_0 z^n + a_1 z^{n-1} + \cdots + a_n$$

    and presume that it has no multiple roots. A central result in a first mathematics course in differential equations is that the solution of any such equation has the form

    $$y(t) = \sum_{j=1}^{n} C_j \exp(r_j x),$$

where the C_j's are constants depending on the initial conditions and the r_j's are the roots of $P(z)$. One can characterize the shapes of exp (rt) according to whether r is positive or negative and whether it has a nonzero imaginary part. We have tried to illustrate this characterization in the accompanying figures.

If r is real and negative, decay:

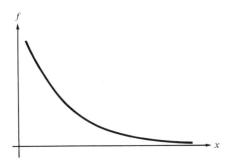

If r is real and positive, growth:

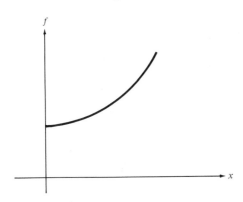

If r is complex with imaginary part, oscillation:

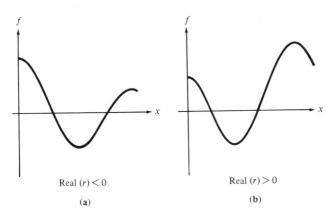

Use the higher-order conversion explained in Section 7.5 and MRUKU to find the solutions of the following equations and explain the shapes in terms of the roots of the associated polynomials.

(a) $y'(t) + y(t) = 0,$ $y(0) = 1.0.$
(b) $y'(t) - y(t) = 0,$ $y(0) = 1.0.$

(c) $y''(t) + 0.2y'(t) + y(t) = 0,$ $y(0) = y'(0) = 1.0.$
(d) $y''(t) - 0.2y'(t) + y(t) = 0,$ $y(0) = y'(0) = 1.0.$
[**HINT:** For parts (c) and (d), it might be easiest to adapt the driver STATEREP (Table 7.19).]

22. The *RLC* circuit shown here is a step beyond the *RL* or *RC* circuits in that for certain ranges of component values, it can exhibit natural oscillatory behavior. The voltage on the capacitor, as a function of time, satisfies the differential equation

$$Lq'' + Rq' + \frac{1}{C}q = 1, \qquad q(0) = q'(0) = 0.$$

If R is 0, the solution should be an undamped sinusoid. As R increases, the oscillations are contained in an envelope shrinking exponentially to 0 as time increases. Verify these assertions by solving the equation using MRUKU. Take $L = C = 1$, and $R = 0, 0.2, 0.5,$ and 2. Plot the solutions over the interval $[0, 10]$.

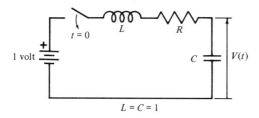

23. The standard model for a pendulum motion (see the accompanying figure) is obtained by equating potential and kinetic energy. It is

$$\theta'' = -\frac{g}{L}\sin(\theta), \qquad \theta(0) = a, \quad \theta'(0) = 0$$

the derivative being with respect to time t. In many expositions, another step is added to make the solution tractable, namely that for small θ,

$$\theta \approx \sin(\theta).$$

[Note that this is the linear Taylor's polynomial for $\sin(\theta)$ about the expansion point $\theta_0 = 0$.] By this approximation, and letting L be the pendulum length and g the acceleration of gravity, one can get the analytic solution

$$\theta(t) = a \cos\left(\sqrt{\frac{g}{L}}\,t\right).$$

Check that this does solve $\theta'' = -(g/L)\theta$. Now use MRUKU to check the accuracy of this linear approximation. Solve the exact model and compare with the approximate solution. Take the interval $[0, 10]$ for testing, and compare the differences at test times $t_j = 0, 2, \ldots, 10$. Take as initial values $a = 0.1, 0.3, 0.5,$ and 1. First check your code by seeing that the approximate solution is recovered exactly if "$\sin(\theta)$" is replaced by θ in your differential equation calling function.

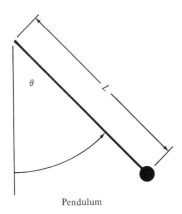

Pendulum

Section 7.6

★**24.**   Find the coordinates of A_{big}, b_{big}, c_{big} of the block diagram shown.

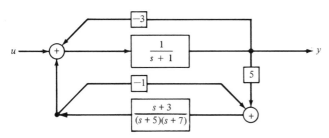

★**25.**   Experimentally assess how large a linear system you can reliably solve for t in the unit interval $[0, 1]$. Choose the coefficients of **A**, **b**, and **c** in Program STATEREP (Table 7.19) by a uniform random number generator and solve with step size $h = 0.002$ and 0.001. Consider the answer accurate if for both runs, the final values are within 0.005 of each other at each state coordinate. Increase the dimension n until this condition is no longer satisfied.

Section 7.7

★**26.**   Reduce the linear boundary-value problems below to initial-value problems.
(a) $y'' + 2y' + y = (x + 2)^2 - 2$, $y(0) = 0$, $y(1) = 2$.
(b) $y'' - 3y' + 2y = 2$, $y(0) = 1$, $y(1) = 3$.
(c) $y'' - xy' + y = -x^2$, $y(0) = -2$, $y(1) = 1$.

★**27.**   (**Continuation of Problem 26**). Solve the boundary-value problems by the shooting method. Compare the results with the exact solutions, which are stated below.
(a) $y(x) = x^2 + xe^{x-1}$.
(b) $y(x) = 1 + 2(e^{2x} - e^x)/(e^2 - e)$.
(c) $y(x) = x^2 + 2x - 2$.

★**28.**   The boundary-value problem

$$y'' - 3y' + 2y = 0,   y(0) = 1,   y(1) = \exp(1),   y(2) = \exp(2)$$

is potentially "overdetermined" since usually an mth-order (here $m = 2$) differential equation solution is uniquely determined by only m conditions. For this case, however, demonstate that the three conditions may be satisfied. But next demonstrate that the equation is not satisfiable if the value for $y(2)$ were replaced by any other number.

References

Abramowitz, M., and I. A. Stegun, eds. (1965), *Handbook of Mathematical Functions with Formulas, Graphs, and Mathematical Tables*, Dover Publications, Inc., New York.

Apostol, T. M. (1957), *Mathematical Analysis: A Modern Approach to Advanced Calculus*, Addison-Wesley Publishing Co., Inc., Reading, Mass.

Bellman, R. (1970), *Introduction to Matrix Analysis*, 2nd ed. McGraw-Hill Book Company, New York.

Bickel, P. J., and K. Doksum (1977), *Mathematical Statistics*, Holden-Day, Inc., San Francisco.

Bloomfield, P. (1976), *Fourier Analysis of Time Series: An Introduction*, John Wiley & Sons, Inc., New York.

Brogan, W. L. (1985), *Modern Control Theory*, 2nd ed., Prentice-Hall, Inc., Englewood Cliffs, N.J.

Butcher, J. C. (1964). On Runge–Kutta Processes of Higher Order, *J. Austral. Math. Soc., 4,* 179–194.

Davis, P., and P. Rabinowitz (1975). *Methods of Numerical Integration*, Academic Press, Inc., New York.

de Boor, C. (1978), *A Practical Guide to Splines*, Springer-Verlag New York, Inc., New York.

Dennis, J. E., and R. B. Schnabel (1983), *Numerical Methods for Unconstrained Optimization*, Prentice-Hall, Inc., Englewood Cliffs, N.J.

Fehlberg, E. (1964), New High-Order Runge–Kutta Formulas with Stepsize Controls for Systems of First and Second Order Differential Equations, *Z. Angew. Math. Mech., 44,* 83–88.

Forsythe, G., M. Malcolm, and C. Moler (1977), *Computer Methods for Mathematical Computations*, Prentice-Hall, Inc., Englewood Cliffs, N.J.

Golub G., and C. Van Loan (1983), *Matrix Computations*, The Johns Hopkins University Press, Baltimore, Md.

Haberman, R. (1977), *Mathematical Models*, Prentice-Hall, Inc., Englewood Cliffs, N.J.

Hart, J. F., et al. (1968), *Computer Approximations*, John Wiley & Sons, Inc., New York.

Henrici, P. (1982), *Essentials of Numerical Analysis*, John Wiley & Sons, Inc., New York.

Herstein, I. (1964), *Topics in Algebra*, Blaisdell Publishing Company, New York.

Huff, D. (1954), *How to Lie with Statistics*, W. W. Norton & Company, Inc., New York.

Isaacson, E., and H. Keller (1966), *Analysis of Numerical Methods*, John Wiley & Sons, Inc., New York.

Johnson, L. W., and R. Riess (1977), *Numerical Analysis*, Addison-Wesley Publishing Co., Inc., Reading, Mass.

Kaplan, W. (1952), *Advanced Calculus,* Addison-Wesley Publishing Co., Inc., Reading, Mass.

Knuth, D. (1969), *Seminumerical Algorithms*, Addison-Wesley Publishing Co., Inc., Reading, Mass.

Lancaster, P. (1969), *Theory of Matrices*, Academic Press, Inc., New York.

Lawson, C. L., and H. J. Hanson (1974), *Solving Least Squares Problems*, Prentice-Hall, Inc., Englewood Cliffs, N.J.

Letcher, J. S., Jr., J. K. Marshall, J. C. Oliver III, and N. Salvesen (1987), Stars and Stripes, *Scientific American*, 257(2), 34–40.

Lin, C. C., and L. A. Segel (1974), *Mathematics Applied to Deterministic Problems in the Natural Sciences*, Macmillan Publishing Company, New York.

Luenberger, D. (1979), *Introduction to Dynamic Systems*, John Wiley & Sons, Inc., New York.

Metropolis, N., J. Howlett, and G. C. Rota, eds. (1980). *A History of Computing in the Twentieth Century*, Academic Press, Inc., New York.

Nering, E. D. (1963), *Linear Algebra and Matrix Theory*, John Wiley & Sons, Inc., New York.

Ortega, J., and W. Poole (1981), *Numerical Methods of Differential Equations*, Pitman Publishing, Inc., Marshfield, Mass.

Ortega, J., and W. Rheinboldt (1970), *Iterative Solution of Nonlinear Equations in Several Variables*, Academic Press, Inc., New York.

Rabenstein, A. L. (1970), *Elementary Differential Equations with Linear Algebra*, Academic Press, Inc., New York.

Ralston, A., and P. Rabinowitz (1978), *A First Course in Numerical Analysis*, 2nd ed., McGraw-Hill Book Company, New York.

Rice, J. (1983), *Numerical Methods, Software, and Analysis*, IMSL Reference Edition, McGraw-Hill Book Company, New York.

S & Y. This is Szidarovszky and Yakowitz (1978). The citation details are listed below.

Savage, L. J. (1954). *The Foundations of Statistics*, John Wiley & Sons, Inc., New York.

Stegun, I., and M. Abramowitz (1956), Pitfalls in Computation, *J. SIAM, 4*, 207–219.

Stewart, G. (1973), *Introduction to Matrix Computations*, Academic Press, Inc., New York.

Stoer, J., and R. Bulirsch (1980), *Introduction to Numerical Analysis*, Springer-Verlag New York, Inc., New York.

Szidarovszky, F., and S. Yakowitz (1978), *Principles and Procedures of Numerical Analysis*, Plenum Press, New York.

U.S. Bureau of the Census (1984), *Statistical Abstract of the United States 1984*, U.S. Government Printing Office, Washington, D.C.

Wilf, H. (1960), The Numerical Solution of Polynomial Equations, in *Mathematical Methods for Digital Computers,* A. Ralston and H. Wilf, eds., John Wiley & Sons, Inc., New York.

Yakowitz, S. (1977), *Computational Probability and Simulation,* Addison-Wesley Publishing Co., Inc., Reading, Mass.

Fundamentals of Matrix Theory

Consider the following simultaneous linear equations

$$2x_1 + x_2 - x_3 = 5$$
$$x_1 + x_2 + x_3 = 5$$
$$-x_1 \qquad + x_3 = -1,$$

where x_1, x_2, and x_3 are the unknowns. The coefficients of the unknowns are conveniently written as a rectangular or, in this special case, a square array,

$$\mathbf{A} = \begin{bmatrix} 2 & 1 & -1 \\ 1 & 1 & 1 \\ -1 & 0 & 1 \end{bmatrix}, \tag{A.1}$$

which is called a matrix of coefficients. For purposes of this book, a *matrix* is any rectangular array of numbers.

$$\mathbf{A} = \begin{bmatrix} a_{11} & a_{12} & \cdots & a_{1n} \\ a_{21} & a_{22} & \cdots & a_{2n} \\ \vdots & \vdots & & \vdots \\ & & \cdots & \\ a_{m1} & a_{m2} & & a_{mn} \end{bmatrix}. \tag{A.2}$$

A matrix with m rows and n columns is said to be of *order* $m \times n$ (pronounced "m by n"). One often designates the coefficient in the ith row and jth column by a subscripted lowercase letter such as a_{ij}. Thus the coefficient a_{32} of the matrix in (A.1) is 0. When we write "the (i, j) coefficient (or coordinate or element) of $\mathbf{A}$," we refer to a_{ij}.

419

Matrices are denoted in this book by boldface capital letters, such as $\mathbf{A}$, $\mathbf{B}$, $\mathbf{C}$. The matrix having coefficients a_{ij} is sometimes denoted by $\mathbf{A} = (a_{ij})$ or by

$$\mathbf{A} = (a_{ij})_{i,j=1}^{m,n}.$$

An $m \times 1$ matrix is called a *column vector*, and a $1 \times n$ matrix is called a *row vector*. Thus vectors are matrices of a special form. In matrix algebra, single numbers are called *scalars*. Vectors are commonly designated by boldface lower-case letters such as $\mathbf{a}$, $\mathbf{b}$, $\mathbf{x}$, and scalars by regular letters such as a, b, and x.

A.1
SPECIAL FORMS AND ALGEBRA
OF MATRICES AND VECTORS

In this section some definitions and properties of vectors and matrices are discussed.

1. For an arbitrary matrix of order $m \times n$, m, of course, need not be equal to n. In the important case that $m = n$, the matrix is called a *square matrix*. In this case, m is the *order* of the matrix. The coefficients $a_{11}, a_{22}, a_{33}, \ldots$ of a square matrix are called *diagonal elements*, and they form the main diagonal or simply the *diagonal* of the matrix.

2. A square matrix with all off-diagonal coefficients equal to zero is a *diagonal matrix*.

Figure A.1 and Example A.1 will help to illustrate the notion of square and diagonal matrices, as well as other special forms given below.

3. A square matrix in which all coefficients below the diagonal are equal to zero is called *upper triangular*; and similarly a square matrix with all zero coefficients above the diagonal is called *lower triangular*.

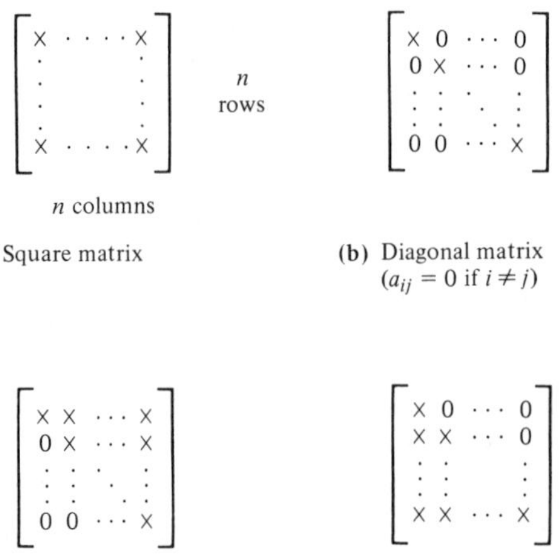

(a) Square matrix

(b) Diagonal matrix
$(a_{ij} = 0$ if $i \neq j)$

(c) Upper triangular matrix
$(a_{ij} = 0$ if $i > j)$

(d) Lower triangular matrix
$(a_{ij} = 0$ if $i < j)$

FIGURE A.1 Some Special Matrix Forms

━━━━━ **EXAMPLE A.1** ━━━━━

Consider the following matrices:

$$A = \begin{bmatrix} 1 & 2 \\ 2 & 3 \\ 4 & 5 \end{bmatrix}, \quad b = [1 \ \ 1 \ \ 0 \ \ 1], \quad c = \begin{bmatrix} 1 \\ 2 \\ 3 \end{bmatrix},$$

$$D = \begin{bmatrix} 1 & 2 & 3 \\ 1 & 1 & 0 \\ 0 & 1 & -1 \end{bmatrix}, \quad E = \begin{bmatrix} 1 & 0 & 0 \\ 0 & 2 & 0 \\ 0 & 0 & -1 \end{bmatrix}, \quad F = \begin{bmatrix} 1 & 2 & 1 \\ 0 & 2 & 4 \\ 0 & 0 & -1 \end{bmatrix},$$

$$G = \begin{bmatrix} 1 & 0 & 0 \\ 1 & 0 & 0 \\ -1 & -5 & 4 \end{bmatrix}.$$

The matrix A is a 3×2 matrix with no special properties, b is a row vector, c is a column vector, D is a square matrix, E is diagonal, F is upper triangular, and G is lower triangular.   ■

Observe that any matrix that is both lower triangular and upper triangular is necessarily diagonal.

4. A matrix composed entirely of zeros is called a *zero* (or *null*) *matrix*, and a vector of zeros is called a *zero* (or *null*) *vector*. We denote them by O and 0, respectively.

5. A diagonal matrix with all diagonal coefficients equal to 1 is called the *identity* (or *unit*) *matrix* and is denoted by I.

━━━━━ **EXAMPLE A.2** ━━━━━

Consider the matrices

$$A = \begin{bmatrix} 0 & 0 & 0 \\ 0 & 0 & 0 \end{bmatrix}, \quad B = \begin{bmatrix} 1 & 0 & 0 \\ 0 & 1 & 0 \\ 0 & 0 & 1 \end{bmatrix}, \quad c = \begin{bmatrix} 0 \\ 0 \\ 0 \end{bmatrix}, \quad d = [0 \ \ 0 \ \ 0].$$

Here A is a zero matrix, B is the identity matrix, and c and d are zero vectors.   ■

6. Matrices A and B are *equal* if they are of the same order $m \times n$ and the corresponding coefficients in the two matrices are equal. That is, $a_{ij} = b_{ij}$ for all i and j. If A and B are equal, we write $A = B$.

7. The *transpose* of an $m \times n$ matrix A is an $n \times m$ matrix, denoted by A^T, and defined so that the (i, j) coefficient of A^T equals a_{ji}, the (j, i) coefficient of A.

8. If a square matrix $\mathbf{A}$ satisfies the relation $\mathbf{A}^T = \mathbf{A}$, then $\mathbf{A}$ is called *symmetric*. A symmetric matrix $\mathbf{A}$ is characterized by the property that $a_{ij} = a_{ji}$ for all i and j.

————— EXAMPLE A.3 —————

An arbitrary diagonal matrix is symmetric. The matrices

$$\mathbf{A} = \begin{bmatrix} 1 & 3 & -4 \\ 3 & 0 & -1 \\ -4 & -1 & 1 \end{bmatrix} \quad \text{and} \quad \mathbf{B} = \begin{bmatrix} 1 & -1 \\ -1 & 1 \end{bmatrix}$$

are also symmetric. Also note that

$$\begin{bmatrix} 1 \\ 1 \\ 1 \end{bmatrix}^T = \begin{bmatrix} 1 & 1 & 1 \end{bmatrix}, \qquad \begin{bmatrix} 0 & 0 & 1 \\ 1 & 1 & 4 \end{bmatrix}^T = \begin{bmatrix} 0 & 1 \\ 0 & 1 \\ 1 & 4 \end{bmatrix}.$$

9. The sum of matrices $\mathbf{A}$ and $\mathbf{B}$ is defined whenever $\mathbf{A}$ and $\mathbf{B}$ have the same number of rows and columns. Each coefficient of the sum $\mathbf{A} + \mathbf{B}$ equals the sum of the two corresponding coefficients of $\mathbf{A}$ and $\mathbf{B}$. In other words, $\mathbf{A} + \mathbf{B}$ is the matrix the (i, j) coefficient of which is $a_{ij} + b_{ij}$, a_{ij} and b_{ij} being the (i, j) coefficients of $\mathbf{A}$ and $\mathbf{B}$, respectively. The difference matrix $\mathbf{A} - \mathbf{B}$ is analogously defined to be the matrix $(a_{ij} - b_{ij})$.

10. A product of a scalar α and a matrix $\mathbf{A}$ is the matrix denoted by $\alpha\mathbf{A}$ and defined so that each coefficient is obtained by multiplying the corresponding coefficient of $\mathbf{A}$ by the constant α. Thus $\alpha\mathbf{A} = (\alpha \cdot a_{ij})$.

————— EXAMPLE A.4 —————

$$\begin{bmatrix} 1 & 1 & 0 \\ 2 & 3 & 4 \end{bmatrix} + \begin{bmatrix} 2 & -1 & 0 \\ 1 & 4 & 5 \end{bmatrix} = \begin{bmatrix} 3 & 0 & 0 \\ 3 & 7 & 9 \end{bmatrix}$$

$$\begin{bmatrix} 1 & 1 & 1 \\ 2 & 3 & 4 \end{bmatrix} - \begin{bmatrix} 2 & -1 & 0 \\ 1 & 4 & 5 \end{bmatrix} = \begin{bmatrix} -1 & 2 & 1 \\ 1 & -1 & -1 \end{bmatrix}$$

$$2\begin{bmatrix} 1 & 0 & 0 \\ 2 & 3 & -1 \end{bmatrix} = \begin{bmatrix} 2 & 0 & 0 \\ 4 & 6 & -2 \end{bmatrix}.$$

11. The matrix operations above satisfy the following relations:

(a) $\mathbf{A} + \mathbf{B} = \mathbf{B} + \mathbf{A}$ (commutative)
(b) $(\mathbf{A} + \mathbf{B}) + \mathbf{C} = \mathbf{A} + (\mathbf{B} + \mathbf{C})$ (associative)

(c) $\mathbf{A} + \mathbf{O} = \mathbf{A}$
(d) $(\mathbf{A}^T)^T = \mathbf{A}$
(e) $(\mathbf{A} + \mathbf{B})^T = \mathbf{A}^T + \mathbf{B}^T$
(f) $a(\mathbf{A} + \mathbf{B}) = a\mathbf{A} + a\mathbf{B}$ (distributive)
(g) $(a + b)\mathbf{A} = a\mathbf{A} + b\mathbf{A}$ (distributive)
(h) For positive integers n,

$$\mathbf{A} + \mathbf{A} + \cdots + \mathbf{A} = n\mathbf{A},$$

where on the left-hand side we presume $\mathbf{A}$ to be added n times. From (b), the order in which addition is done is immaterial. The symbols a and b denote scalars.

12. The product of two matrices $\mathbf{A}$ and $\mathbf{B}$ is defined only when the number of columns of $\mathbf{A}$ equals the number of rows of $\mathbf{B}$. If $\mathbf{A}$ and $\mathbf{B}$ are $m \times n$ and $n \times p$, respectively, the product $\mathbf{C} = \mathbf{A} \cdot \mathbf{B}$ is $m \times p$, and coefficient c_{ij} of $\mathbf{C}$ is defined by

$$c_{ij} = \sum_{k=1}^{n} a_{ik} b_{kj}. \tag{A.3}$$

In other words, the coefficient c_{ij} of $\mathbf{C}$ is obtained by multiplying each coefficient in the ith row of $\mathbf{A}$ by the corresponding element in the jth column of $\mathbf{B}$, and adding these products.

—————— **EXAMPLE A.5** ————————————————————————

$$[1 \quad 1 \quad 3] \begin{bmatrix} 4 \\ 4 \\ 3 \end{bmatrix} = 1 \cdot 4 + 1 \cdot 4 + 3 \cdot 3 = 17$$

$$\begin{bmatrix} 1 \\ 1 \\ 3 \end{bmatrix} [4 \quad 4 \quad 3] = \begin{bmatrix} 4 & 4 & 3 \\ 4 & 4 & 3 \\ 12 & 12 & 9 \end{bmatrix}$$

$$\begin{bmatrix} 1 & 0 \\ 2 & 2 \end{bmatrix} \begin{bmatrix} 1 & 0 & 3 \\ 1 & 1 & 2 \end{bmatrix} = \begin{bmatrix} 1 & 0 & 3 \\ 4 & 2 & 10 \end{bmatrix}.$$

————————————————————————————————————— ∎

13. The multiplication operation satisfies the following properties:

(a) $(\mathbf{AB})\mathbf{C} = \mathbf{A}(\mathbf{BC})$ (associative)
(b) $(\mathbf{A} + \mathbf{B})\mathbf{C} = \mathbf{AC} + \mathbf{BC}$ (distributive)
(c) $\mathbf{A}(\mathbf{B} + \mathbf{C}) = \mathbf{AB} + \mathbf{AC}$ (distributive)
(d) $\mathbf{A} \cdot \mathbf{I} = \mathbf{A}, \mathbf{I} \cdot \mathbf{A} = \mathbf{A}$
(e) $(\mathbf{AB})^T = \mathbf{B}^T \mathbf{A}^T$
(f) $\mathbf{AO} = \mathbf{O}$

14. Note that even if **AB** is defined, the product **BA** may not be defined. Moreover, if both **AB** and **BA** exist, *they are not necessarily the same*. These properties are illustrated next.

────── **EXAMPLE A.6** ──

Let

$$\mathbf{A} = \begin{bmatrix} 1 & 1 & 0 \\ 1 & 0 & 0 \\ 0 & 0 & 0 \end{bmatrix}, \qquad \mathbf{B} = \begin{bmatrix} 1 & 0 \\ 0 & 1 \\ 0 & 0 \end{bmatrix};$$

then

$$\mathbf{AB} = \begin{bmatrix} 1 & 1 & 0 \\ 1 & 0 & 0 \\ 0 & 0 & 0 \end{bmatrix}\begin{bmatrix} 1 & 0 \\ 0 & 1 \\ 0 & 0 \end{bmatrix} = \begin{bmatrix} 1 & 1 \\ 1 & 0 \\ 0 & 0 \end{bmatrix},$$

but the product

$$\mathbf{BA} = \begin{bmatrix} 1 & 0 \\ 0 & 1 \\ 0 & 0 \end{bmatrix}\begin{bmatrix} 1 & 1 & 0 \\ 1 & 0 & 0 \\ 0 & 0 & 0 \end{bmatrix}$$

does not exist. Let

$$\mathbf{C} = \begin{bmatrix} 1 & 1 \\ 1 & 1 \end{bmatrix}, \qquad \mathbf{D} = \begin{bmatrix} 1 & -1 \\ 1 & -1 \end{bmatrix};$$

then

$$\mathbf{CD} = \begin{bmatrix} 1 & 1 \\ 1 & 1 \end{bmatrix}\begin{bmatrix} 1 & -1 \\ 1 & -1 \end{bmatrix} = \begin{bmatrix} 2 & -2 \\ 2 & -2 \end{bmatrix},$$

but

$$\mathbf{DC} = \begin{bmatrix} 1 & -1 \\ 1 & -1 \end{bmatrix}\begin{bmatrix} 1 & 1 \\ 1 & 1 \end{bmatrix} = \begin{bmatrix} 0 & 0 \\ 0 & 0 \end{bmatrix}.$$

The last result shows that the product of two matrices may be the zero matrix, even if neither of the matrices is zero.

── ∎

A.2
LINEAR EQUATIONS AND MATRIX INVERSES

15. Linear equations may be rewritten in a compact form by using matrix and vector notation. Let us consider the linear equations

$$a_{11}x_1 + a_{12}x_2 + \cdots + a_{1n}x_n = b_1$$

$$a_{21}x_1 + a_{22}x_2 + \cdots + a_{2n}x_n = b_2 \tag{A.4}$$

$$\vdots \qquad \vdots \qquad \qquad \vdots \qquad \vdots$$

$$a_{m1}x_1 + a_{m2}x_2 + \cdots + a_{mn}x_n = b_m.$$

Introduce the following notation:

$$\mathbf{A} = (a_{ij})_{i,j=1}^{m,n} = \begin{bmatrix} a_{11} & a_{12} & \cdots & a_{1n} \\ a_{21} & a_{22} & \cdots & a_{2n} \\ \vdots & \vdots & & \vdots \\ & & \cdots & \\ a_{m1} & a_{m2} & & a_{mn} \end{bmatrix},$$

$$\mathbf{x} = (x_j)_{j=1}^{n} = \begin{bmatrix} x_1 \\ x_2 \\ \vdots \\ x_n \end{bmatrix}, \qquad \mathbf{b} = (b_i)_{i=1}^{m} = \begin{bmatrix} b_1 \\ b_2 \\ \vdots \\ b_m \end{bmatrix}.$$

Then equation (A.4) can be written in the compact form

$$\mathbf{Ax} = \mathbf{b}. \tag{A.5}$$

EXAMPLE A.7

In the case of the equations given at the beginning of this appendix, we have $m = n = 3$, and

$$\mathbf{A} = \begin{bmatrix} 2 & 1 & -1 \\ 1 & 1 & 1 \\ -1 & 0 & 1 \end{bmatrix}, \qquad \mathbf{x} = \begin{bmatrix} x_1 \\ x_2 \\ x_3 \end{bmatrix}, \qquad \mathbf{b} = \begin{bmatrix} 5 \\ 5 \\ -1 \end{bmatrix}.$$

---

16. The *powers* or *exponents* of square matrices are defined by the relations $\mathbf{A}^1 = \mathbf{A}$ and $\mathbf{A}^n = \mathbf{A} \times \mathbf{A}^{n-1}(n \geq 2)$. Thus $\mathbf{A}^n = \mathbf{A} \times \mathbf{A} \times \cdots \times \mathbf{A}$, where on the right-hand side the number of factors equals n. Observe that if $\mathbf{A}$ is not a square matrix, then $\mathbf{A} \times \mathbf{A}$ is not defined. Therefore, exponents of matrices are meaningful only for square matrices.

17. The *inverse* of a square matrix $\mathbf{A}$ is that matrix, denoted by $\mathbf{A}^{-1}$, which satisfies the relation

$$\mathbf{A} \cdot \mathbf{A}^{-1} = \mathbf{A}^{-1} \cdot \mathbf{A} = \mathbf{I}.$$

EXAMPLE A.8

Not all squares matrices have inverses. For example, the zero matrix has no inverse, since for any arbitrary matrix $\mathbf{X}$ of the same order, $\mathbf{O} \cdot \mathbf{X} = \mathbf{X} \cdot \mathbf{O} = \mathbf{O} \neq \mathbf{I}$. Consider next the matrix

$$\mathbf{A} = \begin{bmatrix} 2 & 1 & -1 \\ 1 & 1 & 1 \\ -1 & 0 & 1 \end{bmatrix};$$

then one can verify that

$$\mathbf{A}^{-1} = \begin{bmatrix} -1 & 1 & -2 \\ 2 & -1 & 3 \\ -1 & 1 & -1 \end{bmatrix},$$

since

$$\mathbf{A}^{-1}\mathbf{A} = \begin{bmatrix} -1 & 1 & -2 \\ 2 & -1 & 3 \\ -1 & 1 & -1 \end{bmatrix}\begin{bmatrix} 2 & 1 & -1 \\ 1 & 1 & 1 \\ -1 & 0 & 1 \end{bmatrix} = \begin{bmatrix} 1 & 0 & 0 \\ 0 & 1 & 0 \\ 0 & 0 & 1 \end{bmatrix}$$

and

$$\mathbf{A}\mathbf{A}^{-1} = \begin{bmatrix} 2 & 1 & -1 \\ 1 & 1 & 1 \\ -1 & 0 & 1 \end{bmatrix}\begin{bmatrix} -1 & 1 & -2 \\ 2 & -1 & 3 \\ -1 & 1 & -1 \end{bmatrix} = \begin{bmatrix} 1 & 0 & 0 \\ 0 & 1 & 0 \\ 0 & 0 & 1 \end{bmatrix}.$$

18. If $\mathbf{A}$ is a square matrix having an inverse, then (A.5) has a unique solution, which can be written as $\mathbf{x} = \mathbf{A}^{-1}\mathbf{b}$.

This relation can be verified by premultiplying both sides of equation $\mathbf{Ax} = \mathbf{b}$ by the inverse matrix $\mathbf{A}^{-1}$ to get

$$\mathbf{A}^{-1}\mathbf{Ax} = \mathbf{A}^{-1}\mathbf{b},$$

where the left-hand side equals $\mathbf{Ix} = \mathbf{x}$.

The inverse of the matrix of coefficients of the linear equations discussed in Example A.7 has been determined in Example A.8. In view of property 18, this implies that

$$\mathbf{x} = \mathbf{A}^{-1}\mathbf{b} = \begin{bmatrix} -1 & 1 & -2 \\ 2 & -1 & 3 \\ -1 & 1 & -1 \end{bmatrix} \begin{bmatrix} 5 \\ 5 \\ -1 \end{bmatrix} = \begin{bmatrix} 2 \\ 2 \\ 1 \end{bmatrix}.$$

That is, the solutions of the linear equations at the beginning of the appendix are $x_1 = x_2 = 2$ and $x_3 = 1$.

━━━ ■

19. Let $\mathbf{A}$ be a square matrix. If $\mathbf{A}^{-1}$ exists, $\mathbf{A}$ is called *nonsingular*. Otherwise, $\mathbf{A}$ is said to be *singular*.

━━━━━━ **EXAMPLE A.10** ━━━━━━━━━━━━━━━━━━━━━━━━━━━━━━

Consider the matrix

$$\mathbf{A} = \begin{bmatrix} 0 & 1 \\ 0 & 2 \end{bmatrix},$$

and let

$$\mathbf{X} = \begin{bmatrix} x_{11} & x_{12} \\ x_{21} & x_{22} \end{bmatrix}$$

be an arbitrary matrix. Then

$$\mathbf{XA} = \begin{bmatrix} x_{11} & x_{12} \\ x_{21} & x_{22} \end{bmatrix} \begin{bmatrix} 0 & 1 \\ 0 & 2 \end{bmatrix} = \begin{bmatrix} 0 & x_{11} + 2x_{12} \\ 0 & x_{21} + 2x_{22} \end{bmatrix} \neq \mathbf{I}$$

and consequently, no matrix $\mathbf{X}$ satisfies the relation

$$\mathbf{XA} = \mathbf{I}$$

since the first column of $\mathbf{I}$ is not zero. Thus $\mathbf{A}^{-1}$ does not exist. That is, $\mathbf{A}$ is singular.

━━━ ■

20. Let $\mathbf{A}$ and $\mathbf{B}$ be nonsingular $n \times n$ matrices. Then $\mathbf{AB}$ is nonsingular and

$$(\mathbf{AB})^{-1} = \mathbf{B}^{-1}\mathbf{A}^{-1}. \tag{A.6}$$

For notice that in view of the associative law (item 13),

$$(\mathbf{AB})(\mathbf{B}^{-1}\mathbf{A}^{-1}) = \mathbf{A}(\mathbf{BB}^{-1})\mathbf{A}^{-1} = \mathbf{AIA}^{-1} = (\mathbf{AI})\mathbf{A}^{-1} = \mathbf{AA}^{-1} = \mathbf{I}.$$

21. Consider the matrix

$$\mathbf{B} = (\mathbf{b}^{(1)}, \mathbf{b}^{(2)}, \dots, \mathbf{b}^{(n)}), \tag{A.7}$$

where $\mathbf{b}^{(1)}, \mathbf{b}^{(2)}, \dots, \mathbf{b}^{(n)}$ are the columns of $\mathbf{B}$, and let $\mathbf{A}$ be a matrix such that $\mathbf{AB}$ is defined. Then

$$\mathbf{AB} = (\mathbf{Ab}^{(1)}, \mathbf{Ab}^{(2)}, \dots, \mathbf{Ab}^{(n)}). \tag{A.8}$$

That is, the columns of $\mathbf{AB}$ can be obtained by multiplying the matrix $\mathbf{A}$ by each of the columns of $\mathbf{B}$, and then assembling a new matrix column by column from these products. This property is illustrated in the next example.

───── **EXAMPLE A.11** ─────

Define the matrices

$$\mathbf{A} = \begin{bmatrix} 1 & 2 \\ -1 & 1 \end{bmatrix}, \quad \mathbf{B} = \begin{bmatrix} 2 & 0 \\ 1 & 3 \end{bmatrix}.$$

Then

$$\mathbf{AB} = \begin{bmatrix} 1 & 2 \\ -1 & 1 \end{bmatrix}\begin{bmatrix} 2 & 0 \\ 1 & 3 \end{bmatrix} = \begin{bmatrix} 4 & 6 \\ -1 & 3 \end{bmatrix}.$$

But

$$\mathbf{Ab}^{(1)} = \begin{bmatrix} 1 & 2 \\ -1 & 1 \end{bmatrix}\begin{bmatrix} 2 \\ 1 \end{bmatrix} = \begin{bmatrix} 4 \\ -1 \end{bmatrix}$$

$$\mathbf{Ab}^{(2)} = \begin{bmatrix} 1 & 2 \\ -1 & 1 \end{bmatrix}\begin{bmatrix} 0 \\ 3 \end{bmatrix} = \begin{bmatrix} 6 \\ 3 \end{bmatrix}.$$

From inspection we see that $\mathbf{Ab}^{(1)}$ and $\mathbf{Ab}^{(2)}$ are indeed the columns of $\mathbf{AB}$. ∎

22. For any matrices $\mathbf{V}$ and $\mathbf{A}$ such that the product $\mathbf{VA}$ is defined, if $\mathbf{x}$ is a solution of the simultaneous linear equation

$$\mathbf{Ax} = \mathbf{b}, \tag{A.9}$$

then by multiplying both sides on the left by matrix $\mathbf{V}$, we see that it also satisfies

$$\mathbf{VAx} = \mathbf{Vb}. \tag{A.10}$$

If $\mathbf{A}$ and $\mathbf{V}$ are nonsingular, then we may conclude that $\mathbf{x}$ satisfies (A.9) if and only if it satisfies (A.10).

23. The notion of row operation plays a central role in numerical computation procedures for solving simultaneous linear equations. We now consider the operation of adding a multiple α of the jth row of matrix $\mathbf{A}$ to the ith row. If $\mathbf{A} = (a_{ij})$, the resulting matrix will be

$$
\tilde{\mathbf{A}} = \begin{bmatrix}
a_{11} & a_{12} & \cdots & a_{in} \\
\vdots & \vdots & & \vdots \\
a_{i-1,1} & a_{i-1,2} & \cdots & a_{i-1,n} \\
a_{i1} + \alpha a_{j1} & a_{i2} + \alpha a_{j2} & \cdots & a_{in} + \alpha a_{jn}. \\
a_{i+1,1} & a_{1+1,2} & \cdots & a_{i+1,n} \\
\vdots & \vdots & & \vdots \\
a_{n1} & a_{n2} & \cdots & a_{nn}
\end{bmatrix}
$$

This operation is achieved by $\tilde{\mathbf{A}} = \mathbf{VA}$, where

$$
\mathbf{V} = \begin{matrix}
& i & & j & \\
\begin{bmatrix}
1 & & \cdot & & \cdot & & & & \\
& \ddots & \vdots & & \vdots & & & & \\
& & 1 & & & & & & \\
\cdot & \cdots & \cdot 1 \cdot & \cdots & \cdot \alpha \cdot & \cdots & \cdot & & i \\
& & 1 & & & & & & \\
& & \vdots & \ddots & \vdots & & & & \\
& & & & 1 & & & & \\
\cdot & \cdots & \cdot & \cdot & \cdots & \cdot 1 \cdot & \cdots & \cdot & j \\
& & \cdot & & \cdot 1 & & & & \\
& & \vdots & & \vdots & & \cdot & & \\
& & \cdot & & \cdot & & 1 &
\end{bmatrix}
\end{matrix}
$$

That is, $\mathbf{V}$ is the same as the identity matrix $\mathbf{I}$, except that it has an additional element α in the (i, j) position. It is easy to verify that $\mathbf{V}^{-1}$ exists, and, in fact, $\mathbf{V}^{-1}$ equals $\mathbf{V}$, except that α is replaced by $-\alpha$. The reader may check this assertion by evaluating $\mathbf{VV}^{-1}$ and comparing it to $\mathbf{I}$.

24. Another important row operation, the interchange of the ith and jth rows, is obtained from **A** by the product **WA**, where

$$
W = \begin{bmatrix}
1 & & & & \cdot & & & \cdot & & & \\
& 1 & & & \cdot & & & \cdot & & & \\
& & \ddots & & \vdots & & & \vdots & & & \\
& & & 1 & & & & & & & \\
\cdot & \cdots & \cdot & 0 & \cdot & \cdots & \cdot & 1 & \cdot & \cdots & \cdot \\
& & & 1 & & & & & & & \\
& & & & \vdots & \ddots & & \vdots & & & \\
& & & & 1 & & & & & & \\
\cdot & \cdots & \cdot & 1 & \cdot & \cdots & \cdot & 0 & \cdot & \cdots & \cdot \\
& & & \cdot & & & & \cdot & 1 & & \\
& & & \vdots & & & & \vdots & & \ddots & \\
& & & & & & & & & & 1
\end{bmatrix}
$$

The coefficients not shown are presumed to be 0. **W** is diagonal, except for 1's in the (i, j) and (j, i) locations. The diagonal coefficients are all 1's, except for 0's at (i, i) and (j, j). The matrix **W** is its own inverse. An important conclusion we need from this discussion is that if matrix $\tilde{\mathbf{A}}$ differs from a nonsingular matrix **A** only in that a multiple of one row of **A** is added to another, or that rows of **A** are interchanged, then **x** is a solution to

$$\mathbf{Ax} = \mathbf{b}$$

if and only if it is a solution to

$$\tilde{\mathbf{A}}\mathbf{x} = \tilde{\mathbf{b}},$$

where $\tilde{\mathbf{b}}$ is determined from **b** by the same row operation by which $\tilde{\mathbf{A}}$ was constructed.

EXAMPLE A.12

Let

$$
A = \begin{bmatrix} 1 & 2 & 3 \\ 4 & 5 & 6 \\ 7 & 8 & 9 \end{bmatrix}.
$$

The matrix $\tilde{\mathbf{A}}$ obtained by adding $2 \times$ (row 2) to row 1 is

$$\tilde{\mathbf{A}} = \begin{bmatrix} 9 & 12 & 15 \\ 4 & 5 & 6 \\ 7 & 8 & 9 \end{bmatrix}.$$

$\tilde{\mathbf{A}}$ can be obtained by $\tilde{\mathbf{A}} = \mathbf{VA}$, where

$$\mathbf{V} = \begin{bmatrix} 1 & 2 & 0 \\ 0 & 1 & 0 \\ 0 & 0 & 1 \end{bmatrix}.$$

■

Calculus Background

This reference guide summarizes the major definitions, concepts, and results of calculus that are used in this book.

B.1
CONVERGENCE AND CONTINUITY

1. *Convergence* of a sequence is defined as follows: The sequence $\{x_i\}$ of real numbers converges to the limit x^* if, for arbitrary $\varepsilon > 0$, there exists an index $N = N(\varepsilon)$ such that for all $i \geq N$ we have $|x_i - x^*| < \varepsilon$. In other words, for any $i \geq N$ the term x_i approximates the limit x^* with error less than ε. This relation between $\{x_i\}$ and x^* is denoted as

$$\lim_{i \to \infty} x_i = x^*.$$

Convergent sequences have the following properties:

2. $\lim_{i \to \infty} (x_i + y_i) = \lim_{i \to \infty} x_i + \lim_{i \to \infty} y_i.$

3. $\lim_{i \to \infty} (x_i - y_i) = \lim_{i \to \infty} x_i - \lim_{i \to \infty} y_i.$ (B.1)

4. $\lim_{i \to \infty} (x_i y_i) = \lim_{i \to \infty} x_i \cdot \lim_{i \to \infty} y_i.$

5. $\lim_{i \to \infty} (x_i/y_i) = \lim_{i \to \infty} x_i / \lim_{i \to \infty} y_i.$

where in (B.1) we have assumed that sequences $\{x_i\}$ and $\{y_i\}$ are convergent, and in property 5, all y_i's as well as $\lim_{i \to \infty} y_i$ differ from zero.

6. *Convergence of a function* at a point is defined in the following way: The limit of function $f(x)$ at the point x_0 equals A if for arbitrary $\varepsilon > 0$ there exists a $\delta = \delta(\varepsilon) > 0$ such that $|x - x_0| < \delta$ implies that $|f(x) - A| < \varepsilon$. This relation is denoted as

$$\lim_{x \to x_0} f(x) = A.$$

433

A function $f(x)$ is *continuous* at x_0 if and only if

$$\lim_{x \to x_0} f(x) = f(x_0). \qquad (B.2)$$

Continuous real-valued functions have the following properties:

7. Let $f(x)$ be continuous on $[a, b]$ (i.e., $f(x)$ is continuous at each point $x_0 \in [a, b]$). Then there are points $x_1, x_2 \in [a, b]$ such that for all $x \in [a, b]$,

$$f(x_1) \le f(x) \le f(x_2). \qquad (B.3)$$

8. Let $f(x)$ be continuous on $[a, b]$, and let c by any value between $f(a)$ and $f(b)$. Then there exists a point $\xi \in [a, b]$ such that $f(\xi) = c$.

The following consequence is central to the bisection method of Chapter 5: If $f(x)$ is continuous on the interval $[a, b]$, and $f(a)$ and $f(b)$ have different signs, then $f(x)$ has at least one zero in $[a, b]$.

B.2
DERIVATIVES

9. The *derivative* of $f(x)$ at point x_0 is defined by

$$\frac{d}{dx} f(x) \bigg|_{x=x_0} = f'(x_0) = \lim_{h \to 0} \frac{f(x_0 + h) - f(x_0)}{h}, \qquad (B.4)$$

and it gives the slope of the tangent line of function $f(x)$ at x_0 (see Figure B.1). One-sided derivatives, denoted by $f'(x_0 + 0)$ or $f'(x_0 - 0)$, are defined as in (B.4) but with h restricted to positive or negative values, respectively.

The derivatives of functions satisfy the following properties:

10. If $f(x) \equiv c$, c being a constant, then $f'(x) = 0$.

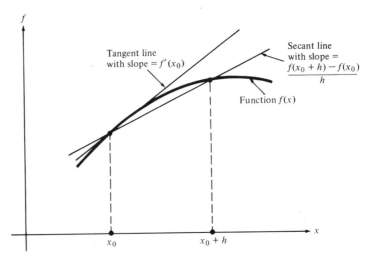

FIGURE B.1   The Derivative and Its Approximation

11. $[cf(x)]' = cf'(x).$

12. $[f(x) + g(x)]' = f'(x) + g'(x).$

13. $[f(x) - g(x)]' = f'(x) - g'(x).$ (B.5)

14. $[f(x)g(x)]' = f'(x)g(x) + f(x)g'(x).$

15. $\left[\dfrac{f(x)}{g(x)}\right]' = \dfrac{f'(x)g(x) - f(x)g'(x)}{(g(x))^2}.$

16. $[f(g(x))]' = f'(g(x))g'(x).$

Property 16 is called the *chain rule* of calculus. The relations listed above are illustrated in the following examples.

───── **EXAMPLE B.1** ─────────────────────────────

By using the definition of derivatives, we shall verify that $(x^3)' = 3x^2$. Note that

$$(x^3)' = \lim_{h \to 0} \frac{(x + h)^3 - x^3}{h} = \lim_{h \to 0} \frac{x^3 + 3x^2 h + 3xh^2 + h^3 - x^3}{h}$$

$$= \lim_{h \to 0} (3x^2 + 3xh + h^2) = \lim_{h \to 0} 3x^2 + \lim_{h \to 0} 3xh + \lim_{h \to 0} h^2.$$

In the limit we have

$$(x^3)' = 3x^2 + 0 + 0 = 3x^2.$$

■

───── **EXAMPLE B.2** ─────────────────────────────

By using relations 12 and 16, we get

$$[\exp (x^2 + x + 1)]' = \exp (x^2 + x + 1)[x^2 + x + 1]'$$
$$= \exp (x^2 + x + 1)(2x + 1)$$
$$[\sin (x^2)]' = \cos (x^2)[x^2]' = \cos (x^2)2x$$
$$[(x + 1)^3]' = 3(x + 1)^2[x + 1]' = 3(x + 1)^2,$$

and by using relations 14 and 15, we have

$$[\sin (x) \cos (x)]' = \cos (x) \cos (x) + \sin (x)[-\sin (x)] = \cos^2(x) - \sin^2(x)$$

$$[\tan (x)]' = \left[\frac{\sin (x)}{\cos (x)}\right]' = \frac{\cos (x) \cos (x) - \sin (x) [-\sin (x)]}{\cos^2(x)} = \frac{1}{\cos^2(x)}.$$

■

17. We say that function $f(x)$ is *differentiable* in the interval $[a, b]$ if for each $x \in (a, b)$ the derivative $f'(x)$ exists, and furthermore, the one-sided derivatives $f'(a + 0)$ and $f'(b - 0)$ exist.

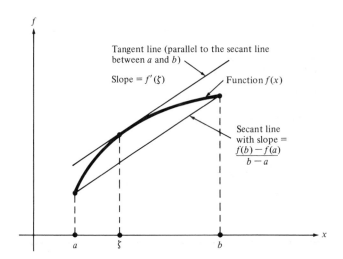

FIGURE B.2   Illustration of Property 19

Differentiable functions have the following properties:

18. (*Rolle's Theorem*) Let $f(x)$ be differentiable on $[a, b]$ and let $f(a) = f(b)$. Then there exists a point ζ between a and b such that

$$f'(\zeta) = 0. \tag{B.6}$$

19. (*Mean-Value Theorem*) Let $f(x)$ be differentiable on $[a, b]$. Then there exists a point ζ between a and b such that

$$f'(\zeta) = \frac{f(b) - f(a)}{b - a}. \tag{B.7}$$

This result is illustrated in Figure B.2.

20. (*Cauchy Mean-Value Theorem*) Let $f(x)$ and $g(x)$ be differentiable on $[a, b]$. Then there exists a point ζ between a and b such that

$$\frac{f'(\zeta)}{g'(\zeta)} = \frac{f(b) - f(a)}{g(b) - g(a)}. \tag{B.8}$$

21. (*Mean-Value Theorem of Derivatives*) If $f(x)$ is differentiable on $[a, b]$, and c is any value between $f'(a)$ and $f'(b)$, there exists a point $\xi \in [a, b]$ such that $f'(\xi) = c$.

22. The *higher-order derivatives* are defined recursively by

$$f^{(n)}(x) = [f^{(n-1)}(x)]', \tag{B.9}$$

where $f^{(n-1)}(x)$ and $f^{(n)}(x)$ denote the $(n - 1)$st-order and nth-order derivatives of function $f(x)$, respectively.

This recursive relation is illustrated in the following example.

━━━━ **EXAMPLE B.3** ━━━

$$[\sin (x)]' = \cos (x)$$

$$[\sin (x)]'' = [\sin (x)']' = [\cos (x)]' = -\sin (x) \qquad \text{(B.10)}$$

$$[\sin (x)]^{(3)} = [\sin (x)'']' = [-\sin (x)]' = -\cos (x),$$

and so on.

━━━ ∎

There are important relations between the signs of the first two derivatives and the fundamental properties of the graphs of functions, which are discussed next.

23. A function $f(x)$ is *locally increasing* (or *decreasing*) at point x_0 if there exists a positive ε such that for all $x_0 - \varepsilon < x < x_0$, $f(x) \le f(x_0)$ [or $f(x) \ge f(x_0)$] and for all $x_0 < x < x_0 + \varepsilon$, $f(x_0) \le f(x)$ [or $f(x_0) \ge f(x)$].

24. The point x_0 is a local *minimum* (or *maximum*) point of function $f(x)$ if there exists a positive ε such that for all $x_0 - \varepsilon < x < x_0 + \varepsilon$, $f(x_0) \le f(x)$ [or $f(x_0) \ge f(x)$].

The relations between the derivative and the foregoing properties are as follows:

25. If $f(x)$ is differentiable in the neighborhood of x_0 [i.e., for $|x - x_0|$ sufficiently small, $f'(x)$ exists], and $f'(x_0) \ge 0$ [or $f'(x_0) \le 0$], then $f(x)$ is locally increasing (or decreasing at x_0).

The converse of this statement is not true in general, as the function $f(x) = x^3$ shows at $x_0 = 0$, but the following statement holds:

26. If $f(x)$ is differentiable in the neighborhood of x_0 and $f(x)$ is locally increasing (or decreasing) at x_0, then $f'(x_0) \ge 0$ [or $f'(x_0) \le 0$].

27. If $f(x)$ is differentiable in the neighborhood of x_0 and x_0 is a local minimum or maximum point of $f(x)$, then $f'(x_0) = 0$.

The converse of this statement is not true in general, as the case of the function $f(x) = x^3$ shows at $x_0 = 0$, but the following holds:

28. Assume that $f(x)$ is twice differentiable in the neighborhood of x_0. If $f'(x_0) = 0$ and $f''(x_0) > 0$ [or $f''(x_0) < 0$], then x_0 is a local minimum (or maximum) point of function $f(x)$. An analogous statement is the following: Assume that $f(x)$ is differentiable in the neighborhood of x_0. If $f'(x_0) = 0$ and for $x < x_0$, $f'(x) < 0$ [$f'(x) > 0$] and for $x > x_0$, $f'(x) > 0$ [$f'(x) < 0$], then $f(x)$ has a local minimum (maximum) at $x = x_0$.

━━━━ **EXAMPLE B.4** ━━━

At $x_0 = 0$:

(a) Function $f_1(x) = 2x$ is locally increasing and function $f_2(x) = -2x + x^2$ is locally decreasing, since $f_1'(0) = 2$ and $f_2'(0) = -2$.

(b) Function $f_3(x) = x^2$ has a local minimum and $f_4(x) = -x^2$ has a local maximum, since $f_3''(0) = 2 > 0$ and $f_4''(0) = -2 < 0$, and $f_3'(0) = f_4'(0) = 0$.

━━━ ∎

B.3
INFINITE SERIES

29. An infinite series

$$s = a_1 + a_2 + \cdots + a_i + \cdots \tag{B.11}$$

is said to be *convergent* if the sequence $\{s_i\}$ of the partial sums defined by

$$s_i = a_1 + a_2 + \cdots + a_i$$

is convergent, and the sum of the infinite series is defined as the limit of the sequence $\{s_i\}$.

Some important properties of infinite series are summarized below.
30. $\Sigma_{i=1}^{\infty} (1/i^{\alpha})$ is convergent for $\alpha > 1$ and divergent for $\alpha \leq 1$.
31. Assume that there exists a convergent infinite series

$$\sum_{i=1}^{\infty} b_i \text{ such that } b_i \geq 0 \ (i \geq 1), \text{ and for all } i, \ |a_i| \leq b_i.$$

Then the series (B.11) is convergent.
32. Assume that in the infinite series

$$s = a_1 - a_2 + a_3 - a_4 + \cdots + (-1)^{i+1}a_i + \cdots$$

all terms a_i have the same sign. Furthermore, suppose that

$$\lim_{i \to \infty} a_i = 0$$

$$|a_{i+1}| \leq |a_i| \qquad (i \geq 1).$$

Then the infinite series is convergent. Also,

$$|s - s_i| \leq |a_{i+1}|, \tag{B.12}$$

where

$$s_i = a_1 - a_2 + a_3 - a_4 + \cdots + (-1)^{i+1}a_i$$

denotes the ith partial sum and s is the limit.

──────── **EXAMPLE B.5** ──

(a) $\Sigma_{i=1}^{\infty} (1/i^2)$ is convergent and $\Sigma_{i=1}^{\infty} (1/i)$ is divergent, since in these cases $\alpha = 2$ and $\alpha = 1$, respectively.
(b) The alternating series

$$1 - \tfrac{1}{2} + \tfrac{1}{3} - \tfrac{1}{4} + \tfrac{1}{5} - \tfrac{1}{6} + \cdots$$

is convergent, since it satisfies the conditons of property 32.

Furthermore, in this case

$$|s - s_i| \leq \frac{1}{i + 1} \, ,$$

since

$$(-1)^{i+2} \frac{1}{i + 1}$$

is the first neglected term in constructing s_i.

∎

33. An infinite series of functions

$$s(x) = f_1(x) + f_2(x) + \cdots + f_i(x) + \cdots$$

is said to be convergent for a given value $x = x_0$ if the sequence $\{s_i(x_0)\}$ is convergent, where for $i = 1, 2, \ldots$, and all x,

$$s_i(x) = f_1(x) + f_2(x) + \cdots + f_i(x).$$

The sum of the series at x_0 is defined as the limit of the sequence $\{s_i(x_0)\}$.

Taylor's polynomials and Taylor's series play important roles in calculus. Their definitions and properties are omitted from this appendix because they are discussed in Section 3.3.

B.4
PARTIAL DERIVATIVES

34. The *partial derivative* of a multivariable function $f(x_1, \ldots, x_n)$, with respect to x_k, is defined as

$$\frac{\partial f}{\partial x_k}(x_1, \ldots, x_n) = f_{x_k}(x_1, \ldots, x_n)$$

$$= \lim_{h \to 0} \frac{f(x_1, \ldots, x_{k-1}, x_k + h, x_{k+1}, \ldots, x_n) - f(x_1, \ldots, x_{k-1}, x_k, x_{k+1}, \ldots, x_n)}{h}.$$

(B.13)

35. *Higher-order partial derivatives* are defined by the recurrent relation

$$\frac{\partial^k f}{\partial x_{i_1} \partial x_{i_2} \cdots \partial x_{i_k}} = \frac{\partial}{\partial x_{i_1}} \frac{\partial^{k-1} f}{\partial x_{i_2} \cdots \partial x_{i_k}}.$$ (B.14)

It is known that if higher-ordered partial derivatives are continuous, their values are independent of the order in which differentiation is done.

───── **EXAMPLE B.6** ──────────────────────────────────────

Consider the bivariable function

$$f(x_1, x_2) = 2x_1^2 - 2x_1x_2 + x_2^2 - 2x_1 + 1.$$

Then

$$\frac{\partial f}{\partial x_1} (x_1, x_2) = 4x_1 - 2x_2 - 2,$$

$$\frac{\partial f}{\partial x_2} (x_1, x_2) = -2x_1 + 2x_2.$$

── ■

36. The *chain rule* for multivariable functions can be stated in the following way: Let $f(x_1, \ldots, x_n)$ be an n-variable differentiable function, and let $g_1(x)$, $\ldots$, $g_n(x)$ be differentiable real functions. Consider now the real function

$$h(x) = f(g_1(x), \ldots, g_n(x)).$$

Then function $h(x)$ is differentiable; furthermore,

$$h'(x) = \frac{\partial f}{\partial g_1} (g_1(x), \ldots, g_n(x))g_1'(x) + \cdots + \frac{\partial f}{\partial g_n} (g_1(x), \ldots, g_n(x))g_n'(x).$$

(B.15)

───── **EXAMPLE B.7** ──────────────────────────────────────

Consider the bivariable function

$$f(x_1, x_2) = x_1^2 + x_2^2$$

and

$$g_1(x) = \sin (x), \qquad g_2(x) = e^x.$$

Then

$$h(x) = f(g_1(x), g_2(x)) = \sin^2 (x) + (e^x)^2.$$

Simple differentiation shows that

$$h'(x) = 2 \sin (x) \cos (x) + 2e^{2x}.$$

On the other hand, by using the chain rule, the same result can be obtained:

$$h'(x) = 2x_1\big|_{x_1 = g_1(x)} g_1'(x) + 2x_2\big|_{x_2 = g_2(x)} g_2'(x)$$

$$= 2g_1(x)g_1'(x) + 2g_2(x)g_2'(x) = 2\sin(x)\cos(x) + 2e^x e^x$$

$$= 2\sin(x)\cos(x) + 2e^{2x}.$$ ■

B.5
INTEGRATION

37. The *primitive function* (or *indefinite integral*) $F(x)$ of a real funciton $f(x)$ is defined by the relation

$$f(x) = F'(x) \tag{B.16}$$

and is denoted as

$$F(x) = \int f(x) \, dx.$$

Some principal properties of primitive functions are summarized as follows:

38. Let $F_1(x)$ and $F_2(x)$ be two primitive functions of $f(x)$. Then $F_1(x) - F_2(x)$ is a constant.

39. If $F(x)$ is a primitive function of $f(x)$, then for arbitrary constant c, $F(x) + c$ is also a primitive function of $f(x)$.

The following relations hold:

40. $\int (f(x) + g(x)) \, dx = \int f(x) \, dx + \int g(x) \, dx.$

41. $\int (f(x) - g(x)) \, dx = \int f(x) \, dx - \int g(x) \, dx.$

42. $\int cf(x) \, dx = c \int f(x) \, dx.$

43. $\int f'(x)g(x) \, dx = f(x)g(x) - \int f(x)g'(x) \, dx$ (integration by parts).

44. $\displaystyle\int f'(x)f^n(x) \, dx = \frac{f^{n+1}(x)}{n+1} + c.$ \hfill (B.17)

45. $\displaystyle\int \frac{f'(x)}{f(x)} \, dx = \ln|f(x)| + c.$

46. If $F(x)$ is a primitive function of $f(x)$, then

$$\int f(g(x))g'(x) \, dx = F(g(x)) + c,$$

and as a special case,

$$\int f(ax + b) \, dx = \frac{F(ax + b)}{a} + c.$$

─────── **EXAMPLE B.8** ───

By using the properties above, we get the following relations (assuming that "log" is to the base e):

(a) $\displaystyle\int \frac{\log (x)}{x} dx = \int \frac{1}{x} [\log (x)] dx = \frac{[\log (x)]^2}{2} + c,$

since the derivative of $\log (x)$ equals $1/x$.

(b) $\displaystyle\int \log (x) dx = \int 1 \log (x) dx = x \log (x) - \int x \frac{1}{x} dx = x \log (x)$

$- x + c$, since we can choose $f(x) = x$ and $g(x) = \log (x)$ in property 43.

(c) $\displaystyle\int \frac{x}{1 + x^2} dx = \frac{1}{2} \int \frac{2x}{1 + x^2} dx = \frac{1}{2} \log (1 + x^2) + c,$

since we may define $f(x) = 1 + x^2$ and use property 45.

■

47. Let $f(x)$ be a bounded function on an interval $[a, b]$, let $a = x_0 < x_1 < \cdots < x_n = b$ be given domain points, and let $\zeta_k \in [x_{k-1}, x_k]$ be arbitrary points for $k = 1, \ldots, n$. Then

$$\sum_{k=1}^{n} f(\zeta_k)(x_k - x_{k-1})$$

is called a *Riemann sum* of function $f(x)$. If the Riemann sums are convergent for any selection of points $\xi_k \in [x_{k-1}, x_k]$ and x_k such that max $\{x_{k+1} - x_k; 0 \le k < n\} \to 0$ as $n \to \infty$, and the limit is always the same, then we say that function $f(x)$ is *integrable* on the interval $[a, b]$, and the *definite integral* of function $f(x)$ on $[a, b]$ is defined by the common limit of the Riemann sums and it is denoted by

$$\int_a^b f(x) \, dx.$$

The relation between primitive functions and definite integrals is given by the following fact:

48. Let $F(x)$ be a primitive function of $f(x)$. Then

$$\int_a^b f(x) \, dx = F(b) - F(a) = F(x)|_a^b. \tag{B.18}$$

49. In applied mathematics there are many applications of the *mean-value theorem for integrals*, which is: Assume that $f(x)$ and $g(x)$ are integrable on $[a, b]$, and in this interval

$$f(x) \ge 0.$$

Then there exists a point $\zeta \in (a, b)$ such that

$$\int_a^b f(x)g(x)\, dx = g(\zeta) \int_a^b f(x)\, dx. \qquad (B.19)$$

50. If either function $f(x)$ is not bounded on $[a, b]$, and/or the interval $[a, b]$ is not finite, then the above definition of definite integrals is inapplicable. These integrals are called *improper*. Some improper integrals can be defined in the following way:

(a) $\int_a^\infty f(x)\, dx = \lim\limits_{b\to\infty} \int_a^b f(x)\, dx.$

(b) $\int_{-\infty}^\infty f(x)\, dx = \lim\limits_{a\to-\infty} \int_a^c f(x)\, dx + \lim\limits_{b\to\infty} \int_c^b f(x)\, dx$, where c is an

　arbitrary number.

──── **EXAMPLE B.9** ──

(a) $\int_0^\pi \sin(x)\, dx = [-\cos(x)]_0^\pi = [-\cos(\pi)] - [-\cos(0)] = 1 + 1 = 2.$

(b) $\int_0^1 x^2\, dx = \left[\dfrac{x^3}{3}\right]_0^1 = \dfrac{1}{3} - \dfrac{0}{3} = \dfrac{1}{3}.$

(c) $\int_1^\infty \dfrac{1}{x^2}\, dx = \lim\limits_{b\to\infty} \int_1^b \dfrac{1}{x^2}\, dx = \lim\limits_{b\to\infty}\left[-\dfrac{1}{x}\right]_1^b = \lim\limits_{b\to\infty}\left(-\dfrac{1}{b} + 1\right) = 0 + 1$

$= 1.$ ∎

──

Answers to Selected Problems

Chapter 1

3. $18,000 \, (2 \cdot 10^2 - 1) + 1 = 3,582,001$
$18,000 = $ number of nonzero mantissas
$(2 \cdot 10^2 - 1) = $ number of exponents
$1 = $ for zero.

4. **(a)**

0	0	0	0	2	5	3	1

1	0	0	0	2	5	3	1

0	0	0	0	0	0	4	8

1	0	0	0	0	0	4	8

6. Ten's complement of $1986 = 99,998,014$.

8. **(a)** 99; 127; 85. **(b)** 5.1875; 0.484375; 1.296875.

9. $(34)_{10} = (100010)_2$.

12. Two's complement of $110011 = (\underbrace{11 \ldots 11}001101)$.

$$26 \text{ 1's}$$

14. **(a)** $(29BC)_{16} = (10,684)_{10}$.

16. In integer representation: 1. In floating-point representation: 0.

18. **(a)** $0.1962 \cdot 10^4$. **(b)** $0.4654 \cdot 10^3$.

22. **(a)** $|1 + 2x - y| \, \delta x + |1 - x + 2y| \, \delta y$.
(c) $|-2 \sin x \cos y + \cos x \sin y| \, \delta x + |-2 \cos x \sin y + \sin x \cos y| \, \delta y$.

23. **(a)** 0.0385. **(b)** 0.0133.

24. **(a)** 0.269%. **(b)** 0.623%.

25. **(a)** $|2x - y| \, \delta x + |-x + 2y| \, \delta y$. **(b)** $\left| \dfrac{x}{\sqrt{x^2 + y^2}} \right| \delta x + \left| \dfrac{y}{\sqrt{x^2 + y^2}} \right| \delta y$.

26. **(a)** 0.0399. **(b)** 0.00706.

27. **(a)** 0.247%. **(b)** 0.125%.

28. $x_1 = \dfrac{-1 + \sqrt{1 - 4 \times 10^{-2n}}}{2 \times 10^{-n}}.$

After rationalizing the numerator of x_1:

$x_1 = \dfrac{-2 \times 10^{-n}}{1 + \sqrt{1 - 4 \times 10^{-2n}}}.$

29. (a) [109.989, 112.211].

31. (a) $\dfrac{x - y}{\sqrt{x} + \sqrt{y}}.$ (b) $\ln\left(\dfrac{x}{y}\right).$

33. $\delta\alpha < \dfrac{2 \cdot 10^{-2}}{10^2[1 - \cos(0.2)]}.$

35. (a) $\delta(x_{k+1}^*) = 5\, \delta(x_k^*) + 0.005.$

37. 1.2%.

Chapter 2

1. (a) $(6, 0, 0)$. (c) $\left(-\frac{20}{3}, \frac{34}{3}, -\frac{8}{3}\right)$.
2. Same as Problem 1.
3. Same as Problem 1.
11. (a) $x_1 = -(\frac{2}{3})x_3 + 1$,
$x_2 = (\frac{1}{3})x_3 - x_4 + 1$, $(1, 1, 0, 0)$, and $(1, 0, 0, 1)$.
(b) $x_1 = 4x_3 + 5x_4 + 1$, $x_2 = -3x_3 - 4x_4 + 2$. $(1, 2, 0, 0)$ and $(6, -2, 0, 1)$

12.

(a) $\begin{pmatrix} \frac{1}{2} & \frac{1}{2} & 0 \\ \frac{3}{4} & -\frac{5}{12} & -\frac{1}{6} \\ -\frac{1}{4} & -\frac{1}{12} & \frac{1}{6} \end{pmatrix}.$ (b) $\begin{pmatrix} 3 & -\frac{3}{2} & -1 \\ -1 & \frac{3}{2} & 2 \\ 0 & -\frac{1}{2} & -1 \end{pmatrix}.$

13. Same as Problem 1.

14. (a) $\begin{pmatrix} 3 & 6 \\ 0 & 0 \\ 0 & 0 \end{pmatrix}.$ (b) $\begin{pmatrix} -18 & -24 \\ 35 & 48 \\ -16 & -22 \end{pmatrix}.$

15. Same as Problem 14.
19. (a) -12. (b) -2.
20. (a) 0. (b) 0. (c) 0.
22. (a) $(-2, 2, 0)$. (b) $(2, 4, 0, 0)$.
23. Same as Problem 22.

25. (a) $\begin{pmatrix} 1 & -1 & -1 \\ -\frac{1}{3} & \frac{2}{3} & \frac{2}{3} \\ -\frac{1}{3} & \frac{2}{3} & -\frac{1}{3} \end{pmatrix}.$ (b) $\begin{pmatrix} 1 & 0 & -1 & -1 \\ 0 & 0 & \frac{1}{2} & \frac{1}{2} \\ -1 & 1 & \frac{3}{2} & \frac{3}{2} \\ -1 & 1 & \frac{3}{2} & \frac{1}{2} \end{pmatrix}.$

(c)
$$\begin{pmatrix} -\frac{3}{5} & \frac{4}{5} & -\frac{1}{5} & -\frac{3}{5} \\ \frac{8}{5} & -\frac{4}{5} & \frac{1}{5} & \frac{3}{5} \\ -\frac{2}{5} & -\frac{1}{5} & \frac{1}{5} & \frac{3}{5} \\ \frac{2}{5} & -\frac{1}{5} & -\frac{1}{5} & \frac{2}{5} \end{pmatrix}.$$

27. (a) 13.33. **(b)** 99.

30. (a)
$$\begin{pmatrix} 1 & 0 & 0 \\ 1 & 1 & 0 \\ 2 & \frac{1}{2} & 1 \end{pmatrix} \begin{pmatrix} 1 & 1 & 1 \\ 0 & -2 & -2 \\ 0 & 0 & 6 \end{pmatrix} \quad (6, 0, 0).$$

(b)
$$\begin{pmatrix} 1 & 0 & 0 \\ 2 & 1 & 0 \\ -1 & -\frac{1}{2} & 1 \end{pmatrix} \begin{pmatrix} 1 & 2 & 3 \\ 0 & 2 & 4 \\ 0 & 0 & -1 \end{pmatrix} \quad (-36, 70, -32).$$

33. (a)
$$\mathbf{U} = \begin{pmatrix} \sqrt{6} & \dfrac{2}{\sqrt{6}} & \dfrac{14}{\sqrt{6}} \\ 0 & \dfrac{\sqrt{7}}{\sqrt{3}} & \dfrac{13}{\sqrt{21}} \\ 0 & 0 & \dfrac{12}{\sqrt{14}} \end{pmatrix}.$$

(b)
$$\mathbf{U} = \begin{pmatrix} \sqrt{6} & \dfrac{17}{\sqrt{6}} & \dfrac{29}{\sqrt{6}} \\ 0 & \dfrac{\sqrt{5}}{\sqrt{6}} & \dfrac{11}{\sqrt{30}} \\ 0 & 0 & \dfrac{2}{\sqrt{5}} \end{pmatrix}.$$

34. (c) $(0.3137, 0.4314, 0.4118)$.
35. Same as Problem 34.
38. $\lambda = 1$, $\mathbf{x} = (1, 1)^T$.

Chapter 3

1. 99.
5. $\delta b_k^* = \delta$, and for $j = k - 1, \ldots, 0$,
$\delta(b_j^*) = |x^*| \, \delta(b_{j+1}^*) + |b_{j+1}^*| \, \hat{\delta} + \delta$,
where $b_k^* = a_k^*$, $b_j^* = x^* b_{j+1}^* + a_j^*$, for $j < k$.
9. $f(x) \approx 1 + \sum_{k=1}^{n} \dfrac{(-1)^{k-1}}{2^k \cdot k!} (1)(3)(5) \cdots (2k - 3)(x - 1)^k$.
For $n = 3$, $f(0.1) \approx 0.40319$, and $\sqrt{0.1} - f(0.1) \approx -0.087$.
For $n = 5$, $f(0.1) \approx 0.36141$, and $\sqrt{0.1} - f(0.1) \approx -0.045$.
At $x = 0$, $f(x)$ is not differentiable.
11. If $0 < y < 2$, then $1/y = 1 + x + x^2 + \ldots$, where $x = 1 - y$.

12. (a) $p_3(x) = 2x - \left(\dfrac{8}{3!}\right) x^3 (x_0 = 0)$

(b) $p_3(x) = 1 + \dfrac{1}{2} (x - 1) - \dfrac{1}{2^2 \cdot 2!} (x - 1)^2 + \dfrac{1 \cdot 3}{2^3 \cdot 3!} (x - 1)^3$.

(c) $p_3(x) = 1 + x^2$. **(d)** $p_3(x) = 1 + x + x^2 + x^3$.

13. **(a)** $1 + \left(\dfrac{2}{1!} + 1\right) x + \left(\dfrac{2^2 x^2}{2!}\right) + \left(\dfrac{2^3}{3!} - \dfrac{1}{3!}\right) x^3 + \cdots$

$$+ \begin{cases} \dfrac{2^n}{n!} x^n, & \text{if } n \text{ is even,} \\[3mm] \left(\dfrac{2^n}{n!} + \dfrac{(-1)^k}{n!}\right) x^n, & \text{if } n \text{ is odd and } k = \dfrac{n-1}{2}. \end{cases}$$

(b) $1 + \dfrac{x^2}{2!} + \dfrac{x^4}{4!} + \cdots + \dfrac{x^{2k}}{(2k)!}. \quad (n = 2k \text{ or } 2k + 1)$

(c) $\dfrac{x}{1!} + \dfrac{x^3}{3!} + \cdots + \dfrac{x^{2k+1}}{(2k+1)!}. \quad (n = 2k + 1 \text{ or } 2k + 2)$

(f) $\displaystyle\sum_{k=0}^{n} \binom{\alpha}{k} x^k$, where $\dbinom{\alpha}{k} = \dfrac{\alpha(\alpha - 1) \cdots (\alpha - k + 1)}{k!}$.

(h) $1 - x + x^2 - x^3 + \cdots + (-1)^n x^n$.

14. $|R_7| \le \dfrac{1}{5040}$.

15. **(b)** $n = 10$.
16. For $f(x) = \cos x$, $n = 6$, $\cos (0.5) \approx 0.877582516$.
  For $f(x) = e^x$, $n = 6$, $e^{0.5} \approx 1.64872127$.
19. $p_0(x) = 0$; $p_1(x) = 4x$; $p_2(x) = x$.
  By selecting $x_2 = 2$, $p_0(x) = 0$; $p_1(x) = x$; $p_2(x) = x^2 + 2x$.
21. $\dfrac{-x^4}{12} + \dfrac{13x^2}{12}$.

25. $p_2(x) = x$.
27. $p_4(x) = x^3 + x + 1$.
28. $p_2(x) = -4x^2 + 4x$, and $|R_2| \le 0.2486$.

30.

x	$p_3(x)$	$\sin (x)$
2.1	0.8546	0.8632
3	−0.2963	0.1411
5	−8.5828	−0.9589

31. $p_3(x) \approx -0.1516x^3 - 0.007884x^2 + x$.
33. $x \approx 0.9168$.
37.

$$g(x) = \begin{cases} -9 + (\tfrac{19}{2})(x + 2) - (\tfrac{3}{2})(x + 2)^3, & \text{if } -2 \le x \le -1; \\[2mm] -1 + 5(x + 1) - (\tfrac{9}{2})(x + 1)^2 + (\tfrac{3}{2})(x + 1)^3, & \text{if } -1 \le x \le 0; \\[2mm] 1 + (\tfrac{1}{2})x + (\tfrac{3}{2})x^3, & \text{if } 0 \le x \le 1; \\[2mm] 3 + 5(x - 1) + (\tfrac{9}{2})(x - 1)^2 - (\tfrac{3}{2})(x - 1)^3, & \text{if } 1 \le x \le 2. \end{cases}$$

39. (a) Yes. (c) No.

40. (a)

$$g(x) = \begin{cases} -x - 2, & \text{if } -3 \le x \le -2; \\ x + 2, & \text{if } -2 \le x \le -1; \\ -x, & \text{if } -1 \le x \le 0; \\ x, & \text{if } 0 \le x \le 1; \\ -x + 2, & \text{if } 1 \le x \le 2. \end{cases}$$

42. (a) $b = 1$, a is arbitrary.

Chapter 4

1. (a) 1. (c) 3. (e) 2.

2. (a) 1.

5. (a) 0.3995. (b) 0.3985.

8. (a) No. (b) Yes.

13. $t_1 \approx 14.8$; $t_2 \approx 10.1$; $s_2 \approx 8.55$.

14. $t_4 = -0.2333$; $s_4 = -0.2$.

15.

n	t_n	s_n
10	0.63138	0.63665
50	0.63641	0.63662

17.

n	t_n	s_n
10	3.1399257	3.1415927
50	3.1415257	3.1415932

22.

n	t_n	s_n
2	0.5	0.6667
4	0.6036	0.6381
6	0.6220	0.6370

The exact value is 0.63662, to the accuracy shown.

25. $n = 4664 > \sqrt{8e} \cdot 10^3$.

26. (b) 8.38906.

27. $I \approx 0.63662$. Between $M = 3$ and $M = 4$, the estimates differed by less than $(\frac{1}{2}) 10^{-5}$.

30.

n	Romberg Estimate
3	8.867362
5	8.840534
10	8.840579
15	8.840601

Note: This problem is subject to considerable roundoff error.

33.

n	Gauss Estimate
1	5.4365
3	8.3878
5	8.3891
7	8.3890

34.

n	I
1	9.6227
3	8.8080
5	8.8277
7	8.8429

36. (c) 1.5708.
37. (a) 1.0.   (b) $0.833\overline{3}$.

Chapter 5
1. $x < 1$ and $x > 3$.
2. $(-10, 10)$.
3. $(4, 5)$.
4. (a) $(0, 1)$.   (b) $(0.7, 1.7)$.   (c) $(0.5, 1.5)$.
9. (a) $(1, 2)$.   (b) $(-2, -1)$ and $(1, 2)$.   (c) $(1, 2)$.
11. $(4, 5), (4, 4.5), (4, 4.25)$.
12. 4.104.
13. 33.
14. (a) 0.860.   (b) 1.05.   (c) 0.785.   (d) 1.11.   (e) 4.10.
15. (a) 0.619 and 1.51.   (b) 1.83.   (c) -1.84 and 1.15.
17. (a) 2.39.   (b) 1.09.   (c) -0.755.
19. $x_0 = 4, x_1 = 5, x_2 = 4.0625, x_3 = 4.08767$.
20. Same as Problem 12.
21. Same as Problem 14.
22. Same as Problem 15.
24. Same as Problem 17.
26. $x_0 = 4, x_1 = 4.11, x_2 \approx 4.103$.
27. Same as Problem 12.
28. Same as Problem 14.
29. Same as Problem 15.
31. Same as Problem 17.
33. 2.8487.
34. 0.78183.
37. $1 - i, 1 + i, i\sqrt{2}, -i\sqrt{2}$.
41. $x \approx 1.5811, y \approx 1.2247$.
42. $x \approx 2.4934, y \approx 0.40106$.
44. $x \approx 0.86066, y \approx 0.63752$.

Chapter 6
1. (a) $p_0 = 3.25$, $p_1 = -1.3x + 2.6$.   (b) $p_0 = 2.5$, $p_1 = 1.4x + 1.8$.

2. Errors least-squares polynomials.

Part (1)

	Degree		
x	1	2	3
0.09	$-0.188E + 00$	$-0.348E - 01$	$-0.297E - 01$
0.18	$0.473E - 01$	$-0.388E - 01$	$-0.290E - 01$
0.27	$0.245E + 00$	$-0.213E - 01$	$-0.112E - 01$
0.36	$0.388E + 00$	$0.225E - 02$	$0.955E - 02$
0.45	$0.466E + 00$	$0.201E - 01$	$0.228E - 01$
0.55	$0.471E + 00$	$0.256E - 01$	$0.229E - 01$
0.64	$0.403E + 00$	$0.172E - 01$	$0.991E - 02$
0.73	$0.265E + 00$	$-0.961E - 03$	$-0.111E - 01$
0.82	$0.664E - 01$	$-0.198E - 01$	$-0.295E - 01$
0.91	$-0.179E + 00$	$-0.255E - 01$	$-0.306E - 01$

Part (2)

	Degree		
x	1	2	3
0.09	$0.306E + 00$	$0.541E - 01$	$-0.171E - 01$
0.18	$-0.221E - 01$	$0.119E + 00$	$-0.172E - 01$
0.27	$-0.303E + 00$	$0.134E + 00$	$-0.712E - 02$
0.36	$-0.527E + 00$	$0.107E + 00$	$0.512E - 02$
0.45	$-0.682E + 00$	$0.505E - 01$	$0.136E - 01$
0.55	$-0.754E + 00$	$-0.223E - 01$	$0.146E - 01$
0.64	$-0.728E + 00$	$-0.948E - 01$	$0.719E - 02$
0.73	$-0.584E + 00$	$-0.147E + 00$	$-0.640E - 02$
0.82	$-0.298E + 00$	$-0.156E + 00$	$-0.199E - 01$
0.91	$0.159E + 00$	$-0.937E - 01$	$-0.225E - 01$

4. $M = 1$.

n	Average Squared Error
5	0.056
10	0.046
15	0.049

$M = 2$.

n	Average Squared Error
5	$0.566 \cdot 10^{-6}$
10	$0.876 \cdot 10^{-6}$
15	$0.472 \cdot 10^{-6}$

$M = 3.$

n	Average Squared Error
5	$0.564 \cdot 10^{-6}$
10	$0.564 \cdot 10^{-6}$
15	$0.473 \cdot 10^{-6}$

8. **(a)** $-0.115 + 1.269x^2$. **(c)** $2x$, which interpolates.

10. $\frac{3}{16} + \frac{15}{16} x^2$.

11. $0.1864 + 0.9329x^2$. Note that this is close to, but not coincident with, the solution to Problem 10.

12. Obviously, if $p(x)$ is the least-squares polynomial, then $p(-x)$ is also a solution of the least-squares problem. The uniqueness implies that $p(x) = p(-x)$; hence $p(x)$ is an even function.

16. $(\mathbf{\Phi}^T\mathbf{\Phi})^T = \mathbf{\Phi}^T(\mathbf{\Phi}^T)^T = \mathbf{\Phi}^T\mathbf{\Phi}$, and so $\mathbf{\Phi}$ is symmetric.

$$\mathbf{u}^T\mathbf{\Phi}^T\mathbf{\Phi}\mathbf{u} = \mathbf{v}^T\mathbf{v} = \Sigma v_i^2 \geq 0, \qquad \text{where } \mathbf{v} = \mathbf{\Phi}\mathbf{u}.$$

17. **(a)** $\phi_0(x) = 1$; $\phi_1(x) = x + (\frac{1}{2})$; $\phi_2(x) = x^2 + x - 1$. **(b)** $\phi_0(x) = 1$; $\phi_1(x) = x - (\frac{1}{2})$; $\phi_2(x) = x^2 - x - 1$.

18. Same as Problem 1.

19. Same as Problem 10.

23. $\displaystyle\int_{-\pi}^{\pi} \sin(kx) = \left.\frac{-\cos(kx)}{k}\right|_{-\pi}^{\pi} = 0.$

$\displaystyle\int_{-\pi}^{\pi} \cos(kx) = \left.\frac{\sin(kx)}{k}\right|_{-\pi}^{\pi} = 0.$

By a trigonometric identity,

$$\int_{-\pi}^{\pi} \sin(kx) \cdot \sin(vx)\, dx = \int_{-\pi}^{\pi} (\tfrac{1}{2}) [\cos((k - v)x) - \cos((k + v)x)]\, dx$$

$$= (\tfrac{1}{2}) \int_{-\pi}^{\pi} \cos((k - v)x)\, dx - (\tfrac{1}{2}) \int_{-\pi}^{\pi} \cos(k + v)x)\, dx = 0, \qquad \text{if } k \neq v.$$

29. **(a)** $\dfrac{2 - 2x}{1 - \frac{2}{3}x - \frac{1}{3}x^2}$, which does not interpolate at $x = 1$.

(b) $\dfrac{1 - 3x}{1 - \frac{7}{3}x + \frac{2}{3}x^2}$. This interpolates all data values.

Chapter 7

1. **(a)** $1 + \dfrac{x^2}{2}$. **(b)** $2 + 2x + x^2 + \frac{1}{3}x^3$.

2. Same as Problem 1.

4.

Problem	$x = h$	$x = 2h$	$x = 10h$	Exact at $x = 10h$
(a)	1.000000	1.010000	1.547110	1.648721
(b)	2.200000	2.42010	5.422122	5.746254

6. For $h = 0.1$, $p(10) = 990.8$; for $h = 0.01$, $P(10) = 991.0$

11. (a)

x	$y(x)$
0	1
0.1	1.005
0.2	1.02015
1.0	1.6415

(b)

x	$y(x)$
0	2
0.1	2.21001
0.2	2.44206
1.0	5.73369

14. $\alpha_2 = \frac{1}{3}$, $\mu_2 = \frac{3}{2}$, $\lambda_{21} = \frac{3}{4}$. It is unique.

15. The computed values of $y(1.0)$ are

	$k = 1$	$k = 2$	$k = 3$
Problem (a) Approximation =	1.6464444	1.648718	1.648713
Problem (b) Approximation =	5.740408	5.746244	5.746252

17.

Problem	$y_1(1)$	$y_2(1)$
(a)	3.07178	3.44777
(b)	-0.539745	1.187362

18. (a) $y_1' = y_2$, $y_1(0) = 1$, $y_2' = (1 - x^2)y_2 + y_1$, $y_2(0) = 1$.

Index ▬▬▬▬▬▬▬▬▬▬▬▬▬▬▬▬▬▬▬▬▬

List of Subroutines